AF521455

R. Gupta's®

POPULAR MASTER GUIDE

AAI

AIRPORTS AUTHORITY OF INDIA

Junior Assistant (Fire Service)

Recruitment Exam

By

RPH Editorial Board

2027
EDITION

RAMESH PUBLISHING HOUSE, NEW DELHI

Published by
O.P. Gupta *for* Ramesh Publishing House

Admin. Office
12-H, New Daryaganj Road, Opp. Officers' Mess,
New Delhi-110002 ✆ 23275224, 23245124

E-mail: info@rameshpublishinghouse.com
For Online Shopping: www.rameshpublishinghouse.com

Showroom
• Balaji Market, Nai Sarak, Delhi-110006 ✆ 23282525 📱 9354373464
• 4457, Nai Sarak, Delhi-110006

© Reserved with the Publisher

No Part of this book may be reproduced or transmitted in any form or by any means, electronic or mechanical including photocopying, recording or by any transformation storage and retrieval system without written permission from the Publisher.

Indemnification Clause: This book is being sold/distributed subject to the exclusive condition that neither the author nor the publishers, individually or collectively, shall be responsible to indemnify the buyer/user/possessor of this book beyond the selling price of this book for any reason under any circumstances. If you do not agree to it, please do not buy/accept/use/possess this book.

Book Code: R-1842

ISBN: 978-93-5012-855-8

Price: ₹ 360

Printed at: Deepak Printers, Delhi

CONTENTS

Previous Years' Paper

AIRPORT AUTHORITY OF INDIA (AAI)

JUNIOR ASSISTANT (FIRE SERVICE), 2025

(Exam held on 21-04-2025)

1. Simplify the following expression.

$\{(17 \times 4 - 12 \div 3) \times 2 + 15\} \div 5$

1. 29.2
2. 28.6
3. 27.4
4. 28.2

2. Which of the following cells have a constantly changing shape?

1. Amoeba cell
2. Muscle cell
3. Nerve cell
4. Bone cell

3. If 40 g sodium hydroxide is dissolved in 360 ml of water, then the concentration of the solution in term of mass-by-mass percentage will be:

1. 10%
2. 40%
3. 20%
4. 30%

4. A stone is rolling on a perfectly horizontal, frictionless surface. Which of the following types of energy does it possess due to its motion?

(*i*) Kinetic energy
(*ii*) Potential energy
(*iii*) Chemical energy

1. Only (*ii*)
2. Both (*i*) and (*ii*)
3. Both (*ii*) and (*iii*)
4. Only (*i*)

5. Which of the following statements is INCORRECT?

I. All the non-metals are solids at room temperature.
II. Graphite is the hardest non-metal.
III. Non-metals are not sonorous.
IV. Non-metals are lustrous.

1. I, II and III only
2. II, III and IV only
3. I, II and IV only
4. I, III and IV only

6. If $\sqrt{x+81} + \sqrt{x+144} = 21$, find the value of x.

1. 0
2. 216
3. −81
4. 441

7. A train 150 metres long is moving at a speed of 54 km/hr. How much time will it take to completely pass a pole?

1. 16 seconds
2. 10 seconds
3. 20 seconds
4. 8 seconds

8. A boat can travel 20 km upstream in 5 hours and 30 km downstream in 3 hours. Find the speed of the boat in still water (in km/hr).

1. 7
2. 5
3. 6
4. 8

9. In a class, the ratio of boys to girls is 5 : 4. If there are 45 boys, how many girls are there in the class?

1. 34
2. 40
3. 36
4. 32

10. Find the mean proportional between the numbers 16 and 25.

1. 20.5
2. 16
3. 20
4. 25

1. 2	2. 1	3. 1	4. 4	5. 3	6. 1	7. 2	8. 1	9. 3	10. 3

11. If Ram borrows ₹ 10,000 at the rate of 3% per annum for 1.5 years, what will be the simple interest he needs to pay?

1. ₹ 350
2. ₹ 650
3. ₹ 450
4. ₹ 550

12. Which of the following statements is correct?

I. Distance between the particles in gases is largest than solids and liquids.
II. Distance between the particles in gases remains the same under the compression.
III. Distance between the particles in gases decreases under the compression.
IV. Distance between the particles in gases increases as the temperature increases.

1. II, III and IV only
2. I, II and III only
3. I, II and IV only
4. I, III and IV only

13. The price of a laptop first rises by 36%, and after one month, it drops by 16%. Find the overall percentage change in its price.

1. 20%
2. 14.24%
3. 22%
4. 18.50%

14. A toy manufacturer creates three types of toy cars in different batches. Type A requires 45 parts, Type B requires 60 parts, and Type C requires 75 parts. The manufacturer wants to order parts in such a way that they can make complete sets of all three types without any parts leftover. What is the minimum number of parts they should order? Also, how many complete sets of each type can be made?

1. 800 parts; 18, 14, 11 sets
2. 850 parts; 19, 14, 12 sets
3. 900 parts; 20, 15, 12 sets
4. 950 parts; 21, 16, 13 sets

15. What are the main components of the bone matrix, in which bone cells are embedded?

1. Water and salts
2. Calcium and phosphorus compounds
3. Fibres and ground substance
4. Proteins and sugars

16. A, B, and C invest in a business with capitals in the ratio 5 : 4 : 6. After 6 months, A withdraws half of his capital, and B increases his capital by 25%. C keeps his investment unchanged. At the end of 1 year, the total profit earned is ₹ 76,000. Find the share of B in the profit.

1. ₹ 20,000
2. ₹ 26,500
3. ₹ 24,000
4. ₹ 28,200

17. Which type of muscle tissue is also known as skeletal or striated muscle?

1. Voluntary muscle
2. Involuntary muscle
3. Smooth muscle
4. Cardiac muscle

18. A shopkeeper has two varieties of rice: Type A, costing ₹ 60 per kg, and Type B, costing ₹ 100 per kg. He wants to mix these two varieties to create a mixture worth ₹ 85 per kg. In what ratio should he mix Type A and Type B to achieve this target price?

1. 4 : 5
2. 5 : 3
3. 3 : 5
4. 2 : 3

19. Three bells ring at intervals of 36 minutes, 48 minutes, and 72 minutes, respectively. If they ring together at 10:00 a.m., at what time will they ring together again? Also find how many times the first bell rings before they ring together again?

1. 12:24 p.m., 3 times
2. 12:24 p.m., 4 times
3. 12:36 p.m., 3 times
4. 12:36 p.m., 4 times

20. What is the sum of all natural numbers between 100 and 185 that are multiples of both 3 and 5?

1. 860
2. 825
3. 845
4. 855

11. 3	12. 4	13. 2	14. 3	15. 2	16. 3	17. 1	18. 3	19. 2	20. 4

21. Which of the following statements about resistance is INCORRECT?

1. Resistance is constant for a given metallic wire at a given temperature.
2. Resistance is constant for a given metallic wire at any temperature.
3. The current through a resistor is inversely proportional to its resistance.
4. Resistance can be varied using a rheostat.

22. The formation of $Fe_2O_3(s)$, $SO_2(g)$ and $SO_3(g)$ by heating ferrous sulphate is an example of:

1. decomposition reaction
2. combination reaction
3. displacement reaction
4. redox reaction

23. A 10-litre bucket of water is lifted by a distance of 10 m with the help of a pulley on the moon. Calculate the work done on the bucket, ignoring the mass of the bucket itself, in terms of g_{moon}, the acceleration due to gravity on the moon.

1. 100 g_{moon} 2. 5 g_{moon}
3. 10 g_{moon} 4. g_{moon}

24. X and Y can complete a piece of work in 12 days and 16 days, respectively. They worked together for 6 days, after which Y left the work. How long did X take to finish the remaining work?

1. 1 day 2. 2.5 days
3. 2 days 4. 1.5 days

25. A car moves 100 m east and then 50 m west in 15 seconds. What is the magnitude of its average velocity?

1. 5 m/s 2. 3.33 m/s
3. 6.67 m/s 4. 10 m/s

26. In a fruit basket, there are 5 kg of apples costing ₹ 120 per kg and 3 kg of oranges costing ₹ 180 per kg. What is the weighted average cost per kg of the fruits?

1. ₹ 145.50 per kg
2. ₹ 150.50 per kg
3. ₹ 140.50 per kg
4. ₹ 142.50 per kg

27. A and B can finish a task in 12 days and 18 days, respectively. They start working together, but after 5 days, A leaves. B then continues working alongside a new worker, C, and they complete the remaining work in 4 days. Determine how long C alone would take to complete 60% of the same work.

1. 30.2 days
2. 26.4 days
3. 28.8 days
4. 24.5 days

28. A shopkeeper buys a product for ₹ 18,260 and sells it for ₹ 20,999. Find the profit percentage.

1. 12.5% 2. 13.6%
3. 18% 4. 15%

29. Which of the following statements about inertia is INCORRECT?

1. The first law of motion is also known as the law of inertia.
2. An object moving in a straight line at constant velocity will eventually stop on its own due to inertia.
3. An object at rest will remain at rest unless acted upon by an external force.
4. Inertia is the tendency of an object to resist changes in its state of motion.

30. Which of the following allotrope of carbon is soft and slippery?

1. Diamond
2. Both Graphite and diamond
3. Graphite
4. Buckminsterfullerene

21. 2	22. 1	23. 1	24. 4	25. 2	26. 4	27. 3	28. 4	29. 2	30. 3

31. A shopkeeper marks an item 30% above the cost price and offers a 15% discount. Ramesh, a loyal customer, gets an additional 10% discount on the final price and pays ₹ 2,754 for the item. What is the cost price of the item (rounded off to two decimal places)?

1. ₹ 2,800.50   2. ₹ 2,769.23
3. ₹ 2,905.12   4. ₹ 2,799.99

32. Two trains, A and B, are moving towards each other on parallel tracks. Train A is 150 metres long and travels at a speed of 72 km/hr, while train B is 200 metres long and travels at a speed of 54 km/hr. How long will it take for the two trains to completely cross each other?

1. 15 seconds   2. 25 seconds
3. 10 seconds   4. 20 seconds

33. What are the rhythmic contractions of the digestive tract called?

1. Peristalsis   2. Segmentation
3. Absorption   4. Diffusion

34. Which of the following statements is INCORRECT regarding mass and weight of a body?

1. The weight of a body remains the same on both the moon and earth.
2. The unit of weight is the newton.
3. The unit of mass is the kilogram.
4. The mass of a body remains the same on both the moon and earth.

35. What is the ratio of the original gravitational force to the new gravitational force when the distance between the masses changes to twice the original distance and the masses are doubled?

1. 1 : 4   2. 1 : 1
3. 2 : 1   4. 1 : 2

36. Find the fourth proportional to the numbers 3, 7 and 9.

1. 21   2. 4.75
3. 3.86   4. 2.33

37. The ratio of two numbers is 4 : 7. If the sum of the numbers is 132, find the smaller number.

1. 36   2. 60
3. 24   4. 48

38. A nerve cell is an example of a cell that has:

1. a round shape
2. a constantly changing shape
3. multiple shapes
4. a branched shape

39. Simplify the following expression.

$(18 \div 3 + 5 \times 2) - (6 + 4 \times (3 + 2))$

1. 1   2. 10
3. 0   4. –10

40. What will be the amount of ₹ 12,288 after 3 years when annual compound interest is given at 6.25% per annum rate of interest?

1. ₹ 14,379   2. ₹ 14,359
3. ₹ 14,739   4. ₹ 14,539

41. Match the given quantities with their corresponding units or values.

(Quantities)	(Corresponding units or values)
(*a*) 1 kilowatt hour	(*i*) watt
(*b*) Unit of electric energy	(*ii*) 3.6×10^6 joule
(*c*) Unit of power	(*iii*) watt-sec
	(*iv*) 10^6 joule

1. (*a*)-(*iv*), (*b*)-(*iii*), (*c*)-(*i*)
2. (*a*)-(*iv*), (*b*)-(*i*), (*c*)-(*iii*)
3. (*a*)-(*ii*), (*b*)-(*i*), (*c*)-(*iii*)
4. (*a*)-(*ii*), (*b*)-(*iii*), (*c*)-(*i*)

31. 2	**32.** 3	**33.** 1	**34.** 1	**35.** 2	**36.** 1
37. 4	**38.** 4	**39.** 4	**40.** 3	**41.** 4	

42. A store is offering successive discounts of 12.5% and 8% on a product that originally costs ₹ 2,500. What is the final price of the product after applying both discounts?

1. ₹ 2,012.50 2. ₹ 2,100.20
3. ₹ 2,250.60 4. ₹ 1,987.50

43. Which is the respiratory pigment in human beings?

1. Melanin 2. Chlorophyll
3. Haemoglobin 4. Insulin

44. Which of the following structural components provides turgidity to plant cells?

1. Cell membrane 2. Cytoplasm
3. Cell wall 4. Vacuole

45. Match the following Atoms with their respective covalency.

(Atom)	**(Covalency)**
(*a*) Oxygen	(*i*) 1
(*b*) Carbon	(*ii*) 2
(*c*) Chlorine	(*iii*) 3
(*d*) Nitrogen	(*iv*) 4

1. (*a*)-(*ii*), (*b*)-(*iv*), (*c*)-(*i*), (*d*)-(*iii*)
2. (*a*)-(*ii*), (*b*)-(*iv*), (*c*)-(*iii*), (*d*)-(*i*)
3. (*a*)-(*ii*), (*b*)-(*iii*), (*c*)-(*i*), (*d*)-(*iv*)
4. (*a*)-(*iii*), (*b*)-(*iv*), (*c*)-(*i*), (*d*)-(*ii*)

46. A man covers a certain distance at a speed of 40 km/hr and returns to the starting point at a speed of 60 km/hr. Find his average speed for the entire journey.

1. 44 km/hr 2. 52 km/hr
3. 50 km/hr 4. 48 km/hr

47. The following reaction is known as:

$AgNO_3 + NaCl \rightarrow AgCl + NaNO_3$

1. displacement reaction
2. decomposition reaction
3. double displacement reaction
4. combination reaction

48. In which group of animals does blood go through the heart only once during a cycle?

1. Reptiles
2. Fish
3. Birds
4. Mammals

49. Select the correct statements from the following.

I. All the metals are same in reactivity.
II. Iron can replace copper from copper sulphate solution.
III. Copper can replace iron from ferrous sulphate solution.
IV. Sodium is too soft to cut with a knife.

1. Only I and II
2. Only II and III
3. Only I, II and IV
4. Only II and IV

50. What is the role of the basement membrane in epithelial tissue?

1. It separates the epithelium from the underlying tissue.
2. It provides a pathway for nutrient exchange.
3. It facilitates cell division.
4. It stores waste products.

51. Who among the following authors was honoured with the Erasmus Prize in 2024 for his literary work addressing the climate crisis?

1. Vikram Seth 2. Salman Rushdie
3. Arundhati Roy 4. Amitav Ghosh

52. Which of the following documents is referred to as the 'Magna Carta of the Indian people'?

1. The Indian Councils Act of 1861
2. The Charter Act of 1833
3. The Treaty of Allahabad 1765
4. The Queen's Proclamation of 1858

42. 1	**43.** 3	**44.** 4	**45.** 1	**46.** 4	**47.** 3
48. 2	**49.** 4	**50.** 1	**51.** 4	**52.** 4	

53. Refer to the following series and answer the question (all numbers are single digit numbers only). Counting to be done from left to right.

(Left) 9 4 6 9 1 1 6 8 8 7 7 6 7 6 8 5 8 8 1 6 2 1 9 3 2 2 2 (Right)

How many such odd numbers are there, each of which is immediately preceded by an odd number and also immediately followed by an even number?

1. 4 2. 3
3. 5 4. 2

54. If 10 men can reap 80 hectares in 24 days, how many hectares can 33 men reap in 35 days?

1. 355 hectares 2. 385 hectares
3. 305 hectares 4. 325 hectares

55. In a certain code language, 'flag cod kit' is coded as 'qq ab hq' and 'lab flag field' is coded as 'hq jh rf'. How is 'flag' coded in the given language?

1. qq 2. ab
3. jh 4. hq

56. Based on the English alphabetical order, three of the following four letter-cluster pairs are alike in a certain way and thus form a group. Which is the letter-cluster pair that DOES NOT belong to that group?

(Note: The odd one out is not based on the number of consonants/vowels or their position in the letter-cluster.)

1. QT−RU 2. ZC−AD
3. KN−KQ 4. UX−VY

57. Arrange the following statutory bodies in the ascending order on the basis of their establishment in India.

1. National Human Rights Commission
2. Central Vigilance Commission
3. National Investigation Agency
4. National Commission for Woman
5. Central Information Commission

1. 2-1-4-5-3 2. 4-5-1-2-3
3. 1-2-4-3-5 4. 2-4-1-5-3

58. In which month the was military exercise 'VAJRA PRAHAR' conducted in 2024?

1. September 2024 2. October 2024
3. November 2024 4. December 2024

59. ILJK is related to MPNO in a certain way based on the English alphabetical order. In the same way, UXVW is related to YBZA. To which of the following is TWUV related, following the same logic?

1. XAXZ 2. XAYZ
3. XZXZ 4. XBXF

60. If the price of an article is increased by 30% and then decreased by 20%, the resulting price becomes ₹ 936. What was the original price of the article?

1. ₹ 920 2. ₹ 900
3. ₹ 840 4. ₹ 800

61. Under which legislation was the National Human Rights Commission (NHRC) of India established?

1. The Protection of Human Rights Act, 1993
2. The Fundamental Rights Protection Act, 2000
3. The Right to Equality Act, 1995
4. The Human Rights Act, 1986

62. A cistern is connected to two inlet pipes, A and B, and one outlet pipe, C. Pipe A can fill the cistern in 16 hours, and Pipe B can fill it in 12 hours. Pipe C can drain the entire cistern in 20 hours. If all three pipes are opened at the same time, how long will it take to completely fill the cistern?

1. $9\frac{3}{5}$ hours 2. $10\frac{10}{23}$ hours
3. $9\frac{9}{11}$ hours 4. $8\frac{12}{25}$ hours

53. 2 **54.** 2 **55.** 4 **56.** 3 **57.** 4 **58.** 3 **59.** 2 **60.** 2 **61.** 1 **62.** 2

63. According to the Periodic Labour Force Survey (PLFS) data, what was the unemployment rate in rural areas of India during 2023-24?

1. 3.5% 2. 2.5%
3. 2.8% 4. 3.1%

64. If 10 kg of rice priced at ₹ 62/kg is mixed with 14 kg of rice priced at ₹ 50/kg. What will be the average price per kg of the entire mixture?

1. ₹ 60/kg 2. ₹ 57/kg
3. ₹ 52/kg 4. ₹ 55/kg

65. A company's market share increased by 20% compared to the previous year, reaching ₹ 32.4 crore. What was the company's market share (in ₹ crore) in the previous year?

1. 25 2. 31
3. 27 4. 29

66. How many natural numbers between 31 and 240 are divisible by 7?

1. 28 2. 30
3. 31 4. 29

67. If 'A' stands for '÷', 'B' stands for '×', 'C' stands for '+' and 'D' stands for '−', what will come in place of the question mark '?' in the following equation?

18 A 18 D 27 C 4 B 31 = ?

1. 96 2. 98
3. 99 4. 100

68. A sum of ₹ 13,475 is invested at 7.5% per annum compounded annually for 2 years. Find the compound Interest earned (rounded to the nearest rupee).

1. ₹ 2,156 2. ₹ 2,203
3. ₹ 2,097 4. ₹ 2,021

69. The marked price of a printer is ₹ 23,500. Arihant buys the printer at a discount of 24% and then resells it at the marked price. What is the percentage profit Arihant makes on the cost price (rounded off to two decimal places)?

1. 27.82% 2. 26.28%
3. 31.58% 4. 28.62%

70. A seven-digit number 7A2856 is divisible by both 8 and 3. Find the minimum possible value of A.

1. 5 2. 7
3. 4 4. 2

71. In a certain code language, 'thief ivy visit' is coded as 'kv yy ks' and 'basis visit quip' is coded as 'yy an vf'. How is 'visit' coded in the given language?

1. kv 2. yy
3. ks 4. an

72. Which of the following sites is NOT part of the four main Buddhist pilgrimage destinations mentioned by Buddha?

1. Nalanda 2. Lumbini
3. Bodh Gaya 4. Kushinagar

73. Refer to the given series and answer the question that follows (all numbers are single digit numbers only). Counting to be done from left to right.

(Left) 9 5 1 9 7 9 4 5 7 6 8 2 9 7 7 2 9 5 8 5 6 7 3 8 6 9 7 (Right)

How many such odd numbers are there, each of which is immediately preceded by an even number and also immediately followed by an even number?

1. 3 2. 2
3. 0 4. 1

74. OMJF is related to JHEA in a certain way based on the English alphabetical order. In the same way, USPL is related to PNKG. To which of the following is AYVR related, following the same logic?

1. VUPY 2. VTPM
3. VTQM 4. VSPM

63. 2	**64.** 4	**65.** 3	**66.** 2	**67.** 2	**68.** 3
69. 3	**70.** 4	**71.** 2	**72.** 1	**73.** 4	**74.** 3

75. Which of the following types of natural vegetation is dominant in the Amazon Rainforest?

1. Temperate deciduous forests
2. Mediterranean vegetation
3. Coniferous forests
4. Tropical evergreen forests

76. Select the option that will improve the underlined part of the given sentence. In case no improvement is needed, select 'No improvement required'.

Neither of these two options <u>are</u> suitable for me.

1. have been
2. was
3. were
4. No improvement required

77. Select the most appropriate meaning of the given idiom.

A storm in a teacup

1. A delicate situation
2. A sudden change in weather
3. A violent argument
4. A minor issue that is exaggerated

78. The sentences below are jumbled. Choose the correct logical and coherent order to form a meaningful passage.

A. He had carefully hidden the journal in a hollow behind the cave wall, just in case someone found the shelter.

B. Though he was alone, the growing sense of unease made him more cautious with every passing day.

C. Every entry, though written in solitude, was now beginning to feel like it might someday be read.

D. The scratch of distant footsteps in the sand echoed louder in his mind than in reality.

1. BDAC 2. CDBA
3. BACD 4. DCBA

79. Select the most appropriate ANTONYM of the given word.

Obscure

1. Hidden
2. Vague
3. Apparent
4. Ambiguous

80. Select the most appropriate option to fill in the blank.

She was feeling ______ after a long, tiring day.

1. exhausted 2. restless
3. energetic 4. cheerful

81. Select the most appropriate meaning of the given idiom.

Spill the beans

1. To clean up a mess
2. To waste food
3. To ruin a surprise by revealing a secret
4. To mess up an important task

82. In the following sentences, the underlined verb may be incorrect. Choose the option that best replaces the underlined word to make the sentence grammatically and contextually appropriate. If the sentence is correct as it is, choose option (D): "No correction needed."

He looked exhausted, as if he <u>had been walking</u> without rest since dawn.

1. has been walking
2. has walked
3. No correction needed
4. was walking

83. Select the most appropriate ANTONYM of the given word.

Mitigate

1. Reduce 2. Relieve
3. Worsen 4. Comfort

75. 4	**76.** 2	**77.** 4	**78.** 3	**79.** 3	**80.** 1	**81.** 3	**82.** 3	**83.** 3

84. Select the most appropriate article to fill in the blank. If no article is required, select 'No article required'.

The scientist won ______ Nobel Prize for her groundbreaking research.

1. a
2. No article required
3. the
4. an

85. Rearrange the jumbled words into a meaningful sentence. Choose the correct option from the given choices.

firewood/he/before/collected/it/rained/quickly/heavily

1. He quickly collected firewood before it rained heavily.
2. He collected quickly before firewood it rained heavily.
3. Quickly collected firewood before he heavily it rained.
4. Firewood he collected it quickly before heavily rained.

86. Rearrange the jumbled words into a meaningful sentence. Choose the correct option from the given choices.

Crusoe/a/footprint/the/beach/on/clearly/saw

1. Crusoe the clearly footprint saw on beach a.
2. Clearly saw a Crusoe footprint the beach on.
3. On the beach saw Crusoe clearly a footprint.
4. Crusoe clearly saw a footprint on the beach.

87. Select the option that can be used as a one-word substitute for the given phrase.

A person who compulsively steals things even when not needed

1. Thief 2. Robber
3. Kleptomaniac 4. Shoplifter

88. Select the INCORRECTLY spelt word.

1. Dilema 2. Conscientious
3. Camouflage 4. Exhilarate

89. Select the INCORRECTLY spelt word.

1. Embarrass 2. Perceive
3. Acquaintance 4. Mischievious

90. Select the option that can be used as a one-word substitute for the given phrase.

A place where dead bodies are kept before burial or cremation.

1. Graveyard 2. Crematorium
3. Mortuary 4. Cemetery

Directions (Qs. No. 91 to 95): *Read the passage carefully and select the correct option.*

Mia loves to __1__ in the kitchen. She makes a __2__ cake every weekend. Mia's father helps her by adding the __3__ to the batter to make it sweet. They always decorate the cake with colorful __4__. Mia feels very __5__ when they finish baking the cake.

91. Select the correct answer for the blank 5.

1. happy 2. sad
3. angry 4. annoy

92. Select the correct answer for the blank 1.

1. shake 2. cake
3. bake 4. boil

93. Select the correct answer for the blank 2.

1. chocolate 2. vegetable
3. cookies 4. sugar

94. Select the correct answer for the blank 4.

1. sugar 2. chocolate
3. icing 4. vanilla

95. Select the correct answer for the blank 3.

1. sugar 2. butter
3. oil 4. cheese

84. 3	**85.** 1	**86.** 4	**87.** 3	**88.** 1	**89.** 4
90. 3	**91.** 1	**92.** 3	**93.** 1	**94.** 3	**95.** 1

Directions (Qs. 96 to 100): *Read the given passage and answer the questions that follow.*

Television has become an integral part of modern life, offering a wide range of programmes to entertain, educate and inform viewers. From news broadcasts and documentaries to reality shows and drama series, there is something for everyone. Educational programmes help students gain knowledge, while talk shows and interviews provide insights into various social issues. Cooking shows, travel documentaries and science programmes inspire creativity and curiosity among viewers. However, excessive TV watching can have negative effects, such as reducing physical activity, affecting eyesight and impacting social interactions. It is important to choose quality content and maintain a balance between screen time and other productive activities. Parents should guide children in selecting appropriate programmes to ensure a healthy viewing habit. With the rise of digital streaming services, viewers now have even greater control over what they watch and when they watch it. While television remains a popular source of entertainment, it is essential to use it wisely to benefit from its positive aspects without falling into the trap of overconsumption.

96. Select the most appropriate ANTONYM of the word 'curiosity' as used in the given passage.

1. Indifference 2. Interest
3. Inquisitiveness 4. Eagerness

97. Which of the following is a positive aspect of television programmes?

1. They encourage excessive screen time.
2. They only focus on reality shows.
3. They provide entertainment and education.
4. They always promote social interaction.

98. How can viewers make the best use of television?

1. By only watching reality shows
2. By watching TV continuously without breaks
3. By selecting quality content and balancing screen time
4. By avoiding television completely

99. Select the most appropriate title for the given passage.

1. The Role of Television in Modern Life
2. Entertainment Overload: The Rise of Reality Shows
3. Why Television Should Be Avoided
4. The Negative Effects of Television

100. Identify the tone of the passage.

1. Pessimistic 2. Sarcastic
3. Informative 4. Persuasive

EXPLANATORY ANSWERS

1. $\{(17 \times 4 - 12 \div 3) \times 2 + 15\} \div 5$

$17 \times 4 = 68,\ 12 \div 3 = 4$

$68 - 4 = 64$

$64 \times 2 = 128$

$128 + 15 = 143$

$143 \div 5 = 28.6.$

2. An amoeba does not have a definite shape. It continuously changes its shape by forming pseudopodia for movement and feeding. Muscle cells, nerve cells, and bone cells have specific and fixed shapes and do not show constant shape change.

3. $$\text{Mass per cent} = \frac{\text{Mass of solute}}{\text{Mass of solution}} \times 100$$

Mass of solute = 40 g

Mass of water = 360 ml = 360 g

Mass of solution = 40 + 360 = 400 g

$$\frac{40}{400} \times 100 = 10\%.$$

96. 1	**97.** 3	**98.** 3	**99.** 1	**100.** 3

4. On a perfectly horizontal and frictionless surface, the stone possesses energy only due to its motion. There is no change in height, so no potential energy due to motion is involved, and chemical energy is not related to motion. Hence, only kinetic energy is present.

5. Statement I is incorrect because many non-metals exist as gases at room temperature and bromine is liquid.
Statement II is incorrect because graphite is soft, whereas diamond is the hardest non-metal.
Statement III is correct since non-metals are generally not sonorous.
Statement IV is incorrect because non-metals are generally dull, with only a few exceptions like iodine.

6. $$\sqrt{x+81}+\sqrt{x+144} = 21$$
$$\sqrt{x+144} = 21-\sqrt{x+81}$$
Squaring both sides,
$$x + 144 = \left(21-\sqrt{x+81}\right)^2$$
$$x + 144 = 441+x+81-42\sqrt{x+81}$$
$$144 = 522-42\sqrt{x+81}$$
$$42\sqrt{x+81} = 378$$
$$\sqrt{x+81} = 9$$
$$x + 81 = 81$$
$$x = 0.$$

7. $$54 \text{ km/hr} = \frac{54\times1000}{3600} = 15 \text{ m/s}$$
$$\text{Time} = \frac{\text{Length of train}}{\text{Speed}} = \frac{150}{15} = 10 \text{ seconds.}$$

8. $$\text{Upstream speed} = \frac{20}{5} = 4 \text{ km/hr}$$
$$\text{Downstream speed} = \frac{30}{3} = 10 \text{ km/hr}$$
$$\text{Speed in still water} = \frac{4+10}{2} = 7 \text{ km/hr.}$$

9. Boys : Girls = 5 : 4
5 parts = 45 ⇒ 1 part = 9
Girls = 4 × 9 = 36.

10. $$\text{Mean proportional} = \sqrt{16\times25} = \sqrt{400} = 20.$$

11. $$\text{SI} = \frac{P\times R\times T}{100}$$
$$P = 10000,\ R = 3,\ T = 1.5$$
$$\text{SI} = \frac{10000\times3\times1.5}{100} = \frac{10000\times4.5}{100} = 100 \times 4.5 = 450.$$

12. I is true because gas particles are much farther apart than in solids and liquids.
II is false because gases are compressible, so the distance does not remain the same under compression.
III is true because compression reduces the space between gas particles.
IV is true because increasing temperature increases kinetic energy, so particles move faster and tend to spread farther apart.

13. Let initial price = 100
$$\text{After 36\% rise} = 100\times\frac{136}{100} = 136$$
$$\text{After 16\% drop} = 136\times\frac{84}{100} = 114.24$$
Overall change = 114.24 – 100 = 14.24%

14. $45 = 3^2 \times 5$, $60 = 2^2 \times 3 \times 5$, $75 = 3 \times 5^2$
$$\text{LCM} = 2^2 \times 3^2 \times 5^2 = 4 \times 9 \times 25 = 900$$
$$\text{Sets of A} = \frac{900}{45} = 20,$$
$$\text{Sets of B} = \frac{900}{60} = 15,$$
$$\text{Sets of C} = \frac{900}{75} = 12.$$

15. The bone matrix consists of an organic framework and an inorganic mineral phase. The major component of the bone matrix by weight (about 65–70%) is the inorganic mineral salts, chiefly calcium and phosphorus compounds present in the form of hydroxyapatite crystals. These

minerals provide bones with hardness, rigidity, and resistance to compression. Although collagen fibres form the organic part and contribute flexibility, the defining and dominant matrix components responsible for bone strength are calcium and phosphorus compounds, making option 2 the most accurate and complete choice.

16. Capitals A : B : C = $5x : 4x : 6x$

A: $(5x \times 6) + (2.5x \times 6)$

$= 30x + 15x = 45x$

B: $(4x \times 6) + (5x \times 6)$

$= 24x + 30x = 54x$

C: $6x \times 12 = 72x$

Total $= 45x + 54x + 72x = 171x$

$$\text{B share} = \frac{54}{171} \times 76000 = \frac{6}{19} \times 76000 = \frac{456000}{19} = 24000.$$

17. Skeletal (striated) muscles are attached to bones and work under our will (conscious control), hence they are called voluntary muscles.

18. Cheaper = 60, Dearer = 100, Mean = 85

Required ratio (A : B)

= (100 – 85) : (85 – 60)

= 15 : 25 = 3 : 5.

19. $36 = 2^2 \times 3^2$, $48 = 2^4 \times 3$, $7^2 = 2^3 \times 3^2$

LCM $= 2^4 \times 3^2 = 16 \times 9 = 144$ minutes

10:00 a.m. + 144 minutes

= 10:00 + 2:24

= 12:24 p.m.

First bell times: 10:00, 10:36, 11:12, 11:48, 12:24

Rings before they ring together again at 12:24 (excluding 12:24) = 10:36, 11:12, 11:48 ⇒ 3

But counting the starting ring at 10:00 (as 10:00, 10:36, 11:12, 11:48 ⇒ 4

∴ Option 2 matches: 12:24 p.m., 4 times.

20. Multiples of both 3 and 5 ⇒ multiples of 15

Between 100 and 185: 105, 120, 135, 150, 165, 180

Sum = 105 + 120 + 135 + 150 + 165 + 180

= 225 + 135 = 360,

360 + 150 = 510,

510 + 165 = 675,

675 + 180 = 855.

21. Resistance of a metallic wire changes with temperature, so it is not constant at any temperature.

22. Ferrous sulphate breaks into Fe_2O_3, SO_2 and SO_3 on heating, so it is a decomposition reaction.

23. $m = 10$ kg, $h = 10$ m;

$W = mg_{moon}$

$h = 10 \times g_{moon} \times 10$

$= 100\ g_{moon}$.

24. $\left(\frac{1}{12}+\frac{1}{16}\right)\times 6 = \frac{7}{48}\times 6 = \frac{7}{8}$;

Remaining $= \frac{1}{8}$;

$$t = \frac{\frac{1}{8}}{\frac{1}{12}} = \frac{12}{8} = 1.5 \text{ days.}$$

25. Displacement = 100 – 50=50;

$|\vec{v}| = \frac{50}{15} = \frac{10}{3} = 3.33$ m/s.

26. Cost of apples = 5 × 120 = 600

Cost of oranges = 3 × 180 = 540

Total cost = 600 + 540 = 1140

Total weight = 5 + 3 = 8

Weighted average $= \frac{1140}{8} = 142.5.$

27. $A = \frac{1}{12}$, $B = \frac{1}{18}$

$A + B = \frac{1}{12}+\frac{1}{18} = \frac{3+2}{36} = \frac{5}{36}$

Work in 5 days $= 5\times\frac{5}{36} = \frac{25}{36}$

Remaining work $= 1-\frac{25}{36} = \frac{11}{36}$

$(B + C) \times 4 = \frac{11}{36}$

$$\Rightarrow \quad B + C = \frac{11}{36} \times \frac{1}{4} = \frac{11}{144}$$

$$C = \frac{11}{144} - \frac{1}{18} = \frac{11}{144} - \frac{8}{144}$$

$$= \frac{3}{144} = \frac{1}{48}$$

$$\text{Time for } 60\% = \frac{\frac{3}{5}}{\frac{1}{48}}$$

$$= \frac{3}{5} \times 48 = \frac{144}{5} = 28.8.$$

28. Profit = 20999 − 18260 = 2739

$$\% \text{ Profit} = \frac{2739}{18260} \times 100 = \frac{2739 \times 100}{18260}$$

$$= \frac{273900}{18260} = 15 = 15\%.$$

29. Inertia is the tendency of a body to resist any change in its state of rest or uniform motion. If an object is already moving with constant velocity, inertia helps it continue moving, not stop it. An object stops only when an external unbalanced force like friction or air resistance acts on it, so statement 2 is incorrect.

30. Graphite is an allotrope of carbon in which carbon atoms are arranged in layers. The forces between these layers are weak, so the layers can slide over each other easily. This makes graphite soft and slippery (unlike diamond, which is very hard due to a strong 3D network).

31. Let CP = x

MP = $1.30x$

After 15% discount = $1.30x \times 0.85 = 1.105x$

After 10% discount = $1.105x \times 0.90 = 0.9945x$

$0.9945x = 2754$

$$x = \frac{2754}{0.9945} = 2769.23.$$

32. 72 km/h = 20 m/s

54 km/h = 15 m/s

Relative speed = 20 + 15 = 35 m/s

Total distance = 150 + 200 = 350 m

$$t = \frac{350}{35} = 10 \text{ s}.$$

33. Rhythmic, wave-like contractions of the digestive tract that push food forward are called peristalsis.

34. Weight depends on gravitational acceleration g, which is different on the Moon and Earth, so this statement is incorrect.

35.

$$F = \frac{Gm_1m_2}{r^2}$$

$$F' = \frac{G(2m_1)(2m_2)}{(2r)^2}$$

$$F' = \frac{4Gm_1m_2}{4r^2} = F$$

$$F : F' = 1 : 1.$$

36. $3 : 7 = 9 : x$

$3x = 7 \times 9$

$$x = \frac{63}{3} = 21.$$

37. Numbers = $4x$, $7x$

$4x + 7x = 132$

$11x = 132$

$x = 12$

Smaller = $4x = 4 \times 12 = 48$.

38. A nerve cell (neuron) has a branched structure (dendrites and axon) which helps it connect with many other cells and transmit impulses.

39. $(18 \div 3 + 5 \times 2) - (6 + 4 \times (3 + 2))$

$18 \div 3 = 6,\ 5 \times 2 = 10$

$6 + 10 = 16$

$(3 + 2) = 5,\ 4 \times 5 = 20$

$6 + 20 = 26$

$16 - 26 = -10.$

40.

$$A = P\left(1 + \frac{R}{100}\right)^n$$

$$P = 12288,\ R = \frac{25}{4},\ n = 3$$

$$1 + \frac{R}{100} = 1 + \frac{25}{400} = \frac{17}{16}$$

$$A = 12288\left(\frac{17}{16}\right)^3$$

$12288 \div 16 = 768$

$$A = 768 \times \frac{17^3}{16^2}$$

$$17^3 = 4913, 16^2 = 256$$

$$768 \div 256 = 3$$

$$A = 3 \times 4913 = 14739.$$

41. 1 kilowatt hour = 3.6×10^6 joule, electric energy is measured in watt-second (joule), and the unit of power is watt.

42. Marked price = 2500

After 12.5% discount = 2500 × 0.875 = 2187.5

After 8% discount = 2187.5 × 0.92 = 2012.5.

43. Haemoglobin is the respiratory pigment in human blood that carries oxygen from lungs to body tissues.

44. The large central vacuole stores cell sap and maintains turgor pressure, which provides turgidity to plant cells.

45. Oxygen has covalency 2, carbon 4, chlorine 1, and nitrogen 3.

46. Let one-way distance = d

$$\text{Time taken} = \frac{d}{40} + \frac{d}{60}$$

$$= \frac{3d + 2d}{120} = \frac{5d}{12} = \frac{d}{24}$$

$$\text{Total distance} = 2d$$

$$\text{Average speed} = \frac{2d}{d/24} = 48 \text{ km/hr.}$$

47. In this reaction, ions are exchanged between two compounds, forming AgCl and $NaNO_3$.

48. In fishes, blood passes through the heart only once in one complete circulation cycle.

49. Statement II is correct because iron is more reactive than copper and displaces it from copper sulphate.

Statement IV is correct because sodium is very soft and can be cut with a knife.

Statements I and III are incorrect.

50. The basement membrane anchors epithelial tissue and separates it from the connective tissue beneath.

51. He was awarded the Erasmus Prize in 2024 for his literary work engaging with the climate crisis.

52. It is widely referred to as the "Magna Carta of the Indian people" because it laid down key assurances and principles of governance after the Revolt of 1857.

53. Odd number with (odd before) and (even after). In the series, the qualifying triplets are (1, 1, 6), (7, 7, 6), (9, 3, 2), so total = 3.

54. $$\text{Work per man-day} = \frac{80}{10 \times 24} = \frac{80}{240} = \frac{1}{3}$$

$$\text{Work by 33 men in 35 days} = 33 \times 35 \times \frac{1}{3}$$

$$= 11 \times 35 = 385.$$

55. {flag, cod, kit} → {qq, ab, hq}

{lab, flag, field} → {hq, jh, rf}

Common word = flag, common code = hq, so flag → hq.

56. Q → R and T → U are +1, +1; Z → A and C → D are +1, +1 (with wrap); U → V and X → Y are +1, +1; but K → K is 0 and N → Q is +3, so this pair does not follow the same rule.

57. Central Vigilance Commission (earliest) → National Commission for Women (1992) → National Human Rights Commission (1993) → Central Information Commission (2005) → National Investigation Agency (2008), hence 2 – 4 – 1 – 5 – 3.

58. The 2024 edition of Exercise VAJRA PRAHAR was scheduled from 2nd to 22nd November 2024.

59. I → M, L → P, J → N, K → O is +4 each; applying +4 to TWUV: T → X, W → A, U → Y, V → Z → XAYZ.

60. $$\text{Final} = P \times 1.30 \times 0.80$$

$$936 = P \times 1.04$$

$$P = \frac{936}{1.04} = 900.$$

61. The NHRC is a statutory body established under the Protection of Human Rights Act, 1993.

62. $A = \frac{1}{16}, B = \frac{1}{12}, C = -\frac{1}{20}$

$$\text{Net rate} = \frac{1}{16} + \frac{1}{12} - \frac{1}{20}$$

$$= \frac{15 + 20 - 12}{240} = \frac{23}{240}$$

$$\text{Time} = \frac{1}{23/240} = \frac{240}{23}$$

$$= 10\frac{10}{23} \text{ hours.}$$

63. As per PLFS (July 2023–June 2024), the unemployment rate in rural areas during 2023–24 is reported as 2.5%.

64.

$$\text{Total cost} = 10 \times 62 + 14 \times 50$$
$$= 620 + 700 = 1320$$
$$\text{Total weight} = 10 + 14 = 24$$
$$\text{Average price} = \frac{1320}{24} = 55.$$

65.

$$\text{Current} = 32.4 = 1.20 \times \text{Previous}$$
$$\text{Previous} = \frac{32.4}{1.2} = 27.$$

66. Smallest multiple of 7 > 31 = 35 = 7 × 5
Largest multiple of 7 < 240 = 238 = 7 × 34
Count = 34 – 5 + 1 = 30.

67. A = ÷, B = ×, C = +, D = –

$18 \div 18 - 27 + 4 \times 31$
$= 1 - 27 + 124 = 98.$

68. $P = 13475, R = 7.5, n = 2$

$$A = 13475\left(1 + \frac{7.5}{100}\right)^2$$
$$= 13475(1.075)^2$$
$$A = 13475 \times 1.155625$$
$$= 15572.05$$
$$CI = 15572.05 - 13475$$
$$= 2097.05 \approx 2097.$$

69.

$$CP = 23500 \times 0.76 = 17860$$
$$SP = 23500$$
$$\text{Profit} = 23500 - 17860 = 5640$$
$$\% \text{ Profit} = \frac{5640}{17860} \times 100 = 31.58\%.$$

70. Divisible by 8: 856 ÷ 8 = 107
Divisible by 3: 7 + A + 2 + 8 + 5 + 6 = 28 + A

$28 + A \equiv 0 \pmod 3$
$A \equiv 2 \pmod 3$
$A \in \{2, 5, 8\} \Rightarrow \min A = 2$

71. "visit" appears in both phrases, and the common code in both codes is "yy", so "visit" → "yy".

72. The four main Buddhist pilgrimage destinations are Lumbini, Bodh Gaya, Sarnath, and Kushinagar; Nalanda is not among these four.

73. Only one odd number is immediately preceded by an even number and immediately followed by an even number (the digit 5 between 8 and 6).

74. O → J, M → H, J → E, F → A is a shift of –5 letters each; applying –5 to A Y V R gives V T Q M.

75. The Amazon Rainforest is dominated by tropical evergreen (rain) forests.

76. With "Neither of these two options", the subject refers to "not one of the two", which is treated as singular in standard grammar. Therefore, the singular verb "was" is the correct improvement.

77. The idiom "a storm in a teacup" means making a big issue out of something small or trivial.

78. Sentence B correctly sets the context by introducing the character's mental state of unease and growing caution. Sentence A logically follows as a concrete action taken due to that unease, showing how he hid the journal. Sentence C then reflects his increasing paranoia and fear that the journal might be read, directly linked to both his unease and his action. Sentence D concludes the passage by presenting a specific sensory trigger—the imagined sound of footsteps—that explains and reinforces the fear and heightened awareness described earlier.

79. "Obscure" means unclear or hidden, while "apparent" means clear or obvious, making it the most appropriate antonym.

80. Since the day is described as long and tiring, "exhausted" best fits the context, indicating extreme tiredness.

81. The idiom "spill the beans" means to disclose a secret or reveal information that was meant to be kept confidential.

82. The sentence correctly uses the past perfect continuous tense ("had been walking") to show an action that began in the past (since dawn) and continued up to another point in the past ("He looked exhausted"). Since the main verb "looked" is in the simple past, using "has been walking" (present perfect continuous) would be grammatically incorrect here.

83. "Mitigate" means to make something less severe or reduce its impact; therefore, its most appropriate antonym is "worsen".

84. "Nobel Prize" is a specific, well-known prize, so the definite article "the" is correctly used before it.

85. This option forms a grammatically correct and logically ordered sentence with proper word placement and clear meaning.

86. This option arranges the words into a grammatically correct and meaningful sentence with proper subject–verb–object order and correct use of adverb and prepositional phrase.

87. A kleptomaniac is a person who has a compulsive urge to steal things even when they are not needed.

88. The correct spelling is dilemma (with double "m"), so "Dilema" is incorrectly spelt.

89. The correct spelling is mischievous, so "Mischievious" is incorrectly spelt.

90. A mortuary is a place where dead bodies are kept before burial or cremation.

91. After finishing baking and decorating the cake together, feeling "happy" best fits the positive context of enjoyment and satisfaction.

92. "Mia loves to bake in the kitchen" is the most natural and meaningful verb used with cakes and cooking activities.

93. "She makes a chocolate cake every weekend" fits logically and grammatically, as chocolate is a common type of cake.

94. Cakes are commonly decorated with colorful icing, making this the most appropriate word for decoration.

95. Sugar is added to the batter to make it sweet, which matches the meaning of the sentence correctly.

96. "Curiosity" means eagerness to know or learn; its most appropriate antonym in the passage's context is "indifference", which means lack of interest.

97. The passage clearly states that television offers programmes that entertain, educate, and inform viewers.

98. The passage emphasizes choosing good programmes and maintaining a balance between screen time and other productive activities.

99. The passage discusses television's benefits, drawbacks, and responsible usage in contemporary life, making this the most suitable title.

100. The passage presents facts, examples, and guidance about television use in a neutral and explanatory manner, without persuasion or negativity.

Previous Paper (Solved)

AIRPORTS AUTHORITY OF INDIA (AAI)
JUNIOR ASSISTANT (FIRE SERVICE)
Online Recruitment Exam, 2022*

1. Let $\Delta ABC \sim \Delta QPR$ and $\frac{\text{area of } \Delta ABC}{\text{area of } \Delta PQR} = \frac{64}{25}$.
If QP = 12 cm, PR = 10 cm and AC = 15 cm, then the length of AB is:
A. 12.8 cm B. 24 cm
C. 16 cm D. 19.2 cm

2. The sum of first 6 terms of an arithmetic progression is 0 and its 4th term is 2. If the sum of its first *n* terms is 1440, then the value of *n* is:
A. 30 B. 28
C. 36 D. 32

3. The cost of 3 pens and 5 pencils is ₹ 74. The cost of 5 pens and 7 pencils exceeds the cost of 4 pens and 3 pencils by ₹ 34. What is the cost of 2 pens and 9 pencils?
A. ₹ 50 B. ₹ 65
C. ₹ 70 D. ₹ 72

4. Which of the following have non-terminating decimal expansions?
(*a*) $\frac{987}{3150}$ (*b*) $\frac{54}{1125}$
(*c*) $\frac{133}{1680}$ (*b*) $\frac{19}{3125}$
A. (*a*) and (*c*) B. (*b*) and (*d*)
C. (*a*) and (*b*) D. (*a*) and (*d*)

5. The radii of the top and bottom circular faces of a bucket in the shape of a frustum of a cone are 35 cm and 28 cm, respectively. Its capacity is 187.88 litres. What is the height of the bucket?
$\left(\text{Take } \pi = \frac{22}{7}\right)$
A. 50 cm B. 80 cm
C. 45 cm D. 60 cm

6. In Δ ABC, ∠B = 135°, AB = $10\sqrt{2}$ cm and BC = 14 cm. What is the length of AC?
A. 26 cm B. $20\sqrt{2}$ cm
C. $24\sqrt{2}$ cm D. 28 cm

7. If $\sqrt{7}\sin\theta = 3\cos\theta$, $0° < \theta < 90°$, then the value of $\sqrt{9\,\text{cosec}^2\theta + 7\sec^2\theta}$ is:
A. $4\sqrt{2}$ B. 4
C. 2 D. $2\sqrt{2}$

8. If the ratio of the sums of the first 9 terms to the first 15 terms of an arithmetic progression is 9 : 25, then the ratio of the 9th term to the 15th term is:
A. 14 : 19 B. 3 : 5
C. 19 : 31 D. 17 : 29

9. In the given figure, in Δ PQR, PQ = 8 cm, ∠P = 90° and median PS is perpendicular to median QT at X. What is the length of QT?

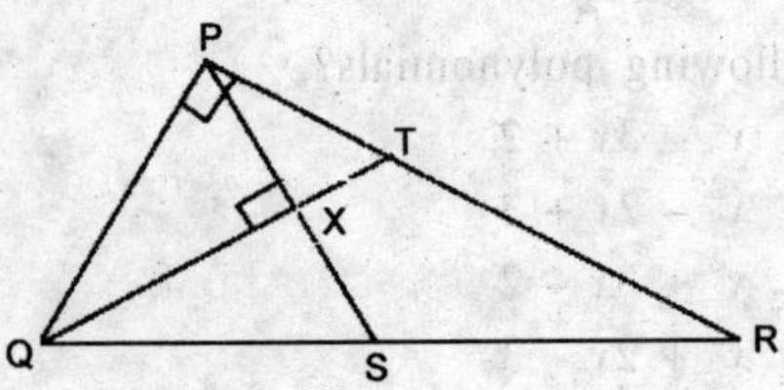

A. $4\sqrt{6}$ cm B. $6\sqrt{6}$ cm
C. $8\sqrt{3}$ cm D. $6\sqrt{3}$ cm

*Exam held on 15-11-2022.

10. The LCM of two numbers is 240 times their HCF, and the sum of their LCM and HCF is 17593. One of these two numbers, when divided by 125, the quotient is 8 and the remainder is 95. The other number is:

A. 1314 B. 1095
C. 1168 D. 1241

11. The weights (in g) of packets received in a post office in one day are given below. If the modal weight of the packets is 31.6 g, then what is the value of x?

Weight (in g)	16-22	22-28	28-34	34-40	40-46
Number of packets	13	16	25	x	20

A. 17 B. 18
C. 19 D. 21

12. The value of

$$\frac{(\sec\theta + \tan\theta)(1 - \sin\theta)}{\cot\theta(1 + \tan\theta + \sec\theta)(1 + \cot\theta - \operatorname{cosec}\theta)},$$

$0° < \theta < 90°$, is equal to:

A. $2 \sin \theta$ B. $\frac{1}{2}\sin\theta$
C. $\frac{1}{2}\cos\theta$ D. $\cos \theta$

13. If the points P(–2, 1), Q (α, β) and R(4, –1) are collinear and $\alpha - \beta = -3$, then the value of ($\alpha + \beta$) is:

A. 2 B. 1
C. 0 D. –1

14. If α and β, $\alpha > \beta$, are the zeroes of the polynomial $p(x) = 2x^2 - 5x + k$ such that $\alpha - \beta = -\frac{7}{2}$, then k is a zero of which of the following polynomials?

A. $x^2 - 3x + 2$
B. $x^2 - 2x + 3$
C. $x^2 + 3x - 2$
D. $x^2 + 2x - 3$

15. ABCD is a cyclic quadrilateral such that $\angle B = 112°$. The tangents at A and C meet at a point P. What is the measure of $\angle APC$?

A. 44° B. 42°
C. 68° D. 38°

16. In Δ ABC, AB = 12 cm, BC = 16 cm and AC = 20 cm. A circle is inscribed inside the triangle. What is the radius (in cm) of the circle?

A. 5 B. 6
C. 3 D. 4

17. Water is flowing at the rate of 1.68 km/h through a cylindrical pipe into a cylindrical tank, whose diameter of the base is 60 cm. If the water level in the tank rises by 2.1 m in 30 minutes, the internal radius of the pipe is (assuming no overflow):

A. 1.6 cm B. 1.8 cm
C. 1.2 cm D. 1.5 cm

18. A beam of white light passes through a glass prism and a spectrum is observed. The .... light bends the least.

A. violet B. yellow
C. blue D. red

19. How does the following organism reproduce?

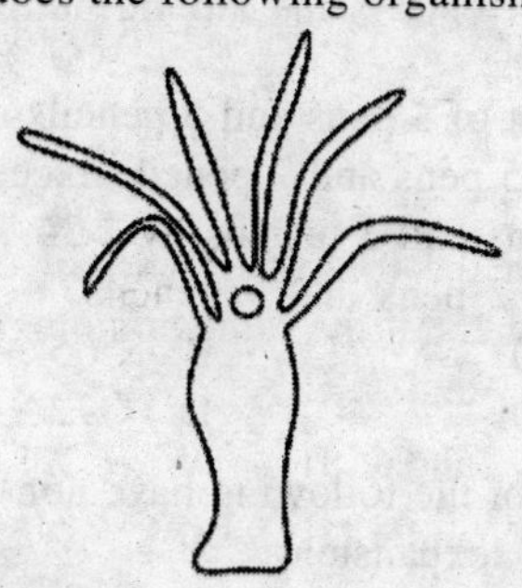

A. Sporulation B. Binary fission
C. Budding D. Multiple fission

20. In the modern periodic table, element 'X' belongs to a period for which $n = 4$ and element 'Y' belongs to a period for which $n = 2$, but both the elements belong to the same group. Which of the following statements is true about these elements?

A. 'X' and 'Y' are equally non-metallic
B. 'X' is more metallic than 'Y'
C. 'Y' is more metallic than 'X'
D. 'X' and 'Y' are equally metallic

21. A ray of light passes from the air (refractive index 1.00) to water (refractive index 1.33). The ratio (v_1/v_2) of the speed of light in the

air (v_1) to that in water (v_2) is .... and the ray bends .... the normal after refraction.

A. 1.33; away from B. 0.75; towards
C. 1.33; towards D. 0.75; away from

22. Which of the following practices is an example of 'Reuse' to protect and preserve our environment?

A. Using cloth bags instead of paper bags
B. Using mud cups instead of metal cups
C. Using paper straws for drinks instead of plastic straws
D. Using metal lunch box instead of plastic lunch box

23. How many moles of CO_2 are present in a gas jar containing 1.506×10^{23} molecules of carbon dioxide?

A. 2 B. 0.5
C. 0.25 D. 1

24. The atom of an element has 3 electrons in the M-shell. What is the atomic number of this element?

A. 13 B. 5
C. 10 D. 3

25. Which of the following pairs of compounds are members of the same homologous series?

A. C_9H_{18} and C_7H_{16}
B. C_9H_{20} and C_7H_{14}
C. C_9H_{20} and C_7H_{16}
D. C_9H_{16} and C_7H_{16}

26. An element 'X', when burnt in oxygen, forms a compound 'Z'. Solution of compound 'Z' in water turns blue litmus red. Which of the following is correct about 'X' and 'Z'?

A. 'X' is a non-metal and 'Z' is basic in nature
B. 'X' is a metal and 'Z' is basic in nature
C. 'X' is a non-metal and 'Z' is acidic in nature
D. 'X' is a metal and 'Z' is acidic in nature

27. Two resistors, each of 10 Ω are connected in parallel. The combination is connected in series to a third resistor of 10 Ω. The equivalent resistance of this arrangement is:

A. $\left[\frac{10}{3}\right]\Omega$ B. 15 Ω
C. $\left[\frac{20}{3}\right]\Omega$ D. 30 Ω

28. An object is placed at 15 cm in front of a concave mirror with a focal length of 20 cm. Following the new Cartesian sign convention, the image formed at v = ...

A. –60 cm B. +60 cm
C. $-\left(\frac{60}{7}\right)$ cm D. $+\left(\frac{60}{7}\right)$ cm

29. Consider the following statements about magnetic field at a point due to a current carrying straight conductor.

(*a*) It increases as the current in the conductor increases.
(*b*) It decreases as the distance of the point from the conductor increases.
(*c*) Its direction can be determined by 'Right-hand Thumb rule'.

Which of the statement(s) is/are correct?

A. Only (*a*)
B. Only (*b*)
C. All (*a*), (*b*) and (*c*)
D. Both (*a*) and (*b*)

30. In the following figure, which label points to a dendrite?

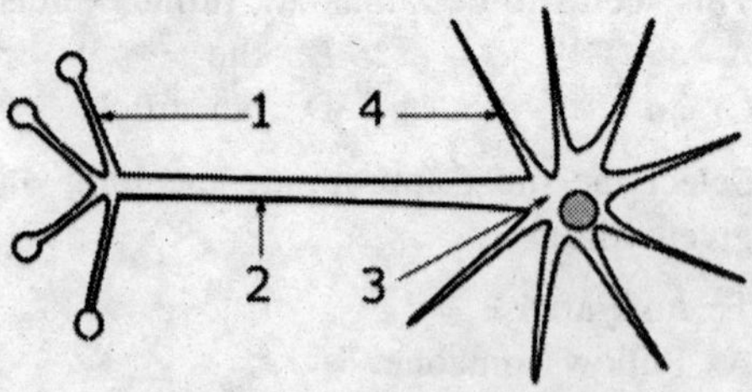

A. Arrow 4 B. Arrow 1
C. Arrow 3 D. Arrow 2

31. Identify the true statement.

A. An oxygen molecule is split by UV radiation, which then generates ozone molecules
B. Oxygen and ozone are both colourless and hence do not absorb any radiation

C. Oxygen and ozone can both absorb UV radiation to protect us from cancer
D. An ozone molecule is split by UV radiation, which then generates oxygen molecules

32. In an angiospermic flower, going from outside to inside, which of the following organs do we find in sequence?
A. Petals – Sepals – Stamens – Pistils
B. Leaves – Petals – Pistils – Stamens
C. Petals – Stamens – Sepals – Pistils
D. Sepals – Petals – Stamens – Pistils

33. The pH values of two solutions 'I' and 'II' are 8 and 10, respectively. Which of the following statements is true about these solutions?
A. 'II' is more acidic than 'I'
B. 'I' is more acidic than 'II'
C. 'I' is basic and 'II' is acidic
D. 'II' is more basic than 'I'

34. How can we know if two organs are homologous?
A. By comparing their functions
B. By comparing the appearance
C. By comparing the size
D. By comparing the anatomy

35. Select the most appropriate article to fill in the blank.

This seems to be .... futile exercise.

A. a　　B. the
C. an　　D. No article

36. Select the most appropriate meaning of the given Idiom.

To take after

A. Follow someone
B. Wait for something
C. Resemble someone
D. Borrow something

37. Select the most appropriate option to fill in the blank.

He usually .... to his office.

A. drove　　B. is driving
C. drive　　D. drives

38. Select the option that can be used as a one-word substitute for the given group of words.

A doctor who attends to bone problems.

A. Orthopaedist
B. Obstetrician
C. Ophthalmologist
D. Orthodontist

39. Sentences of a paragraph are given below in jumbled order. Arrange the sentences in the correct order to form a meaningful and coherent paragraph.

(*a*) He runs away to live with his friends to escape the tyranny of his guardian.
(*b*) The novel had a strong autobiographical element.
(*c*) It tells the story of an orphaned Anglo-Indian teenager.
(*d*) Ruskin bond started writing his first novel at the age of 17.

A. (*d*)(*b*)(*c*)(*a*)　　B. (*d*)(*c*)(*b*)(*a*)
C. (*c*)(*a*)(*d*)(*b*)　　D. (*b*)(*c*)(*d*)(*a*)

40. Select the most appropriate option to fill in the blank.

We need a .... ladder than this one to reach the top.

A. longer　　B. longest
C. long　　D. more long

41. Select the most appropriate option to fill in the blank.

He .... a picture of the Buddha in his living room.

A. hanged　　B. hung
C. hang　　D. had hanged

42. Select the most appropriate article to fill in the blank.

She is .... only student in the class who can speak five languages.

A. the　　B. No article
C. an　　D. a

43. Select the most appropriate meaning of the given idiom.

Give it a shot

A. Give a chance to someone
B. Try to do something
C. Give orders
D. Shoot someone

44. Select the most appropriate ANTONYM of the given word.

Caution

A. Watchfulness B. Rashness
C. Restraint D. Attention

45. Select the most appropriate option to fill in the blank.

Chew your food .... for proper digestion.

A. noisily B. slowly
C. softly D. strongly

46. Select the most appropriate synonym of the given word.

Arrogant

A. Humble B. Haughty
C. Hasty D. Hungry

47. Select the option that can be used as a one-word substitute for the given group of words.

People who work together in an organisation.

A. Colleagues B. Companions
C. Collaborators D. Comperes

Directions (Qs. No. 48-50): *Read the given passage and answer the questions that follow.*

The worst days of any summer are the rainy ones. We spend all year looking forward to nice weather and long, hot days. All of winter, with its dreary grey days and bitter cold, we dream of those endless days at the beach, laying on the sand and soaking in the bright and burning sun. And then, summer comes, and it rains.

As a child, I would wake up to rainy summer days and come close to crying. It wasn't fair. We suffered through months of school and miserable weather for those scant ten weeks of freedom and balmy weather. Any day that I could not spend at the beach or playing ball with my friends seemed like a punishment for something I didn't even do. On those rainy summer days, I had nothing to do and could only sit inside, staring out at the rain like a Dickensian orphan. I was an only child, so there was no one else to play with.

My father worked from home, so I was not truly alone, but he could not actively play with me since he was technically at work. It was those days that I would resign myself to whatever was on television or any books that I could find lying around. I'd crawl through the day and pray each night that the rain would not be there the next day.

48. '... staring out at the rain like a Dickensian orphan'. What feelings of the narrator are conveyed by this comparison?

A. Misery B. Curiosity
C. Fear D. Anger

49. Which of the following statements is NOT true?

A. The narrator prayed for a clear day with no rain.
B. The narrator passed his time watching TV or reading when it was raining outside.
C. The pleasant weather lasts for only ten days, according to the narrator.
D. Rain plays the spoilsport on summer days.

50. Why does the narrator look forward to summer?

A. To soak in the rain
B. To relax indoors
C. To enjoy at the beach
D. To walk in scorching heat

51. In which of the following months, a leftover piece of a rocket hit the lunar surface and created a new crater on the Moon that may be up to 65 feet wide?

A. March 2022 B. December 2021
C. January 2022 D. February 2022

52. In February 2022, the Union Cabinet permitted up to .... foreign direct investment (FDI) under automatic route in Life Insurance Corporation of India (LIC).

A. 15% B. 10%
C. 25% D. 20%

53. Smart Cities Mission was launched by Prime Minister Narendra Modi in the year:

A. 2017 B. 2018
C. 2016 D. 2015

54. Sayyid dynasty ruled in India between:
A. 1390 AD and 1406 AD
B. 1414 AD and 1451 AD
C. 1380 AD and 1440 AD
D. 1406 AD and 1490 AD

55. In March 2022, who among the following players broke Kapil Dev's 36-year old record for most runs at number 7?
A. David Warner B. Neil Wagner
C. Chris Gayle D. Ravindra Jadeja

56. 'Namami Gange Programme', is an integrated conservation mission, approved as 'Flagship Programme' by the Union Government in June 2014 with budget outlay of .... Crores.
A. ₹ 20,000 B. ₹ 15,000
C. ₹ 25,000 D. ₹ 10,000

57. Slave dynasty ruled in India between:
A. 1201 AD and 1304 AD
B. 1206 AD and 1290 AD
C. 1190 AD and 1260 AD
D. 1160 AD and 1201 AD

58. Vilayat Khan was known for which of the following musical instruments?
A. Sarangi B. Sahnai
C. Sitar D. Tabla

59. Who is the chairman of the Inter-State-Council as per the present composition?
A. Vice President of India
B. Home Minister
C. President of India
D. Prime Minister

60. Which of the following technologies was invented by Jaap Haartsen?
A. WiMAX B. Bluetooth
C. 3G D. 4G

61. Task Force on "Projections of Minimum Needs and Effective Consumption Demand" which was headed by Dr. Y K. Alagh was constituted in the year ....
A. 1977 B. 1978
C. 1980 D. 1979

62. Which of the following articles of the Indian Constitution deals with the abolition of untouchability?
A. 16 B. 15
C. 18 D. 17

63. Ancient city Harappa is located in which of the following provinces of Pakistan?
A. Khyber Pakhtunkhwa
B. Punjab
C. Balochistan
D. Sindh

64. In 2022, on which of the following dates did Virat Kohli play his 100th Test?
A. 2nd March B. 3rd March
C. 5th March D. 4th March

65. In which of the following years did the Ministry of Environment and Forests, Government of India, constitute a Committee on 'Prevention of Illegal Trade in Wildlife and Wildlife Products'?
A. 1994 B. 1995
C. 1997 D. 1996

66. Which of the following animals is NOT an amphibian?
A. Salamanders B. Python
C. Caecilian D. Frogs

67. Mehmet Ilker Ayci, who was named as the new Air India CEO-MD, and later declined the position, was from which country?
A. Iran B. UAE
C. Turkey D. Chechnya

68. In a certain code language:
'A + B' means 'A is the daughter of B'
'A – B' means 'A is the sister of B'
'A × B' means 'A is the brother of B'
'A & B' means 'A is the son of B'
Based on the above, how is S related to V if 'R – S & Q × T + V'?
A. Son B. Brother's son
C. Brother D. Son's son

69. Select the combination of letters that when sequentially placed in the blanks of the given series will complete the series.
S _ P K_ _ P _ S L _ K S _ _ K
A. KLKPPK B. KLSPLK
C. LSLKPLP D. SLSKPLP

70. Read the given statements and conclusions carefully. Find out which of the given conclusions is/are true based on the statements.

Statements: $A \leq M < R = S$

$T > M$

$T \geq U$

Conclusions: I. $A < U$

II. $U < M$

A. Neither conclusion I nor II is true
B. Both conclusions I and II are true
C. Only conclusion II is true
D. Only conclusion I is true

71. In a certain code language, 'ANT' is written as 35, and 'ZEBRA' is written as 52. How will 'OCTOPUS' be written in that language?

A. 98 B. 86
C. 72 D. 109

72. Select the option that is related to the fifth letter-cluster in the same way as the first letter-cluster is related to the second letter-cluster and the third letter-cluster is related to the fourth letter-cluster.

JRPI : FPLG :: WFPM : SDLK :: TIWO : ?

A. PGSM B. QGSM
C. PGTM D. PHSN

73. Six friends Anoop, Kailash, Vikas, Darshit, Eshan and Lalit live on different floors of a six-floor building, having floor numbers from 1 to 6. The lowermost floor is numbered 1, the floor above it is numbered 2, and so on. Only two friends live above Vikas's floor and only four friends live below Darshit's floor. Only Anoop lives between the floors of Kailash and Eshan.

Who lives on the 6th floor?

A. Lalit B. Kailash
C. Vikas D. Eshan

74. What approximate value should come in place of the question mark (?) in the following expression?

$7.999^{3.001} + 3.001^{1.999} + 19.002 = ?$

A. 534 B. 568
C. 540 D. 520

75. Three of the following four number-triads follow a certain rule/logic/relation and therefore are alike in a certain way. Select the ODD one out from the given options.

A. (48, 56, 208) B. (36, 54, 180)
C. (22, 48, 140) D. (44, 62, 214)

76. Read the given statements and conclusions carefully. Assuming that the information given in the statements is true, even if it appears to be at variance with commonly known facts, decide which of the given conclusions logically follow(s) from the statements.

Statements: Some mobiles are watches.

All watches are clocks.

All mobiles are pen drives.

Conclusions: I. Some clocks are mobiles.

II. All pen drives are watches.

A. Only conclusion II follows
B. Neither conclusion I nor II follows
C. Both conclusions I and II follow
D. Only conclusion I follows

77. Select the correct mirror image of the given figure when the mirror is placed at 'AB' as shown.

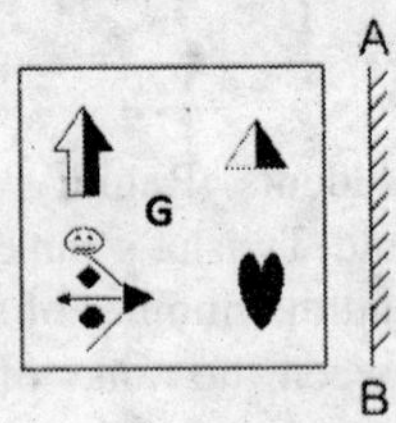

A. 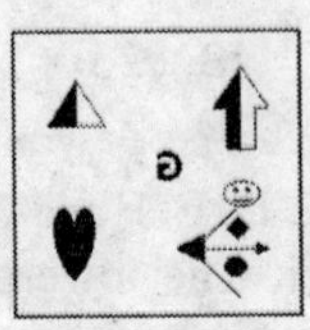

B. 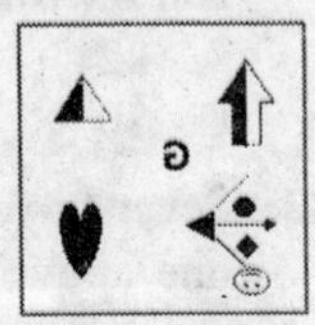

C. 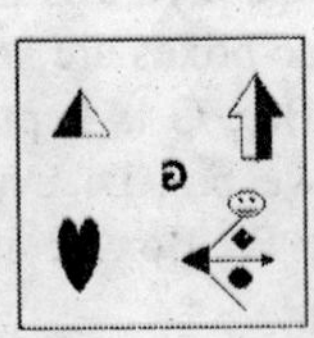

D. 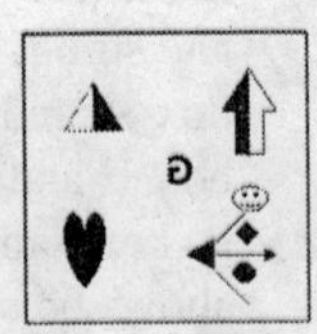

78. Select the option that is related to the fifth letter-cluster in the same way as the first letter-cluster is related to the second letter-cluster and the third letter-cluster is related to the fourth letter-cluster.

NTLG : UOHM :: PGUR : HQSV :: HTPM : ?

A. UKNR B. VIQN
C. UINQ D. UJQN

79. Which two signs should be interchanged to make the following equation correct?

$143 + 13 - 8 \div 2 \times 5 = 13$

A. + and × B. ÷ and +
C. ÷ and × D. − and +

80. Select the figure from among the given options that can replace the question mark (?) in the following series.

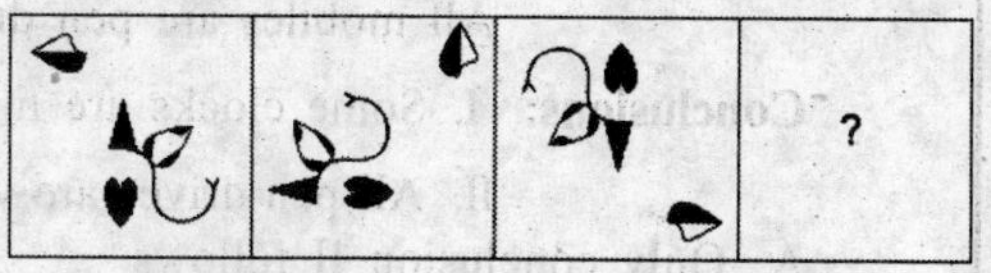

A.  B. 

C.  D. 

81. In a class of 48 students, Ragini's rank is 12th from the top and Twisha's rank is 14th from the bottom. Find the number of students whose ranks lie between the ranks of Ragini and Twisha.

A. 22 B. 23
C. 20 D. 21

82. Seven boxes A, B, C, D, E, F and G are placed one above the other. The lowermost box is numbered 1, the box above it is numbered 2, and so on. Only three boxes are kept between box A and box F. Box G is kept just below box F and just above box D. Only one box is kept above box B. Box C is kept just above box E.

Which box is kept at the middle position?

A. Box E B. Box F
C. Box C D. Box G

83. Select the number from among the given options that can replace the question mark (?) in the following series:

148, 149, 153, 162, ?

A. 178 B. 176
C. 172 D. 182

84. Six friends Kriss, Donald, Mac, John, Farhan and Romio are sitting around a circular table facing towards the center. Romio is sitting third to the right of Donald. Kriss and Mac are not immediate neighbours of Romio. Kriss is sitting to the immediate left of John.

Who is sitting third to the left of Kriss?

A. Farhan B. Romio
C. Mac D. Donald

85. Select the most appropriate option to fill in the blank.

The patient was complaining .... pain in the chest.

A. from B. for
C. against D. of

86. Select the most appropriate option to fill in the blank.

She was tired as she .... alone since morning.

A. was working
B. has been working
C. had been working
D. worked

87. Select the most appropriate option to fill in the blank.

The children sat indoors .... while it was raining.

A. gloomily B. slowly
C. hastily D. cleverly

88. Select the option that can be used as a one-word substitute for the given group of words.

Main character in a story or play

A. Idol B. Antagonist
C. Protagonist D. Model

89. Sentences of a paragraph are given below in jumbled order. Arrange the sentences in the correct order to form a meaningful and coherent paragraph.

(*a*) It helps in the balanced development of a person's mind, body and soul.

(*b*) Yoga is derived from the Sanskrit word 'Yuj'.

(*c*) It is not merely the art of body-postures but a scientific a way of living.

(*d*) It means to connect with the universe around.

A. (*c*)(*a*)(*b*)(*d*) B. (*b*)(*d*)(*c*)(*a*)
C. (*b*)(*a*)(*c*)(*d*) D. (*d*)(*b*)(*a*)(*c*)

90. Select the most appropriate synonym of the given word.

Deface

A. Deride B. Deform
C. Degrade D. Deplete

91. Select the most appropriate ANTONYM of the given word.

Valid

A. Lawful B. Good
C. False D. Right

92. Select the most appropriate meaning of the given proverb.

Penny wise pound foolish

A. Saving small sums is beneficial in the long run
B. Saving every penny leads to wealth creation
C. Stingy with small amounts but wasteful with large sums
D. Wise people do not spend money on foolish things

93. Select the most appropriate meaning of the given idiom.

Once in a blue moon

A. Monthly B. Rarely
C. Often D. Daily

94. Select the option that can be used as a one-word substitute for the given group of words.

Something which is no longer in use

A. Extinct B. Obscure
C. Obsolete D. Extinguished

95. Select the most appropriate option to fill in the blank.

Why are you .... an umbrella today?

A. carry B. carried
C. carries D. carrying

Directions (Qs. No. 96-100): *Read the given passage and answer the questions that follow.*

The sage of science, Einstein, was sitting in a pensive mood one evening. His eyes were brimming with tears. The pain was evident on his face. He peeped out of the window of his room. The sun had set a few minutes back. The sky was filled with a reddish glow. At this sunset, he felt that it was humanity that had sunk into devilish darkness and the reddish glow in the sky was the blood of humanity spilling all over the sky from earth. With tired steps, he walked back to his chair and settled down. It was the 9th of August 1945. Three days back, he had been torn apart when he had heard on the radio that America had dropped an atom bomb on the Japanese city, Hiroshima. Today, within three days, another bomb was dropped on another city, Nagasaki; and, lakhs of people had been killed.

He had heard that the blast released so much energy that it had paled all past destructions in comparison and death had played out a pitiable dance of destruction. The flames that broke out of the bomb were burning, melting and exploding buildings. Scared of the heat of the bomb, people had jumped into lakes and rivers, but the water was boiling, and the people too were burnt and killed. The animals in the water were already boiled to death. Animals, trees, herbs, fragrant flowering plants were all turned into ashes. The atomic energy destruction had just not stopped there. It had entered the atmosphere there and had spread radiation that would affect people for generations to come and would also ring about destructive irreversible biological changes in animals and plants.

As the news of the atomic attack reached Einstein, and he became aware of the glaring horror of the abuse of atomic energy, his distress and restlessness knew no bounds. He could not control

himself and picked up his violin to turn his mind on to other things. While playing the violin, his heart was filled with an ocean of agony and tears just continued streaming uncontrollably out of his eyes.

96. Which of the following statements does NOT depict the destruction caused by the atom bomb?
A. Burning and exploding buildings
B. Boiling of the lakes and rivers
C. Darkness descending from the sky
D. Animals and plants reduced to ashes

97. Select the most appropriate meaning of 'pensive' as used in the passage.
A. Aggressive B. Shocked
C. Thoughtful D. Restless

98. What did Einstein associate the red glow in the sky with?
A. The blast of bombs
B. The setting sun
C. The agony of war
D. The blood of humanity

99. What had shattered Einstein on the 6th of August 1945?
A. The bombing of all Japanese cities
B. The bombing of Nagasaki
C. The bombing of America
D. The bombing of Hiroshima

100. Einstein was horrified at the:
A. sudden rise in temperatures
B. environmental pollution
C. abuse of atomic energy
D. biological changes in animals

ANSWERS

1	2	3	4	5	6	7	8	9	10
D	A	D	A	D	A	A	D	A	C
11	**12**	**13**	**14**	**15**	**16**	**17**	**18**	**19**	**20**
C	B	D	D	A	D	D	D	C	B
21	**22**	**23**	**24**	**25**	**26**	**27**	**28**	**29**	**30**
C	A	C	A	C	C	B	B	C	A
31	**32**	**33**	**34**	**35**	**36**	**37**	**38**	**39**	**40**
A	D	D	D	A	C	D	A	A	A
41	**42**	**43**	**44**	**45**	**46**	**47**	**48**	**49**	**50**
B	A	B	B	B	B	A	A	C	C
51	**52**	**53**	**54**	**55**	**56**	**57**	**58**	**59**	**60**
A	D	D	B	D	A	B	C	D	B
61	**62**	**63**	**64**	**65**	**66**	**67**	**68**	**69**	**70**
A	D	B	D	A	B	C	D	C	A
71	**72**	**73**	**74**	**75**	**76**	**77**	**78**	**79**	**80**
D	A	A	C	D	D	A	C	B	B
81	**82**	**83**	**84**	**85**	**86**	**87**	**88**	**89**	**90**
A	A	A	A	D	C	A	C	B	B
91	**92**	**93**	**94**	**95**	**96**	**97**	**98**	**99**	**100**
C	C	B	C	D	C	C	D	D	C

EXPLANATORY ANSWERS

1. $\because \Delta ABC \sim \Delta QPR$

$$\frac{\text{ar } \Delta ABC}{\text{ar } \Delta PQR} = \frac{AB^2}{PQ^2} = \frac{BC^2}{QR^2} = \frac{AC^2}{PR^2}$$

$$\Rightarrow \quad \frac{64}{25} = \frac{AB^2}{12^2}$$

$$\Rightarrow \quad \left(\frac{8}{5}\right)^2 = \left(\frac{AB}{12}\right)^2$$

$$\Rightarrow \quad \frac{8}{5} = \frac{AB}{12}$$

$$\Rightarrow \quad AB = \frac{96}{5}$$

$$\Rightarrow \quad AB = 19.2 \text{ cm}$$

Hence, the length of AB = 19.2 cm.

2. $\because$ 4th term of A.P. = 2

$\Rightarrow \quad a + 3d = 2$

$\Rightarrow \quad a = 2 - 3d \quad$ ...(*i*)

Again sum of 6th term = 0

$$\Rightarrow \quad 0 = \frac{6}{2}\{2a + (6-1)d\}$$

$\Rightarrow \quad 0 = 3\{2a + 5d\}$

$\Rightarrow \quad 2a + 5d = 0$

$\Rightarrow \quad 2a = -5d$

$$\Rightarrow \quad a = \frac{-5d}{2} \quad \text{...}(ii)$$

From (*i*) and (*ii*)

$$2 - 3d = \frac{-5d}{2}$$

$\Rightarrow \quad d = 4$

$a = -10$

$$1440 = \frac{n}{2}\{2a + (n-1)d\}$$

$\Rightarrow \quad 2 \times 1440 = n\{-20 + (n-1)4\}$

$= n\{4n - 24\}$

$\Rightarrow \quad 2880 = 4n^2 - 24n$

$\Rightarrow 4n^2 - 24n - 2880 = 0$

$\Rightarrow n^2 - 6n - 720 = 0$

$\Rightarrow n^2 - 30n + 24n - 720 = 0$

$\Rightarrow n(n - 30) + 24(n - 30) = 0$

$\Rightarrow (n - 30) + (n + 24) = 0$

$\Rightarrow n = 30$ or $n = -24$

$\therefore n = 30.$

3. $\because 3x + 5y =$ ₹ 74 $\quad$ ...(*i*)]×1

$5x + 7y - (4x + 3y) =$ ₹ 34

$\Rightarrow x + 4y = 34 \quad$ ...(*ii*)]×3

$$\begin{array}{r} 3x + 5y = 74 \\ 3x + 12y = 102 \\ - \quad - \quad - \\ \hline 7y = 28 \end{array}$$

$\Rightarrow y = 4, x = 18$

$2x + 9y = 2 \times 18 + 9 \times 4$

$= 36 + 36$

$= 72$

Hence, the cost of 2 pens and 9 pencils = ₹ 72.

4. (*a*) $\frac{987}{3150} = 0.31333...$

(*b*) $\frac{54}{1125} = 0.048$

(*c*) $\frac{133}{1680} = 0.0791666...$

(*d*) $\frac{19}{3125} = 0.00608$

Hence, (*a*) and (*c*) have non-terminating decimal expansions.

5. Volume of frustum $= \frac{1}{3}\pi h(R^2 + Rr + r^2)$

$$\Rightarrow \frac{18788}{100} \times 1000 \text{ cm}^3$$

$$= \frac{1}{3} \times \frac{22}{7} \times h(1225 + 980 + 784)$$

$$\Rightarrow h = \frac{18788 \times 210}{22 \times 2989} = \frac{3945480}{65758} = 60$$

Hence, height of the bucket = 60 cm.

6.

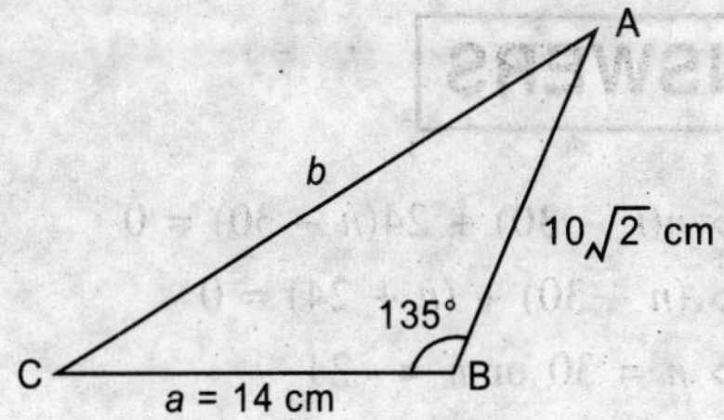

We have, $\cos B = \dfrac{a^2 + c^2 - b^2}{2ac}$

$$\Rightarrow \cos 135° = \frac{(14)^2 + \left(10\sqrt{2}\right)^2 - b^2}{2 \times 14 \times 10\sqrt{2}}$$

$$\Rightarrow -\frac{1}{\sqrt{2}} = \frac{196 + 200 - b^2}{280\sqrt{2}}$$

$\Rightarrow -280 = 196 + 200 - b^2$

$\Rightarrow -280 = 396 - b^2$

$\Rightarrow b^2 = 396 + 280 = 676$

$\Rightarrow b = 26$

Hence, the length of AC = 26 cm.

7. $\sqrt{7}\sin\theta = 3\cos\theta$

$$\frac{\sin\theta}{\cos\theta} = \frac{3}{\sqrt{7}}$$

$$\Rightarrow \quad \tan\theta = \frac{3}{\sqrt{7}}$$

$$\tan^2\theta = \frac{9}{7}$$

$$1 + \tan^2\theta = 1 + \frac{9}{7} = \frac{16}{7}$$

$$\sec^2\theta = \frac{16}{7}$$

$\Rightarrow \quad 7\sec^2\theta = 16$ ...(*i*)

$$\frac{\cos\theta}{\sin\theta} = \frac{\sqrt{7}}{3}$$

$$\Rightarrow \quad \cot\theta = \frac{\sqrt{7}}{3}$$

$$\cot^2\theta = \frac{7}{9}$$

$$1 + \cot^2\theta = 1 + \frac{7}{9} = \frac{16}{9}$$

$9\,\text{cosec}^2\theta = 16$ ...(*ii*)

Adding (*i*) and (*ii*)

$9\,\text{cosec}^2\,\theta + 7\sec^2\,\theta = 32$

$$\sqrt{9\,\text{cosec}^2\theta + 7\sec^2\theta} = \sqrt{32} = 4\sqrt{2}$$

Hence, the value of $\sqrt{9\,\text{cosec}^2\theta + 7\sec^2\theta}$

$= 4\sqrt{2}$

8. Let first term = a

and common difference = d

$$S_9 = \frac{9}{2}[2a + (9-1)d]$$

$$S_{15} = \frac{15}{2}[2a + (15-1)d]$$

$$\frac{\frac{9}{2}[2a + (8)d]}{\frac{15}{2}[2a + (14)d]} = \frac{3^2}{5^2}$$

$$\Rightarrow \quad \frac{2a + 8d}{2a + 14d} = \frac{3}{5}$$

$[10a + 40d = 6a + 42d]$

$\Rightarrow \quad 4a = 2d$

$\Rightarrow \quad d = 2a$

$$\therefore \quad \frac{T_9}{T_{15}} = \frac{a + (9-1)d}{a + (15-1)d}$$

$$= \frac{a + 8d}{a + 14d}$$

$$= \frac{a + 8(2a)}{a + 14(2a)}$$

$$= \frac{a + 16a}{a + 28a}$$

$$= \frac{17a}{29a}$$

$= 17 : 29$

Hence, the ratio of the 9th term to the 15th term = 17 : 29.

10. Let HCF = x

$\therefore$ LCM = $240x$

Sum of LCM + HCF = 17593

$\Rightarrow 240x + x = 17593$

$\Rightarrow 241x = 17593$

$\Rightarrow x = \frac{17593}{241} = 73$

$\therefore$ HCF = 73

LCM = 17593 − 73

= 17520

One number = 125 × 8 + 95

= 1095

$\therefore$ Other number = $\frac{\text{LCM} \times \text{HCF}}{\text{One number}}$

$= \frac{17520 \times 73}{1095}$

= 1168.

12. $$\frac{\left(\frac{1}{\cos\theta}+\frac{\sin\theta}{\cos\theta}\right)(1-\sin\theta)}{\frac{\cos\theta}{\sin\theta}\left(1+\frac{\sin\theta}{\cos\theta}+\frac{1}{\cos\theta}\right)\left(1+\frac{\cos\theta}{\sin\theta}-\frac{1}{\sin\theta}\right)}$$

$$= \frac{\left(\frac{1+\sin\theta}{\cos\theta}\right)(1-\sin\theta)}{\frac{\cos\theta}{\sin\theta}\left(1+\frac{\cos\theta+\sin\theta+1}{\cos\theta}\right)\left(1+\frac{\sin\theta+\cos\theta-1}{\sin\theta}\right)}$$

$$= \frac{\frac{\cos^2\theta}{\cos\theta}}{\frac{\cos\theta}{\sin\theta}\left[\frac{(\cos\theta+\sin\theta)^2-(1)^2}{\cos\theta.\sin\theta}\right]}$$

$$= \frac{\cos\theta}{\frac{\cos\theta}{\sin\theta}\left[\frac{\cos^2\theta+\sin^2\theta+2\cos\theta.\sin\theta-1}{\cos\theta.\sin\theta}\right]}$$

$$= \frac{\cos\theta}{\frac{\cos\theta}{\sin\theta}\left[\frac{2\sin\theta.\cos\theta}{\cos\theta.\sin\theta}\right]}$$

$$= \frac{\cos\theta \times \sin\theta}{2\cos\theta}$$

$$= \frac{1}{2}\sin\theta.$$

13. $\because$ Points P(−2, 1), Q(α, β), R(4, −1) are collinear

$\therefore$ Area of triangle = 0

Area of triangle

$$= \frac{1}{2}[x_1(y_2-y_3)+x_2(y_3-y_1)+x_3(y_1-y_2)]$$

$$\Rightarrow 0 = \frac{1}{2}[-2(\beta+1)+\alpha(-1-1)+4(1-\beta)]$$

$\Rightarrow 0 = [-2\beta - 2 - 2\alpha + 4 - 4\beta]$

$\Rightarrow 0 = -2\alpha - 6\beta + 2$

$\Rightarrow 0 = -2(\alpha + 3\beta - 1)$

$\Rightarrow \alpha + 3\beta = 1$

$\alpha - \beta = -3$

− + +

$4\beta = 4$

$\Rightarrow \beta = 1$

$\alpha = -3 + \beta$

$\alpha = -3 + 1$

$= -2$

$\therefore$ Value of $\alpha + \beta = -2 + 1 = -1$.

14. $2x^2 - 5x + k = 0$

$$\Rightarrow \alpha + \beta = -\left(\frac{-5}{2}\right)$$

$$= \frac{5}{2}$$

$$\Rightarrow \alpha \times \beta = \frac{k}{2}$$

$\because (\alpha - \beta)^2 = (\alpha + \beta)^2 - 4\alpha\beta$

$$\left(\frac{-7}{2}\right) = \left(\frac{5}{2}\right)^2 - 4\left(\frac{k}{2}\right)$$

$$\Rightarrow \frac{49}{4} = \frac{25}{4} - 2k$$

$$\Rightarrow 2k = \frac{25}{4} - \frac{49}{4}$$

$$= \frac{-24}{4}$$

$$= -6$$

$$\Rightarrow \quad k = -3$$

Hence, the required polynomial is $x^2 + 2x - 3$.

15.

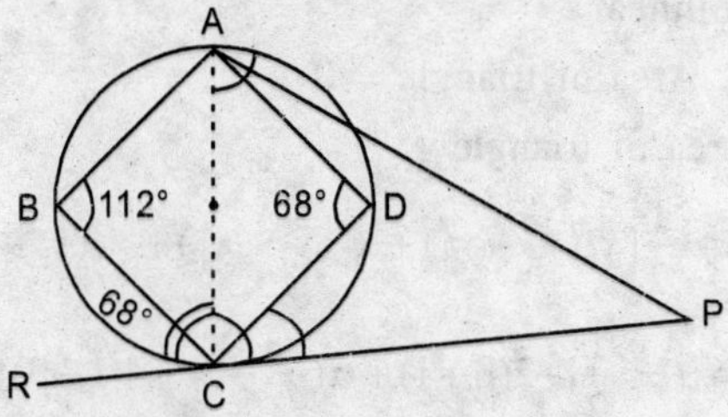

$\because$ ABCD is cyclic

$\therefore$ $\angle A + \angle C = 180°$ and $\angle B + \angle D = 180°$

In Δ ABC,

$$\angle A + \angle C + \angle P = 180°$$

$$\Rightarrow 68° + 68° + \angle P = 180°$$

$$\Rightarrow \quad 136° + \angle P = 180°$$

$$\Rightarrow \quad \angle P = 180° - 136°$$

$$= 44°$$

Hence, $\angle APC = 44°$.

16.

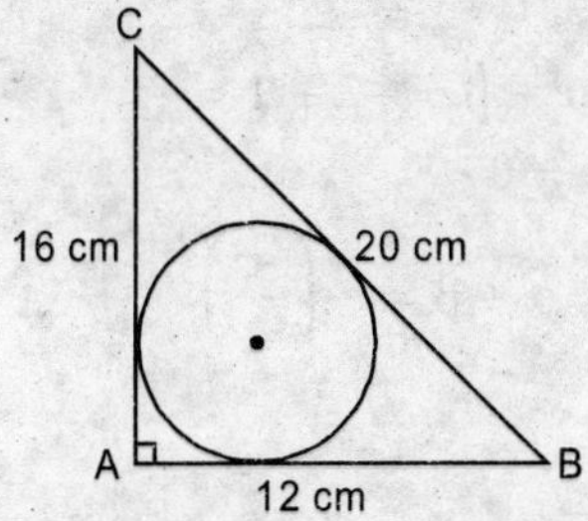

Area of triangle ABC $= \frac{1}{2} \times 12 \times 16 = 96 \text{ cm}^2$

$$S = \frac{a+b+c}{2}$$

$$= \frac{12+16+20}{2}$$

$$= \frac{48}{2}$$

$$= 24 \text{ cm}$$

Radius of the circle $= \dfrac{\text{area of } \Delta}{\text{semiperimeter of } \Delta}$

$$= \frac{96}{24}$$

$$= 4 \text{ cm.}$$

17. Volume of pipe = Volume of tank

$$\Rightarrow \pi r^2 h = \pi R^2 H$$

$$\Rightarrow r^2 \times h = R^2 \times H$$

$$\Rightarrow r^2 \times \frac{168}{100} \times \frac{1000}{60 \times 60} = 30 \times 30 \times \frac{21}{10 \times 30 \times 60}$$

$$\Rightarrow r^2 = \frac{9 \times 21}{180} \times \frac{360}{168}$$

$$\Rightarrow r^2 = \frac{9 \times 21 \times 2}{168} = \frac{9}{4}$$

$$\Rightarrow r = \frac{3}{2} = 1.5 \text{ cm}$$

Hence, radius of the pipe = 1.5 cm.

68. In a certain code language:

'A + B' means 'A is the daughter of B'
'A – B' means 'A is the sister of B'
'A × B' means 'A is the brother of B'
'A & B' means 'A is the son of B'

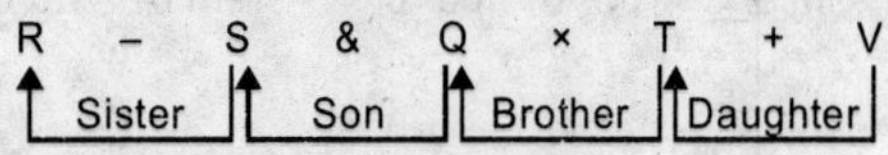

Hence, S related to V as Son's son.

69. S L P K S L P K S L P K S L P K

Hence, LSLKPLP will be written in the blank space then the given series will complete the series: SLPK, SLPK, SLPK, ...

71. Given,

A N T
↓ ↓ ↓
1 14 20 → Position is English alphabet

1 + 14 + 20 = 35

and

Z E B R A
↓ ↓ ↓ ↓ ↓
26 5 2 18 1

26 + 5 + 2 + 18 + 1 = 52

Similarly,

O C T O P U S

↓ ↓ ↓ ↓ ↓ ↓ ↓

15 3 20 15 16 21 19

$15 + 3 + 20 + 15 + 16 + 21 + 19 = 109$

72. Given,

J R P I

–4↓ –2↓ –4↓ –2↓

F P L G

and

W F P M

–4↓ –2↓ –4↓ –2↓

S D L K

Similarly,

T I W O

–4↓ –2↓ –4↓ –2↓

P G S M

Hence, PGSM will come at the place of question mark.

73.

6th	Lalit
5th	Dakshit
4th	Vikas
3rd	Kailash
2nd	Anup
1st	Eshan

Clearly, Lalit lives on the 6th floor.

74. Approximate value of

$7.999^{3.001} + 3.001^{1.999} + 19.002$

$= (8)^3 + (3)^2 + 19$

$= 512 + 9 + 19$

$= 540.$

75. (A) (48, 56, 208)

$48 + 56 = 104 \times 2 = 208$

(B) (36, 54, 180)

$36 + 54 = 90 \times 2 = 180$

(C) (22, 48, 140)

$22 + 48 = 70 \times 2 = 140$

(D) (44, 62, 214)

$44 + 62 = 106 \times 2 = 212$

(44 62 214) is unlike

Hence, option (D) is odd one out.

78. Given,

N T L G

↓ ↓ ↓ ↓

14 20 12 7 → Position is English alphabet

$14 + 20 + 12 + 7 = 53$

or U O H M

↓ ↓ ↓ ↓

21 15 8 13

$21 + 15 + 8 + 13 = 57$

Difference $= 57 - 53 = 4$

and

P G U R

↓ ↓ ↓ ↓

16 7 21 18

$16 + 7 + 21 + 18 = 62$

or H Q S V

↓ ↓ ↓ ↓

8 17 19 22

$8 + 17 + 19 + 22 = 66$

Difference $= 66 - 62 = 4$

Similarly,

H T P M

↓ ↓ ↓ ↓

8 20 16 13

$8 + 20 + 16 + 13 = 57$

or U I N Q

↓ ↓ ↓ ↓

21 9 14 17

$21 + 9 + 14 + 17 = 61$

Difference $= 61 - 57 = 4$

Hence, UINQ will come at the place of question mark.

79. $143 + 13 - 8 \div 2 \times 5 = 13$

$143 \div 13 - 8 + 2 \times 5$

$= 11 - 8 + 10$

$= 21 - 8$

$= 13$

Hence, two signs ÷ and + should be interchanged, then the equation is correct.

81.

Total no. of students = 48

Hence, no. of students whose rank lie between the ranks of Ragini and Twisha

$= 48 - (12 + 14)$

$= 48 - 26$

$= 22.$

82.

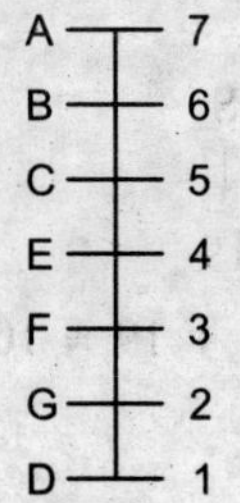

Clearly, box E is kept at the middle position.

83.

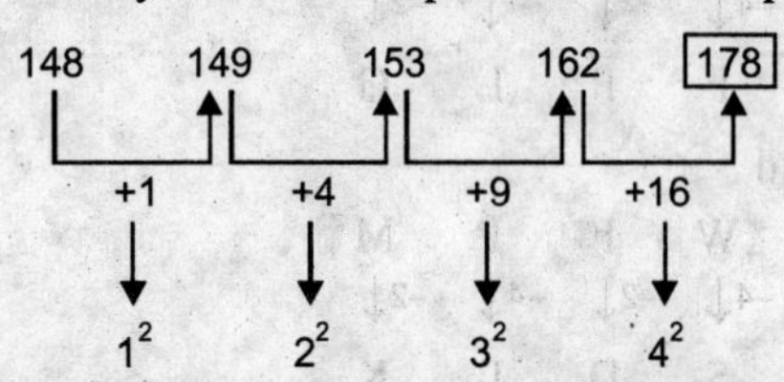

Hence, 178 will come at the place of question mark.

84.

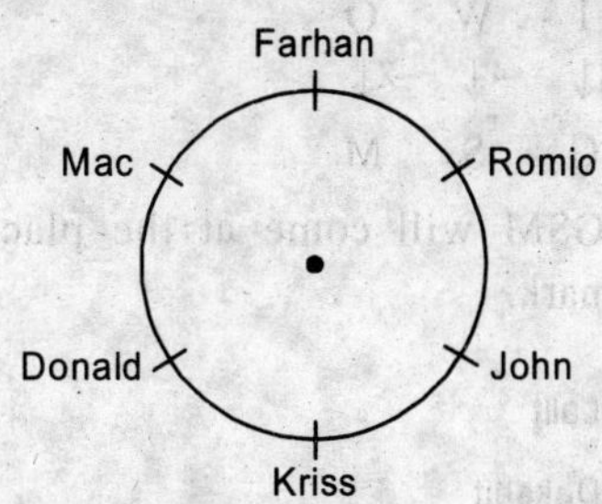

Farhan is sitting third to the left of Kriss.

Previous Paper (Solved)

Airports Authority of India (AAI)

Junior Assistant (Fire Service), Online Recruitment Exam

Basic Arithmetic

1. The value of $\dfrac{\sqrt[6]{2}\left[(625)^{\frac{3}{5}} \times (1024)^{-\frac{6}{5}} \div (25)^{\frac{3}{5}}\right]^{\frac{1}{2}}}{\left(\sqrt[3]{128}\right)^{\frac{-5}{2}} \times (125)^{\frac{1}{5}}}$ is:

A. 10 B. 5

C. 2 D. 1

2. On simplification $\dfrac{4.669 \times 4.669 - 2.331 \times 2.331}{(4.669)^2 + (2.331)^2 + 4.669 \times 4.662}$ is equal to:

A. 0.331 B. 0.334

C. 1.669 D. 2.338

3. The value of 25 – 5 [2 + 3 {2 – 2 (5 – 3) + 5} – 10] ÷ 5 is:

A. 0 B. 1

C. 24 D. 25

4. If $1 + \dfrac{1}{\sqrt{5} + \dfrac{1}{\sqrt{5} + \dfrac{1}{\sqrt{5}}}} = a + b\sqrt{5}$, where a and b are rational numbers, then $(a - b)$ equals:

A. $\dfrac{29}{35}$ B. $\dfrac{6}{35}$

C. $\dfrac{19}{35}$ D. $\dfrac{41}{35}$

5. Let x be the least number which when divided by 5, 10, 12 and 15 leaves a remainder 2 in each case, but is divisible by 7. The sum of digits of x is:

A. 8 B. 9

C. 11 D. 13

6. H.C.F. of two numbers each of four digits is 103 and their L.C.M. is 187 times their H.C.F. The sum of the numbers is:

A. 4882 B. 4288

C. 2488 D. 2884

7. A person saves 40% of his income. His expenditure increases by 25% and his income also increases by 10%. Now his per cent saving are approximately:

A. 28 B. 30

C. 32 D. 35

8. The freight of machine amounts to 20% of its price. Had the price been 10% less than what it is, the total cost of machine would have been ₹ 4800 less. What is the price of the machine?

A. ₹ 40000 B. ₹ 42000

C. ₹ 45000 D. ₹ 48000

9. At an examination in which full marks were 1000, A got 10% less marks than B; B got 25% more than C and C got 20% less than D. If A got 720 marks, what percentage of full marks was obtained by D?

A. 70 B. 72

C. 75 D. 80

10. A dealer buys a table listed at ₹ 1200 and gets two successive discounts of 10% and 20%. He spends 10% of his cost price on transportation. At what price should he sell it to earn a profit of 20%?

A. ₹ 1045.44

B. ₹ 1140.48

C. ₹ 1150.56

D. ₹ 1164.52

11. The catalogue price of an article is ₹ 720. If it is sold at a discount of $16\frac{2}{3}$% of the catalogue price, the gain is 25%. If it is sold ₹ 160 below catalogue price, then what is the gain/loss per cent?

A. $16\frac{2}{3}$% gain   B. $16\frac{2}{3}$% loss

C. $6\frac{2}{3}$% gain   D. $6\frac{2}{3}$% loss

12. A vessel is full of a solution of alcohol and water in which their ratio is 4 : 3. If 14 litres of the solution are taken out and replaced by the same amount of water, then the ratio of alcohol and water in the resulting solution becomes 3 : 4. The capacity of the vessel, in litres, was:

A. 28   B. 35

C. 42   D. 56

13. A sum of ₹ 3535 is divided among A, B, C and D such that A : B = 1 : 2, B : C = 3 : 2 and C : D = 8 : 9. The difference in shares of B and D is:

A. ₹ 202   B. ₹ 303

C. ₹ 404   D. ₹ 505

14. A bag contains coins of one rupee, 50 paise and 25 paise. If these coins are in the ratio of 2 : 3 : 10 and the total amount of money in the bag is ₹ 288, then the number of 50 paise coin exceeds the number of one rupee coin by:

A. 48   B. 136

C. 184   D. 336

15. If $(x^2 - y^2) : (x^2 + y^2) = 3 : 5$, then $(x^2 + 2y^2) : (2x^2 - y^2)$ is equal to:

A. 4 : 3   B. 3 : 4

C. 7 : 6   D. 6 : 7

16. Two equal sums are lent out at the same time at 6% and 5% per annum simple interest respectively. The first is received 2 years earlier than the other and the amount in each case is ₹ 6400. Each sum is:

A. ₹ 3200   B. ₹ 4000

C. ₹ 4200   D. ₹ 4500

17. A certain sum amounts to ₹ 5832 in 2 years at 8% compound interest. The same sum will amount to ₹ x in 4 years at the same rate at simple interest. The value of x is:

A. ₹ 6200   B. ₹ 6400

C. ₹ 6600   D. ₹ 6800

18. A sum of ₹ 3903 is distributed between A and B such that A's share at 4% compound interest per annum in 7 years equals B's share at the same rate of compound interest in 9 years. The difference of shares of A and B is:

A. ₹ 153   B. ₹ 154

C. ₹ 253   D. ₹ 254

19. A batsman has a certain average runs for 16 innings. In the 17th innings he made a score of 85 runs thereby increasing his average by 3. What is his average after 17th innings?

A. 34   B. 35

C. 36   D. 37

20. The average age of 24 boys and x girls is 12 years 8 months. The average age of boys is 13 years and that of girls is 12 years. The difference of the number of boys and x is:

A. 7   B. 8

C. 9   D. 12

21. A person has to cover a distance of 240 km in 6 hours. If he covers one-third of the distance in two-third of the time, what must be his speed (in km/hour) to cover the remaining distance in the remaining time?

A. $33\frac{1}{3}$ B. $66\frac{2}{3}$

C. 40   D. 80

22. The difference between the time taken by two cars to travel a distance of 350 km is 2 hours 20 minutes. If the difference between their speeds is 5 km/hour, the speed (in km/h) of the car that takes less time to travel is:

A. 25   B. 30

C. 32   D. 40

23. Two motor-boats are approaching each other. One of them is moving downstream with a speed of u km/hour and the other upstream with a speed of w km/hour. In one hour, the

total distance covered by them is s km. If the speed of each boat in still water is x km/hour, then:

A. $x = \frac{s}{2}$　　B. $x = \frac{s}{3}$
C. $2x = 3s$　　D. $3x = 2s$

24. A can do $\frac{1}{4}$ of a work in 5 days, while B can do $\frac{5}{6}$ of the same work in 25 days. They worked together for some time, then B left. If A completed the remaining work in 10 days, then B worked for:

A. 12 days　　B. 10 days
C. 9 days　　D. 6 days

25. A can do a piece of work in 9 days, B in $13\frac{1}{2}$ days and C in 18 days. They start working together, but A leaves 2 days and B 3 days before completion of work and C alone continues till the work is finished. In what time is the entire work completed?

A. 6 days　　B. 8 days
C. 9 days　　D. 10 days

Basic Science

26. Salts formed from strong acids and weak bases are:

A. Acidic　　B. Basic
C. Neutral　　D. Amphoteric

27. Aqueous solution of sodium chloride is called:

A. Brine　　B. Aqua regia
C. Aerosol　　D. Emulsion

28. The first shell or orbit in an atom is designated as:

A. K-shell　　B. L-shell
C. M-shell　　D. N-shell

29. Eka-Aluminium refers to:

A. Scandium　　B. Gallium
C. Silicon　　D. Germanium

30. The most electronegative atom in the modern periodic table is:

A. Fluorine　　B. Chlorine
C. Bromine　　D. Iodine

31. Carbon participates in bonding by:

A. Losing 4 electrons
B. Gaining 2 electrons
C. Gaining 4 electrons
D. Sharing 4 electrons

32. If in a solution, the OH^- concentration is greater than H^+ ion concentration, the solution will have pH:

A. less than 7　　B. greater than 7
C. equal to 7　　D. greater than 14

33. Electrical energy changes into chemical energy when current passes:

A. Electrolyte　　B. Heater
C. Motor　　D. Generator

34. The work done in taking a test charge 'q' around the complete circuit of the cell is called:

A. Potential difference
B. E.M.F
C. Volt
D. Ampere

35. The reciprocal of the resistance is ....

A. conductance　　B. resistivity
C. capacitance　　D. inductance

36. The temperature of an object is 60°C. Its value in Fahrenheit scale is:

A. 120° F　　B. 130° F
C. 140° F　　D. 110° F

37. The elements having same mass number but different atomic numbers are:

A. isobars　　B. isomers
C. isotones　　D. isotopes

38. Which is the longest part in the alimentary canal of human being?

A. Small intestine
B. Large intestine
C. Oesophagus
D. Stomach

39. How many pairs of legs are found in insects?

A. 02 B. 03

C. 04 D. 19

40. Identify the water-soluble vitamin from the following:

A. Vitamin A B. Vitamin B_1

C. Vitamin D D. Vitamin E

41. Which of the following activity is not responsible for greenhouse effect?

A. Use of solar car for transport

B. Use of wood as fuel

C. Emission from thermal power plant

D. Use of petrol vehicles for transport

42. Which cell organelle utilizes light energy during photosynthesis?

A. Mitochondria B. Golgi body

C. Ribosome D. Plastid

43. Identify the correctly matched pair from the following options:

A. Colon – Small Intestine

B. Bronchi – Lungs

C. Pons – Adrenal gland

D. Alveoli – Liver

44. Identify the micronutrients of crop plants from the following:

A. Magnesium B. Manganese

C. Potassium D. Sulphur

45. Number of Coliform is a measure for:

A. pH of water

B. chemical pollution in water

C. turbidity of water

D. microbial contamination of water

46. Which of the following substances is used to remove permanent hardness of water?

A. Gypsum B. Plaster of paris

C. Washing soda D. Benzene

47. Which of the following Metals will burn in air with dazzling brilliant light?

A. Copper B. Iron

C. Magnesium D. Zinc

48. The direction of induced current is obtained by:

A. Flemings right hand rule

B. Elock rule

C. Faraday's law

D. Fleming's left hand rule

49. The necessary condition for a conductor to obey Ohm's law:

A. voltage remains constant

B. current remains constant

C. temperature remains constant

D. nature of material

50. A particle having no charge and no mass is:

A. positron B. neutron

C. electron D. neutrino

General Knowledge

51. Which of the following is the highest peak of Vindhya range in India?

A. Kalumar B. Duphgarh

C. Lushai D. Guru Shikhar

52. Which of the following River's source is Mahabaleshwar in Maharashtra?

A. Mahanadi B. Krishna

C. Narmada D. Godavari

53. Which of the following Dam is built in Kerala?

A. Tungbhadra B. Cheruthoni

C. Koyna D. Mettur

54. Which of the following belongs from Kharif crop in India?

A. Wheat B. Barley

C. Cotton D. Sesame

55. Which of the following Two-wheeler manufacturing units situated at Waluj, Aurangabad?

A. Bajaj B. Hero

C. TVS D. Honda

56. Who founded the Mughal empire in India?

A. Ibrahim Lodi B. Babur

C. Nadir Shah D. Shershah Suri

57. During First war of Independence, 1857, Kanpur region rose to oppose the British rule where Nana Saheb's Palace at ____ served as its headquarters.
A. Bithoor B. Pokhraya
C. Fatehgarh D. Bibighar

58. Gandhiji was imprisoned at ______ jail following 'Quit India' resolution in 1942.
A. Yervada B. Aga Khan Palace
C. Transvaal D. Bombay

59. Which of the following King did not belong to Mauryan dynasty?
A. Bindusar B. Ashoka the great
C. Brihadratha D. Harshvardhan

60. Which Film won the best Film award at 63rd National Film awards in year 2016?
A. Piku B. Bajarangi Bhaijan
C. Bahubali D. Bajirao Mastani

61. Who is appointed as new cricket coach of Indian Men's cricket team in year 2016?
A. Ravi Shastri B. Anil Kumble
C. Rahul Dravid D. Saurav Ganguly

62. Vijayanagara's Empire ancient city of Hampi is situated in _______ state of southern India.
A. Tamil Nadu B. Andhra Pradesh
C. Kerala D. Karnataka

63. Which of the following Articles of Indian Constitution describes the abolition of untouchability?
A. Article 14 B. Article 15
C. Article 16 D. Article 17

64. Which of the following Indian state have the maximum representation in Lok Sabha?
A. Maharashtra B. Uttar Pradesh
C. Tamil Nadu D. Bihar

65. Who is the current deputy speaker of the Lok Sabha?
A. Sumitra Mahajan B. M Thambidurai
C. G.V. Mavalankar D. Karia Munda

66. Which of the following folk dance belongs from Karnataka?
A. Balakat B. Kolattam
C. Kargam D. Padayani

67. Which of the following painting forms have been originated in Western Ghats of India?
A. Warli B. Phad
C. Patachitra D. Kalighat

68. "Losar" festival is celebrated in ______ State of India.
A. Assam
B. Manipur
C. Arunachal Pradesh
D. Meghalya

69. Which of the following type of new overnight double-decker trains are announced in Union Railway Budget 2016?
A. Tejas B. Humsafar
C. Antyodaya D. Uday

70. According to Union Budget, 2016, which of the following state have university of Disability studies?
A. Karnataka B. Tamil Nadu
C. Kerala D. Andhra Pradesh

71. As per Union Budget, 2016 An IIT to be set up in the state of ______ .
A. Kerala B. Karnataka
C. Maharashtra D. Uttar Pradesh

72. Which of the following sportsperson is not the recipient of Rajiv Gandhi Khel Ratna Award in year 2016?
A. P.V. Sindhu B. Sakshi Malik
C. Jitu Rai D. Abhinav Bindra

73. Which among the following countries is not the member of ASEAN?
A. Singapore B. Thailand
C. Indonesia D. India

74. Which among the following place's Atomic Power station is newest one?
A. Kaiga B. Tarapore
C. Kudankulam D. Kakrapar

75. Dugong, a vulnerable marine mammal is found in the _____ Marine wildlife Sanctuary.
A. Malvan
B. Gihirmatha
C. Gulf of Mannar
D. Gulf of Kutch

Elementary English/Grammar

Directions (Qs. No. 76-77): *Fill in the blank with the appropriate word.*

76. The government is trying to _____ information about Chikungunya through the media and awareness campaigns.

A. disseminate B. capitulate
C. habituate D. culminate

77. My teacher's words made an _____ mark on my mind and I changed my ways completely.

A. inimitable B. immaculate
C. incredible D. indelible

Directions (Qs. No. 78-79): *Identify the grammatically incorrect words underlined in the following sentence.*

78. It's the festival season, and all the college students want to visit their hometown to be with their familiar and friends.

A. It's the festival season
B. want to visit
C. to be with
D. familiar and friends.

79. I am told that solar energy is the energy of the future and will save depletion of naturally resources from this earth.

A. I am told B. of the future
C. depletion of D. naturally resources

Directions (Q. No. 80): *Choose the sentence structure that is grammatically correct.*

80. next year in my summer vacation (1)/ that our family will (2)/ my father and I have decided (3)/ not go on a European holiday (4).

A. 3241 B. 3421
C. 4324 D. 1324

Directions (Qs. No. 81-82): *Choose the word that is misspelt.*

81. A. gorgeous B. gregarous
C. gigantic D. gargantuan

82. A. smuolder B. simile
C. smoother D. smoothie

Directions (Qs. No. 83-84): *Find the meaning of the underlined idiom/phrase.*

83. "Let me save this for a rainy day", I told my friend, when I earned money after my internship.

A. for the day I am out in the rain
B. for the day when I can enjoy the rain
C. for a sunny day when it may rain
D. for a day when I need it the most

84. "All work and no play will take its toll on your health", my father told me as I was neglecting exercise.

A. have a bad effect on health
B. become difficult for you
C. be better for your health
D. be very beneficial for you

Directions (Qs. No. 85-87): *Find the meaning of the underlined phrase.*

85. "By taking my parents on a holiday I killed two birds with one stone. I managed to go on a holiday and also made them spend time together."

A. solve two problems by taking one action
B. make two people do something together
C. kill two birds and enjoy it
D. aim at having a lot of fun

86. My business partner and I finally saw eye to eye and agreed upon a new business model.

A. became friends with each other
B. sat facing each other
C. agreed with each other
D. understood the plan well

87. The speaker was able to drive home the point he wanted to make with the help of examples from day to day life.

A. emphasize B. empathize
C. enumerate D. encounter

Directions (Qs. No. 88-89): *Choose the word which is synonym of the given word.*

88. Congenital

A. convenient B. inherited
C. physical D. genuine

89. Dissertation
A. treatise   B. development
C. combination   D. displeasure

Directions (Qs. No. 90-91): *Choose the word which is antonym of the given word.*

90. Poignant
A. astringent   B. eloquent
C. unimpressive   D. imaginative

91. Surly
A. pleasant   B. hopeful
C. brilliant   D. surprising

Directions (Qs. No. 92-94) : *Fill in the blanks with the correct words.*

92. It's a pleasure watching the dolphins, who _____ many tricks and are now performing in the pool.
A. are being learning   B. are learned
C. have learned   D. having learnt

93. Our new house ______ in Gurgaon. We hope to move into it by December this year.
A. was constructing
B. is constructing
C. is being constructed
D. was been constructed

94. There was a huge fire in the busy marketplace. The firemen _______ it within an hour, thus saving many lives.
A. were extinguished
B. extinguished
C. were extinguishing
D. had been extinguished

Directions (Q. No. 95): *Choose the sentence structure that is grammatically correct.*

95. therefore immediate steps must be taken to reverse the situation (1)/ a noted economist who has spent years studying world economics (2)/ is going through a difficult phase (3)/ has said that the global economy (4).
A. 2431   B. 2134
C. 4312   D. 4132

Directions (Qs. No. 96-100): *Read the following passage and answer the questions.*

Why do most of us have to struggle so much to be empathetic to others? Is it because we are so different from them? Or is it because we cannot understand their behaviour patterns? We go around carrying a load of guilt and uneasiness that we may have failed others – not through lack of trying, but because that was all we were really able to do in those circumstances. Introspection is necessary for growth, but not of the kind where we examine all that we did through a microscope and find faults. Admittedly, even with all the wisdom we may have acquired over the years, we could still make wrong choices. The subjective and the objective have a way of crisscrossing our lives. Detachment is an attitude that prevents us from getting too involved with a situation; it helps us take decisions with a cool mind. When we are passionately attached to something, our emotions get coloured and we begin to grow dissatisfied with ourselves and constantly think,' if only I had done this; or 'if only I had done that....'

When we are able to look at ourselves with compassion, we become less harsh and judgemental of ourselves, our actions and our motives, and so we are also able to treat others with compassion.

This means that we are able to flow with time and not allow all the mistakes we made and the weaknesses we have – that led us to do certain things in unsatisfactory ways – to stop us short. When we realise that life is all about imperfection and that perfection is a short-lived ideal we start looking at the whole of life differently.

Life is both success and failure. It is about mismanagement and disorder as well as smooth running and order. Once this realisation dawns, we begin to accept our limitations, we see how insignificant we really are and yet, are also important contributors to society. We remain contented with all of life, not just its most positive aspects.

96. Most of us go around feeling guilty of _____ in need of support.
A. troubling other people
B. not even trying to help those
C. not being helpful enough to those
D. being empathetic to people around us

97. Not getting too attached to something:
A. is an unhealthy habit

B. helps us take better decisions.
C. is good for our emotions.
D. is a sign of our dissatisfaction.

98. If we understand our own selves, we will:
A. be more successful in our lives.
B. understand others also.
C. be able to judge our actions.
D. find our emotions getting affected.

99. We need to understand that:
A. no one is perfect in this world.
B. making mistakes is not expected.
C. life is short and we have to take quick actions.
D. we must stop acting in unsatisfactory ways.

100. When the writer says, 'perfection is a short-lived ideal,' he means that:
A. we desire perfection but it is temporary.
B. ideally, we must all try to be perfect.
C. perfection once achieved, stays for a limited time.
D. we are all perfect in our short lives.

ANSWERS

1	**2**	**3**	**4**	**5**	**6**	**7**	**8**	**9**	**10**
D	B	C	A	C	D	C	A	D	B
11	**12**	**13**	**14**	**15**	**16**	**17**	**18**	**19**	**20**
A	D	B	A	D	B	C	A	D	D
21	**22**	**23**	**24**	**25**	**26**	**27**	**28**	**29**	**30**
D	B	A	D	A	A	A	A	B	A
31	**32**	**33**	**34**	**35**	**36**	**37**	**38**	**39**	**40**
D	B	A	A	A	C	A	A	B	B
41	**42**	**43**	**44**	**45**	**46**	**47**	**48**	**49**	**50**
A	D	B	B	D	C	C	A	C	D
51	**52**	**53**	**54**	**55**	**56**	**57**	**58**	**59**	**60**
A	B	B	C	A	B	A	B	D	C
61	**62**	**63**	**64**	**65**	**66**	**67**	**68**	**69**	**70**
B	D	D	B	B	A	A	C	D	C
71	**72**	**73**	**74**	**75**	**76**	**77**	**78**	**79**	**80**
B	D	D	C	C	A	D	D	D	A
81	**82**	**83**	**84**	**85**	**86**	**87**	**88**	**89**	**90**
B	A	D	A	A	C	A	B	A	C
91	**92**	**93**	**94**	**95**	**96**	**97**	**98**	**99**	**100**
A	C	C	B	A	C	B	B	A	A

EXPLANATORY ANSWERS

1. $$\frac{\sqrt[6]{2}\left[\left(5^4\right)^{\frac{3}{5}}\times\left(2^{10}\right)^{\frac{-6}{5}}\div\left(5^2\right)^{\frac{3}{5}}\right]^{\frac{1}{2}}}{\left(2^{\frac{7}{3}}\right)^{\frac{-5}{2}}\times\left(5^3\right)^{\frac{1}{5}}}$$

$$=\frac{\sqrt[6]{2}\left[5^{\frac{12}{5}-\frac{6}{5}}\times2^{-12}\right]^{\frac{1}{2}}}{2^{\frac{-35}{6}}\times5^{\frac{3}{5}}}=\frac{\sqrt[6]{2}\left[5^{\frac{6}{5}\times\frac{1}{2}}\times2^{-6}\right]}{2^{\frac{-35}{6}}\times5^{\frac{3}{5}}}$$

$$=\sqrt[6]{2}\left[5^{\frac{3}{5}-\frac{3}{5}}\times2^{-6+\frac{35}{6}}\right]=\sqrt[6]{2}\left[5^{0}\times2^{\frac{-1}{6}}\right]$$

$$= 2^{\frac{1}{6}} \times 2^{\frac{-1}{6}} \times 1 = 2^{\frac{1}{6}-\frac{1}{6}} \times 1$$
$$= 2^0 \times 1 = 1 \times 1 = 1.$$

2. Let $4.669 = a$ and $2.331 = b$

The given expression is

$$= \frac{a \times a - b \times b}{a^2 + b^2 + 2ab} = \frac{a^2 - b^2}{(a+b)^2}$$
$$= \frac{(a+b)(a-b)}{(a+b)(a+b)} = \frac{a-b}{a+b}$$
$$= \frac{4.669 - 2.331}{4.669 + 2.331} = \frac{2.338}{7} = 0.334.$$

3. $25 - 5\,[2 + 3\{2 - 2(5 - 3) + 5\} - 10] \div 5$
$= 25 - 5[2 + 3\{2 - 2 \times 2 + 5\} - 10] \div 5$
$= 25 - 5\,[2 + 3\{7 - 4\} - 10] \div 5$
$= 25 - 5\,[2 + 9 - 10] \div 5$
$= 25 - 5[1] \div 5$
$= 25 - 5 \div 5 = 25 - 1 = 24.$

4. $$1+\frac{1}{\sqrt{5}+\frac{1}{\frac{5+1}{\sqrt{5}}}} = 1+\frac{1}{\sqrt{5}+\frac{\sqrt{5}}{6}} = 1+\frac{1}{\frac{7\sqrt{5}}{6}}$$
$$= 1+\frac{6}{7\sqrt{5}}\times\frac{\sqrt{5}}{\sqrt{5}} = 1+\frac{6\sqrt{5}}{35}$$
$$1+\frac{6\sqrt{5}}{35} = a+b\sqrt{5}$$
$$\Rightarrow \quad a = 1 \text{ and } b = \frac{6}{35}$$
$$\therefore \quad a - b = 1-\frac{6}{35} = \frac{35-6}{35} = \frac{29}{35}.$$

5. L.C.M. of 5, 10, 12 and 15 = 60

Least no. = 60 + 2 = 62

But 62 is not divisible by 7

$\therefore$ $60 \times 2 = 120 + 2 = 122$

which is not divisible by 7

$\therefore$ $60 \times 3 = 180 + 2 = 182$

which is divisible by 7

Hence, required value of $x = 182$

Sum of the digits of $x = 1 + 8 + 2 = 11.$

6. $\because$ H.C.F. = 103

and L.C.M. = 103 × 187 = 19261

Let the numbers are $103x$ and $103y$

L.C.M. = $103xy$

$103xy = 19261$

$$\Rightarrow \quad xy = \frac{19261}{103} = 187$$

$187 = 1 \times 187$ $\quad (x = 1, y = 187)$

or $187 = 11$ and $y = 17$

$(\because 11 \times 17 = 187)$

when $x = 11$ then first no. = 103 × 11 = 1133

when $y = 17$ then 2nd no. = 103 × 17 = 1751

Sum of the numbers = 1133 + 1751 = 2884.

7. Let Man's income = ₹ 100

$$\text{Saving} = \frac{40}{100}\times 100 = ₹\ 40$$

Expenditure = 100 – 40 = ₹ 60

$$\text{Now,}\quad \text{his income} = 100+\frac{10}{100}\times 100 = ₹\ 110$$
$$\text{Expenditure} = 60+\frac{25}{100}\times 60 = ₹\ 75$$

His saving = 110 – 75 = ₹ 35

$$\text{Required \% saving} = \frac{35}{110}\times 100 = \frac{350}{11}$$
$= 32\%$ (Approx.)

8. Let the price of machine = ₹ x

$$\text{Freight} = \frac{20}{100}\times x = \frac{x}{5}$$
$$\text{C.P.} = x+\frac{x}{5} = \frac{6x}{5}$$

According to the question,

$$\frac{10}{100} \text{ of } \frac{6x}{5} = 4800$$
$$\Rightarrow \quad 6x = 4800 \times 50$$
$$x = \frac{4800 \times 50}{6}$$
$$= 800 \times 50 = 40000$$

Hence, the price of machine = ₹ 40000.

9. Let D got 100 marks

$$\text{C got marks} = 100 - \frac{20}{100} \times 100 = 80$$

$$\text{Marks obtained by B} = 80 + \frac{25}{100} \times 80$$

$$= 80 + 20 = 100$$

$$\text{Marks obtained by A} = 100 - \frac{10}{100} \times 100$$

$$= 100 - 10 = 90$$

When A got 90 marks then D got 100

When A got 720 marks then D got

$$= \frac{100}{90} \times 720 = 800$$

$$\% \text{ of D} = \frac{800}{1000} \times 100 = 80\%$$

Hence, marks obtained by D = 80%.

10. $\frac{10}{100} \times 1200 = ₹\ 120$

$1200 - 120 = ₹\ 1080$

Again, $\frac{20}{100} \times 1080 = ₹\ 216$

$1080 - 216 = ₹\ 864$

$$\text{Transportation} = \frac{10}{100} \times 864 = ₹\ 86.4$$

$$\text{C.P.} = 864 + 86.4 = 950.4$$

$$\text{Profit} = \frac{20}{100} \times 950.4$$

$$= 190.08$$

$$\text{S.P.} = 950.4 + 190.08$$

$$= ₹\ 1140.48.$$

11. $\text{Discount} = 16\frac{2}{3}\% \text{ of } 720$

$$= \frac{50}{3 \times 100} \times 720 = ₹\ 120$$

$$\text{S.P.} = 720 - 120 = ₹\ 600$$

$$100 + 25 = 125$$

When S.P. ₹ 125 then C.P. = ₹ 100

When S.P. ₹ 600 then C.P. = $\frac{100}{125} \times 600$

$$\text{C.P.} = 4 \times 120 = ₹\ 480$$

$$\text{Now S.P.} = 720 - 160 = ₹\ 560$$

$$\text{Profit} = 560 - 480 = ₹\ 80$$

$$\text{Profit \%} = \frac{80}{480} \times 100 = \frac{50}{3} = 16\frac{2}{3}\%.$$

12. Let the vessel contains $4x\ l$ and $3x\ l$ of alcohol and water respectively

Amount of alcohol in 14 l solution

$$= \frac{4}{7} \times 14 = 8l$$

$$\text{Amount of water} = \frac{3}{7} \times 14 = 6l$$

According to the question,

$$\frac{4x - 8}{3x - 6 + 14} = \frac{3}{4}$$

$$\Rightarrow \frac{4x - 8}{3x + 8} = \frac{3}{4}$$

$$\Rightarrow 16x - 32 = 9x + 24$$

$$\Rightarrow 7x = 56 \Rightarrow x = 8$$

∴ Capacity of vessel = $7x = 7 \times 8 = 56\ l$.

13. $\frac{A}{B} = \frac{1}{2} \Rightarrow A = \frac{B}{2}$

$$\frac{B}{C} = \frac{3}{2} \Rightarrow C = \frac{2B}{3}$$

$$\frac{C}{D} = \frac{8}{9} \Rightarrow D = \frac{9C}{8} = \frac{9}{8} \times \frac{2B}{3} = \frac{3B}{4}$$

$$A + B + C + D = 3535$$

$$\Rightarrow \frac{B}{2} + B + \frac{2B}{3} + \frac{3B}{4} = 3535$$

$$\Rightarrow \frac{6B + 12B + 8B + 9B}{12} = 3535$$

$$\Rightarrow 35B = 12 \times 3535$$

$$\Rightarrow B = \frac{12 \times 3535}{35}$$

$$= 12 \times 101 = 1212$$

$$D = \frac{3B}{4} = \frac{3}{4} \times 1212$$

$$= 3 \times 303 = 909$$

$$B - D = 1212 - 909 = 303$$

Hence, the difference in shares of B and D $= 303$.

14. Let the number of ₹ 1, 50 paise and 25 paise coins be $2x$, $3x$ and $10x$ respectively.

According to the question,

$$\frac{2x}{1}+\frac{3x}{2}+\frac{10x}{4} = 288$$

$$\Rightarrow \quad \frac{8x+6x+10x}{4} = 288$$

$$\Rightarrow \quad 24x = 4 \times 288$$

$$\Rightarrow \quad x = \frac{4\times 288}{24}$$

$$= 4 \times 12 = 48$$

Number of ₹ 1 coins $= 2x = 2 \times 48 = 96$

Number of 50 paise coins

$$= 3x = 3 \times 48 = 144$$

Difference $= 144 - 96 = 48$.

15. $\because \quad \frac{x^2 - y^2}{x^2 + y^2} = \frac{3}{5}$

$$\Rightarrow \quad 5x^2 - 5y^2 = 3x^2 + 3y^2$$

$$\Rightarrow \quad 2x^2 = 8y^2$$

$$\Rightarrow \quad x^2 = 4y^2$$

Now, $\frac{x^2+2y^2}{2x^2-y^2} = \frac{4y^2+2y^2}{8y^2-y^2} = \frac{6y^2}{7y^2} = \frac{6}{7}$

Hence, $(x^2 + 2y^2) : (2x^2 - y^2) = 6 : 7$.

16. $\frac{P\times r_1 \times (t-2)}{100} = \frac{P\times r_2 \times t}{100}$

$$\Rightarrow \quad 6 \times (t - 2) = 5t$$

$$\Rightarrow \quad 6t - 12 = 5t$$

$$\Rightarrow \quad t = 12 \text{ years}$$

$$\text{S.I.} = \frac{P\times 6\times 10}{100} = \frac{3P}{5}$$

$$P + \text{S.I.} = 6400$$

$$P+\frac{3P}{5} = 6400$$

$$\Rightarrow \quad 8P = 6400 \times 5$$

$$\Rightarrow \quad P = \frac{6400\times 5}{8} = 4000$$

Hence, each sum = ₹ 4000.

17. Let, $P = ₹\ 100$

$$A = 100\left(1+\frac{8}{100}\right)^2$$

$$= 100\times\frac{27}{25}\times\frac{27}{25} = \frac{2916}{25}$$

When amount ₹ $\frac{2916}{25}$ then P = ₹ 100

When amount ₹ 5832 then P

$$= \frac{100\times 25}{2916}\times 5832$$

$$\therefore \quad P = ₹\ 5000$$

Now, $\text{S.I.} = \frac{5000\times 8\times 4}{100} = 1600$

$\therefore$ Amount = 5000 + 1600 = ₹ 6600.

18. Let A's share = ₹ x and B's share = $3903 - x$

According to the question,

$$\frac{\left(1+\frac{4}{100}\right)^9}{\left(1+\frac{4}{100}\right)^7} = \frac{x}{3903-x}$$

$$\Rightarrow \quad \left(1+\frac{4}{100}\right)^2 = \frac{x}{3903-x}$$

$$\Rightarrow \quad \left(\frac{26}{25}\right)^2 = \frac{x}{3903-x}$$

$$\frac{676}{625} = \frac{x}{3903-x}$$

$$\Rightarrow 676 \times 3903 - 676x = 625x$$

$$\Rightarrow \quad 1301x = 676 \times 3903$$

$$\Rightarrow \quad x = \frac{676\times 3903}{1301}$$

$$= 676 \times 3 = 2028$$

A's Share = ₹ 2028

B's Share = 3903 – 2028 = ₹ 1875

The difference of shares of A and B

= 2028 – 1875 = ₹ 153.

19. Let average for 16 innings be x

then, $\frac{16x+85}{17} = x + 3$

$\Rightarrow \quad 16x + 85 = 17x + 51$

$\Rightarrow \quad 17x - 16x = 85 - 51 \Rightarrow x = 34$

Hence, average after 17 innings

$= 34 + 3 = 37.$

20. Total age of 24 boys and x girls

$= (24+x)\times 12\frac{8}{12} = (24+x)\times\frac{38}{3}$

Total age of 24 boys $= 24 \times 13$

Total age of x girls $= 12 \times x$

$$(24+x)\times\frac{38}{3} = 24 \times 13 + 12x$$

$\Rightarrow \quad 24 \times 38 + 38x = 24 \times 13 \times 3 + 36x$

$\Rightarrow \quad 2x = 24 \times 39 - 24 \times 38$

$= 24\ (39 - 38)$

$\Rightarrow \quad 2x = 24 \times 1 = 24$

$\Rightarrow \quad x = 12$

Required difference $= 24 - 12 = 12.$

21. 240 km travelled in 6 hours

$\frac{1}{3}$ of 240 km $= 80$ km and $\frac{2}{3}$ of 6 hours

$= \frac{2}{3}\times 6 = 4$ hours

Remaining distance $= 240 - 80 = 160$ km

Remaining time $= 6 - 4 = 2$ hours

Speed $= \frac{160}{2} = 80$ km/hour.

22. Let speed of slow car $= x$ km/hr

and speed of fast car $= (x + 5)$ km/hr

According to the question,

$$\frac{350}{x} - \frac{350}{x+5} = 2\frac{20}{60}$$

$\Rightarrow \quad 350\left(\frac{x+5-x}{x(x+5)}\right) = \frac{7}{3}$

$\Rightarrow \quad x^2 + 5x = 750$

$\Rightarrow \quad x^2 + 5x - 750 = 0$

$\Rightarrow \quad x^2 + 30x - 25x - 750 = 0$

$\Rightarrow \quad x(x + 30) - 25(x + 30) = 0$

$\Rightarrow \quad (x - 25)\ (x + 30) = 0$

$\Rightarrow \quad x = 25$ or $x = -30$

Hence, speed of slow car $= 25$ km/hr

Speed of fast car $= (25 + 5) = 30$ km/hr.

23. Average speed $= \frac{\text{Total distance}}{\text{Total time}}$

$\Rightarrow \quad x = \frac{S}{2}.$

24. A can do full work in 20 days

and B can do this work in 30 days

$\because$ A works alone for 10 days

$\therefore$ Work done by A in 10 days $= \frac{10}{20}$ work

$\therefore$ A + B do together $1-\frac{10}{20} = \frac{10}{20}$ work

Now, A + B do 1 work in

$$\frac{20\times 30}{20+30} = \frac{600}{50} = 12 \text{ days}$$

$\therefore$ A + B do $\frac{10}{20}$ work in $12\times\frac{10}{20} = 6$ days

Hence, B worked for 6 days.

25. Let the work be finished in x days

According to the question,

$$\frac{x-2}{9} + \frac{2(x-3)}{27} + \frac{x}{18} = 1$$

$\Rightarrow \quad \frac{x-2}{9} + \frac{2x-6}{27} + \frac{x}{18} = 1$

$\Rightarrow \quad \frac{6(x-2)+2(2x-6)+3x}{54} = 1$

$\Rightarrow \quad 6x - 12 + 4x - 12 + 3x = 54$

$\Rightarrow \quad 13x - 24 = 54$

$\Rightarrow \quad 13x = 78$

$\Rightarrow \quad x = 6$

Hence, the work be finished in 6 days.

ENGLISH LANGUAGE

1. Comprehension Passages

ENGLISH LANGUAGE COMPREHENSION

The objective of language comprehension test is to ascertain the ability of the candidates to understand the passage properly. Therefore candidates are required to take notice of the following points:

1. Read the full passage very attentively and intelligently.
2. Try to comprehend the gist of it.
3. Make a mental note of all the important details and points given in the passage.
4. Read the passage for the second time in case you have not been able to understand it satisfactorily.
5. Divide the time proportionately for all the passages.
6. Answer the questions on the basis of facts, as given in the paragraph.
7. Don't waste much time in answering the questions of any one passage.
8. Check all the answers once again, very carefully, to see whether any question is left unanswered by mistake.

MODEL QUESTIONS (FOR PRACTICE)

Directions: *Each of the following passages is followed by five questions. Read the passage carefully and then answer the questions that follow each. For each question, four probable answers A, B, C and D are given. Only one out of these is correct. Choose the correct answer.*

PASSAGE-1

The use of words like 'welcome', 'thank you', 'please', etc., at the right moment reflects a polite nature. The civic sense also lies within the scope of good manners. We should not shout or talk loudly in public places like hospitals and libraries and create disturbance. We should not cheat people or make fun of them. Cleanliness is also necessary. We must not throw the waste on roads and make use of dustbins. We should not harm the public property as it belongs to all of us. While in a queue, discipline should be maintained. We must give fair chance to others.

1. Expressions like 'welcome' 'thank you' and 'please' reflect
   A. happiness B. discipline
   C. civic sense D. polite nature
2. While in a library, we should
   A. respect others B. avoid arguments
   C. talk in low tone D. be courteous
3. A public property belongs to
   A. nobody
   B. all of us
   C. government
   D. one who maintains it

4. Discipline is
   A. the rule of proper conduct or action
   B. the rule of road sense
   C. making use of dustbins
   D. forming a queue
5. The most appropriate title for this passage would be
   A. Polite Nature
   B. Courtesy
   C. Good Manners
   D. Civic Sense

PASSAGE-2

There is an old proverb 'Early to bed and early to rise makes a man healthy and wise.' I am in the habit of getting up early in the morning and have formed the habit of taking long morning walks in the past two years. It is a light exercise and best for physical fitness. The morning air which is fresh and pure is beneficial for the lungs. The early rays of the rising sun are good for healthy skin. 'Health is wealth' and doctors also recommend morning walk to their patients for gaining sound health and freshness of energy.

1. What is good for lungs?
   A. Sunrays B. Fresh air
   C. Sound sleep D. Light exercise
2. What is a light exercise?
   A. Early to bed
   B. Early to rise
   C. Morning walk
   D. Gaining sound health
3. What is good for skin?
   A. Fresh air
   B. Morning air
   C. Morning walk
   D. Rising sun's rays
4. What is best for physical fitness?
   A. Light exercise
   B. Long morning walk
   C. Early to rise
   D. Fresh and pure air
5. Long morning walk
   A. bring sound sleep
   B. ensures physical fitness
   C. ensures healthy skin
   D. keeps healthy, wealthy and wise

PASSAGE-3

Mahatma Gandhi lived a splendid long life and has set great moral standards before us. He showed to the world the true way to peace. He wished to see India prosper but he became a martyr for the noble cause of Hindu-Muslim unity at the time of partition when a religious fanatic, Nathuram Godse, shot him dead on January 30, 1948. His last words were 'Hey Ram'. He lived and died for his country and countryman.

1. Mahatma Gandhi showed the world the true way to
   A. prosperity B. love
   C. truth D. peace
2. Mahatma Gandhi became a martyr for the noble cause of
   A. truth
   B. non-violence
   C. freedom of India
   D. Hindu-Muslim unity
3. Mahatma Gandhi was shot dead
   A. before India achieved independence
   B. by a mad man
   C. by an intolerant religious person
   D. by a non-religious person
4. Mahatma Gandhi set great moral standards. It means
   A. he was a great religious teacher
   B. he was a great moralist
   C. he made India morally stronger
   D. moral was everything to him
5. Gandhiji lived and died for his country and countryman. It means
   A. he was born in India and died in India
   B. he was a patriot
   C. he was a great moralist
   D. he sacrified his life for India and her people

PASSAGE-4

On one hot day a crow felt very thirsty. He flew from one place to another in search of water. After long hours of labour he found a pitcher. Eagerly, he perched on the mouth of the pitcher. He found that

the water was at the bottom of the vessel. He tried his best to dip his beak but did not succeed. He did not know what to do. Suddenly some pebbles lying nearby gave him an idea. One by one he dropped the pebbles with his beak into the pitcher. The level of water slowly came up to the mouth of the pitcher. The crow then drank the water and quenched his thirst.

1. The crow found a pitcher
   A. as it flew
   B. after many hours of labour
   C. full of water
   D. which was empty

2. What is the moral of the passage?
   A. No pains, no gains
   B. God helps those who help themselves
   C. Necessity is the mother of invention
   D. Try and try again, you will succeed at last

3. The crow flew from place to place
   A. in search of pitcher
   B. in search of pebbles
   C. in search of water
   D. in search of a vessel

4. The pitcher, the crow found
   A. was full of water
   B. was dry
   C. had little water in the bottom
   D. had water up to its mouth

5. As the crow dropped pebbles into the pitcher, what happend?
   A. The pitcher broke down
   B. The water leaked one of the pitcher
   C. The level of water into the pitcher rose up slowly
   D. Water level immediately rose to the mouth of the pitcher

PASSAGE-5

Once upon a time a crane and a fox lived in a forest. They were good friend. One day the fox invited the crane to a feast. He made a tasty food and served it before the crane on a plate. The crane could not eat anything because of the long beak. But the fox licked all his food. The crane felt insulted. He decided to teach the fox a lesson. Next day he invited the fox. He prepared the same tasty food and placed it in front of the fox inside a narrow glass. The crane ate easily while the fox looked on. Now, it was the fox's turn to remain hungry.

1. What is the moral of the passage?
   A. Beware of the wicked
   B. One good turn deserves another
   C. Be contented with what you have
   D. Tit for tat

2. The crane could not eat tasty food because the
   A. food was served in a shallow plate
   B. food was very hot
   C. food was served in a long jar
   D. crane was not hungry

3. The fox had to remain hungry because
   A. the food served was not enough in quantity
   B. the food was served inside a narrow glass
   C. the food served was not tasty
   D. the food was all liquid

4. Why did the crane feel insulted?
   A. Because he was invited to feast but he could not eat anything
   B. Because the food was served in a shallow plate and he could not eat
   C. Because the food was too hot
   D. Because the fox gulped all the food quickly

5. The crane successfully taught a lesson to the fox when he invited the fox to a feast and served the food
   A. in a narrow glass
   B. in a large plate
   C. in a broken plate
   D. in a long jar

PASSAGE-6

The family set down at the table and began to talk about the summer holidays. They had to decide a place to visit during the vacation. Should they go to their village or to a hill station? The parents preferred the village while the children wished to go the hill station. After few moments of discussion the elders decided to visit both the places. First they shall go to the village for a week and then stay at the hill station for the remaining days. For the first

time the family shall be together during the holidays. The children were happy with the holiday plan.

1. The purpose for which the family set down at the table was
   A. to decide a place to visit during the vacation
   B. to educate the children how to carry articles during a visit to a hill station
   C. to decide the date when they should start their journey
   D. to tell the children that they will visit a hill station during this vacation
2. The final plan was to visit
   A. their village
   B. a hill station
   C. their village as well as a hill station
   D. their home town
3. The final decision was made by
   A. the boys   B. the girls
   C. the women   D. the elders
4. They decided first to go to their village and stay there for
   A. a day   B. a week
   C. ten days   D. a fortnight
5. Why were children happy?
   A. Because a hill station was included in their holiday plan
   B. Because a visit to their village was excluded from their holiday plan
   C. Because their choice prevailed
   D. Because they were going all alone to the hill station

PASSAGE-7

Once Govind intended to go on pilgrimage with his family. He asked Mirind to accompany. But for his trade's reason, he did not go with him. So Govind thought it safe to leave the box of his jewellery with him, as it was dangerous to leave it in a lone house or take it on the journey. So he went to him with the box. He took him to a lonely place under a tree and handed it over to him. He told Mirind, "Keep it safe with you. I shall return from the journey after six month then I shall take it back from you." Mirind said, "Don't worry, I shall keep it as safe as own."

1. Govind intended to go
   A. for a business trip
   B. to a hill station
   C. on a long journey to a sacred place
   D. to his home town for a long period
2. Why did Govind leave his box of jewellery with Mirind?
   A. Because it was not safe to take the box with him on a long journey
   B. Because Mirind was his fast friend
   C. Because the box was very heavy
   D. Because his house was unsafe
3. Why did Govind take Mirind to a lonely place?
   A. To tell him that the box contained valuable jewellery
   B. So that no third person could see box
   C. To show him what was within the box
   D. To tell him that the box will remain with him
4. Where did Govind hand over the box of jewellery to Mirind?
   A. At Mirind's house
   B. At his own house
   C. In a lonely place
   D. In a lonely place under a tree
5. It was not safe to leave the box in a lone house. Here the word 'lone house' means
   A. a house in a deserted place
   B. a house where none lives
   C. a house without door and lock
   D. a house near the forest

PASSAGE-8

Zahir-ud-din Babar was the first Mughal emperor of India. A descendent of Timur on father's side and Changez Khan on his mother's side, Babar was a brave warrior. After defeating Ibrahim Lodhi in the First Battle of Panipat in 1526 he entered Delhi and soon gained control over Agra. After many more battles with Rajputs he extended his empire over Punjab, Uttar Pradesh and north Bihar. He died at a young age of 48 years in 1530 at his capital Agra without getting much time to consolidate his victories.

1. Zahir-ud-din Babar was the first
A. Muslim ruler of India
B. Mughal ruler of India
C. Afghan ruler of India
D. Turk ruler of India

2. Babar was born in the years
A. 1480 B. 1482
C. 1492 D. 1962

3. Babar first occupied
A. Punjab B. Agra
C. Delhi D. Panipat

4. Babar was a brave warrior. Here brave warrior means
A. courageous soldier
B. a kind hearted soldier
C. a clever fighter
D. a victorious general

5. Babar extended his empire over Punjab and Uttar Pradesh after many more battles with the
A. Afghans B. Rajputs
C. Mughals D. Lodhies

PASSAGE-9

Our National Flag is tricolour. It has three equal horizontal strips. The strip at the top is saffron, in the middle is white and at the bottom is green. The ratio of width to length of the flag is 2 : 3. In the centre of the white strip is a wheel in navy blue. The wheel represents the *chakra.* Its design is similar to the wheel which appears on the abacus of the Sarnath Lion Capital of Ashoka. Its diameter approximates to the width of the white strip. The wheel has 24 spokes. It was adopted by Constituent Assembly on July 22, 1947. We love our national flag. We respect it. We are ready to sacrifice our life to protect its honour. It represents the nation. So it is a symbol of national honour.

1. In our national flag the wheel is located in the centre of
A. saffron strip B. white strip
C. green strip D. blue strip

2. In our national flag which of the strips is at the bottom in our national flag
A. blue C. saffron
B. white D. green

3. Why do we love our national flag?
A. Because it is tricolour
B. Because it has three strips
C. Because it has a wheel at the centre
D. Because it is a symbol of national honour

4. Our national flag was approved by
A. President
B. Lok Sabha
C. Parliament
D. Constituent Assembly

5. The diameter approximates to the width of the white strip. Here the word 'approximates' means
A. is more or less equal
B. is exactly equal
C. is not equal
D. is related

PASSAGE-10

Distance in large cities are long. All the people do not have their own means of transport. They have to depend upon the state or private buses. The number of bus users is very large. Every bus stop is, therefore, crowded. The number of buses is not adequate. Thus people suffer the torture of long wait at the bus stop. Some bus stops are quite orderly. People form queues and get into the buses turn by turn. However, often this order is forgotten and confusion spreads when the bus comes and the law of jungle prevails.

1. Why are the bus stops crowded?
A. Because they are small is size
B. Because the number of passengers is very large
C. Because they are situated at some busy centre
D. Because people do not form queues

2. Long wait at the bus stop is the result of
A. over-crowding in the buses
B. late running of buses
C. shortage of buses
D. slow speed of buses

3. Some bus stops are quite orderly where
A. there is no crowd
B. the number of buses is adequate

C. people do not have to wait for long
D. people form queues and enter the buses one by one

4. Most of the people who travel by buses are
A. non-working
B. do not have their own vehicles
C. have to go a long distance
D. live in large cities

5. What happens when people do not have their own transport?
A. They have to wait for a bus at a bus stop
B. They have to depend upon the state or private buses
C. They have to travel long distances
D. They form queues and get into buses one by one

PASSAGE-11

A certain king once fell ill and doctors said that only a sudden fright would restore his health but the king was not a man for anyone to play tricks on, except his fool. One day, when the fool was with him in his boat he cleverly pushed the king into water but he was rescued and put to bed. The fright, the bath and bed cured the diseased king, but he was so angry with the fool that he turned him out of the country.

1. What did the doctor say about the king?
A. Only a sudden fright would restore the king's health
B. Only fool would cure the king
C. Only a boat trick could cure the king
D. The king had suffered a sudden fright

2. He cleverly pushed the king into water but *he* was rescued and put to bed. In this sentence *he* refers to
A. the king B. the fool
C. the doctor D. the river

3. When the fool pushed the king into water they were
A. in the palace B. in the bed
C. in the garden D. in a boat

4. Who played the trick on the king?
A. The doctor B. The boatman
C. The fool D. The fright

5. The fool who cured the king was
A. rewarded
B. thrown into water
C. turned out of the country
D. put into jail

ANSWERS

Passage	1	2	3	4	5
Passage 1.	D	C	B	A	C
Passage 2.	B	C	D	B	B
Passage 3.	D	D	C	B	D
Passage 4.	B	C	C	C	C
Passage 5.	D	A	B	B	A
Passage 6.	A	C	D	B	A
Passage 7.	C	A	B	D	B
Passage 8.	B	B	C	A	B
Passage 9.	B	D	D	D	A
Passage 10.	B	C	D	B	B
Passage 11.	A	A	D	C	C

2. English Grammar

PARTS OF SPEECH

Part of speech	Definition or Function	Examples
Noun	Name of a person, place, animal, quality or thing	Ram, boy, dog pen, sun, Delhi, truth, honesty
Pronoun	Used in place of a noun	I, you, he she, they
Articles & Determiners	Points out indefinite and definite nouns	a, an, the, few, some
Adjective	Describes a noun or pronoun	big, honest, wooden valuable, quiet, deep, soft, narrow
Adverb	Describes a verb, an adjective or another adverb	silently, widely, softly, quietly, very, carefully
Verb	Tells about action or state of something or someone	is, am, was, have, do, like, walk, work, make, throw, tell
Conjuction	Joins words, clauses or sentences	and, but, when, yet, while, else
Preposition	Links a noun or pronoun to another word	at, to, after, on for, under, over, with
Interjection	Expresses sudden feelings or emotions	Ah!, Alas!, oh!, ouch!, hi!, well!, Hurrah!

NOUNS

A word which denotes a person, a thing, an animal or a place is said to be a noun.

There are two noun numbers in English — the *Singular* and the *Plural*.

Singular Numbers : A noun that denotes one person or one thing, is said to be in the Singular number. For example — book, pencil, bird, dog, hen etc. are in singular number.

Plural Number : A noun that denotes more than one person or one thing is said to be in plural number. For example — boys, pens, lions, girls, men etc. are in plural number.

REMEMBER

Singular	*Plural*
Cat	Cats
Book	Books
Pen	Pens
Room	Rooms
Tree	Trees
Bus	Buses
Bush	Bushes
Box	Boxes
Glass	Glasses
Dish	Dishes
Judge	Judges
Tax	Taxes
Watch	Watches
Calf	Calves
Thief	Thieves
Knife	Knives

Singular	*Plural*
Scarf	Scarves
Wife	Wives
Leaf	Leaves
Wolf	Wolves
Half	Halves
Monarch	Monarchs
Roof	Roofs
Hoof	Hoofs
Gulf	Gulfs
Staff	Staffs
Radio	Radios
Bamboo	Bamboos
Folio	Folios
Hero	Heroes
Volcano	Volcanoes
Mango	Mangoes
Potato	Potatoes
Photo	Photos
Piano	Pianos
Baby	Babies
Fly	Flies
Country	Countries
Lady	Ladies
Boy	Boys
Monkey	Monkeys
Ox	Oxen
Child	Children
Man	Men
Woman	Women
Tooth	Teeth
Axis	Axes
Basis	Bases
Foot	Feet
Goose	Geese
Englishman	Englishmen
Radius	Radii
Vertex	Vertices
Stimulus	Stimuli

1. Note the plurals of the following nouns:

Singular	*Plural*	*Singular*	*Plural*
copy	copies	cry	cries
baby	babies	duty	duties
body	bodies	country	countries
family	families	diary	diaries
fly	flies	fairy	fairies
city	cities	spy	spies
army	armies	storey	storeys
bay	bays	monkey	monkeys

2. The following nouns do not undergo any change in plural form, in general.

Singular	*Plural*	*Singular*	*Plural*
deer	deer	sheep	sheep
thousand	thousand	pair	pair
hundred	hundred	score	score
dozen	dozen	gross	gross

Note: We can write—

(*a*) thousands of men; (*b*) two pairs of shoes; (*c*) dozens of mangoes; (*d*) scores of people etc.

But—

(*a*) two thousand rupees; (*b*) three hundred men; (*c*) five dozen eggs, etc.

3. The following nouns are usually used in plural forms. They take a plural verb after them—

eatables	fetters	surroundings
riches	alms	spectacles
trousers	pants	scissors
premises	thanks	annals
congratulations	goods	shorts
tongs	pains	arms
breeches	(for troubles)	

4. The following are the nouns which are plural in appearance but are usually used in singular number. They are followed by a singular verb—

news	politics	physics
mathematics	economics	ethics
politics	classics	gallows
statistics	athletics	innings
mechanics	summons	mumps

5. Collective nouns often used as plurals—

public	police	cattle
audience	clergy	folk
people	poultry	nation
elite	gentry	glitterati

6. The nouns that are usually used in singular forms—

advice	hair	rice
fuel	alphabet	machinery
offspring	issue	furniture
mischief	stationery	luggage
bedding	information	abuse

7. Material nouns are always used in singular number—

gold	copper	milk
water	silk	wool

Note: They may be used in plural with a different meaning.

copper coins (coppers), chains or fetters (irons), cans made of tin (tins).

GENDERS

The difference in sex is denoted by Gender in grammar. The various genders are as follows :

1. **Masculine Gender :** A noun that denotes a male is said to be of the masculine gender, as man, uncle, ox, boy etc.
2. **Feminine Gender :** A noun that denotes a female is said to be of feminine gender, as woman, aunt, princess, cow etc.
3. **Common Gender :** Nouns which denote both males and females are said to be of the common gender, as friend, cousin, person, parent, baby etc.
4. **Neuter Gender :** A noun that denotes the name of object without life is said to be of neuter gender, as file, table, pencil.

REMEMBER

Masculine	*Feminine*
Boy	Girl
Son	Daughter
Brother	Sister
Murderer	Murderess
Sorcerer	Sorceress
Son-in-law	Daughter-in-law
Father-in-law	Mother-in-law
Man-servant	Maid-servant
Land-lord	Land-lady
Bachelor	Maid
Gentleman	Lady
Monk	Nun
Earl	Countess
Lad	Lass
Sir	Madam
Duke	Dutchess
Emperor	Empress
Milk-man	Milk-maid
Pea-cock	Pea-hen
Step-father	Step-mother
Hero	Heroine
Viceroy	Vicerine
Mr.	Mrs.
Governor	Governess
Master	Mistress
Wizard	Witch
Heir	Heiress
Host	Hostess
Lion	Lioness
Mayor	Mayoress
Actor	Actress
Buck	Doe
Colt	Filly
Dog	Bitch
Horse	Mare
Count	Countess
Hunter	Huntress
Prince	Princess
Abbot	Abbess
God	Goddess
Author	Authoress
Ox	Cow
Widower	Widow
Grand-father	Grand-mother
He-goat	She-goat
Milk-man	Milk-woman
Bridegroom	Bride
Tiger	Tigress
Priest	Priestess
Poet	Poetess
Shepherd	Shepherdess
Nephew	Niece
Stag	Hind

PRONOUNS

The repetition of a noun in a sentence or a set of sentences is really boring. So, instead of repeating the noun, we can use a word (for that noun) called the pronoun.

"A pronoun is a word that we use instead of a noun".

Example:

This is *Sachin. He* plays cricket.

Note: *He* is the pronoun used in place of *Sachin.*

Kinds of Pronouns

1. **Personal pronouns :** A pronoun which is used instead of the name of a person is known as a 'Personal Pronoun'. A list of the 'Personal pronouns' is listed below :

   I, my, mine, me, we (First Person)
   You, your, yours (Second Person)
   He, his, him, she, her, hers, it,
   its, they, their, theirs, them (Third Person)

2. **Demonstrative, Indefinite and Distributive Pronouns :**

   (a) Demonstrative Pronouns : Pronouns used to point out the objects to which they refer are called Demonstrative Pronouns.

   Examples :
   (i) *This* is a present from my uncle.
   (ii) *These* are merely excuses.
   (iii) Bembay mangoes are better than *those* of Bangaluru.

   (b) Indefinite Pronouns : All pronouns which refer to persons or things in a general way and do not refer to any particular person or thing are called Indefinite Pronouns.

   Examples :
   (i) *Somebody* has stolen my watch.
   (ii) *Few* escaped unhurt.
   (iii) Did you ask *anybody* to come?

   (c) Distributive Pronouns : Each, either, neither are called distributive pronouns because they refer to persons or things one at a time. For this reason they are always singular and followed by the verb in singular.

   Examples :
   (i) *Each* of the men received a reward.
   (ii) *These* men received *each* a reward.
   (iii) *Either* of you can go.

3. **Relative Pronouns :** A relative pronoun refers or relates to some noun going before, which is called its Antecedent.

   Examples :
   (i) I met Hari *who* used to live here.
   (ii) I have found the pen *which* I had lost.
   (iii) Here is the book *that* you lent me.

4. **Interrogative Pronouns :** These pronouns, are used for asking questions.

   Examples :
   (i) *Whose* book is this?
   (ii) *What* will all the neighbours say?
   (iii) *Which* do you prefer, tea or coffee?

Note : Interrogative pronouns can also be used in asking indirect questions. Consider the following examples :
(i) I asked *who* was speaking.
(ii) Tell me *what* you have done.
(iii) Say *which* you would like best.

Behaviour of the Pronouns

1. If three pronouns are used together in the same sentence they are arranged in the following order :

   2 + 3 + 1
   ↓ ↓ ↓
   Second Person, Third Person, First Person

   Examples :
   I, you and he must help *that* poor man. (Incorrect)
   You, he and I must help *that* poor man. (Correct)

2. When two or more singular nouns are joined by and, the pronoun used for them should be plural.

   Examples :
   Mohan and Sohan are friends. *They* play football. *They* live at Lajpat Nagar.

3. But if these nouns joined by and refer to the same person or thing, the pronoun used should be singular.

   Examples :
   (i) Delhi, the beautiful city and the capital of India, is famous for *its* historical monuments.
   (ii) The manager and owner of the firm expressed *his* views on the demands of the workers.

4. When two nouns are used with as well as, the pronoun agrees with the first subject.

Examples :

(a) Mohan as well as his friends is doing *his* work.

(b) The students as well as their teachers are doing *their* work.

5. When two singular nouns joined by 'and' are preceded by *each* or *every,* the pronoun used must be singular and should agree in gender with the second noun.

Examples :

(a) Every man and every woman will do *her* best for the nation.

(b) Each boy and each girl went to *her* house.

6. When two nouns are joined by using 'with', the pronoun agrees with the noun coming before 'with'.

Examples :

(a) The boy with *his* parents has gone to see a movie.

(b) The children with *their* parents have gone to picnic.

7. When two different nouns are joined by either.......... or; neither .... nor, the pronoun is used according to the number and gender of the second noun.

Examples :

(a) Either your sister or you have done *your* work.

(b) Neither the students nor the teacher was in *his* class.

8. The pronoun coming after '*than*' must be in the same case as that coming before '*than*'.

Examples :

(a) She plays better than *me.* (Incorrect)
She plays better than *I.* (Correct)

(b) His elder brother is more intelligent than *him.* (Incorrect)
His elder brother is more intelligent than *he.* (Correct)

9. 'Many a' always takes a singular pronoun and singular verb.

Example :

Many a soldier has met *his* death in the battle field.

10. 'Who', 'Whose', 'Whom' are used only for persons.

Examples :

(a) *Who* is knocking at the door?

(b) *Whose* pen is this?

(c) *What* do you want?

11. 'Which' is used for things.

Example :

Which game do you like?

MULTIPLE CHOICE QUESTIONS

Directions: *In the following questions choose the correct options to fill the blanks.*

1. The place was so dirty that ..... wished to run away from there.
A. everybody B. anybody
C. few D. some

2. ..... was there to help me.
A. Somebody B. Anything
C. Anybody D. Nobody

3. Is there .... to eat?
A. some B. something
C. any D. few

4. ..... of the students were making a great noise.
A. Anyone B. Somebody
C. Many D. Nobody

5. ..... of the students can solve this sum.
A. Someone B. Anybody
C. Somebody D. None

6. ...... of us should try our best to make India a heaven.
A. Any B. Somebody
C. Anybody D. All

7. ...... of us do not know the real meaning of our lives.
A. Any B. Something
C. Several D. Many

8. My .... black.
A. hairs are B. hair is
C. hairs shall D. hair will

9. She saw two .... on the last Sunday.
A. thiefs B. theifs
C. thieves D. theives

10. My sister is a ....
A. bacheloress B. bachelor
C. unmaried D. spinster

11. One is supposed to do ....
A. our duty B. their duty
C. one's duty D. his duty

12. Take anything .... you want.
A. that B. which
C. than D. then

13. I cannot tolerate ....
A. separated you
B. your separation
C. separation from you
D. you separated

14. He is .... faithful partner.
A. Yours B. You
C. Your D. Your's

15. Ajay is more smart than ....
A. her B. hers
C. herself D. she

16. Vivek works harder than ....
A. me B. I
C. her D. his

17. They should help ....
A. the poor people B. the poor
C. the poor persons D. the poor peoples

18. .... are mad.
A. All his sons B. His all sons
C. Sons all his D. All sons his

19. The poor fellow .... to fate.
A. resigned
B. resigned himself
C. resigned itself
D. resigned themselves

20. Nobody will help you but ....
A. I B. me
C. ours D. his

21. It is a good chance, You must avail .... this opportunity.
A. of B. yourself of
C. for D. from

22. The person who is elected .... my relative.
A. is B. he is
C. his D. him

23. He made ....
A. yours mention B. mention of you
C. mention for you D. mention about you

24. .... I know, he is quite faithful.
A. As far as B. So far as
C. So far this D. So far so

25. It is a duty of a person to take .... for his family.
A. pain B. pains
C. pain-killers D. pained

26. She does not love .... husband.
A. his B. her
C. its D. their

27. Let .... work together.
A. him and me B. he and I
C. he and him D. I and me

28. Copper, Silver and Gold ....
A. each will do B. either will do
C. any one will do D. any will do

29. Jessica and Roma are very irregular .... habits.
A. in her B. in their
C. in its D. in every

30. One likes to enjoy .... who was a great poet.
A. The sonnets of Shakespeare
B. Shakespeare's sonnets
C. Sonnets
D. Shakespeare

31. That is the boy .... everybody loves.
A. whom B. who
C. that D. whose

32. That is the girl .... won the first prize.
A. whom B. who
C. whose D. which

33. That is the man .... purse was lost.
A. who B. whom
C. whose D. their

ANSWERS

1	2	3	4	5	6	7	8	9	10
A	D	B	C	D	D	D	B	C	D
11	**12**	**13**	**14**	**15**	**16**	**17**	**18**	**19**	**20**
C	A	C	C	D	B	B	A	B	B
21	**22**	**23**	**24**	**25**	**26**	**27**	**28**	**29**	**30**
B	A	B	A	B	B	A	C	B	A
31	**32**	**33**							
A	B	C							

ARTICLES

The family of the articles has only three members. They are : A, An and The. However, they fall under two groups :

(a) Definite Article *(b)* Indefinite Article

'The' is known as definite article whereas 'a' and 'an' are known as indefinite articles.

Use of the Definite Article 'The'

'The' is used before

1. The superlative degree :
   He is the ablest man of the town.
   (ablest is a superlative degree)
2. The name of states, countries etc. having a descriptive name :
   (i) The J & K is a small state. (J & K is a descriptive name)
   (ii) He lives in the U.S.A. (U.S.A. is a descriptive name)
   (But the Delhi and the America are wrong because neither Delhi nor America is a descriptive name)
3. The names of the scriptures :
   The Gita is a holy book. (Gita is a scripture)
4. Name of newspapers :
   The Tribune is published from Chandigarh.
5. Name of rivers, canals, seas, oceans, bays, gulfs, groups of islands etc. :
   (i) The Ganga is a holy river.
   (ii) The Indian Ocean is the deepest ocean.
   (iii) The Persian Gulf is a narrow gulf.
6. The name of famous buildings :
   The Taj is one of the best buildings in India.
7. The names of nationals, sects and communities:
   (i) The English defeated the Germans in the World War.
   (ii) The rich should help the poor.
   (iii) The Hindus believe in the caste system.
8. Proper nouns used as common nouns :
   (i) Kalidas is the Shakespeare of India.
   (ii) Delhi is the London of India.
9. Famous historical events :
   The Industrial Revolution changed the face of England.
10. The directions and the celestial bodies:
    The sun rises in the east.
11. Titles :
    Akbar, the Great was loved by his subjects.

Do not use 'the'

1. Before languages :
   The English is an international language. (Incorrect)
   English is an international language. (Correct)
2. Before the names of games :
   The hockey is a popular game. (Incorrect)
   Hockey is a popular game. (Correct)

Use of the Indefinite Articles 'A' and 'An'

'A' is used before :

1. All singular common nouns beginning with a consonant :
   (i) A boy sings a song.

(ii) A black and a white cow were grazing in the field.

2. If a word begins with a vowel but gives the sound of a consonant, 'a' should be used before it :
   (i) He was helped in his work by a European.
   (ii) He is a one-eyed man.
   (iii) It is a useful work.

'An' is used as follows :

1. All singular common nouns beginning with a vowel (*i.e.*, a, e, i, o, u) :
   (i) He is an artist.
   (ii) He is an old man.
   (iii) I intend to buy an umbrella.
2. If a word starts with a consonant but gives the sound of a vowel, "an" should be used before it :
   (i) Brutus is an honourable man.
   (ii) He is an honour to his profession.
   (iii) He is an L.L.B.
   (iv) He is an M.A.
   (v) You will reach there in an hour.

Demonstratives, that, these and those

1. The demonstrative adjectives and pronouns are for objects nearby the speaker:
   this (singular) those (plural)
   and for objects far away from the speaker.
   That (singular) those (plural)
2. Demonstratives are the only adjectives that agree in number with their nouns.
   That hat is nice.
   Those hats are nice.
3. When there is the idea of selection, the pronoun "one" (or "ones") often follows the demonstrative.
   I want a book. I'll get this (one).
   If the demonstrative is followed by an adjective, "one"(or "ones") must be used.
   I want a book. I'll get this big one.

MULTIPLE CHOICE QUESTIONS

Directions: *In the following questions choose the correct options to fill the blanks.*

1. .... will have to be paid for this material.
A. Half rupee B. Half a rupee
C. A half rupee D. An half rupee

2. .... is taking keen interest in India.
A. The USA B. USA
C. An USA D. A USA

3. Only .... can save our country.
A. the Hitler B. a Hitier
C. Hitler D. an Hitler

4. I can run for ....
A. hundred miles B. the hundred miles
C. a hundred miles D. an hundred miles.

5. .... man-eater has been killed.
A. The B. A
C. An D. Either A or B

6. What .... fine idea!
A. the B. an
C. a D. No article

7. .... earth is moving around the sun.
A. An B. A
C. The D. No article

8. This is .... first example while I got.
A. the B. a
C. an D. No article

9. This is .... house which was built during earthquake.
A. a B. an
C. the D. No article

10. .... America is a rich country.
A. The B. An
C. A D. No article

11. .... U.S.A. is a developed country.
A. A B. An
C. The D. No article

12. .... Bible is a holy book.
A. A B. The
C. An D. No article

13. .... rich should help the poor.
A. The B. A
C. An D. No article

14. .... Gold is a costly metal.
A. The B. A
C. An D. No article

15. Kalidas is .... Shakespeare of India.
A. a B. an
C. the D. No article

16. I cannot do .... difficult work.
A. a such B. the such
C. such the D. such a

17. How foolish .... plan it is!
A. a B. an
C. the D. No article

18. An ink is .... useful article.
A. an B. a
C. the D. No article

19. There are .... husband and wife.
A. a B. an
C. the D. No article

20. He is learning .... French
A. the B. a
C. an D. No article

ANSWERS

1	2	3	4	5	6	7	8	9	10
B	A	B	C	D	C	C	A	C	D
11	**12**	**13**	**14**	**15**	**16**	**17**	**18**	**19**	**20**
C	B	A	D	C	D	A	B	D	D

ADJECTIVES & ADVERBS

An Adjective is a word which adds something to the meaning of a noun or a pronoun.

Mridula is an *intelligent* girl.
He has a *black* goat.
He is a *brilliant* student.
She is a *clever* girl.
It is a *beautiful* picture.

In the sentences given above, the words in italics are adjectives.

An Adverb is a word which qualifies the meaning of a Verb, an Adjective or another Adverb.

(*i*) He talks *slowly.*
(*ii*) He is a *very* good student.
(*iii*) He talks *very* slowly.

In sentence (*i*), *slowly* qualifies the verb *talks.*

In sentence (*ii*), *very* qualifies the adjective *good.*

In sentence (*iii*), *very* qualifies the adverb *slowly.*

Adjectives have three degrees of comparison :

1. **Positive Degree :** It expresses the common form of an adjective.
   Example :
   Ram is a *tall* boy.
   In the above sentence *tall* is an adjective and expresses the common form.
2. **Comparative Degree :** It expresses the more of the same form.
   Example :
   Ram is *taller* than Mahesh.
   In the above sentence *taller* is an adjective that expresses the more of the common form of the adjective *tall.*

"When and How to Use" Comparative Degree?

(a) Comparative Degree is used when two persons or two groups of persons or things are compared.
Examples :
(a) He is *wiser* than his younger brother.
(b) This glass is *cleaner* than the other.

(b) When two different qualities in the same person are compared, more is used instead of 'er' to form the comparative. The formula used in this case should be :
More + Positive Degree
She is *fairer* than polite. (Incorrect)
She is *more fair* than polite. (Correct)

(c) When selection of one out of two persons or things is meant, the degree of comparison is followed by of and *the* is used before it.
Example :
Zia is abler of *the* two sisters.

(d) If two comparatives are used in the same sentence to impress upon an idea, both should be preceded by the definite article.

Examples :

(i) The higher you go, the cooler it is.

(ii) The more we get, the more we desire.

(e) When one person or thing is compared with another of the same kind, other is used after the comparative degree. In such sentences other is normally preceded by any or all.

Examples :

(i) Kalidas is greater than any dramatist. (Incorrect)

Kalidas is greater than any other dramatist. (Correct)

(ii) Lead is heavier than all metals. (Incorrect)

Lead is heavier than all other metals. (Correct)

(f) Senior, junior, superior, inferior, prior, anterior (earlier than) and posterior (later than) are always followed by 'to'.

Examples :

(i) Ram is senior *to* Mohan by three years.

(ii) That pen is inferior *to* that.

(iii) He is junior *to* me in rank.

(iv) This event was posterior *to* that.

Note: Never use *than* after the above mentioned adjectives.

Important Information

(a) 'Preferable' is also used as an adjective of the comparative degree. As such, it is always followed by *to* and not *a*.

Death is preferable than dishonour. (Incorrect)

Death is preferable *to* dishonour. (Correct)

(b) To intensify the Degree of comparison, we use *far* or *much* before the comparative.

Examples :

(i) This book is *far* better than that.

(ii) His performance was *much* better than Mohan's.

Warning : Always avoid the use of double comparatives.

Don't say : Ram is more cleverer than his younger brother.

Say: Ram is cleverer than his younger brother.

3. Superlative Degree : It expresses the most of the common form of an adjective.

Example :

He is the ablest man of the town.

How and when to use the Superlative Degree?

(a) The Superlative Degree is used when more than two persons or things are compared.

(b) The Superlative Degree is generally preceded by 'the' and followed by 'of' in most of the cases or otherwise.

(c) When an adjective of the superlative degree is preceded by a Possessive Adjective or a Noun in the Possessive case, 'the' should not be used before it.

Example :

Which is Kalidas' best play?

It will be a blunder to use 'the' before the Superlative Degree in such cases.

Don't say : Which is Kalidas' the best play.

(d) To intensify the degree of comparison, *by far* is used before the superlative degree.

Example :

India is *by far* the most beautiful country of the world.

Note: Always avoid the use of double superlatives.

Don't say : He is the most strongest boy in the class.

Say : He is the strongest boy in the class.

Use of some Important Adjectives

1. (a) **'Some'** is used as follows :

(i) With countable nouns where it means—a little, a small quantity.

(ii) In a question which shows some request.

Examples :

(i) There is some water in the bottle.

(ii) Some of the students were absent yesterday.

(iii) Will you have some milk?

(iv) Will you buy some fruit for me?

(b) **'Any'** is used as follows :

(i) In negative sentences.

(ii) In interrogative sentences.

(iii) After 'Hardly', 'Scarcely' and 'Barely'.
(iv) After 'If'.

Examples :

(i) There is not any sugar in the pot.
(ii) We haven't any rice in the house.
(iii) I have hardly any money.
(iv) There are scarcely any plants in this field.
(v) If there is any danger, blow the whistle.

2. (a) **Older :** Older (and oldest) are used for persons animals and things. But 'Older' and 'Oldest' refer to the persons who do not belong to the same family.

Examples :

(i) Radha is older than Shyama.
(ii) John is the oldest member of the staff. 'Older' and 'Oldest' refer to the persons who do not belong to the same family.

(b) **Elder** (and **eldest**) are used in respect of the members of the same family like sons, daughters, brothers, sisters.

Examples :

(i) My elder sister is a lecturer.
(ii) Meenakshi is the eldest of the three sisters.

Note :

(i) 'Elder' is not followed by 'than'.
(ii) 'Elder' and 'Eldest' cannot be used for things.

3. (a) **'Few'** is negative and is the opposite of 'Many'. It means 'not many'.

(b) **'A few'** is positive and means 'some at least'. It is the opposite of 'None'.

(c) **'The few'** means 'minority' and suggests 'whether there is'.

Examples :

(i) We have few holidays in school.
(ii) Only a few boys will fail in the examination.
(iii) The few poems that he wrote are very popular.

4. (a) **Further** means 'something additional'.

(b) **Farther** means 'a greater distance'.

Examples :

(i) Further discussion will be held in the office of the principal.
(ii) Amritsar is farther from Delhi than Ambala.

5. (a) **Little** is negative. It means, 'not much', or 'hardly any'.

(b) **A little** is positive. It means 'some quantity'.

(c) **The little** denotes quantity. It means, 'not much but all that is, or whatever quantity there is'.

Examples :

(i) There is little hope of his success.
(ii) He knows a little of everything.
(iii) I have spent the little money I had.
(iv) The little knowledge of shoe-making proved very useful to me.

6. (a) '**Much**' expresses 'quantity'.

(b) '**Many**' expresses 'number'.

(c) **'Many a'**—'Singular noun' and 'Singular verb' are used with 'many a'.

Examples :

(i) There is not *much* water in the jug.
(ii) *Many* boys are absent today.
(iii) *Many* a battle has been fought on the soil of India.

7. (a) '**Less**' denotes 'in a small degree'.

(b) '**Fewer**' denotes 'number'.

Examples :

(i) He devotes less time to his studies.
(ii) There are no fewer than ten chairs in this room.

8. (a) '**Each**' is used for a single number of 'two persons' or 'things'.

(b) '**Every**' is used for a single number of 'many persons' or 'things'.

Examples :

(i) Each boy must take part in games.
(ii) There are only two poets. Each poet recited his poem.
(iii) Every man dies in this world.
(iv) Every man is expected to do his duty.

9. (a) '**Either**' means one of the two or both.

(b) '**Neither**' is negative of the either.

Examples :

(i) You may buy either of these two chairs.
(ii) Neither of them could speak on the stage.

10. (a) '**Later**' expresses 'late in time'.
(b) '**Latter**' means 'second in position or order'.
Examples :
(i) My father reached later than I expected.
(ii) The latter position was better than the former.

Use of some Important Adverbs

1. (a) Also, too, enough:
(i) He taught English. Also, he edited the school magazine
(ii) He is a writer and also he is a painter.
(iii) He is too obstinate to listen to any reason.
(iv) This is too difficult a piece for the junior students.
(v) Sarla was kind enough to help the poor.
(vi) He is brave enough to help the truth.
Note; 'Too' is used in a negative sense, but enough is used in a positive sense.
(b) Fairly and rather: Both suggest the meaning 'moderately'. But, mainly 'fairly' is used with the words that denote a positive meaning and rather is used with the words that denote a negative meaning:
(i) Rita did fairly well in that competition, but her performance was rather poor in sports.
(ii) Mona is fairly rich, but she is rather stingy.
Note: 'Rather' can also be used in a positive sense.
(i) This is a rather interesting job.
(ii) That boy is rather smart.
(c) Hardly, barely, scarcely: These words mostly convey the negative suggestions and are almost similar.
(i) I have hardly any strength now.
(ii) There was barely any supply to the township,
(iii) There were scarcely a hundred guests present.
Note: With slight variance in the meaning, the words given above convey the idea of 'very little', 'not enough', 'lack of quantity and number'.
(d) Yet, Still: These adverbs can often be used to connect the sentence units:
(i) He has been defeated many times in the contest; still he wants to be a competitor.
(ii) Mona was sick; yet she went on doing her work.
(e) Alone:
(i) He alone (none else) is capable of handling that fire,
(ii) He hunted all alone in the forest. (not in any company)

Special Note:
(a) Apart from their conventional positions the adverbs might be used in different positions with different meanings and angles.
(i) He had only four books.
(ii) John only contacted his friend in need.
(iii) He greeted me only.
(iv) Only he greeted me there.
(b) Inversion: Some adverbs can be inverted *i.e.* placed in the beginning of the sentence and then be followed by an interrogative form. The most common of these adverb are: so, seldom, never, nowhere, under no circumstances, hardly, scarcely etc.
(i) So big was the bus that it could not enter the narrow lane.
(ii) Hardly had he reached the station when he received the message.

MULTIPLE CHOICE QUESTIONS

Directions: *In the following questions choose the correct options to fill the blanks.*

1. The girl whom you met is the .... sister of Ravi.
A. eldest B. elder
C. older D. oldest

2. The historical place is ....
A. seeing worth

B. worthy of seeing
C. worth seeing
D. worthy seeing

3. These flowers smell ....
A. sweet B. sweetly
C. more sweetly D. sweetest

4. .... aspirant cannot pass the entrance examination.
A. Each B. Every
C. All D. No

5. Harivansh Rai .... second Shakespeare.
A. is a B. is
C. is the D. is an

6. .... student in the class got prizes.
A. Each and every B. Every and each
C. Every D. Never

7. It is .... picture than the one we saw last Monday.
A. interesting B. much interesting
C. more interesting D. most interesting

8. She is clever ....
A. that her mother is
B. as her mother is
C. to her mother is
D. than her mother is

9. They will get ....
A. Red, green and black paper
B. Red, green black paper
C. Red and green and black paper
D. Red green black paper

10. Health is .... wealth.
A. preferable to
B. more preferable than
C. more preferable to
D. most preferable then

11. .... water that was in the jug evaporated.
A. Little B. The little
C. Small D. A small

12. He has not sung .... songs.
A. much B. most
C. more D. many

13. Srishti has searched .... office.
A. whole the B. the whole
C. a whole D. some whole

14. Premchand was .... best and .... famous writer.
A. a, the most B. the, a most
C. the, more D. the, the most

15. William Shakespeare is famous as ....
A. a poet and a dramatist
B. a poet and dramatist
C. the poet and the dramatist
D. a poet and the dramatist

16. What does .... leader suggest?
A. other B. another
C. others D. anothers

17. He .... money.
A. has few B. have few
C. has little D. have little

18. The .... boys are rewarded.
A. first two B. two first
C. firsts two D. two's first

19. He is .... brave.
A. stronger than
B. stronger then
C. more strong then
D. more strong than

20. No sooner said ....
A. so done B. and done
C. then done D. but done

21. She returned .... than I had thought.
A. quickly B. more quicker
C. more quickly D. quicker

22. He is .... foolish person.
A. rather the B. a rather
C. rather a D. rather

23. This pen .... rupees.
A. costs twenty
B. twenty costs only
C. costs only twenty
D. only costs twenty

24. It is .... pride.
A. nothing else but
B. nothing else than
C. else nothing than
D. but

25. This tea is .... to drink.
A. too hot B. very hot
C. enough hot D. much hot

ANSWERS

1	2	3	4	5	6	7	8	9	10
A	C	A	B	A	C	C	C	A	A
11	**12**	**13**	**14**	**15**	**16**	**17**	**18**	**19**	**20**
B	D	B	D	B	B	C	A	D	C
21	**22**	**23**	**24**	**25**					
C	C	C	A	A					

DETERMINERS

Determiners are actually Adjectives. They are always followed by nouns.

Determiners are of the following kinds:

1. **Demonstrative Determiners**
   this, that, these, those
2. **Possessive Determiners**
   my, our, your, his, her, its, their
3. **Quantitative Determiners**
   some, any, much, enough, sufficient, whole, a little, the little, little, all, both
4. **Numerical Determiners**
   a few, some, few, the few, any, several, many, no, etc.
   One, two, three ... (Cardinals)
   First, second, third ... (Ordinals)
5. **Distributive Determiners**
   either, neither
6. **Articles**
   Indefinite: a, an
   Definite: the

MULTIPLE CHOICE QUESTIONS

Directions: *In the following questions choose the correct options to fill the blanks.*

1. Give me .... rice.
A. some B. few
C. a few D. any

2. .... sheep grazing on the slope of the hill had gone away.
A. Any B. The few
C. This D. Much

3. Have you got .... magazines to read?
A. all B. much
C. some D. little

4. I have .... money that I want to spend on shares.
A. any B. much
C. less D. some

5. There is .... owl on the branch of the tree.
A. a B. the
C. an D. some

6. My brother is .... MBA.
A. a B. an
C. the D. any

7. Have you got .... cheese?
A. some B. many
C. a few D. few

8. No, I have not got .... cheese.
A. many B. few
C. any D. some

9. There is only .... milk left in the bottle.
A. enough B. few
C. much D. a little

10. There is .... hope of his recovery.
A. any B. little
C. many D. few

11. .... dogs were barking at the strangers.
A. Some B. Any
C. Much D. Less

12. The girl bought her father .... juice.
A. few B. some
C. any D. many

13. You should take .... honey everyday.
A. any B. many
C. a little D. a few

14. .... boy was punished by the teacher.
A. Either B. All
C. Any D. Many

15. .... girl was asked to join the army.
A. None B. Neither
C. All D. Any

16. .... water in the jug has been drunk by Mohan.
A. The little B. The few
C. A few D. Few

17. I shall play .... piano at the party.
A. some B. any
C. the D. few

18. .... labourers were found dead in the mine.
A. Any B. Fewer
C. Many D. Less

19. Could I borrow .... umbrella?
A. our B. your
C. yours D. my

20. My brother is standing in the .... row.
A. any B. many
C. some D. first

ANSWERS

1	2	3	4	5	6	7	8	9	10
A	B	C	D	C	B	A	C	D	B
11	**12**	**13**	**14**	**15**	**16**	**17**	**18**	**19**	**20**
A	B	C	A	B	A	C	C	B	D

THE VERB

A Verb is a word that tells something about the action or state of or happenning to a person or thing.

A Verb tells the following:

1. What a person or thing does.
Sachin goes to school daily.
The bell *rang* loudly.
Many birds fly in the sky.
She *sang* a song.

2. What a person or thing is.
India *is* the biggest democracy in the world.
Ram Mehar *is* very rich.
They *are* happy.

3. What is done to a person or thing.
You *are liked* by all.
Two thieves *were arrested.*
Four students *were punished* by the teacher.

4. What happens to a person or thing.
His maternal uncle *died* last week.
Two ships *sank* yesterday.
Leaves *turn* yellow in autumn.

5. What a person or thing has, had, and so on.
I *have* a new car.
He *had* a scooter last year.
He *has* several cows and goats.

It goes without saying that a verb is the most important part of a sentence. No sentence is complete without a Verb.

Important Information

1. If two or more singular nouns are joined by 'and' the verb used will be plural.

   Example:
   (i) He and I were going to the market.
   (ii) Ram and Mohan are friends.

2. If two singular nouns joined by 'and' points out to the same thing or person, the verb used must be singular.

   Example:
   (i) Rice and curry is the favourite food of the Punjabis.
   (ii) The Collector and District Magistrate is away.

3. In case two subjects are joined by 'as well as' the verb agrees with the first subject.

   Example :
   (i) Kanta as well as her children is playing.
   (ii) Children as well as their mother are playing.

In the case of first sentence the verb (is) agrees with Kanta and in the case of second sentence the verb (are) agrees with the children.

4. 'Neither', 'Either', 'Every', 'Each', 'Everyone', and 'Many a' are followed by a singular verb.
   Example :
   (i) Either of the plans is to be adopted.
   (ii) Neither of the two brothers is sure to pass.
   (iii) Every student is expected to be obedient.
   (iv) Everyone of them desires this.
   (v) Many a person is drowned in the sea.
5. If two subjects are joined by 'Either .... or' / 'Neither .... nor', the verb agrees with the subject near to it.
   Example :
   (i) Either my brother or I am to do this work.
   (ii) Neither he nor they are prepared to do this work.
6. 'A great many' is always followed by a 'plural noun' and a 'plural verb'. For example :
   A great many students have been declared successful.
7. Similarly if two subjects are joined by 'with', 'together with', 'no less than', in addition to 'and not', etc. the verb agrees with the first subject.
   Example :
   (i) The boy with his parents has arrived.
   (ii) He, no less than I, is to blame.
8. Nouns, plural in form, but singular in meaning, take a singular verb.
   Example :
   This news was broadcast from television yesterday.

MULTIPLE CHOICE QUESTIONS

Directions: *In the following questions choose the correct options to fill the blanks.*

1. The bus with all its passengers .... lost.
A. were B. was
C. are D. would

2. You as well as I .... responsible for this work.
A. am B. are
C. was D. is

3. Raghava like all his companions .... a spoiled child.
A. are B. were
C. is D. will be

4. Pen and ink .... required for me.
A. are B. were
C. is D. has required

5. Every girl and every boy .... attended the seminar.
A. have B. has
C. is D. are

6. Not only she but all her sisters ...... been married.
A. has B. have
C. is D. are

7. There .... nothing but miseries in life.
A. is B. are
C. were D. will be

8. Neither prose nor poem .... given.
A. were B. was
C. has D. have

9. Either he or I .... wrong.
A. is B. are
C. am D. were

10. Either Sulekha or Rekha .... coming here.
A. are B. is
C. were D. have

11. .... the child or his parents to blame?
A. Is B. Are
C. Were D. Has

12. You and I .... neighbours.
A. am B. are
C. was D. has

13. The house with all its belongings ..... sold away.
A. were B. are
C. was D. must

14. Either water or juice .... required.
A. is B. are
C. were D. has

15. There were not as many tables as .... required.
A. was B. were
C. is D. are

16. They each .... a book.
A. have B. are
C. has D. is

17. He and I .... class friends.
A. is B. am
C. was D. are

18. She as well as I .... guilty.
A. is B. are
C. am D. must be

19. Purushottam .... not read more on this chapter.
A. needs B. has been need
C. need D. had been need

20. He came .... to his aunt.
A. run B. running
C. to run D. in run

21. She dislikes .... meat.
A. eat to B. to eat
C. eating D. to eating

22. He likes ....
A. sing to B. singing
C. to sing D. to singing

23. We are ready .... the match.
A. play to B. to playing
C. playing D. to play

24. .... is injurious to health.
A. Smoking B. To smoke
C. To smoking D. Smoke to

25. He loves .... raw vegetables.
A. eaten B. eating
C. to eating D. eat to

26. He seemed .... finished his homework.
A. have to B. to have
C. having D. to having

ANSWERS

1	2	3	4	5	6	7	8	9	10
B	B	C	C	B	B	A	B	C	B
11	**12**	**13**	**14**	**15**	**16**	**17**	**18**	**19**	**20**
A	B	C	A	B	A	D	A	C	B
21	**22**	**23**	**24**	**25**	**26**				
C	B	D	A	B	B				

CONJUNCTIONS

A conjunction is a word which connects words, clauses or sentences:

Look at the following sentences.

(i) He bought apples *and* mangoes.

(ii) God made the country *and* man made the town.

(iii) The door was open *but* there was no one in the house.

(iv) He knows that I am here *and* that I want to see him.

In the sentence (i), *and* connects two words—*apples* and *mangoes.*

In the sentence (ii), *and* connects two sentences—*God made the country* and *man made the town.*

In the sentence (iii), *but* connects two sentences—*The door was open* and *there was no one in the house.*

In the sentence (iv), *and* connects two clauses—*that I am here* and *that I want to see him.*

The main coordinating conjunctions are:

and, but, for, or, nor, also, either ..... or, neither ..... nor.

There are some conjunctions which are used in pairs. They are:

either .... or, ... neither .... nor, both .... and, though .... yet, whether .... or, not only .... but also.

Example: *Either* take it *or* leave it.

It is *neither* useful *nor* ornamental.

They *both* like *and* respect me.

Though he is suffering from high fever, *yet* he does not cry.

He does not care *whether* you go *or* stay.

He is *not only* doltish, *but also* obstinate.

The conjunctions which are used in pairs in this way, are called correlative conjunctions, or merely correlatives.

Use of Important Conjunctions

1. **As soon as :** As soon as denotes simultaneous time.
   Example : As soon as he saw his enemy, he took to his heels.
2. **No sooner .... than :**
   (a) 'No sooner' is always followed by 'than'.
   (b) Please remember that 'No sooner' is always followed by do/does/did. As such only first form of the verb should be used after the subject.
   Example :
   No sooner did he see his enemy than he took to his heels.
3. **Hardly :** Hardly is followed by when.
   Examples :
   (i) Hardly had I left the house when it started raining.
   (ii) We had hardly come into the room when his father began chastising him.
   Note :
   A. Hardly is never followed by than.
   B. 'Scarcely' can also be used in the sense and manner of 'Hardly'.
4. **Lest :** Lest is used in the sense of so that .... not. It is always followed by should. Lest is negative in sense. Hence 'not' should never be used with it.
   Example :
   Work hard lest you should fail.
   Note : 'Lest' is always followed by 'should' and not 'may'.
5. **Unless :** Unless expresses condition. It is also used in the negative sense. Use of 'not' is not allowed with unless because unless is already in the negative sense.
   Example :
   Unless you labour hard you will not pass.
6. **Until :** 'Until' expresses time. It means 'till not'.
   Example :
   Wait here until I return.
   Note : Until is in the negative sense. So 'not' should not be used with it. Example :
   Wait here until I do not return. (Incorrect)
   Wait here until I return. (Correct)
7. **As well as :** When two subjects are joined by 'as well as', the verb always agrees with the first subject.
   Examples :
   (i) The teacher as well as students is playing.
   (ii) Students as well as the teacher are playing.
   Note : 'Both' and 'as well as' cannot be used together in the same sentence.
   Examples :
   Both Sita as well as Kanta are beautiful. (Incorrect)
   Sita as well as Kanta is beautiful. (Correct)
   Both Sita and Kanta are beautiful. (Correct)
8. **As if :** 'As if' is used in the sense of pretension. While using 'as if' in a sentence, we should see that even the third person singular subject gets 'were'.
   Example :
   He talks as if he were mad.
9. **Till :** Till expresses time. Till is always used in the affirmative.
   Example :
   We did not come back till sunset.
10. **Rather than :** 'Rather than' is used in the sense of 'preference'. 'Rather' is always followed by 'than'.
    Example :
    I would rather die than submit.
11. **As long as/so long as :** Both express time during which an action or event takes place.
    Example :
    As long as there is life, there is hope.
12. **However :** It is both a subordinate and co-ordinate clause.
    Examples :
    (a) Mala worked hard, she however, failed.
    (b) However hard he may work, he cannot pass.
13. **Such as :** 'Such as' gives us the sense of 'like'. Such is always followed by 'as'.
    Example :
    Life is such a puzzle as cannot be solved.

MULTIPLE CHOICE QUESTIONS

Directions: *In the following questions choose the correct options to fill the blanks.*

1. Neither he .... his friend is good.
A. or B. and
C. but D. nor

2. The officer asked the peon .... why he was late.
A. that B. if
C. but D. No word needed

3. Both Ajay .... Vijay are intelligent.
A. or B. nor
C. and D. No word needed

4. No Sooner did the thief see the public .... he ran away.
A. then B. and
C. but D. than

5. Abhinav .... his brothers was going to Mumbai.
A. but B. yet
C. No word needed D. together with

6. He behaves .... he were the captain of the team.
A. as if B. as
C. No word needed D. that

7. Either Rupali .... Sonali is going to attend the meeting.
A. and B. but
C. nor D. or

8. Neither Nirmal .... Ashwinee is going to listen the speech.
A. and B. but
C. nor D. or

9. Ravi .... Prakash are going to Kolkata.
A. or B. nor
C. but D. and

10. Rice .... curry is my usual breakfast.
A. and B. but
C. then D. than

11. Hardly had he left .... his brother came.
A. then B. than
C. when D. that

12. I would rather have a copy .... a book.
A. then B. than
C. when D. that

13. He is no other .... my friend.
A. then B. than
C. when D. but

14. He saw a snake ....he awoke.
A. then B. when
C. than D. No word needed

15. Ten years have passed .... my grandmother died.
A. since B. when
C. then D. than

16. She is .... good .... bad.
A. either, not B. neither, or
C. neither, nor D. neither, than

17. The cellphone is both cheap .... best.
A. than B. and
C. then D. or

18. No sooner did the rogue see the police .... he disappeared.
A. then B. than
C. so D. because

19. Srishti will go .... Sanju goes.
A. if B. than
C. then D. although

20. She is wise .... timid.
A. and B. yet
C. but D. however

21. Make hay .... the sun shines.
A. though B. while
C. after D. before

22. He is so weak .... he cannot walk.
A. but B. that
C. then D. so

23. Although he is rich, ... he is unhappy.
A. but B. yet
C. so D. still

24. Wait here .... I come back.
A. till B. until
C. before D. after

25. He is my friend .... I shall help him.
A. so
B. hence
C. that is why
D. therefore

26. He must go away .... he will be beaten.
A. otherwise B. and
C. or D. else

27. God loves good men .... good men love God.
A. and B. or
C. that D. those

28. He was late .... he was not punished.
A. but B. yet
C. still D. therefore

29. Walk slowly ...., you may fall.
A. and B. or
C. so D. otherwise

30. Work hard, ... you will fail.
A. and B. or
C. otherwise D. else

ANSWERS

1	2	3	4	5	6	7	8	9	10
D	D	C	D	D	A	D	C	D	A
11	**12**	**13**	**14**	**15**	**16**	**17**	**18**	**19**	**20**
C	B	B	B	A	C	B	B	A	C
21	**22**	**23**	**24**	**25**	**26**	**27**	**28**	**29**	**30**
B	B	B	A	B	C	A	C	D	D

PREPOSITIONS

A *Preposition* is a word which is placed before a noun or a pronoun to show its relation to some other word in the sentence.

1. I saw a goat *in* the field.
2. I am fond *of* hot coffee.

In sentence 1, the word *in* shows the relation between two things—*goat* and *field.*

In sentence 2, the word *of* shows the relation between the attribute expressed by the adjective *found* and *tea.*

The words *in* and *of* are here used as prepositions.

The noun or pronoun which is used with a preposition is called its object. The noun or pronoun is in the objective case. It is governed by the preposition. Now it is absolutely clear that in sentence 1, the noun *field* is in the objective case. The word *field* is governed by the preposition *in.*

A preposition may have two or more objects.

The road runs over *hill* and *plain.*

Here, the words *hill* and *plain* are used as objects.

Use of Important Prepositions

1. Among, Between

'**Among**' is used for more than two persons or things; '**Between**' is used only for two.

Examples :

(i) Distribute these sweets *among* the poor students of the class.

(ii) Distribute these books *between* Ram and Shyam.

2. Among, In

'**Among**' is used before collective plural nouns

'**In**' is used before collective singular nouns.

Examples :

(i) I found him standing *among* the crowd.

(ii) I saw him in the crowd.

3. Beside, Besides

'**Beside**' means 'by the side of'. '**Besides**' means 'in addition to'.

Examples :

(i) The daughter was sitting *beside* her mother.

(ii) *Besidcs* his relatives, he invited his friends also.

4. In, Within

'**In**' means at the expiry of a period of time in future, '**Within**' means before the expiry of a period of time in any tense.

Examples :

(i) She will return *in* a week.

(ii) I shall finish my work *within* a weak.

5. On, Upon

'**On**' is used for things at rest; '**Upon**' is used for things in motion.

Examples :

(i) He is sitting *on* the floor.

(ii) The dog sprang *upon* the table.

6. By, With

'**By**' denotes the agent or doer, '**With**' denotes the instrument with which anything is done.

Examples :

(i) The bird was killed *by* the hunter with an arrow.

(ii) He beat the dog *with* a stick.

(iii) I shall reach here *by* five o'clock.

7. After, In

'**After**' means at the end of a period of time in the past. '**In**' means at the end of a period of time in future.

Examples :

(i) I shall return your book *in* a week.

(ii) He returned the book *after* a week.

8. For, From, Since

'**For**' is used before a noun denoting a period of time with all the tenses. '**From**' is used before a noun or phrase denoting a point of time, it is used in all the tenses. '**Since**' is used before a noun or phrase denoting some point of time and is always produced by a verb in the perfect continuous tense or third form of a verb.

Examples :

(i) We have been playing cards *for* two hours.

(ii) She stayed with her uncle *from* the 15th of March to the 15th of May.

(iii) I have been reading this book *since* morning.

9. Above, Over

'Above' means 'higher from', **Over** is used in the following four senses :

(i) In the sense of 'above' :
At noon, the sun is *over* our heads.

(ii) In the sense of 'beyond' :
I cannot get *over* my disappointment.

(iii) In the sense of 'Superiority' :
God *over* all blesses for ever more.

(iv) In the sense of 'Conclusion' :
It is all *over* with me.

10. At, Towards

'**At**' denotes the idea of aim, **'Towards'** denotes the idea of destination.

Examples :

(i) He threw the stone *at* the cat.

(ii) He went *towards* the house.

11. At, In, On

'At' is used as follows :

(i) **'At'** is used with small towns and villages.

Examples :

(a) He was born *at* Sonepat.

(b) He lives *at* village Bangra. (Bangra is a village)

(ii) **'At'** is used before a noun denoting a definite point of time.

Example :

He called on me *at* 9 p.m. yesterday.

'In' is used as follows :

(iii) **'In'** is used with the names of big cities, provinces and countries.

Examples :

(a) His father lives *in* England.

(b) His younger brother lives *in* Calcutta.

(iv) **'In'** is used before the names of months and years.

Example :

His elder sister was born *in* 1972 *in* the month of May.

'On' is used with dates and names of days.

Examples :

(a) I joined college *on* the 26th April.

(b) He will leave for Kolkata *on* Wednesday next.

Important Information

1. **'In'** is also used in the following phrases :
In the morning; In the evening, In winter, In summer.

2. '**In**' also denotes a place inside anything.
He travelled *in* a crowded bus.
3. '**At**' is used in the following phrases :
At home, *At* the station, *At* work, *At* play.

12. Below, Beneath

Below means 'of lower level in position, dignity and expectation' etc. *Beneath* means 'under'.

Examples :

(i) It is *below* my dignity to talk to her.
(ii) They rested *beneath* the shade of a tree.

13. In, Into, To

'**In**' expresses Rest or Motion inside anything. '**Into**' expresses Motion towards the inside of anything or change from one medium to another. '**To**' denotes motion from one place to another.

Examples :

(i) The boys are *in* the room.
(ii) Translate this passage from English *into* Hindi.
(iii) Every morning he goes *to* the temple.

14. Till, By, Of, Off

- 'Till' means upto or not earlier than.
- 'By' means not later than.
- 'Of' shows cause, source, separation, quality, contents, possession, apposition, point of reference, space in time etc.
- 'Off' shows separation at a near distance, and detached condition.

Consider the following examples:

(i) I shall work *till* 5 a.m.
(ii) Madhu died *of* cancer.
(iii) The nib *of* the pen is made *of* gold.
(iv) He presented me a bottle *of* perfume.
(v) Our principal is a man *of* principle.
(vi) He lived in the house *of* his friend.
(vii) *By* this time tomorrow, I'll have finished my job.
(viii) My house is *off* the road.
(ix) The book fell *off* the table.

MULTIPLE CHOICE QUESTIONS

Directions: *Tick the correct preposition for the blank in each of the following sentences.*

1. He applied ...... the manager.
A. for B. to
C. with D. by

2. Trust ...... God and do the right.
A. in B. for
C. to D. with

3. She is worthy ...... a prize.
A. with B. for
C. to D. of

4. Mr. Gomes has no taste ...... music.
A. of B. for
C. with D. to

5. You are hard ...... hearing.
A. at B. of
C. with D. for

6. He is sure ...... his success
A. for B. with
C. on D. of

7. Preeti was warned ...... the danger ahead.
A. for B. at
C. of D. about

8. I am thankful ...... you for a good advice.
A. for B. with
C. to D. of

9. Deepak would not surrender ...... the police.
A. with B. to
C. for D. on

10. The small plant in your lawn is very sensitive ...... touch.
A. on B. with
C. to D. about

11. Divya was sure to succeed ..... the examination.
A. for B. in
C. to D. with

12. Geeta was jealous ...... Ravina's beauty.
A. to B. with
C. for D. of

13. He was ignorant ..... what was happening there.

A. for B. of

C. to D. with

14. Your pen is inferior ...... mine.

A. than B. with

C. from D. to

15. Reenu is no match ...... Meenu.

A. to B. for

C. with D. upon

16. It is necessary ...... you to apply for this job.

A. on B. with

C. for D. to

17. Be loyal ...... your country.

A. for B. to

C. on D. with

18. Mukesh is junior ...... me.

A. than B. to

C. from D. of

19. Deepika was innocent ...... the crime.

A. of B. with

C. from D. to

20. I am desirous.... joining the Indian cricket team.

A. for B. of

C. to D. on

ANSWERS

1	2	3	4	5	6	7	8	9	10
B	A	D	B	B	D	D	D	B	D
11	**12**	**13**	**14**	**15**	**16**	**17**	**18**	**19**	**20**
B	D	B	D	B	D	B	B	A	B

SYNONYMS

A synonym is a word which conveys a meaning similar to the given word.

REMEMBER

Words	*Synonyms*
Add	Increase
Adequate	Enough
Adjust	Adapt
All	Aggregate
Allow	Permit
Abode	Dwelling
Apt	Proper
Assess	Appraise
Accuse	Calumniate
Abashed	Timid
Annoy	Displease
Ample	Enough, Sufficient
Amplify	Increase
Apathetic	Unenthusiastic
Accost	Address
Authentic	True

Words	*Synonyms*
Adjust	Fit
Approve	Assent, Allow, Accept
Adapt	Conform
Adversary	Opponent, Rival, Competitor
Beat	Whack
Benign	Kind
Breeze	Zephyr
Baffle	Puzzle
Booty	Spoil
Beauty	Charm
Beast	Animal
Bandit	Robber
Blaze	Shine
Bond	Tie
Bend	Twist
Bate	Diminish
Beg	Plead
Barbaric	Wild, Savage
Bashful	Shy, Reserved

Words	Synonyms
Begin	Start
Blend	Mix, Mingle
Bizarre	Funny
Below	Under
Bedevil	Confuse
Bemoan	Lament
Babble	Nonsense
Blame	Fault
Behaviour	Demeanour
Call	Accost
Copy	Imitate
Close	Shut
Caress	Love
Camp	Stay
Connect	Attach
Cut	Injure, Curtail
Cling	Stick
Conical	Funny
Convey	Carry
Conspicuous	Prominent
Cheerful	Happy, Pleasant
Curtail	Decrease
Cheerless	Sad, Dejected
Curious	Strange
Circumstance	Factor, Situation, Condition
Competent	Capable
Congruent	Overlapping
Cope	Deal, Endure
Confident	Sure
Complex	Intricate
Cajole	Coax, Flatter
Cunning	Crafty
Delectable	Joyful, Delightful
Devilish	Diabolical
Delicate	Soft
Devil	Fiend
Delay	Postpone
Dislike	Repugnance
Destroy	Ruin

Words	Synonyms
Dwell	Live, Dilate
Declare	Pronounce
Drunk	Flushed
Deficient	Lacking
Damn	Condemn, Curse
Decrease	Diminish
Destruction	Devastation
Efficient	Competent
Ethnic	Racial
Enthral	Enslave
Earnest	Serious
Envious	Jealous
Ending	Final
Egg	Incite
Extempore	At once
Extensive	Far-ranging
Extra	Surplus
Existence	Life
Exceed	Overstep
Enormous	Vast
Excessive	Superfluous
Free	Unhindered
Frigid	Cold
Feed	Cater
Fame	Reputation
Frame	Make
First	Initial
Frighten	Terrorise, Intimidate
Fervent	Fervid
Fall	Decline
Feeble	Frail
Fickle	Changeable
Finish	Conclude
Fraud	Deception
Forgiving	Placable
Grow	Develop
Greed	Avidity
Greet	Welcome
Grave	Serious
Group	Constellation

Words	*Synonyms*
Given	Bestowed
Gratitude	Thankfulness
Have	Possess
Hire	Rent
Hit	Strike
Handsome	Beautiful
Hinder	Prevent
Heap	Pile
Hope	Expect
Hard	Harsh
Help	Aid
Hymn	Song
Henpecked	Enslaved
Hoodwink	Mystify, Cheat
Humble	Polite, Urbane, Modest
Harass	Vex, Trouble
Impart	Instil
Intact	Untouched
Instal	Establish
Indict	Impeach
Imitate	Ape
Instigate	Incite
Initiate	Start, Introduce
Inimical	Unfriendly
Insufferable	Intolerable
Impartiality	Justice
Jolly	Merry
Joyful	Delectable
Join	Conjoin
Kind	Benign
Kill	Murder
Kindred	Similar
Kinship	Relationship
Keen	Sharp
Knowledge	Scholarship
Lazy	Slothful
Large	Substantial, Gargantuan
Listless	Careless, Lackadaisical
Lax	Loose
Little	Small
Lifelike	Realistic

Words	*Synonyms*
Lofty	High
Lenient	Soft, Gentle
Lacking	Deficient, Wanting
Lessen	Decrease
Middleclass	Bourgeois
Mitigate	Lessen, Abate
Modesty	Humility, Lowliness
Mix	Mingle, Blend
Mixture	Mingling
Mixed	Assorted
Modify	Decrease
Mean	Imply
Multifarious	Varied
Miscarry	Abort
Note	Notice
Noble	Stately
Native	Indigenous
Needful	Necessary
Notify	Declare
Nervous	Shaky, Tremulous, Timid
Natural	Spontaneous
Near	Close
Normal	Natural
Offend	Displease
Oppress	Persecute, Tyrannize
Opponent	Adversary
Obstruct	Hinder, Check
Offence	Fault
Offender	Villain
Overstep	Exceed
Overlapping	Congruent
Occult	Mystic
Profane	Unholy
Patience	Forbearance
Pornographic	Obscene
Plenitude	Abundance
Prominent	Important
Prodigal	Spender
Procrastinate	Postpone
Promote	Develop, Honour
Persecute	Tyrannise

Words	*Synonyms*
Profess	Claim
Pliant	Flexible
Plebian	Common
Polished	Sophisticated
Quake	Shake
Quit	Leave
Queer	Eccentric
Quell	Suppress
Quantify	Allot
Reply	Answer
Relinquish	Retire
Read	Peruse
Relation	Reference
Render	Do
Remainder	Residuals
Repeat	Reiterate
Repentant	Contrite
Retaliative	Retaliatory
Rumour	Hearsay
Reveal	Divulge
Ritualistic	Ceremonious
Soft	Delicate
Sort	Kind, Choose, Select
Selfish	Egoistic
Sensual	Earthly
Suppress	Quell, Check
Stimulate	Provoke
Tasteless	Insipid
Travel	Journey
True	Authentic, Faithful, Truthful
Turbulence	Turmoil
Tragedy	Calamity
Tasteful	Tasty, Delicious
Touching	Painful
Thankful	Grateful
Tremendous	Great, Huge
Tough	Strong
Terminate	Conclude, End
Theory	Doctrine
Tell	Relate
Tremble	Shake, Shiver
Urge	Spur

Words	*Synonyms*
Unbeaten	Unsubdued
Use	Utilize, Practise
Underhand	Unfair, Undue
Unfair	Unjust
Unravel	Reveal, Divulge
Unimportant	Common
Unconcerned	Apathetic
Unimitated	Inimitable
Unfortunate	Unlucky
Understand	Perceive, Comprehend
Vain	Proud, Haughty, Conceited, Shameless
Vale	Valley, Dale, Dell
Vice	Fault
Virtue	Quality
Veracity	Reality
Value	Price, Prize
Vex	Tease
Vibrate	Quiver, Shake
Violent	Excessive
Vivid	Clear, Lucid
Victory	Triumph
Vulgar	Indecent
Virtuous	Honest
Variegated	Varied, Multifarious
Well	Good
Yell	Cry, Shout
Yonder	There
Yearn	Wish, Desire
Yoke	Slavery
Zest	Earnestness, Enthusiasm
Zealous	Earnest

ANTONYMS

A antonym is a word which conveys a meaning opposite to the given word.

REMEMBER

Words	*Antonyms*
Abhor	Love
Abnormal	Normal
Able	Unable
Acceptable	Unacceptable
Adequate	Inadequate
Amusing	Boring

Words	*Antonyms*	*Words*	*Antonyms*
Angry	Calm	Hard	Soft
Apex	Bottom	Hate	Love
Attract	Repel	Honest	Dishonest
Bad	Good	Idle	Busy
Barren	Fertile	Immoral	Moral
Beautiful	Ugly	Include	Exclude
Bitter	Sweet	Incorrect	Correct
Brave	Cowardly	Intelligent	Unintelligent
Brief	Lengthy	Kind	Cruel
Bright	Dull	Like	Dislike
Calm	Violent	Long	Short
Careful	Careless	Lucid	Vague
Clear	Vague, Cloudy	Major	Minor
Cold	Hot	Naive	Experienced
Cruel	Kind	Nadir	Apex
Dear	Cheap	Neat	Clumsy
Deep	Shallow	Obedient	Disobedient
Difficult	Easy	Obscure	Clear
Direct	Indirect	Oppose	Support
Dishonest	Honest	Optimistic	Pessimistic
Disobey	Obey	Out	In
Encourage	Discourage	Patience	Impatience
Enormous	Tiny	Peaceful	Belligerent
Excellent	Bad	Pious	Impious
Expensive	Cheap	Polite	Impolite
Eat	Fast	Potent	Impotent
Fair	Unfair	Prominent	Unimportant
Fake	Authentic	Proper	Improper
False	True	Pure	Impure
Famous	Notorious	Quick	Slow
Fool	Genius	Quiet	Disturbance
Generous	Miserly	Real	False, Unreal
Genius	Fool	Reject	Select, Choose
Genuine	Unauthentic	Reliable	Unreliable
Gigantic	Tiny	Respect	Disrespect
Glad	Depressed	Right	Wrong
Good	Bad	Robust	Feeble, Weak
Great	Little	Sad	Happy
Happy	Sad		

Words	Antonyms
Secret	Open
Sensible	Insensible
Severe	Mild
Sharp	Blunt
Simple	Complex
Sociable	Unsociable
Tall	Short
Tidy	Untidy
Uncanny	Canny
Violent	Calm
Vivid	Vague

Words	Antonyms
Strong	Weak
Big	Small
Easy	Difficult
Fast	Slow
High	Low
Catchy	Unattractive
Ugly	Handsome, Beautiful, Tidy
Tasty	Insipid
Sonorous	Harsh

MULTIPLE CHOICE QUESTIONS

Directions (Qs. 1 to 20): *In the following questions choose the word which best expresses the meaning of the given word.*

1. ABSURD
A. Foolish B. Simple
C. Courageous D. Silly

2. ABANDON
A. Lose B. Profit
C. Vacate D. Foil

3. CAJOLE
A. Pause B. Lenient
C. Blast D. Lure

4. COMBAT
A. Fight B. Conflict
C. Shoot D. Quarrel

5. LAMENT
A. Condone B. Console
C. Complain D. Contribution

6. DEBACLE
A. Disgrace B. Defeat
C. Collapse D. Decline

7. SHIVER
A. Fear B. Tremble
C. Shake D. Ache

8. TORTURE
A. Terror B. Harassment
C. Torment D. Tranquility

9. LAUDABLE
A. Lovable B. Commendable
C. Profitable D. Oblivious

10. FIXED
A. Sterile B. Static
C. Stubborn D. Parennial

11. QUEER
A. Unfamiliar B. Cute
C. Curious D. Strange

12. SUFFICIENT
A. Fit B. Proper
C. Adequate D. Vast

13. GLOSS
A. Brightness B. Soothing
C. Rubbing D. Miracle

14. LONGING
A. Prune B. Apathy
C. Curtail D. Craving

15. JEER
A. Applaud B. Magnanimity
C. Avoid D. Scoff

16. ZENITH
A. Minimum B. Nadir
C. Plant D. Peak

17. GARB
A. Distort B. Dress
C. Trivial D. Rage

18. ABHOR
A. Rude B. Reconcile
C. Crave D. Detest

19. YIELD
A. Shum B. Incisive
C. Retain D. Surrender

20. YOKE
A. Twist B. Release
C. Link D. Extra

Directions (Qs. 21 to 38): *In the following questions choose the word which best expresses the opposite of the given word.*

21. TRAGIC
A. Dramatic B. Strong
C. Gentle D. Comic

22. ORAL
A. Verbal B. Sane
C. Minor D. Written

23. ADMIRE
A. Hate B. Unlike
C. Dislike D. Enough

24. VIOLENT
A. Gentle B. Savage
C. Haughty D. Decline

25. ADVERSITY
A. Windfall B. Inprosperity
C. Prosperity D. Slave

26. GENUINE
A. Spurious B. Obscure
C. Countless D. Apathetic

27. GRUDGE
A. Essence B. Guile
C. Goodwill D. Ill-will

28. STIFF
A. Soft B. Courteous
C. Lively D. Flexible

29. VANITY
A. Conceit B. Pride
C. Ostentious D. Humility

30. FRONT
A. Upper B. Unusual
C. Back D. Rear

31. ATTRACT
A. Lured B. Longing
C. Repel D. Disguise

32. COMFORT
A. Discomfort B. Discontent
C. Uncomfort D. Miscomfort

33. WELCOME
A. Repel B. Accept
C. Resist D. Fight

34. TACTFUL
A. Naive B. Loose
C. Strict D. Uncivilized

35. DUTIFUL
A. Harmful B. Watchful
C. Forgetful D. Remiss

36. RIGID
A. Flux B. Adoptable
C. Yielding D. Adaptable

37. RARE
A. Petty B. Poor
C. Small D. Common

38. ZEAL
A. Despair B. Calmness
C. Passiveness D. Indifference

ANSWERS

1	2	3	4	5	6	7	8	9	10
D	C	D	A	C	C	B	C	B	B
11	**12**	**13**	**14**	**15**	**16**	**17**	**18**	**19**	**20**
D	C	A	D	D	D	B	D	D	C
21	**22**	**23**	**24**	**25**	**26**	**27**	**28**	**29**	**30**
D	D	C	A	C	A	C	D	D	D
31	**32**	**33**	**34**	**35**	**36**	**37**	**38**		
C	A	C	A	D	D	D	D		

3. Sentence Completion

It is such an exercise which starts with the primary schools and continues in the highest level of competitive examinations. One must practise it regularly to score well.

Directions (Qs. 1 to 15): *Pick out the most effective word(s) from the given words to fill in the blanks to make the sentence meaningfully complete.*

1. The student ...... that book from the library to study at home.
A. issued B. borrowed
C. hired D. lent

2. I wish I ...... a king.
A. was B. am
C. should be D. were

3. He ...... to listen to my arguments and walked away.
A. denied B. disliked
C. objected D. refused

4. The flow of blood was so ...... that the patient died.
A. intense B. adequate
C. profuse D. extensive

5. When I met her yesterday, it was the first time I ...... her since Christmas.
A. saw B. have seen
C. had seen D. have been seing

6. Can you pay ...... all these articles?
A. for B. of
C. off D. out

7. I ...... you to be at the party this evening.
A. expect B. hope
C. look forward to D. desire

8. ...... being a handicapped person, he is very cooperative and self-reliant.
A. Because B. Although
C. Since D. Despite

9. The child broke ...... from his mother and ran towards the painting.
A. away B. after
C. down D. with

10. With his ...... income, he finds it difficult to live a comfortable life.
A. brief B. sufficient
C. meagre D. huge

11. He could ...... a lot of money in such a short time by using his intelligence and working hard.
A. spend B. spoil
C. exchange D. accumulate

12. Though the brothers are twins, they look ......
A. alike B. handsome
C. indifferent D. different

13. Unfavourable weather conditions can ..... illness.
A. cure B. detect
C. treat D. enhance

14. No sooner did the bell ring, ... the actor started singing.
A. when B. than
C. after D. before

15. If I ...... realised it, I would not have acted on his advice.
A. was B. had
C. were D. have

Directions (Qs. 16 to 25): *In each question, an incomplete statement (Stem) followed by four fillers*

is given. Pi:k out the best one which can complete the incomplete stem correctly and meaningfully.

16. Unless you work harder you will fail, means .....

A. if you fail you will work harder.
B. you must at least plan well than you will not fail.
C. hardly you will fail if you do not desire so.
D. if you do not put more efforts, then you will fail.

17. Even if it rains I shall come, means .....

A. if I come it will not rain.
B. if it rains I shall not come.
C. I will certainly come whether it rains or not.
D. whenever there is rain I shall come.

18. Dinesh is as stupid as he is lazy means .....

A. Dinesh is stupid because he is lazy.
B. Dinesh is lazy because he is stupid.
C. Dinesh is either stupid or lazy.
D. Dinesh is equally stupid and lazy.

19. He is so lazy that he .....

A. cannot depend on others for getting his work done.
B. cannot delay the schedule of completing the work.
C. can seldom complete his work on time.
D. dislike to postpone the work that he undertakes to do.

20. He always stammers in public meetings, but his today's speech .....

A. was fairly audible to everyone present in the hall.
B. was not received satisfactorily.
C. could not be understood properly.
D. was free from that defect.

21. In order to raise the company's profit, the employees .....

A. demanded two additional increments.
B. decided to go on paid holidays.
C. requested the management to implement new welfare schemes.
D. offered to work overtime without any compensation.

22. Although, he is reputed for making very candid statements, ...

A. his today's speech was not fairly audible.
B. his promises had always been realistic.
C. his speech was very interesting.
D. his today's statements were very ambiguous.

23. I felt somewhat more relaxed .....

A. but tense as compared to earlier.
B. and tense as compared to earlier.
C. as there was already no tension at all.
D. and tension-free as compared to earlier.

24. With great efforts his son succeeded in convincing him not to donate his entire wealth to an orphanage .....

A. and lead the life of a wealthy merchant.
B. but to a home for the forsaken children.
C. and make an orphan of himself.
D. as the orphanage needed a lot of donations.

25. Even though it is a very large house, ...

A. there is a lot of space available in it for children.
B. there is hardly any space available for children.
C. there is no dearth of space for children.
D. the servants take a long time to clean it.

ANSWERS

1	2	3	4	5	6	7	8	9	10
B	D	D	C	C	A	A	D	A	C
11	**12**	**13**	**14**	**15**	**16**	**17**	**18**	**19**	**20**
D	D	D	B	B	D	C	D	C	D
21	**22**	**23**	**24**	**25**					
D	D	D	C	B					

4. Spotting Errors

The most common errors in English are of spellings, grammar and usage of words. By regular practice, the errors can be easily spotted and minimised.

MULTIPLE CHOICE QUESTIONS

Directions: *In the following questions some of the sentences have errors and some are correct. Find out which part of a sentence has an error, the number of that part is your answer. If a sentence is free from errors, then your answer is D i.e., No error.*

1. (A) Either Ram or/(B) you is responsible/(C) for this action./(D) No error.

2. (A) The student flatly denied/(B) that he had copied/(C) in the examination hall./(D) No error.

3. (A) By the time you arrive tomorrow/(B) I have finished/(C) my work./(D) No error.

4. (A) The captain with the members of his team/ (B) are returning/(C) after a fortnight./(D) No error.

5. (A) After returning from/(B) an all-India tour/ (C) I had to describe about it./(D) No error.

6. (A) The teacher asked his students/(B) if they had gone through/(C) either of the three chapters included in the prescribed text./(D) No error.

7. (A) Do you know/(B) how old were you/(C) when you came here?/(D) No error.

8. (A) Beware of/(B) a fair-weather friend/(C) who is neither a friend in need nor a friend indeed./ (D) No error.

9. (A) Copernicus proved/(B) that Earth/(C) moves round the Sun./(D) No error.

10. (A) The property/(B) was divided/(C) among the two brothers./(D) No error.

11. (A) I am quite certain/(B) that the lady is not only greedy/(C) but miserly./(D) No error.

12. (A) The brilliant success in the examination/ (B) as well as his record in sports/(C) deserves high praise./(D) No error.

13. (A) I cannot find/(B) where has he gone/(C) though I have tried may best./(D) No error.

14. (A) If I was/(B) the Prime Minister of India/(C) I would work wonders/(D) No error.

15. (A) If it weren't/(B) for you,/(C) I wouldn't be alive today./(D) No error.

16. (A) He looked like a lion/(B) baulked from/ (C) its prey./(D) No error.

17. (A) Widespread flooding/(B) is affecting/(C) large areas of the villages./(D) No error.

18. (A) If we really set to/(B) we can get the whole house/(C) cleaned in an afternoon./(D) No error.

19. (A) It's arrogant for you/(B) to assume you'll/ (C)win every time./(D) No error.

20. (A) The two books are the same/(B) except for the fact that this/(C) has an answer in the back./(D) No error.

21. (A) Your husband doesn't/(B) believe that you are older/(C) than I./(D) No error.

22. (A) I could not/(B) answer to/(C) the question./(D) No error.

23. (A) Two years passed/(B) since/(C) my cousin died./(D) No error.

24. (A) I am learning English/(B) for ten years/(C) without much effect./(D) No error.

25. (A) Ramesh has agreed/(B) to marry with the girl/(C) of his parent's choice./ (D) No error.

26. (A) When he was arriving./(B) the party was/(C) in full swing./(D) No error.

27. (A) The most studious boy/(B) in the class/(C) was made as the captain./(D) No error.

28. (A) I am participating/(B) in the two-miles race/(C) tomorrow morning./(D) No error.

29. (A) When the boy committed a mistake/(B) the teacher made him to do/(C) the sum again./(D) No error.

30. (A) Whenever a person lost anything/(B) the poor folk around/(C) are suspected./(D) No error.

ANSWERS

1	2	3	4	5	6	7	8	9	10
B	D	B	B	C	C	D	D	B	C
11	**12**	**13**	**14**	**15**	**16**	**17**	**18**	**19**	**20**
C	D	B	A	C	C	C	A	A	C
21	**22**	**23**	**24**	**25**	**26**	**27**	**28**	**29**	**30**
C	B	A	A	B	A	C	B	B	A

EXPLANATORY ANSWERS

1. Replace 'is' by 'are'.
2. No error.
3. Replace 'have' by 'would have'.
4. Replace 'are' by 'is'.
5. Replace 'had to describe' by 'described'.
6. Replace 'either' by 'any'.
7. No error.
8. No error.
9. Omit 'that'.
10. Replace 'among' by 'between'.
11. Add 'also'.
12. No error.
13. Replace 'has he' by 'he has'.
14. Replace 'was' by 'were'.
15. Replace 'wouldn't be' by 'would not have been'.
16. Replace 'its' by 'his'.
17. Replace 'areas' by 'area'.
18. Replace 'set to' by 'set on'.
19. Replace 'for' by 'of'.
20. Replace 'in' by 'on'.
21. Replace 'I' by 'me'.
22. Omit 'to'.
23. Replace 'passed' by 'have passed'.
24. Replace 'am' by 'have been'.
25. Omit 'with'.
26. Replace 'was arriving' by 'arrived'.
27. Omit 'as'.
28. Replace 'in' by 'at'.
29. Omit 'to'.
30. Replace 'lost' by 'loses'.

5. One Word Substitution

There are many single words in English language which can be perfectly used for a number of words. These words help in expressing ideas in a short and correct manner for the right occasion. Such words not only increase the vocabulary but also enable you to economise in the use of words to a great extent.

Multiple Word Expression	*Substitution*
One who always looks towards the bright side of things	Optimist
One who always looks towards the dark side of things	Pessimist
The time when one develops from a child into an adult	Adolescence
The process of growing more plants in order to form a forest.	Afforestation
The science which deals with farming	Agriculture
From some other country or place etc.	Alien
A term, etc. giving more than one meaning	Ambiguous
A vehicle which is used to carry sick persons	Ambulance
An animal which can live both in water and on land	Amphibian
A lawless situation when there is no government	Anarchy
Belonging to the history of thousands of years old	Ancient
Once a year	Annual
A very old object but still valuable	Antique
Words of opposite meanings	Antonyms
Words of similar meanings	Synonyms
Signatures of a famous person	Autograph
A government led by one person with absolute authority	Autocracy
A written work of one's own life history	Autobiography
A person who has never been married	Bachelor
A person usually having no hair on his head	Bald
A place where one can deposit money and get interest	Bank
A person who cuts our hair	Barber
A building/group of buildings where soldiers live	Barracks
A person who makes buns and biscuits	Baker
A person who lives by asking people for food and money without doing any useful job	Beggar
The crime of having married to two persons at the same time	Bigamy
The branch of science which deals with the study of plants	Botany
Able to speak two languages	Bilingual

Multiple Word Expression	*Substitution*
Able to speak more than two languages	Polyglot
The branch of science which deals with the living organisms	Biology
A powerful snow storm	Blizzard
A great successful book or movie	Blockbuster
A short news on the radio or TV	Bulletin
A system in which the most important works are organised by the government officials	Bureaucracy
A person who has no vision in his eyes	Blind
A page or a series of pages on which the information of days, weeks, months, etc. is given	Calendar
A person who eats human flesh	Cannibal
A complete list of items often arranged alphabetically	Catalogue
A sudden disaster	Catastrophe
A period of 100 years	Century
A branch of science which deals with chemicals	Chemistry
A printed leaf usually issued by banks that we sign to carry certain financial deal	Cheque
A person who makes or mends shoes	Cobbler
A group of people who has been chosen by others to make decisions on their own	Committee
A building in which nuns live	Convent
An animal which feeds on other animals	Carnivorous
A person who does criticism	Critic
A person who cannot hear	Deaf
A condition in which one loses a lot of water from one's body because of vomiting, etc.	Dehydration
A system of government in which the people cast their votes to elect their leaders	Democracy
The study of skin problems	Dermatology
A long piece of land covered with sand	Desert
The art of managing relationships between countries	Diplomacy
A piece of information about the words in a book form	Dictionary
A piece of information about the telephone numbers of the people in a book from	Directory
A person in charge of a newspapers, magazine etc.	Editor
A person who thinks he is better than the others	Egoist
To leave your country and settle in some other country	Emigrate
A book or series of books giving almost all knowledge about an area or some persons etc.	Encyclopaedia
Study of insects	Entomology
Time when day and night are of the same duration	Equinox
To sell things out of the country	Export
To purchase things from some other country	Import
A plant or animal no longer in existence	Extinct
A situation when there is a shortage of food for a long period of time	Famine
An amount of money that we pay for some action or services	Fee
Related to women	Feminine
An animal strong and aggressive	Ferocious

Multiple Word Expression	*Substitution*
A piece of land where plants grow easily from the soil that is favourable to them	Fertile
A work of literature having some imaginary events	Fiction
A large amount of water covering certain area	Flood
A person who sells flowers	Florist
A religious ceremony for burying or cremating a dead person	Funeral
A substance which kills fungus	Fungicide
A person studying or having studied the diseases and the related things of female reproductory system	Gynaecologist
The murder of the person of the same group race or country	Genocide
A substance which kills germs	Germicide
A situation in which many people die because of fire during war	Holocaust
The act of killing a person deliberately	Homicide
A word having the pronunciation as the other one does but it differs in meaning	Homophone
A word having the same spelling as the other one does but it is pronounced in some other way	Homonym
A person who is attracted towards the person of the same sex	Homosexual
Go across and parallel to the ground	Horizontal
A substance which kills the insects	Insecticide
That cannot be corrected	Incorrigible
That cannot be defeated	Invincible
That cannot be eaten	Inedible
That cannot be seen	Invisible
A place in a school or college where books are kept for the benefit of students, teachers etc.	Library
A place in a school or college where scientific experiments are performed	Laboratory
An official who is a judge in the lowest court	Magistrate
A piece of music or a book before it is printed	Manuscript
Related to men	Masculine
One who believes in the existence of God	A theist
One who does not believe in the existence of good	An atheist
That can be believed	Credible
That cannot be believed	Incredible
That which dissolves in a solvent	Soluble
That which does not dissolves in a solvent	Insoluble
Hard writing that can be read	Legible
Hard writing that cannot be read	Illegible
A person who does jobs beneficial to mankind	Philanthropist
A person who goes on foot	Pedestrian
A person who fights for his own country	Patriot
An act of killing oneself	Suicide
A woman whose husband is dead	Widow
A man whose wife is dead	Widower
A person who eats vegetarian and non-vegetarian diets	Omnivorous

Multiple Word Expression	*Substitution*
Something which is everywhere at the same time	Omnipresent
One who knows everything	Omniscient
A child who does not have parents	Orphan
An award etc. given after the death of the person	Posthumous
The place where animals are kept for amusement and to increase the knowledge of the public	Zoo
The science which deals with the study of animals	Zoology

MULTIPLE CHOICE QUESTIONS

Directions: *In questions given below, out of the four alternatives, choose the one which can be substituted for the given words/sentences.*

1. Something that relates to everyone in the world
A. General B. Common
C. Usual D. Universal

2. An expression of mild disapproval
A. Warning B. Denigration
C. Impertinence D. Reproof

3. One who is not easily pleased by anything
A. Maiden B. Medieval
C. Precarious D. Fastidious

4. Murder of a king
A. Infanticide B. Matricide
C. Genocide D. Regicide

5. A remedy for all diseases
A. Stoic B. Marvel
C. Panacea D. Recompense

6. A dramatic performance
A. Mask B. Mosque
C. Masque D. Mascot

7. Study of birds
A. Orology B. Optology
C. Ophthalmology D. Ornithology

8. Ready to believe
A. Credulous B. Credible
C. Creditable D. Incredible

9. Incapable of being seen through
A. Ductile B. Opaque
C. Obsolete D. Potable

10. One who eats everything
A. Omnivorous B. Omniscient
C. Irresistible D. Insolvent

11. A place where bees are kept is called
A. An apiary B. A mole
C. A hive D. A sanctuary

12. One who cannot be corrected
A. Incurable B. Incorrigible
C. Hardened D. Invulnerable

13. One who is in charge of a museum
A. Curator B. Supervisor
C. Caretaker D. Warden

14. Continuing fight between parties, families, clans, etc.
A. Enmity B. Feud
C. Quarrel D. Skirmish

15. A voice loud enough to be heard
A. Audible B. Applaudable
C. Laudable D. Oral

16. A paper written by hand
A. Handicraft B. Manuscript
C. Handiwork D. Thesis

17. Habitually silent or talking little
A. Serville B. Unequivocal
C. Taciturn D. Synoptic

18. To slap with a flat object
A. Chop B. Hew
C. Gnaw D. Swat

19. A person who speaks many languages
A. Linguist B. Monolingual
C. Polyglot D. Bilingual

20. A light sailing-boat built specially for racing
A. Canoe B. Yacht
C. Frigate D. Dinghy

21. A fixed orbit in space in relation to earth
A. Geological B. Geo-synchronous
C. Geo-centric D. Geo-stationary

22. A style in which a writer makes a display of his knowledge
A. Pedantic B. Verbose
C. Pompous D. Ornate

23. A religious discourse
A. Preach B. Stanza
C. Sanctorum D. Sermon

24. A place that provides refuge
A. Asylum B. Sanatorium
C. Shelter D. Orphanage

25. Detailed plan of a journey
A. Travelogue B. Travelkit
C. Schedule D. Itinerary

26. A person who insists on something
A. Disciplinarian B. Stickler
C. Instantaneous D. Boaster

27. A drawing on transparent paper
A. Red print B. Blue print
C. Negative D. Transparency

28. One who believes that all things and events in life are predetermined is a
A. Fatalist B. Puritan
C. Egoist D. Tyrant

29. A school boy who cuts classes frequently is a
A. Defeatist B. Sycophant
C. Truant D. Martinet

30. The act of violating the sanctity of the church is
A. Blasphemy B. Heresy
C. Sacrilege D. Desecration

31. A place where monks live as a secluded community
A. Cathedral B. Diocese
C. Convent D. Monastery

32. One who is fond of fighting
A. Bellicose B. Aggressive
C. Belligerent D. Militant

33. Tending to move away from the centre or axis
A. Centrifugal B. Centripetal
C. Axiomatic D. Awry

34. Words inscribed on tomb
A. Epitome B. Epistle
C. Epilogue D. Epitaph

35. Leave or remove from a place considered dangerous
A. Evade B. Evacuate
C. Avoid D. Exterminate

36. Original inhabitants of a country
A. Abroge B. Aborger
C. Aborgory D. Aborigins

37. Government by the officials
A. Theocracy B. Plutocracy
C. Bureaucracy D. Democracy

38. Incapable of being exhausted
A. Inexhaustible B. Inaexhaustible
C. Exhaustable D. Non-tired

39. A person of good understanding, knowledge and reasoning power
A. Expert B. Intellectual
C. Snob D. Literate

40. One absorbed in his own thoughts and feelings rather than in things outside
A. Scholar B. Recluse
C. Introvert D. Intellectual

ANSWERS

1	2	3	4	5	6	7	8	9	10
D	D	D	D	C	C	D	A	B	A
11	**12**	**13**	**14**	**15**	**16**	**17**	**18**	**19**	**20**
A	B	A	B	A	B	C	D	A	B
21	**22**	**23**	**24**	**25**	**26**	**27**	**28**	**29**	**30**
D	A	D	A	D	B	D	A	C	C
31	**32**	**33**	**34**	**35**	**36**	**37**	**38**	**39**	**40**
D	A	A	D	B	B	C	A	B	C

6. Spelling Errors

There are thousands of words in English language. It is difficult to remember the spellings and meanings of all at once. Try to learn as many as you can. Use a dictionary regularly.

Directions: *Find the correctly spelt words.*

1. A. Damage B. Dammage C. Damaige D. Dammege

2. A. Efficiant B. Effecient C. Efficient D. Eficient

3. A. Schedule B. Schdule C. Schedale D. Schedeule

4. A. Occurad B. Occurred C. Ocurred D. Occured

5. A. Grieff B. Grief C. Grieef D. Grrief

6. A. Guarantee B. Garuntee C. Guaruntee D. Gaurantee

7. A. Meddicine B. Medicine C. Medicene D. Medicinne

8. A. Benefeted B. Benefitted C. Benifited D. Benefited

9. A. Acommodation B. Acomodation C. Accomodation D. Accommodation

10. A. Querrelsome B. Quarrelsame C. Quarrelsome D. Querralsome

11. A. Sympathetic B. Smypathetic C. Sympothetic D. Sympethetic

12. A. Prograssive B. Progressive C. Progresive D. Prograsive

13. A. Uncivilized B. Uncevilized C. Uncivillized D. Uncevelized

14. A. Extravagant B. Extreragent C. Extreregant D. Extravegent

15. A. Missunderstood B. Miesunderstood C. Misunderstood D. Misunderstod

16. A. Belligerent B. Beligirent C. Belligarant D. Belligerrent

17. A. Astonished B. Astronished C. Astoneshed D. Asstonished

18. A. Sincerely B. Sencerely C. Sincerelly D. Sincerrely

19. A. Rigourous B. Rigerous C. Rigorous D. Regerous

20. A. Satellite B. Sattellite C. Satelite D. Sattelite

21. A. Pesanger B. Passenger C. Pessenger D. Pasanger

22. A. Humurous B. Humorous C. Humoreus D. Humorrous

23. A. Exeggerate B. Exaggerate C. Exadgerate D. Exagerate

24. A. Fariegn B. Forein C. Foriegn D. Foreign

25. A. Excesive B. Excessive C. Exccessive D. Exccesive

26. A. Forcaust B. Forcast C. Forecast D. Forecaste

27. A. Paralleted B. Paralelled C. Parralleled D. Parallelled

28. A. Ocasion B. Occassion
C. Occasion D. Ocassion

29. A. Boquet B. Bouquet
C. Bouquete D. Bouquette

30. A. Chettering B. Chaterring
C. Chattering D. Chatering

31. A. Discourage B. Disscourage
C. Discourege D. Discaurage

32. A. Curageous B. Courageous
C. Courrageous D. Couregeous

33. A. Abandon B. Abanddon
C. Abendon D. Abbandon

34. A. Embarassment
B. Emberrassement
C. Embarrassment
D. Embbaresment

35. A. Eccintric B. Eccentrie
C. Eccentric D. Eccintrie

36. A. Occasional B. Occassional
C. Occesional D. Occessional

37. A. Querrel B. Querral
C. Quarrel D. Quarel

38. A. Contrebution B. Contribution
C. Contributtion D. Conterbution

39. A. Desgrace B. Disgrece
C. Disgrice D. Disgrace

40. A. Harassment B. Herassment
C. Harasment D. Harassmient

41. A. Imaginative B. Imeginative
C. Imagenative D. Imaginetive

42. A. Suficient B. Suficiant
C. Sufficient D. Sufficiant

43. A. Adequate B. Edequate
C. Adaquete D. Edaquete

44. A. Exparienced B. Experianced
C. Experienced D. Experrienced

45. A. Flatering B. Fletering
C. Flattering D. Fletaring

46. A. Cuttiveted B. Culltrivated
C. Cultivated D. Caltivated

47. A. Praiceworthy B. Peiseworthy
C. Praiseworthy D. Praisaworthy

48. A. Profesional B. Professionel
C. Professional D. Profissional

49. A. Ameteur B. Amateur
C. Amataur D. Amateor

50. A. Unfevourable B. Unfevaurable
C. Unfavourable D. Unfivourable

ANSWERS

1	2	3	4	5	6	7	8	9	10
A	C	A	B	B	A	B	B	D	C
11	**12**	**13**	**14**	**15**	**16**	**17**	**18**	**19**	**20**
A	B	A	A	C	A	A	A	C	A
21	**22**	**23**	**24**	**25**	**26**	**27**	**28**	**29**	**30**
B	B	B	D	B	C	A	C	B	C
31	**32**	**33**	**34**	**35**	**36**	**37**	**38**	**39**	**40**
A	B	A	C	C	A	C	B	D	A
41	**42**	**43**	**44**	**45**	**46**	**47**	**48**	**49**	**50**
A	C	A	C	A	C	C	C	B	C

ARITHMETIC

1. NUMBERS

The development of the number system started with natural numbers. These are generally known as counting numbers.

Natural Numbers

Numbers which start from 1 are known as natural numbers. It is denoted by N. The smallest natural number is 1. It is written as,

$$N = \{1, 2, 3, ..., \infty\}$$

Whole Numbers

A number which starts from zero (0) is known as whole number. It is denoted by W. It is written as,

$$W = \{0, 1, 2, 3, ..., \infty\}$$

Integers

Natural numbers along with 0 and their negatives are known as integers. It is denoted by I. It is written as,

$$I = \{..., -4, -3, -2, -1, 0, 1, 2, 3, 4, ...\}$$

Even Numbers

A number which is divisible by 2 is known as even numbers.

Such as, 2, 4, 6, 10, 12, 128, 432 etc.

Odd Numbers

A number which is not divisible by 2 is known as odd numbers:

Such as, 1, 3, 5, 7, 9, 11, 13, 21, 29, 123 etc.

Prime Numbers

A number which is divided by itself is known as prime numbers. The smallest prime number is 2.

Such as, 2, 3, 5, 7, 11, 13, 17, 19, 23, ... etc.

Composite Numbers

A number which is divided by itself and others also is known as composite numbers. The smallest composite number is 4.

Such as, 4, 6, 8, 9, 10, 12, 14, 15, 16, 18, ... etc.

There are 25 prime numbers between 1 tc 100.

Such as, 2, 3, 5, 7, 11, 13, 17, 19, 23, 29, 31, 37, 41, 43, 47, 53, 59, 61, 67, 71, 73, 79, 83, 89, 97.

Test, whether a given number is prime or composite: If we want to test any number more than 100, whether it is prime or not, take an integer larger than the approximate square root of that number. Let it be x. Test the divisibility of the given number by every prime number less than x. If it is not divisible by any of them, then it is prime; otherwise it is composite number.

EXAMPLE: Which of the following numbers are prime numbers?

(*i*) 421 (*ii*) 671

SOLUTION:

(*i*) The square root of 421 is nearly 21.
Prime numbers less than 21 are 2, 3, 5, 7, 11, 13, 17, 19. Clearly, 421 is not divisible by any of them. So, 421 is a prime number.

(*ii*) The square root of 671 is nearly 26.
Prime numbers less than 26 are 2, 3, 5, 7, 11, 13, 17, 19, 23. Out of these, 671 is divisible by 11. So, 671 is not a prime number. Hence it is composite number.

The formulae given below are quite useful for quick multiplication:

(*i*) $(a + b)^2 = a^2 + 2ab + b^2$

(*ii*) $(a - b)^2 = a^2 - 2ab + b^2$

(iii) $a^2 - b^2 = (a+b)(a-b)$

(iv) $a^2 + b^2 = (a+b)^2 - 2ab$

(v) $(a+b)^3 = a^3 + b^3 + 3ab(a+b)$

(vi) $(a-b)^3 = a^3 - b^3 - 3ab(a-b)$

(vii) $a^3 + b^3 = (a+b)(a^2 - ab + b^2)$

(viii) $a^3 - b^3 = (a-b)(a^2 + ab + b^2)$

EXAMPLE: Simplify the following.

(i) $\dfrac{348 \times 348 \times 348 + 252 \times 252 \times 252}{348 \times 348 - 348 \times 252 + 252 \times 252}$

(ii) $\dfrac{261 \times 261 \times 261 - 77 \times 77 \times 77}{261 \times 261 + 261 \times 77 + 77 \times 77}$

SOLUTION:

(i) $\dfrac{348 \times 348 \times 348 + 252 \times 252 \times 252}{348 \times 348 - 348 \times 252 + 252 \times 252}$

Let $348 = a$

and $252 = b$

$\therefore$ Given expression is written as

$$\frac{a \times a \times a + b \times b \times b}{a \times a - a \times b + b \times b} = \frac{a^3 + b^3}{a^2 - ab + b^2}$$

$$= \frac{(a+b)(a^2 - ab + b^2)}{(a^2 - ab + b^2)} = a + b$$

$= 348 + 252 = 600.$

(ii) $\dfrac{261 \times 261 \times 261 - 77 \times 77 \times 77}{261 \times 261 + 261 \times 77 + 77 \times 77}$

Let $261 = a$

and $77 = b$

$$\therefore \frac{a^3 - b^3}{a^2 + ab + b^2} = \frac{(a-b)(a^2 + ab + b^2)}{(a^2 + ab + b^2)} = a - b$$

$\therefore$ $261 - 77 = 184.$

If we divide a given number by another number, then

Dividend = (Divisor × Quotient) + Remainder

EXAMPLE: On dividing 18254 by a certain number, the quotient is 289 and the remainder is 47. Find the divisor.

SOLUTION: Here, Dividend = 18254

quotient = 289

remainder = 47

$$\therefore \quad \text{Divisor} = \frac{\text{Dividend} - \text{Remainder}}{\text{Quotient}}$$

$$= \frac{18254 - 47}{289} = \frac{18207}{289} = 63$$

Hence, divisor = 63.

EXAMPLE: What least number must be subtracted from 862 to get a number exactly divisible by 31?

SOLUTION: On dividing 862 by 31, the remainder obtained is 25.

Hence, the required number = 25.

MULTIPLE CHOICE QUESTIONS

1. The face value of 8 in the numeral 458926 is:

A. 8000 B. 8

C. 1000 D. 458000

2. $106 \times 106 + 94 \times 94 = x$, the value of x is:

A. 21032 B. 20032

C. 23032 D. 20072

3. If $m \times 48 = 173 \times 240$ then the value of m is:

A. 545 B. 685

C. 865 D. 495

4. $\left(1-\frac{1}{3}\right)\left(1-\frac{1}{4}\right)\left(1-\frac{1}{5}\right)\ldots\left(1-\frac{1}{n}\right) = x$

then the value of x is:

A. $\dfrac{1}{n}$ B. $\dfrac{2}{n}$

C. $\dfrac{2(n-1)}{n}$ D. $\dfrac{2}{n(n+1)}$

5. When simplified the product

$\left(2-\frac{1}{3}\right)\left(2-\frac{3}{5}\right)\left(2-\frac{5}{7}\right)\ldots\left(2-\frac{997}{999}\right)$ is

equal to:

A. $\dfrac{5}{999}$ B. $\dfrac{1001}{999}$

C. $\dfrac{1001}{3}$ D. None of these

6. Which number should replace both the asterisks in $\left(\frac{*}{21}\right)\times\left(\frac{*}{189}\right)=1$?

A. 21 B. 63
C. 3969 D. 147

7. In a division sum, the divisor is 12 times the quotient and 5 times the remainder. If the remainder be 48, then the dividend is:

A. 240 B. 576
C. 4800 D. 4848

8. What least number must be subtracted from 1294 so that the remainder when divided by 9, 11, 13 will leave in each case the same remainder 6?

A. 0 B. 1
C. 2 D. 3

9. If $\sqrt{\left(1+\frac{27}{169}\right)}=\left(1+\frac{x}{13}\right)$, then the value of x is:

A. 1 B. 3
C. 5 D. 7

10. If $\frac{x}{y}=\frac{3}{4}$, then the value of $\left(\frac{6}{7}+\frac{y-x}{y+x}\right)$ equals:

A. $\frac{5}{7}$ B. $1\frac{1}{7}$
C. 1 D. 2

11. The largest natural number by which the product of three consecutive even natural numbers is always divisible, is:

A. 16 B. 24
C. 48 D. 96

12. The least number of five digits which is exactly divisible by 12, 15 and 18 is:

A. 10080 B. 10800
C. 18000 D. 81000

13. The least number which when divided by 8, 9, 12, 16 and 20 leaves the same remainder 1 in each case is:

A. 712 B. 271
C. 721 D. 720

14. The value of 0.8693 + 0.092 + 0.87 + 0.4 equals:

A. 2.3213 B. 2.2331
C. 3.2313 D. 2.2313

15. The prime numbers between 1 to 50 are:

A. 8 B. 12
C. 15 D. 10

ANSWERS

1	2	3	4	5	6	7	8	9	10
B	D	C	B	C	B	D	B	A	C
11	**12**	**13**	**14**	**15**					
C	A	C	D	C					

EXPLANATORY ANSWERS

1. The face value of 8 in the numeral 458926 is 8.

2. $106 \times 106 + 94 \times 94 = x$

$\Rightarrow (106)^2 + (94)^2 = x$

$\Rightarrow (100 + 6)^2 + (100 - 6)^2 = x$

$\Rightarrow 10000 + 1200 + 36 + 10000 - 1200 + 36 = x$

$\Rightarrow 20072 = x$

$\Rightarrow x = 20072.$

3. $\because m = \frac{173 \times 240}{48} = 865.$

4. $\left(1-\frac{1}{3}\right)\left(1-\frac{1}{4}\right)\left(1-\frac{1}{5}\right)\ldots\left(1-\frac{1}{n}\right) = x$

$\because \quad 1-\frac{1}{3} = \frac{3-1}{3} = \frac{2}{3}$

$$1-\frac{1}{4}=\frac{4-1}{4}=\frac{3}{4}$$

$$1-\frac{1}{5}=\frac{5-1}{5}=\frac{4}{5}$$

$$\vdots$$

$$1-\frac{1}{n}=\frac{n-1}{n}$$

$$\therefore \frac{2}{3}\times\frac{3}{4}\times\frac{4}{5}\times\ldots\times\frac{n-2}{n-1}\times\frac{n-1}{n}=\frac{2}{n}$$

5. $\left(2-\frac{1}{3}\right)\left(2-\frac{3}{5}\right)\left(2-\frac{5}{7}\right)\ldots\left(2-\frac{997}{999}\right)$

$$2-\frac{1}{3}=\frac{6-1}{3}=\frac{5}{3}$$

$$2-\frac{3}{5}=\frac{10-3}{5}=\frac{7}{5}$$

$$2-\frac{5}{7}=\frac{14-5}{7}=\frac{9}{7}$$

$$2-\frac{997}{999}=\frac{1998-997}{999}=\frac{1001}{999}$$

$$\therefore \frac{5}{3}\times\frac{7}{5}\times\frac{9}{7}\times\ldots\times\frac{999}{997}\times\frac{1001}{999}=\frac{1001}{3}$$

6. $\frac{*}{21}\times\frac{*}{189}=1$

$$\frac{x^2}{21\times189}=1$$

$\Rightarrow \quad x^2 = 21 \times 189 = 21 \times 21 \times 9$

$\Rightarrow \quad x^2 = 21 \times 21 \times 3 \times 3$

$\Rightarrow \quad x = 21 \times 3 = 63$

7. Let quotient = Q and remainder = R
Then, divisor = 12Q = 5R
Now, R = 48
$\Rightarrow$ 12Q = 5 × 48 $\Rightarrow$ Q = 20
$\therefore$ Dividend = (20 × 240 + 48) = 4848

8. The number when divided by 9, 11, 13 leaving remainder 6 = (LCM of 9, 11, 13) + 6 = 1293
$\therefore$ Required number = (1294 – 1293) = 1

9. $\sqrt{\left(1+\frac{27}{169}\right)}=\left(1+\frac{x}{13}\right)$

$\Rightarrow \quad \sqrt{\frac{169+27}{169}}=\frac{13+x}{13}$

$\Rightarrow \quad \sqrt{\frac{196}{169}}=\frac{x+13}{13}$

$\Rightarrow \quad \frac{14}{13}=\frac{x+13}{13}$

$\Rightarrow \quad x+13=14$

$\Rightarrow \quad x=1$

10. $\because \frac{x}{y}=\frac{3}{4}$ then,

$$\frac{6}{7}+\frac{y-x}{y+x}=\frac{6}{7}+\frac{\frac{y}{y}-\frac{x}{y}}{\frac{y}{y}+\frac{x}{y}}$$

[Divide numerator and denominator by y.]

$$=\frac{6}{7}+\frac{1-\frac{3}{4}}{1+\frac{3}{4}}=\frac{6}{7}+\frac{\frac{1}{4}}{\frac{7}{4}}=\frac{6}{7}+\frac{1}{7}=\frac{7}{7}=1$$

11. It is 2 × 4 × 6 = 48

12. Least number of 5 digits is 10000.
LCM of 12, 15, 18 is 180.
On dividing 10000 by 180, the remainder is 100.
$\therefore$ The least number = 10000 + (180 – 100)
= 10080.

13. Least number = (LCM of 8, 9, 12, 16, 20) + 1

2	8,	9,	12,	16,	20
2	4,	9,	6,	8,	10
2	2,	9,	3,	4,	5
3	1,	9,	3,	2,	5
	1,	3,	1,	2,	5

$\therefore$ LCM = $2^4 \times 3^2 \times 5 = 720$
Hence, least number = (720 + 1) = 721.

14.
```
   0.8693
   0.092
   0.87
 + 0.4
   2.2313
```

$\therefore$ The value of 0.8693 + 0.092 + 0.87 + 0.4
= 2.2313.

15. The prime numbers between 1 to 50 are 2, 3, 5, 7, 11, 13, 17, 19, 23, 29, 31, 37, 41, 43, 47.
Hence, there are 15 prime numbers between 1 to 50.

2. HCF AND LCM

FACTORS

The numbers are said to be factors of a given number when they exactly divide that number.

Example: Factors of 15 are 1, 3, 5 and 15 because each of these completely divides 15.

Highest Common Factor

The HCF of two or more than two numbers is the greatest number that divides each of them exactly. The highest common factor is also known as Greatest Common Divisor or Greatest Common Measure.

EXAMPLE: Let us consider two numbers 24 and 36. All possible factors of 24 are 1, 2, 3, 4, 6, 8, 12 and 24. All possible factors of 36 are 1, 2, 3, 4, 6, 9, 12, 18 and 36. The common factors of 24 and 36 are 1, 2, 3, 4, 6, 12. The greatest factor among these common factors is 12.

Hence, 12 is the HCF of 24 and 36.

EXAMPLE: Let us consider two numbers 18 and 30.

Now, $18 = 2 \times 3 \times 3$

and $30 = 2 \times 3 \times 5$

The factors common to the two numbers are 2 and 3. Hence the required HCF $= 2 \times 3 = 6$.

There are two methods of determining the HCF of two or more numbers.

(*i*) HCF by Factorization method

(*ii*) HCF by Division method.

HCF by Factorization Method

Express each one of the given number as the product of prime factors. Now choose common factors and take the product of these factors to obtain the required HCF.

EXAMPLE: Find the HCF of 126, 396 and 5400.

SOLUTION: $126 = 2 \times 3 \times 3 \times 7$

$396 = 2 \times 2 \times 3 \times 3 \times 11$

$5400 = 2 \times 2 \times 2 \times 3 \times 3 \times 3 \times 5 \times 5$

Common factors are 2, 3 and 3.

Hence, the HCF $= 2 \times 3 \times 3 = 18$.

EXAMPLE: Find the HCF of 1056, 1584 and 2178.

SOLUTION: $1056 = 2^5 \times 3 \times 11$

$1584 = 2^4 \times 3^2 \times 11$

and $2178 = 2 \times 3^2 \times 11^2$

Hence, HCF $= (2 \times 3 \times 11) = 66$.

HCF by Division Method

Suppose we have to find the HCF of two given numbers. Divide the larger number by the smaller one. Now, divide the divisor by the remainder. Repeat the process of dividing the preceding divisor by the remainder last obtained till zero is obtained as remainder. The last divisor is the required HCF.

Suppose we have to find the HCF of three numbers. Then HCF of [(HCF of any two numbers) and (the third number)] gives the HCF of three given numbers. Similarly, the HCF of more than three numbers may be obtained.

EXAMPLE: Find the HCF of 48, 168 and 324.

SOLUTION: Firstly, we find the HCF of 48 and 168.

```
48) 1 6 8 (3
  – 1 4 4
    ------
      2 4) 4 8 (2
           4 8
           ---
            0
           ---
```

Thus, HCF of 48 and 168 = 24.

Now, we find the HCF of 24 and 324.

24) 3 2 4 (13
− 2 4
8 4
− 7 2
1 2) 2 4 (2
2 4
0

Thus, the HCF of 48, 168 and 324 is 12.

Lowest Common Multiple

The LCM of two or more numbers is the lowest or least number which is exactly divisible by each of them. In other words, it is the lowest number which contains each of them as a factor.

LCM by Factorization

Resolve each one of the given numbers into a product of prime factors. Then LCM is the product of highest powers of all the factors.

EXAMPLE: Find the LCM of 72, 189 and 1026.

SOLUTION: $72 = 2^3 \times 3^2$

$189 = 3^3 \times 7$

and $1026 = 2 \times 3^3 \times 19$

$\therefore$ $\text{LCM} = 2^3 \times 3^3 \times 7 \times 19$

$= 8 \times 27 \times 7 \times 19 = 28728$

EXAMPLE: Find the LCM of 12, 15, 20 and 54 by short cut method.

SOLUTION:

2	12,	15,	20,	54
2	6,	15,	10,	27
3	3,	15,	5,	27
5	1,	5,	5,	9
	1,	1,	1,	9

$\therefore \text{LCM} = 2 \times 2 \times 3 \times 5 \times 9 = 540$

FORMULA

Product of two numbers = HCF × LCM.

$$\text{LCM} = \frac{\text{Product of numbers}}{\text{HCF}}$$

$$\text{HCF} = \frac{\text{Product of numbers}}{\text{LCM}}$$

$$\text{First number} = \frac{\text{LCM} \times \text{HCF}}{\text{2nd number}}$$

$$\text{2nd number} = \frac{\text{LCM} \times \text{HCF}}{\text{First number}}$$

HCF and LCM of Fractions

(*i*) $\text{HCF} = \dfrac{\text{HCF of numerators}}{\text{LCM of denominators}}$

(*ii*) $\text{LCM} = \dfrac{\text{LCM of numerators}}{\text{HCF of denominators}}$

EXAMPLE: Find the HCF and LCM of $\frac{3}{4}, \frac{6}{8}, \frac{15}{64}$ and $\frac{12}{32}$.

SOLUTION: $\text{HCF} = \dfrac{\text{HCF of 3, 6, 15, 12}}{\text{LCM of 4, 8, 64, 32}} = \dfrac{3}{64}$

$\text{LCM} = \dfrac{\text{LCM of 3, 6, 15, 12}}{\text{HCF of 4, 8, 64, 32}} = \dfrac{60}{4}$.

MULTIPLE CHOICE QUESTIONS

1. HCF of 1485 and 4356 is:
   A. 189 B. 89
   C. 99 D. 83
2. LCM of 18, 24, 42, 63 is:
   A. 302 B. 604
   C. 504 D. 404
3. Which of the following fractions is the greatest of all?

   $\frac{7}{8}, \frac{6}{7}, \frac{4}{5}, \frac{5}{6}$

   A. $\frac{6}{7}$ B. $\frac{4}{5}$
   C. $\frac{5}{6}$ D. $\frac{7}{8}$
4. Which of the following is in ascending order?
   A. $\frac{5}{7}, \frac{7}{8}, \frac{9}{11}$ B. $\frac{5}{7}, \frac{9}{11}, \frac{7}{8}$
   C. $\frac{7}{8}, \frac{5}{7}, \frac{9}{11}$ D. $\frac{9}{11}, \frac{7}{8}, \frac{5}{7}$

5. HCF of three numbers is 12. If they be in the ratio 1 : 2 : 3, the numbers are:
A. 12, 24, 36 B. 10, 20, 30
C. 5, 10, 15 D. 4, 8, 12

6. The largest natural number which exactly divides the product of any four consecutive natural numbers is:
A. 6 B. 12
C. 24 D. 120

7. The traffic lights at three different road crossings change after every 48 seconds, 72 seconds and 108 seconds respectively. If they all change simultaneously at 8 : 20 : 00 hrs; then they will again change simultaneously at:
A. 8 : 27 : 12 hrs B. 8 : 27 : 24 hrs
C. 8 : 27 : 36 hrs D. 8 : 27 : 48 hrs

8. The HCF of two numbers is 16 and their LCM is 160. If one of the number is 32, then the other number is:
A. 48 B. 80
C. 96 D. 112

9. The HCF of two numbers is 12 and their difference is also 12. The numbers are:
A. 66, 78 B. 70, 82
C. 94, 106 D. 84, 96

10. The largest number which exactly divides 210, 315, 147 and 161 is:
A. 3 B. 7
C. 21 D. 4410

11. The least perfect square number which is divisible by 3, 4, 5, 6 and 8 is:
A. 900 B. 1200
C. 2500 D. 3600

12. The smallest number which is divisible by 12, 15, 20 and is a perfect square, is:
A. 400 B. 900
C. 1600 D. 3600

13. The sum of two numbers is 216 and their HCF is 27. The numbers are:
A. 54, 162 B. 108, 108
C. 27, 189 D. None of these

14. The HCF and LCM of two numbers are 44 and 264 respectively. If the first number is divided by 2, the quotient is 44. The other number is:
A. 33 B. 66
C. 132 D. 264

15. The number of prime factors in $2^{222} \times 3^{333} \times 5^{555}$ is:
A. 3 B. 1107
C. 1110 D. 1272

16. The number of prime factors in the expression $(6)^{10} \times (7)^{17} \times (11)^{27}$ is:
A. 54 B. 64
C. 71 D. 81

17. Three measuring rods are 64 cm, 80 cm and 96 cm in length. The least length of cloth that can be measured exact number of times using any one of the above rod is:
A. 0.96 m B. 19.20 m
C. 9.60 m D. 96.00 m

18. The product of two numbers is 1600 and their HCF is 5. The LCM of the numbers is:
A. 320 B. 1605
C. 1595 D. 8000

19. About the number of pairs which have 16 as their HCF and 136 as their LCM, we can definitely say that:
A. Only one such pair exists
B. Only two such pairs exist
C. Many such pairs exist
D. No such pair exist

20. The total number of prime factors of the product $(8)^{20} \times (15)^{24} \times (7)^{15}$ is:
A. 59 B. 98
C. 123 D. 138

ANSWERS

1	2	3	4	5	6	7	8	9	10
C	C	D	B	A	C	A	B	D	B
11	**12**	**13**	**14**	**15**	**16**	**17**	**18**	**19**	**20**
D	D	C	C	C	B	C	A	D	C

EXPLANATORY ANSWERS

1.
```
1485) 4 3 5 6 (2
      2 9 7 0
      -------
      1 3 8 6) 1 4 8 5 (1
               1 3 8 6
               -------
                  9 9) 1 3 8 6 (14
                         9 9
                         -----
                         3 9 6
                         3 9 6
                         -----
                           0
```
$\therefore$ HCF of 1485 and 4356 is 99.

2.

2	18,	24,	42,	63
3	9,	12,	21,	63
3	3,	4,	7,	21
7	1,	4,	7,	7
	1,	4,	1,	1

LCM of 18, 24, 42, 63 = $2 \times 3^2 \times 7 \times 4 = 504$.

3. $\frac{7}{8} = 0.875$, $\frac{6}{7} = 0.857$, $\frac{4}{5} = 0.8$

$\frac{5}{6} = 0.833$

Clearly, 0.875 is the greatest of all.

Hence, $\frac{7}{8}$ is the greatest of all.

4. $\frac{5}{7} = 0.714$, $\frac{7}{8} = 0.875$, $\frac{9}{11} = 0.818$

Now, $0.714 < 0.818 < 0.875$

Hence, $\frac{5}{7} < \frac{9}{11} < \frac{7}{8}$.

5. Let the numbers be x, $2x$ and $3x$.
Then, their HCF = x
According to the question, $x = 12$
$\therefore$ The numbers are 12, 24, 36.

6. $1 \times 2 \times 3 \times 4 = 24$
$\therefore$ Required number = 24.

7. LCM of 48, 72, 108 = 432
432 seconds = 7 min 12 seconds.
So, the next simultaneous change will take place at 8 : 27 : 12 hrs.

8. Other number = $\frac{\text{LCM} \times \text{HCF}}{\text{One number}} = \frac{160 \times 16}{32} = 80$
Hence, other number = 80.

9. 12 is not the HCF of given options A, B and C. Hence, D is correct answer.
In 84, 96, 12 is HCF of 84 and 96
Difference of 96 – 84 = 12
So, required numbers are 84 and 96.

10. HCF of 210, 315, 147 and 161 = 7
Hence, the required number = 7.

11.

2	3,	4,	5,	6,	8
2	3,	2,	5,	3,	4
3	3,	1,	5,	3,	2
	1,	1,	5,	1,	2

LCM of 3, 4, 5, 6, 8 = $2 \times 2 \times 3 \times 5 \times 2$
Required number
$= (2 \times 2 \times 3 \times 3 \times 5 \times 5 \times 2 \times 2) = 3600$

12. LCM of 12, 15 and 20 = 60
Hence, required number = $60 \times 60 = 3600$.

13. HCF of 54, 162 = 54
HCF of 108, 108 = 108
HCF of 27, 189 = 27
Hence, required numbers are 27 and 189.

14. According to the question,
First number = $2 \times 44 = 88$
Other number
$= \frac{\text{LCM} \times \text{HCF}}{\text{First number}} = \frac{264 \times 44}{88} = 132$

15. The number of prime factors in the given product = (222 + 333 + 555) = 1110

16. 2, 3, 7, 11 are prime numbers in the given expression. The number of prime factors in the given expression (10 + 10 + 17 + 27) = 64

17. Required length = (LCM of 64, 80, 96) cm
= 960 cm = 9.60 m.

18. LCM = $\frac{\text{Product of numbers}}{\text{HCF}} = \frac{1600}{5} = 320$

19. HCF is always a factor of LCM. So no two numbers exist with HCF = 16 and LCM = 136.

20. Since 2, 3, 5, 7 are prime numbers and the given expression is $(2^3)^{20} \times (3 \times 5)^{24} \times (7)^{15}$ *i.e.* $2^{60} \times 3^{24} \times 5^{24} \times 7^{15}$, so the number of prime factors in the given expression
$= (60 + 24 + 24 + 15) = 123$

3. SIMPLIFICATION

Simplification means expressing in a simpler form. In order to simplify an expression we use the operations in the following order which is easily remembered as "BODMAS".

(*i*) Bracket (*ii*) Of (*iii*) Division (*iv*) Multiplication (*v*) Addition (*vi*) Subtraction.

'Of' means multiplication but it is operated even before division.

While removing brackets, first of all bar bracket '—' and after that small bracket '( )' is removed. Thereafter curley bracket '{ }' and at last square bracket '[ ]' is removed.

EXAMPLE: Simplify: $100 \div 25 \times 6 + 16 - 32$

SOLUTION: $100 \div 25 \times 6 + 16 - 32$

$= 4 \times 6 + 16 - 32$

$= 24 + 16 - 32$

$= 40 - 32 = 8$

EXAMPLE: Simplify: $54 + 24 \div 4 - 8 \times 5 + 4 \times 3$

SOLUTION: $54 + 24 \div 4 - 8 \times 5 + 4 \times 3$

$= 54 + 6 - 40 + 12$

$= 72 - 40 = 32$

EXAMPLE: Simplify: $10 - \left[6 - \left\{7 - \left(6 - \overline{8-5}\right)\right\}\right]$

SOLUTION: $10 - \left[6 - \left\{7 - (6 - 3)\right\}\right]$

$= 10 - [6 - \{7 - 3\}]$

$= 10 - [6 - 4] = 10 - 2 = 8.$

EXAMPLE: Simplify: $\dfrac{12 \times 12 \times 12 - 1 \times 1 \times 1}{12 \times 12 + 12 \times 1 + 1 \times 1}$

SOLUTION: Let $a = 12$ and $b = 1$

$$\therefore \quad \frac{a \times a \times a - b \times b \times b}{a \times a + a \times b + b \times b} = \frac{a^3 - b^3}{a^2 + ab + b^2}$$

$$= \frac{(a-b)(a^2 + ab + b^2)}{(a^2 + ab + b^2)}$$

$$= a - b = 12 - 1 = 11$$

EXAMPLE: Simplify:

$$\frac{2.33 \times 2.33 \times 2.33 + 7.67 \times 7.67 \times 7.67}{2.33 \times 2.33 - 2.33 \times 7.67 + 7.67 \times 7.67}$$

SOLUTION: Let $a = 2.33$ and $b = 7.67$

$$\frac{a^3 + b^3}{a^2 - ab + b^2} = \frac{(a+b)(a^2 - ab + b^2)}{(a^2 - ab + b^2)} = (a+b)$$

$$= 2.33 + 7.67 = 10$$

MULTIPLE CHOICE QUESTIONS

1. $\dfrac{48 - 12 \times 3 + 9}{12 - 9 \div 3}$ equals:

A. 3 B. 21

C. $\dfrac{7}{3}$ D. $\dfrac{1}{3}$

2. $\dfrac{69 - 14 \times 3 + 2}{9 \times 5 - (5)^2}$ equals:

A. 1.45 B. 2.75

C. 26.5 D. 265

3. If $\frac{17.28 \div x}{3.6 \times 0.2} = 2$ then, the value of x is:

A. 120 B. 1.20

C. 12 D. 0.12

4. $171 \div 19 \times 9$ equals:

A. 0 B. 1

C. 18 D. 81

5. $3120 \div 26 + 13 \times 30$ equals:

A. 2400 B. 3900

C. 536 D. None of these

6. $\frac{31}{10} \times \frac{3}{10} + \frac{7}{5} \div 20$ equals:

A. 0 B. 1

C. 100 D. $\frac{107}{200}$

7. The simplification of $1 + \cfrac{1}{2 + \cfrac{1}{1 - \cfrac{1}{3}}}$ yields the result:

A. $\frac{2}{7}$ B. $\frac{7}{9}$

C. $\frac{9}{7}$ D. $\frac{13}{7}$

8. The value of $1 + \frac{1}{4 \times 3} + \frac{1}{4 \times 3^2} + \frac{1}{4 \times 3^3}$ up to four places of decimals is:

A. 1.1202 B. 1.1203

C. 1.1204 D. None of these

9. $\dfrac{\frac{1}{2} \div 4 + 20}{\frac{1}{2} \times 4 + 20}$ equals:

A. $\frac{81}{88}$ B. $2\frac{3}{11}$

C. $\frac{161}{176}$ D. 1

10. $3 \div \left[(8-5) \div \left\{(4-2) \div \left(2 + \frac{8}{13}\right)\right\}\right]$ equals:

A. $\frac{13}{17}$ B. $\frac{68}{13}$

C. $\frac{17}{13}$ D. $\frac{13}{68}$

11. $10 - [9 - \{8 - (7 - 6)\}] - 5$ is equal to:

A. –5 B. 1

C. 3 D. 9

12. $\dfrac{\frac{1}{5} \div \frac{1}{5} \text{ of } \frac{1}{5}}{\frac{1}{5} \text{ of } \frac{1}{5} \div \frac{1}{5}}$ is equal to:

A. 1 B. 5

C. $\frac{1}{5}$ D. 25

13. The value of $1 + \cfrac{1}{1 + \cfrac{1}{1 + \cfrac{1}{9}}}$ is:

A. $\frac{29}{19}$ B. $\frac{10}{19}$

C. $\frac{29}{10}$ D. $\frac{10}{9}$

14. $\frac{3}{48}$ is what part of $\frac{1}{12}$?

A. $\frac{3}{7}$ B. $\frac{1}{12}$

C. $\frac{4}{3}$ D. None of these

15. How many $\frac{1}{8}$ s are there in $37\frac{1}{2}$?

A. 300 B. 400

C. 500 D. None of these

ANSWERS

1	2	3	4	5	6	7	8	9	10
C	A	C	D	D	B	C	B	C	A
11	**12**	**13**	**14**	**15**					
C	D	A	D	A					

EXPLANATORY ANSWERS

1. $\dfrac{48-12\times3+9}{12-9\div3} = \dfrac{48-36+9}{12-3}$

$= \dfrac{57-36}{9} = \dfrac{21}{9} = \dfrac{7}{3}.$

2. $\dfrac{69-14\times3+2}{9\times5-5^2} = \dfrac{69-42+2}{45-25}$

$= \dfrac{71-42}{20} = \dfrac{29}{20} = 1.45.$

3. $17.28 \div x = 2\times3.6\times0.2$

$\Rightarrow \dfrac{17.28}{x} = 1.44 \Rightarrow 1.44\,x = 17.28$

$\Rightarrow x = \dfrac{17.28}{1.44} = \dfrac{1728}{144} = 12.$

4. $171 \div 19 \times 9 = 9 \times 9 = 81.$

5. $3120 \div 26 + 13 \times 30 = 120 + 390 = 510.$

6. $\dfrac{31}{10}\times\dfrac{3}{10}+\dfrac{7}{5}\div20 = \dfrac{31}{10}\times\dfrac{3}{10}+\dfrac{7}{5}\times\dfrac{1}{20}$

$= \dfrac{93}{100}+\dfrac{7}{100} = \dfrac{93+7}{100} = \dfrac{100}{100} = 1$

7. $1+\dfrac{1}{2+\dfrac{1}{1-\dfrac{1}{3}}} = 1+\dfrac{1}{2+\dfrac{1}{\dfrac{3-1}{3}}}$

$=1+\dfrac{1}{2+\dfrac{1}{\dfrac{2}{3}}} = 1+\dfrac{1}{2+\dfrac{3}{2}} = 1+\dfrac{1}{\dfrac{7}{2}} = 1+\dfrac{2}{7} = \dfrac{9}{7}$

8. $1+\dfrac{1}{4\times3}+\dfrac{1}{4\times3^2}+\dfrac{1}{4\times3^3}$

$= 1+\dfrac{1}{12}+\dfrac{1}{36}+\dfrac{1}{108} = \dfrac{108+9+3+1}{108}$

$= \dfrac{121}{108} = 1.1203$

9. $\dfrac{\dfrac{1}{2}\div4+20}{\dfrac{1}{2}\times4+20} = \dfrac{\dfrac{1}{8}+20}{2+20} = \dfrac{\dfrac{1+160}{8}}{22}$

$= \dfrac{161}{8\times22} = \dfrac{161}{176}$

10. $3\div\left[(8-5)\div\left\{(4-2)\div\left(2+\dfrac{8}{13}\right)\right\}\right]$

$= 3\div\left[3\div\left\{2\div\dfrac{34}{13}\right\}\right]$

$= 3\div\left[3\div\left\{2\times\dfrac{13}{34}\right\}\right] = 3\div\left[3\div\dfrac{13}{17}\right]$

$= 3\div\left[3\times\dfrac{17}{13}\right] = 3\div\dfrac{51}{13} = 3\times\dfrac{13}{51} = \dfrac{13}{17}$

11. $10-[9-\{8-(7-6)\}]-5$

$= 10-[9-\{8-1\}]-5$

$= 10-[9-7]-5 = 10-2-5 = 10-7 = 3$

12. $\dfrac{\dfrac{1}{5}\div\dfrac{1}{5}\text{ of }\dfrac{1}{5}}{\dfrac{1}{5}\text{ of }\dfrac{1}{5}\div\dfrac{1}{5}} = \dfrac{\dfrac{1}{5}\div\dfrac{1}{25}}{\dfrac{1}{25}\div\dfrac{1}{5}} = \dfrac{\dfrac{1}{5}\times\dfrac{25}{1}}{\dfrac{1}{25}\times\dfrac{5}{1}} = \dfrac{\dfrac{5}{1}}{\dfrac{1}{5}}$

$= \dfrac{5}{1}\times\dfrac{5}{1} = 25$

13. $1+\dfrac{1}{1+\dfrac{1}{1+\dfrac{1}{9}}} = 1+\dfrac{1}{1+\dfrac{1}{\dfrac{10}{9}}} = 1+\dfrac{1}{1+\dfrac{9}{10}}$

$= 1+\dfrac{1}{\dfrac{19}{10}} = 1+\dfrac{10}{19} = \dfrac{29}{19}$

14. Let x of $\dfrac{1}{12} = \dfrac{3}{48}$

$\Rightarrow \dfrac{x}{12} = \dfrac{3}{48} \Rightarrow 48x = 36$

$\Rightarrow x = \dfrac{36}{48} = \dfrac{3}{4}.$

15. Let n times $\dfrac{1}{8} = 37\dfrac{1}{2}$

$\Rightarrow \dfrac{n}{8} = \dfrac{75}{2} \Rightarrow 2n = 8\times75$

$\Rightarrow n = \dfrac{8\times75}{2} = 4\times75 = 300.$

4. SURDS AND INDICES

SURDS

If 'a' is a rational number and n is a positive integer such that nth root of 'a', *i.e.*, $a^{1/n}$ or $\sqrt[n]{a}$ is an irrational number, then $a^{1/n}$ is called a surd or radical.

In other words, an irrational root of a rational number is called a surd. The symbol '√' is known as surd sign or radical.

For example, $\sqrt{2} = 2^{1/2}$ = Square root of 2

$\sqrt[3]{5} = 5^{1/3}$ = Cube root of 5

Pure and Mixed Surds

Pure Surd: A surd which has unity only as rational factor, the other factor being irrational, is called a pure surd.

For example, $\sqrt{2}$, $\sqrt[3]{3}$, $\sqrt[5]{3}$ are pure surds.

Mixed Surd: A surd which has a rational factor other than unity, the other factor being irrational, is called a mixed surds.

For example, $2\sqrt{5}$ $3\sqrt[4]{7}$, $5\sqrt[3]{11}$ are mixed surds.

Rationalising Factor: When the product of two surds is a rational number, then each of them is called the rationalising factor (R.F.) of the other.

For example, $3\sqrt{5} \times \sqrt{5} = 3 \times 5 = 15$

$\therefore$ $\sqrt{5}$ is a rationalising factor of $3\sqrt{5}$.

Important Formulae Based on Surds

$\sqrt[n]{a} = a^{1/n}$ and it is called a surd of order n.

(*i*) $\sqrt[n]{a^n} = a$

(*ii*) $\sqrt[n]{ab} = \sqrt[n]{a}\,\sqrt[n]{b}$

(*iii*) $\sqrt{a} \times \sqrt{a} = a$

(*iv*) $\sqrt{a} \times \sqrt{b} = \sqrt{ab}$

(*v*) $\sqrt{a^2 b} = a\sqrt{b}$

(*vi*) $\left(\sqrt{a} + \sqrt{b}\right)^2 = a + b + 2\sqrt{ab}$

(*vii*) $\left(\sqrt{a} - \sqrt{b}\right)^2 = a + b - 2\sqrt{ab}$

(*viii*) $\left(\sqrt{a} + \sqrt{b}\right)\left(\sqrt{a} - \sqrt{b}\right) = a - b$ where a and b are positive rational numbers.

INDICES

Let n be a positive integer and 'a' be a real number. The continued product of n factors each equal to a *e.g.*, $a \times a \times a \times \ldots \times n$ times is written as a^n and is called "n^{th} power of a" or "a raised to the power n".

The expression a^n is termed as power function or simply power, a is called the base and n is called index or exponent of the power a^n.

For example, 2^2 = square of 2, 2^3 = cube of 2, etc.

Laws of Indices

(*i*) $a^m \times a^n = a^{m+n}$

(*ii*) $a^m \times a^n \times a^p \times \ldots = a^{m+n+p+\ldots}$

(*iii*) $\dfrac{a^m}{a^n} = a^{m-n}$, if $m > n$

(*iv*) $\dfrac{a^m}{a^n} = \dfrac{1}{a^{n-m}}$, if $m < n$

(*v*) $(a^m)^n = a^{mn}$

(*vi*) $(ab)^n = a^n b^n$

(*vii*) $a^0 = 1$

(*viii*) If $a^m = a^n$ then $m = n$

(*ix*) If $a^m = b^m$ then $a = b$

(*x*) $\dfrac{a^m}{a^m} = a^{m-m} = a^0 = 1$

MULTIPLE CHOICE QUESTIONS

1. If the infinite series is $x = \sqrt{6+\sqrt{6+\sqrt{6+...}}}$ then the value of x is:

A. 2.5 B. 3
C. 6 D. 8

2. If $\frac{9^n \cdot 3^2 \cdot 3^n - (27)^n}{3^{3m} \cdot 2^3} = \frac{1}{27}$, then the value of $(m-n)$ is:

A. 1 B. 2
C. $\sqrt{3}$ D. $\sqrt{\frac{2}{3}}$

3. If $x = \frac{\sqrt{5}+\sqrt{3}}{\sqrt{5}-\sqrt{3}}$ and $y = \frac{\sqrt{5}-\sqrt{3}}{\sqrt{5}+\sqrt{3}}$, then $(x+y)$ is equal to:

A. 8 B. 6
C. $2\sqrt{15}$ D. $2\left(\sqrt{5}+\sqrt{3}\right)$

4. $2^{x+1} + 2^{x+3} = 2560$, then x is equal to:

A. 12 B. 11
C. 8 D. 6

5. If $\frac{5+2\sqrt{3}}{7+4\sqrt{3}} = a + b\sqrt{3}$, then b is equal to:

A. –6 B. 6
C. –11 D. 11

6. If $\frac{(21)^{5.36}}{(21)^{3.47}} = (21)^x$, then the value of x is:

A. 8.88 B. 1.54
C. 9.32 D. 1.89

7. $\sqrt{24} + \sqrt{12}$ equal to:

A. $\sqrt{36}$ B. $2\sqrt{6} + 2\sqrt{3}$
C. $6\sqrt{2}$ D. $\sqrt{288}$

8. If $a^b = 64$, where a and b are positive integers then $(a-b)^{a+b-4}$ is:

A. 0 B. 1
C. 2 D. $\frac{1}{2}$

9. The value of $\frac{5^{10+n} \cdot 25^{3n-4}}{5^{7n}}$ is:

A. 5 B. 8
C. 25 D. 16

10. $3^x - 3^{x-1} = 18$, then the value of x^x is:

A. 3 B. 8
C. 27 D. 216

11. If $x = \sqrt{10+\sqrt{25+\sqrt{121}}}$, then x is equal to:

A. –2 only B. 2 only
C. ±4 D. 4 only

12. If $a^x = b^y = c^z$ and $b^2 = ac$, then y is equal to:

A. $\frac{xz}{x+z}$ B. $\frac{xz}{2(x-z)}$
C. $\frac{xz}{2(z-x)}$ D. $\frac{2xz}{x+z}$

13. $\frac{5^{n+3} - 6 \times 5^{n+1}}{9 \times 5^n - 5^n \times 2^2}$ is equal to:

A. 5 B. 19
C. 25 D. 95

14. The value of $\left(\frac{x^a}{x^b}\right)^{(a+b)} \times \left(\frac{x^b}{x^c}\right)^{(b+c)} \times \left(\frac{x^c}{x^a}\right)^{(c+a)}$ is equal to:

A. 0 B. 2
C. 1 D. 3

15. If $\sqrt{3^n} = 729$, then the value of n is:

A. 12 B. 8
C. 10 D. 6

ANSWERS

1	2	3	4	5	6	7	8	9	10
B	A	A	C	A	D	B	B	C	C
11	**12**	**13**	**14**	**15**					
D	D	B	C	A					

EXPLANATORY ANSWERS

1. $x = \sqrt{6+x}$

Squaring both sides

$$x^2 = 6 + x$$
$$\Rightarrow x^2 - x - 6 = 0$$
$$\Rightarrow x^2 - 3x + 2x - 6 = 0$$
$$\Rightarrow x(x-3) + 2(x-3) = 0$$
$$\Rightarrow (x-3)(x+2) = 0$$
$$\Rightarrow x = 3 \text{ or } x = -2$$

But x cannot be -2.

Hence, the required value of x is 3.

2. $$\frac{9^n \cdot 3^2 \cdot 3^n - (27)^n}{3^{3m} \cdot 2^3} = \frac{1}{27}$$

$$\Rightarrow \frac{3^{2n} \times 9 \times 3^n - 3^{3n}}{8 \times 3^{3m}} = \frac{1}{3^3}$$

$$\Rightarrow \frac{3^{3n}(9-1)}{8\ 3^{3m}} = 3^{-3}$$

$$\Rightarrow 3^{3n-3m} = (3)^{-3}$$
$$\Rightarrow 3m - 3n = 3$$
$$\Rightarrow 3(m-n) = 3$$
$$\Rightarrow m - n = \frac{3}{3} = 1$$

3. $$x = \frac{\sqrt{5}+\sqrt{3}}{\sqrt{5}-\sqrt{3}} \times \frac{\sqrt{5}+\sqrt{3}}{\sqrt{5}+\sqrt{3}} = \frac{\left(\sqrt{5}+\sqrt{3}\right)^2}{5-3}$$

$$\Rightarrow x = \frac{5+3+2\sqrt{15}}{2} = \frac{8+2\sqrt{15}}{2} = \frac{2\left(4+\sqrt{15}\right)}{2}$$

$$\therefore x = 4 + \sqrt{15}$$

Again, $$y = \frac{\sqrt{5}-\sqrt{3}}{\sqrt{5}+\sqrt{3}} \times \frac{\sqrt{5}-\sqrt{3}}{\sqrt{5}-\sqrt{3}}$$

$$= \frac{\left(\sqrt{5}-\sqrt{3}\right)^2}{5-3}$$

$$\Rightarrow y = \frac{5+3-2\sqrt{15}}{2}$$

$$= \frac{8-2\sqrt{15}}{2} = \frac{2\left(4-\sqrt{15}\right)}{2}$$

$$\Rightarrow y = 4 - \sqrt{15}$$

$$\therefore x + y = 4 + \sqrt{15} + 4 - \sqrt{15} = 8$$

4. $$2^{x+1} + 2^{x+3} = 2560$$
$$\Rightarrow 2^x \times 2 + 2^x \times 2^3 = 2560$$
$$\Rightarrow 2 \times 2^x + 8 \times 2^x = 2560$$
$$\Rightarrow 2^x (2+8) = 2560$$
$$\Rightarrow 2^x = 256 = 2^8$$
$$\Rightarrow x = 8$$

5. $\because$ $$\frac{5+2\sqrt{3}}{7+4\sqrt{3}} = a + b\sqrt{3}$$

$$\frac{5+2\sqrt{3}}{7+4\sqrt{3}} \times \frac{7-4\sqrt{3}}{7-4\sqrt{3}} = \frac{35-20\sqrt{3}+14\sqrt{3}-24}{49-48}$$

$$= \frac{11-6\sqrt{3}}{1}$$

Comparing then we get,

$a = 11$, $b = -6$

Hence, $b = -6$.

6. $$\frac{(21)^{5.36}}{(21)^{3.47}} = (21)^x$$

$$\Rightarrow (21)^{5.36-3.47} = (21)^x$$
$$\Rightarrow x = 1.89$$

7. $\sqrt{24} + \sqrt{12} = 2\sqrt{6} + 2\sqrt{3}$

8. $a^b = 64 = (4)^3 \Rightarrow a = 4, b = 3$

$\therefore (a-b)^{a+b-4} = (4-3)^{4+3-4} = (1)^3 = 1$

9. $$\frac{5^{10+n} \cdot 25^{3n-4}}{5^{7n}} = \frac{5^{10} \times 5^n \times (5^2)^{3n-4}}{5^{7n}}$$

$$= \frac{5^{10} \times 5^n \times 5^{6n} \times 5^{-8}}{5^{7n}}$$

$$= \frac{5^{10-8} \times 5^{7n}}{5^{7n}} = 5^2 \times 5^{7n-7n}$$

$$= 25 \times 5^0 = 25 \times 1 = 25$$

10. $$3^x - 3^{x-1} = 18$$
$$\Rightarrow 3^x - 3^x \times 3^{-1} = 18$$
$$\Rightarrow 3^x\left(1 - \frac{1}{3}\right) = 18$$
$$\Rightarrow 3^x\left(\frac{2}{3}\right) = 18$$

$$\Rightarrow \quad 3^x = \frac{18 \times 3}{2} = 27$$

$$\Rightarrow \quad 3^x = (3)^3 \Rightarrow x = 3$$

$$\therefore \quad x^x = (3)^3 = 27$$

11. $x = \sqrt{10 + \sqrt{25 + \sqrt{121}}}$

$$\Rightarrow \quad x = \sqrt{10 + \sqrt{25 + 11}}$$

$$\Rightarrow \quad x = \sqrt{10 + \sqrt{36}}$$

$$\Rightarrow \quad x = \sqrt{10 + 6} = \sqrt{16}$$

$$\Rightarrow \quad x = 4$$

12. Let $a^x = b^y = c^z = k$

then $a = k^{\frac{1}{x}}$, $b = k^{\frac{1}{y}}$, $c = k^{\frac{1}{z}}$

Now, $b^2 = ac$

$$\Rightarrow \quad \left(k^{\frac{1}{y}}\right)^2 = k^{\frac{1}{x}} \cdot k^{\frac{1}{z}}$$

$$\Rightarrow \quad k^{\frac{2}{y}} = k^{\frac{1}{x}+\frac{1}{z}}$$

$$\Rightarrow \quad \frac{2}{y} = \frac{z + x}{xz}$$

$$\Rightarrow \quad 2xz = y(x + z)$$

$$\Rightarrow \quad y = \frac{2xz}{x + z}$$

13. $\dfrac{5^{n+3} - 6 \times 5^{n+1}}{9 \times 5^n - 5^n \times 2^2} = \dfrac{5^n \times 5^3 - 6 \times 5^n \times 5}{9 \times 5^n - 4 \times 5^n}$

$$= \frac{5^n(125 - 30)}{5^n(9 - 4)} = 5^0 \times \frac{95}{5}$$

$$= 1 \times 19 = 19.$$

14. $\left(\dfrac{x^a}{x^b}\right)^{(a+b)} \times \left(\dfrac{x^b}{x^c}\right)^{(b+c)} \times \left(\dfrac{x^c}{x^a}\right)^{(c+a)}$

$$= \left(x^{a-b}\right)^{(a+b)} \times \left(x^{b-c}\right)^{(b+c)} \times \left(x^{c-a}\right)^{c+a}$$

$$= x^{a^2-b^2} \times x^{b^2-c^2} \times x^{c^2-a^2}$$

$$= x^{a^2-b^2+b^2-c^2+c^2-a^2}$$

$$= x^0 = 1$$

15. $\sqrt{3^n} = 729 \Rightarrow 3^{n/2} = 3^6$

$$\Rightarrow \quad \frac{n}{2} = 6$$

$$\Rightarrow \quad n = 12.$$

5. RATIO AND PROPORTION

RATIO

When comparison is made by dividing one quantity by another of the same kind, the result is called ratio. If a and b are two numbers, ratio of a to b is denoted by $a : b$ or $\frac{a}{b}$. Here a is called first term and b is called the second term. The first term is also called antecedent and the second term is also called consequent.

EXAMPLE: The ratio 3 : 10 represents $\frac{3}{10}$ with antecedent 3 and consequent 10.

The multiplication or division of each term of a ratio by a same non-zero number does not effect the ratio.

PROPORTION

Equality of two ratios is called proportion. If $a : b = c : d$, then a, b, c, d are called in proportion. In a proportion $a : b : : c : d$, then a and d are called extremes and b and c are called means.

Product of extremes = Product of means

Comparison of Ratio: Suppose $\frac{a}{b} > \frac{c}{d}$ then we say that $a : b > c : d$.

Compounded Ratio: The compound ratio of the ratios $a : b$, $c : d$ and $e : f$ is $ace : bdf$.

Duplicate Ratio: The duplicate ratio of $a : b$ is $a^2 : b^2$.

Triplicate Ratio: The triplicate ratio of $a : b$ is $a^3 : b^3$.

Sub-duplicate and Sub-triplicate ratios

The sub-duplicate and Sub-triplicate ratios of ratio $a : b$ are $a^{1/2} : b^{1/2}$ and $a^{1/3} : b^{1/3}$ respectively.

Mean Proportional: Mean proportional between a and b is $\sqrt{ab}$.

Third Proportional: The third proportional to a, b is the fourth proportional to a, b, b.

Fourth Proportional: If $a : b : : c : d$ is a proportion, then d is called the fourth proportional to a, b, c.

EXAMPLE: If A : B = 3 : 4 and B : C = 8 : 9 then find A : C.

SOLUTION: $A : B = 3 : 4 \Rightarrow \frac{A}{B} = \frac{3}{4}$

$B : C = 8 : 9 \Rightarrow \frac{B}{C} = \frac{8}{9}$

$$\frac{A}{C} = \frac{A}{B} \times \frac{B}{C} = \frac{3}{4} \times \frac{8}{9} = \frac{2}{3}$$

$\Rightarrow$ A : C = 2 : 3

EXAMPLE: If 15% of A is the same as 20% of B, then find A : B.

SOLUTION: Given : 15% of A = 20% of B

$$\Rightarrow \frac{15}{100} \times A = \frac{20}{100} \times B$$

$$\Rightarrow 3A = 4B$$

$$\Rightarrow \frac{A}{B} = \frac{4}{3}$$

$\Rightarrow$ A : B = 4 : 3

EXAMPLE: A stick 1.4 m long casts a shadow 1.3 m long at the same time when a pole casts a shadow 5.2 m long. Find the length of the pole.

SOLUTION: Clearly, more is the length of shadow, more is the length of the object.

Let the length of the pole be x metres.

Then, 1.3 : 5.2 : : 1.4 : x

$$\Rightarrow \quad \frac{1.3}{5.2} = \frac{1.4}{x}$$

$$\Rightarrow \quad \frac{1}{4} = \frac{1.4}{x}$$

$$\Rightarrow \quad x = 1.4 \times 4 = 5.6$$

Hence, the length of the pole is 5.6 m.

MULTIPLE CHOICE QUESTIONS

1. If A : B = 2 : 3 and B : C = 4 : 5, then C : A is equal to:

A. 15 : 8 B. 12 : 10
C. 8 : 5 D. 8 : 15

2. If 10% of x is the same as 20% of y, then $x : y$ is equal to:

A. 1 : 2 B. 2 : 1
C. 5 : 1 D. 10 : 1

3. The mean proportional to $6+\sqrt{27}$ and $6-\sqrt{27}$ is:

A. 3 B. 9
C. 10 D. $\sqrt{10}$

4. If $x : y = 9 : 11$, the value of $\frac{5x+3y}{3x+5y}$ is:

A. 45 : 55 B. 18 : 22
C. 37 : 41 D. 39 : 41

5. If $a + b : b + c : c + a = 6 : 7 : 8$ and $a + b + c = 14$, then the value of c is:

A. 14 B. 7
C. 8 D. 6

6. Two numbers are in the ratio 2 : 3. If 5 is added to each number, the ratio becomes 5 : 7. The bigger number is:

A. 30 B. 40
C. 60 D. 20

7. What should be added to each of the numbers 12, 30, 40 and 86, so that they are in proportion?

A. 6 B. 4
C. –6 D. –4

8. The ratio of males and females of a village is 5 : 3. If there are 800 males in the village, females are:

A. 240 B. 480
C. 840 D. 488

9. In a mixture of 60 litres, the ratio of ethanol to ether is 4 : 1. How much ether must be added to the mixture to make this ratio 2 : 1?

A. 10 litres B. 12 litres
C. 18 litres D. 24 litres

10. The proportion of zinc and copper in a brass piece is 4 : 5. How much zinc will be there in 180 kg of such a piece?

A. 40 kg B. 80 kg
C. 100 kg D. 120 kg

11. The prices of a scooter and a television set are in the ratio 3 : 2. If a scooter costs ₹ 6000 more than the television set, the price of the television set is:

A. ₹ 18000 B. ₹ 12000
C. ₹ 10000 D. ₹ 6000

12. The weight of a 13 metres long iron rod be 23.4 kg. The weight of 6 metres long of such rod will be:

A. 7.2 kg B. 12.4 kg
C. 10.8 kg D. 18 kg

13. The ratio between the ages of Gayatri and Savitri is 6 : 5 and the sum of their ages is 44 years. The ratio of their ages after 8 years will be:

A. 5 : 6 B. 7 : 8
C. 8 : 7 D. 14 : 13

14. Two numbers are such that the ratio between them is 3 : 5 but if each is increased by 10, the ratio between them becomes 5 : 7. The numbers are:

A. 3, 5 B. 7, 9
C. 13, 22 D. 15, 25

15. In a factory the ratio of male workers to female workers was 5 : 3. If the number of female workers was less by 40, the total number of workers in the factory was:

A. 100
B. 500
C. 160
D. 200

ANSWERS

1	2	3	4	5	6	7	8	9	10
A	B	A	D	D	A	A	B	B	B
11	**12**	**13**	**14**	**15**					
B	C	C	D	C					

EXPLANATORY ANSWERS

1. $\frac{A}{B} = \frac{2}{3}$ and $\frac{B}{C} = \frac{4}{5}$

$\Rightarrow \quad \frac{A}{B} \times \frac{B}{C} = \frac{2}{3} \times \frac{4}{5} \Rightarrow \frac{A}{C} = \frac{8}{15}$

$\Rightarrow \quad \frac{C}{A} = \frac{15}{8}$

Hence, $\quad$ C : A = 15 : 8.

2. 10% of x = 20% of y

$\Rightarrow \quad \frac{10}{100}x = \frac{20}{100}y \Rightarrow \frac{x}{10} = \frac{y}{5}$

$\Rightarrow \quad \frac{x}{y} = \frac{10}{5} \Rightarrow x : y = 2 : 1$

3. Mean proportional = $\sqrt{(6+\sqrt{27})(6-\sqrt{27})}$

$= \sqrt{36-27} = \sqrt{9} = 3$

4. $\because \quad \frac{x}{y} = \frac{9}{11}$

$$\frac{5x+3y}{3x+5y} = \frac{\frac{5x}{y}+\frac{3y}{y}}{\frac{3x}{y}+\frac{5y}{y}} = \frac{5\left(\frac{x}{y}\right)+3}{3\left(\frac{x}{y}\right)+5}$$

$$= \frac{5\times\frac{9}{11}+3}{3\times\frac{9}{11}+5} = \frac{\frac{45+33}{11}}{\frac{27+55}{11}} = \frac{78}{82} = \frac{39}{41}$$

Hence, the value of $\frac{5x+3y}{3x+5y} = \frac{39}{41}$.

5. Given : $\quad a+b = 6x,\ b+c = 7x$

and $\quad c+a = 8x \quad ...(i)$

and $\quad a+b+c = 14 \quad ...(ii)$

Adding Eq. (*i*)

$a+b+b+c+c+a = 6x+7x+8x$

$\Rightarrow \quad 2(a+b+c) = 21x$

$\Rightarrow \quad 2 \times 14 = 21x \quad$ [from Eq. (*ii*)]

$\Rightarrow \quad x = \frac{28}{21} = \frac{4}{3}$

$\therefore \quad a+b = 6x = 6\times\frac{4}{3} = 8$

$\because \quad a+b+c = 14 \Rightarrow c = 14-8 = 6$

6. Let the two numbers are a and b

According to the question,

$\frac{a}{b} = \frac{2}{3} \Rightarrow 3a = 2b \Rightarrow b = \frac{3a}{2}$

Now, $\quad \frac{a+5}{b+5} = \frac{5}{7} \Rightarrow 7a+35 = 5b+25$

$\Rightarrow \quad 7a-5b = -10$

$\Rightarrow \quad 7a-5\left(\frac{3a}{2}\right) = -10$

$\Rightarrow \quad 14a-15a = -20 \Rightarrow -a = -20$

$\Rightarrow \quad a = 20,\ b = 3\times\frac{20}{2} = 30$

Hence, the bigger number is 30.

7. Let x be added to each of the numbers.

Then, $(12+x) : (30+x) :: (40+x) : (86+x)$

$\Rightarrow \quad \frac{12+x}{30+x} = \frac{40+x}{86+x}$

$\Rightarrow (12+x)(86+x) = (30+x)(40+x)$

$\Rightarrow 12\times86+12x+86x+x^2 = 30\times40+30x+40x+x^2$

$\Rightarrow \quad 1032+98x = 1200+70x$

$\Rightarrow \quad 28x = 168 \Rightarrow x = 6$

8. Ratio of Males : Females = 5 : 3

$\Rightarrow \quad \frac{800}{x} = \frac{5}{3} \Rightarrow 5x = 3\times800$

$\Rightarrow \quad x = \frac{3\times800}{5} = 3\times160 = 480$

Hence, number of females = 480.

9. Let ethanol = $4x$ and ether = $1x$

$4x + 1x = 60 \Rightarrow 5x = 60 \Rightarrow x = 12$

Quantity of ethanol = $12 \times 4 = 48$ litres

Quantity of ether = $1 \times 12 = 12$ litres

Let m litres of ether be added to mixture to get the desired ratio. Then,

$$\frac{48}{12+m} = \frac{2}{1} \quad \Rightarrow \quad 24 + 2m = 48$$

$$\Rightarrow \quad 2m = 24 \quad \Rightarrow \quad m = 12$$

Hence, 12 litres of ether is to be added.

10. In 9 kg of brass, zinc = 4 kg

$\therefore$ In 180 kg of brass, zinc = $\frac{4}{9} \times 180 = 80$ kg.

11. Let the prices of a scooter and a television be ₹ $3x$ and $2x$ respectively.

According to the question,

$3x - 2x = 6000 \Rightarrow x = 6000$

$\therefore$ Price of a television = 2×6000 = ₹ 12000.

12. Weight of 13 m long iron rod = 23.4 kg

Weight of 6 m long iron rod

$= \frac{23.4}{13} \times 6 \text{ kg} = 1.8 \times 6 = 10.8$ kg.

13. Let present age of Gayatri = $6x$ years and present age of Savitri = $5x$ years.

According to the question,

$$6x + 5x = 44 \Rightarrow 11x = 44 \Rightarrow x = 4$$

Gayatri's age = $6 \times 4 = 24$ years

Savitri's age = $5 \times 4 = 20$ years

After 8 years their ages will be 32 years and 28 years.

Ratio of their ages after 8 years = $\frac{32}{28} = 8 : 7$.

14. Let numbers are x and y

$$\frac{x}{y} = \frac{3}{5}$$

$$\Rightarrow \quad 5x = 3y \Rightarrow x = \frac{3y}{5}$$

According to the question,

$$\frac{x+10}{y+10} = \frac{5}{7} \Rightarrow 7x + 70 = 5y + 50$$

$$\Rightarrow \quad 7x - 5y = -20$$

$$\Rightarrow \quad 7\left(\frac{3y}{5}\right) - 5y = -20$$

$$\Rightarrow \quad 21y - 25y = -100$$

$$\Rightarrow \quad 4y = 100 \Rightarrow y = 25$$

$$\therefore \quad x = \frac{3 \times 25}{5} = 15$$

Hence, numbers are 15 and 25.

15. Let the number of male and female workers be $5x$ and $3x$ respectively.

According to the question,

$5x - 3x = 40 \Rightarrow 2x = 40 \Rightarrow x = 20$

$\therefore$ Number of male = $5 \times 20 = 100$

and number of female = $3 \times 20 = 60$

Hence, total number of workers = $100 + 60 = 160$.

6. PARTNERSHIP

Partnership is a form of association of two or more persons who contribute resources like money together in order to carry on a business. It may be of simple or compound type.

Simple partnership is one in which the capitals of the partners are invested for the same time. The profits or losses are divided among the partners in the ratio of their investments.

Compound partnership is one in which the capitals of the partners are invested for different periods. In such cases, equivalent capitals are calculated for each partner by multiplying their capital contributions with time. The profits or losses are then divided in the ratio of these equivalent capitals. Thus, the ratio of profits is directly proportional to both capital invested as well as time.

The partner who invests the money in the business as well as takes part in its management, is known as **Working partner**.

The partner who only invests the money in the business and does not work, is known as **Sleeping partner**.

A working partner gets either monthly payment or a share in the profit for his contribution in the management of the business. This payment is deducted from the total profit before its distribution.

EXAMPLE: A, B and C invest ₹ 15000, ₹ 20000 and ₹ 25000 respectively in a business. The profit earned is ₹ 1200. Find the share of each in the profit.

SOLUTION: This is a case of simple partnership

Ratio of investments, A : B : C

= 15000 : 20000 : 25000

= 3 : 4 : 5

Sum of the ratios = 3 + 4 + 5 = 12

Share in the profit

$$\text{For A} = \frac{3}{12} \times 1200 = ₹\,300$$

$$\text{For B} = \frac{4}{12} \times 1200 = ₹\,400$$

$$\text{For C} = \frac{5}{12} \times 1200 = ₹\,500$$

EXAMPLE: A and B are partners in a firm. A invests ₹ 15000 and B ₹ 25000. A is the working partner and gets 20% of the profit for his contribution in the management of the firm. B is the sleeping partner. If the profit is ₹ 475, find the share of each.

SOLUTION: First we have to deduct the payment to be made to A from the total profit for his contribution in the management of the firm.

20% of ₹ 475 = ₹ 95

Balance profit = 475 – 95 = ₹ 380

This has to be divided between A and B in the ratio of their investments *i.e.,* ₹ 15000 : ₹ 25000 = 3 : 5

$$\text{A's share} = ₹\,380 \times \frac{3}{8} = ₹\,142.5$$

$$\text{B's share} = ₹\,380 \times \frac{5}{8} = ₹\,237.5$$

Finally, A gets a total of (95 + 142.5) = ₹ 237.5 and B gets = ₹ 237.5

EXAMPLE: In a business A and B gained some amount in a certain ratio. B and C received the profit in the ratio as that of A and B. If B received ₹ 6400 and C received ₹ 10,000 then find the amount invested by B.

SOLUTION: Let the ratio of A's and B's profit be $\frac{a}{b}$.

Hence, the ratio of B's and C's profit = $\frac{a}{b}$

Thus, $A : B : C = a : b : \frac{b^2}{a}$

when A's profit, a = ₹ 6400

and C's profit, $\frac{b^2}{a}$ = ₹ 10,000

$\Rightarrow$ $b^2 = 10{,}000 \times 6400 = 100 \times 100 \times 80 \times 80$

$\Rightarrow$ $b = 100 \times 80 = 8000$

Hence, the amount invested by B = ₹ 8000.

MULTIPLE CHOICE QUESTIONS

1. A, B and C share the profit in the ratio of 3 : 5 : 7. If the gain is ₹ 2040, then C's share is:
A. ₹ 360 B. ₹ 600
C. ₹ 952 D. ₹ 120

2. A, B and C started a business with ₹ 47000. A puts in ₹ 5000 more than B and B ₹ 3000 more than C. The share of A out of the profit of ₹ 14100 will be:
A. ₹ 3600 B. ₹ 4500
C. ₹ 6000 D. ₹ 6300

3. A starts a business with ₹ 5000. After 4 months B joins him with a sum of ₹ 4000. In the end of the year there is a profit of ₹ 8970. The share of A in the profit will be:
A. ₹ 3120 B. ₹ 4020
C. ₹ 5850 D. ₹ 6360

4. A, B, C are three partners in a business. The profit share of A is $\frac{3}{16}$ of the profit and B's share is $\frac{1}{4}$ of the profit. If C receives ₹ 243, then the amount received by B will be:
A. ₹ 90 B. ₹ 96
C. ₹ 108 D. ₹ 120

5. A, B and C share the profit in the ratio 2 : 3 : 7. If the average gain is ₹ 8000, then B's share is:
A. ₹ 2000 B. ₹ 1000
C. ₹ 1500 D. ₹ 3000

6. Ashok started a business investing ₹ 90,000. After 3 months Shabir joined him with a capital of ₹ 1,20,000. If at the end of one year the total profit made by them was ₹ 96,000, what will be the difference between their shares?
A. ₹ 24000 B. ₹ 8000
C. ₹ 20000 D. None of these

7. Mahesh received ₹ 6000 as his share out of the total profit of ₹ 9000 which he and Ram entered at the end of one year. If Mahesh invested ₹ 20,000 for 6 months, whereas Ram invested his amount for the whole year, what was the amount invested by Ram?
A. ₹ 4000 B. ₹ 5000
C. ₹ 3000 D. ₹ 6000

8. A and B started a business jointly. A's investment was thrice the investment of B and the period of his investment was two times the period of investment of B. If B received ₹ 40,000 as profit, then their total profit is:
A. ₹ 2,40,000 B. ₹ 28000
C. ₹ 24000 D. ₹ 2,80,000

9. Anil started a business investing ₹ 70,000. After 8 months Vimal joined him with a capital of ₹ 1,80,000. In what ratio should Anil and Vimal share the profit after two years?
A. 8 : 7 B. 7 : 5
C. 7 : 6 D. None of these

10. A, B and C starts a business. A invests ₹ 3,20,000 for four months. B invests ₹ 5,10,000 for three months and C invests ₹ 2,70,000 for five months. If at the end of year there is a profit of ₹ 1,24,800, then share of B is:
A. ₹ 79000 B. ₹ 49200
C. ₹ 50000 D. ₹ 45900

11. A, B and C contract a work for ₹ 550. Together A and B are to do $\frac{7}{11}$ of the work. The share of C should be:
A. ₹ 400 B. ₹ 300
C. ₹ 200 D. ₹ $183\frac{1}{3}$

12. Jagmohan, Rooplal and Pankaj rented a video cassette for one week at a rent of ₹ 350. If they use it for 6 hrs, 10 hrs and 12 hrs respectively, the rent to be paid by Pankaj is:
A. ₹ 75 B. ₹ 125
C. ₹ 35 D. ₹ 150

13. Manoj got ₹ 6000 as his share out of the total profit of ₹ 9000 which he and Ramesh earned at the end of one year. If Manoj invested ₹ 20,000 for 6 months, whereas Ramesh invested his amount for the whole year, the amount invested by Ramesh was:

A. ₹ 60,000 B. ₹ 10,000
C. ₹ 4000 D. ₹ 5000

14. A, B and C invest ₹ 2000, ₹ 3000 and ₹ 4000 in a business. After one year A removed his money, B and C continued the business for one more year. If the net profit after 2 years be ₹ 3200, then A's share in the profit is:

A. ₹ 1000 B. ₹ 600
C. ₹ 800 D. ₹ 400

15. A and B enter into partnership investing ₹ 12000 and ₹ 16000 respectively. After 8 months, C also joins the business with a capital of ₹ 15000. The share of C in a profit of ₹ 46500 after 2 years will be:

A. ₹ 12000 B. ₹ 14400
C. ₹ 19200 D. ₹ 21200

ANSWERS

1	2	3	4	5	6	7	8	9	10
C	C	C	C	A	D	B	D	D	D
11	**12**	**13**	**14**	**15**					
C	D	D	D	A					

EXPLANATORY ANSWERS

1. C's share $= \frac{7}{15} \times 2040 =$ ₹ 952.

2. Let C's capital be ₹ x

Then B's capital = ₹ $(x + 3000)$

and A's capital = ₹ $(x + 3000 + 5000) = x + 8000$

$\Rightarrow \quad x + (x + 3000) + (x + 8000) = 47000$

$\Rightarrow \quad 3x + 11000 = 47000$

$\Rightarrow \quad 3x = 47000 - 11000 = 36000$

$\Rightarrow \quad x = 12000$

Thus, capital of A, B and C are ₹ 20000, ₹ 15000 and ₹ 12000 respectively.

∴ Profit sharing ratio = 20 : 15 : 12

∴ Profit of A $= \frac{20}{47} \times 14100 =$ ₹ 6000

3. ₹ 5000 × 12 = ₹ 60,000 for A

₹ 4000 × (12 – 4) = 4000 × 8 = ₹ 32000 for B

Ratio of profit sharing = 60000 : 32000 = 60 : 32 = 15 : 8

∴ Share of A in the profit $= \frac{15}{23} \times 8970$

= 15 × 390 = ₹ 5850

4. Let the profit be ₹ 1. Then,

$$A : B : C = \frac{3}{16} : \frac{1}{4} : \left[1 - \left(\frac{3}{16} + \frac{1}{4}\right)\right]$$

$$= \frac{3}{16} : \frac{1}{4} : \frac{9}{16}$$

$$= \frac{3}{16} : \frac{4}{16} : \frac{9}{16} \text{ i.e., } 3 : 4 : 9$$

when C's share is ₹ 9, then B's share = ₹ 4

when C's share is ₹ 243, then B's share

$$= \frac{4 \times 243}{9} = ₹\ 108$$

5. B's share $= \frac{3}{2+3+7} \times 8000$

$= \frac{3 \times 8000}{12} =$ ₹ 2000

6. The ratio of their investment

$= 12 \times 90000 : (12 - 3) \times 120000$

$= 12 \times 9 : 9 \times 12 = 1 : 1$

Ashok's share $= \frac{1}{1+1} \times 96000 =$ ₹ 48000

Shabir's share $= \frac{1}{1+1} \times 96000 =$ ₹ 48000

Difference between their shares

$= ₹\ 48000 - ₹\ 48000 = 0.$

7. The ratio of their profit

$= ₹\ 6000 : ₹\ (9000 - 6000)$

$= ₹\ 6000 : ₹\ 3000 = 2 : 1$

Let ₹ x be the amount invested by Ram.

The ratio of their profit = The ratio of their investment

$\Rightarrow \quad 2 : 1 = 6 \times 20000 : 12 \times x$

$\Rightarrow \quad \frac{2}{1} = \frac{6 \times 20000}{12 \times x} \Rightarrow 2x = 10000$

$\Rightarrow \quad x = 5000$

$\therefore$ The investment of Ram is ₹ 5000.

8. Let ₹ x be the investment of B and n years be the period of investment of B.

Given : A's investment $= 3 \times ₹\ x = ₹\ 3x$

and period of investment of A = $2n$ years

$\therefore$ The ratio of investment of A and B

$= 2n \times 3x : n \times x$

$= 6nx : nx = 6 : 1$

Let the total profit be ₹ y

Given B's share in profit = ₹ 40,000

$\Rightarrow \frac{1}{6+1} \times y = ₹\ 40,000 \Rightarrow y = ₹\ 2,80,000$

$\therefore$ Total profit is ₹ 2,80,000.

9. The ratio of Anil's and Vimal's share in the profit

= Ratio of their investments

$= 24 \times 70000 : 16 \times 180000$

$= 24 \times 7 : 16 \times 18 = 7 : 12$

10. The ratio of investments of A, B and C

$= 4 \times 320000 : 3 \times 510000 : 5 \times 270000$

$= 4 \times 32 : 3 \times 51 : 5 \times 27$

$= 128 : 153 : 135$

Total profit after 1 year = ₹ 124800

$\text{Share of B} = ₹\ \frac{153}{128+153+135} \times 124800$

$= ₹\ \frac{153}{416} \times 124800 = ₹\ 45900$

11. $\text{C's share} = ₹\left(550 \times \frac{4}{11}\right) = ₹\ 200$

12. Ratio of rents $= 6 : 10 : 12 = 3 : 5 : 6$

$\therefore \text{Pankaj's share of rent} = ₹\left(350 \times \frac{6}{14}\right) = ₹\ 150$

13. Let amount invested by Ramesh be ₹ x

$\therefore 20000 \times 6 : 12x = 6000 : 3000$

i.e., $\frac{12x}{120000} = \frac{3000}{6000}$ or $x = ₹\ 5000$

14. Ratio of investments

$= (2000 \times 1) : (3000 \times 2) : (4000 \times 2)$

$= 1 : 3 : 4$

$\therefore \text{A's share} = ₹\left(3200 \times \frac{1}{8}\right) = ₹\ 400.$

15. Ratio of investments

$= (12000 \times 24) : (16000 \times 24) : (15000 \times 16)$

$= 6 : 8 : 5$

$\text{C's share of profit} = ₹\left(45600 \times \frac{5}{19}\right) = ₹\ 12000$

7. AVERAGE

The sum of all the quantities of same kind divided by their number is called average (or mean) of those quantities.

FORMULAE

1. Average $= \left(\dfrac{\text{Sum of observations}}{\text{Number of observations}}\right)$
2. Sum of the first n natural numbers
$= 1 + 2 + 3 + ... + n = \dfrac{n(n+1)}{2}$
3. Sum of the squares of the first n natural numbers
$= 1^2 + 2^2 + ... + n^2 = \dfrac{n(n+1)(2n+1)}{6}$
4. Sum of the cubes of the first n natural numbers
$= 1^3 + 2^3 + ... + n^3 = \left\{\dfrac{n(n+1)}{2}\right\}^2$
5. Sum of the first n odd numbers
$= 1 + 3 + 5 + ... + (2n-1) = n^2$
6. Distance between two stations P and Q is x km. A person covers the journey from P to Q at 'a' km/hr and returns back to P with a uniform speed of 'b' km/hr. Then the average speed of the person during the whole journey
$= \dfrac{2ab}{a+b}$ km/hr.

Different kinds of mean or average:

(*a*) Arithmetic mean
(*b*) Geometric mean
(*c*) Harmonic mean

(*a*) **Arithmetic Mean:** It is most popularly used of all the averages. For example, average income, average profit, average mileage etc. As defined earlier, it is the sum total of all values of items divided by the total number of items. For detailed discussion we will confine ourselves to Arithmetic Mean only because this is the most relevant of all the average for us.

Let $x_1, x_2, x_3, ..., x_n$ be the n values of x.

Their average is denoted by $\overline{x}$ and given by

$$\overline{x} = \frac{\text{Sum of observations}}{\text{Total number of observations}}$$

or $$\overline{x} = \frac{x_1 + x_2 + x_3 + ... + x_n}{n}$$

(*b*) **Geometric Mean :** For observations $x_1, x_2, x_3, ..., x_n$ the geometric mean denoted by G.M. is defined as:

$$\text{G.M.} = (x_1 . x_2 . x_3 ... x_n)^{1/n}$$

It is useful in calculating averages of ratios such as average population, growth rate, average percentage increase etc.

(*c*) **Harmonic Mean:** It is defined as

$$\text{H.M.} = \frac{n}{\frac{1}{x_1} + \frac{1}{x_2} + ... + \frac{1}{x_n}}.$$

EXAMPLE: Find the average of first ten prime numbers.

SOLUTION: First ten prime numbers are 2, 3, 5, 7, 11, 13, 17, 19, 23 and 29.

$$\therefore \text{Average} = \frac{2+3+5+7+11+13+17+19+23+29}{10}$$

$$= \frac{129}{10} = 12.9$$

EXAMPLE: If x_1, x_2, x_3, x_4, x_5 are five consecutive odd numbers then find the average of these numbers.

SOLUTION: Since x_1 is the first odd number.

$$\therefore \quad x_2 = x_1 + 2$$
$$x_3 = x_2 + 2 = x_1 + 4$$
$$x_4 = x_3 + 2 = x_1 + 6$$
$$x_5 = x_4 + 2 = x_1 + 8$$

$$\therefore \text{ Average} = \frac{x_1 + x_1 + 2 + x_1 + 4 + x_1 + 6 + x_1 + 8}{5}$$

$$= \frac{5x_1 + 20}{5} = \frac{5(x_1 + 4)}{5} = x_1 + 4$$

EXAMPLE: If the average of four consecutive even numbers is 27, then find the largest of these numbers.

SOLUTION: Let x be the first even number in the series of four consecutive even numbers.

$\therefore$ 2nd even number $= x + 2$

3rd even number $= x + 4$

4th even number $= x + 6$

$$\text{Average} = \frac{x + x + 2 + x + 4 + x + 6}{4}$$

$$\Rightarrow \quad 27 = \frac{4x + 12}{4}$$

$$\Rightarrow \quad 4x + 12 = 27 \times 4 = 108$$

$$\Rightarrow \quad 4x = 96$$

$$\Rightarrow \quad x = 24$$

Largest number in this series is $x + 6$

i.e., $24 + 6 = 30$

EXAMPLE: The average of eight numbers is 14. The average of six of these numbers is 16. What is the average of the remaining two numbers?

SOLUTION: Sum of the eight numbers $= 14 \times 8 = 112$

Sum of six of these eight numbers $= 16 \times 6 = 96$

$\therefore$ Sum of the remaining two numbers $= 112 - 96 = 16$

$\therefore$ Average of the remaining two numbers $= \frac{16}{2} = 8$

EXAMPLE: What is the average of first 30 multiples of 7?

SOLUTION: Required Average

$$= \frac{7 + 14 + 21 + ... + 210}{30}$$

$$= \frac{7(1 + 2 + 3 + ... + 30)}{30}$$

$$= \frac{7 \times 30(30 + 1)}{2 \times 30}$$

$$= \frac{7 \times 31}{2} = \frac{217}{2} = 108.5$$

EXAMPLE: The average of 11 results is 50. If the average of first six results is 49 and that of last six is 52, find the sixth result.

SOLUTION: Sum of 11 results $= 11 \times 50 = 550$

Sum of first 6 results $6 \times 49 = 294$

Sum of last 6 results $= 6 \times 52 = 312$

$\therefore$ 6th result $= 294 + 312 - 550$

$= 56$

EXAMPLE: The average age of three boys is 15 years. If their ages are in the ratio 3 : 5 : 7. What is the age of the youngest boy?

SOLUTION: Let the ages of the three boys be $3x$, $5x$ and $7x$.

$$\text{Average age} = \frac{3x + 5x + 7x}{3} = 5x$$

and $5x = 15 \Rightarrow x = 3$

The age of the youngest boy $= 3x = 3 \times 3 = 9$ years.

EXAMPLE: The average of 100 observations is 45. It was later found that two observations 19 and 31 were incorrectly recorded as 91 and 13. Find the correct average.

SOLUTION: Sum of 100 observations

$= 100 \times 45 = 4500$

New sum of 100 observations

$= 4500 + (19 + 31) - (91 + 13)$

$= 4500 + 50 - 104 = 4446$

$$\text{Correct average} = \frac{4446}{100} = 44.46$$

MULTIPLE CHOICE QUESTIONS

1. The average of first five multiples of 3 is:
A. 3 B. 9
C. 12 D. 15

2. The average of 25 results is 18, that of first 12 is 14 and of the last 12 is 17. Thirteenth result is:
A. 78 B. 85
C. 28 D. 72

3. Out of three numbers, the first is twice the second and is half of the third. If the average of the three numbers is 56, the three numbers in order are:
A. 48, 96, 24 B. 48, 24, 96
C. 96, 24, 48 D. 96, 48, 24

4. The sum of three numbers is 98. If the ratio between first and second be 2 : 3 and that between second and third be 5 : 8, then the second number is:
A. 30 B. 20
C. 58 D. 48

5. The average age of a committee of seven trustees is the same as it was 5 years ago; a young man having been substituted for one of them. The new man compared to the replaced old man, is younger in age by:
A. 5 years B. 7 years
C. 12 years D. 35 years

6. The average expenditure of a man for the first five months is ₹ 120 and for the next seven months is ₹ 130. His monthly average income if he saves ₹ 290 in that year, is:
A. ₹ 160 B. ₹ 170
C. ₹ 150 D. ₹ 140

7. The average salary of 20 workers in an office is ₹ 1900 per month. If the manager's salary is added, the average becomes ₹ 2000 per month. The manager's salary is:
A. ₹ 24000 B. ₹ 25200
C. ₹ 45600 D. None of these

8. The average temperature of first 3 days is 27°C and of the next 3 days is 29°C. If the average of the whole week is 28.5°C, the temperature of the last day is:
A. 31.5°C B. 10.5°C
C. 21°C D. 42°C

9. A cricketer scored 180 runs in the first test and 258 runs in the second. How many runs should he score in the third test so that his average score in the three tests would be 230 runs?
A. 219 B. 242
C. 334 D. None of these

10. The average of first five prime numbers is:
A. 5.0 B. 5.2
C. 5.6 D. 6.0

11. The average weight of 3 men A, B and C is 84 kg. Another man D joins the group and the average now becomes 80 kg. If another man E, whose weight is 3 kg more than that of D, replaces A, then average weight of B, C, D and E becomes 79 kg. The weight of A is:
A. 70 kg B. 72 kg
C. 75 kg D. 80 kg

12. The average age of A, B, C, D 5 years ago was 45 years. By including x, the present average of all the five is 49 years. The present age of x is:
A. 64 years B. 48 years
C. 45 years D. 40 years

13. The average height of 30 boys, out of a class of 50, is 160 cm. If the average height of the remaining boys is 165 cm, the average height of the whole class (in cm) is:
A. 161 B. 162
C. 163 D. 164

14. The average age of an adult class is 40 years. 12 new students with an average age of 32 years join the class, thereby decreasing the average of the class by 4 years. The original strength of the class was:
A. 10 B. 11
C. 12 D. 15

15. If a, b, c, d, e are five consecutive odd numbers, their average is:
A. $5(a+4)$ B. $\frac{abcde}{5}$
C. $5(a+b+c+d+e)$ D. None of these

16. Of the three numbers, second is twice the first and is also thrice the third. If the average of the three numbers is 44, the largest number is:
A. 24 B. 36
C. 72 D. 108

17. The average of 50 numbers is 38. If two numbers namely, 45 and 55 are discarded, the average of remaining number is:

A. 36.50 B. 37.00
C. 37.50 D. 37.52

18. The average height of 30 girls out of a class of 40 is 160 cm and that of the remaining girls is 156 cm. The average height of the whole class is:

A. 158 cm B. 158.5 cm
C. 159 cm D. 159.5 cm

19. The average of n numbers is x. If 36 is subtracted from any two numbers each, then new average is $(x - 8)$. The value of n is:

A. 6 B. 8
C. 9 D. 72

20. The average salary of male employees in a firm is ₹ 520 and that of female employees is ₹ 420. The mean salary of all the employees is ₹ 500. The percentage of female employees is:

A. 40% B. 30%
C. 25% D. 20%

ANSWERS

1	2	3	4	5	6	7	8	9	10
B	A	B	A	D	C	D	A	D	C
11	**12**	**13**	**14**	**15**	**16**	**17**	**18**	**19**	**20**
C	C	B	C	D	C	C	C	C	D

EXPLANATORY ANSWERS

1. Average $= \frac{3(1+2+3+4+5)}{5} = \frac{(3\times15)}{5} = 9$

2. Thirteenth result

$= [(25 \times 18) - (12 \times 14 + 12 \times 17)]$

$= [450 - (168 + 204)]$

$= 450 - 372 = 78.$

3. Let the numbers be $2x$, x and $4x$.

Average $= \frac{2x+x+4x}{3} = \frac{7x}{3}$

According to the question,

$\frac{7x}{3} = 56$

$\Rightarrow \quad 7x = 3 \times 56$

$\Rightarrow \quad x = \frac{3\times56}{7} = 24$

Hence, the numbers in order are 48, 24 and 96.

4. Let the numbers be x, y, z, then

$x + y + z = 98$

$\frac{x}{y} = \frac{2}{3}$ and $\frac{y}{z} = \frac{5}{8}$

$\therefore \quad x = \frac{2y}{3}$ and $z = \frac{8y}{5}$

So, $\frac{2y}{3} + y + \frac{8y}{5} = 98$

$\Rightarrow \quad \frac{10y+15y+24y}{15} = 98$

$\Rightarrow \quad 49y = 15 \times 98$

$\Rightarrow \quad y = \frac{15\times98}{49} = 30$

5. During these five years, the total age would have increased by $(7 \times 5) = 35$ years. But, it remains the same as it was 5 years ago.

$\therefore$ The new man is younger than the replaced old man by 35 years.

6. Total income for 12 months

$= ₹\ (120 \times 5 + 130 \times 7 + 290)$

$= ₹\ 1800$

Average monthly income $= ₹\frac{1800}{12} = ₹150$

7. Total salary of 20 workers

$= 20 \times 1900 = ₹\ 38000$

Total salary of 20 workers and manager

$= 21 \times 2000 = ₹\ 42000$

Monthly salary of the manager

$= 42000 - 38000 = ₹\ 4000.$

8. Total temperature of first 3 days

$= 27 \times 3 = 81°C$

Total temperature of next 3 days

$= 29 \times 3 = 87°C$

Total temperature of 7 days

$= 28.5 \times 7 = 199.5°C$

Temperature of the last day

$= 199.5 - (81 + 87)$

$= 199.5 - 168 = 31.5°C$

9. Let runs he should score in third test be x :

Then, $\dfrac{180+258+x}{3} = 230$

$\Rightarrow$ $x = 690 - 438 = 252.$

10. Average $= \dfrac{2+3+5+7+11}{5} = \dfrac{28}{5} = 5.6.$

11. Weight of D = $(80 \times 4 - 84 \times 3)$ kg = 68 kg

Weight of E = $(68 + 3)$ kg = 71 kg

(B + C + D + E)'s weight = (79×4) kg = 316 kg

$\therefore$ (B + C)'s weight

= [316 – (68 + 71)] kg = 177 kg

Hence, A's weight

= [(84 × 3) – 177]kg = 75 kg

12. Total age of A, B, C and D 5 years ago

= (45 × 4) years = 180 years.

Total present age of A, B, C, D and x

= (49 × 5) years = 245 years.

Present age of A, B, C and D

= (180 + 5 × 4) years = 200 years.

$\therefore$ Present age of x = 45 years.

13. Total height of 30 boys = 30 × 160 = 4800

Total height of 20 boys = 20 × 165 = 3300

Total height of 50 boys = 8100

Average height of 50 boys $= \dfrac{8100}{50} = 162.$

14. $40x + 12 \times 32 = (12 + x) \times 36$

$\Rightarrow$ $40x + 384 = 432 + 36x$

$\Rightarrow$ $4x = 432 - 384 = 48$

$\Rightarrow$ $x = \dfrac{48}{4} = 12$

Hence, the original strength of the class was 12.

15. Average $= \dfrac{a+a+2+a+4+a+6+a+8}{5}$

$= \dfrac{5a+20}{5} = \dfrac{5(a+4)}{5} = a+4$

16. Let the numbers be x, $2x$ and $\dfrac{2x}{3}$.

Average $= \dfrac{x+2x+\dfrac{2x}{3}}{3}$

$\Rightarrow$ $\dfrac{11x}{9} = 44$

$\Rightarrow$ $x = \dfrac{44\times 9}{11} = 36$

So, the numbers are 36, 72 and 24.

Hence, the largest one is 72.

17. Total of 50 numbers = 50 × 38 = 1900

Average of 48 numbers $= \dfrac{1900-(45+55)}{48}$

$= \dfrac{1800}{48} = 37.50$

18. The average of the whole class

$= \dfrac{(30\times 160+10\times 156)}{40} = \dfrac{4800+1560}{40}$

$= \dfrac{6360}{40} = 159$ cm

19. $\dfrac{nx-36-36}{n} = x - 8$

$\Rightarrow$ $nx - 72 = nx - 8n$

$\Rightarrow$ $8n = 72$

$\Rightarrow$ $n = 9$

20. Let the total employees be 100.

n_1 = number of females = x

n_2 = number of males = $100 - x$

$\bar{x} = \dfrac{n_1\bar{x}_1 + n_2\bar{x}_2}{n_1 + n_2}$

$\Rightarrow$ $500 = \dfrac{x\times 420+(100-x)\times 520}{100}$

$\Rightarrow$ $500 = \dfrac{42x+5200-52x}{10}$

$\Rightarrow$ $5000 = 5200 - 10x$

$\Rightarrow$ $10x = 200$

$\Rightarrow$ $x = 20$ *i.e.,* 20%.

8. PROFIT AND LOSS

Cost Price (CP)

The price at which an article is purchased is called the cost price of the article.

Selling Price (SP)

The price at which an article is sold is called the selling price of the article.

Profit or Gain

If SP is greater than the CP, the seller is said to have a profit or gain.

Clearly, $\text{Gain} = \text{SP} - \text{CP}$

Loss

If SP is less than CP, the seller is said to have a loss.

Clearly, $\text{Loss} = \text{CP} - \text{SP}$

Profit or loss per cent is calculated on cost price.

$$\text{Profit \%} = \frac{\text{Profit}}{\text{CP}} \times 100$$

$$\text{Loss \%} = \frac{\text{Loss}}{\text{CP}} \times 100$$

$$\text{SP} = \frac{\text{CP} \times (100 + \text{Profit\%})}{100}, \text{ if there is gain}$$

$$\text{SP} = \frac{\text{CP} \times (100 - \text{Loss\%})}{100}, \text{ if there is loss}$$

$$\text{CP} = \text{SP} \times \left(\frac{100}{100 + \text{Profit\%}}\right), \text{ if there is gain}$$

$$\text{CP} = \text{SP} \times \left(\frac{100}{100 - \text{Loss\%}}\right), \text{ if there is loss}$$

If an article is sold at a gain of 20%,

then, $\text{SP} = (120\% \text{ of CP})$

If an article is sold at a loss of 20%,

then, $\text{SP} = (80\% \text{ of CP})$

Overheads

The expenses incurred on transportation, rent, personnel salary, maintenance, packaging, advertisements and the like are included under the general heading of overheads. These overhead and the profit when added to the cost price determine the selling price. If the overheads are not separately mentioned in the problem, we assume it to be zero or else these have been included in the cost price itself.

Discount

It is an offer made by the seller to the buyer for reduction in price to be paid. There are several cases where discounts are allowed. For instance, to dispose off old goods, to increase its market share when the customer is ready to pay the whole amount in cash instead of instalment and so on. It is subtracted from the original price and is usually expressed as per cent or a fraction of the marked price. The price obtained after deducting the discount from the original price is the selling price which the customer has to pay.

Example: If an article is purchased for ₹ 570 and sold for ₹ 518.70, find the lost per cent.

Solution: CP = ₹ 570

SP = ₹ 518.70

∴ Loss = CP – SP

= 570 – 518.70 = ₹ 51.30

$$\text{Loss \%} = \frac{\text{Loss}}{\text{CP}} \times 100 = \frac{51.30}{570} \times 100$$

$$= \frac{5130}{570} = \frac{513}{57} = 9\%$$

EXAMPLE: A man buys a TV for ₹ 16,000. After two years he sells it for ₹ 12800. Find his loss per cent.

SOLUTION: $$\text{Loss \%} = \frac{\text{Loss}}{\text{CP}} \times 100$$

$$= \frac{16000 - 12800}{16000} \times 100$$

$$= \frac{3200}{16000} \times 100 = 20\%$$

EXAMPLE: Mohan sells his watch at a loss of ₹ 500 for ₹ 1000. Find the cost price and loss per cent.

SOLUTION: $$\text{CP} = \text{SP} + \text{Loss}$$

$$= 1000 + 500 = ₹\ 1500$$

$$\text{Loss \%} = \frac{\text{Loss}}{\text{CP}} \times 100 = \frac{500}{1500} \times 100$$

$$= \frac{100}{3} = 33\frac{1}{3}\%$$

EXAMPLE: Ravi buys an article for ₹ 5000 and sells it at 20% gain. Find it selling price.

SOLUTION: $$\text{Profit} = 20\% \text{ of CP} = \frac{20}{100} \times 5000$$

$$\Rightarrow \quad \text{Profit} = ₹\ 1000$$

$$\text{SP} = \text{CP} + \text{Profit}$$

$$= 5000 + 1000$$

$$= ₹\ 6000$$

EXAMPLE: A man sells an article at 20% gain for ₹ 3600. Find its cost price.

SOLUTION: Let CP = ₹ 100

then SP = 100 + 20 = ₹ 120

When SP ₹ 120 then CP = ₹ 100

When SP ₹ 3600 then CP = $\frac{100}{120} \times 3600$

Hence CP = ₹ 3000

EXAMPLE: The cost price of 6 pens is equal to the selling price of 4 pens. Find the profit per cent.

SOLUTION: SP of 4 pens = CP of 6 pens

$$\text{SP of 2 pens} = \text{CP of } \frac{6}{4} \times 2 = 3 \text{ pens}$$

Profit = CP of 3 pens

investment = CP of 6 pens

$$\text{Profit \%} = \frac{3}{6} \times 100 = 50\%$$

Alternatively:

Let the CP of 1 pen be ₹ x.

$\therefore$ CP of 6 pens = ₹ $6x$

Also, SP of 4 pens = ₹ $6x$

$$\therefore \quad \text{SP of 6 pens} = \frac{6x}{4} \times 6 = ₹\ 9x$$

$$\text{Profit} = \text{SP} - \text{CP} = 9x - 6x = 3x$$

$$\text{Profit \%} = \frac{3x}{6x} \times 100 = 50\%$$

EXAMPLE: If CP of 20 tables is equal to the SP of 25 tables. Find the loss percent.

SOLUTION: Let the CP of 1 table be ₹ x.

$\therefore$ CP of 20 tables = ₹ $20x$

Also, SP of 25 tables = ₹ $20x$

$$\therefore \quad \text{SP of 20 tables} = ₹\ \frac{20x}{25} \times 20 = ₹\ 16x$$

$$\text{Loss} = 20x - 16x = 4x$$

$$\text{Loss \%} = \frac{\text{Loss}}{\text{CP}} \times 100$$

$$= \frac{4x}{20x} \times 100 = 20\%$$

EXAMPLE: Ram sold a book at a profit of 6%. Had he sold it for ₹ 2 more he would have gained 10%. Find the cost price of the book.

SOLUTION: (10% – 6%) of CP = 4% of CP = ₹ 2

$$\Rightarrow \quad \frac{4}{100} \times \text{CP} = 2$$

$$\Rightarrow \quad \text{CP} = \frac{200}{4} = ₹\ 50$$

EXAMPLE: An article is sold for ₹ 4600 at a gain of 15%. What would be the profit or loss per cent if it is sold for ₹ 3600?

SOLUTION: $$\text{CP} = 4600 \times \frac{100}{115} = ₹\ 4000$$

$$\text{Loss \%} = \frac{4000 - 3600}{4000} \times 100 = 10\%$$

MULTIPLE CHOICE QUESTIONS

1. A loss of 5% was suffered by selling a plot for ₹ 4085. The cost price of the plot was:
A. ₹ 4350 B. ₹ 4259.25
C. ₹ 4200 D. ₹ 4300

2. On selling an article for ₹ 240, a trader loses 4%. In order to gain 10%, he must sell that article for:
A. ₹ 264.00 B. ₹ 273.20
C. ₹ 275.00 D. ₹ 280.00

3. A man purchased a watch for ₹ 400 and sold it at a gain of 20% of the selling price. The selling price of the watch is:
A. ₹ 300 B. ₹ 320
C. ₹ 440 D. ₹ 500

4. If 5% more is gained by selling an article for ₹ 350 than by selling it for ₹ 340, the cost of the article is:
A. ₹ 50 B. ₹ 160
C. ₹ 200 D. ₹ 225

5. Profit after selling a commodity for ₹ 425 is same as loss after selling it for ₹ 355. The cost of the commodity is:
A. ₹ 385 B. ₹ 390
C. ₹ 395 D. ₹ 400

6. The cost price of an article, which on being sold at a gain of 12% yields ₹ 6 more than when it is sold at a loss of 12%, is:
A. ₹ 30 B. ₹ 25
C. ₹ 20 D. ₹ 24

7. The CP of an article which is sold at a loss of 25% for ₹150, is:
A. ₹ 125 B. ₹ 175
C. ₹ 200 D. ₹ 225

8. When the price of pressure cooker was increased by 15%, its sale fell down by 15%. The effect on the money receipt was:
A. no effect B. 15% decrease
C. 7.5% increase D. 2.25% decrease

9. A man sells 320 mangoes at the cost price of 400 mangoes. His gain per cent is:
A. 10% B. 25%
C. 15% D. 20%

10. By selling 12 oranges for one rupee a man loses 20%. How many for a rupee should he sell to get a gain of 20%?
A. 5 B. 8
C. 10 D. 15

11. A man sells a car to his friend at 10% loss. If the friend sells it for ₹ 54000 and gains 20%, the original CP of the car was:
A. ₹ 25000 B. ₹ 37500
C. ₹ 50000 D. ₹ 60000

12. The loss incurred on selling an article for ₹ 270 is as much as the profit made after selling it at 10% profit. The CP of the article is:
A. ₹ 90 B. ₹ 110
C. ₹ 363 D. ₹ 300

13. An item costing ₹ 200 is being sold at 10% loss. If the price is further reduced by 5%, the selling price will be:
A. ₹ 179 B. ₹ 175
C. ₹ 171 D. ₹ 170

14. A trader lists his articles 20% above CP and allows a discount of 10% on cash payment. His gain per cent is:
A. 10% B. 6%
C. 8% D. 5%

15. A discount series of 10%, 20% and 40% is equal to a single discount of:
A. 50% B. 56.80%
C. 70% D. 70.28%

ANSWERS

1	2	3	4	5	6	7	8	9	10
D	C	D	C	B	B	C	D	B	B
11	**12**	**13**	**14**	**15**					
C	D	C	C	B					

EXPLANATORY ANSWERS

1. Loss = 5%, SP = ₹ 4085

Let CP = ₹ 100

$\therefore$ SP = ₹ 100 − 5 = ₹ 95

When SP ₹ 95 then CP = ₹ 100

When SP ₹ 4085 then CP = $\frac{100}{95} \times 4085$

$= 4300$

Hence, the cost price of the plot was ₹ 4300.

2. Loss = 4%, SP = ₹ 240

Let CP = ₹ 100

$\therefore$ SP = 100 − 4 = 96

When SP ₹ 96 then CP = ₹ 100

When SP ₹ 240 then CP = $\frac{100}{96} \times 240 =$ ₹ 250

Again 100 + 10 = 110

When CP 100 then SP = ₹ 110

When CP 250 then SP = $\frac{110}{100} \times 250 =$ ₹ 275

3. Let SP = ₹ x

then, profit = $\frac{20}{100} \times x =$ ₹ $\frac{x}{5}$

CP = SP − profit = $x - \frac{x}{5} =$ ₹ $\frac{4x}{5}$

According to the question,

$\frac{4x}{5} = 400 \Rightarrow 4x = 2000$

$\Rightarrow \quad x = 500$

Hence, selling price of the watch = ₹ 500.

4. Let CP = ₹ x

Then, if SP = ₹350

Profit = SP − CP = ₹ $(350 - x)$

if SP = ₹ 340 then, profit = ₹ $(340 - x)$

$\therefore (350 - x) - (340 - x) = \frac{5}{100}x$

$\Rightarrow 10 = \frac{5}{100}x \quad \Rightarrow x = 200$

Hence, the cost of the article = ₹ 200.

5. Let CP = ₹ x,

then, $425 - x = x - 355 \Rightarrow 2x = 780$

$\Rightarrow x = 390$

Hence, the cost of commodity is ₹ 390.

6. Let CP of the article = ₹ x

Then, SP when profit is 12%

$= \left(\frac{12x}{100} + x\right) = \frac{112x}{100}$

$\therefore \quad \frac{112x}{100} - \frac{88x}{100} = 6$

$\Rightarrow \quad 24x = 600$

$\Rightarrow \quad x = \frac{600}{24} = 25$

$\therefore$ CP of the article is ₹ 25.

7. 100 − 25 = 75

When SP 75 then CP = ₹ 100

When SP 150 then CP = ₹ $\frac{100}{75} \times 150 =$ ₹ 200

8. Let the original cost of each cooker be ₹ 1 and let the number sold originally be 100.

Total sale proceed = ₹ (100 × 1) = ₹ 100

New rate = (115% of ₹ 1) = ₹ 1.15

Number sold now = 85

$\therefore$ Sale proceed now = ₹(1.15 × 85) = ₹ 97.75

So, there is a decrease of 2.25% in the money receipt.

9. Let CP of each mango be ₹ 1.

Then, CP of 400 mangoes = ₹ 400

$\therefore$ CP of 320 mangoes = ₹ 320

SP of 320 mangoes = ₹ 400

Profit = 400 − 320 = ₹ 80

Profit% = $\frac{80}{320} \times 100 = 25\%$

10. SP = ₹ 1, Loss = 20%

$\Rightarrow$ CP = $\left(\frac{100}{80} \times 1\right) \Rightarrow$ CP = ₹ $\frac{5}{4}$

Now, CP = ₹ $\frac{5}{4}$, gain, 20%

$\Rightarrow$ SP = $\frac{120}{100} \times \frac{5}{4} =$ ₹ $\frac{3}{2}$

For ₹$\frac{3}{2}$, he must sell 12 oranges

For ₹ 1, he must sell $\left(12 \times \frac{2}{3}\right)$ = 8 oranges.

11. SP = ₹ 54000 and gain earned = 20%

CP = ₹$\left(\frac{100}{120} \times 54000\right)$ = ₹ 45000

Now, SP = ₹ 45000 and Loss = 10%

∴ CP = ₹$\left(\frac{100}{90} \times 45000\right)$ = ₹ 50000

12. Let CP be ₹ x. Then,

$x - 270 = 10\%$ of $x = \frac{x}{10}$

$\Rightarrow \quad x - \frac{x}{10} = 270$

$\Rightarrow \quad 9x = 10 \times 270$

$\Rightarrow \quad x = \frac{10 \times 270}{9}$

$\Rightarrow \quad x = 300$

∴ CP of the article is ₹ 300.

13. SP = 90% of ₹ 200 = ₹ 180

Further, SP = (95% of ₹180) = ₹ 171

14. Let CP = ₹ 100. Then, MP = ₹ 120.

SP = 90% of ₹ 120 = $\frac{90}{100} \times 120$ = ₹ 108

Profit = SP – CP = 108 – 100 = ₹ 8

Profit % = $\frac{\text{Profit}}{\text{CP}} \times 100 = \frac{8}{100} \times 100 = 8\%$

15. Let original price = ₹ 100

Price after 1st discount = ₹ 90

Price after 2nd discount

= ₹$\left(\frac{80}{100} \times 90\right)$ = ₹ 72

Price after 3rd discount

= ₹$\left(\frac{60}{100} \times 72\right)$ = ₹ 43.20

∴ Single discount = 100 – 43.20 = 56.8%.

9. SIMPLE AND COMPOUND INTEREST

In any money transaction there is a **lender** who gives money, and a **borrower** who receives money. The amount of loan borrowed, is called the principal (P). The borrower pays a certain amount for the use of this money. This is called **Interest (I)**. Interest is always calculated on the principal borrowed. The borrowing is for a specified **Time (t)** and on specified terms. The specified term is expressed as per cent of the principal and is called rate of interest.

The sum of the principal and the interest is called the **Amount (A)**. In general, the rate of interest may be yearly, half yearly, quarterly or monthly as mutually agreed upon by both parties at the time of transaction. Depending upon the period of rate of interest, time is expressed in multiples of this period.

Interest is of two kinds—**Simple Interest and compound Interest**. If the interest is calculated only, on a certain sum borrowed it is called Simple Interest.

The simple interest (SI) on a principal P at R% per annum for T years is given by:

$$SI = \frac{P \times R \times T}{100}$$

$$\therefore \quad P = \frac{SI \times 100}{R \times T}$$

$$\therefore \quad R = \frac{SI \times 100}{P \times T}$$

$$\therefore \quad T = \frac{SI \times 100}{P \times R}$$

Compound Interest differs from Simple Interest that in CI the interest for the future period is calculated not only on the principal but also on the interest earned until the previous period. Thus, the total interest earned in case of CI is not uniformly distributed over time units whereas in Simple Interest it is uniformly distributed. The interest due at the end of the first unit of time is added to the principal and the amount so obtained becomes the principal for the second unit. Similarly, the amount after the 2nd unit of time becomes the principal for the third unit of time and continues till the last unit of time.

The difference between the final amount (A) obtained at the last unit of time and the original principal is called the **Compound Interest**.

Important Relations

Principal = ₹ P (in rupees)

Rate = R % (in per cent per annum)

Time period = T years (in years)

Amount = ₹ A (in rupees)

I. When interest is compounded annually,

$$A = P\left[1 + \frac{R}{100}\right]^T$$

II. When interest is compounded half-yearly,

$$A = P\left[1 + \frac{R/2}{100}\right]^{2T} = P\left[1 + \frac{R}{200}\right]^{2T}$$

[R is divided by 2 and T is multiplied by 2.]

III. When interest is compounded quarterly,

$$A = P\left[1+\frac{R/4}{100}\right]^{4T} = P\left[1+\frac{R}{400}\right]^{4T}$$

[R is divided by 4 and T is multiplied by 4.]

IV. When interest is $R_1\%$ for first year, $R_2\%$ for 2nd year and $R_3\%$ for third year;

$$A = P\left[1+\frac{R_1}{100}\right]\left[1+\frac{R_2}{100}\right]\left[1+\frac{R_3}{100}\right]$$

V. $CI = A - P$

Example: Find the simple interest on ₹ 1000 for 3 years at 10% p.a.

Solution: $SI = \frac{P \times R \times T}{100} = \frac{1000 \times 10 \times 3}{100} = ₹\,300$

Example: Find the amount of ₹ 600 in 4 years at 3% p.a.

Solution: $SI = \frac{P \times R \times T}{100} = \frac{600 \times 3 \times 4}{100} = ₹\,72$

$\therefore$ Amount = P + SI = 600 + 72 = ₹ 672

Example: In what time will ₹ 7000 give ₹ 3675 as interest at the rate of 7% p.a. simple interest?

Solution: $T = \frac{SI \times 100}{P \times R} = \frac{3675 \times 100}{7000 \times 7}$

$= \frac{15}{2} = 7\frac{1}{2}$ years.

Example: At what rate per annum will a sum of ₹ 5000 amount to ₹ 6000 in 4 years?

Solution: SI = A – P = 6000 – 5000 = ₹ 1000

$$R = \frac{SI \times 100}{P \times T} = \frac{1000 \times 100}{5000 \times 4} = 5\%$$

Example: In how many years will a sum of money double itself at 5% rate of interest?

Solution: A sum doubles itself when amount of interest becomes equal to the principal

SI = P, R = 5%

$$\therefore \quad T = \frac{100 \times P}{P \times 5} = 20 \text{ years}$$

Example: A certain sum amounts to ₹ 115200 in 2 years and to ₹ 165888 in 4 years. Find the sum and rate per cent.

Solution: Here, amount on ₹ 115200 for 2 years at CI is ₹ 165888

$$\therefore \quad 115200\left(1+\frac{R}{100}\right)^2 = 165888$$

$$\left(1+\frac{R}{100}\right)^2 = \frac{165888}{115200} = 1.44$$

$$\therefore \quad 1+\frac{R}{100} = 1.2$$

$$\frac{R}{100} = 1.2 - 1 = 0.2$$

$$\Rightarrow \quad R = 0.2 \times 100 = 20\%$$

Amount after 2 years is ₹ 115200

$$\therefore \quad P\left(1+\frac{20}{100}\right)^2 = 115200$$

$$\Rightarrow \quad P = \frac{115200}{\left(1+\frac{20}{100}\right)^2} = \frac{115200}{1.44} = 80000$$

$\therefore$ Principal = ₹ 80000

Example: A sum of money doubles itself at CI in 15 years. In how many years will it become eight times?

Solution: $P\left(1+\frac{R}{100}\right)^{15} = 2P$

$$\Rightarrow \quad \left(1+\frac{R}{100}\right)^{15} = 2$$

Let T be the required number of years that makes the principal 8 times of it.

$$\therefore \quad P\left(1+\frac{R}{100}\right)^{T} = 8P$$

$$\Rightarrow \quad \left(1+\frac{R}{100}\right)^{T} = 8 = (2)^3$$

$$\Rightarrow \quad \left(1+\frac{R}{100}\right)^{T} = \left[\left(1+\frac{R}{100}\right)^{15}\right]^3$$

$$\Rightarrow \quad \left(1+\frac{R}{100}\right)^{T} = \left(1+\frac{R}{100}\right)^{45}$$

$$\Rightarrow \quad T = 45 \text{ years}$$

Hence, required number of years is 45 years.

EXAMPLE: The difference between simple and compound interest on a sum of money at 5% p.a. for 2 years is ₹ 25. Find the sum.

SOLUTION: Let P = ₹ 100

$$SI = \frac{P \times R \times T}{100} = \frac{100 \times 5 \times 2}{100} = ₹\ 10$$

$$A = P\left(1+\frac{R}{100}\right)^T = 100\left(1+\frac{5}{100}\right)^2$$

$$= \frac{100 \times 21 \times 21}{400} = ₹\frac{441}{4}$$

$$CI = A - P = \frac{441}{4} - 100 = ₹\frac{41}{4}$$

$$CI - SI = \frac{41}{4} - 10 = \frac{41-40}{4} = ₹\frac{1}{4}$$

When difference ₹ $\frac{1}{4}$ then P = ₹ 100

When difference ₹ 25 then P = 100 × 4 × 25 = ₹ 10000

Hence, sum = ₹ 10000.

MULTIPLE CHOICE QUESTIONS

1. The simple interest on ₹ 500 for 6 years at 5% p.a. is:
   A. ₹ 250 B. ₹ 150
   C. ₹ 140 D. ₹ 120
2. A certain sum of money at SI amounts to ₹ 1012 in $2\frac{1}{2}$ years and to ₹ 1067.20 in 4 years. The rate of interest per annum is:
   A. 2.5% B. 3%
   C. 4% D. 5%
3. ₹ 1200 amounts to ₹ 1632 in 4 years at a certain rate of simple interest. If the rate of interest is increased by 1%, it would amount to how much?
   A. ₹ 1635 B. ₹ 1644
   C. ₹ 1670 D. ₹ 1680
4. A man will get ₹ 87 as simple interest on ₹ 725 at 4% per annum in:
   A. 3 years B. 3½ years
   C. 4 years D. 5 years
5. At simple interest, a sum doubles after 20 years. The rate of interest per annum is:
   A. 5% B. 10%
   C. 20% D. Data inadequate
6. A lent ₹ 600 to B for 2 years and ₹ 150 to C for 4 years and received altogether from both ₹ 90 as simple interest. The rate of interest is:
   A. 12% B. 10%
   C. 5% D. 4%
7. Interest on a certain sum of money for $2\frac{1}{3}$ years at $3\frac{3}{4}$% per annum is ₹ 210. The sum is:
   A. ₹ 2800 B. ₹ 1580
   C. ₹ 2400 D. None of these
8. A certain sum of money at simple interest amounts to ₹ 1260 in 2 years and to ₹ 1350 in 5 years. The rate per cent per annum is:
   A. 2.5% B. 3.75%
   C. 5% D. 7.5%
9. A sum of money doubles itself in 5 years. It will become 4 times itself in:
   A. 10 years B. 12 years
   C. 15 years D. 20 years
10. The simple interest on a sum of money will be ₹ 600 after 10 years. If the principal is trebled after 5 years, the total interest at the end of 10 years will be:
    A. ₹ 600 B. ₹ 900
    C. ₹ 1200 D. Data inadequate
11. ₹ 800 amounts to ₹ 920 in 3 years at simple interest. If the interest rate is increased by 3%, it would amount to how much?
    A. ₹ 1056 B. ₹ 1112
    C. ₹ 1182 D. ₹ 992
12. A sum of money at simple interest amounts to ₹ 2240 in 2 years and ₹ 2600 in 5 years. The sum is:
    A. ₹ 1880 B. ₹ 2000
    C. ₹ 2120 D. Data inadequate

13. If ₹ 7500 are borrowed at CI at the rate of 4% per annum, then after 2 years the amount to be paid is:

A. ₹ 8082 B. ₹ 7800
C. ₹ 8100 D. ₹ 8112

14. Simple interest on a sum at 4% per annum is ₹ 80 in 2 years. The compound interest on the same sum for the same period is:

A. ₹ 81.60 B. ₹ 160
C. ₹ 1081.60 D. None of these

15. ₹ 800 at 5% per annum compound interest will amount to ₹ 882 in:

A. 1 year B. 2 years
C. 3 years D. 4 years

ANSWERS

1	2	3	4	5	6	7	8	9	10
B	C	D	A	A	C	C	A	C	C
11	**12**	**13**	**14**	**15**					
D	B	D	A	B					

EXPLANATORY ANSWERS

1. $SI = \frac{P \times R \times T}{100} = \frac{500 \times 5 \times 6}{100} = ₹\, 150$

2. SI for $1\frac{1}{2}$ years = 1067.20 – 1012 = ₹ 55.20

SI for $2\frac{1}{2}$ years = $55.20 \times \frac{2}{3} \times \frac{5}{2} = ₹\, 92$

∴ Principal = ₹ (1012 – 92) = ₹ 920

$R = \frac{SI \times 100}{P \times T} = \frac{92 \times 100 \times 2}{920 \times 5} = 4\%$

3. $R = \frac{SI \times 100}{P \times T} = \frac{432 \times 100}{1200 \times 4} = 9\%$

New rate = (9 + 1)% = 10%

$SI = \frac{P \times R \times T}{100} = \frac{1200 \times 10 \times 4}{100} = ₹\, 480$

Amount = P + SI = 1200 + 480 = ₹ 1680

4. $T = \frac{SI \times 100}{P \times R} = \frac{87 \times 100}{725 \times 4} = 3$ years

5. Let P be ₹ x then A = ₹ $2x$

SI = A – P = $2x - x$ = ₹ x

$R = \frac{SI \times 100}{P \times T} = \frac{x \times 100}{x \times 20} = 5\%$

6. $SI = \frac{P \times R \times T}{100} = \frac{600 \times R \times 2}{100} = 12R$

Again $SI = \frac{P \times R \times T}{100} = \frac{150 \times R \times 4}{100} = 6R$

Total SI = 12R + 6R = 18R

According to the question,

$18R = 90 \Rightarrow R = \frac{90}{18} = 5\%$

7. $T = 2\frac{1}{3} = \frac{7}{3}$ years,

$R = 3\frac{3}{4}\% = \frac{15}{4}\%$

$P = \frac{SI \times 100}{P \times T} = \frac{210 \times 100}{\frac{15}{4} \times \frac{7}{3}}$

$= \frac{210 \times 100 \times 4 \times 3}{15 \times 7} = ₹\, 2400$

8. SI for 3 years = ₹ 1350 – ₹ 1260 = ₹ 90

SI for 1 year = $\frac{90}{3}$ = ₹ 30

SI for 2 years = ₹ 30 × 2 = ₹ 60

P = A – SI = 1260 – 60 = ₹ 1200

$R = \frac{SI \times 100}{P \times T} = \frac{60 \times 100}{1200 \times 2} = \frac{5}{2} = 2.5\%$

9. Let P be ₹ x, A = ₹ $2x$,
SI = $2x - x$ = ₹ x

$$R = \frac{SI \times 100}{P \times T} = \frac{x \times 100}{x \times 5} = 20\%$$

Again, P = ₹ x, A = $4x$,
SI = $4x - x = 3x$

$$T = \frac{SI \times 100}{P \times R} = \frac{3x \times 100}{x \times 20} = 15 \text{ years}$$

10. Let P be ₹ x
SI = ₹ 600, T = 10 years.

$$R = \frac{SI \times 100}{P \times T} = \frac{600 \times 100}{x \times 10} = \frac{6000}{x}\%$$

$$\text{SI for first 5 years} = \frac{x \times 5 \times 6000}{100 \times x} = ₹\ 300$$

$$\text{SI for last 5 years} = \frac{3x \times 5 \times 6000}{100 \times x} = ₹\ 900$$

Total interest at the end of 10 years
= 900 + 300 = ₹ 1200.

11. P = ₹ 800, SI = 920 – 800 = ₹ 120
T = 3 years

$$R = \frac{SI \times 100}{P \times T} = \frac{120 \times 100}{800 \times 3} = 5\%$$

New rate = 8% (increase 3%)

$$SI = \frac{P \times R \times T}{100} = \frac{800 \times 8 \times 3}{100} = ₹\ 192$$

∴ A = P + SI = 800 + 192 = ₹ 992.

12. SI for 3 years = 2600 – 2240 = ₹ 360

$$\text{SI for 2 years} = \frac{360}{3} \times 2 = ₹\ 240$$

∴ Sum = 2240 – 240 = ₹ 2000

13. $$A = P\left(1 + \frac{R}{100}\right)^T = 7500\left(1 + \frac{4}{100}\right)^2$$

$$= 7500 \times \frac{26}{25} \times \frac{26}{25} = ₹\ 8112$$

14. $$P = \frac{SI \times 100}{T \times R} = \frac{80 \times 100}{4 \times 2} = ₹\ 1000$$

$$A = P\left(1 + \frac{R}{100}\right)^T = 1000\left(1 + \frac{4}{100}\right)^2$$

$$= 1000 \times \frac{26}{25} \times \frac{26}{25} = 1081.60$$

CI = A – P = 1081.60 – 1000 = ₹ 81.60

15. Let time = x years

$$A = P\left(1 + \frac{R}{100}\right)^T$$

$$882 = 800\left(1 + \frac{5}{100}\right)^x$$

$$\Rightarrow \frac{882}{800} = \left(\frac{21}{20}\right)^x$$

$$\Rightarrow \left(\frac{21}{20}\right)^2 = \left(\frac{21}{20}\right)^x \Rightarrow x = 2$$

∴ Time = 2 years

10. TIME AND WORK

Performing or doing work of any amount involves efforts of person (S) over a period of time. Therefore, the number of persons (P), the quantity of work (W) and the period of time (T) are important variables in problems related to "Time and Work". Moreover time (T) taken to do a work depends not only on how many persons are employed to do it but also on how efficient they are. Efficiency here means rate of doing same work. This aspect comes into picture when the problem involves comparison of work done by different categories of persons. For instance, efficiencies of man, woman, boy, girl in general are different. Even efficiency of one man may not be same as that of other; but unless otherwise specifically stated in the problem, all men or women working in a group are assumed to do work with equal efficiency.

The problems on Time and Work can be solved by following two methods:

(*i*) Ratio and proportion method

(*ii*) Unitary method

(*i*) **Ratio and Proportion Method:** Since problems concerning to Time and Work have proportional relation, these can be solved by this method. We have tried to solve questions based on Time and Work in the chapter mentioned.

(*ii*) **Unitary Method:** This is a very simple and useful method. The term 'Unitary' is self-evident. In this method, we first proceed to reduce the problem to either work done by one person or work done in 1 day and so on as per the requirement of the problem. Let us try to understand it.

(*a*) If a man can do a piece of work in 10 days he will do $\frac{1}{10}$ of the work in 1 day. Conversely, if a man can do $\frac{1}{10}$ of the work in 1 day, he will do the work in 10 days.

(*b*) If the number of men engaged to do a piece of work be changed in the ratio 5 : 4, the time required for the work will be changed in the ratio 4 : 5.

(*c*) If A is x times as good a workman as B, then A will take $\frac{1}{x}$ of the time that B takes to do a certain work.

All the above points can be summarised into one and can be written in the following form:

If M_1 persons can do W_1 works in D_1 days and M_2 persons can do W_2 works in D_2 days then we have a very general formula in the relationship of

$$M_1 D_1 W_2 = M_2 D_2 W_1$$

The above relationship can be taken as a very basic and all-in-one formula we also derive:

(*i*) More men less days and conversely more days less men.

(*ii*) More men more work and conversely more work more men.

(*iii*) More days more work and conversely more work more days.

$$M_1 D_1 T_1 W_2 = M_2 D_2 T_2 W_1$$

EXAMPLE: 5 men can prepare 10 toys in 6 days working 6 hrs a day. How many days can 12 men prepare 16 toys working 8 hrs a day?

SOLUTION: $M_1 D_1 T_1 W_2 = M_2 D_2 T_2 W_1$

$$5 \times 6 \times 6 \times 16 = 12 \times D_2 \times 8 \times 10$$

$$D_2 = \frac{5 \times 6 \times 6 \times 16}{12 \times 8 \times 10} = 3 \text{ days.}$$

EXAMPLE: A can reap a field in 8 days, which B alone can reap in 12 days. In how many days, both together, can reap this field?

SOLUTION: A's 1 day's work $= \frac{1}{8}$

B's 1 day's work $= \frac{1}{12}$

(A + B)'s 1 day's work $= \left(\frac{1}{8}+\frac{1}{12}\right)$

$= \frac{3+2}{24} = \frac{5}{24}$

$\therefore$ Both together can reap the field in $\frac{24}{5}$ days

$= 4\frac{4}{5}$ days.

EXAMPLE: A and B together can do a piece of work in 12 days, B alone can finish it in 30 days. In how many days can A alone finish the work?

SOLUTION: (A + B)'s 1 day's work $= \frac{1}{12}$

B's 1 day's work $= \frac{1}{30}$

$\therefore$ A's 1 day's work $= \frac{1}{12}-\frac{1}{30}$

$= \frac{5-2}{60} = \frac{3}{60} = \frac{1}{20}$

Hence, A alone can finish the work in 20 days.

EXAMPLE: A and B can do a piece of work in 12 days, C and A in 20 days and B and C in 15 days. In how many days will they finish it together and separately?

SOLUTION: (A + B)'s 1 day's work $= \frac{1}{12}$

(B + C)'s 1 day's work $= \frac{1}{15}$

(C + A)'s 1 day's work $= \frac{1}{20}$

Adding, 2(A + B + C)'s 1 day's work

$= \left(\frac{1}{12}+\frac{1}{15}+\frac{1}{20}\right) = \frac{5+4+3}{60}$

$= \frac{12}{60} = \frac{1}{5}$

or (A + B + C)'s 1 day's work $= \frac{1}{10}$

$\therefore$ A, B, C together can finish the work in 10 days.

Now, C's 1 day's work $= \frac{1}{10}-\frac{1}{12} = \frac{1}{60}$

$\therefore$ C alone can finish the work in 60 days.

Similarly B's 1 day's work $= \frac{1}{10}-\frac{1}{20} = \frac{1}{20}$

$\therefore$ B alone can finish the work in 20 days.

A's 1 day's work $= \frac{1}{10}-\frac{1}{15} = \frac{1}{30}$

$\therefore$ A alone can finish the work in 30 days.

EXAMPLE: A can do a piece of work in 25 days and B can finish it in 20 days. They work together for 5 days and then A goes away. In how many days will B finish the work?

SOLUTION: (A + B)'s 5 days work $= 5\left(\frac{1}{25}+\frac{1}{20}\right) = \frac{9}{20}$

Remaining work $= 1-\frac{9}{20} = \frac{11}{20}$

Now, $\frac{1}{20}$ work is finished by B in 1 day

$\therefore$ $\frac{11}{20}$ work will be finished by B in $\left(\frac{20\times 11}{20}\right)$ = 11 days.

EXAMPLE: A is thrice as good a workman as B and is therefore able to finish a piece of work in 60 days less than B. Find the time in which they can do it, working together.

SOLUTION: Ratio of work done by A and B in the same time = 3 : 1

Ratio of time taken by A and B = 1 : 3

Suppose B takes x days to finish a work

then, A takes $(x - 60)$ days

$\therefore$ $\frac{x-60}{x} = \frac{1}{3}$ or $3(x-60) = x \Rightarrow x = 90$

$\therefore$ B can finish the work in 90 days.

A can finish the work in (90 – 60) = 30 days

Both finish the work $= \left[\frac{1}{30}+\frac{1}{90} = \frac{2}{45}\right]$

$= \frac{45}{2} = 22\frac{1}{2}$ days.

EXAMPLE: A certain number of men complete a piece of work in 60 days. If there were 8 men more, the work could be finished in 10 days less. How many men were originally there?

SOLUTION: Let the original number of men be x.

Now, x men can finish the work in 60 days

and $(x + 8)$ men can finish it in $(60 - 10)$ *i.e.*, 50 days.

$$\therefore \quad x + 8 : x :: 60 : 50$$

$$\Rightarrow \quad \frac{x+8}{x} = \frac{60}{50} = \frac{6}{5}$$

$$\Rightarrow \quad 6x = 5x + 40 \Rightarrow x = 40$$

Hence, the original number of men = 40.

EXAMPLE: If 4 men or 6 boys can finish a piece of work in 20 days, in how many days can 6 men and 11 boys finish it?

SOLUTION: 4 men = 6 boys

$$\therefore \quad 6 \text{ men} = \frac{6}{4} \times 6 = \frac{36}{4} = 9 \text{ boys}$$

6 men + 11 boys = 9 + 11 = 20 boys

Now, 6 boys can finish a work in 20 days.

1 boy can finish the same work in 6 × 20 days.

20 boys can finish the same work in $\frac{6 \times 20}{20}$

= 6 days.

EXAMPLE: If 12 men can build a wall 360 m long in 54 days, how many days will it take to build a similar wall 160 m long, if 16 men working on it?

SOLUTION: 12 men can build 360 m long wall in 54 days.

1 man can build 360 m long wall in 54 × 12 days.

1 man can build 1 m long wall in $\frac{54 \times 12}{360}$ days

16 men can build 1 m long wall in $\frac{54 \times 12}{360 \times 16}$ days

16 men can build 160 m long wall in $\frac{54 \times 12 \times 160}{360 \times 16}$ days

= 18 days.

EXAMPLE: If 3 persons weave 168 carpets in 7 days, how many carpets will 8 persons weave in 5 days?

SOLUTION: 3 persons can weave in 7 days 168 carpets

1 person can weave in 7 days = $\frac{168}{3}$ carpets

1 person can weave in 1 day = $\frac{168}{3 \times 7}$ carpets

8 persons can weave in 1 day = $\frac{168 \times 8}{3 \times 7}$ carpets

8 persons can weave in 5 days = $\frac{168 \times 8 \times 5}{3 \times 7}$ carpets

= 320 carpets

EXAMPLE: Mukesh can do a job in 12 days while Manoj can do the same job in 15 days. They undertake to complete the job for ₹ 5400. What will be the share of each in the income?

SOLUTION: Mukesh's 1 day's work = $\frac{1}{12}$

Manoj's 1 day's work = $\frac{1}{15}$

Ratio of their 1 day's work = $\frac{1}{12} : \frac{1}{15} = 5 : 4$

$\therefore$ Mukesh's share = ₹ $\frac{5}{9} \times 5400$ = ₹ 3000

Manoj's share = ₹ $\frac{4}{9} \times 5400$ = ₹ 2400

MULTIPLE CHOICE QUESTIONS

1. A and B can together do a piece of work in 15 days. B alone can do it in 20 days. In how many days can A alone do it?

A. 30 days B. 40 days

C. 45 days D. 60 days

2. A can do a piece of work in 30 days while B can do it in 40 days. A and B working together can do it in:

A. 70 days B. $42\frac{3}{4}$ days

C. $27\frac{1}{7}$ days D. $17\frac{1}{7}$ days

3. A can do $\frac{1}{3}$ of the work in 5 days and B can do $\frac{2}{5}$ of the work in 10 days. In how many days both A and B together can do the work?

A. $7\frac{3}{4}$ days B. $8\frac{4}{5}$ days

C. $9\frac{3}{8}$ days D. 10 days

4. A, B and C can do a piece of work in 6, 12 and 24 days respectively. They altogether will complete the work in:

A. $3\frac{3}{7}$ days B. $\frac{7}{24}$ days

C. $4\frac{4}{5}$ days D. $\frac{5}{24}$ days

5. A, B and C contract a work for ₹ 550. Together A and B are to do $\frac{7}{11}$ of the work. The share of C should be:

A. ₹ $183\frac{1}{3}$ B. ₹ 200

C. ₹ 300 D. ₹ 400

6. A and B finish a job in 12 days while A, B and C can finish it in 8 days. C alone will finish the job in:

A. 20 days B. 14 days

C. 24 days D. 16 days

7. 12 men can complete a work in 8 days. Three days after they started the work, 3 more men joined them. In how many days will all of them together complete the remaining work?

A. 2 B. 4

C. 5 D. 6

8. Mahesh and Umesh can complete a work in 10 and 15 days respectively. Umesh starts the work and after 5 days Mahesh joins him. In all, the work would be completed in:

A. 9 days B. 7 days

C. 11 days D. None of these

9. Sunil completes a work in 4 days whereas Dinesh completes the work in 6 days. Ramesh works $1\frac{1}{2}$ times as fast as Sunil. How many days it will take for the three together to complete the work?

A. $\frac{7}{12}$ B. $1\frac{5}{12}$

C. $1\frac{5}{7}$ D. None of these

10. A can complete a work in 6 days and B in 5 days. They work together, finish the job and receive ₹ 220 as wages. B's share should be:

A. ₹ 120 B. ₹ 110

C. ₹ 100 D. ₹ 90

11. 12 men and 8 children can finish a piece of work in 9 days. If each child takes twice the time taken by a man to finish the work, in how many days will 12 men finish the same work?

A. 8 days B. 15 days

C. 9 days D. 12 days

12. A, B and C together earn ₹ 150 per day while A and C together earn ₹ 94 and B and C together earn ₹ 76. The daily earning of C is:

A. ₹ 75 B. ₹ 56

C. ₹ 34 D. ₹ 20

13. If 5 men or 9 women can finish a piece of work in 19 days, 3 men and 6 women will do the same work in:

A. 10 days B. 12 days

C. 13 days D. 15 days

14. A can do a piece of work in 12 days. B is 60% more efficient than A. The number of days, it takes B to do the same piece of work, is:

A. $7\frac{1}{2}$ days B. $6\frac{1}{4}$ days

C. 8 days D. 6 days

15. A and B can do a piece of work in 45 and 40 days respectively. They began the work together, but A leaves after some days and B finished the remaining work in 23 days. After how many days did A leave?

A. 6 days B. 8 days

C. 9 days D. 12 days

ANSWERS

1	2	3	4	5	6	7	8	9	10
D	D	C	A	B	C	B	A	D	A
11	**12**	**13**	**14**	**15**					
D	D	D	A	C					

EXPLANATORY ANSWERS

1. (A + B)'s 1 day's work $= \frac{1}{15}$

B's 1 day's work $= \frac{1}{20}$

A's 1 day's work $= \frac{1}{15} - \frac{1}{20} = \frac{4-3}{60} = \frac{1}{60}$

$\therefore$ A can do this work alone in 60 days.

2. A's 1 day's work $= \frac{1}{30}$

B's 1 day's work $= \frac{1}{40}$

(A + B)'s 1 day's work

$$= \frac{1}{30} + \frac{1}{40} = \frac{4+3}{120} = \frac{7}{120}$$

$\therefore$ Both together will finish the work in $\frac{120}{7}$

$$= 17\frac{1}{7} \text{ days.}$$

3. $\frac{1}{3}$ of the work is done by A in 5 days.

$\therefore$ Whole work will be done by A in 3×5 = 15 days

$\frac{2}{5}$ of the work is done by B in 10 days.

Whole work will be done by B in $\left(10 \times \frac{5}{2}\right)$ = 25 days

(A + B)'s 1 day's work $= \frac{1}{15} + \frac{1}{25} = \frac{5+3}{75} = \frac{8}{75}$

$\therefore$ Both together can finish it in $\frac{75}{8} = 9\frac{3}{8}$ days.

4. A's 1 day's work $= \frac{1}{6}$

B's 1 day's work $= \frac{1}{12}$

C's 1 day's work $= \frac{1}{24}$

(A + B + C)'s 1 day's work $= \frac{1}{6} + \frac{1}{12} + \frac{1}{24}$

$$= \frac{4+2+1}{24} = \frac{7}{24}$$

$\therefore$ They all together will complete the work in

$\frac{24}{7}$ days $= 3\frac{3}{7}$ days

5. Work to be done by C $= \left(1 - \frac{7}{11}\right) = \frac{4}{11}$

$\therefore$ (A + B) : C $= \frac{7}{11} : \frac{4}{11} = 7 : 4$

$\therefore$ C's share = ₹ $\frac{4}{11} \times 550$ = ₹ 200

6. (A + B)'s 1 day's work $= \frac{1}{12}$

(A + B + C)'s 1 day's work $= \frac{1}{8}$

C's 1 day's work $= \frac{1}{8} - \frac{1}{12} = \frac{3-2}{24} = \frac{1}{24}$

Hence, C will complete the work in 24 days.

7. 1 man's 1 day's work $= \frac{1}{96}$

12 men's 3 day's work $= \frac{12}{96} \times 3 = \frac{3}{8}$

Remaining work = $\left(1-\frac{3}{8}\right) = \frac{5}{8}$

15 men's 1 day's work = $\frac{15}{96}$

Now, $\frac{15}{96}$ work is done by them in 1 day

$\therefore$ $\frac{5}{8}$ work will be done by them in $\frac{96}{15}\times\frac{5}{8}$
= 4 days

8. Umesh's 5 day's work = $\frac{5}{15} = \frac{1}{3}$

Remaining work = $\left(1-\frac{1}{3}\right) = \frac{2}{3}$

Now, $\left(\frac{1}{10}+\frac{1}{15}\right)$ work is done by A and B in 1 day.

$\therefore$ $\frac{2}{3}$ work will be done by A and B in $6\times\frac{2}{3}$
= 4 days.

So, the work would be completed in (5 + 4)
= 9 days.

9. Time taken by Ramesh alone = $\frac{2}{3}\times 4 = \frac{8}{3}$ days

$\therefore$ Their 1 day's work = $\left(\frac{1}{4}+\frac{1}{6}+\frac{3}{8}\right)$

$= \frac{6+4+9}{24} = \frac{19}{24}$

So, together they can finish the work in $\frac{24}{19}$ days

$= 1\frac{5}{19}$ days.

10. Ratio of time taken by A and B = 6 : 5
Ratio of work done in same time = 5 : 6
So, the money is to be divided among A and B in the ratio 5 : 6.

$\therefore$ B's share = ₹$\frac{6}{11}\times 220$ = ₹ 120

11. 2 children = 1 man
$\therefore$ 8 children + 12 men = 4 + 12 = 16 men
Now, less men, more days

$12 : 16 : : 9 : x \Rightarrow \frac{12}{16} = \frac{9}{x} \Rightarrow x = 12$ days

12. B's daily earning = ₹ (150 – 94) = ₹ 56
A's daily earning = ₹ (150 – 76) = ₹ 74
C's daily earning = ₹ [150 – (56 + 74)] = ₹ 20

13. 5 men = 9 women ⇒ 1 man = $\frac{9}{5}$ women

$\therefore$ 3 men + 6 women = $\left(3\times\frac{9}{5}+6\right) = \frac{57}{5}$ women

Now, 9 women can do the work in 19 days

$\therefore$ $\frac{57}{5}$ women can do it in $\frac{9\times 19\times 5}{57}$ = 15 days

14. A's 1 day's work = $\frac{1}{12}$

B's 1 day's work = $\frac{1}{12}$ + 60% of $\frac{1}{12} = \frac{2}{15}$

Hence, B can do the whole work in $\frac{15}{2}$

$= 7\frac{1}{2}$ days.

15. B's 23 day's work = $\frac{23}{40}$

Remaining work = $\left(1-\frac{23}{40}\right) = \frac{17}{40}$

Now, (A + B)'s 1 day's work = $\left(\frac{1}{45}+\frac{1}{40}\right) = \frac{17}{360}$

$\frac{17}{360}$ work is done by A and B in 1 day

$\frac{17}{40}$ work is done by A and B in $\frac{360}{17}\times\frac{17}{40}$
= 9 days.

Hence, A left after 9 days.

11. AREA AND PERIMETER

The area of any figure is the amount of surface enclosed within its boundary lines. It is measured by the number of square metres or square centimetres or square inches (or some other units of square measure) it contains.

Perimeter

Perimeter of a geometrical figure is the total length of the sides enclosing the figure.

Triangle

A triangle is a plane figure bounded by three sides. It includes three angles. It is denoted by the symbol Δ. The sum of angles of a triangle is 180°.

(*i*) **Equilateral Triangle:** A triangle in which all sides are equal is called an equilateral triangle.

(*ii*) **Isosceles Triangle:** A triangle in which two sides are equal is called an isosceles triangle.

(*iii*) **Scalene Triangle:** A triangle in which all sides are different or unequal is called scalene triangle.

(*iv*) **Right Angled Triangle:** A triangle having one of the angles equal to 90° is called a right angled triangle. The side opposite to the right angle of a triangle is called its hypotenuse.

Quadrilateral

A plane figure bounded by four straight lines is called a quadrilateral.

Various Types of Quadrilaterals:

(*i*) **Rectangle:** A quadrilateral whose opposite sides are equal and all angles are at right angles. The diagonals of a rectangle are equal.

(*ii*) **Square:** A rectangle having all sides are equal is called a square.

(*iii*) **Parallelogram:** A quadrilateral whose opposite sides are equal and parallel is called parallelogram.

(*iv*) **Rhombus:** A parallelogram having all the sides equal is called a rhombus. Diagonals of a rhombus are not equal and they bisect each other at right angles.

(*v*) **Trapezium:** A quadrilateral having one pair of opposite sides parallel, is called a trapezium.

Circle

The path traced by a point which moves in such a way that its distance from a fixed point is always same, is called a circle. The fixed point is called its centre and fixed distance is called its radius. The length of the whole path of a circle is called its circumference.

(*i*) **Arc:** Any part of the circumference of a circle is called an arc.

(*ii*) **Chord:** The straight line joining the ends of an arc of a circle is called a chord.

(*iii*) **Diameter:** The chord passing through the centre of a circle is called its diameter.

The diameter of a circle divides the circle into two equal parts, each one of which is called a semi-circle.

(*iv*) **Segment:** The area enclosed by an arc and a chord is called a segment.

(*v*) **Sector:** The area bounded by an arc and two radii is called a sector.

Formulae for Area of Various Figures:

(*i*) **Rectangle:**

Area of rectangle = $l \times b$

Perimeter of rectangle = $2\ (l + b)$.

(ii) Square:

Area of square = $(\text{side})^2$

Perimeter of square = $4 \times \text{side}$

Area of room = $l \times b$

Area of 4 walls of a room = $2(l + b) \times h$

(iii) Parallelogram:

Area of $11^{gm} = b \times h$

Area of rhombus = $\frac{1}{2} \times d_1 \times d_2$.

(iv) Trapezium:

Area of trapezium = $\frac{1}{2}$(sum of parallel sides) × (distance between them)

(v) Triangle:

(a) Area of right triangle = $\frac{1}{2} \times b \times h$

(b) Area of equilateral triangle = $\frac{\sqrt{3}}{4} \times (\text{side})^2$

(c) Area of scalene triangle

$$= \sqrt{s(s-a)(s-b)(s-c)}$$

where, $s = \frac{a+b+c}{2}$

(vi) Circle:

(a) Area of circle = πr^2

(b) Circumference of a circle = $2\pi r$

(c) Length of arc = $\frac{\theta}{360} \times 2\pi r$

(d) Area of sector = $\frac{\theta}{360} \times \pi r^2$

Polygon

A polygon is plane figure bounded by multiple number of sides. Normally, it is used for figures enclosed by more than four sides: *e.g.*, pentagon, hexagon, octagon etc.

Regular Polygon

It is a polygon whose all sides are equal.

For a regular polygon of n equal sides, its vertex angle θ is given by

$$\theta = \left(\frac{n-2}{n}\right) \times 180°$$

Example: Find the area and perimeter of a rectangle whose length is 25 m and breadth is 15 m.

Solution: Area of rectangle $= l \times b$

$= 25 \times 15 = 375 \text{ m}^2$

Perimeter of rectangle $= 2(l + b)$

$= 2(25 + 15) = 80$ m

Example: Find the area of a rectangle whose one side is 6 m and the diagonal is 10 m.

Solution: Another side of rectangle = $\sqrt{(10)^2 - (6)^2}$

$= \sqrt{100-36} = \sqrt{64} = 8$ m

Area of rectangle = $l \times b = 8 \times 6 = 48 \text{ m}^2$

Example: Find area and perimeter of a square whose each side is 12 cm.

Solution: Area of square = $(\text{side})^2 = (12)^2 = 144 \text{ cm}^2$

Perimeter of square = $4 \times \text{side} = 4 \times 12 = 48$ cm

Example: Find the area of a parallelogram whose base is 35 m and altitude 18 m.

Solution: Area of parallelogram = $b \times h$

$= 35 \times 18 = 630 \text{ m}^2$

Example: Find the area of a rhombus one side of which measures 20 cm and one diagonal 24 cm.

Solution: Since the diagonals of a rhombus bisect at right angles, so one side and half of each of the diagonals form a right angled triangle. In this right angled triangle,

One side = 20 cm, another side = $\frac{24}{2} = 12$ cm

Third side = $\sqrt{(20)^2 - (12)^2} = \sqrt{400-144}$

$= \sqrt{256} = 16$ cm

Hence other diagonal = $16 \times 2 = 32$ cm

Area of rhombus = $\frac{1}{2} \times d_1 \times d_2$

$= \frac{1}{2} \times 24 \times 32 = 12 \times 32$

$= 384 \text{ cm}^2$

Example: Find the area of an equilateral triangle each of whose sides measures 12 cm.

Solution: Area of equilateral triangle

$= \frac{\sqrt{3}}{4}(\text{side})^2 = \frac{\sqrt{3}}{4} \times (12)^2$

$$= \frac{\sqrt{3}}{4} \times 144 = 36\sqrt{3} \text{ cm}^2$$
$$= 36 \times 1.73 = 62.28 \text{ cm}^2$$

EXAMPLE: Find the area of a triangle whose sides are 40 cm, 41 cm and 9 cm respectively.

SOLUTION: $s = \frac{a+b+c}{2} = \frac{9+40+41}{2}$

$$= \frac{90}{2} = 45 \text{ cm}$$

$$\text{Area of triangle} = \sqrt{s(s-a)(s-b)(s-c)}$$
$$= \sqrt{45(45-9)(45-40)(45-41)}$$
$$= \sqrt{45 \times 36 \times 5 \times 4}$$
$$= \sqrt{225 \times 144}$$
$$= 15 \times 12 = 180 \text{ cm}^2$$

EXAMPLE: Find the circumference and the area of a circle of radius 3.5 cm.

SOLUTION: Circumference $= 2\pi r$

$$= 2 \times \frac{22}{7} \times 3.5 = 22 \text{ cm}$$

$$\text{Area of circle} = \pi r^2 = \frac{22}{7} \times 3.5 \times 3.5$$
$$= 38.5 \text{ cm}^2$$

EXAMPLE: In a circle of radius 35 cm, an arc subtends an angle of 72° at the centre. Find the length of the arc and the area of the sector.

SOLUTION: Length of arc $= \frac{\theta}{360} \times 2\pi r$

$$= \frac{72}{360} \times 2 \times \frac{22}{7} \times 35$$
$$= 44 \text{ cm}$$

$$\text{Area of the sector} = \frac{\theta}{360} \times \pi r^2$$
$$= \frac{72}{360} \times \frac{22}{7} \times 35 \times 35$$
$$= 770 \text{ cm}^2$$

EXAMPLE: Find the area of a trapezium whose parallel sides are 77 cm, 60 cm and the other sides are 25 cm and 26 cm.

SOLUTION:

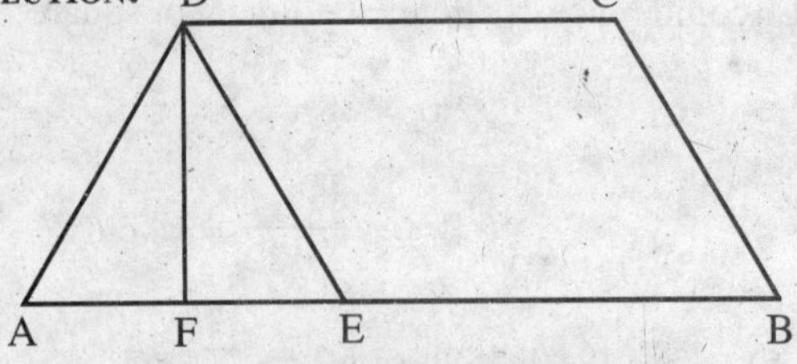

Let ABCD be the given trapezium in which AB = 77 cm, CD = 60 cm, BC = 25 cm, AD = 26 cm.

Draw DE || BC and DF ⊥ AB

Now, DE = BC = 25 cm

$$AE = AB - EB = AB - CD$$
$$= 77 - 60 = 17 \text{ cm}$$

In ΔDAE, $s = \frac{17+25+26}{2} = \frac{68}{2} = 34 \text{ cm}$

$$\text{Area of } \Delta DAE = \sqrt{34(34-17)(34-25)(34-26)}$$
$$= \sqrt{34 \times 17 \times 9 \times 8} = 204 \text{ cm}^2$$

$$\text{Again area of } \Delta DAE = \frac{1}{2} \times AE \times DF$$
$$204 = \frac{1}{2} \times 17 \times DF$$
$$\Rightarrow \quad DF = \frac{2 \times 204}{17} = 24 \text{ cm}$$

$$\therefore \text{ Area of trapezium ABCD} = \frac{1}{2}(AB + CD) \times DF$$
$$= \frac{1}{2}(77+60) \times 24$$
$$= \frac{1}{2} \times 137 \times 24$$
$$= 1644 \text{ cm}^2$$

EXAMPLE: A copper wire when bent in the form of a square, encloses an area of 484 cm². If the same wire is bent in the form of circle, find the area enclosed by it.

SOLUTION: Area of the square = 484 cm²

$$\text{Side} = \sqrt{484} = 22 \text{ cm}$$

$$\text{Length of wire} = \text{Perimeter of square}$$
$$= 4 \times \text{side} = 4 \times 22$$
$$= 88 \text{ cm}$$

Let r be the radius of the circle.

$\therefore$ Circumference of circle = Perimeter of square

$$\therefore \quad 2\pi r = 88 \Rightarrow r = \frac{88}{2\pi}$$

$$= \frac{88 \times 7}{2 \times 22} = 14 \text{ cm}$$

$$\text{Area of circle} = \pi r^2 = \frac{22}{7} \times 14 \times 14$$

$$= 616 \text{ cm}^2$$

EXAMPLE: A bicycle wheel makes 5000 revolutions in moving 11 km. Find the diameter of the wheel.

SOLUTION: Distance covered by the wheel in 1 revolution

$$= \frac{\text{Distance covered}}{\text{Number of revolutions}} = \frac{11}{5000} \text{ km}$$

$$= \frac{11 \times 1000 \times 100}{5000} \text{ cm} = 220 \text{ cm}$$

$\therefore$ Circumference of the wheel = 220 cm

$$2\pi r = 220 \Rightarrow 2 \times \frac{22}{7} \times r = 220$$

$$\Rightarrow \quad r = \frac{220 \times 7}{44} = 35 \text{ cm}$$

Hence, diameter of the wheel = 35 × 2 = 70 cm

EXAMPLE: The perimeter of a square is 44 cm and circumference of a circle is 44 cm. Which area is greater and by how much?

SOLUTION: Side of square $= \frac{44}{4} = 11$ cm

Area of square $= (11)^2 = 121 \text{ cm}^2$

Circumference of a circle $= 2\pi r$

$$\Rightarrow \quad 44 = 2 \times \frac{22}{7} \times r$$

$$\Rightarrow \quad r = \frac{44 \times 7}{44} = 7 \text{ cm}$$

Area of circle $= \pi r^2$

$$= \frac{22}{7} \times 7 \times 7 = 154 \text{ cm}^2$$

Clearly, area of circle > area of square

Difference = 154 – 121 = 33 cm^2.

EXAMPLE: A sheet of paper is in the form of a rectangle ABCD in which AB = 40 cm and AD = 28 cm. A semi-circular portion with BC as diameter is cut off. Find the area of the remaining paper.

SOLUTION:

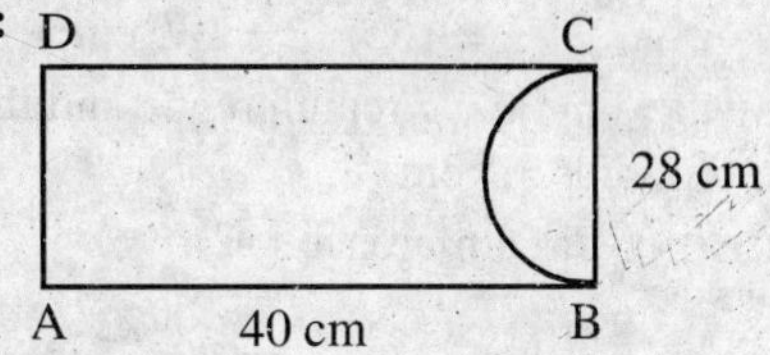

Area of ABCD = 40 × 28 = 1120 cm^2

$$\text{Area of semicircle} = \frac{1}{2}\pi r^2$$

$$= \frac{1}{2} \times \frac{22}{7} \times 14 \times 14$$

$$= 22 \times 14 = 308 \text{ cm}^2$$

Area of the remaining paper = 1120 – 308 = 812 cm^2

MULTIPLE CHOICE QUESTIONS

1. The length of a plot is four times its breadth. A playground measuring 1200 square metres occupies a third of the total area of the plot. What is the length of the plot, in metres?

A. 20 B. 30
C. 60 D. None of these

2. The width of a rectangular hall is $\frac{3}{4}$ of its length. If the area of the hall is 300 m^2, then the difference between its length and width is:

A. 3 m B. 4 m
C. 5 m D. 15 m

3. The length and breadth of a rectangular piece of land are in ratio of 5 : 3. The owner spent ₹ 3000 for surrounding it from all the sides at ₹ 7.50 per metre. The difference between its length and breadth is:

A. 50 m
B. 100 m
C. 150 m
D. 200 m

4. A room 8 m × 6 m is to be carpeted by a carpet 2 m wide. The length of carpet required is:

A. 12 m B. 36 m
C. 24 m D. 48 m

5. The length of a rectangle is increased by 60%. By what per cent would the width have to be decreased to maintain the same area?

A. $37\frac{1}{2}\%$ B. 60%
C. 75% D. 120%

6. A man walked 20 m to cross a rectangular field diagonally. If the length of the field is 16 m, the breadth of the rectangle is:

A. 4 m
B. 16 m
C. 12 m
D. Cannot be determined

7. If the ratio of the areas of two squares is 9 : 1, the ratio of their perimeters is:

A. 9 : 1 B. 3 : 1
C. 3 : 4 D. 1 : 3

8. The perimeter of both, a square and a rectangle are each equal to 48 m and the difference between their areas is 4 m^2. The breadth of the rectangle is:

A. 10 m B. 12 m
C. 14 m D. None of these

9. Area of a square with side x is equal to the area of a triangle with base x. The altitude of the triangle is:

A. $\frac{x}{2}$ B. x
C. $2x$ D. $4x$

10. If only the length of the rectangular plot is reduced to $\frac{2}{3}$rd of its original length, the ratio of original area to reduced area is:

A. 2 : 3 B. 3 : 2
C. 1 : 2 D. None of these

11. If the radius of a circle be reduced by 50%, its area is reduced by:

A. 25% B. 50%
C. 75% D. 100%

12. The perimeter of a rhombus is 52 m while its longer diagonal is 24 m. Its other diagonal is:

A. 5 m B. 10 m
C. 20 m D. 28 m

13. The circumference of a circle is 352 m, then its area in m^2 is:

A. 9856 B. 8956
C. 6589 D. 5986

ANSWERS

1	2	3	4	5	6	7	8	9	10
D	C	A	C	A	C	B	A	C	B
11	**12**	**13**							
C	B	A							

EXPLANATORY ANSWERS

1. Area of the plot = 3 × 1200 = 3600 m^2

Let breadth be x m. Then length = $4x$ m

According to the question,

$4x \times x = 3600 \Rightarrow x^2 = 900 \Rightarrow x = 30$

Hence, length of the plot = 4 × 30 = 120 m.

2. Let length be x m, then breadth = $\frac{3x}{4}$ m

Area of the hall = $x \times \frac{3x}{4} = \frac{3x^2}{4}$

According to the question,

$\frac{3x^2}{4} = 300 \Rightarrow x^2 = 400 \Rightarrow x = 20$

Length = 20 m and breadth = $\frac{3}{4} \times 20$ = 15 m

Difference = 20 – 15 = 5 m

3. Let length = $5x$ m and breadth = $3x$ m

Perimeter of rectangle = $2(5x + 3x) = 16x$ m

But perimeter = $\frac{\text{Total cost}}{\text{Rate}} = \frac{3000}{7.50}$ = 400 m

Now, $16x = 400 \Rightarrow x = 25$

$\text{length} = 5x = 5 \times 25 = 125$ m

$\text{breadth} = 3x = 25 \times 3 = 75$ m

$\text{Difference} = 125 - 75 = 50$ m

4. Length of the carpet $= \dfrac{8 \times 6}{2} = 24$ m.

5. Initially, let length $= x$ and breadth $= y$
Let new breadth $= z$.

Then new length $= \dfrac{160x}{100} = \dfrac{8x}{5}$

$\therefore \quad \dfrac{8x}{5} \times z = xy \Rightarrow z = \dfrac{5y}{8}$

Decrease in breadth $= \left(y - \dfrac{5y}{8}\right) = \dfrac{3y}{8}$

$\therefore$ Decrease per cent $= \dfrac{3y}{8} \times \dfrac{1}{y} \times 100$

$= \dfrac{75}{2} = 37.5\% =$

6. Breadth $= \sqrt{(20)^2 - (16)^2}$

$= \sqrt{400 - 256} = \sqrt{144} = 12$ m.

7. Let the areas of the squares be $(9x^2)$ m^2 and (x^2) m^2
Then, their sides are $3x$ m and x m respectively

Ratio of their perimeters $= \dfrac{12x}{4x} = 3 : 1$

8. Let length of rectangle $= x$ m
and breadth of rectangle $= y$ m
Also, let the side of the square be z m
According to the question,

$2(x + y) = 4z = 48$

$x + y = 24$ and $z = 12$

Also, $z^2 - xy = 4$

$\Rightarrow \quad (12)^2 - 4 = xy$

$\Rightarrow \quad xy = 140$

$\because \quad x + y = 24$ and $xy = 140$

$(x - y)^2 = (x + y)^2 - 4xy$

$\Rightarrow \quad (x - y)^2 = (24)^2 - 4(140)$

$\Rightarrow \quad (x - y)^2 = 576 - 560 = 16$

$\Rightarrow \quad x - y = 4$

Now, $x + y = 24$

$x - y = 4$

Solving and get $x = 14$, $y = 10$
Hence, breadth of rectangle = 10 m.

9. According to the question,

$x^2 = \dfrac{1}{2} \times x \times h$

$\Rightarrow \quad h = \dfrac{2x^2}{x} = 2x$

10. Let length $= x$ and breadth $= y$

New length $= \dfrac{2}{3}x$

$\therefore \quad \dfrac{\text{Original area}}{\text{Reduced area}} = \dfrac{xy}{\frac{2}{3}xy} = \dfrac{3}{2} = 3 : 2$

11. Original area $= \pi r^2$, New area $= \pi\left(\dfrac{r}{2}\right)^2 = \dfrac{\pi r^2}{4}$

Reduction in area $= \pi r^2 - \dfrac{\pi r^2}{4} = \dfrac{3\pi r^2}{4}$

Reduction per cent $= \dfrac{3\pi r^2}{4} \times \dfrac{1}{\pi r^2} \times 100 = 75\%$

12. Side of rhombus $= \dfrac{52}{4} = 13$ m

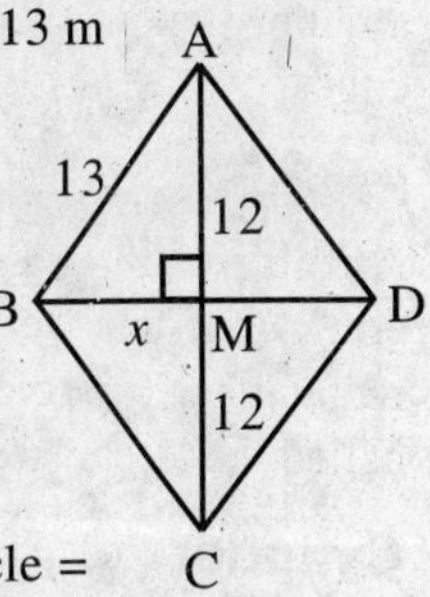

In ΔABM,

$x^2 = (13)^2 - (12)^2$

$x^2 = 169 - 144$

$x^2 = 25$

$\Rightarrow \quad x = 5$ m

$\therefore$ Another diagonal

$= 2 \times 5 = 10$ m

13. Circumference of a circle $= 2\pi r$

$\Rightarrow \quad 352 = 2 \times \dfrac{22}{7} \times r$

$\Rightarrow \quad r = \dfrac{352 \times 7}{44} = 56$ m

Area of circle $= \pi r^2 = \dfrac{22}{7} \times 56 \times 56$

$= 9856$ m^2

12. VOLUME AND SURFACE AREA

We know that every real object occupies some space. It is usually specified by its three dimensions—length, breadth and depth (or height or thickness). It may be a solid or a hollow object. In case of circular, cylindrical and spherical object the specifying dimensions may change to radius, angle etc. The amount of space occupied by the object is called its volume. Its unit of measurement is m^3, cm^3, $(\text{inches})^3$ etc. The area of the surfaces (plane/curved) of the object is called its surface area.

A Cuboid and A Cube

The solid like wooden boxes, tea containers, match box etc. which have six faces, each of which is a rectangle, are called cuboids. It has 12 edges.

A cuboid in which every face is a square is called a cube. Length of each face of a cube is called its edge.

Prism

A right prism is a solid in which the two ends are congruent parallel figures and the side faces are rectangles. The total area of side faces of a prism is called the lateral surface of the prism.

Cylinder

The solid generated by the revolution of a rectangle about one of its sides as axis is called a cylinder.

Pyramid

A solid whose base is a plane rectilinear figure having the side faces as triangles meeting at a common vertex is called a pyramid. When the base of a pyramid is a triangle, the pyramid is called a tetrahedron.

Cone

The solid generated by the revolution of a right angled triangle about one of the sides containing the right angle as the axis is called a right circular cone.

The perpendicular distance from the vertex to the base is called the height of the cone and the length of slant face from vertex to the base is called the slant height of the cone.

Frustum

If a cone is cut by a plane parallel to the base so as to divide the cone into two parts, then the lower part is called the frustum of the cone.

Sphere

When a semicircle moves about its diameter, the solid generated is called a sphere.

Formulae

Cuboid:

Volume of cuboid $= l \times b \times h$ cubic units

Whole surface area $= 2(lb + bh + hl)$ square units

Diagonal of cuboid $= \sqrt{l^2 + b^2 + h^2}$ units

Area of 4 walls of a room $= 2(l + b) \times h$ square units

Cube:

Volume of cube $= a^3$ cubic units

Side of cube $= \sqrt[3]{\text{Volume}}$

Lateral surface area $= 4a^2$ square units

Total surface area $= 6a^2$ square units

Diagonal of the cube $= \left(\sqrt{3}\,a\right)$ units

Cylinder:

Volume of cylinder = $\pi r^2 h$ cubic units

Lateral surface area = $2\pi rh$ square units

Total surface area = $2\pi r(h + r)$ square units

Cone:

Volume of cone = $\frac{1}{3}\pi r^2 h$ cubic units

Lateral surface area = πrl square units

Total surface area = $\pi r(l + r)$ square units

Slant height $(l) = \sqrt{r^2 + h^2}$

Sphere:

Volume of sphere = $\frac{4}{3}\pi r^3$ cubic units

Surface area = $4\pi r^2$ square units

Hemisphere:

Volume = $\frac{2}{3}\pi r^3$ cubic units

Lateral surface area = $2\pi r^2$ square units

Total surface area = $3\pi r^2$ square units

Frustum:

Volume = $\frac{1}{3}\pi h(r_1^2 + r_1 r_2 + r_2^2)$ cubic units

Curved surface area = $\pi(r_1 + r_2) \times l$ square units

Total surface area = $\pi\left[r_1^2 + r_2^2 + (r_1 + r_2)l\right]$ square units

Pyramid:

Volume = $\frac{1}{2} \times$ (area of base) $\times$ height cubic units

Example: The dimensions of a metallic cuboid are 100 cm × 80 cm × 64 cm. It is melted and recast into cube. Find the total surface area of the cube.

Solution: Volume of cuboid = $l \times b \times h$

$= 100 \times 80 \times 64$

$= 512000$ cm^3

Volume of cube = a^3

According to the question,

$a^3 = 512000$

$\Rightarrow \quad a^3 = 8 \times 8 \times 8 \times 10 \times 10 \times 10$

$\Rightarrow \quad a = 8 \times 10 = 80$ cm

Total surface area of cube = $6a^2 = 6 \times 80 \times 80 = 38400$

Hence, total surface area of cube is 38400 cm^2.

Example: Three cubes whose edges measure 3 cm, 4 cm and 5 cm respectively form a single cube. Find the total surface area of the new cube.

Solution: Let the edge of new cube = x cm

$x^3 = 3^3 + 4^3 + 5^3$

$= 27 + 64 + 125 = 216$ cm^3

$\Rightarrow \quad x^3 = 6 \times 6 \times 6 \Rightarrow x = 6$ cm

Total surface area of cube = $6(x)^2 = 6 \times 6 \times 6 = 216$ cm^2

Hence, total surface area of new cube = 216 cm^2.

Example: The capacity of a cylindrical tank is 6160 m^3. If the radius of its base is 14 m, find the depth of the tank.

Solution: Volume of cylinder = $\pi r^2 h$

$\pi r^2 h = 6160$

$\Rightarrow \quad \frac{22}{7} \times 14 \times 14 \times h = 6160$

$\Rightarrow \quad h = \frac{6160}{44 \times 14} = 10$ m

Hence, depth of the tank is 10 m.

Example: How many bullets can be made out of a lead cylinder 28 cm high and 6 cm radius, each bullet being 1.5 cm in diameter?

Solution: Number of bullets

$$= \frac{\text{Volume of cylinder}}{\text{Volume of 1 bullet}}$$

$$= \frac{\pi \times 6 \times 6 \times 28}{\frac{4}{3} \times \pi \times 0.75 \times 0.75 \times 0.75}$$

$$= \frac{6 \times 6 \times 28 \times 3}{4 \times \frac{3}{4} \times \frac{3}{4} \times \frac{3}{4}} = \frac{6 \times 6 \times 28 \times 4 \times 4 \times 3}{3 \times 3 \times 3}$$

$= 1792$

Example: A metal sphere of diameter 42 cm is dropped into a cylindrical vessel, which is partly filled with water. The diameter of the vessel is 1.68 metres. If the sphere is completely submerged, find by how much the surface of water will rise.

Solution: Radius of the sphere = 21 cm

Volume of sphere = $\frac{4}{3}\pi r^3$

$= \frac{4}{3} \times \frac{22}{7} \times 21 \times 21 \times 21$

$= 38808$ cm^3

Volume of water displaced by sphere = 38808 cm^3

Let water rise by h cm.

Volume of cylinder = $\pi r^2 h$

$$\frac{22}{7} \times 84 \times 84 \times h = 38808$$

$$\Rightarrow \quad h = \frac{38808 \times 7}{22 \times 84 \times 84} = \frac{7}{4} = 1.75 \text{ cm}$$

EXAMPLE: A tent is in the form of a right circular cylinder surmounted by a cone. The diameter of cylinder is 24 m. The height of the cylindrical portion is 11 m while the vertex of the cone is 16 m above the ground. Find the area of the canvas required for the tent.

SOLUTION: Lateral surface area of cylinder = $2\pi rh$

$$= 2 \times \frac{22}{7} \times 12 \times 11 = \frac{5808}{7} \text{ m}^2$$

Height of cone = 16 – 11 = 5 m

Radius of cone = 12 m

$$\text{Slant height } l = \sqrt{r^2 + h^2} = \sqrt{12^2 + 5^2}$$

$$= \sqrt{169} = 13 \text{ m}$$

Lateral surface area of cone = πrl

$$= \frac{22}{7} \times 12 \times 13 = \frac{3432}{7} \text{ m}^2$$

$$\text{Area of canvas} = \frac{5808}{7} + \frac{3432}{7}$$

$$= \frac{9240}{7} = 1320 \text{ m}^2$$

EXAMPLE: The slant height of the frustum of a cone is 20 cm and the height of the frustum is 16 cm. The radius of the smaller circle is 8 cm. Find the volume and total surface area of the frustum.

SOLUTION: $l = \sqrt{h^2 + (R - r)^2} = \sqrt{16^2 + (R - 8)^2}$

$$\Rightarrow \quad 20 = \sqrt{256 + R^2 - 16R + 64}$$

$$= \sqrt{R^2 - 16R + 320}$$

$\Rightarrow$ $R^2 - 16R + 320 = 400$

$\Rightarrow$ $R^2 - 16R - 80 = 0 \Rightarrow R = 20$ cm

$$\text{Volume of frustum} = \frac{1}{3}\pi h(R^2 + r^2 + Rr)$$

$$= \frac{1}{3} \times \frac{22}{7} \times 16(400 + 64 + 160)$$

$$= \frac{73216}{7} \text{ cm}^3$$

$$\text{Total surface area} = \pi(R^2 + r^2 + Rl + rl)$$

$$= \frac{22}{7}(400 + 64 + 400 + 160)$$

$$= \frac{22}{7} \times 1024 = \frac{22528}{7}$$

$$= 3218.28 \text{ cm}^2$$

EXAMPLE: The length of a garden roller is 2 m and diameter is 1.4 m. How much area will it cover in 10 revolutions?

SOLUTION: Area covered

= Curved surface × no. of revolutions

= $2\pi rh \times 10$

$$= 2 \times \frac{22}{7} \times 0.7 \times 2 \times 10 = 88 \text{ m}^2$$

EXAMPLE: A cylinder is made by lead whose radius is 4 cm and height is 10 cm. By melting it how many spheres of radius 2 cm can be made?

SOLUTION: Given, radius of the cylinder = 4 cm

and height of the cylinder = 10 cm

$\therefore$ Volume of the cylinder = $\pi r^2 h = \pi(4)^2 \times 10$

= 160π cm^3

$$\text{Volume of sphere} = \frac{4}{3}\pi r^3 = \frac{4}{3}\pi(2)^3$$

$$= \frac{32}{3}\pi \text{ cm}^3$$

$$\therefore \quad \text{Number of spheres} = \frac{\text{Volume of cylinder}}{\text{Volume of one sphere}}$$

$$= \frac{160\pi}{\frac{32}{3}\pi} = \frac{160 \times 3}{32} = 15$$

Hence, number of spheres that can be made are 15.

MULTIPLE CHOICE QUESTIONS

1. The surface area of a cube is 726 m^2. The volume of cube is:

A. 1300 m^3 B. 1331 m^3
C. 1452 m^3 D. 1542 m^3

2. Sum of the length, width and depth of a cuboid is s and its diagonal is d. Its surface area is:

A. s^2 B. d^2
C. $s^2 - d^2$ D. $s^2 + d^2$

3. A wooden box of dimensions 8 m × 7 m × 6 m is to carry rectangular boxes of dimensions 8 cm × 7 cm × 6 cm. The maximum number of boxes that can be carried in 1 wooden box is:

A. 1200000 B. 1000000
C. 9800000 D. 7500000

4. The length of the longest rod that can be placed in a room 30 m long, 24 m broad and 18 m high is:

A. 30 m B. $15\sqrt{2}$ m
C. 60 m D. $30\sqrt{2}$ m

5. If the volume of two cubes are in the ratio 8 : 1, the ratio of their edges is:

A. 8 : 1 B. $2\sqrt{2} : 1$
C. 2 : 1 D. None of these

6. A metal sheet 27 cm long 8 cm broad and 1 cm thick is melted into a cube. The difference between the surface areas of two solids will be:

A. 284 cm^2 B. 296 cm^2
C. 286 cm^2 D. 300 cm^2

7. If each edge of a cube is increased by 50%, the percentage increase in surface area is:

A. 50% B. 75%
C. 100% D. 125%

8. If a right circular cone of vertical height 24 cm has a volume of 1232 cm^3, then the area of its curved surface in cm^2 is:

A. 1254 B. 704
C. 550 D. 154

9. Two cubes have volumes in the ratio 1 : 27. The ratio of their surface areas is:

A. 1 : 3 B. 1 : 8
C. 1 : 9 D. 1 : 18

10. If the volumes of two cones are in the ratio 1 : 4 and their diameters are in the ratio 4 : 5, then the ratio of their heights is:

A. 1 : 5 B. 5 : 4
C. 5 : 16 D. 25 : 64

11. The radius of a wire is decreased to one-third. If volumes remains the same, length will increase:

A. 1 time B. 3 times
C. 6 times D. 9 times

12. A cylindrical piece of metal of radius 2 cm and height 6 cm is shaped into a cone of same radius. The height of cone is:

A. 18 cm B. 14 cm
C. 12 cm D. 8 cm

13. If 1 cubic cm of cast iron weight 21 g then the weight of a cast iron pipe of length 1 m with a bore of 3 cm and in which the thickness of the metal is 1 cm, is:

A. 21 kg B. 24.2 kg
C. 26.4 kg D. 18.6 kg

14. The number of solid spheres, each of diameter 6 cm, that could be moulded to form a solid metal cylinder of height 45 cm and diameter 4 cms, is:

A. 3 B. 4
C. 5 D. 6

15. A right cylinder and a right circular cone have the same radius and the same volume. The ratio of the height of the cylinder to that of the cone is:

A. 3 : 5 B. 2 : 5
C. 3 : 1 D. 1 : 3

ANSWERS

1	2	3	4	5	6	7	8	9	10
B	C	B	D	C	C	D	C	C	D
11	**12**	**13**	**14**	**15**					
D	A	C	C	D					

EXPLANATORY ANSWERS

1. Surface area of cube = $6a^2$

$6a^2 = 726 \Rightarrow a^2 = \frac{726}{6} = 121 \Rightarrow a = 11$ m

Volume of cube = $a^3 = 11 \times 11 \times 11 = 1331$ m^3

2. $l + b + h = s$

and $\sqrt{l^2 + b^2 + h^2} = d \Rightarrow l^2 + b^2 + h^2 = d^2$

$(l + b + h)^2 = s^2$

$\Rightarrow l^2 + b^2 + h^2 + 2(lb + bh + hl) = s^2$

$\Rightarrow d^2 + 2(lb + bh + hl) = s^2$

$\Rightarrow 2(lb + bh + hl) = s^2 - d^2$

$\therefore$ Surface area = $(s^2 - d^2)$.

3. Number of boxes = $\frac{800 \times 700 \times 600}{8 \times 7 \times 6} = 1000000$

4. Diagonal of cuboid = $\sqrt{l^2 + b^2 + h^2}$

$\therefore$ Length of longest rod = $\sqrt{30^2 + 24^2 + 18^2}$

$= \sqrt{900 + 576 + 324} = \sqrt{1800}$

$= \sqrt{30 \times 30 \times 2} = 30\sqrt{2}$ m

5. Let their volumes be $8x^3$ and x^3.
Then, their sides are $2x$ and x
$\therefore$ Ratio of their edges = 2 : 1

6. Volume of sheet = $27 \times 8 \times 1 = 216$ cm^3
Volume of cube formed = 216 cm^3

Side of cube = $\sqrt[3]{216} = 6$ cm
Surface area of cuboid = $2(lb + bh + hl)$
$= 2(27 \times 8 + 8 \times 1 + 1 \times 27) = 502$ cm^2
Surface area of cube = $6(\text{side})^2 = 6 \times 36 = 216$ cm^2
Difference in areas = $502 - 216 = 286$ cm^2

7. Let original length of cube = x
then, its surface area = $6x^2$

New edge = $\left(\frac{150}{100}x\right) = \frac{3}{2}x$

New surface area = $6 \times \left(\frac{3}{2}x\right)^2$

$= 6 \times \frac{9}{4}x^2 = \frac{27}{2}x^2$

Increase in surface area = $\left(\frac{27}{2} - 6\right)x^2 = \frac{15}{2}x^2$

$\therefore$ Increase % = $\frac{15x^2/2}{6x^2} \times 100$

$= \frac{15x^2}{12x^2} \times 100 = 125\%$

8. Volume of cone = 1232

$\Rightarrow \frac{1}{3}\pi r^2 h = 1232$

$\Rightarrow \frac{1}{3} \times \frac{22}{7} \times r^2 \times 24 = 1232$

$\Rightarrow r^2 = \frac{3 \times 7 \times 1232}{22 \times 24} = 49 \Rightarrow r = 7$ cm

$\Rightarrow l = \sqrt{r^2 + h^2} = \sqrt{7^2 + 24^2} = \sqrt{625} = 25$ cm

Lateral surface area of cone = πrl

$= \frac{22}{7} \times 7 \times 25 = 22 \times 25 = 550$ cm^2

9. Let their volumes are x^3 and $27x^3$.
Then, their sides are x and $3x$.

Ratio of their surface areas = $\frac{6x^2}{6(3x)^2} = \frac{x^2}{9x^2}$

$= 1 : 9$

10. Let the diameters of the bases of the cones be $4r$ and $5r$. Let their heights be h and H.

then, $\frac{\frac{1}{3}\pi \times \left(\frac{4r}{2}\right)^2 \times h}{\frac{1}{3}\pi\left(\frac{5r}{2}\right)^2 \times H} = \frac{1}{4}$

$\Rightarrow \frac{16}{25} \times \frac{h}{H} = \frac{1}{4}$

$\Rightarrow \frac{h}{H} = \frac{25}{64}$

11. Let original radius = r

and original length = h

$$\text{New radius} = \frac{1}{3}r$$

Let new length = H

then, $$\pi r^2 h = \pi\left(\frac{1}{3}r\right)^2 \times H = \frac{\pi r^2 H}{9}$$

$\therefore$ $$H = 9h$$

Thus length becomes 9 times.

12. Volume of cone = Volume of cylinder

$$\frac{1}{3}\pi r^2 h = \pi r^2 h$$

$$\Rightarrow \quad \frac{1}{3}\times\frac{22}{7}\times 2\times 2\times h = \frac{22}{7}\times 2\times 2\times 6$$

$$\Rightarrow \quad \frac{h}{3} = 6 \Rightarrow h = 18 \text{ cm}$$

$\therefore$ Height of cone = 18 cm

13. Diameter = 3 cm, h = 1 m = 100 cm

$\therefore$ Radius $= \frac{3}{2}$ cm = 1.5 cm

thickness = 1 cm

$\therefore$ R = 1.5 + 1 = 2.5 cm

r = 1.5 cm

$$\begin{aligned}\text{Volume of metal} &= \pi(R^2 - r^2)\times h \\ &= \pi[(2.5)^2 - (1.5)^2]\times 100 \\ &= \pi[4]\times 100 = \pi\times 400 \text{ cm}^3\end{aligned}$$

$\because$ 1 cm^3 = 21 g

$\therefore$ $\pi\times 400$ cm^3 = $21\times\pi\times 400$ g

$$= 21\times\frac{22}{7}\times\frac{400}{1000} \text{ kg}$$

$$= 26.4 \text{ kg}$$

14. $$\text{Number of spheres} = \frac{\text{Volume of cylinder}}{\text{Volume of sphere}}$$

$$= \frac{\pi\times 2\times 2\times 45}{\frac{4}{3}\pi\times(3)^3} = \frac{4\times 45\times 3}{4\times 27} = 5$$

15. Volume of cylinder = Volume of cone

$$\pi r^2 h = \frac{1}{3}\pi r^2 H$$

$$\Rightarrow \quad 3h = H \Rightarrow \frac{h}{H} = \frac{1}{3}$$

13. DATA INTERPRETATION

The collection of figures and facts in every field is called the statistical data. There are three types of statistical data.

(*a*) **Primary data:** The data collected by the investigator or the statistician to be used or integrated himself are called primary data. It is more reliable and relevant because it is collected by the investigator himself for the first time for his study.

(*b*) **Secondary data:** The data which are collected originally by someone else and used and interpreted by others for statistical analysis are called secondary data.

(*c*) **Grouped data:** When primary data is arranged in classes or groups to bring out certain sailent feature of the data is called grouped data.

Graphical Representation of Data

A graph is a visual form for presentation of data, highlighting their basic facts and relationship.

The word graph, chart and diagram are used interchangeably for the pictorial representation of data. However, the visual form made by using rectangular coordinate system is called a graph. In general, the other pictorial representation in which the coordinate system is not used are called diagrams or charts.

Variate: The quantity that we measure from observation-to-observation is called a variate.

Class-Interval: Every data is generally divided into small group using some interval is said to be in class-interval, *e.g.,* 0–5, 5–10, 10–15 etc.

Class-Size: The difference between the true upper limit and true lower limit of a class gives the size of a class-interval, *e.g.,* class-size of the class-interval 0–5 is 5.

Mid Value: The variable value which is mid-way between the lower and upper limit of a class is called its mid-value, *e.g.,* mid-value of class-interval 0–5 is $\frac{0+5}{2} = 2.5$.

Frequency: The number of observations corresponding to particular class is said to be the frequency of that class, *e.g.,* frequency of the interval 5–10 is 6. It means 6 persons have got 5 or more articles but less than 10.

Cumulative Frequency: The sum of the preceding frequencies is called cumulative frequency. Last frequency of cumulative frequency column is equal to the sum of the frequencies.

Class Limit: Every interval has two limits. Lower number of the interval is called lower limit while upper number of the interval is called upper limit, *e.g.,* in class-interval 0–5, 0 is lower limit while 5 is the upper limit.

Histogram

A statistical graph that represents by the height of a rectangular column the number of times that each class of result occurs in a sample or experiment, *e.g.,* the following table represents the number of matured persons in age group (15–20) in a city.

Age Group	Number of persons
15–20	200
20–25	350
25–30	475
30–35	600
35–40	750
40–45	900
45–50	100

Then the histogram of the data is given below:

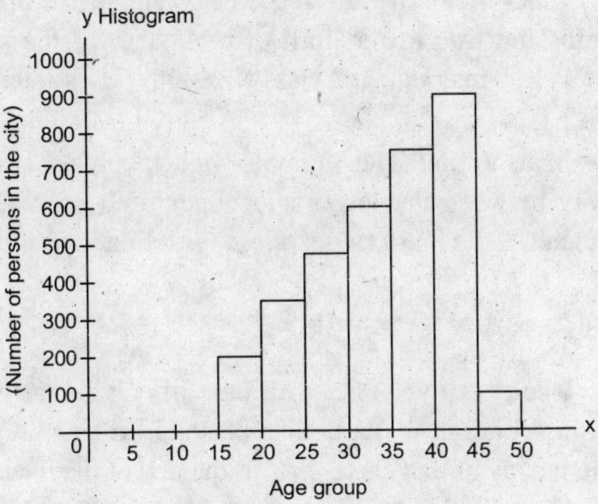

Bar Chart

A graph consisting of bars whose lengths are proportional to quantities in a set of data. It can be used when one axis cannot have a numerical scale, *e.g.*, to show how many different columns of flowers grow from a packet of mixed seeds, *e.g.*,

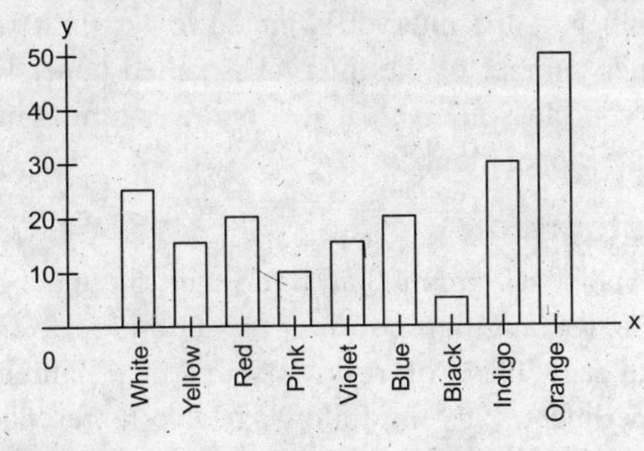

Pie Chart

A diagram in which proportions are illustrated as sectors of a circle. The relative area of the sectors representing the different proportions, *e.g.*, if out of 100 military personnels 25 personnels use tank, 30 personnels use warship, 40 personnels use aircraft and rest of them use rifles. Then pie-chart of the above data is

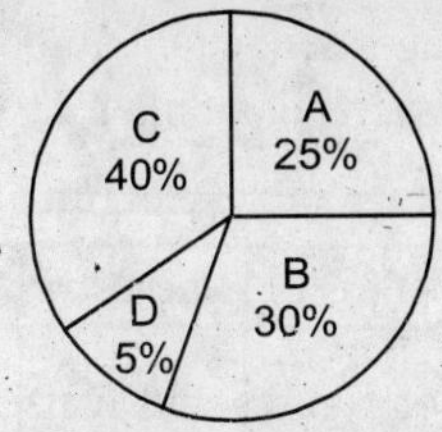

$$\text{A uses tank} = \frac{25}{100} \times 360 = 90^\circ$$

$$\text{B uses warship} = \frac{30}{100} \times 360 = 108^\circ$$

$$\text{C uses aircraft} = \frac{40}{100} \times 360 = 144^\circ$$

$$\text{D uses rifles} = \frac{5}{100} \times 360 = 18^\circ$$

EXAMPLE: Find out the marks obtained in different subjects from the following pie-diagram, if the total marks be 540.

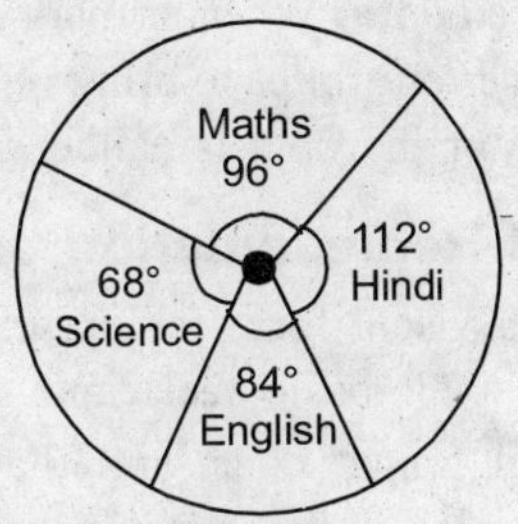

SOLUTION: Sum of the angles at the centre of circle = 360°

Total marks = 540

$$\therefore \text{ Marks obtained in Hindi} = \frac{112}{360} \times 540 = 168$$

$$\text{Marks obtained in English} = \frac{84}{360} \times 540 = 126$$

$$\text{Marks obtained in Science} = \frac{68}{360} \times 540 = 102$$

$$\text{Marks obtained in Maths} = \frac{96}{360} \times 540 = 144$$

MULTIPLE CHOICE QUESTIONS

Directions (Qs. 1 to 5): *Answers the questions on the basis of the following table:*

Assume all colleges sent equal number of candidates in all subjects for the examination.

Percentage of results for Subjects

College	Maths	Physics	Chemistry	Zoology	Botany
A	52	65	62	47	40
B	47	62	52	35	38
C	53	70	46	54	39
D	35	72	58	62	57

1. Taking all the colleges into account which subject has shown highest percentage result?

A. Chemistry
B. Maths
C. Zoology
D. Physics

2. Taking the performance in all the subjects into account which college has shown highest level of percentage results?

A. D B. A
C. B D. C

3. Seeing the performance of all the four colleges together which combination of groups has shown lowest level of percentage results?

A. Zoology and Botany
B. Physics and Chemistry
C. Maths and Physics
D. Chemistry and Botany

4. Taking all the colleges into account which subject has shown lowest percentage result?

A. Maths
B. Physics
C. Chemistry
D. Botany

5. Taking the performance in all subjects into account which college has shown lowest level?

A. A B. B
C. C D. D

Directions (Qs. 6 to 10): *These questions refer to the following circle graph showing the expenditure distribution of a certain family. The family spends ₹6500 per month.*

Expenditure Distribution of a Certain Family

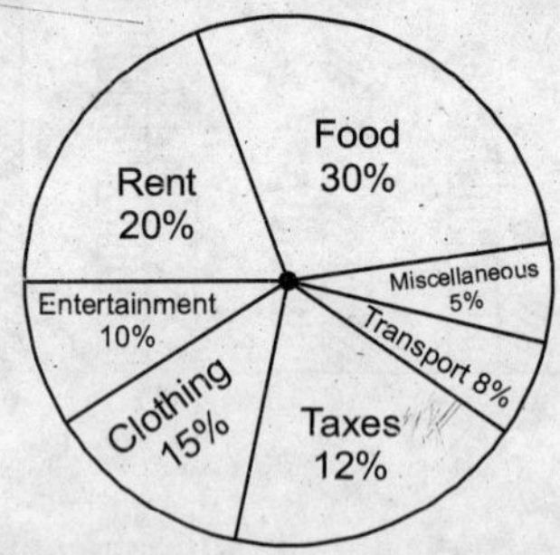

6. How much it spends on food per month?

A. ₹ 1950
B. ₹ 2950
C. ₹ 4850
D. ₹ 850

7. How much are its annual taxes?

A. ₹ 6500 B. ₹ 9360
C. ₹ 8900 D. ₹ 9500

8. How many degrees should there be in the central angle showing clothing, taxes and transportation combined?

A. 100 B. 115
C. 118 D. 126

9. How much more money per month is spent by the family on food as compared to the rent?

A. ₹ 650 B. ₹ 750
C. ₹ 550 D. ₹ 850

10. If the expenditure budget of the family is raised to ₹ 8000 per month and distribution on various items remain the same, then the monthly expenses on both, the entertainment and the transport, will be:

A. ₹ 1700
B. ₹ 1650
C. ₹ 1440
D. ₹ 1320

Directions (Qs. 11 to 15): *Study the following graph carefully and answer the following questions.*

Demand and Production of Colour TV sets of Five Companies for October 1988

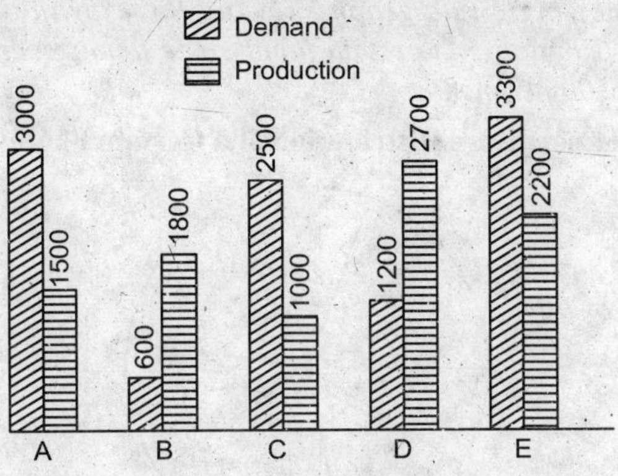

11. What is the ratio of companies having more demand than production of those having more production than demand?

A. 2 : 3 B. 4 : 1
C. 2 : 2 D. 3 : 2

12. What is the difference between average demand and average production of the five companies taken together?

A. 1400 B. 400
C. 280 D. 138

13. The production of Company 'D' is approximately how many times that of the production of the Company A?

A. 1.8 B. 4.5
C. 2.5 D. 4.9

14. The demand for Company 'B' is approximately what per cent of the demand for Company 'C'?

A. 4% B. 24%
C. 20% D. 60%

15. If Company A desires to meet the demand by purchasing surplus TV sets from a single company, which one of the following companies can meet the need adequately?

A. B B. C
C. D D. None of these

Directions (Qs. 16 to 20): *Study the following graph to answer the given questions.*

Per cent profit earned by two companies over the given years

$$\% \text{ Profit} = \frac{\text{Income} - \text{Expenditure}}{\text{Expenditure}} \times 100$$

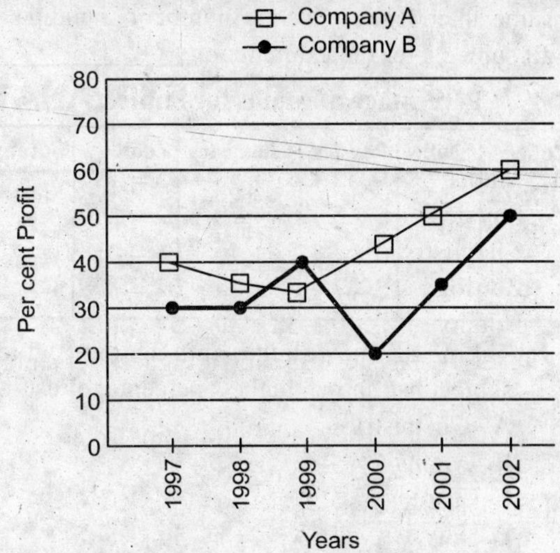

16. If the expenditure of Company B in 2000 was ₹ 200 crores, what was its income?

A. ₹ 240 crores B. ₹ 220 crores
C. ₹ 160 crores D. ₹ 180 crores

17. If the income of Company A in 2002 was ₹ 600 crores, what was its expenditure?

A. ₹ 360 crores B. ₹ 480 crores
C. ₹ 375 crores D. ₹ 320 crores

18. If the income of Company B in 1998 was ₹ 200 crores, what was its profit in 1999?

A. ₹ 21.5 crores
B. ₹ 153 crores
C. ₹ 46.15 crores
D. Cannot be determined

19. If the incomes of the two companies in 1998 were equal, what was the ratio of their expenditure?

A. 1 : 2 B. 26 : 27
C. 4 : 5 D. 100 : 67

20. What is the per cent increase in per cent profit for Company B from year 2000 to 2001?

A. 75 B. 175
C. 160 D. 150

ANSWERS

1	2	3	4	5	6	7	8	9	10
D	A	A	D	B	A	B	D	A	C
11	**12**	**13**	**14**	**15**	**16**	**17**	**18**	**19**	**20**
D	C	A	B	C	A	C	D	B	A

EXPLANATORY ANSWERS

1. Maths : $52 + 47 + 53 + 35 = 187$
Physics : $65 + 62 + 70 + 72 = 269$
Chemistry : $62 + 52 + 46 + 58 = 218$
Zoology : $47 + 35 + 54 + 62 = 198$
Botany : $40 + 38 + 39 + 57 = 174$
Clearly, Physics has shown highest percentage result.

2. A : $52 + 65 + 62 + 47 + 40 = 266$
B : $47 + 62 + 52 + 35 + 38 = 234$
C : $53 + 70 + 46 + 54 + 39 = 262$
D : $35 + 72 + 58 + 62 + 57 = 284$
Clearly, college D has shown highest level of percentage result.

3. Zoology and Botany of groups has shown lowest level of percentage result.

4. Total marks of Botany = 174 which shows lowest percentage result.

5. College B has shown lowest level because its total percentage result in all five subjects is 234 which is lowest.

6. Food 30% of ₹ 6500 = $\frac{30}{100} \times 6500$ = ₹ 1950

7. Taxes = 12% of ₹ 6500

= $\frac{12}{100} \times 6500$ = ₹ 780/month

= ₹ 780 × 12 = ₹ 9360/year

∴ Annual taxes = ₹ 9360

8. Clothing, taxes and transportation combined are 35%.

Now, $100\% = 360^\circ$

$$35\% = \frac{360^\circ}{100} \times 35 = 126^\circ$$

9. 10% of ₹ 6500 = $\frac{10}{100} \times 6500$ = ₹ 650/month

10. 18% of ₹ 8000 = $\frac{18}{100} \times 8000$ = ₹ 1440

11. The companies having more demand than production are A, C and E *i.e.* their number is 3. The companies having more production than demand are B and D *i.e.* their number is 2.
So, the required ratio is 3 : 2.

12. Average demand

$$= \frac{1}{5}(3000 + 600 + 2500 + 1200 + 3300)$$

$$= \frac{10600}{5} = 2120$$

Average production

$$= \frac{1500 + 1800 + 1000 + 2700 + 2200}{5}$$

$$= \frac{9200}{5} = 1840$$

∴ Difference between average demand and average production = 2120 – 1840 = 280

13. Let $K(1500) = 2700$

$$\Rightarrow \quad K = \frac{2700}{1500} = \frac{9}{5} = 1.8.$$

14. Let $x\%$ of (demand for C) = (demand for B)

$$\Rightarrow \quad \frac{x}{100} \times 2500 = 600$$

$$\Rightarrow \quad x = \frac{600 \times 100}{2500} = 24\%$$

15. Since Company D produces highest number of TV sets and Company A desires to meet the demand by purchasing surplus TV sets from a single Company.
Clearly, D can meet the demand of A.
∴ Correct answer is C.

16. Let the income be ₹ x crores

$\therefore \quad 20 = \frac{x - 200}{200} \times 100$

$\Rightarrow \quad 40 = x - 200$

$\Rightarrow \quad x = 240$

$\therefore$ Income = ₹ 240 crores

17. The income of Company A in 2002 = ₹ 600 crores

% Profit = 60

Let the expenditure be ₹ x crores.

$\therefore \quad 60 = \frac{600 - x}{x} \times 100$

$\Rightarrow \quad x = \frac{600 - x}{60} \times 100$

$\Rightarrow \quad x = \frac{(600 - x)5}{3}$

$\Rightarrow \quad 3x = 3000 - 5x$

$\Rightarrow \quad 8x = 3000$

$\Rightarrow \quad x = \frac{3000}{8} = 375$

Hence, expenditure = ₹ 375 crores.

18. It cannot be determined as Income and Expenditure of respective year is not known.

19. Let their equal incomes be ₹ 1 crore. Also, let expenditure of Company A be ₹ E_1 crores and that of Company B be ₹ E_2 crores.

Now, $\quad 35 = \frac{1 - E_1}{E_1} \times 100$

$35 E_1 = 100 - 100 E_1$

$135 E_1 = 100 \quad$ ...(*i*)

Similarly $\quad 30 = \frac{1 - E_2}{E_2} \times 100$

$130 E_2 = 100 \quad$ ...(*ii*)

From (*i*) and (*ii*)

$135 E_1 = 130 E_2$

$\Rightarrow \quad \frac{E_1}{E_2} = \frac{130}{135} = \frac{26}{27}$

$\therefore \quad E_1 : E_2 = 26 : 27$

20. Required percentage $= \frac{35 - 20}{20} \times 100$

$= \frac{15}{20} \times 100 = 75.$

GENERAL SCIENCE

PHYSICS

Physical Quantities

- Physical quantities may be divided in two classes:
  1. Scalar Quantities
  2. Vector Quantities
- A scalar quantity is one which has only magnitude.
- A vector quantity has both magnitude and direction.
- Force, Velocity, Momentum, Acceleration are examples of vector quantities.
- Mass, length, time, volume, speed, energy, work are examples of scalar quantities.

Units

- All measurements in physics require standard units.
- In 1960, the General Conference of Weights and Measures recommended that a metric system of measurements called the International System of Units, abbreviated as SI units, be used.

Some Important Units

S. No.	Units	Quantity
1.	Metre	Length
2.	Kilogram	Mass
3.	Second	Time
4.	Ampere	Electric Current
5.	Candela	Luminous Intensity
6.	Newton	Force
7.	Joule	Workdone
8.	Watt	Power
9.	Coulomb	Quantity of Electricity
10.	Volt	Potential Difference
11.	Ohm	Electrical Resistance
12.	Farad	Capacitance
13.	Henry	Inductance
14.	Lumen	Luminous Flux

- Very small distances are measured in micrometers or (microns) (μm), angstroms (Å), nanometers (nm) and femtometres (fm).
- $1 \text{ m} = 10^6 \text{ μm} = 10^9 \text{ nm} = 10^{10} \text{ Å} = 10^{15} \text{ fm}$
- $1 \text{ micron } (1\mu) = 10^{-4} \text{ cm} = 10^{-6} \text{ m}$
- $1 \text{ Angstrom } (1 \text{ Å}) = 10^{-8} \text{ cm} = 10^{-10} \text{ m}$
- $1 \text{ Fermi } (1\text{F}) = 10^{-13} \text{ cm} = 10^{-15} \text{ m}$

Motion

- When a body changes its position with respect to something else as time goes on, we say the body is in motion.
- There are two types of motion— translational (linear) and rotational (spin).
- The motion of a car on a road is translational whereas the motion of a top, spinning on its axis is rotational.

Speed

- It is a scalar form of velocity and is defined as the distance travelled irrespective of direction in one second.
- $\text{Speed} = \dfrac{\text{distance travelled}}{\text{time required}}$
- SI unit of speed is meters per second (m/s).

Velocity

- The distance covered by an object in a specified direction in unit time interval is called velocity.
- The SI unit of velocity is m/s.
- Velocity is a vector quantity.

Acceleration

- The velocity of a body changes due to change in its speed or direction or both. The rate of change of the velocity of a body is called its acceleration.

- Acceleration = $\frac{\text{change in velocity}}{\text{time}}$
- Negative acceleration is known as retardation. It indicates that the velocity of the object is decreasing with respect to time.
- Acceleration is uniform when neither its direction nor magnitude changes with respect to time.

Acceleration Due to Gravity

- When a body falls freely, then the increase in velocity per second is called acceleration due to gravity. It is represented by 'g'.

$$g = \frac{GMe}{Re^2}$$

where G = Universal Gravitational Constant
Me = Mass of Earth
Re = Radius of the Earth

- Value of 'g' depends upon the radius of the earth as $g \propto \frac{1}{R}$.
- Value of 'g' is maximum at poles and minimum at equator.

Equations of Motion

1. $V = u + at$
2. $S = ut + \frac{1}{2}at^2$
3. $V^2 = u^2 + 2as$

where u is initial velocity
V is final velocity
t is time
a is acceleration
s is distance

FORCE

Gravitational Force

- It is the force of attraction between two masses.
- The gravitational force exists between all bodies, even between two apples lying on a table.
- It is gravitational force that holds the moon in its orbit round the earth and the earth in its orbit round the sun.
- **Newton's Law of Universal Gravitation** states that every particle in the universe attracts every other particle with a force that is directly proportional to the product of their masses and inversely proportional to the square of the distance between them.
- In equation form, the gravitational force

$$F = G\frac{m_1 m_2}{r^2}$$

where r is the distnace between two particles of masses m_1 and m_2 and G the universal gravitational constant.

- The value of G is 6.67×10^{-11} SI units.

Centripetal Force

- The force acting towards the centre on a particle executing uniform circular motion is called centripetal force and is given by

$$F = \frac{mv^2}{r}$$

where m = Mass of the object
v = Speed
r = Radius of the Circular Path

- In case of the moon, gravitational force between the earth and the moon acts as the centripetal force.
- When a stone tied at one end of a string is whirled in a circle, the pull in the string provides the centripetal force.
- Without centripetal force there can be no circular motion.
- Centripetal force always acts on the particle performing circular motion.

Centrifugal Force

- The pseudo force that balances the centripetal force in uniform circular motion is called centrifugal force.
- Centrifugal force is directed away from the centre along the radius.
- The centrifugal force is zero exactly at the poles and maximum at the equator.

WEIGHT

- The weight of a body is the force with which the earth attracts the body towards its centre.
- The weight of a body should not be confused with its mass, which is a measure of the quantity of matter contained in it. When we say that a person weighs 60 kg, we are actually describing his mass and not weight.
- The mass of a body is a constant quantity whereas its weight varies slightly from place-to-place on the earth.
- The weight of a body is maximum at the poles and minimum at the equator. This variation in weight is due to:
  1. the shape of the earth.
  2. the rotation of the earth about its axis.
- The weight of an object is less at high elevations them at sea level.
- At the centre of the earth, the weight of a body would be zero.
- The weight of a body can also be expressed in terms of the acceleration due to gravity (g). The weight (w) of a body of mass m is given by the product of m and g, *i.e.*,

$$w = mg$$

- On the surface of the moon the value of the acceleration due to gravity is nearly one-sixth of that on earth and, therefore, an object on the moon would weigh only one-sixth its weight on the earth. The mass of an object on the moon would be the same as on earth.
- The weight of a body would be more if the earth stopped rotating. Conversely, if the speed of rotation were higher, the weight would be lesser.
- A person weighs more in a lift, which is accelerating upward.
- An astronaut feels weightlessness in a spaceship because he is not pushing against anything.

FRICTION

- Friction is the force which opposes the relative motion of two surfaces in contact.
- It is friction between the ground and the soles of our shoes that makes walking possible and it is lack of friction that makes our feet slip on highly polished surfaces.
- The force of friction that acts when a body is moving (sliding) on a surface is called sliding friction.
- When a cylindrical or spherical body rolls over a surface, the force opposing the motion is called rolling friction. For the same pair of materials rolling friction is much smaller than sliding friction.
- Friction in machines wastes energy and also causes wear and tear. This friction is reduced by using (1) lubricants, and (2) ball bearings.
- Rolling friction is always lesser than the sliding friction and hence it is easier to move a heavy object on rollers rather than to slide it. This property can be attributed to the fact that in case of rolling friction, the area of contact between the two surfaces is far less.

NEWTON'S LAWS OF MOTION

FIRST LAW

- Every object continues in its state of rest or of uniform motion in a straight line if no net force acts upon it. It is also known as **law of inertia.**
- **Examples:** 1. An unwary passenger in a fast-moving bus falls forward when it stops suddenly. This happens because the feet of the passenger come to rest suddenly whereas his body continues to be in motion.

  2. A person getting down from a moving bus has to run some distance, in the direction of the bus, before stopping. If he does not run he is bound to fall because his feet come to rest whereas his body continues to be in motion.

Momentum

- The momentum of a body is defined as the product of its mass and velocity.

SECOND LAW

- This law states that "the rate of change of momentum of a body is proportional to the applied force and takes place in the direction of the force."
- If we express force (F) in Newtons, mass (m) in kilograms and acceleration (a) in metres per second squared, we can write the second law as

$$F = ma$$

- In travelling the same distance, a car consumes more fuel on a crowded road than on a free road. This happens because the car has to stop and start quite often on a crowded road. The repeated acceleration requires a force (second law), which ultimately comes from the fuel. On a free road the car runs at almost uniform speed requiring fewer accelerations and hence less fuel consumption.

THIRD LAW

- This law states that "to every action there is an equal and opposite reaction." The statement means that if body A exerts a force on body B, then B exerts an equal and opposite force on A along the same line of action.
- When a bullet is fired from a gun, equal and opposite forces are exerted on the bullet and the gun.
- A rocket contains solid chemicals which burn to produce a high velocity blast of hot gases. Space rockets have liquid fuel together with a supply of liquid oxygen to enable the fuel to burn. In either case, the large force created by chemical reaction propels out hot gases through the tail nozzle with a very high velocity. The reaction to this force propels the rocket forward.
- The engine in a jet aeroplane works on the same principle as a rocket but there is a difference in the method of obtaining the high velocity gas jet.
- The fuel used in a jet engine in Kerosene (paraffin).

IMPULSE

- If a force acts on a body for a very short time, then the product of force and time is called the impulse.

$$\text{Impulse} = \text{Change in momentum} = \text{Force} \times \text{Time}$$

Application of Impulse

1. A cricket player draws his hand back while catching.
2. A person jumping on hard cement floor receives more injuries than a person jumping on muddy or sandy floor.

WORK, POWER AND ENERGY

WORK

- Whenever a force acting on a body displaces it, work is said to be done.
  Work = Force × Distance moved in the direction of force.
- Work is a scalar quantity and its SI unit is Joule (J).

POWER

- Power is defined as the rate of doing work.

$$\text{Power} = \frac{\text{Work done}}{\text{Time taken}}$$

- The SI unit of power is Watt (W) and is also measured in horse power.

$$1 \text{ HP} = 746 \text{ W}$$

ENERGY

- Energy is defined as the capacity to do work.
- The SI unit of energy is Joule (J).
- There are two forms of mechanical energy—Kinetic and Potential.

Kinetic Energy

- The energy possessed by an object due to its motion is called kinetic energy and is described by the expression

$$KE = \frac{1}{2}mv^2$$

where m = mass of the object

v = speed

Potential Energy

- Potential energy is the energy possessed by the body by virtue of its position, configuration or any condition of stress or strain.
- One of the commonest forms of potential energy is that possessed by an object when it is above the level of the earth's surface. This is called gravitational potential energy and is described by the expression

$$PE = mgh$$

where m is the mass of the object, g the acceleration due to gravity and h the height of the object above the earth's surface.

- There are many examples of potential energy. A stone held at some height above the ground has potential energy. Water in an elevated reservoir possesses potential energy.

Conservation of Energy

- Energy can neither be created nor destroyed; it can only be transformed from one form into another, but the total amount of energy remains constant.

Transformation of Energy

S.No.	Equipment	Transformation
1.	Dynemo	Mechanical energy into electrical energy
2.	Microphone	Sound energy into electrical energy
3.	Loud Speaker	Electrical energy into sound energy
4.	Electric Bulb	Electrical energy into light and heat energy
5.	Battery	Chemical energy into electrical energy
6.	Electrical Motor	Electrical energy into mechanical energy

Einstein Relation

- According to Einstein, mass can be converted into energy and energy can be converted into mass. One can be obtained at the cost of the other. The equivalence between mass and energy is expressed in terms of Einstein Relations:

$$E = mc^2$$

where m is the mass that disappears, E is the energy that appears and c is the velocity of light in vacuum ($c = 3 \times 10^8$ m/s)

CENTRE OF GRAVITY

- The centre of gravity of a body is the point where the whole weight of the body can be considered to act.
- The centre of gravity of a body may even lie outside the actual material of the body. For example, the centre of gravity of a ring lies at its centre, which is outside its material.
- The stability of an object is connected with the position of its centre of gravity (CG).
- If the vertical through the CG passes through the base of an object, then it is stable, otherwise it is unstable and topples down.
- Racing cars are built low and with wide wheel bases to reduce the risk of overturning at sharp bends.
- While crossing a river in a boat, passengers are not allowed to stand. This keeps the CG of the system (boat and passengers) low and ensures stability.
- A porter carrying a load on his back leans forward to keep the vertical line passing through the CG of the system between his feet.

ARTIFICIAL SATELLITES

- In the case of a satellite, the centripetal force is provided by the gravitational pull of the earth.
- The speed of the satellite does not depend on its mass. It means that at a particular distance from the earth, all objects would have the same speed of revolution.

- If a satellite moves from a higher orbit to a lower orbit, its speed increases.
- If the speed of a satellite is more than 11.2 km/s or 25,000 miles/hour, the satellite would escape the earth entirely and would never come back. This is called escape velocity.
- The existence of gaseous atmosphere on the earth is due to the high value of its escape velocity.
- On the moon the value of the escape velocity is 1.9 km/s (nearly one-sixth of that on earth). If any gases are formed on the moon, the molecules would have velocities greater than 1.9 km/s and would therefore escape, leaving the moon bare.
- The value of escape velocity does not depend upon the mass of the projected body, instead it depends on the mass and radius of the planet from which it is being projected.
- The value of escape velocity does not depend on the angle and direction of projection.
- The root mean square velocity of hydrogen is more than that of the escape velocity of earth, therefore, hydrogen is not found in earth's lower atmosphere.

Geostationary Satellites

- Geostationary satellites are stationary with respect to an observer on the earth. Their time period is 24-hour. There height above the surface of earth is 36,000 km. They are always in equatorial plane and their orbits are circular. They are also called parking orbits.

DENSITY AND RELATIVE DENSITY

- The mass per unit volume of a substance is called its density.

$$\text{Density} = \frac{\text{Mass}}{\text{Volume}}$$

- The SI unit of density is kilogram per metre cubed (kg/m^3).

Densities of Some Common Substances

Sr. No.	Substance	Density in kg/m^3
1.	Alcohol	790
2.	Water	1,000
3.	Aluminium	2,700
4.	Steel (vories)	7,800
5.	Copper	8,900
6.	Lead	11,300
7.	Mercury	13,600
8.	Gold	19,300
9.	Platinum	21,500

- The relative density of a substance is the ratio of the density of the substance to the density of water.
- Relative density has no unit.

PRESSURE

- Pressure is defined as force acting per unit area.

$$\text{Pressure} = \frac{\text{Force}}{\text{Area}}$$

- The SI unit of pressure is newton per metre squared or pascal.
- There is a inverse relationship between magnitude of pressure and area of contact.
- It is much easier to cut fruit with a sharp knife than with a blunt one. In the case of a sharp knife the blade makes such a small area of contact with the fruit that the pressure below it, is very high and easily cuts the fruit.
- Broad wooden sleepers are placed below the rails to reduce the pressure exerted by the weight of a train.
- The pressure of water increases with depth, therefore bottom of a dam is made much thicken than the top.
- The pressure exerted on an enclosed liquid at one place is transmitted equally throughout the liquid. This is called Pascal's Principle.

- Hydraulic presses, hydraulic brakes, hydraulic door closers, etc. are applications of the Pascal's Principle.
- At high attitudes where atmosphere pressure is less nose bleeding may occur due to the greater pressure of blood.
- It is due to the pressure of the atmosphere that ink rises in the tube of a fountain pen or liquid rises in a syringe when the piston is pulled.
- In an aircraft flying at high altitude, normal atmospheric pressure is maintained by the use of air pumps. If this were not done, the crew and passengers would experience difficulty in breathing and consequently face dangers.
- Atmospheric pressure is measured with an instrument called the **Barometer.**
- Aneroid barometer does not use any liquid.
- If the barometric height falls suddenly, it indicates the coming of a storm. A gradual fall in the barometric height indicates the possibility of rain. A gradual increase in the barometric height indicates fair weather.

ARCHIMEDE'S PRINCIPLE

- This principle states that when a body is wholly or partially immersed in a fluid, it experiences an upthrust (upward force) equal to the weight of the fluid displaced.
- When an object is immersed in a fluid, two forces act on it: (*i*) the weight of the object acting downward, and (*ii*) upthrust acting upward.
- It is due to upthrust that objects apparently weightless when immersed in fluids.

LAW OF FLOATATION

- When a body is immersed in a fluid then if—
  1. the weight of body is equal to upthrust, the body floats with whole of its volume inside the liquid.
  2. the weight of body is more than the upthrust, the body will sink.
  3. the weight of body is less than the upthrust, the body will float with some of its part outside the liquid.
- An iron nail sinks in water whereas a ship made of iron and steel floats. This is due to the fact that a ship is hollow and contains air and, therefore, its density is less than that of water.
- The density of sea water is more than that of river water, due to this a ship sinks less in sea water. It is for this reason that a ship rises a little when it enters a sea from a river.
- It is because of the higher density of sea water that it is easier to swim in the sea.
- A solid chunk of iron will sink in the water but float in mercury because the density of iron is more than that of water but less than that of mercury.
- A balloon filled with a light gas, such as hydrogen, rises because the average density of the balloon and the gas is less than that of air. The balloon cannot rise indefinitely because the density of the air decreases with increasing altitude. At a certain height, where the density of air is equal to the average density of the balloon, it ceases to rise and drifts sideways with the wind.
- When an ice block floats in water the water level will remain the same when all the ice melts into water.
- A **hydrometer** is an instrument used for measuring the relative density of liquids.
- A special type of a hydrometer called **Lactometer** is used for testing milk by measuring its density.

SURFACE TENSION

- Surface tension is that property of liquids owing to which they tend to acquire minimum surface area.
- Surface tension is caused by molecular attractions.
- When a paint brush is dipped in water all its hair spread out but when it is taken out it is

covered with a thin film of water which contracts due to surface tension and pulls the hair together.

- Liquid drops, such as raindrops, oildrops, drops of molten metals, dewdrops etc. are all spherical because their surface tend to contract in order to have minimum surface area. For a given volume, a sphere has the minimum surface area.
- Soaps and detergents lower the surface tension of water. This increases the wetting power of water or its ability to detach dirt particles from clothes and untensils.
- Cohesive forces are the forces of attraction acting between molecules of same substance. The liquids for which cohesive forces are large do not wet the walls of the vessel, *e.g.*, mercury. Surface tension forces arise due to cohesive forces.
- Adhesive forces are the forces of attraction acting between the molecules of different substances. If adhesive forces are greater than cohesive force then the liquid wets the walls of the vessel, *e.g.*, water wets the walls of a glass-capillary.
- The force of attraction between unlike molecules is called **adhesion** and that between like molecules **cohesion.**
- The melted wax of a candle is drawn up into the wick by capillary action. Oil rises up a lamp wick for the same reason.
- If one end of a sugar cube is dipped into tea, the entire cube is quickly wet on account of capillary action.
- The fine pores of a blotting paper act as tiny capillary tubes. The ink rises into the blotting paper through these pores.

VISCOSITY

- The force which opposes the relative motion between different layers of liquid or gases is called viscous force.
- Viscosity is the property of liquids and gases both.
- The viscosity of a liquid is due to cohesive force between its molecules.
- The viscosity of a gas is due to diffusion of its molecules from one layer to other layer.

Bernoulli's Theorem

- According to Bernoulli's theorem, in case of streamline flow of incompressible and non-viscous fluid (ideal fluid) through a tube, total energy (sum of pressure energy, potential energy and kinetic energy) per unit volume of fluid is same at all points.
- An important corollary of this theorem is: pressure in a fluid decreases with increased velocity of the fluid. Examples :
  1. When a bowler spins a ball, it changes its direction (swings) in the air due to unequal pressure acting on it.
  2. The shape of the wings of an aeroplane is such that wind velocity above the wings is higher than that below them. Consequently, there is higher pressure below the wings and this lifts the aeroplane.
  3. When the piston of a sprayer is pushed, air is forced past the upper end of a tube, whose lower end dips in the liquid to be sprayed. Due to the increased velocity of air, the pressure near the upper end of the tube is reduced. The atmospheric pressure in the container, therefore, pushes the liquid to the top, from where it is carried away by the stream of air.

HEAT

- Heat is that form of energy which flows from one body to other body due to difference in temperature between the bodies. The amount of heat contained in a body depends upon the mass of the body.

Temperature and Heat

- The temperature of a body is the quantity that tells how hot or cold it is with respect to some standard body.

- Heat is the internal energy transferred from one body to another due to temperature difference.

Measurement of Temperature

- Temperature is measured by a thermometer.
- To measure temperature two fixed points are taken on each thermometer. One of the fixed points is the freezing point of water or ice point as lower fixed point (LFP). The other fixed point is the boiling point of water or steam point as upper fixed point.
- A thermometer may be graduated in following scales—
  1. The upper and lower points of centigrade scale are 100°C and 0°C.
  2. The upper and lower points of Fahrenheit scale are 212°F and 32°F.
  3. The upper and lower points of Reaumur scale are 80°R and 0°R.
  4. The upper and lower points of Kelvin scale are 373K and 273K.
  5. The upper and lower points of Rankine scale are 672° Ra and 460° Ra.
- Relation between different temperature scales

$$\frac{C}{100} = \frac{F - 32}{180} = \frac{R}{80} = \frac{K - 273}{100} = \frac{Ra - 460}{212}.$$

- At – 40 degrees both celsius and Fahrenheit scales will show identical readings.
- **Pyrometer** is a instrument for measuring high temperatures.
- Weather reports in newspapers carry the maximum and the minimum temperatures recorded during the last 24 hours.
- Mercury is used in thermometers because—
  1. It is opaque and shining and, therefore, temperature can be read conveniently.
  2. It is a good conductor of heat, and, therefore, records temperatures rapidly.
  3. It does not stick to glass and also does not vaporise much and therefore yields correct readings.
- Water cannot be used in a thermometer becaues it freezes at 0°C and also becaue of its irregular expansion.
- In cold countries where winter temperatures of –40°C are not uncommon, mercury thermometers cannot be used because mercury freezes at –39°C. In such countries, alcohol thermometers are useful, since alcohol freezes at –115°C.

THERMAL EXPANSION

- Solids, liquids and gases generally expand when heated and contract when cooled.
- Gaps have to be left in railway tracks to make allowance for expansion, otherwise the rails will buckle. Allowance is made for the expansion of long steel bridges. One end of such bridge is fixed while the other rests on rollers.
- Telephone wires sag more in summer than in winter due to thermal expansion.

Expansion of Water

- Water has its minimum volume and maximum density at 4°C.
- Water shows unusual expansion. If we take a cube of ice at –5°C and heat it, it expands till ice starts melting. During melting its temperature remains 0°C but its volume decreases. If heat is continuously supplied to water at 0°C, it further contracts up to 4°C and then it starts expanding.
- Anomalous expansion of water helps preserve aquatic life during very cold weather. When temperature falls, the top layer of water in a pond contracts, becomes denser and sinks to the bottom. A circulation is thus set up until the entire water in the pond reaches maximum density at 4°C. If the temperature falls further, the top layer expands and remains on top till it freezes. Thus, even though the upper layers are frozen the water near the bottom is at 4°C and the fishes etc., can survive in it easily.

TRANSMISSION OF HEAT

- There are three ways of heat transmission:
  1. Conduction
  2. Convection
  3. Radiation

Conduction

- In this process, heat is transferred from one place to other place by the successive vibration of the particles of the medium without bodily movement of the particles of the medium.
- Conduction takes place mainly in solids.
- Air is a very bad conductor of heat. The good insulating properties of wool, cotton, etc. are mainly due to the air spaces they contain.
- Sawdust is a bad conductor of heat. Therefore, ice slabs are covered with sawdust to minimise melting.
- On a cold night two thin blankets are preferred to a single thick blanket because the layer of air between the two blankets serves as a better insulator.

Convection

- In this process, heat is transferred by the actual movement of particles of the medium from one place to other place.
- In liquids and gases heat is transmitted by convection.

Radiation

- It is the fastest means of heat transfer.
- In this mode of heat transmission heat is transferred from one place to another without effecting the intervening medium.
- Both conduction and convection require a material medium for conveying heat from one part to another. Radiation, on the other hand, does not require any medium.

Newton's Law of Cooling

- This law states that the rate of which a hot body loses heat is directly proportional to the difference between its temperature and the surrounding temperature.
- **Example:** Hot water takes much less time in cooling from 90°C to 80°C than in cooling from 40°C to 30°C.

Kirchhoff's Law

- According to Kirchhoff's law, the ratio of emissive power to absorptive power is same for all surfaces at the same temperature and is equal to emissive power of black body at that temperature.

Greenhouse Effect

- A greenhouse acts like a radiation trap.
- In a greenhouse, heat radiation from the sun passes through the glass and keeps the plants and the air inside warm. The glass prevents warm air from escaping.
- A car parked in the sun with its windows closed gets terribly warm due to the greenhouse effect.

Heat Capacity

- The heat capacity of a body is defined as the heat required to raise the temperature of the body by 1 K. Its SI unit is J/K.

Specific Heat Capacity

- The specific heat capacity of a substance is the heat required to raise the temperature of a unit mass of the substance by 1 K.
- Its SI unit is J/kg K.
- Water has a very high specific heat capacity.
- It is because of its high specific heat capacity that water is used as a cooling liquid in car engine.

Latent Heat

- It is defined as the amount of heat absorbed or given out by a body during the change of state.
- The latent heat of fusion of a substance is defined as the heat required to convert a unit mass of the substance from the solid to the liquid state without change of temperature.

- The latent heat of vaporization of a substance is the heat required to change a unit mass of the substance from liquid to the vapour state without change of temperature.
- The latent heat of steam is 2260000 J/kg or 2260 J/g.
- Each gram of ice that melts abrosbs 336 J of heat.
- Scalding (burning) with steam is more severe than that caused by boiling water because steam contains more energy than boiling water at the same temperature.
- Latent heat of vapourisation is maximum at 0°C and decreases on increasing temperature.
- Melting point decreases on adding impurity.
- Boiling point increases on adding impurity.
- Boiling point increases on increasing pressure.
- Bottled drinks are cooled more effectively when surrounded with lumps of ice than with iced water because ice absorbs more heat than does the same amount of iced water.

Evaporation

- Water can change into the vapour state either by boiling or by evaporation at lower temperatures.
- When evaporation takes place at room temperature, the energy required for evaporation is taken from the liquid itself, which cools as a consequence.
- When sweat evaporates from the skin it draws much heat from the body and produces a cooling sensation.
- In summer, water is stored in pitchers for cooling. Water oozes out of the pores of the pitchers and cools on evaporation.
- The rate of evaporation increases with increase in temperature.
- Evaporation increases with increase in surface area.

Refrigerator

- In a refrigerator, cooling is produced by the evaporation of a volatile liquid, freon, inside a copper coil (evaporator), which surrounds the freezer.
- The cooling unit (freezer) in a refrigerator is fitted near the top to cool the whole of the interior.
- A thermostat switch regulates the temperature inside the refrigerator by switching the pump on and off at intervals.

Relative Humidity

- Relative humidity is defined as the ratio of the mass of water vapour in a given volume of air to the mass required for saturating the same volume of air at the same temperature.
- The weather report in newspapers expresses relative humidity as percentage.
- Relative humidity is measured with an instrument called the hygrometer.

Pressure Cooker

- The boiling point of a liquid depends on external pressure.
- When the atmospheric pressure is 76 cm of mercury, water boils at 100°C. But when the pressure is increased, the boiling point of water is raised.
- In a pressure cooker, water boils at temperatures higher than 100°C due to increased pressure. The increased boiling temperature allows water to hold more heat which cooks food faster.
- At higher altitudes, atmospheric pressure is reduced. This lowers the boiling point of water and food takes much longer to cook.

WAVE MOTION

- Wave motion may be defined as the transfer of energy without the net transfer of matter.
- If the particles of the medium vibrate perpendicular to the direction of propagation of wave, the wave is called transverse wave.
- Light waves are transverse waves.
- The terms **crest** and **trough** refer to the highest and the lowest parts of the wave respectively.

- If the particles of the medium vibrate in the direction of propagation of wave, the wave is called longitudinal wave.
- Sound waves are longitudinal waves.
- **Amplitude** is defined as the maximum displacement of the vibrating particle on either side from the equilibrium position.
- The wavelength (λ) of a wave is the distance between adjacent crests (or troughs) in the case of transverse waves, or between adjacent compressions (or rarefactions), in the case of longitudinal waves.
- The frequency (n) of a wave is the number of waves that pass a given point per second.
- The unit of frequency is vibrations/second or hertz (Hz).
- Relation between wavelength, frequency and speed of wave is—

  Speed of wave = Frequency × wavelength

  or $V = n\lambda$

Electromagnetic Wave

- Electromagnetic waves include an enormous range of frequencies—from radio waves with frequencies less than 10^5 Hz to gamma rays having frequencies greater than 10^{20} Hz.
- Visible light is simply electromagnetic radiation in the range of frequencies 4.3×10^{14} to 7×10^{14} Hz.
- All electromagnetic wave have the same speed (3×10^8 m/s) in vacuum. The relation $V = n\lambda$ holds good for all electromagnetic waves.
- If the frequency of radio waves sent out by a radio station is known, the wavelength can be calculated by dividing 3×10^8 m/s by the given frequency.

Radio and Television Transmission

- Radio waves sent out by radio stations are reflected by the ionosphere and can be received anywhere on the earth.
- At night the radio reception improves because the layers of the ionosphere are not exposed to sunlight and are more settled.
- High-frequency waves carrying television signals penetrate the ionosphere and are not received like radio signals.
- The curvature of the earth limits the range of television reception.

Radar

- Radar (Radio detection and ranging) employs high frequency radio waves for detecting objects like ships and aeroplanes.

Microwave Oven

- Microwave oven cooks food using microwaves. Microwaves are generated in the over at a frequency of about 2450 MHz by means of a magnetron.
- In microwave oven, when the waves fall on the food, these are absorbed by water, fats, sugars and certain other molecules whose consequent vibrations produce heat. Since heating occurs inside the food, without warming the surrounding air, the cooking time is greatly reduced.
- In microwave oven, food cannot be cooked in metal vessels because the metal blocks out the microwaves.

LIGHT

- Light is a form of energy which is propagated as electromagnetic waves.
- Light travels fastest.
- Light is a transverse wave.
- Speed of light in vacuum is 3×10^8 m/s.
- Light takes 8 minute 19 second to reach from sun to earth.

Reflection

- When light is incident upon a surface, part of it is reflected. But certain surfaces like mirrors and polished metals reflect almost all the light incident upon them.
- The law of reflection states that the angle of incidence is equal to the angle of reflection.
- An image formed in a plane mirror has the following characteristics—

1. The image is of the same size as the object.
2. It is as far behind the mirror as the object is in front of it.
3. It is virtual.
4. It is laterally inverted, *i.e.,* if a person is wearing a watch on his left hand, the watch appears to be on right hand of the image.

- To see his full image in a plane mirror, a person requires a mirror of at least half of his height.

Inclined Mirror (No. of Images)

- When an object is placed between two inclined mirrors, several images of the object are formed.
- The number of images depends on the angle between the mirrors and can be determined by using the following formula

$$\text{No. of images} = \frac{360}{\text{angle between mirrors}} - 1$$

- If an object is placed between two mirrors inclined at 90°, there will be a total of three images.
- In the case of parallel mirrors, there will be an infinite number of images.
- The Kaleidoscope is a toy in which multiple images are formed by two strips of plane mirrors placed at an angle of 60° inside a tube.

Curved Mirrors

- There are two types of curved spherical mirrors—
  1. Concave Mirror
  2. Convex Mirror
- Curved mirrors are made by depositing vaporized aluminium on a glass surface which would form a part of a sphere.
- Deposition on the outside of the glass makes a concave (or converging) mirror, while deposition on the inside makes a convex (or diverging) mirror.
- Concave mirror can concentrate the sun's radiation falling on it at one point, it can be used as a burning glass.
- Concave mirrors are also used in solar cookers.
- Large concave mirrors are used in reflecting telescopes for observing and photographing distant stars and other heavenly bodies.
- Concave mirror forms a virtual or real image depending on the position of the object. When an object is placed close to the mirror, *i.e.,* at a distance less than the focal length of the mirror the image formed is virtual, erect and larger than the object.
- Concave mirror is also used as a shaving or make-up mirror.
- Small concave mirrors are used by dentists for examining teeth.
- Concave parabolic mirrors are used in searchlight and headlamps of cars.
- Convex mirror always produces virtual images. These images are erect and smaller than the objects.
- Convex mirrors are also used as rear view mirrors in vehicles.

Refraction

- When a ray of light passes from one medium to other it suffers a change in direction at the boundary of separation of two media. This phenomenon is called refraction.
- When a ray of light travels from one medium to another the wavelength and velocity of light change but the frequency does not change.
- When a ray passes from one medium to another optically denser medium, *e.g.,* from air to water or glass, it bends towards the normal. Conversely, a ray passing from water or glass into air is bent away from the normal.
- **Examples of Refraction:**
  - Rivers appear shallow, coin in a beaker filled with water appears raised, due to refraction.

- Another effect of refraction is the apparent upward bending of the immersed portion of a stick when dipped in water.
- The refractive index of a medium = $\frac{\text{speed of light in vacuum}}{\text{speed of light in the medium}}$
- It is due to refraction, produced by the earth's atmosphere, that the sun is visible for several minutes after it has set below the horizon. Thus, atmospheric refraction tends to lengthen the day.
- When the sun (or moon) is near the horizon, it appears elliptical, *i.e.*, with the vertical diameter less than the horizontal diameter. This happens because rays from the lower edge of the sun are bent more then those from the upper edge (Atmospheric Refraction).
- One of the most interesting effects of atmospheric refraction and Mirage is a combined effect of atmospheric refraction and total internal reflection.

Dispersion

- White light consists of seven colours—violet, indigo, blue, green, yellow, orange and red. These colours are called the spectrum of the white light.
- Violet has the minimum wavelength (or maximum frequency) and red the maximum wavelength (or minimum frequency).
- In the vacuum, all colours of white light travel with the same speed but in a transparent medium they have different speeds. Violet travels the slowest through glass while red travels the fastest. This is why it is used as traffic STOP sign throughout the world.
- Due to different speeds, the colours are refracted through different angles and therefore, when a narrow beam of white light passes through a glass prism, it is split up into its constituent colours. This separation of light into colours is called dispersion.
- Dispersion takes place because the light rays of different colours are deviated at different angles, so an angular separation is produced between them.
- The most spectacular illustration of dispersion and total internal reflection is the dispersion.

Colour of Objects

- We see objects because of the light they reflect.
- When a rose is viewed in white light, its petals appear red and the leaves appear green, because the petals reflect the red part of the white light and leaves reflect the green part. The remaining colours are absorbed. When the same rose is viewed in green light, the petals will appear black and the leaves green. In blue or yellow light both the petals and leaves will appear black.
- Red, blue and green are primary colours.

LENSES

- Lenses are used in optical instrument that produce images, *e.g.*, cameras, projectors, telescopes, microscopes, etc. lenses are also used in spectacles to correct defects of vision.
- There are mainly two types of lenses:
  1. Convex or Converging Lens
  2. Concave or Diverging Lens
- If a parallel beam is incident on a convex lens, all the rays, after passing through the lens, converge to a point called the principal focus.
- In the case of a concave lens the rays will spread out after passing through the lens.
- Converging or convex lens is used as a magnifying glass.
- Power of a lens is its capacity to deviate a ray. Power of a lens is measured as the reciprocal of the focal length.

$$P = \frac{1}{f}$$

- SI unit of power of lens is dioptre (D).

- The power of a converging lens is positive and that of a diverging lens is negative.
- If a converging lens is held near an object so that the object lies within the principal focus, an erect, magnified and virtual image will be seen. If the object is outside the principal focus of a converging lens, it forms a real image.
- For all positions of the object, the images formed by diverging (concave) lens are virtual, erect and diminished.

EYE

- The light entering the eye is focused by the eye-lens to form an image on the retina.
- In front of the eye lens is the coloured part of eye, called the iris, which automatically adjusts the size of the pupil to the intensity of light falling on it.
- In bright light the iris automatically shuts tighter, reducing the amount of light entering the pupil. This protects the retina from getting damaged.
- When a person enters a dark room after being in bright light, he is not able to see clearly for a while because the iris is unable to dilate the pupil immediately.
- Least distance of distinct vision is 25 cm.

Defects of Vision

- A person suffering from long sight (hypermetropia) can clearly see objects at infinity but cannot see near objects clearly. This defect is caused by the eyeball being too short and can be corrected by wearing converging lenses.
- In the case of a person suffering from short sight (myopia), the eye ball is too long and distant objects are focused in front of the retina. This defect can be corrected by wearing diverging lenses.
- **Astigmatism:** Curvature of cornea becomes irregular and image is not clear. Cylindrical lens is used.
- With advancing age, people lose their power of accommodation and cannot focus near objects. Such people wear spectacles with converging lenses for reading and writing etc.

Scattering of Light

- When light falls on atoms and molecules, it is scattered in all directions.
- Scattering of light is maximum for violet colour and minimum for red colour.
- Blue colour of sky is due to scattering of light.
- In the evening, the sun is lower in the sky and its light has to traverse a longer path through the atmosphere to reach an observer. Thus, at sunset, blue, green and other colours having been scattered only red and some orange light reach us and the sun appears a deep orange-red.
- In outerspace, *i.e.,* beyond the atmosphere, then is nothing to scatter the sunlight and therefore the sky appears dark and stars are visible even in the presence of the sun.

Interference of Light

- The superposition of two (or more) waves of the same kind that pass the same point in space at the same time is called interference.
- Beautiful colours seen in soap bubbles and oil films on water are produced due to the interference of white light reflected by these surfaces.
- LASER (Light Amplification by Stimulated Emission of Radiation) is an optical device which produces an intense beam of coherent monochromatic light.
- **Examples of Interference of Light:** Holography, Laser.

Diffraction of Light

- When a beam of light passes through a narrow slit or an aperture, it spreads out to a certain extent into the region of geometrical shadow. This is an example of diffraction, *i.e.,* of the failure of light to travel in a straight line.

SOUND

- Sound waves are longitudinal and cannot travel in vacuum. The transmission of sound requires a medium: air, liquid or solid.
- The longitudinal mechanical waves which lie in the frequency range 20 Hz to 20,000 Hz are called audible or sound waves. These waves are sensitive to human ear.
- The longitudinal mechanical waves having frequencies less than 20 Hz are called Infrasonic. These waves are produced by sources of bigger size such as earthquakes, volcanic eruptions, ocean waves etc.
- The longitudinal waves having frequencies greater than 20,000 Hz are called ultrasonic waves. Human ear cannot detect these waves. But some animals such as cats, dogs, bats can detect these waves.

Pitch and Frequency

- The pitch (shrillness of a sound depends on its frequency.
- A sound of higher frequency has a higher pitch.
- The pitch of a woman's voice is higher than that of a man.

Loudness

- The loudness of sound is related to the energy of the waves and depends on amplitude.
- The relative loudness of sound is measured in decibels (db).
- All stringed instruments, such as the violin, sitar, guitar, etc. have sound boxes attached to increase the loudness.

Speed of Sound

- The pitch and loudness of sound have no effect on their speed.
- The presence of water vapour in the air increases the speed of sound.
- Sound travels faster through warm air than through cold air. The speed of sound is higher on a hot day than on a cold day.
- The speed of sound in air increases by 0.61 metre per second for each degree rise in temperature above 0°C.

In Different Medium

S.No.	Medium	Speed (m/s)
1.	Air	331
2.	Water	1450
3.	Steel	5000

- Thunder is heard much after the flash of lighting is seen because of the wide difference in the speeds of light and sound.

Reflection of Sound

- When a sound wave is reflected by a distant obstacle, such as a wall or a cliff, an echo is heard.
- To hear echo, the minimum distance between the observer and reflector should be 17 m.
- Exploration of underwater gas and oil is done by detecting the echoes of shock waves produced by explosions on the water surface.
- Echoes of ultrasonic waves are used for measuring the depth of sea-beds or locating submerged objects. An apparatus called Sonar (Sound Navigation Ranging) is used for this purpose.
- Bats emit ultrasonic waves of frequencies up to 80,000 Hz and use the reflection of these waves (echoes) to determine the presence and distance of objects on their way and from them respectively.

Resonance

- If the frequency of imposed periodic force is equal to the natural frequency of a body, the body oscillates with a very large amplitude. This phenomenon is called resonance.
- Sometimes the amplitudes that result from resonance can be disastrous. While crossing a suspension bridge soldiers are ordered to break step as otherwise the resonant vibrations caused by their marching can severely damage the bridge.

Doppler Effect

- The Doppler effect is the change in frequency of a wave (sound or light) due to the motion of the source or observer.
- It is due to the Doppler effect that the whistle of a train appears shriller when it approaches a listener than when it moves away from him.

ELECTRICITY

- Electricity produced by friction between two dissimilar objects is known as static electricity. Depending on the nature of the objects, one acquires a positive charge and the other an equal negative charge. For example, if a glass rod is rubbed with silk, the rod acquires positive charge and the silk an equal negative charge.
- When a hollow metallic conductor is charged with static electricity it is found experimentally that the charge resides entirely on the outside of the conductor; the inner surface remains uncharged.
- If a car is struck by lighting, persons sitting inside are shielded from the electricity and not harmed at all since the charge remains on the outer surface and may arc to the ground through the lowest metallic part of the car.
- **Lightning** is a gigantic electric discharge occurring between two charged clouds or between a charged cloud and the earth.

Conductor

- Conductors are those materials which allow electricity (charge) to pass through themselves.
- Metals conduct electricity because they have a large number of conduction or free electrons.

Insulators

- Insulators are those materials which do not allow electricity to flow through themselves. Insulators have no free electrons.
- Wood, cork, glass and air are poor conductors but good insulators.

Super Conductors

- The resistance of metals to flow of electricity reduces with decreasing temperature. At temperatures near absolute zero, metals have almost zero resistance and became super conductors.

Semi-conductors

- Certain materials, such as silicon and germanium, have electrical resistivity intermediate between those of conductors and insulators. These materials are termed as semi-conductors.
- Semi-conductors are good insulators in their pure crystalline form but their conductivity increases when small amounts of impurities are added to them.

Integrated Circuits (IC)

- An integrated circuit can be defined generally as an arrangement of multifunction semi-conductor devices.
- 'IC chips' for computers are usually made of silicon.

Electric Current

- Electric current is simply the flow of electric charge. In solid conductors the flow of electrons and in fluids the flow of ions as well as electrons constitute the current.
- SI units of electric current is Ampere (A).

Electrical Resistance

- When electric current flows through a conductor, *e.g.*, a metallic wire, it offers some obstruction to the current. This obstruction offered by the wire is called its electrical resistance.
- SI unit of Resistance is Ohm.
- The resistance (R) of a wire of a given material depends on its length (l) and area of cross-section (a)

$$R = P\frac{l}{a}$$

where P is a constant called the resistivity of the material of wire.

Ohm's Law

- If physical conditions like temperature, intensity of light etc. remains unchanged then electric current flowing through a conductor is directly proportional to the potential difference across its ends.

Combination of Resistance

- In series combination, the equivalent resistance is equal to the sum of the resistances of individual conductors. ($R = R_1 + R_2 + ... R_n$)
- In parallel combination, the reciprocal of equivalent resistance is equal to the sum of the reciprocal of individual resistances.

$$\left[\frac{1}{R} = \frac{1}{R_1} + \frac{1}{R_2} + ... + \frac{1}{R_n}\right]$$

Electric Cell

- In a cell, chemical energy is converted into electric energy.
- There are two types of cells—Primary and Secondary.
- In **primary cell** electrical energy is obtained from the irreversible chemical reaction taking place inside the cell.
- Voltaic cell, Leclanche cell, Daniel cell and Dry cell are the examples of primary cell.
- **Secondary cells** are known as storage cells or accumulators. Because of their low internal resistance, secondary cells are capable of giving large currents. Such cells are rechargable.
- Production of electricity by chemical reaction (first source of continuous current) was first discovered by Italian physicist count Alessandro Volta (1745-1827) (Voltaic cell is named after him) in 1794.
- In voltaic cell zinc rod is used as cathode and copper rod is used as anode. These rods are placed in sulphuric acid kept in a glass vessel.
- In a laclanche cell, carbon rod acts as anode and zinc rod acts as cathode. These rods are placed in amonium chloride kept in a glass vessel.
- In a dry cell, mixture of MnO_2, NH_4Cl and carbon is kept in a zinc vesse!. A carbon rod is placed in this mixture which acts as anode. The zinc vessel itself acts as cathode.

Electrolysis

- An electric current passed through a solution results in the decomposition of the solution into negative and positive ions. Negative ions collect at the positive electrode (anode) and the positive ions collect at the negative electrode (cathode). This phenomenon is known as electrolysis.
- Electrolysis is widely used in electroplating, *i.e.,* coating of a base metal with a layer of more expensive metal.

Heating Effect

- When a charge moves in a conductor it does work, which results in heating the conductor. Thus electric energy in the form of electric current is converted into heat energy.
- If the resistance of a wire is R Ohms and the current flowing through it, is I Amperes, the heat produced per second in the wire is I^2R Joules. Heat produced, H, in time *t* is given by

$$H = I^2Rt$$

- The heating effect of electric current is made use of in a variety of appliances, such as a geyser, iron, toaster, oven and room heater. These appliances have coils of nichrome (an alloy of nickel and chromium), which are heated when current is passed.

Electric Motor

- In an electric motor, electrical energy is converted into mechanical energy.
- Electric fans, mixers, washing machines, etc. work on electric motors.

Inverter

- An inverter is a device which converts DC to AC. The inverters used in homes and offices are specially designed to:
  1. Convert DC from a battery to AC, and
  2. Charge the battery.

Ammeter

- Ammeter is a device which is used to measure electric current in a circuit. It is connected in series in the circuit.
- The resistance of an ideal ammeter is zero.

Voltmeter

- Voltmeter is a device used to measure the potential difference between two points in a circuit. It is connected in parallel to the circuit.
- The resistance of an ideal voltmeter is infinite.

Galvanometer

- Galvanometer is a device used to detect and measure electric current in a circuit.
- A galvanometer can be converted into an ammeter by connecting a shunt parallel to it.
- A galvanometer can be converted into voltmeter by connecting a very high resistance in its series.

Transformer

- Transformer is a device which converts low voltage A.C. into high voltage A.C. and high voltage A.C. into low voltage A.C. It is based on electromagnetic induction and can be used only in case of alternating current.

Fuse

- Electric fuse is a protective device used in series with an electric appliance to save it from being damaged due to high current.
- A fuse is a short piece of wire made of a tin-lead alloy, which has a low melting point.
- Fuses are always connected in the live wire.

Incondescent Lamp or Filament Lamp

- An electric lamp produces light energy from electrical energy.
- Electric lamp has a tungsten filament connected between two lead in-wires. When current is passed, the tungsten filament is heated and emits light.
- In electric lamp tungsten is used because it has a high melting point of 3,400°C. The lamp contains a small quantity of organ (an inert gas) to prevent evaporation of tungsten.

Fluorescent Tubes

- A fluorescent tube contains mercury vapours at low pressure. When the tube is switched on, the mercury vapours emit invisible ultraviolet rays. These ultraviolet rays fall on the fluorescent coating on the inside of the tube and emit visible light.

Light-Emitting Diode (LED)

- It is a ritifying semicunductor device that converts electrical energy into light or infrared radiation. LEDs are extensively used for displaying letters and numbers in digital instruments in which a self-luminous display is required.

Cost of Electricity

- The consumption of electrical energy in a house is measured in the unit kWh.
- Kilowatt hour is equal to the energy consumed in the circuit at the rate of 1 kilowatt for 1 hour.

MAGNETISM

- A magnet attracts and holds pieces of iron but does not attract pieces of copper.
- Substances attracted by a magnet are described as magnetic and those not attracted are called as non-magnetic.
- Iron, cobalt, nickel and certain alloys are strongly magnetic whereas copper, wood, glass, etc. are non-magnetic.
- A lodestone is a natural magnet.
- When a bar magnet is suspended with a thread tied exactly in its middle, the magnet oscillates for a little while and then comes to rest pointing approximately in the north-south direction. The end pointing towards the north is called the north-seeking or simply north pole of the magnet and that pointing towards the south is called the south seeking or south pole of the magnet.
- If two bar magnets are brought near each other so that their north poles are close, the magnets repel. If the north pole of one magnet is brought near the south pole of the other; the two attracts.
- Our earth behaves as a powerful magnet whose south pole is near the geographical north pole and whose north pole is near the geographical south pole.
- At a particular place on the earth, the magnetic north is not usually in the direction of the geographic north. The angle between the two directions is called the **declinations.**
- The angle, which a freely suspended bar magnet makes with the horizontal, is called the **dip** of the place. Thus, on the equator, the value of the dip is zero and that on the poles is 90°.

ATOMIC AND NUCLEAR PHYSICS

- Atomic physics deals with the study of the atom.
- Atom consists of three fundamental particles electron, proton and neutron. All the protons and neutrons are present in the central core of atom called nucleus. Electrons revolve around the nucleus.
- Protons and electrons both carry electric charge. Protons have positive charge and electrons negative. Neutrons have no charge.
- Protons and neutrons are dumped together.

Properties of Fundamental Particles

S.No.	Particle	Mass (Kg)	Charge (Coulomb)	Discoverer
1.	Proton	1.672×10^{-27}	$+1.6 \times 10^{-19}$	Ernest Rutherford
2.	Neutron	1.675×10^{-27}	neutral	James Chadwick
3.	Elect	9.108×10^{-31}	-1.6×10^{-19}	J.J. Thomson

- The total number of protons in the nucleus is called atomic number (Z).
- The total number of proton and neutrons in the nucleus is called mass number (A).
- Ernest Rutherford, discovered nucleus by the scattering of α-particles from gold foil.

RADIOACTIVITY

- Henry Bacquerel (1896) observed that a photographic plate blackened, when placed near double sulphate of potassium and uranium. He further observed that uranium emitted special kind of rays. They were called Becqueral rays.
- Pierre and Marie Curie observed that the radiation from pitchblende was four times stronger than uranium. In 1898, they finally discovered two new substances—Polonium and Radium. These newly discovered substances were called radioactive substances and this property of these substances was named radioactivity.
- All nuclei having 83 or more protons are unstable. In order to achieve greater stability, these unstable nuclei disintegrate spontaneously with emission of alpha (α), beta (β) and gamma (γ) rays.
- Alpha rays are positively charged helium nuclei, beta rays are negatively charged electrons and gamma rays are chargeless photons.
- No radioactive substance emits both α and β particles simultaneously. Some substances emit α-particles while some other emit β-particles. γ-rays are emitted along with both α- and β-particles.
- The effect on the mass number and atomic number with the emission of α, β and γ rays is decided by Group-displacement law or **Sody-Fajan Law.**

X-RAYS

- X-rays are electromagnetic radiations having wavelength from a fraction of an Angestrom to about 100 Å. They were discovered by Rontgen during his studies on the electrical discharge phenomena in gases—he found that an unknown radiation was produced when electrons collided with the walls of the tubes.

Properties of X-Rays

1. They ionize the material through which they pass.
2. The affect photographic plates in the same manner as visible light.
3. They penetrate matter and are obsorbed as they pass through it.

Half-Life

- The half-life of a radioactive element is defined as the time taken for half of the number of atoms of the element to disintegrate.

CHEMISTRY

ELEMENTS

- An element may be defined as a substance which is made by same type of atoms and it can neither be broken into, nor built from two or more simpler substances by any known physical or chemical methods, *e.g.*, copper, silver, hydrogen, carbon, oxygen, nitrogen, gold, iron etc.

COMPOUNDS

- A compound may be defined as a substance which contains two or more elements combined in some fixed proportion by weight and which can be decomposed into two or more elements by any suitable method.
- The properties of a compound are entirely different from those of the elements from which it is made.
- Some common examples of compounds are water, sugar, salt, aspirin, chloroform, alcohol and ether.

MIXTURES

- A material containing two or more elements or compounds in any proportion is a mixture.
- The components of a mixture can be separated by physical means like filtration, sublimation and distillation.

SEPARATION OF MIXTURES

Sublimation

In this process, a solid substance passes directly into its vapours on application of heat. The vapours when cooled, give back the original substance. This method can be used for substances which are sublimable in their separation from non-sublimable materials.

- Some examples of compounds that are sublimable are naphthalene, iodine and ammonium chloride.

Sedimentation and Decantation

This method is used when one component is a liquid and other an insoluble solid.

Crystallisation

This method is based on the difference in solubility of the various compounds in a solvent, *e.g.*, mixture of KNO_3 and NaCl can be separated by this process.

- For the separation of more complex mixtures, fractional crystallisation is used, in which the components of the mixture crystalline out at different intervals of time.

Filtration

This is a process for quick and complete removal of solid suspended particles from a liquid (or gas) by passing the suspension through a filter.

- The industrial and common applications of this process are purification of the domestic water supply by filtering river water through a layer of sand and gravel in a filter fed; removal of solid particles in the engine oil in car engines by air filters; filtration of tea from tea leaves in the preparation of tea, etc.

Distillation

The conversion of a liquid into its vapour on heating and then cooling the vapour back into the liquid is called distillation. In this process, both evaporation and condensation to the place.

Fractional Distillation

The process is used if both the components of a mixture are volatile. It is based on the difference of boiling points.

- The industrial applications of fractional distillation are: separation of petrol, diesel oil, kerosene oil, heavy oil, etc. from crude petroleum; separation of oxygen, nitrogen, inert gases and carbon dioxide from liquid air.

Chromatography

This is the most versatile separation method which can be applied to solid, liquid or gas. This process is used to separate and identify substances. In this method the components of a mixture are adsorbed on a suitable adsorbent at different rates and thus get separated. Some common examples are the separation of coloured materials from green vegetables, ink and the plants.

ATOMIC STRUCTURE

Atom

- Atom is the smallest part of the element that takes part in a chemical reaction. Atom of an element can not be changed into that of another element by a chemical or physical means. It odes not exist in free state.

Molecule

- A molecule is the smallest part of an element or compound that is capable of existing independently.

Atomic Weight (or Atomic Mass)

- The atomic mass of an element is the number of times its atom is heavier than 1/12th of the mass of carbon (C^{12}) atom.
- The unit used to measure atomic mass called atomic mass unit, *i.e.*, amu.

Molecular Weight

Molecular weight of a substance is the number which represents how many times a molecule of that substance is heavier than $\frac{1}{12}$th of an atom of C^{12} isotope.

Mole

- One mole is equal to the number of atoms present in 12 g of C^{12} isotope.
- 4 mole = 6.022×10^{23}
  Here 6.022×10^{23} is known as Avogadro's number.

Atomic Number

- Number of proton present in the nucleus of an atom is known as atomic number (z).

Atomic Mass and Mass Number

- The sum of number of proton and neutron present in the nucleus of an atom is known as atomic mass or mass number.

Electron

- The electron is a fundamental particle of an atom which carries a unit negative charge. It was discovered by J.J. Thomson in 1897.

Proton

- It is a fundamental particle of an atom carrying a unit positive charge. It was discovered by Rutherford and Goldstein in 1886.

Neutron

- It is a fundamental particle of an atom carrying no charge. It was discovered by Chadwick in 1932.

Isotopes

- The atoms of the same element having different mass numbers are called isotopes.
- Isotopes have same atomic numbers (hence, same number of electrons and protons) but different mass numbers because they differ in the number of neutrons that they contain, *e.g.*, hydrogen has three isotopes, that is Protium, Deuterium and Tritium.

Isobars

- Elements having the same atomic mass but differ in atomic number are called isobars.

Isotones

- Elements having the same number of neutrons are called isotones.

Quantum Numbers

- The set of four numbers which give complete information about the electron in an atom, *i.e.*, energy, angular momentum, orientation and spin of electron as well as the size and shape of orbit and orbital respectively.

Quantum Numbers

1. **Principal Quantum Number** (n)
   - It gives the major energy level to which the electron belongs. Thus, $n = 1, 2, 3$ ..... etc. depending upon whether the electron belongs to first, second, third etc. energy levels.
2. **Azimuthal Quantum Number** (l)
   - It gives the energy level of subshells.
   - It also gives the following information—
     (*a*) Shapes of subshells.
     (*b*) Number of subshells present within a main shell.
     (*c*) Contribution of energy due to angular momentum towards the total energy of the electron.
   - For a given value of n, l can have values from 0 to $(n - 1)$.
3. **Magnetic Quantum Number** (m)
   - It tells the number of orbitals present within the same subshell. For a given value of l, m can have values from $-l$ to $+l$ including zero, making a total of $(2l + 1)$ values. These quantum numbers also give the orientation of the orbital. The number of orbital in a shell with principal quantum number n is equal to n^2.
4. **Spin Quantum Number** (s)
   - This arises due to the spinning of the electron about its own axis. It can be clockwise represented by $+\frac{1}{2}$ or ↑ or anti-clockwise represented by $-\frac{1}{2}$ or ↓. This is the only quantum number that has non-integral values.

Pauli's Exclusion Principle

- It states that "No two electrons in an atom can have the same set of four quantum numbers." In other words "An orbital can have a maximum two electrons and these must have opposite signs."

Aufbau Principle

- It states that "Orbital of lowest energy is filled first, before the filling of orbitals having a higher energy states following $(n + l)$ rule.

$(n + l)$ Rule

- Lower the value of $(n + l)$ for an orbital, the lower is its energy. If two orbitals have the same $(n + l)$ value, the orbital with lower value of n has lower energy and hence is filled first.

Hund's Rule of Maximum Multiplicity

- It states that "Electron pairing in any orbital (s, p, d, f) cannot take place until each orbital of the same sublevel contains one electron."

Dalton's Atomic Theory

- Dalton proposed his atomic theory in 1808, according to which—
  1. Matter is made up of extremely small particles called atoms.
  2. The atom can neither be created nor destroyed.
  3. The atoms of a particular element are similar in all respects and have the same mass. The atoms of an element remain unchanged in all chemical processes.
  4. The atoms of different elements differ from each other and have different masses.
  5. In a chemical reaction between two or more elements, the atoms of these elements combine to form compound atoms of molecules.

Rutherford's Atomic Model

- Rutherford proposed the atomic model in the following manner:
  1. Most of the mass and all of the positive charge of an atom is present in a very

small region called the 'nucleus' of the atom.

2. The magnitude of the charge on the nucleus is different in atoms of different elements.
3. There are electrons outside the nucleus and their number is equal to the number of the units of positive charge in the nucleus. The electrons revolve around the nucleus in 'orbits' or 'shells' have different energy levels.

Thomson's Atomic Model

- J.J. Thomson proposed a model of atomic structure according to which an atom consists of a positively charged sphere where the charge is distributed uniformly over the entire body of the atom. The electrons are embedded in the positively charged body just like seeds in a water melon. The number of electrons is sufficient so that the atom as a whole is electrically neutral.

PERIODIC TABLE

Mandeleev's Periodic Law

- Physical and Chemical properties of the elements are the periodic function of their atomic weights.

Modern Periodic Law

- The physical and chemical properties of the elements are a periodic function of their atomic numbers.

Main Features of Modern Periodic Table

- It has 7 horizontal rows called periods and 18 vertical columns called groups or families.
- The first period is the shortest period consisting of 2 elements.
- The elements of second period are known as bridge elements.
- The elements of XVIII group are known as inert gases or noble gases.
- The elements of III group to XII group are known as transition elements.

CHEMICAL BONDING

- The chemical reactions between atoms of different elements take place as a result of bond formation between them to give new molecules. When two or more atoms come together and react with each other, a chemical bond of some kind is formed between them. This bond is formed between the electrons in the outermost orbit of the atom (only electrons of the outermost orbit take part in chemical reactions and chemical bonding).
- There are three types of bond—
  1. Electrovalent Bond
  2. Covalent Bond
  3. Co-ordinate Bond

Electrovalent Bond

- When a bond is formed by the complete transfer of electron known as ionic or electrovalent bond.
- These types of bonds are mainly formed between metals and non-metals.

Covalent Bond

- When a bond is formed by the mutual sharing of electron is known as covalent bond.
- This type of bond is mainly formed between non-metals.

Co-ordinate or Dative or Semipolar Bond

- A special type of covalent bond in which a pair of electron is donated by one atom only called co-ordinate bond.
- This bond is also called as semipolar bond since, it involves electrovalency and covalency both.

OXIDATION AND REDUCTION

- Oxidation is a process in which a substance adds on oxygen or loses hydrogen. In modern terms, oxidation is the process in which a substance loses electrons.
- Reduction is a process in which a substance adds on hydrogen or loses oxygen. In modern terms, reduction is the process in which a substance gains electrons.

- Oxidation and reduction always occur simultaneously. If one substance is oxidised, another is reduced. The reaction in which this oxidation-reduction process occurs is called a redox reaction.
- Oxidising agents are substances which bring about the oxidation of other substances, *e.g.* Potassium Permanganate, Potassium Dichromate, Nitric Acid, Hydrogen Peroxide, etc.
- Reducing agents are substances which bring about the reduction of other substances, *e.g.* hydrogen sulphide, hydrogen, carbon, sulphur dioxide, etc.

ACIDS, BASES AND SALTS

Acids

- An acid is any compound that can react with a base to form a salt, the hydrogen of the acid being replaced by positive metallic ion. According to modern theory, an acid is a compound which yields hydrogen ions (protons) to a base in a chemical reaction. In a water solution, an acid tastes sour, turns blue litmus red and produces free hydrogen ions.

S. No.	Acid	Sources
1.	Citric acid	Lemons or Oranges (Citrus Fruits)
2.	Lactic acid	Sour milk
3.	Tartaric acid	Grapes
4.	Acetic acid	Vinegar
5.	Maleic acid	Apples
6.	Oxalic acid	Tomato
7.	Formic acid	Red ants

Bases

- Such compounds which gives salt and water with acid known as bases. Bitter in taste, turns red litmus paper into blue, contains replaceable hydroxyl group.
- Some important bases are sodium hydroxide, potassium hydroxide, sodium carbonate and ammonium hydroxide.
- An alkali is a basse which is soluble in maters.
- All alkalies are bases but all bases are not alkalies because all bases are not soluble in water.

Salts

- Salts are ionic compounds containing a positive ion (cation) and a negative ion (anion).

Neutralisation

- When an acid reacts with a base, a salt and water are formed. This reaction is called neutralization since the acid and base neutralize each other's effect.

pH Scale

- pH is a scale of acidity and alkalinity.
- pH scale is defined as the negative logarithm of the hydrogen ion concentration in grass ion per litre of a solution.

$$pH = -\log_{10}[H^+]$$

- The acidities and basicities of compounds are denoted by the pH values of their aqueous solutions.
- pH value is just a number (from 0 to 14) without any units.
- A solution with a pH between 0 and 6.99 is acidic, while any solution with pH between 7.01 and 14 is basic.
- A solution with a pH of 7 is neutral.

Buffer Solution

- A solution whose pH is not changed even by in addition of strong acid or base known as buffer solution.

ELECTROLYSIS

- The process of decomposition of an electrolyte by the passage of an electric current through its molten state or its aqueous solution is called electrolysis.
- Device through which electric current is passed known as electrodes.

Anode

- Positively charged electrode is known as anode.
- It is impure metal and thick rod.
- Loss of electron takes place at anode (oxidation).

Cathode

- Negatively charged electrode is known as cathode.
- It is pure rod and thin.
- Reduction takes place at Cathode (gain of electron)

Ions

- Electrically charged particles are called ions.
- Cations are positively charged ions.
- Anions are negatively charged ions.

CARBON AND ITS COMPOUNDS

Allotropy

- Such substances which having the same chemical properties, but differ in physical properties, known as allotropes and this property is called allotropy.

Diamond

- Diamond is the purest form of carbon.
- It is non-conductor of heat and electricity.
- It is the hardest natural substance.
- It burns in air at 900°C and gives out CO_2.

Graphite (Black Lead)

- It is good conductor of heat and electricity.
- Graphite is used in making lead pencils.
- Graphite is also used as electrodes, lubricant, moderators, electrotyping and carbon arc.

Amorphous Forms of Carbon

1. Wood Charcoal – Obtained from wood
2. Sugar Charcoal – Obtained from cane sugar
3. Bone or Animal Charcoal – Obtained from animal bones
4. Coke Charcoal – Obtained from coal

Carbon Monoxide (CO)

- Carbon monoxide is an active poison and is very dangerous as it is a colourless and odourless gas and cannot, therefore, be easily detected.
- The extremely poisonous nature of carbon monoxide is a result of its combining with the haemoglobin of the blood to form carboxyhaemoglobin, which is not decompassed by any of the processes in the body. Its formation thus stops the regular activity of haemoglobin of combining with oxygen and carrying it to the tissues.

HYDROCARBONS

- Compounds of carbon and hydrogen are called hydrocarbon.
- A natural source of hydrocarbon is petroleum obtained from sedimentary rocks.
- Compounds having the same molecular formula but differ in properties due to different structural formula known as isomers and this property is called isomerism.

Examples: C_4H_{10} have following two structures:

$CH_3 - CH_2 - CH_2 - CH_3$

n-butane

$$\begin{array}{c} CH_3 \\ | \\ CH_3 - CH - CH_3 \end{array}$$

isobutane

- On the basis of type of bonds present in the hydrocarbons, they are classified as—
  1. Saturated Hydrocarbon
  2. Unsaturated Hydrocarbon

Saturated Hydrocarbons (Alkanes)

- Containing single covalent bonds only.
- Such compounds are, in general, called alkanes for instance, Methane, Ethane, Propane, Butane.

Unsaturated Hydrocarbons

- Containing multiple bonds.
- Compounds with double bonds are called alkenes, *e.g.*, ethylene, propyene etc. and triple bond containing compounds are called alkynes, *e.g.*, acetylene, propyne etc.
- Benzene is an unsaturated cyclic hydrocarbon with the structure.
- Compounds derived from benzene are called aromatic compounds.

FUELS

Solid Fuels

- These contain carbon and, during combustion, form mainly carbon dioxide and carbon monoxide with a large amount of heat.

- Examples of solid fuels are wood, coal, coke and paraffin wax.

Liquid Fuels

- These are basically mixtures of several hydrocarbons. During combustion, they form carbon dioxide and water.
- Liquid fuels are obtained as different fractions during the distillation of petroleum.
- Examples of liquid fuels are kerosene oil, petrol, diesel oil and alcohol.

Gaseous Fuels

- Gaseous fuels do not leave ash on burning and have high content of heat.
- The main gaseous fuels are liquefied petroleum gas (LPG, mainly a mixture of propane and butane and used in homes for cooking, water gas ($CO + H_2$), producer gas ($CO + N_2$), coal gas (mixture of hydrogen, methane ethylene, carbon monoxide, nitrogen, oxygen and carbon dioxide) and natural gas (mixture of methane, ethane, propane and butane with traces of higher hydrocarbons obtained from oil well, above petroleum).

METALLURGY

- Metals occur in nature, in the native (in free state) as well as in the combined state.
- Naturally occurring materials containing metals are called minerals.
- A mineral from which a given metal is obtained economically is called an ore.
- The process of extraction of a metal in a pure state on a large scale from its ore by Physical and Chemical means is called metallurgy.
- The rocky and siliceous matter that associated with the ore is known as gauge.
- Substance that is added to ore to remove the gangue is known as flux.
- The process of removal of gangue from the ore is known as concentration.
- Calcination is the heating of the ore in the absence of air. This method is employed for obtaining the metal oxides from carbonates and hydroxides.
- Roasting is the heating of the ore in the presence of air. On roasting, part of the ore is oxidised to form an oxide. This oxide is then reduced to the metal.
- The industrial reduction process for obtaining metal from the treated ore is called smelting.

AMALGUM

- An alloy in which one of the component metals is mercury is known as amalgum.

PETROLEUM AND NATURAL GAS

- Natural gas contains about 80% methane and 10% ethane, the remaining 10% being a mixture of higher gaseous hydrocarbons.
- Compressed Natural Gas (CNG) is natural gas filled in cylinders under high pressure.
- The refining of crude oil involves separation into fractions with different boiling points.
- All chemicals derived from petroleum fractions are called petrochemicals.
- The quality of petrol for use in car engines is denoted by their anti-knock properties. The anti-knock property of petrol samples are measured by the values of their octane numbers. The higher the octane number of a petrol sample, the more anti-knocking property it has and more useful it is.
- To increase octane number, tetra ethyl lead (TEL) is added to petrol.

IRON AND STEEL

- Iron is extracted from its ores by the blast furnace process.
- Iron obtained from blast furnace is called pig iron or cast iron containing about 5% carbon.
- Pure iron is called wrought iron which does not contain carbon more than 0.2%, or any other impurities or constituents.
- Steel contains 0.25% – 2% carbon and varying amounts of other elements. Depending upon the carbon content and other metals present in it, different varieties of steel are classified as chrome steel, tungsten steel, stainless steel, manganese steel and nickel steel.

- Stainless steel contains 18% chromium and nickel.

Rusting of Iron

- If iron objects are left exposed to the atmosphere, they are covered with a brown powdery layer known as rust. This process is called rusting or corrosion. The brown powdery material is a mixture of ferric hydroxide and ferric oxide, formed as a result of the oxidation of iron in the presence of oxygen and moisture present in the air.

WATER

- Chemically heavy water is deuterium oxide.
- Heavy water is used in nuclear reactors as a moderator because it slows the fast moving neutrons.

Hard and Soft Water

- Water which produces lather with soap solution readily is called soft water.
- Water which does not produce lather with soap solution readily is called hard water.
- The hardness of water is due to presence of the bicarbonates, chlorides and sulphates of calcium and magnesium.
- Temporary hardness of water is due to the presence of bicarbonates of calcium and magnesium.
- Permanent hardness of water is due to presence of bicarbonates of calcium and magnesium.

GLASS

- Ordinary glass is solid mixture of silica, sodium silicate and calcium silicate.
- Soft glass is a soda-lime silicate glass. It melts at low temperature. It is used in manufacturing of bottles, test tubes etc.
- Hard glass is potash lime silicate and melts at high temperature in comparison to soft glass and is used in manufacturing of flask etc.
- Flint glass is a lead potash silicate and is used in manufacturing of prism and lens optical instruments.
- Pyrex glass is a mixture of sodium aluminium borosilicates. It is used in manufacturing of high quality equipments in laboratory because it does not melt at very high temperature.
- Safety glass is prepared by placing a layer of transparent plastic glass between two layers of glass by means of a suitable adhesive. It is used in making wind screen of automobiles, aeroplanes, trains etc.

CEMENT

- The approximate composition of Portland cement is:
  1. Calcium Oxide → 62%
  2. Silica → 22%
  3. Alumina → 7.5%
  4. Magnesia → 2.5%
  5. Ferric Oxide → 2.5%
- A small amount of gypsum is added to slow down the setting of cement.
- Cement containing excess amount of lime cracks during setting while cement containing less amount of lime is weak in strength.
- Cement containing no iron is white but hard to burn.
- Cement with excess of silica shows slow setting and that having an excess of alumina shows quick setting.
- Concrete is a mixture of cement, sand, gravel and approximate amount of water.

COMMON DRUGS

Analgesics

- These are drugs used for relieving pain, aspirin, paracetamol and some other antipyretics act as analgesics.
- Certain narcotics are also used as analgesics, *e.g.*, morphine, marijuana, coceine and heroin.

Antibiotics

- These are chemotherapeutic substances which are obtained as metabolic products from some specific organisms (bacteria, fungi and moulds) and can be used to kill or inhibit the growth of other micro-organisms.

- The first of the antibiotics discovered was penicillin by Alexander Fleming in 1929.

Antipyretics

- Antipyretics are substances used to bring down body temperature during high fever. Common examples are aspirin, phenacetin, paracetamol and novalgin.

Antiseptics

- These are chemicals that prevent growth of micro-organisms or kill them, but are safe to be applied to living human tissues. They can be applied on wounds, ulcers and diseased skin surfaces.
- Chlorine is used for making water fit for drinking.
- Low concentrations of sulphur dioxide are used for sterilizing squashes for preservation.
- Commonly used antiseptic-detol is a mixture of chloroxylenol and terpeneol in a suitable solvent.
- Bithional is added to soap to impart antiseptic properties, it also reduces undesirable odour.
- Tranquilizers are drugs used for the treatment of mental diseases.

POLYMERS AND PLASTICS

- A polymer is a large molecule, built up from many hundreds of thousands of small unit called monomeric units or monomers.
- The process of formation of polymers from monomers is called polymerization.
- Plastics are cross-linked polymers and very tough.
- Some examples of plastics are — Celluloid, Bakelite and Vinyl Plastics.

Rubber

- Natural and Synthetic rubbers are examples of polymers.
- Natural rubber is isomer of isoprene.
- When the natural rubber is heated along with sulphur called vulcanisation. The resulting rubber is elastic, hard and strong.
- Synthetic rubbers are made by polymerisation of chloroprene, styrene and butadiene mixtures and isobutylene.

DYES

- Coloured substances used for colouring textiles, foodstuffs, silk, wool etc. are called dyes. But all coloured substances are not dyes. For a substance to act as a dye, it most fulfil the following requirements:

  It must have a suitable attractive colour, *i.e.*, it should absorb light in the visible region; it must be able to fix itself to the fabrics by either physical or chemical bonding; it must be fast to light; it must not be affected either by water, dilute acids or alkalies.
- Nitro dyes are polynitro derivatives of phenol when nitro group acts as a chromophore and hydroxyl group as auxochrome.
- Azo dyes are an important class of dyes and are characterised by the presence of azo group ($-N \equiv N-$) as the chromophore. The groups like NH_2, NR_2 or $-OH$, etc., present in the molecule containing one or more azo groups act as the auxochromes.

SOAPS

- The soaps are sodium salts of higher fatty acids. They are useful only in soft water as they form an insoluble precipitate in hard water. This precipitate consists of salts of calcium and magnesium of higher fatty acids. No lather or emulsion is formed and washing is not possible.
- Detergents are sodium salts of alkyl or aryl sulphonic acids or sulphonates of aliphatic alcohols. Detergents can be used for washing purposes even in hard water as the calcium and magnesium salts of sulphonic acids are water soluble.

BIOLOGY

The term *biology* derived from the Greek work, bios, "life" and the suffix-*logia*, "study of." **Biology** is a natural science concerned with the study of life and living organisms.

BRANCHES OF BIOLOGY

Apiculture	Culture of Bee
Cytology	Study of Cells
Dermatology	Study of Skin
Entomology	Study of Insects
Evolution	Study of Origin of new from old
Floriculture	Study of Flower Yielding Plants
Genetics	Study of heredity and Variations
Gynaecology	Study of Female Reproductive Organ
Horticulture	Study of Garden Cultivation
Haematology	Study of Blood
Mycology	Study of Fungi
Nephrology	Study of Kidneys
Neurology	Study of Nervous System
Obstetrics	Branch of Medicine Dealing with Pregnancy
Ophthalmology	Study of Eyes
Ornithology	Study of Birds
Osteology	Study of Bones
Palaeontology	Study of Fossils
Phycology	Study of Algae
Pisciculture	Study of Fish
Pomology	Study of Fruits
Sericulture	Culture of Silk Moth and Pupa
Serpentology	Study of Snakes
Virology	Study of Virus

CELL

1. **Cell Membrane:** Cells are enclosed by a thin film like membrane called plasma membrane, cytoplasmic membrane or plasma lemma.

   Endocytosis: Taking substance inside the cell by the plasma membrane. It is of two types : *Phagocytosis* : Cell Eating. *Pinocytosis* : Cell drinking. *Exocytosis:* Reverse of Endocytosis.

2. **Cytoplasm:** It is a part of protoplasm lying between plasma membrane and nucleus.
3. **Cell Wall :** Cells of most fungi, prokaryotes (bacteria and blue - green algae) and plants (except gametes) are surrounded by the cell wall. It is absent in animals.
4. **Nucleus:** Discovered by Robert Brown. Nucleus controls the metabolic activities of the cell by controlling the synthesis of enzymes.
   - Contains nucleoplasm (nuclear sap) which contains chromatin.
   - Chromatin organizes itself into thread like structures called Chromosomes.
   - The function of chromosomes is to carry genetic information from one cell generation to another.
   - Nucleolus is also present which helps in the production of ribosomes.
5. **Chromosomes :** Waldeyer coined the term chromosome. Each chromosome is made up of DNA.
   - Chromosome number is constant for a particular species. Diploid number (2n) of chromosomes are present in somatic cells and haploid number (n) of chromosomes are there in gametes.
   - In humans, the diploid number is 46.
6. **Mitochondria :** Powerhouse of the cell and energy is stored as ATP
   - They are semi-autonomous organelles. They contain DNA.

- Mitochondria is enclosed by a double-membraned envelope.

7. **Endoplasmic Reticulum :** Provides an increased surface area for various metabolic activities within the cell. Types: Rough ER and smooth ER.
8. **Golgi Complex :** Main function is secretion. Secretions are in the form of granules in cytoplasm.
9. **Lysosomes :** Also called Suicidal bags. Contain enzymes acid hydrolases which digest worn - out or unnecessary parts of the cell, or even whole cells by process called 'Autophagy'.
10. **Ribosomes :** Made of RNA and proteins in equal amounts. Sites of protein synthesis.
11. **Vacuoles :** Large vacuole found in plant cells. Membrane surrounding the vacuole is tonoplast. Regulation of water, in osmoregulation, in storage and in digestion.
12. **Plastids :** Found only in plant cells.
    - ***Chloroplast :*** Green contains the pigment chlorophyll.
    - ***Leucoplasts :*** Colorless, occur in large no in cells of fruits, seeds, etc. They store nutrients (e.g., amyloplasts of potato store starch).
    - ***Chromoplasts :*** Colored, containing fat soluble yellow, orange and red pigments. Found in flowers and fruits.
13. **Centrosome :** Found in animal cells and cells of lower plants (e.g., Algae) only. The first indication that the cell is about to divide is generally given by the centrosome.

BALANCED DIET

A Balanced Diet comprising of healthy and diverse foods is key to promoting good health. The components of food are:

1. **Carbohydrates:** Constitutes 3 elements : Carbon, Hydrogen and Oxygen. 1 gm gives 17 kJ of energy (or 4.1 kcal of energy). Carbohydrates form a better fuel than proteins and fats because their molecules have relatively more oxygen.
    - Cellulose is present in the cell - wall of plants.
    - D - fructose is the sweetest of sugars. It is found in Fruit Juices, Honey, etc.
    - Excess Sugar is stored as Glycogen in liver.
    - ***Sources of Carbohydrates are :*** Cereals (Wheat, Rice and Maize), Sugarcane, Milk (contains Lactose - a type of Sugar), Fruits, Honey, Beet, etc.
    - ***Types of Carbohydrates:*** **(i) Monosaccharides :** They are the simplest carbohydrates consist of one unit (eg: glucose, fructose, galactose). **(ii) Disaccharides :** Consist of 2 units of monosaccharides (eg : sucrose, lactose and 1 maltose). **(iii) Polysaccharides :** Consist of more than three monosaccharide units (eg: starch in plants and glycogen in animals).
2. **Fats:** Provides twice the energy of carbohydrates (1 gm provides 37 kJ or 9 kcal of energy). Acts as the reserve food material, excess fat is stored in the liver and adipose tissue.
    - ***Types of fatty acids :*** Saturated and Unsaturated. **(i) Saturated Fatty Acids :** Solids at room temperature. **(ii) Unsaturated Fatty Acids :** Liquids at room temperature.
    - Excess of saturated fats increases the blood — cholesterol level and may cause arteriosclerosis (hardening of arteries). This may lead to heart attack.
    - Essential Fatty Acids include Linoleic, Linolenic and Arachidonic Acids are present in Groundnut Oil, Sunflower Oil.
    - ***Hydrogenation :*** Process by which unsaturated fatty acids are converted into saturated fatty acids by the addition of Hydrogen.
3. **Proteins :** Made up of Carbon, Hydrogen, Oxygen, Nitrogen and Sulphur. Important for growth and repair of the body (75% of our body is proteins only).
    - ***Types of Amino acids are: (i)*** **Essential Amino Acids :** They cannot be synthesised in the body. eg. isoleucine, leucine, lysine, methionine, phenylalanine, threonine, tryptophan and valine. ***(ii)*** **Non - Essential Amino Acids :** They are synthesized in the

body. eg. Alanine, Arginine, Asparagine, Aspartic Acid, Cysteine, Glutamine, Glutamic Acid, Glycine, Histidine, Proline, Serine and Tyrosine.

- ***Some important Proteins are: Enzymes:*** eg. Pepsin, Trypsin. **Hormone:** eg. Insulin, Glucogon, **Carrier:** eg. Haemoglobin - Transports O_2 in blood, Myoglobin - Stores O_2 in muscles. **Contractile Proteins:** eg. Actin and Myosin. **Structural Proteins:** eg. Collagen – Component of Bones, Tendons, Cartilage. Keratin – Component of Skin, Feathers, Nails, Hair, Horn. **Protective Proteins:** eg. Gamma globulins. **Visual Proteins** : Rhodopsin and Iodopsin of rods and cones. (present in Retina of the eye).
- ***Protein Energy Malnutrition: (i) Kwashiorkar:*** Due to deficiency of protein. Abdomen and feet swells, Skin becomes Dark and Scaly, Enlarged Liver, Anaemia. ***(ii)*** **Marasmus:** Deficiency of Proteins. Losing of body weight, wasting of muscles, ribs look prominent. (Oedema and skin pigmentation absent).

4. Minerals: Minerals maintain water balance and nutrition in the body

- ***Types of mineral nutritution:*** *(i)* Macro-elements (required in amount more than 1 gm). ***(ii)*** Microelements (required in trace amounts less than 1 gm)

MINERALS REQUIRED IN HUMAN BEINGS

Minerals	Sources	Functions	Deficiency
Macro Elements			
Calcium	Milk, Cheese	Formation of Teeth and Bones	Weak Teeth and Bones
Phosphorus	Milk, Meat, DNA, RNA	Component of ATP, Bones; Retarded Growth	Weak Teeth &
Sulphur	Proteins of Food	Component of Amino Acids	Disturbed Protein Metabolism.
Potassium	Meat, Milk, Cereals, Fruits	Water Regulation.	Weak Muscles; Risk of Paralysis
Chlorine	Table salt	Acid-Base Balance	Loss of Appetite; Muscle Cramps.
Sodium	Table salt	Acid - Base and Water Balances	Low Blood Pressure, Loss of Appetite;
Magnesium	Cereals, Green Vegetables	Cofactor of Enzymes	Affects Nervous Functions.
Iron	Meat, Eggs, Cereals	Component of haemoglobin	Anaemia, Weakness
Iodine	Sea Food, Iodized Salt	Component of Thyroxine	Goitre, Cretinism
Micro Elements			
Flourine	Drinking Water, Tea, Sea Food	Maintenance of Bones and Teeth	Weak Teeth,
Manganese	Dry Fruits, Cereals,	Cofactor of some Enzymes	Irregular Growth of Bones, Cartilages

VITAMINS REQUIRED IN HUMAN BEINGS

Vitamins : Discovered by Funk. It do not provide energy but help in different physiological processes.

Vitamin	Sources	Effect of Deficiency
Water - Soluble Vitamins		
B_1 (Thiamine)	Rice Bran, Whole Wheat Flour	Beri - beri
B_2 (Riboflavin)	Cheese, Eggs, Yeast,	Cheilosis Keratitis of Cornea
B_3 (Nicotinic Acid)	Fresh Meat, Liver, Fish,	Pellagra, Muscle Atrophy,
B_6 (Pyridoxine)	Milk, Cereals, Fish, Meat Liver,	Dermatitis, Convulsions, Nausea, Mental Disorders
B_5 (Pantothenic Acid)	Yeast, Liver, Kidneys, Eggs, Meat,	Dermatitis, Anaemia, Fatigue, Nausea.
H (Biotin)	Yeast, Vegetables, Fruits, Eggs,	Skin Lesions, Loss of Appetite, Hair Fall.
Folic Acid Group	Green Vegetables, Soyabean,	Retarded Growth.
B_{12} (Cyanocobabmine)	Meat, Fish, Liver, Eggs,	Pernicious Anaemia
C (Ascorbic acid)	Lemon, Orange, and	Scurvy
Fat - Soluble Vitamins		
A (Retinol)	Milk, Butter, Egg Yolk, Liver,	Xerophthalmia
D (Cholecalciferol)	Synthesized in skin cells	Rickets, Osteomalacia.
E (Tocopherol)	Green Vegetables	Causes sterility, Muscular dystrophy,
K (Phylloauinone)	Carrots, Lettuce,	Haemorrhages, delayed blood clotting.

DIGESTIVE SYSTEM OF HUMANS

The process of converting food into energy giving substances is carried out by this system.

1. **Buccal Cavity :** In the mouth salivary glands secrete saliva which contains the enzyme Ptyalin
   - ***Teeth :*** They are produced in two sets - Temporary and Permanent. The teeth are of four types : Incisors, Canines, Premolars and Molars.
   - ***Structure of a Tooth :*** A tooth consists of 3 Regions : Crown, Neck and Root. Enamel is the hardest substance in the human body.
   - ***Dental Formula :*** 2123 / 2123, means that there are 2 incisors, 1 canine, 2 Premolars and 3 molars in half of the upper jaw and exactly the same arrangement in half of the lower jaw.
   - In elephants, incisors of the upper jaw grow into huge tusks.
   - Canines are very large in predators such as cat, dog and lion.
   - Rabbit and squirrel lack canines. In walrus, the upper canines are enlarged into projecting tusks.
   - The last molars are called the wisdom teeth.
2. **Pharynx :** Links Buccal Cavity to Oesophagus. Food is carried by peristaltic movement. Trachea opens into Pharynx through an aperture called Glottis.
3. **Oesophagus :** 25 cm Long Tube. Longitudinal folds keep its cavity almost closed, except during swallowing of food.
4. **Stomach :** Oesophagus opens into it. In stomach, the food is called chyme. Has 3 Parts : Fundus, Cardiac and Pyloric. Gastric juices produced in the stomach help in digestion of

food. Also contains HCI which provides acidic medium. Besides it activates pepsinogen to pepsin and prorennin to rennin.

- Ruminents (Cattle, Buffaloes, Goats, Sheep, Deer, Camel) have their stomach consisting of 4 Chambers : Rumen, Reticulum, Omasum and Abomasum.

5. **Small Intestine :** Here the food from the stomach is mixed with bile and pancreatic juice.
   - Duodenum receives the bile - pancreatic duct formed by the union of bile duct and pancreatic duct.
   - Both jejunum and ileum have numerous figure like projections called the villi. The villi contain blood vessels to absorbe digested food.
6. **Large Intestine:** It receives undigested material from the small intestine and absorbs water.
   - Caecum is the diverted part of intestine. Cellulose digestion takes place in it. It is very large in herbivores.
   - Vermiform appendix is a part of caecum. Both caecum and appendix are vestigial in humans.

BLOOD IN HUMAN BODY

Blood is a fluid connective tissue. It is 6.8 litres in man and 500 ml less in woman. 6 - 8% of body weight (pH 7.4)

1. **Red Blood Corpuscles:** Also called Erythrocytes, disc - shaped (for increased Surface Area), no nucleus contains a pigment called Haemoglobin, which gives blood its Red Color.
   - ***Amount of Haemoglobin*** is 14-15.6 gm/100 cc of blood (11 - 14 in woman).
   - Life of RBC is 120 days after which they are broken down in spleen or liver.
   - Product of breakdown of haemoglobin is a pigment (yellow colour), called bilirubin. Retention of bilirubin leads to jaundice.
2. **White Blood Corpuscles:** Also called Leucocytes, rounded, with a nucleus, far less numerous than RBCs, life 3 - 4 days.
   - ***Types :*** Granulocytes (Basophils, Eosinophils, Neutrophils) and Agranulocytes (Monocytes, Lymphocytes)
   - ***Basophils :*** Take up basic stains. Have an S-shaped nucleus. Secrete an anti - coagulant Heparin, which prevents clots within the blood vessels.
   - ***Eosinophils or Acidophils :*** Take up acidic stains. Assists in defence mechanism.
   - ***Neutrophils :*** Most numerous of the WBCs (65 - 70%). Defence.
   - ***Monocytes:*** Largest of all. Very motile. Defence.
   - ***Lymphocytes :*** 25% of the WBC. Takes part in antigen and antibody formation.
3. **Platelets :** Also called Thrombocytes, formed in bone marrow, life 3 - 7 days, sets off blood clotting.

   Plasma (65%) : Watery part of blood, clear, yellow fluid. Contains about 90% water, proteins and organic salts.
   - ***Lymph :*** Lymph = Blood - RBC, i.e., Plasma + WBC. All interchanges of nutrients and waste products between blood and tissue takes place through lymph only.
   - Spleen produces lymph. At the same time it also acts as the graveyard of lymph.

Blood Groupings

- ***Father of Blood Grouping:*** Karl Landsteiner. He discovered A, B and O blood groups in 1900.
- Decastello and Sturle in 1902 discovered AB blood group.
- ABO system of blood groups is based on antigens and antibodies.
- AB: Universal recipient
- O: Universal donor

RH Factor: It is based on Rh antigen. Discovered in 1940 by Landsteiner and A.S. Veiner. It discovered in Rhesus monkey. A person can be Rh+ or Rh-.

- In world population Rh+ are 85% and Rh- are 15% only.
- Blood transfusion technique was first developed by James Blundell in 1825.

EXCRETORY SYSTEM OF HUMANS

Waste materials excreted in animals are of many kinds : Nitrogenous Substances, Carbon - Dioxide, Pigments, Excess Water, etc.

The Nitrogenous Waste can be excreted in the following forms :

- **Ammonia :** Highly Toxic. In aquatic animals (called Ammoniotelic).
- **Urea :** Far less toxic than ammonia In Mammals, Alligators, Turtles (called Ureotelic).
- **Uric Acid :** In animals where conservation of water is needed. In Birds, Insects, Land Reptiles (called Uricotelic).

Excretory System of Mammals

1. **Kidneys :** A kidney is composed of 1.2 million microscopic structural and functional units called nephrons or uriniferous tubules.
2. **Ureters :** Open into Urinary Bladder
3. **Urinary Bladder :** Size depends upon the amount of mine in it (up to 700 - 800 ml).

   The lower part is guarded by 2 Sphinctors : inner involuntary and outer voluntary.
4. **Urethra :** Leads to the exterior. In females, it carries only urine. In males it carries urine as well as spermatic fluid.

Nephron

Functional unit of kidney. It is a long tube differentiated into 4 regions.

1. **Bowman's Capsule :** Contains a globular bunch of capillaries, the glomerulus. In glomerular filtrate: water (99%), inorganic salts, amino acids, fatty acids, glucose, urea, uric acid, hormones, vitamins are present.
2. **Proximal Convoluted Tubule :** Starts from the neck of Bowman's capsule and is highly twisted. Almost whole of the glucose and vitamins, amino acids, Na and K, Ca and Mg and water is absorbed.
3. **Loop of Henle:** U-shaped. Consist of 2 straight limbs: descending and ascending. No water is absorbed in ascending limb.
4. **Distal Convoluted Tubule :** Greatly twisted. Reabsorbs some Na and Cl.Leads to Collecting Tubules which lead to ureters.

   - The yellow colour of urine is caused by the pigment urochrome, which is a breakdown product of haemoglobin from worn out RBCs.
   - The urine gives a pungent smell due to conversion of urea into ammonia by bacteria.
   - Kidney stones: Calcium Oxalate

RESPIRATORY SYSTEM OF HUMANS

I. Anaerobic Respiration : When nutrients are oxidized without using O_2 (also called fermentation). eg. Ascaris, Fasciola, Taenia also respire anaerobically.

It is a low energy yielding process.

II. Aerobic Respiration : Cells utilize O_2 for oxidizing nutrients. It is found in most plants and animals. It involves:

1. **External Respiration:** Gaseous exchange of O_2 and CO_2 between blood and air (or water).
2. **Internal Respiration:** Gaseous exchange between blood and tissues.
3. **Cellular Respiration:** Oxidation of nutrients in the cells and liberation of energy.

ENDOCRINE SYSTEM OF HUMANS

Formed by endocrine glands (or Ductless Glands). They secrete hormones directly into the blood stream.

Hypothalamus : Forms a part of fore - brain, secretes neurohormones, which effect the release of hormones from pituitary.

Pituitary Gland: Also called Master Gland. It is the smallest endocrine gland. It secretes:

1. ***Somatotrophic Hormone :*** Controls the general growth of the body. Hypersecretion leads to acromegaly and gigantism and hyposecretion leads to dwarfness.

2. ***Gonadotrophic Hormone:*** Stimulates the primary sex hormones, *i.e.* ovaries and testes.
3. ***Lactogenic Hormone :*** Initiates milk production in the pregnant females.
4. ***Thyrotrophic Hormone :*** Aids in the regulation of thyroid secretion.
5. ***Adrenocorticotrophic Hormone :*** Influences the secretion from the cortex of adrenal glands.
6. ***Oxytocin or Pitocin :*** Stimulates smooth muscle contractions during child birth. Also helps in the secretion of milk in females.
8. ***Vasopressin (Anti - Diuretic Hormone) :*** Regulates reabsorption of water from the kidney tubules, causing increase in Blood Pressure.

Thyroid Gland : It is the largest endocrine gland located in the neck between the trachea and larynx.

1. ***Thyroxine :*** Regulates physical, mental and sexual development.
   - Poor in iodine is insufficient for the synthesis of thyroxin, leads to simple goitre.
2. ***Thyrocalcitonin :*** It controls the amount of calcium in the body.
   - *Hashimoto Disease :* Due to age factor or injury in thyroid gland secretion of thyroid reduces.

Parathyroid Gland : Secretes Parathormone. It influences calcium and phosphorus metabolism.

Thymus Gland: Situated near the heart. Produces Thymine. Preventing development of gonads.

Pancreas : It is an exocrine as well as an endocrine gland. Its endocrine part is known as Islets of Langerhans. Beta cells secrete Insulin which controls the amount of sugar in the blood.

Adrenal Glands : Consists of 2 Distinct Parts : Outer cortex and inner medulla.

1. Adrenal Medulla secretes Adrenaline or epinephrine which effects liberation of glucose from glycogen stored in liver.
2. Adrenal Cortex secretes two types of Hormones :
   (*a*) ***Mineralo Corticoids :*** Maintain electrolyte balance. Its hyposecretion results in Addison's disease
   (*b*) ***Gluco Corticoids:*** It influences carbohydrate metabolism. Its hypersecretion leads to Cushing Disease.

REPRODUCTIVE SYSTEM OF HUMANS

It is the process by which an individual multiplies in number by producing more individuals of its own type.

I. Asexual Reproduction : Asexual Reproduction is the process of multiplication of individuals without the formation or fusion of gametes.

Binary Fission : It involves the division of the nucleus followed by that of the cytoplasm, breaking the body into two young ones. *e.g.*, Amoeba, Euglena, Paramecium, etc.

II. Sexual Reproduction : The process of sexual reproduction involves the formation and fusion of gametes (Syngamy) and results in the formation of a new organism genetically different from parent.

Mammalian Reproductive System: The reproductive system of sexually reproducing animals consists of:

Sex Organs	Primary Sex Organs	Secondary Sex
Male	Testes	Epididymis, Vas deferens, Ejaculatory duct, Urethra Seminal vesicle Prostate Gland Cowper's gland Penis
Female	Ovary	Fallopian tubes, Uterus, Vagina External Genitalia / Vulva Bartholian's Gland Mammary glands

SENSORY ORGANS OF HUMANS

Eye : Eye is made up of 3 Layers : Upper Sclerotic, Middle Choroids, Inner Retina

1. ***Sclerotic Layer:*** The Transparent bulging, circular part of sclerotic layer which lies in the front is called cornea. Cornea is covered by the thin Conjunctiva.

2. ***Choroid Layer :*** Choroid layer starts from iris which is next to cornea. The circular aperture of iris is called pupil.

- Lens is a proteinous. It is biconvex in nature.

3. ***Retina :*** Image of the object is formed on retina. Retina is composed of 2 types of Cells :

- *Rod Cells :* Sensitive to dim light and contain the pigment Rhodopsin (in nocturnal animals more)
- *Cone Cells :* Color sensitive for 3 primary colors (Red, Blue and Green). They are found more in diurnal animals.

Yellow Spot (Macula Lutea) : On retina, finest image is formed here. Favea centralis is the depression in the middle of yellow spot.

Blind Spot : No image formation takes place here as the optic nerves innervate the eyeball here.

- Cornea is donated in Eye Donation.
- Eyes glow in animals due to tapetum.

Defects of Eye

1. ***Myopia:*** Cannot see distant objects, image formed before retina, concave lens is used.
2. ***Hypermetropia :*** Cannot see near objects, image formed behind retina, convex lens is used.
3. ***Astigmatism :*** Curvature of cornea becomes irregular and image is not clear cylindrical lens is used.
4. ***Cataract :*** Due to defective protein metabolism the lens becomes opaque Operation is needed.
5. ***Gloucoma :*** Due to defect in aqueous humour.
6. ***Presbiopia :*** In this, power of accommodation of lens decreases due to age factor and defected metabolism. Can be removed by bifocal lens.

Ear : Divided into 3 Parts :

1. ***External Ear :*** Pinna + External Auditary Meatus

- Has wax glands which produce cerumen to trap dust particles.

2. ***Middle Ear :*** It encloses 3 Ear Ossicles : Malleus (Hammer - Shaped), Incus (Anvil - Shaped), Stapes (Stirrup - Shaped)

Fanastra Ovalis : Connects middle ear to internal ear. Middle ear is connected to the pharynx by Eustachian tube.

3. ***Internal Ear (Membranous Labyrinth) :*** Most delicate part. Enclosed by parotic bone. It perform two functions : Maintenance of balance and hearing.

- In the internal ear are 3 semi - circular canals and utriculus which are filled with a fluid, endolymph.

DISEASES IN HUMAN

Human Viral Diseases

Chickenpox	Measles
Polio	Rabies
Mumps	Influenza
Hepatitis	Herpes
AIDS	Trachoma (of Cornea)

Human Bacterial Diseases

Cholera	Diphtheria
Tuberculosis	Leprosy
Tetanus	Typhoid
Plague	Whooping Cough
Sore Throat	Pneumonia
Gonorrhoea	Syphilis
Botulism	

Human Protozoans Diseases

Amoebiasis	Malaria
Sleeping Sickness	Kalazar
Diarrhoea	Piarrhoea

Human Fungal Diseases

Ringworm	Athlete's foot
Dhobie itch	

SOME IMPORTANT FACTS OF HUMAN BODY

Length of Alimentary Canal	Approximately 8 metres
Number of Cells in Body	75 trillion
Longest Bone	Femur (Thigh bone)
Smallest Bone	Ear ossicle, stapes
Weight of Brain	1400 gms
Blood Volume	6.8 litres (in 70 kg body)
Normal B.P	120/80 mm Hg
Number of R.B.C	(*a*) In Male : 4.5 - 5.0 million/cubic mm. (*b*) In Female : 4.0 - 4.5 million/cubic mm
Life Span of R.B.C	120 days
Normal W.B.C Count	5000 - 1000/cubic mm
Life Span of W.B.C	3 - 4 days
D.L.C. (Differential Leucocyte Count)	(*a*) Basophils : 0.5 - 1% (*b*) Eosinophils : 1 - 3% (*c*) Monocytes : 3 - 8% (*d*) Neutrophils : 40 - 70% (*e*) Lymphocytes : 2 - 25%
Blood Platelets Count	2,00,000 - 4,00,000/cubic mm
Haemoglobin	(*a*) In Male : 14 - 15.6 gm/100 c.c. of blood (*b*) In Female : 11 - 14 gm/100 c.c. of blood
Hb Content in Body	500 - 700 gm
Universal Blood Donor	O Rh-ve
Universal Blood Recipient	AB
Blood Clotting Time	2 - 5 minutes
Average Body Weight	70 kg
Normal Body Temperature	98.4° F or 37°C
Breathing Rate	16 - 20/minute
Dental Formula	Adult : 2123 / 2123 = 32; Child : 2120 / 2120 = 22 Milk Teeth
Number of Cranial Nerves	12 pairs
Number of Spinal Nerves	31 pairs
Largest Endocrine Gland	Thyroid
Gestation Period	9 months (253 - 266 days)
Normal Heart Beat	72 - 75/minute
Largest Gland	Liver
Largest Muscle in the Body	Gluteus maximus (Buttock Muscle)
Smallest Muscle in the Body	Stapedius
Largest Artery	Abdominal Aorta
Largest Vein	Inferior Venacava
Greatest Regeneration Power	In liver
Longest Nerve	Sciatic
Longest Cell	Neuron (Nerve Cell)
Minimum Regeneration Power	In Brain Cells
pH of Gastric Juice	1.4
pH of Urine	6.0
pH of Blood	7.35 - 7.45
Total Number of Muscles in the Body	639
Total Number of Bones in the Body	206

EVERYDAY SCIENCE

VARIOUS SCIENCES

Acoustics: The study of sound and sound waves.

Aerodynamics: The study of forces acting upon bodies in motion in the air (e.g., aircraft, missiles, etc.).

Aeronautics: Concerned with all activities of aerial locomotion (art of flying).

Agronomy: The science of soil management and the production of field crops.

Agrostology: The study of grasses.

Anatomy: The science of the structure of the animal/human body learnt by dissection.

Anaesthesiology: A branch of medicine concerned with administration of anaesthetics and the condition of the patient while under anaesthesia.

Anthropology: The study of the origin and physical and cultural development of mankind.

Archaeology: A scientific study of the material remains of the past as evidence of man's life, culture and history.

Astronautics: A science dealing with space travel and space vehicles.

Astrophysics: A branch of astronomy dealing with the physical nature of heavenly bodies.

Astronomy: The science of heavenly bodies (planets).

Astrogeology: The study of structures and formation of rocks and minerals on other planets.

Bacteriology: A branch of microbiology dealing with bacteria.

Biology: The science of living organisms; subdivided into Botany and Zoology.

Biophysics: The physics of the vital processes of living organisms.

Botany: The science of the plant kingdom.

Bryology: The study of mosses.

Cardiology: A branch of medicine dealing with heart.

Carpology: The study of fruits and seeds.

Ceramics: The art of making objects from clay.

Cetology: The study of acquatic mammals, especially whales.

Chemistry: The study of elements, their behaviour and laws of their combination etc.

Chorology: The study of geographical areas; plants and animal distribution.

Cosmetology: The study of cosmetics and their use.

Cosmology: The study of the universe—its origin, nature, structure and evolution.

Craniology: The study of skulls (not to be confused with phrenology which is not a science).

Cryogenics: Concerned with the production, control and application of extremely low temperatures.

Cytology: A branch of biology dealing with structure and function of cells.

Cytopathology: The study of diseased cells.

Dactylogy: The study of fingerprints.

Dermatology: A branch of medicine dealing with skin.

Dietetics: The science of diet and nutrition.

Ecology: The study of relationship between organisms and their environment.

Entomology: Deals with study of insects.

Endocrinology: The study of glands.

Etymology: A study of the origin and history of words.

Genetics: A branch of biology dealing with heredity and the laws that govern it.

Geology: A study of the chemical composition of the earth's crust.

Gerontology: A branch of medicine studying the ageing process, problems and diseases.

Gynaecology: A branch of medicine dealing with female diseases of the reproduction system.

Haematology: A branch of medicine studying blood and its disorders.

Hepatology: A branch of medicine dealing with the liver.

Histology: The study of tissues.

Horticulture: A branch of agricultural science dealing with flowers, fruits, vegetables, etc.

Hydrology: The science of water with reference to its occurrence and properties in the hydrosphere and atmosphere.

Hygiene: A branch of medicine dealing with health and its preservation.

Immunology: A branch of medicine dealing with the immune system of the body.

Lithology: The study of the characteristics of rocks.

Morphology: A biological study of external form and structure of living organisms and their parts.

Mycology: Concerned with fungi and fungal diseases.

Nephrology: A branch of medicine dealing with kidney diseases.

Neuropathology: A branch of medicine dealing with changes produced by diseases in the nervous system.

Obstetrics: A branch of medicine dealing with pregnancy, labour and child birth.

Oncology: A branch of medicine dealing with tumours.

Ophthalmology: A branch of medicine dealing with eyes and related diseases.

Orology: The study of mountains.

Ornithology: The science of birds.

Orthopaedics: A branch of medicine dealing with diagnosis and treatment of diseases of the skeletal system (bones).

Osteology: A study of bones.

Paediatrics: A branch of medicine dealing with child disease (infants).

Palaeontology: The study of fossils and ancient life-forms.

Parasitology: The science of parasites, especially those connected with diseases.

Pathology: A branch of medicine that deals with etiologies, mechanisms and manifestation of diseases.

Pharmacology: A branch of medicine dealing with drugs, their chemistry, effects on body, etc.

Physiology: A study of the life processes of various organs of living organisms.

Psychiatry: The study and treatment of mental and emotional disorders.

Radiology: A branch of medical science dealing with the use of x-rays for diagnosis and treatment.

Semiology: The science dealing with signs, sign language or system of signalling.

Seismology: The study of earthquakes and related phenomena.

Theology: The study of religions.

Toxicology: A branch of pharmacology dealing with poisons and other toxic substances.

Urology: The study of the physiology and pathology of the urogenital tract.

Virology: The science that deals with viruses.

Zoology: A branch of biology that deals with animal life.

Zymology: A study that deals with the process of fermentation.

SCIENTIFIC INSTRUMENTS

Name of Instrument	Use
Altimeter	Measures altitude (used in aircraft)
Ammeter	Measures strength of electric current
Anemometer	Measures force and velocity of wind and determines its direction
Audiometer	Measures intensity of sound
Barometer	Measures atmospheric pressure
Balometer	Measures heat radiation
Callipers	Measures inner and outer diameters of solids
Calorimeter	Measures quantities of heat
Cardiogram (ECG)	Traces movements of the heat; recorded on a cardiograph
Chronometer	Determines longitude of a vessel at sea
Cryometer	Measures very low temperatures, usually below 0°C
Dynamo	Converts mechanical energy into electrical energy
Dynamometer	Measures electrical power
Electroencephalograph (EEC)	Records and interprets the electrical waves of the brain recorded on electroencephalograms
Electrometer	Measures very small, potential difference in electric current
Electroscope	Detects presence of an electric current
Endoscope	Examines internal organs of the body
Fathometer	Measures depth of the ocean
Fluxmeter	Measures magnetic flux
Galvanometer	Measures the electric current
Hydrometer	Measures the relative density of liquids
Hygrometer	Measures level of humidity
Hydrophone	Measures sound under water
Kymograph	Graphically records physiological movement (e.g., blood pressure/ heartbeat)
Lactometer	Measures the relative density of milk to determine purity (fat content)
Manometer	Measures the pressure of gases
Microphone	Converts sound waves into electrical vibrations
Microscope	To obtain a magnified view of small objects
Nephetometer	Measures the scattering of light by particles suspended in a liquid
Ohmmeter	Measures electrical resistance in ohms
Ondometer	Measures the frequency of electromagnetic waves
Periscope	To view objects above sea level (used in submarines)
Polygraph	Instrument that simultaneously records changes a physiological process such as heartbeat, blood pressure and respiration—used as a lie detector
Pyknometer	Determines the density and coefficient of expansion of liquids
Pyrheliometer	Measures components of solar radiation
Pyrometer	Measures very high temperature
Quadrant	Measures altitudes and angles in navigation and astronomy. Detects the direction and range of an approaching aeroplane by means of radiowaves (Radio, Angle, Detection and Range)

Name of Instrument	Use
Refractometer	Measures refractive indices
Resistance Thermometer	An accurate type of thermometer in which temperature is measured by determining the electrical resistance of a coil of thin wire
Salinometer	Determines salinity of solutions
Sextant	Used by navigators to find the latitude of a place by measuring the elevation above the horizon of the sun or another star—also measures the height of distant objects
Sphygmomanometer	Measures blood pressure
Stereoscope	To view two-dimensional pictures
Stethoscope	Used by doctors to hear and analyze heart and lung sounds
Stroboscope	To view rapidly moving objects
Tachometer	To determine speed, especially the rotational speed of a shaft (used in aeroplanes and motor-boats)
Tacheometer	Used to measure distances, elevations and bearings during survey
Tangent	Galvanometer measures the strength of direct current
Telescope	To view distant objects in space
Theodolite	Measures horizontal and vertical angles
Tonometer	Measures the pitch of sound
Transponder	Used to receive a signal and transmit a reply immediately
Udometer	Rain gauge
Venturimeter	Measures rate of flow of liquids
Viscometer	Measures the viscosity of liquids
Voltmeter	Used to measure potential difference between two points
Wattmeter	Measures the power of an electric circuit
Wavemeter	Measures the wavelength of a radiowave

SCIENTIFIC INVENTIONS AND DISCOVERIES

Invention	Inventor(s)
Adding Machine	Pascal
Aeroplane	Wright brothers
Ballpoint Pen	C. Biro
Barometer	E. Torricelli
Bicycle	K. Macmillan
Bicyle Tyre	J. B. Dunlop
Centigrade Scale	A. Celsius
Cinematograph	Thomas Alva Edison
Computer	Charles Babbage
Cine Camera	Friese-Greene
Cinema	A.L. and J. L. Lumiere
Clock (Mechanical)	Hsing and Ling-Tsan
Clock (Pendulum)	C. Hugyens
Diesel Engine	Rudolf Diesel
Dynamite	Alfred Nobel
Dynamo	Michael Faraday
Electric Iron	H.W. Seeley
Electric Lamp	Thomas Alva Edison
Electromagnet	W. Sturgeon
Film (with sound)	Dr Lee de Forest
Fountain Pen	LE. Waterman
Gas Lighting	William Murdoch
Gramophone	Thomas Alva Edison
Jet Engine	Sir Frank Whittle
Lift	E. G. Otis
Locomotive	Richard Trevithick
Machine Gun	Richard Gatling
Match (safety)	J.E. Lundstrom
Microphone	David Hughes
Microscope	Z. Janssen

Invention	Inventor(s)	Invention	Inventor(s)
Motor Car (petrol)	Karl Benz	Shorthand (modern)	Sir Isaac Pitman
Motorcycle	Edward Butler	Spinning Frame	Sir Richard Arkwright
Neon-Lemp	G. Claude	Stream Engine (piston)	Thomas Newcombe
Nylon	Dr W. H. Carothers	Stream Engine	James Watt
Parachute	Louis Lenormand	Stainless Steel	Harry Brearley
Photography (paper)	W.H. Fox Talbot	Submarine	D. Bushnell
Printing Press	J. Gutenberg	Tank	Sir Ernest Swington
Radar	Dr A.H. Taylor and L.C. Young	Telegraph Code	Samuel F. B. Morse
Radium	Marie and Pierre Curie	Telephone	Alexander Graham Bell
Rayon	Viscos Co.	Telescope	Hans Lippershey
Razor (safety)	K. C. Gillette	Television	John Logie Baird
Razor (electric)	Col. J. Schick	Terylene	J. Whinfield and H. Dickson
Refrigerator	J. Harrison and A. Catlin	Thermometer	Galileo Galilei
Revolver	Samuel Colt	Tractor	J. Froelich
Rubber (vulcanised)	Charles Goodyear	Transistor	Bardeen, Shockley and Brattain
Rubber (waterproof)	Charles Macintosh	Typewriter	C. Sholes
Safety Lamp	Sir Humphry Davy	Radio Valve	Sir J. A. Fleming
Safety Pin	William Hurst	Watch	A. L. Brequet
Sewing Machine	B. Thimmonnier	X-ray	Wilhelm Roentgen
Scooter	G. Bradshaw	Zip Fastener	W. L. Judson
Ship (stream)	J.C. Perier		
Ship (turbine)	Sir Charles Parsons		

MEDICAL DISCOVERIES

Discovery	Made by	Discovery	Made by
Antibiotic (Penicillin)	Alexander Fleming	Hypodermic Syringe	Charles Gabriel Pravaz
Antiseptic	Joseph Lister	Heart Transplant	Christian Barnard
Aspirin	Felix Hoffmann	Kidney Machine	W. J. Kolff
Blood Circulation	William harvey	Malaria Germs	A. Laveran
Blood Group	K. Landsteiner	Organ Transplant	John P. Merril
Blood Transfusion	James Blundell	Scan (CAT)	Godrey Hounsfield
Cholera and TB Germs	Robert Koch	Sphygomomanometer	Scipione Riva-Rocci
Diphtheria Germs	Klebs & Loffler	Stethoscope	Rene Laennec
Electro cardiogram (ECG)	William Einthoven	Thermometer (Clinical)	Sir Thomas
Heart-Lung Machine	John Heynsham Gibbon	Ultrasound	Ian Donald
		X-ray	W. Roentgen

IMPORTANT VACCINES

Vaccine	Discovered by	Vaccine	Discovered by
Small Pox	Edward Jenner	TB Vaccine	Leon Calmette and Camille Guerin
Cholera	Louis Pasteur	Polio Vaccine	Jonas E. Salk
Diphtheria and Tetanus	Emil Adolf Von Belming and Shibasaburo Kitasato	Measles Vaccine	John F. Enders
		Rabies Vaccine	Louis Pasteur
		Typhus Vaccine	J. Niccolle

CLASSIFICATION OF BLOOD GROUPS

Blood Group	Can donate blood to	Can receive blood from
A	A, AB	A and O
B	B, AB	B and O
AB	Only AB	AB, A, B and O
O	AB, A, B and O	Only O

DISEASES AFFECTING DIFFERENT PARTS OF BODY

Disease	Part of the Human Body Affected
AIDS	Immune system of the body (resistance)
Arthritis	Joints
Asthma	Bronchial muscles (lungs)
Cataract	Eyes
Conjunctivitis	Eyes
Glaucoma	Eyes
Trachoma	Eyes
Diabetes	Pancreas, blood
Dermatitis	Skin
Diphtheria	Throat
Eczema	Skin
Goitre	Joints
Hepatitis, Jaundice	Liver
Malaria	Spleen
Meningitis	Spinal cord and brain
Polio	Legs
Pyrrhoea	Teeth and gums
Pleurisy	Lungs
Rheumatism	Joints
Pneumonia	Lungs
Sinusitis	Facial bones
Typhoid	Intestines, whole body
Tuberculosis	Lungs
Tonsillitis	Glands in throat (tonsils)

CHEMICAL NAMES AND FORMULAE OF SOME COMMONLY KNOWN COMPOUNDS

Chemical Name	Formulae
Alum	Potassium aluminium sulphate $K_2SO_4Al_2(SO_4)_3$, $24H_2O$
Edible soda	Sodium bicarbonate $NaHCO_3$
Bleaching powder	Calcium hypochloride $Ca(OCl)Cl_2$
Caustic Soda	Sodium hydroxide NaOH
Blue vitriol	Copper sulphate $CuSO_4$, $5H_2O$
Chalk	Calcium Carbonate $CaCo_3$
Borax	Sodium borate $Na_2B_4O_7$, $10H_2O$
Galena	Lead sulphide PbS
Gypsum	Calcium sulphate $2CaSO_4$, H_2O
Formalin	Formaldehyde HCHO
Green vitriol	Ferrous sulphate $FeSO_4$
Dry ice	Solid carbon dioxide CO_2
Grape juice	Glucose $C_2H_{12}O_6$
Common salt	Sodium chloride NaCl
Caustic potash	Potassium hydroxide KOH
Chile salt peter	Sodium Nitrate or Soda nitre $NaNO_3$
Carbolic acid	Fenol C_6H_5OH
Alcohol	Ethyl alcohol C_2H_5OH
Bauxite	Hydrated aluminium oxide Al_2O_3, $2H_2O$
Washing soda	Sodium carbonate Na_2CO_3, $10H_2O$
Acid salt	Hydrogen chloride HCl
Salt peter	Potassium nitrate KNO_3

Chemical Name	Formulae
Litharge	Lead oxide PbO_2
Lime water	Calcium hydroxide $Ca(OH)_2$
Laughing gas	Nitrous oxide N_2O
Red solution	Potassium permanganate $KMNO_4$
Lime (unhydrated)	Calcium oxide CaO
Red sindoor	Lead peroxide Pb_3O_4
Acid of saltpeter	Nitric acid HNO_3
Muratic acid	Hydrochloric acid HCl
Limestone	Calcium carbonate $CaCO_3$
Sal ammoniac (Nausadar)	Ammonium chloride NH_4Cl
Soda ash	Anhydrous sodium carbonate Na_2CO_3
Silica	Silicon oxide SiO_2
T.N.T.	Trinitrotoluene $C_6H_2CH_3(NO_2)_3$
Calomel	Mercurous Chloride Hg_2Cl_2
Vinegar	Solution of dilute acetic acid CH_3COOH
White lead	Basic lead carbonate $2Pb_2CO_3.Pb(OH)_2$
Starch	Polysaccharide $C_6H_{10}O_5$
Plaster of Paris	Calcium sulphate hemihydrate $(CaSO_4)_2H_2O$
Hypo	Sodium Thiosulphate $Na_2S_2O_3.5H_2O$
Butanal	Butyraldehyde C_3H_9CHO
Butanone	Methyl ethyl ketone $CH_3COC_2H_5$
Aniline	Phenylamine, Amino benzene $C_6H_5NH_2$
Alum stone	Alunite $KAl_3[SO_4(OH)_2]_3$
Aspirin	Acetyl salicylic acid $CH_3COOC_6H_4COOH$
Arsine	Arsenic hydride AsH_3
Epsom salt	Magnesium sulphate $MgSO_4.7H_2O$
Furan	Furfuran C_4H_4O
Fruit Sugar	Fructose $C_5H_{12}O_6$
Pyrite	Ferrous Sulphate (FeS_2)
Urea	$CO(NH_2)_2$
Zinc Sulphate	Hepta hydrate $ZnSO_4.7H_2O$ and Monohydrate $ZnSO_4.H_2O$

IMPORTANT ALLOYS

Alloy	Components	Percent quantity
Brass	Copper	60-80
	Zinc	40-20
Bronze	Copper	80
	Zinc	10
	Tin	10
Gun metal	Copper	88
	Zinc	01
	Tin	10
	Lead	01
German Silver	Copper	30-60
	Zinc	25-35
	Nickel	15-35
Duralumin	Aluminium	95.0
	Copper	04.0
	Magnesium	0.5
	Manganese	0.5
Magnelium	Aluminium	90-95
	Magnesium	05-10
Nickel Steel	Iron	96-98
	Nickel	02-04
Stainless Steel	Iron	74
	Chromium	18
	Nickel	08
Electrum	Silver	55-88
	Gold	22-45
Solder	Tin	50
	Lead	50

Multiple Choice Questions

PHYSICS

1. When a body is stationary
- A. there is no force acting on it
- B. the combination of forces acting on it balance each other
- C. the force acting on it are not in contact with it
- D. the body is in vacuum

2. Newton's first law of motion gives the concept of
- A. energy B. work
- C. momentum D. inertia

3. Newton's second law gives a measure of
- A. acceleration
- B. force
- C. momentum
- D. angular momentum

4. A man in a lift will weigh more when
- A. lift accelerated upward
- B. lift accelerates downward
- C. lift descends freely
- D. the lift going up in slowing down

5. Three equal weights of mass 2 kg. each are hanging on a string passing over a fixed pully as shown in figure. What is the tension in the string connecting the weight *B* and *C*?

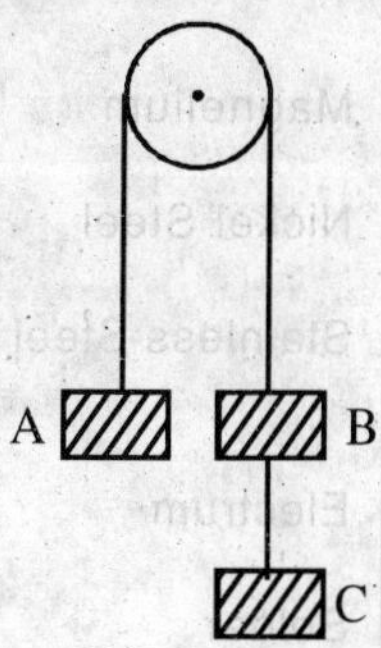

- A. zero
- B. 13 N
- C. 3.3 N
- D. 19.6 N

6. A body is accelerated by applying a force of 30 N. The momentum of the body after 2 sec.
- A. 7.5 kg-m/s B. 30 kg-m/s
- C. 120 kg-m/s D. 60 kg-m/s

7. With what minimum acceleration can a fireman slide down a rope whose breaking strength is 3/4th of his weight?
- A. 1/4 g B. 1/2 g
- C. 3/4 g D. zero

8. Conservation of linear momentum is equivalent to
- A. Newton's 1st law of motion
- B. Newton's 2nd law of motion
- C. Newton's 3rd law of motion
- D. None of the above

9. If the net force acting on a body is doubled, the acceleration of the body is
- A. halved B. doubled
- C. unchanged D. quadrupled

10. A jet plane flies in air because
- A. the thrust of the jet compensates the force of gravity
- B. the weight of air whose volume is equal to the volume of the plane is more than the weight of the plane
- C. the flow of air and the wings causes an upward force which compensates for the force of gravity
- D. the gravity does not act on body moving with high speed

11. The passengers in a boat are not allowed to stand because:

A. this will raise the centre of gravity and the boat will be rocked
B. this will lower centre of gravity and the boat will rocked
C. the effective weight of system increases
D. of surface tension effects

12. A person presses the earth least where he is:

A. sitting
B. standing
C. running
D. lying on the ground

13. One litre of cool air weighs heavier than one litre of hot air because of the:

A. increased number of collisions between the molecules
B. increased number of molecules at high temperature
C. greater energy of molecules at high temperature
D. lower energy of molecules at high temperature

14. A bomb is dropped from an aeroplane moving horizontal at constant speed. When air resistance is taken into consideration, then the bomb:

A. flies with the aeroplane
B. falls on earth ahead of the aeroplane
C. falls on earth behind aeroplane
D. falls on earth exactly below the aeroplane.

15. A ball is thrown upwards in a train which is accelerating. The ball will fall

A. Ahead of the thrower
B. Behind the thrower
C. In the hands of thrower
D. Data inadequate

16. The flying of birds is a proof of Newton's:

A. first law
B. second law
C. third law of motion
D. both second and third law

17. A moving bullet hits a solid target resting on a frictionless surface and gets embedded in it. What is conserved in this process?

A. both momentum and kinetic energy
B. kinetic energy alone
C. momentum alone
D. neither momentum nor kinetic energy

18. Fat can be separated from milk in a cream-separator because of:

A. cohesive force
B. gravitational force
C. centrifugal force
D. centripetal force

19. A cricket player while taking a catch lowers his hands to

A. Increase time of impulse
B. Decrease time of impulse
C. Take catch safely
D. Increase the area of impact

20. Where should be the centre of gravity of a body?

A. It must lie within the body
B. It may be near but not essentially within the body
C. It changes its position from time to time
D. It must be outside the body

21. The process of walking involves

A. Newton's first law of motion
B. Newton's second law of motion
C. Newton's third law of motion
D. Conservation of momentum

22. Which of the following is used to reduce friction

1. Streamlines
2. Use of ball bearings
3. Lubrication

A. 1 & 2 only B. 1 & 3 only
C. 2 & 3 only D. 1, 2 & 3

23. Which law is involved in the act of cleaning a carpet by beating it with a stick?

A. First law of motion.
B. Second law of motion.
C. Law of conservation of energy.
D. Law of conservation of mass.

24. When a body is taken from the earth to the moon:
A. Its weight increases
B. Its weight decreases
C. Its weight remains unchanged
D. It becomes completely weightless

25. Which of the following is the cause of weightlessness experienced while orbiting around earth on a spaceship ?
A. Inertia B. Zero gravity
C. Acceleration D. Centre of gravity

26. The weight of an object would be minimum when it is placed:
A. at the North Pole
B. at the South Pole
C. at the Equator
D. at the Centre of the Earth

27. As the train starts moving, a man sitting inside leans backwards because of:
A. inertia of rest
B. inertia of motion
C. moment of inertia
D. conservation of mass

28. Electrons revolve round the nucleus because of:
A. cohesive force B. adhesive force
C. centripetal force D. centrifugal force

29. If the speed of a particle in circular motion is doubled and its radius is halved, then the centripetal force will
A. increase six times
B. increase eight times
C. increase four times
D. remain the same

30. If velocity of a particle is uniform, then its acceleration would be
A. positive B. negative
C. very low D. zero

31. The speed of the earth is highest when it is
A. farthest from the sun
B. nearest to the sun
C. passing through the month of September
D. none of the above

32. Slopes are made on the road in order to
A. help the driver to drive slowly
B. reduce friction
C. help the vehicle to get the centripetal force
D. help the driver to retain balance while driving

33. If a body is sent with a velocity of ....km sec^{-1}, it would leave the earth forever.
A. 11.9 B. 11.6
C. 11.4 D. 11.2

34. In the motion of the planets,
A. the angular velocity is constant
B. the linear momentum is constant
C. the angular momentum is constant
D. none of the above

35. The value of g
A. increases with increase in depth
B. decreases with decrease in depth
C. remains same regardless of the depth
D. depends upon the mass of the object

36. The path traced by a satellite launch vehicle is
A. a hyperbola B. a circle
C. a parabola D. none of these

37. If the speed of rotation of the Earth increases, the weight of the body at the equator will
A. increase
B. remain the same as before
C. be zero
D. decrease

38. If the distance of the Sun from the Earth is doubled, then the gravitational attraction between the Sun and the Earth will be
A. 1/3rd of the value at present
B. 1/4th of the value at present
C. 1/6th of the value at present
D. none of the above

39. An iron ball and a wooden ball are released from a height in vacuum. The speed of the iron ball would be
A. same to the speed of the wooden ball
B. more than the speed of the wooden ball
C. lesser than the speed of the wooden ball
D. none of these

40. A freely falling body
A. is weightless
B. has double the weight, which it actually possesses
C. is likely to gain weight as it moves towards the Earth
D. none of the above

41. Moment of inertia of thin uniform rod of length l is equal to
A. $\frac{ml^2}{6}$ B. $\frac{ml^2}{12}$
C. $\frac{ml^2}{4}$ D. $\frac{ml^2}{24}$

42. The inertial force acts in a
A. opposite direction to that of acceleration force
B. same direction as that of accelerating force
C. perpendicular direction to that accelerating force
D. none of the above

43. The earth's gravitational force field is said to be conservative force field because
A. the value of gravitational force rise fixed
B. the direction of gravitational force is fixed
C. the work acted by the earth's gravitational field on a particle is independent on the path traced out by the particle
D. the work acted by the earth's gravitational field will cause same path for all particles irrespective of their mass

44. The maximum frictional force that comes into play when a body just begins to slide over the surface of another body is known as
A. Dynamic friction
B. Rolling friction
C. Kinetic friction
D. Limiting friction

45. The limiting force of friction is
A. the value of frictional force which stops the movement of the body
B. the value of frictional force which can not exceed under a situation
C. the frictional force acting when the body is just about to move
D. the frictional force acting on a body when it is in motion

46. A car is moving at 100 km/h. If the mass of the car is 950 kg, its kinetic energy is:
A. 367 J B. 0.367 J
C. 3.67 MJ D. 3.67 J

47. Einstein got his Nobel Prize for:
A. His theory of relativity
B. Explanation of Photoelectric effect
C. His theory of atomic heats of solids
D. None of the above

48. If a body moves along a frictionless horizontal surface its weight:
A. does work B. does not work
C. work partially D. none of these

49. A car and a lorry both are moving with equal kinetic energies. If equal breaking force is applied on both, then before coming to rest:
A. the car will cover a greater distance
B. lorry will cover a greater distance
C. both will cover the same distance
D. the distance covered by them will depend only on their respective velocities.

50. The work done by a force:
A. is independent of the frame of reference
B. is same in all reference-frames
C. is same in all inertial frames
D. none of these

51. Identify the correct statement of Work-Energy Theorem:
A. Work done by all the forces on a particle to displace it is equal to its change in kinetic energy.
B. Work done by all the forces on a particle is equal to its change in mechanical energy.
C. Work done by all the forces acting on a particle is equal to change in its potential energy.
D. Work done by a force on a particle is equal to change in its kinetic energy.

52. Which of the following statement is true?
A. Kinetic energy and momentum both are conserved in all types of motion.
B. Momentum is conserved in elastic collision but not in inelastic collision.
C. Total kinetic energy is not conserved but momentum is conserved in inelastic collision.
D. Kinetic energy is conserved in elastic collision but not in inelastic collision.

53. Thermal energy is a energy due to:
A. Kinetic energy of molecules
B. Potential energy of molecules
C. Both (A) and (B)
D. None of these

54. The internal energy of a gas:
A. is the sum total of kinetic and potential energies.
B. is the total transitional kinetic energies.
C. is the total kinetic energy of randomly moving molecules.
D. is the total kinetic energy of gas molecules.

55. Power is measured in—
A. Joules per second
B. Joules per minute
C. Joules per square second
D. None of these

56. A rifle bullet loses 1/20th of its velocity in passing through a plank. Assuming constant resistive force, the least number of such planks required just to stop the bullet is:
A. 5 B. 10
C. 11 D. 20

57. Absolute zero is
A. –273°C B. –273°F
C. –273°K D. none of these

58. Which one of the following statements is correct.
A. It is the temperature at which, saturated vapour pressure of a liquid equals the atmospheric pressure
B. It is the temperature below which, evaporation of the liquid occurs very rapidly
C. It is the temperature above which, a gas cannot be liquified.
D. It is the temperature at which the states of solid, liquid and gas co-exit.

59. When the temperature of body is equal to that of atmosphere, then
A. heat transfer between body and atmosphere continues
B. there is no exchange of heat
C. the body is in unstable equilibrium
D. none of the above

60. Good absorbers of heat are
A. poor emitters of heat
B. good emitters of heat
C. only black bodies
D. none of these

61. How many calories of heat are required by 1 gram of water at 99°C to boil off?
A. 530 B. 640
C. 540 D. 500

62. The mean kinetic energy of a gas molecule is proportional to
A. $\sqrt{T}$ B. T^2
C. T D. None of the above

63. The temperature, to which a gas must be cooled before it can be liquified by pressure alone, is known as its
A. saturation point
B. freezing point
C. liquification temperature
D. critical temperature

64. What is Latent Heat?
A. It is the heat given to a body and simultaneously the body releases it to the atmosphere
B. It is the heat given to a body to heat it by 1°C
C. It is the heat given to body to change its state at constant temperature
D. None of the above

65. In case of negative work, the angle between the force and displacement is:
A. 0° B. 45°
C. 90° D. 180°

66. The work done on an object does not depend on the:
A. displacement
B. angle between force and displacement
C. force applied
D. initial velocity of the object

67. Water stored in a dam possesses:
A. no energy B. electrical energy
C. kinetic energy D. potential energy

68. Which of the following does not possess the ability to do work not because of motion?
A. a sparrow flying in the sky
B. a sparrow moving slowly on the ground
C. a sparrow in the nest on a tree
D. a squirrel going up a tree

69. When an object falls freely towards the earth, then its total energy:
A. increases
B. decreases
C. remains constant
D. first increases and then decreases

70. Which one of the following is not the unit of energy?
A. joule B. newton-metre
C. kilowatt D. kilowatt-hour

71. Which of the following energy change involves frictional force?
A. chemical energy to heat energy
B. kinetic energy to heat energy
C. potential energy to sound energy
D. chemical energy to kinetic energy

72. An object is falling freely from a height x. After it has fallen a height $x/2$, it will possess:
A. only potential energy
B. only kinetic energy
C. half potential and half kinetic energy
D. less potential and more kinetic energy

73. The commercial unit of energy is:
A. watt B. watt-hour
C. kilowatt-hour D. kilowatt

74. The device which converts mechanical energy into energy which runs our microwave oven is:
A. electric motor B. alternator
C. turbine D. electric heater

75. Kinetic energy of a body is directly proportion to its:
A. Weight B. Speed
C. Mass D. Velocity

76. Internal energy of a gas increases when
A. the change is cyclic
B. it absorbs heat
C. the change is adiabatic
D. none of these

77. The power of a water jet flowing through an office of radius 10 cm with a velocity 5 ms^{-1} is
A. 196 watt B. 1960 watt
C. 19.6 watt D. 1.96 watt

78. Which of the following statements is wrong?
A. Sound travels in straight line
B. Sound travels as waves
C. Sound is a form of energy
D. Sound travels faster in vacuum than in air

79. Sound waves do not show in air:
A. polarisation B. diffraction
C. refraction D. reflection

80. With the rise of temperature, the velocity of sound:
A. decreases
B. remains the same
C. increases
D. is independent of temperature

81. Velocity of sound will be:
A. smaller in moist air than in dry air
B. greater in moist air than in dry air
C. same in moist and dry air
D. independent of its density

82. The apparent wavelength of light from a star moving away from the earth is 0.02% more than actual wavelength. What is the velocity of the star.
A. 30 kms^{-1} B. 60 kms^{-1}
C. 90 kms^{-1} D. none of these

83. Buzzing of a mosquito is:
A. loud sound B. shrill sound
C. flat sound D. sweet sound

84. The frequency of the third harmonic of a closed organ pipe is equal to which of the overtone

A. first B. second
C. fourth D. none of these

85. Pitch of sound depends upon it:

A. wavelength
B. frequency
C. amplitude
D. periodicity and regularity

86. Doppler's effect of sound is produced when the source and the observer are:

A. moving
B. in relative motion
C. stationary
D. resonance phenomenon

87. The Doppler effect is applicable for:

A. light waves only
B. sound waves only
C. both light and sound waves
D. none of the above

88. To a stationary man the frequency of a sound source moving towards the man appears to be:

A. lower than the original frequency
B. same as the original frequency
C. higher than the original frequency
D. lower as well higher than the original frequency depending upon the speed of the source

89. The same notes being played on the Sitar and Veena differ in:

A. pitch
B. quality
C. both pitch and quality
D. neither pitch nor quality

90. Two closed organ pipes, when sounded together give five beats per second. Their lengths are in the ratio of 100 : 101. The fundamental notes (in Hz.) produced by them are

A. 245, 250 B. 250, 255
C. 495, 500 D. 500, 505

91. When we hear a sound, we can identify its source from:

A. amplitude of sound
B. intensity of sound
C. wavelength of sound
D. absorb sound

92. Consider the following statements:

Assertion A: The velocity of sound in the air increases due to presence of moisture in it.

Reason R: The presence of moisture in air lowers the density of air.

Of these statements,

A. both (A) and (R) are true and (R) is the correct explanation of (A).
B. both (A) and (R) are true but (R) is not the correct explanation of (A).
C. (A) is true but (R) is false.
D. (A) is false but (R) is true.

93. To hear a clear echo what should be the minimum distance between the reflecting surface and the observer?

A. 165 metre B. 165 feet
C. 16.5 metre D. 16.5 feet

94. Why does radio reception improve slightly during the night?

A. The outside noise is reduced very much at night.
B. Unlike the daytime, only a few radio stations broadcast during the night.
C. Sunlight affects radio broadcasts to some extent during the day.
D. The magnetic field of the earth acts with reduced intensity during the night, thereby reducing its impact on broadcasts.

95. An air-box attached to a musical instrument increases the:

A. pitch of the sound
B. intensity of the sound
C. quality of the sound
D. shrillness of the sound

96. An astronaut can't hear his companion at the surface of the moon because:
A. produced frequencies are above the audio frequency
B. there is no medium for sound propagation
C. temperature is too low during night and too high during day.
D. there are too many craters on the surface of the moon

97. The difference between musical sound and noise is due to:
A. musical instruments
B. wave lengths
C. pitch
D. intensity

98. Why the auditorium walls are provided with cardboard panels and porons wall furnishings?
A. So that the sound from the stage may be heard properly
B. So that the echo effect may be minimised
C. So that the sound may appear to be pleasing on the ears of the listeners
D. All of the above

99. A musical sound is the one that is produced
A. at regular intervals
B. in quick succession
C. Both (A) and (B)
D. None of (A) and (B)

100. Which relationship, out of those given below, represents the velocity of sound wave?

A. $v = \frac{\lambda}{n}$ B. $v = nl$

C. $v = \frac{n}{\lambda}$ D. $v = nl + 1$

101. The loudness of sound depends upon
A. its velocity
B. its pitch
C. its amplitude
D. its frequency

102. The audible range of a person is 20 to 18,000 Hz. If speed of sound in air is 330 ms^{-1}, calculate the longest wavelength of sound, which he can detect?

A. $\frac{18000}{330}$ m B. $\frac{330}{18000}$ m

C. $\frac{20}{330}$ m D. $\frac{330}{20}$ m

103. A thunder is heard 4 seconds after the lighting. At what distance, the lightning occurred?
A. 1,480 m B. 1,380 m
C. 2,380 m D. 1,000 m

104. The ratio of velocity of sound in air at 4 atmospheric pressure and that at 1 atmospheric pressure would be
A. 2 :1 B. 1 : 2
C. 1 : 1 D. 1: 4

105. For an organ pipe, the wavelength of the fundamental note is
A. equal to the length of the pipe
B. half the length of the pipe
C. one-fourth the length of the pipe
D. twice the length of the pipe

106. The frequency of sound can remain unchanged even if we double the length of the wire, provided
A. tension of the wire is doubled
B. tension of the wire is decreased four-fold
C. tension of the wire is halved
D. tension of the wire is increased four-fold

107. Which characteristic of sound enables us to distinguish two musical notes coming from different sources but having the same frequency and loudness?
A. Timber B. Pitch
C. Loudness D. None of the above

108. As the length of a vibrating column increases, its frequency
A. decreases
B. increases
C. remains the same
D. increases if the vibrating column is not in air

109. For a sound wave in air, the vibrations of the particles of a medium
A. are parallel to the direction of propagation
B. are perpendicular to the direction of propagation
C. may either be parallel or perpendicular to the direction of propagation
D. None of the above

110. For sound waves in air, the vibration are
A. electromagnetic B. longitudinal
C. transverse D. None of the above

111. If two vibrating systems are in resonance, then
A. their amplitudes are equal
B. their frequencies are equal
C. their temperatures are equal
D. their intensities are equal

112. If the temperature of a room is 30°C, what will be the velocity of sound?
A. 350 ms^{-1} B. 333 ms^{-1}
C. 380 ms^{-1} D. 300 ms^{-1}

113. How many nodes and antinodes are there in a tuning fork?
A. 6 B. 5
C. 3 D. 4

114. The phenomenon of echo of sound waves is due to
A. reflection B. interference
C. diffraction D. all of the above

115. The musical interval between two tone is determined by
A. the actual difference of their frequencies
B. the difference of square roots of their frequencies
C. the ratio of their frequencies
D. the ratio of square of their frequencies

116. Velocity of sound in a medium is
A. independent of its density
B. inversely proportional to its density
C. directly proportional to its density
D. inversely proportional to the square root of its density

117. The maximum speed of vibrations which produce audible sound will be in
A. dry air B. sea water
C. ground D. human blood

118. What is the audible range of sound?
A. 0 – 200 Hz B. 0 – 20,000 Hz
C. 20 – 2000 Hz D. 30.0 to 2000 Hz

119. Which one of the following has the longest wavelength?
A. Radio waves B. Sound waves
C. X-rays D. Infra-red ray

120. The velocity of sound in the air (vacuum) is
A. 330 m/sec B. 220 m/sec
C. 110 m/sec D. 232 m/sec

121. Sound wave is
A. transverse and mechanical
B. longitudinal and mechanical
C. transverse and non-mechanical
D. longitudinal and non-mechanical

122. If the guitar and the flute be tunned in the unison then the produced sound can be distinguished by
A. pitch, timber and quality
B. only pitch and timber
C. only timber
D. only quality

123. Decibel is the unit of physical quantity used for:
A. the speed of light
B. the intensity of heat
C. the intensity of sound
D. the frequency of radiowaves

124. Which of the following can produce longitudinal waves as well as transverse waves under different conditions?
A. water B. slinky
C. tuning fork D. TV transmitter

125. SONAR is frequently used by
A. Austronauts B. Doctors
C. Engineers D. Navigators

126. The pitch or frequency of the siren of the coming train appears to be increasing because of

A. Big-bang theory
B. Doppler's effect
C. Charle's law
D. Archemedies' principle

127. In a resonance tube the first resonance occurs at 16 cm and the second resonance occurs at 49 cm. The end corrections will be

A. 0.3 cm B. 0.5 cm
C. 0.8 cm D. 1.0 cm

128. When light travels from one medium to another medium which are separated by a sharp boundary, the characteristic which does not change is:

A. velocity B. wavelength
C. frequency D. amplitude

129. Identify the incorrect statement about light rays:

A. light always propagate along a straight line
B. two light rays donot disturb each other upon intersection
C. object and its image are inter-changeable
D. none of these

130. The refractive index of a given piece of transparent quartz is the greatest for:

A. red light B. violet light
C. green light D. yellow light

131. The ratio of refractive index of red light to blue light in air is:

A. less than unity
B. equal to unity
C. greater than unity
D. less as well as greater than unity depending upon the experimental arrangements.

132. A virtual image is formed by a plane mirror, when the pencil of light is incident on the mirror, then the incident ray on the mirrors:

A. diverging B. parallel
C. converging D. all of the above

133. Choose the correct statement related to the image formed by a plane mirror

A. a plane mirror always forms a virtual image
B. the image formed by a plane mirror may be magnified or diminished
C. the image formed by a plane mirror is always unmagnified and inverted
D. the image formed by a plane mirror is always unmagnified and erect

134. A person of height *h* standing at the centre of room looking towards a plane mirror hung on a wall, can see the whole height of the wall behind him if the length of the mirror is:

A. h B. $h/2$
C. $h/3$ D. $h/4$

135. Aperture of the human eye is 2 mm. Assuming the mean wavelength of light to be 5000 Å, the angular resolution limit of the eye is:

A. 2 min B. 1 min
C. 0.5 min D. 1.5 m

136. Mirages are observed in atmosphere due to the phenomenon of:

A. interference of light
B. total internal reflection of light
C. scattering of light
D. double refraction of light

137. In the double-slit experiment, the distance of the second dark fringe from the central line is 3 mm. The distance of the fourth bright fringe from the central line is:

A. 6 mm B. 8 mm
C. 12 mm D. 16 mm

138. Brilliance of diamond is due to:

A. shape
B. cutting
C. reflection
D. total internal reflection

139. Colour of sky appears blue because:

A. all the blue colour of solar spectrum is absorbed
B. it is its natural colour

C. blue colour of solar spectrum is scattered
D. all red colour of solar spectrum is absorbed

140. An air bubble in water shines because of the phenomenon of:
A. reflection
B. refraction
C. diffraction
D. total internal reflection

141. Rising or setting sun appears to be reddish because:
A. the sun is colder at sunrise or at sunset
B. diffraction sends red rays to the earth at these times
C. refraction is responsible for this effect
D. scattering due to dust particles and air molecules is responsible for this effect

142. The disease of astigmatism in human eye is because of:
A. unequal and uneven curvature of eye lens
B. eye lens being of organic matter
C. eye lens being thick
D. opacity development in eye lens

143. A disorder of vision in which lines in one plane of an object appear in focus while those in another plane are out of focus is called:
A. astigmatism B. distortion
C. myopia D. hypermetropia

144. Who among the following is able to see the ultra-violet light?
A. Bee B. Monkey
C. Fish D. Bird

145. Surface of a CD is coded with
A. Silver B. Aluminium
C. Gold D. Silver and Gold

146. The audio/video system or a computer reads the CD using—
A. Laser beam
B. Radio wave
C. Electromagnetic wave
D. None of these

147. Image formed by plane mirror is:
A. Vertual B. Inverted
C. Magnified D. Real

148. Which type of lens is used to treat myopia:
A. Concave lens B. Convex lens
C. Cylindrical lens D. Bifocal lens

149. By which instrument we collect the space information:
A. Convex lens
B. Microscope
C. Hubble Telescope
D. None of these

150. An object is placed at 20 cm from a convex mirror of focal length 20 cm. The distance of the image from the pole of the mirror is
A. 15 cm B. 10 cm
C. 40 cm D. infinity

151. When light passes from one medium to another, the physical quantity that remains unchanged is
A. velocity B. wavelength
C. frequency D. None of these

152. What is the unit of power of a lens?
A. Candela B. Dioptre
C. Metre D. Lux

153. Astigmatism for a human eye can be removed by using
A. concave lens
B. convex lens
C. cylindrical lens
D. prismatic lens

154. Which one of the following mirrors is free from spherical aberration?
A. convex B. concave
C. parabolic D. none of these

155. The image of an object formed by a device is always virtual and small. The device may be
A. canvex lens B. concave mirror
C. glass plate D. concave lens

156. Focal length of a convex lens is maximum for
A. blue light B. yellow light
C. green light D. red light

157. A photographer changes the aperture of his camera and reduces it to half of the original aperture. The exposure time now should be
A. same as before
B. double than before
C. four times than before
D. half than before

158. The magnifying power of a simple microscope can be increased if we use eye piece of
A. higher focal length
B. smaller focal length
C. higher diameter
D. smaller diameter

159. In which mirror a diminished virtual image can be obtained?
A. A plane mirror B. Convex mirror
C. Concave mirror D. None of these

160. Which of the following lights has maximum wavelength?
A. g-rays B. X-rays
C. UV-rays D. Visible rays

161. In which form does the Light propagates?
A. Electric waves
B. Magnetic waves
C. Electromagnetic waves
D. Sound wave

162. Light can pass through
A. Vacuum B. Glass
C. Air D. All of these

163. The wavelength of light visible to eye is of the order of
A. 10^{-4} m B. 10^{-8} m
C. 10^{-10} m D. 10^{-7} m

164. Which mirror is used in movie projectors?
A. Convex mirror B. Concave mirror
C. Plane mirror D. Parabolic mirror

165. If image is formed behind the mirror, it is
A. Real and inverted
B. Virtual and erect
C. Virtual and inverted
D. Real and erect

166. Which among the following is a group of primary colours?
A. Red, blue and green
B. Red, green and violet
C. Yellow, blue and green
D. Yellow, green and orange

167. Name the body which absorbs all colours.
A. Black B. White
C. Red D. Yellow

168. Among the following which part of spectrum of white light produces maximum visibility:
A. Red B. Yellow green
C. Yellow D. Blue

169. When green and red colours are mixed, the colour produced is
A. Yellow B. Magenta
C. Indigo D. Black

170. A converging lens is that which
A. Collects rays
B. Canverse rays
C. Reflect rays
D. Forms virtual image

171. If image is real and inverted, magnification will be
A. Two B. Negative
C. One D. Zero

172. In which mirror image appears erect?
A. Plane B. Parabolic
C. Convex D. Concave

173. When reflection takes place from a spherical mirror, positions of the object and its image are known as
A. Poles B. Conjugate foci
C. Focal length D. Centre of focus

174. When rays of light fall on a convex lens, it
A. Converges them
B. Does not bend them
C. Diverges them
D. Enlarge them

175. If magnification is positive, the nature of the image is
A. Real and inverted
B. Virtual and erect
C. Real
D. None of these

176. Which one of the following is more monocromatic?
A. Laser beam
B. White light
C. Sodium light
D. Mercury light

177. A person can see clearly up to 3 metres what should be the power of the lens in his spectacles so that he could see clearly up to 12 metres.
A. 0.25 D B. –0.25 D
C. 0.5 D D. –0.75 D

178. Who named positive and negative charges?
A. Faraday
B. Gauss
C. Benjamin Franklin
D. Madam Curie

179. Choose the incorrect statement about electric charge:
A. charge is a point.
B. charge is a property of matter.
C. The SI unit of charge is coulomb.
D. Two types of charge exist in nature.

180. Choose the correct statement about electric charges:
A. Two charges exert only electrical force on each other.
B. Two charges exert only magnetic forces on each other.
C. Two charges interact electromagnetically.
D. Two charges interact either electrically or magnetically

181. An electric cell does 5 joule of work in carrying 10 coulomb charge around the closed circuit. The electromotive force of the cell is:
A. 2 volt B. 1/2 volt
C. 4 volt D. 1 volt

182. A soap bubble is given a negative charge, then its radius:
A. decreases
B. increases
C. remains unchanged
D. nothing can be said

183. Current in a conductor is due to:
A. motion of the free electrons in it
B. motion of the positive ions
C. free electrons and holes
D. protons

184. When the temperature of a metallic conductor is increased its resistance:
A. always decreases
B. always increases
C. may increase or decrease
D. remains the same

185. If an electric current is passed through a nerve, the man:
A. begins to laugh
B. begins to weep
C. is excited
D. becomes insensitive to pain

186. In which of the following substances the resistance decreases with increase of temperature?
A. carbon B. constantan
C. copper D. silver

187. Which of the following statement is true?
A. insulators do not have electrons.
B. some of the electrons in a conductor are free to move through the material.
C. conductors always contain more electrons than insulators.
D. the atoms in a conductor move about but those in an insulator cannot move.

188. The function of a fuse wire is independent of:
A. Its specific resistance
B. Its radius
C. Its length
D. Current flowing through it

189. The resistance can be increased by:
A. increasing the area
B. changing the resistivity
C. decreasing the length
D. none of these

190. The temperature of a metal wire rises when an electric current is passed through it because:
A. collision of conduction electrons with the atoms of metal gives them energy which appears as heat
B. when electrons fall from higher energy level to lower energy level, heat energy is released
C. collisions of metal atoms with each other releases heat energy.
D. collisions of conduction electrons with each other releases heat energy.

191. The heating element in an electric iron is made up of:
A. nichrome B. iron
C. constantan D. tungsten

192. The potential difference between two points if 2J of work must be done to move a 4 mC charge from one point to another is:
A. 50 V B. 500 V
C. 5 V D. 5000 V

193. Of the two bulbs in a house, one glows brighter than the other. Which of the two has a larger resistance?
A. the bright bulb
B. the dim bulb
C. both have the same resistance
D. the brightness does not depend upon the resistance.

194. The conversion of heat into electrical energy may be achieved by using:
A. Hydrometer
B. Thermo-couple
C. Voltmeter
D. Photo-electric tube

195. In an electrolyte solution, current is maintained by the flow of:
A. electrons only
B. negative ions only
C. positive ions only
D. negative and positive ions both.

196. A dynamo:
A. creates electrical energy
B. converts mechanical energy into electrical energy
C. converts electrical energy into mechanical energy
D. creates mechanical energy

197. A transformer:
A. transforms energy
B. transforms frequency
C. transforms voltage
D. generates e.m.f.

198. Alternating current is one which changes in its:
A. direction
B. magnitude
C. magnitude and direction both
D. none of the above

199. A.C. can be measured with the help of:
A. moving coil galvanometer
B. hot-wire ammeter
C. tangent galvanometer
D. hot-wire voltmeter

200. A transformer is employed to:
A. convert A.C. into A.C.
B. convert D.C. into A.C.
C. obtain a suitable A.C. voltage
D. obtain a suitable D.C. voltage

201. The best material for the core of a transformer is:
A. stainless steel B. wild steel
C. hard steel D. soft iron

202. A device which converts electrical energy into mechanical energy is:
A. dynamo B. generator
C. motor D. induction coil

203. The freezer in a refrigerator is fitted near the top:
A. to keep it away from the hot compressor which is near the bottom
B. because of convenience
C. so that it can cool the whole interior by setting up convection currents
D. without any specific purpose

204. One should not connect a number of electrical appliances to the same power sockets because:
A. this can damage the appliances
B. this can damage the domestic wiring due to overheating
C. the appliances will not get full voltage
D. the appliances will not get proper current

205. Short circuit means:
A. direct flow of current between two points of different potentials
B. indirect flow of current between two points
C. direct flow of current between points of the same potentials
D. none of the above

206. The wire of an electric lamp has a:
A. high resistance and a high melting-point
B. high resistance and low melting-point
C. low resistance and low melting-point
D. low resistance

207. Fuses are connected in ..... to the live wire:
A. parallel B. series
C. either way D. both ways

208. Name the unit of electrical potential:
A. Coulomb B. Watt
C. Joule/sec D. Volt

209. The element of an electric heater is made of:
A. Tin B. Copper
C. Nichrome D. Tungsten

210. In an electric circuit, a fuse is connected:
A. in the live wire
B. in the neutral wire
C. in the earth wire
D. None of these

211. For what a voltmeter is used to measure?
A. Electric power
B. Consumption of energy
C. Potential difference
D. Voltage

212. What is called the rate of doing work in an electric circuit?
A. Power B. Energy
C. Current D. Voltage

213. Which one of the following is the unit of electric power/sec?
A. Joule B. Coulomb
C. Volt/m D. Watt

214. Which among the following is measured in Kilowatt hour?
A. Energy B. Power
C. Resistance D. Electric current

215. An electric bulb is rated 220 volt and 100 watt, Power consumed by it when operated on 110 volt is:
A. 50 W B. 85 W
C. 90 W D. 35 W

216. Which among the following is the commercial unit of electric power?
A. Volt B. Watt
C. Ampere D. kWh

217. Name the instrument which converts sound energy into electric energy.
A. Loudspeaker B. Microphone
C. Dynamo D. Bell

218. When an electric bulb breaks, there is a mild bang due to:
A. The photo-chemical reaction between the enclosed gases.
B. The compressed gases rushing out suddenly.
C. The air rushing into fill the evacuated space.
D. None of these

219. In 220 V ac, the value of 220 represents:
A. normal voltage B. effective voltage
C. constant voltage D. peak voltage

220. The advantage of ac over dc is that:
A. its generation costs much less.
B. it contains more electric energy.
C. it is free from voltage fluctuations.
D. it can be transmitted over long distances with minimum power loss.

221. An electric fan marked 60 watt consumes 3 units for the duration:
A. 50 hours B. 150 hours
C. 100 hours D. 15 hours

222. Which is represented by the electric current?
A. Charge per unit volume
B. Charge per unit time
C. Charge per unit area
D. Both A and B

223. On which does the current in a wire depend:
A. On the potential difference applied
B. On the resistance of the wire
C. Both A and B
D. None of these

224. In an electrolytic cell, the electrode connected to the positive terminal of the battery is called the:
A. Cathode B. Anode
C. Cation D. None of these

225. An electric field can deflect:
A. X rays B. Neutrons
C. a-rays D. g-rays

226. No current flows between two charged bodies connected together when they have the same:
A. charge B. potential
C. capacitance D. resistance

227. If an electron has an initial velocity in a direction different from that of an electric field, the path of the electron is:
A. a straight line B. a circle
C. an ellipse D. a parabola

228. The radius of a nucleus with mass number 16 is 3 fm. The radius of another nucleus with mass number 128 is
A. 6 fm B. 12 fm
C. 18 fm D. 24 fm

229. Hydrogen is not used as a household fuel because
A. it is highly combustible gas
B. its transportation is difficult
C. it is costly
D. All of these

230. Fuels that provide most of the energy need of the world:
A. petroleum and coal
B. petroleum and wood
C. coal and wood
D. wood and petroleum

231. The end product of the decay of $^{232}_{90}\text{Th}$ is $^{208}_{82}\text{Pb}$. The number of alpha and beta particles emitted are
A. 3, 3 B. 6, 4
C. 6, 0 D. 4, 6

232. All are solid fuels except
A. alcohol B. wood and coal
C. coke D. charcoal

233. Which of the following is not a gaseous fuel?
A. LPG
B. Coal gas and water gas
C. Gobar gas and acetylene
D. Liquid hydrogen.

234. All are processed fuels except
A. charcoal and coke
B. petrol and diesel
C. wood and coal
D. coal gas and water gas

235. If 200 MeV of energy is released in the fission of one nucleus of $^{235}_{92}\text{U}$, how many nuclei must fission per second to produce a power of 1 kW.
A. 3.125×10^{13} B. 3.125×10^{11}
C. 3.215×10^{13} D. 3.215×10^{11}

236. The efficiency of traditional chulhas is
A. 8% B. 12%
C. 20% D. 25%

237. Which of the following substances is smokeless?
A. Charcoal
B. Bio gas and LPG
C. Coke
D. All of these

238. Animal dung contains
A. phosphorus B. nitrogen
C. both A and B D. None of these

239. Gas obtained from animal dung and human excreta is called

A. bio gas B. water gas
C. waste gas D. All of these

240. In bio gas methane is
A. 65%
B. 60%
C. 50%
D. more than 30%

241. Gasoline is the name given to the some substance as
A. diesel oil
B. petrol
C. natural gas
D. crude oil

242. All of the following are the examples of fossil fuels except
A. petroleum
B. coal
C. natural gas
D. charcoal

243. Coal can be converted into
A. synthetic petrol
B. coal gas
C. electricity
D. All of these

244. Varieties of coal differ in
A. moisture
B. volatile motter
C. their carbon content
D. All of these

245. When a neutron collides with a quasi free proton, it loses half of its energy on the average in the every collission. How many collisions, on the average, are required to reduce a 2 MeV neutron to a thermal energy of 0.04 eV.
A. 30 B. 22
C. 35 D. 26

246. What is the power output of ${}_{92}U^{235}$ reactor if it takes 30 days to use 2 kg of fuel, and if each fission gives 185 MeV of usable energy
A. 50.48 MW
B. 46.58 MW
C. 58.46 MW
D. 46.58 MW

247. Petroleum gas is used in
A. the production of carbon black needed in tyre industry
B. the production of hydrogen needed in fertilizer industry
C. manufacturing gasoline
D. All of these

248. When coal is mixed with a hot solvent and heated with hydrogen, it forms
A. ammonia
B. liquid hydrocarbon
C. synthetic rubber
D. None of these

249. When coal is burnt in an insufficient supply of oxygen which gas is given out?
A. CO_2 B. NO
C. CO D. O_2

250. All of the following are the pollutants produced by burning petrols except
A. CO
B. alcohol and acids
C. lead compound and carbon particles
D. SO_2

251. When a burning candle is covered with a glass it extinguishes because
A. supply of oxygen is cut off
B. supply of hydrogen is cut off
C. supply of nitrogen is cut off
D. supply of CO_2 is cut off

252. Combustion of a fuel produces heat because
A. bonds of CO_2 + H_2O are formed which causes the energy to release
B. of the electro-magnetic charges
C. of the infra-red radiation
D. All of these

253. Atoms having the highest electronegativity (attraction of elements) value is
A. H_2
B. fluorine
C. ethane
D. O_2

254. The removal of electrons from an atom is called
A. fusion B. fission
C. reduction D. oxidation

255. The addition of electrons in an atom is called
A. reduction B. fusion
C. magnetization D. None of these

256. The heat produced by one gram of charcoal is
A. 30 kJ B. 33 kJ
C. 38 kJ D. 40 kJ

257. Combustion is
A. exothermic reaction
B. endothermic reaction
C. addition reaction
D. None of these

258. Efficiency of gasoline is adjudged in terms of
A. butane number
B. octane number
C. hexane number
D. None of these

259. Which is the main constituent of petroleum gas?
A. methane B. ethane
C. butane D. propane

260. Which is abundantly found in natural gas?
A. methane B. ethane
C. propane D. butane

261. Which product of petroleum is used to drive heavy vehicles like trucks?
A. petrol B. kerosene
C. diesel D. None of these

262. The source of energy which is stored in fossil fuels is
A. sea B. earth
C. sun D. None of these

263. Coke is more valuable when used
A. as a fuel for industrial boilers
B. as an oxidising agent
C. as a reducing agent
D. as a fuel in domestic ovens

264. Which of the following does not contribute to acid rain?
A. nitrogen monoxide
B. sulphur dioxide
C. carbon monoxide
D. carbon dioxide

265. In solar cooker which is responsible for producing greenhouse effect
A. utensils placed in the cooker box
B. black coating inside the cooker
C. glass sheet cover
D. plane mirror reflector

266. By which solar cells are made of?
A. conductors
B. insulators
C. semi-conductors
D. None of these

267. The radiations present in sunlight which make a solar cooker work are
A. g-rays
B. ultraviolet rays
C. cosmic rays
D. infrared rays

268. In an efficient solar cooker, the cover of cooker box should be made of
A. transparent plastic sheet
B. coated aluminium sheet
C. coated glass sheet
D. transparent glass sheet

269. The minimum speed of wind necessary for the satisfactory working of a wind generator to produce electricity is about
A. 15 km/h
B. 20 km/h
C. 12 km/h
D. 18 km/h

270. If the solar constant is 1.4 kW/m^2, then the solar energy received by 1m^2 area in one hour is:
A. 4080 J B. 504.0 kJ
C. 5040 kJ D. 5.04 kJ

CHEMISTRY

1. Volume of a gas at NTP is 1.12×10^{-7} cc. Calculate the number of molecules in it.
A. 3.01×10^{12} B. 3.01×10^{20}
C. 3.01×10^{24} D. 30.1×10^{23}

2. The element present in the largest amount in rocks and minerals is
A. Silicon B. Carbon
C. Hydrogen D. Gold

3. The average K.E. of an ideal gas per molecule in SI units at 25°C will be
A. 6.17×10^{-21} kJ B. 6.17×10^{-21} J
C. 6.17×10^{-20} J D. 7.16×10^{-20} J

4. The alloy of steel containing chromium to resist rusting, is known as:
A. wrought iron B. cast iron
C. hard steel D. stainless steel

5. The number of atoms in 100 g of an F.C.C. crystal with density d = 10 gm cm^{-3} and cell edge as 200 pm is equal to
A. 3×10^{25} B. 5×10^{24}
C. 1×10^{25} D. 2×10^{25}

6. Which of the following is a chemical change?
A. Evaporation B. Precipitation
C. Dissolution D. Oxidation

7. Which of the following substance consists of only one element?
A. Diamond B. Glass
C. Marble D. Sand

8. Why is tungsten used in the manufacture of electric bulbs?
A. It is cheaper than other metals
B. It is both durable and economical
C. It has high melting-point
D. It makes the bulb light brighter

9. If rate of diffusion of A is 5 times that of B, what will be the density ratio of A and B?
A. $\frac{1}{25}$ B. $\frac{1}{5}$
C. 25 D. 5

10. Which is the lightest element in the universe?
A. Helium B. Hydrogen
C. Nitrogen D. Silicon

11. Gun-powder is a mixture of:
A. nitrates of potassium and sodium
B. sulphates of potassium and mangnesium
C. charcoal, sulphur and potassium nitrate
D. potassium sulphate and charcoal

12. For protection against gamma radiations, the shields should be made of:
A. Iron B. Lead
C. Copper D. Tin

13. Which of the following statement is correct?
I. German silver is an alloy of silver and copper and zinc.
II. There is no zinc in brass
III. Bronze is an alloy of copper and tin
A. I, II and III B. Only III
C. I and III D. I and II

14. The metal generally mixed with gold while making ornaments is:
A. zinc B. iron
C. silver D. copper

15. Magnalium is an alloy of
A. Magnesium and Copper
B. Aluminium and Copper
C. Magnesium and Aluminium
D. None of these

16. When a crystal of potassium permanganate is placed at the bottom of water in a beaker, the water in the whole beaker turns purple on its own, even without stirring. This is an example of:
A. distribution B. intrusion
C. diffusion D. effusion

17. Choose the correct statement in respect of fluids.
A. only gases behave as fluids
B. gases and solids behave as fluids
C. gases and liquids behave as fluids
D. None of these

18. Which one of the following represents the correct arrangement in the increasing order of forces of attraction between their particles?
A. water, air, oxygen
B. air, sugar, oil
C. oxygen, water, sugar
D. None of these

19. If 4 g of oxygen diffuse through a very narrow hole, how much hydrogen would have diffused under identical conditions?
A. 16 g   B. 1 g
C. $\frac{1}{4}$g   D. 64 g

20. The best evidence for the existence and movement of particles in liquids was provided by:
A. John Dalton   B. Thomas Edyson
C. J.J. Thomson   D. Robert Brown

21. Which form of matter has no fixed shape but it has a fixed volume?
A. krypton   B. kerosene
C. carbon steel   D. oxygen

22. When a gas jar full of air is placed upside down on a gas jar full of bromine vapours, the red-brown vapours of bromine from the lower jar go upward into the jar containing air. In this experiment:
A. bromine cannot be heavier than air because it is going upwards against gravity
B. both air and bromine have the same density
C. bromine is heavier than air
D. air is heavier than bromine

23. Which one of the following statements is not true?
A. the molecules in a solid vibrate about a fixed position
B. the molecules in a liquid are arranged in a regular pattern
C. the molecules in a gas exert negligibly small forces on each other, except during collisions
D. the molecules of a gas occupy all the space available

24. Which one of the following does not undergo sublimation?
A. iodine
B. sodium chloride
C. ammonium chloride
D. None of these

25. If the temperature of an object of 268 K, it will be equivalent to:
A. –5°C   B. –50°C
C. –15°C   D. –25°C

26. The boiling point of ethane is, –88°C. This temperature will be equivalent to:
A. 285 K   B. 218 K
C. 185 K   D. –185 K

27. When heat is constantly supplied by a gas burner with small flame to melt ice, then the temperature of ice during melting:
A. increases very slowly
B. does not increase at all
C. first remain constants then decreases
D. None of these

28. When water at 0°C freezes to form ice at the same temperature of 0°C, then it:
A. absorbs some heat
B. releases some heat
C. neither absorbs nor releases heat
D. Both A and B

29. The latent heat of vaporisation of water is:
A. 2.25×10^6 J/kg   B. 2.25×10^8 J/kg
C. 22.5×10^4 J/kg   D. 22.5×10^{-6} J/kg

30. Which of the following represent the suitable conditions for the liquefaction of gases?
A. low temperature, low pressure
B. high temperature, low pressure
C. low temperature, high pressure
D. high temperature, high pressure

31. During summer days, water kept in an earthen pot (pitcher) becomes cool because of the phenomenon of:
A. radiation   B. transpiration
C. osmosis   D. evaporation

32. The conversion of a solid vapours without passing through the liquid state is called:
A. osmosis B. fusion
C. sublimation D. evaporation

33. Which of the following energy is absorbed during the change of state of a substance?
A. specific heat B. latent heat
C. heat capacity D. heat of solution

34. During respiration, glucose and oxygen enter our body cells and waste products carbon dioxide and water leave the body cells by the process of:
A. evaporation B. osmosis
C. diffusion D. plasmolysis

35. Which of the following is not an element?
A. graphite B. germanium
C. silica D. silicon

36. Which one of the following substances is neither a good conductor of electricity nor an insulator?
A. gallium B. germanium
C. chromium D. potassium

37. The element which is not common between the compounds called baking soda and soda ash is
A. nitrogen B. hydrogen
C. oxygen D. sulphur

38. Which elements are normally exist in the liquid state?
A. iodine and mercury
B. mercury and chlorine
C. bromine and iodine
D. bromine and mercury

39. On the basis of composition of matter, milk is considered to be:
A. a pure substance
B. an impure substance
C. an element
D. a compound

40. Which of the following does not have fixed melting point/boiling point?
A. gold B. ethanol
C. air D. oxygen

41. Which is the most effective method of separating mixtures of miscible volatile liquids?
A. Fractional distilliation
B. Simple distillation
C. Chromatography
D. Filtration

42. Brittleness is a property of solid due to which—
A. they break into small pieces
B. the solid does not back to its original shape
C. solid regains its original shape
D. None of these

43. The purification of a substance in which it eva-porates without melting can be carried out by:
A. Crystallization
B. Distillation
C. Steam distillation
D. Sublimation

44. Stainless steel is an alloy of:
A. Iron and nickel
B. Iron, chromium and nickel
C. Iron, chromium and zinc
D. Iron and manganese

45. Out of the following, an example of matter which can be termed as fluid is:
A. carbon B. sulphur
C. oxygen D. phosphorus

46. An aqueous solution of an acid is characterised by the presence of
A. H^+ ions B. H_2^+ ions
C. H_4O^+ ions D. H_3O^+ ions

47. Which of the following acid is used as a dehydrating and drying agent?
A. Acetic B. Hydrochloric
C. Nitric D. Sulphuric

48. A substance which behaves both as an acid and base is
A. Amphoteric B. Alkali
C. Salt D. Hygroscope

49. Soda water contains:
A. Carbonic acid B. Sulphuric acid
C. Carboxylic acid D. Nitrous acid

50. The main use of salt in the diet is to:
A. make the taste of food better
B. produce in small amounts the hydrochloric acid required for the digestion of food.
C. ease the process of cooking
D. increase the solubility of food particles in water

51. The acid that can be used as a hypnotic is:
A. tartaric acid B. benzoic acid
C. barbituric acid D. butanoic acid

52. When milk is converted into curd, the sour taste is due to:
A. Acetic acid B. Citric acid
C. Lactic acid D. Tartaric acid

53. Match the following :

	List-I		**List-II**
I.	Sodium bicarbonate	a.	Double salt
II.	Alum	b.	Mixed salt
III.	Bleaching Powder	c.	Acidic salt
IV.	Sodium chloride	d.	Normal salt

A. I-c, II-a, III-b, IV-d
B. I-a, II-d, III-b, IV-c
C. I-d, II-a, III-c, 1V-b
D. I-c, II-b, III-a, IV-d

54. All acids essentially contain the element:
A. oxygen B. chlorine
C. sulphur D. hydrogen

55. The acid generally stored in batteries is:
A. sulphuric acid B. nitric acid
C. hydrochloric acid D. acetic acid

56. Ants have .... acid.
A. glutaric B. citric
C. acetic D. formic

57. Acid precipitation is now regarded as a serious problem in some European and Asian countries. Its major cause or source is:
A. discharge of acidic effluents onto neutral or slightly alkaline land where the acidic components precipitate.
B. emission of sulphur oxides and nitrogen oxides from thermal power plants and burning of fossil fuels; these oxides dissolve in atmospheric water vapour and fall back on earth as acid rain.
C. natural carbon dioxide released during respiration of living organisms dissolves in water, forming carbonic acid which is the chief contributor to acidity in rain water.
D. None of the above

58. Weakest acid among the following is:
A. CH_3COOH B. C_6H_5OH
C. H_2O D. C_2H_2

59. Vinegar contains:
A. 10 to 20% acetic acid
B. 10% acetic acid
C. 6 to 10% acetic acid
D. 100% acetic acid

60. Formic acid is not representative member of carboxylic acids because
A. it does not contain alkyl group
B. it contains an aldehydic group while the other acids do not
C. it is the first member of the series
D. it is a gas

61. Baking soda is a/an:
A. Acidic substance
B. Basic substance
C. Neutral substance
D. None of these

62. Which of the following is acidic:
A. Milk B. Lemon
C. Salt solution D. Sugar solution

63. Which of the following substance has bitter taste?
A. Milk B. Amla
C. Soap solution D. Salt solution

64. Which of the following is a base according to Lowry-Bronsted concept?
A. I^- B. H_3O^-
C. HCl D. NH_4^+

65. Name the substance which makes the fruits sour:
A. Acids B. Bases
C. Salts D. None of these

66. When a particular quantity of a hydrochloric acid solution is mixed with a particular quantity of sodium hydroxide solution, one gets a:
A. Half acidic solution
B. Acidic solution
C. Neutral solution
D. Basic solution

67. Acids and bases react to produce:
A. Water and oxygen gas
B. Salt and hydrogen gas
C. Salt and water
D. None of these

68. What happens when bases are dissolved in water?
A. H^+ ions are formed
B. OH^- ions are formed
C. O^- ions are formed
D. None of these

69. What does the acid in water contain?
A. H^+ ions B. OH^- ions
C. O^- ions D. 2OH ions

70. For an acidic solution:
A. $[H^+] = [OH^-]$ B. $[H^+] < [OH^-]$
C. $[H^+] > [OH^-]$ D. $[H^+] = 2OH$

71. Which compound is used as an antacid?
A. Soda ash
B. Baking soda
C. Nitrous oxide
D. Magnesium carbonate

72. Which compound is used for disinfecting water?
A. Soda ash B. Sodium carbonate
C. Bleaching powder D. Hydrogen oxide

73. A salt whose aqueous solution will have a pH of more than 7 will be:
A. K_2CO_3 B. K_2SO_4
C. NaCl D. NH_4Cl

74. Chemical formula of baking soda is:
A. Na_2CO_3 B. $Na_2CO_3 10H_2O$
C. $Na_2CO_3 . 2H_2O$ D. $NaHCO_3$

75. Which of the following salts will give an aqueous solution having pH of almost 7?
A. NH_4NO_3 B. NH_4Cl
C. $CaCl_2$ D. KCl

76. According to Arrhenius theory acids are those compounds which give
A. Oxygen ions B. Hydrogen ions
C. Hydroxide ions D. None of these

77. Which is the strong base?
A. NaOH B. $Mg(OH)_2$
C. NH_4OH D. None of these

78. According to Bronsted Lowry concept, the relative strengths of the bases CH_3COO^-, OH^- and Cl^- are in the order
A. $OH^- > CH_3COO^- > Cl^-$
B. $Cl^- > OH^- > CH_3OO^-$
C. $CH_3COO^- > OH^- > Cl^-$
D. $OH^- > Cl^- > CH_3COO^-$

79. A solution reacts with marble chips to produce a gas which turns lime water milky. The solution contains:
A. Na_2SO_4 B. $CaSO_4$
C. H_2SO_4 D. K_2SO_4

80. Which one of the following is not an organic acid?
A. ethanoic acid B. formic acid
C. citric acid D. carbonic acid

81. Which property is not shown by acids?
A. they have sour taste
B. they feel soapy
C. they turn litmus red
D. None of these

82. The discomfort caused by indigestion due to over-eating can be cured by taking:
A. vinegar B. lemon juice
C. baking soda D. caustic soda

83. Which property is common between vinegar and curd?
A. have sweet taste B. have bitter taste
C. are tasteless D. have sour taste

84. Which indicator produces a pink colour in an alkaline solution?
A. methyl orange B. turmeric paper
C. phenolphthalein D. litmus paper

85. Fresh milk has pH of 6. When milk changes into curd, the pH value will:
A. become 7
B. become less than 6
C. become more than 7
D. remain unchanged

86. Wasp stings can be treated with:
A. baking soda B. vinegar
C. washing soda D. milk of magnesia

87. The colour of methyl orange indicator in a solution is yellow. The pH of this solution is likely to be:
A. 7 B. less than 7
C. 0 D. more than 7

88. Which of the following is a Lewis acid?
A. Cl^- B. H_3O^+
C. BF_3 D. C_2H_5OH

89. Bee sting contains:
A. an acidic liquid
B. a salt solution
C. an alkaline liquid
D. an alcohol

90. Wasp sting contains:
A. a sugar solution B. an acidic liquid
C. a salt solution D. an alkaline liquid

91. One of the following does not inject an acidic liquid into the skin through its sting. This is:
A. honey bee B. ant
C. wasp D. nettle leaf hair

92. The salt which will give an acidic solution on dissolving in water is:
A. KCl B. NH_4Cl
C. Na_2CO_3 D. CH_3COONa

93. One of the following salts will give an alkaline solution on dissolving in water. This is:
A. Na_2CO_3 B. Na_2SO_4
C. NaCl D. $(NH_4)_2SO_4$

94. The number of molecules of water of crystallisation present in washing soda crystals is:
A. five B. two
C. ten D. seven

95. The aqueous solution of one of the following salts will turn phenolphthalein indicator pink. This salt is:
A. KCl B. K_2SO_4
C. K_2CO_3 D. KNO_3

96. Which of the following can adsorb largest volume of hydrogen gas?
A. Finely divided platinum
B. Finely divided nickel
C. Colloidal solution of palladium
D. Colloidal Hydroxide

97. A basic oxide will be formed by the element:
A. K B. S
C. P D. Kr

98. An acidic oxide is produced by the element:
A. Na B. C
C. Ca D. H

99. Which among the following is most reactive metal:
A. aluminium B. copper
C. tin D. calcium

100. The least reactive metal among the following is:
A. sodium B. silver
C. copper D. lead

101. The metals which can produce amphoteric oxides are:
A. sodium and aluminium
B. zinc and potassium
C. calcium and sodium
D. aluminium and zinc

102. The elements whose oxides can turn litmus solution blue are:
A. carbon and sulphur
B. sodium and carbon
C. potassium and magnesium
D. magnesium and sulphur

103. A metal less reactive and another metal more reactive than hydrogen are:
A. aluminium and lead
B. iron and magnesium
C. copper and tin
D. copper and mercury

104. An element reacts with oxygen to give a compound with a high melting point. This compound is also soluble in water. The element is likely to be:
A. calcium B. carbon
C. silicon D. iron

105. Which of the following metal exists in the liquid state?
A. Na B. Ag
C. Cr D. Hg

106. Two metals lighter than water are
A. Al, Mg B. Al, Mn
C. Pb, Mg D. CO, Mn

107. Temporary hardness of water is due to the presence of
A. Magnesium bicarbonate
B. Calcium chloride
C. Magnesium sulphate
D. Calcium carbonate

108. Which statement is true?
A. Aluminium is the most abundant metal in the earth's crust.
B. Oxygen is the most abundant non-metal in the earth's crust.
C. Ammonia (NH_3) and methane (CH_4) are covalent hydrides
D. All of these

109. Which of the following is a metal?
A. Potassium B. Sulphur
C. Argon D. Diamond

110. Which of the following has metallic as well as non-metallic character?
(*i*) Arsenic (*ii*) Antimony
(*iii*) Lead
A. (*i*) Only B. (*ii*) Only
C. (*i*) and (*ii*) Only D. (*i*), (*ii*) and (*iii*)

111. Malachite is an ore of
A. copper B. iron
C. zinc D. silver

112. Cryolite is an ore of
A. aluminium B. iron
C. silicon D. None of these

113. Copper glance is represented by
A. Cu_2S B. Cu_2O
C. $CuCO_3$ D. None of these

114. Saturated solution of sodium chloride is
A. crystal B. brine
C. lime stone D. soda ash

115. Which metal can melt even in our hand?
A. Gallium B. Sodium
C. Nickel D. None of these

116. The metal which shows variable valencies is
A. Iron B. Aluminium
C. Nickel D. Cobalt

117. All are non-metals except
A. hydrogen (H_2) and carbon (C)
B. potassium (K)
C. inert gases (helium, neon and argon)
D. sulphur (S), phosphorus (P), and fluorine (F)

118. Which of the following is not true?
A. Hardness of water depends on its behaviour towards soap.
B. The temporary hardness is due to the presence of Ca and Mg bicarbonates.
C. Permanent hardness is due to the presence of soluble Ca and Mg sulphates.
D. Permanent hardness can be removed by boiling the water.

119. Which of the following metal is a good conductor of electricity?
A. Silver and Gold
B. Copper and Aluminium
C. Tungsten
D. All of these

120. The metal which displaces hydrogen from a boiling caustic soda solution is
A. As B. Zn
C. Mg D. Fe

121. Metals oxides are
A. basic in nature
B. electrovalent (ionic) in nature
C. able to turn red litmus solution blue
D. all of these

122. When a metal reacts with water it forms
A. alkalies B. basic oxide
C. dilute acid D. neutral oxide

123. Metals which loses electrons more easily than hydrogen are more reactive than H_2 and they can
A. not displace H_2 from dilute acids
B. displace hydrogen from dilute acids
C. not react with water easily
D. None of these

124. Which metal can react with hydrogen?
A. Na and Ca B. Mg
C. K D. All of these

125. Non-metals do not displace hydrogen from acids. It means that they do not react with
A. neutral oxides B. acidic oxides
C. dilute acids D. liquid solution

126. Oxides of which of the following metals is reduced by aluminium powder?
A. Magnesium B. Potassium
C. Chromium D. All of the above

127. Distillation method is used for the purification of volatile metals like
A. Hg B. Fe
C. Ca D. All of these

128. If impurities can be oxidized more easily than the metal itself, which method is used?
A. Liquation method
B. Distillation method
C. Oxidation method
D. None of these

129. Iron is used as catalyst in the preparation of ammonia gas by
A. Bayer's process
B. Haber's process
C. Froth floatation process
D. None of these

130. Calcium hydroxide ($Ca(OH)_2$) in water is used for
A. white-washing
B. preparing ammonia, caustic soda and bleaching powder
C. reducing the activities of the soil
D. All of the above purposes

131. Lead pipes are not used for carrying drinking water because
A. they are covered with a coating of lead carbonate
B. they are corroded by air and moisture
C. water containing dissolved air attacks lead forming soluble hydroxide
D. none of the above

132. SiO_2 (Silica) occurs in the form of
A. sand B. quartz
C. opal D. All of these

133. Which is not the property of silicon?
A. It has a high melting point of 1410°C
B. It has a low electrical conductivity
C. Its atomic arrangement is similar to that of diamond
D. It is a soft and ductile metal

134. Red phosphorus is more stable than white phosphorus because
A. its melting point is high
B. of its colour
C. it has strong bonds in its atoms
D. All of these

135. On strong heating sulphur burns in the air with blue flame and gives out
A. SO_2 B. SO_3
C. Both of these D. Neither of these

136. Sulphur is used for preparing
A. dyes, drugs, detergents, fertilizer etc.
B. vulcanized rubber
C. antiseptic cream and ointments
D. All of these

137. Quick silver is now known as
A. lead B. mercury
C. tin D. brass

138. Which of the following metals can occur in free state?
A. Gold B. Lead
C. Sodium D. Iron

139. Blistered copper contains
A. 88% Cu B. 98% Cu
C. 90% Cu D. 81% Cu

140. Which of the two metals are most malleable?
A. Gold, Silver
B. Iron, Magnesium
C. Tungsten, Mercury
D. Aluminium, Copper

141. Which one of the following is not a neutral oxide?
A. CO B. H_2O
C. N_2O D. Na_2O

142. Which of the following metals will not displace hydrogen from dilute hydrochloric acid?
A. Silver (Ag) B. Copper (Cu)
C. Gold (Au) D. All of these

143. Pb is
A. the poorest conductor of heat
B. poor conductor of electricity
C. a good conductor of electricity
D. a good conductor of heat

144. Sodium and potassium are the only
A. soft metals
B. metals of low densities
C. metals having low melting and boiling points
D. (A) and (B) both

145. $NaHCO_3$ is used in
A. fire extinguisher
B. medicines
C. preparing bleaching powder
D. All of these

BIOLOGY

1. The structure which constitutes the basic structural and functional unit of living beings is:
A. Atoms B. Cell
C. Molecule D. None of the above

2. Chloroplast is a/an:
A. organelle B. cell
C. tissue D. organ

3. The scientist who stated that plants and animal's body is consisted of cells was:
A. Leeuwenhoek B. Robert Brown
C. Dutrochet D. None of the above

4. Cell theory was proposed by:
A. Einstein
B. J. Schwann & R. Schleiden
C. Robert Hooke
D. All the above

5. Largest cell in the human body is:
A. Nerve cell B. Liver cell
C. Epithelial cell D. None of the above

6. Cell of Amoeba is:
A. Spindle shaped B. Broad shaped
C. Spherical in shape D. Indefinite in shape

7. The factor which influences unicellular organisms to keep spherical shape is:
A. Surface tension B. Osmosis
C. Viscosity D. Protoplasm

8. Which unicellular organism of the following does not possess the organised nucleus?
A. Bacteria B. Amoeba
C. Chlamydomonas D. None of the above

9. Cells of multicellular organism are usually:
A. Triangular B. Rectangular
C. Polyhedral D. None of the above

10. The difference between protoplasm and cell sap was given by:
A. Huxley B. Purkinje
C. Hugo Von Mohl D. None of these

11. Nucleolus mainly contain:
A. RNA B. DNA
C. ADP D. ATP

12. Which is substitution of mitochondria in *E.coli?*
A. Mesomes B. Golgi body
C. Ribosome D. Glyoxysomes

13. Middle lamella is mainly made up of:
A. Chlorophyll
B. Na, H_2 and P compounds
C. NaCl
D. Calcium pectate compounds

14. Cell membrane surrounds the:
A. Nucleoplasm B. Cell wall
C. Protoplasm D. None of the above

15. Which is present in a bacterial cell?
A. Nucleoid B. Prochromosome
C. Genophore D. All above

16. In plants, respiration occurs in:
A. growing tissues B. all living cells
C. cell wall D. xylem and phloem

17. The longest cell in the plant kingdom is:
A. sieve tube B. vessel
C. sclerenchyma fibre D. tracheid

18. Plastids are present only in:
A. Animal cells B. Animals
C. Plant cells D. None of the above

19. Centrosome is found only in:
A. Animal cells B. Plant cells
C. Both A and B D. None of the above

20. The living matter of an organism is:
A. Nucleus B. Protoplasm
C. Cell D. Nucleoplasm

21. *Amoeba* consists of:
A. Many cells B. One cell
C. Two cells D. Four cells

22. The power house of a cell is:
A. Golgi complex B. Ribosomes
C. Mitochondria D. None of the above

23. The organelle of a cell concerned digestion is:
A. Golgi Complex B. Mitochondria
C. Ribosomes D. Lysosomes

24. The organelle associated with protein synthesis in a cell is:
A. Mitochondria B. Lysosomes
C. Ribosomes D. Chromosomes

25. Biological oxidation of enzymes occur in:
A. Golgi complex B. Ribosomes
C. Mitochondria D. None of the above

26. Golgi bodies are the sites of a cellular:
A. respiration B. digestion
C. secretion D. diamorphism

27. The plasma membrane of animal cells is elastic due to the presence of:
A. lipids B. carbohydrates
C. proteins D. water

28. The group of cells having similar origin, structure and function are called:
A. Organ B. Tissues
C. Cell membrane D. None of the above

29. The meristematic tissue is found in:
A. growing regions B. vascular bundles
C. leaves D. None of the above

30. Vascular layers of plant body shows:
A. Protective tissue B. Epithelia tissue
C. Meristematic tissue D. None of the above

31. Which tissue is found in pith and cortex of stem and roots?
A. Sclerenchyma B. Parenchyma
C. Collenchyma D. None of the above

32. In higher animals, the skin is made up of:
A. Epithelial tissue B. Connective tissue
C. Nerve tissue D. None of the above

33. Blood is a:
A. Connective tissue B. Muscular tissue
C. Epithelial tissue D. None of the above

34. Connective tissues are present in:
A. Spinal cord
B. Nerves
C. Bones and cartilage
D. None of the above

35. Which of the following is cell wall protein?
A. HRGP B. PRP
C. GRP D. All the above

36. Which of the following have cartilaginous skeleton?
A. Man B. Dear
C. Shark D. None of the above

37. Bacteria is an example of:
A. Eukaryotic cell B. Prokaryotic cell
C. Connective tissue D. Muscular tissue

38. Which of the following cellular organelles extracts energy from carbohydrates and form ATP molecules?
A. Mitochondria B. Chloroplast
C. Ribosomes D. Nucleus

39. The outermost part of a plant cell is:
A. Plasma membrane B. Cell wall
C. Epidermis D. Cuticle

40. True nucleus is absent in:
A. Bacteria B. Algae
C. Fungi D. None of the above

41. Centre of autonomic nervous system is located in:
A. hypothalamus B. medulla oblongata
C. cerebellum D. both A and B

42. Central nervous system is consists of:
A. Brain
B. Spinal cord
C. Nerves and ganglia
D. Both A and B

43. The centre for the control of all activities of an animal is:
A. Heart B. Brain
C. Liver D. Stomach

44. Diencephalon has centres for the control of:
A. Metabolism of fats and carbohydrates
B. Regulation of genital function
C. Sleep
D. All the above

45. When the person is alert, with open eyes and actively trying to solve some complex problem, the EEG shows-waves:
A. alpha B. beta
C. delta D. gamma

46. The system which consists of nerves arising from the brain the spinal cord is called:
A. Peripheral nervous system
B. Central nervous system
C. Autonomous nervous system
D. None of the above

47. The number of cranial nerves in a frog are:
A. 10 pairs B. 15 pairs
C. 12 pairs D. 4 pairs

48. In frog the auditory nerve arises from:
A. Medulla B. Pharynx
C. Internal ear D. Tongue

49. Which one of the following is a motor nerve?
A. Facial B. Abducens
C. Vagus D. Olfactory

50. Which of the following cranial nerve of man is both sensory and motor?
A. Optic B. Auditory
C. Olfactory D. Trigeminal

51. Which structure helps a person to maintain his equilibrium?
A. Cochlea B. Hammer
C. Semicircular canals D. None of these

52. Receptors for hearing and balance are called:
A. Photoreceptors
B. Tangoreceptors
C. Statoacoustic receptors
D. Olfactoreceptors

53. Sclerotic, cloroid and retina are the layers of:
A. Intestine B. Eyeball
C. Stomach D. Oesophagus

54. Which of the following have solid optic lobes?
A. Frog B. Snake
C. Man D. Bird

55. Deficiency of vitamin A in the body results in insufficient rhodopsin in the rods which leads to:
A. colour blindness B. total blindness
C. night blindness D. myopia

56. Human temperature is set at:
A. 47.5°C B. 37°C
C. 37°F D. 98.4°C

57. The sensory ganglion concerned with spinal reflex is located in:

A. Dorsal root of spinal nerve
B. Ventral root of spinal nerve
C. Both A and B
D. None of the above

58. Jacobson's organs are concerned with .... in amphibians:
A. taste B. smell
C. touch D. taste and vision

59. Constriction of the pupil is function of:
A. Parasympathetic system
B. Hypothalamus
C. Thalamus
D. None of the above

60. Brain is produced by:
A. mesoderm
B. ectoderm
C. endoderm
D. both mesoderm and ectoderm

61. Which among the following nerves carry the impulse to the spinal cord?
A. Reflex Action B. Central Nerves
C. Motor D. Sensory nerves

62. The stimulus of the plant due to certain chemicals is called:
A. Phototropism B. Chemotropism
C. Geotropism D. Arthrotopism

63. Memory is related to
A. Cerebellum B. Cerebrum
C. Medulla D. Olfactory lobes

64. Plant hormones are:
A. Physical substances
B. Chemical substances
C. Photo Chemical substances
D. Both A and B

65. Central nervous system consists of:
A. Brain and spinal cord
B. Brain and visceral nerves
C. Cranial and sympathetic nervous system
D. Spinal and visceral nerves

66. The function of control and coordination performed in plants by:
A. Plant hormones B. Photosynthesis
C. Respiration D. Osmosis

67. Which of the following is the bony cover box in the skull that protects the brain?
A. Outer Brain B. Mid brain
C. Cranium D. Fore brain

68. Reflex actions in man are controlled by:
A. Brain B. Spinal cord
C. Sense glands D. Hormones

69. What is the other name of the endocrine glands?
A. Ducting gland B. Normal
C. Ductless gland D. Oesophagus

70. Which of the following is the regulating centre for swallowing, coughing, sneezing and vomiting?
A. Cerebellum
B. Medulla oblongata
C. Pons
D. Spinal cord

71. Which of the following is a gaseous hormone:
A. Gibberellin B. Ethylene
C. Cytokinin D. Auxin

72. Name the instrument which can record electrical activity of brain:
A. X-ray B. ECG
C. EEG D. Ultrasound

73. The endocrine gland situated on the top of the either side of kidney is:
A. Thymus gland B. Pituitary gland
C. Adrenal gland D. Parathyroid gland

74. Insulin and glucagon hormone is secreted by:
A. Pituitary gland B. Adrenal gland
C. Pancreas D. Thyroid gland

75. Calcitrin is secreted from:
A. Thyroid gland B. Adrenal gland
C. Parathyroid gland D. Pituitary gland

76. Nervous tissue is made up of:
A. Neurons B. Nerve fibres
C. Neuroglia D. All the above

77. A nerve is composed of:
A. Muscular tissue
B. Nerve fibre bundles

C. Bundle sheaths
D. None of the above

78. The secretion of adrenal glands called:
A. Aldrin B. Adrenalin
C. Sympathin D. None of these

79. Temperature control centre is located in the:
A. Hypophysis B. Hypothalamus
C. Diencephalon D. None of these

80. Number of spinal nerves in rabbit are:
A. 32 pairs B. 23 pairs
C. 73 pairs D. 37 pairs

81. Semon consists of an enzyme:
A. seminase B. hyaluronidase
C. vasciulase D. ligase

82. Vernalization is related to:
A. Plant growth B. Flowers
C. Stems D. Leaves

83. Auxin promotes:
A. Growth of stems
B. Elongation and growth of stems and roots
C. Enlargement of fruits
D. Both A and C

84. Which of the following promotes cell division in vascular cambium?
A. Gibberellin B. Cytokinin
C. Auxin D. None of the above

85. Which of the following can retard the ageing of plant organs?
A. Auxin B. Ethylene
C. Cytokinin D. None of the above

86. Which of the following growth hormone is act as a stress hromone?
A. IAA B. 2, 4 D
C. ABA D. None of the above

87. Which of the following is capable of delaying yellowish of leaves?
A. Gibberelic acid B. IAA
C. ABA D. Cytokinins

88. Phytochrome is found in:
A. Fungi B. Algae
C. Pteridophytes D. Angiosperms

89. Corpus luteum is developed from:
A. left over oocyte
B. nephrostome
C. left over Graafian follicle after release of ovum
D. none of these

90. The development of embryo inside an egg is called:
A. Vivipery B. Carnivorous
C. Omnivorous D. Ovipery

91. The type of fertilization occur in frog is:
A. Internal B. External
C. Both A and B D. None of the above

92. The only haploid stage in an animal life cycle is the:
A. Zoospores B. Spores
C. Gametes D. None of the above

93. The common method of reproduction in yeast is:
A. Fission
B. Binary fission
C. Budding
D. Sexual reproduction

94. Oblique ovary is found in:
A. Solanaceae B. Palmaceae
C. Poaceae D. Liliaceae

95. Most of the plant's auxin is produced in its:
A. Root tips B. Buds
C. Leaves D. Shot apex

96. A fruit developed from the wall of the:
A. Style B. Androecium
C. Ovary D. None of these

97. The rate of cleavage in a zygote depends upon:
A. amount of yolk
B. amount of cytoplasm
C. size of nucleus
D. all above

98. The meiotic process by which homologous are paired during prophase I is called:
A. Chasma B. Crossing over
C. Duplication D. Synapsis

99. Growth is maximum in the zone of:
A. Tracheds B. Sieve tubes
C. Cell elongation D. Companion cells

100. At what stage does cytokinesis begin?
A. Anaphase B. Prophase
C. Telephase D. None of the above

101. The fertilizations takes place in mammals in:
A. Water B. Ovary
C. Uterus D. Fallopian tube

102. The sexual reproduction in protozoa is caused by:
A. Binary fission B. Conjugation
C. Fregmentation D. None of the above

103. The hormones playing important role in growth of man are:
A. thymosin and thyroxine
B. testosterone and glucagon
C. aldesterone and calcitonin
D. all above

104. Two successive cell division occurs in the process of:
A. Amitosis
B. Meiosis
C. Mitosis
D. Somatic cell division

105. Sexual reproduction through gametic fusion is absent in:
A. Angiosperms B. Eukaryotes
C. Prokaryotes D. Gymnosperms

106. The sexual phase in its life history is not determined in:
A. *Rihzopus* B. *Opedogonium*
C. *Spirogyra* D. *Amoeba*

107. In *Spirogyra* the sexual reproduction takes palce by:
A. Binary fission
B. Spore formation
C. Conjugation
D. Aplanospore formation

108. Reparative regeneration is common in:
A. invertebrates B. vertebrates
C. both above D. none of these

109. In mammals the fertilization and entire embryonic development takes place within the:
A. Uterus of female
B. Uterus of male
C. Fellopian tube of female
D. Ovary of female

110. In plants part developing into seeds is:
A. Ovary B. Pollen grain
C. Ovules D. None of these

111. Gametes are produced in gonads by the process of:
A. Mitosis B. Meiosis
C. None of these D. Both A and B

112. The attachment of embryo with the uterus is called:
A. Implantation B. Parturation
C. Gestation D. None of these

113. Mature ova are released by:
A. Uterus B. Ovary
C. Fallopian tube D. Oviduct

114. The male reproductive organs in plants are:
A. Sepals B. Stamens
C. Petals D. Carpel

115. Normal menstrual cycle is completed in:
A. 32 days B. 82 days
C. 28 days D. 38 days

116. Pollen grains are produced in:
A. Sepals B. Petals
C. Anthers D. Carpel

117. Which surgical operation is undertaken in a women for planned family?
A. Vasectomy B. Prostatectomy
C. Tubectomy D. None of the above

118. Which part of flower changes into fruit?
A. Stamen B. Pistil
C. Ovary D. Seed

119. Premenstrual syndrome is related to:
A. Women B. Men
C. Microorganisms D. None of the above

120. Which of the following organisms is reproduced by the mode of budding?

A. Amoeba B. Fungi
C. Plasmodium D. Yeast

121. In which animal the fertilization occurs externally?
A. Frog B. Woman
C. Earthworm D. None of the above

122. The gestation period of elephant is about:
A. 15 months B. 10 months
C. 22 months D. 30 months

123. The female gamete ovum is produced by:
A. Testis B. Uterus
C. Ovary D. None of these

124. The head cap of sperm is called :
A. Acrosome B. Centrosome
C. Lysosome D. Ribosome

125. The male gamete sperm is produced in:
A. Ovary B. Penis
C. Testis D. Uterus

126. Identical twins are born when:
A. Two ova crosses with two sperms
B. One ovum crosses with one sperm
C. Two sperms crosses with one ovum
D. None of the above

127. Sex linked inheritance was discovered by:
A. Mendel B. Johnsen
C. Morgan D. Darwin

128. Continuous variation is attributed to:
A. mutation
B. crossing over
C. chromosomal aberration
D. polyploidy

129. A co-ordinated unit which controls the genetic expression is:
A. cistron B. recon
C. muton D. operon

130. Animals of similar genetic constitution are called:
A. Heterozygous B. Homozygous
C. Genotypes D. Phenotypes

131. Rarely observed phenotype in population is called:
A. wild type B. mutant type
C. variant type D. all of these

132. Crossing over generally takes place during:
A. Amitosis B. Mitosis
C. Meiosis D. None of the above

133. Haemophilia is:
A. Enzyme B. Disease
C. Sex linked disease D. None of the above

134. Polydipsia and Polyuria is related to:
A. Haemophilia
B. Colour blindness
C. Nephrogenic diabetes insipidus
D. None of the above

135. Factors which can induce genetic mutations in organisms are called:
A. Mutants B. Mutagens
C. Muton D. None of these

136. William Shockley is related to:
A. Eugenics B. Mutation
C. Haemoglobin D. Blood groups

137. The first person who induce mutations by using X-rays was?
A. Hugo de Vries B. Muller
C. Mendel D. None of these

138. The chromosome number in plants can be increased by:
A. Hormone treatment
B. Colchicine treatment
C. Heat treatment
D. None of the above

139. Colchicine can induce polyploidy in:
A. Animals only B. Plants only
C. Both A. and B. D. None of these

140. The human chromosomes number i.e., 46 were discovered by:
A. Mendel B. H.J. Mullar
C. Tijo and Laren D. Watson and Crick

141. The basis of Klinefelter's syndrome and supermale are the following characteristic of sex chromosomes:
A. XXY and XYY B. XO and XXX
C. XXX and YYY D. None of these

142. The basis of Turner's syndrome and super-females are the following characteristic of sex chromosomes:
A. XO and XXX B. XXX and XYY
C. XXXY and XXYY D. None of these

143. In Down's syndrome one extra chromosome is added to:
A. 20th pair B. 21st pair
C. 22th pair D. None of these

144. Which genes are present on sex chromosomes?
A. Sex linked genes
B. Autosomal genes
C. Chromosomes genes
D. None of these

145. Which among the following are the components of nucleotides?
A. Sugar, Phosphate and Nucleic acid
B. Pyrimidine, Purine and Nucleic acid
C. Nitrogenous base, Sugar and Phosphate
D. None of these

146. Find the two pyrimidines in DNA:
A. Cytosine and Thymine
B. Cytosine and Gaunine
C. Adenine and Cytosine
D. None of these

147. Adenine and Guanine are two:
A. Cytosines C. Salts
C. Nucleotides D. Purines

148. For a female human being:
A. 44 + XX B. 42 + YY
C. 44 + XXY D. 44 + YY

149. If taster male and female in heterozygous form are crossed the % of male tasters in progeny will be:
A. 18 B. 45
C. 0 D. 75

150. According to position of centromere, chromosome are of .... type:
A. 2 B. 4
C. 3 D. 5

151. What is called the arrangement of chromosomes?
A. Kryotype B. Phenotype
C. Xerotype D. None of these

152. In which cell chromosomes are found in pairs?
A. Ovum B. Sperm
C. Haploid cell D. Diploid cell

153. Who wrote the book 'Origin of Species'?
A. Linneus B. Lamark
C. Darwin D. None of these

154. Which one of the following supports theory of evolutions?
A. Morphological evidence
B. Psephological evidence
C. Embroyological evidence
D. Both A and C

155. The average estimated age of mother giving birth to children with Down syndrome is:
A. 25 years B. 34 years
C. 21 years D. 45 years

156. Duckbilled paltypus is a link between:
A. Reptiles and birds
B. Birds and mammals
C. Reptiles and mammals
D. Reptiles and Humen

157. Theory of natural selection was given by:
A. Ernst Haccket
B. Jean Baptist Lamark
C. Carolus Linneus
D. Charles Robert Darwin

158. Which among the following deals with study of Heredity?
A. Resemblances and differences between the parents and offsprings
B. Differences between the parents and the offsprings
C. Resemblances between the parents and the offsprings
D. None of these

159. By which chromosomes are made of?
A. DNA and RNA B. DNA and Protein
C. DNA only D. Protein only

160. Which among the following represents female human chromosomes?
A. XX B. XY
C. YY D. XXY

ANSWERS

PHYSICS

1	2	3	4	5	6	7	8	9	10
B	D	B	A	B	D	A	C	B	A
11	**12**	**13**	**14**	**15**	**16**	**17**	**18**	**19**	**20**
A	D	B	C	B	C	C	C	A	C
21	**22**	**23**	**24**	**25**	**26**	**27**	**28**	**29**	**30**
C	D	A	B	B	D	A	C	B	D
31	**32**	**33**	**34**	**35**	**36**	**37**	**38**	**39**	**40**
B	C	D	C	B	C	D	B	A	A
41	**42**	**43**	**44**	**45**	**46**	**47**	**48**	**49**	**50**
B	A	C	D	C	B	B	B	C	D
51	**52**	**53**	**54**	**55**	**56**	**57**	**58**	**59**	**60**
A	D	C	C	A	C	B	C	A	B
61	**62**	**63**	**64**	**65**	**66**	**67**	**68**	**69**	**70**
C	C	D	A	D	D	D	C	C	C
71	**72**	**73**	**74**	**75**	**76**	**77**	**78**	**79**	**80**
B	C	C	B	C	C	B	D	A	C
81	**82**	**83**	**84**	**85**	**86**	**87**	**88**	**89**	**90**
B	B	B	A	B	B	C	C	B	D
91	**92**	**93**	**94**	**95**	**96**	**97**	**98**	**99**	**100**
D	A	A	C	B	B	C	B	D	A
101	**102**	**103**	**104**	**105**	**106**	**107**	**108**	**109**	**110**
C	A	B	C	D	C	A	A	A	B
111	**112**	**113**	**114**	**115**	**116**	**117**	**118**	**119**	**120**
B	A	D	A	C	D	C	C	B	A
121	**122**	**123**	**124**	**125**	**126**	**127**	**128**	**129**	**130**
B	B	C	B	D	B	B	C	A	B
131	**132**	**133**	**134**	**135**	**136**	**137**	**138**	**139**	**140**
A	A	B	B	B	B	B	D	C	D
141	**142**	**143**	**144**	**145**	**146**	**147**	**148**	**149**	**150**
D	C	A	A	D	A	A	A	C	B
151	**152**	**153**	**154**	**155**	**156**	**157**	**158**	**159**	**160**
C	B	C	B	D	D	C	B	C	D
161	**162**	**163**	**164**	**165**	**166**	**167**	**168**	**169**	**170**
C	D	D	B	B	A	A	B	A	A
171	**172**	**173**	**174**	**175**	**176**	**177**	**178**	**179**	**180**
B	C	B	A	B	B	B	C	A	C
181	**182**	**183**	**184**	**185**	**186**	**187**	**188**	**189**	**190**
B	B	A	B	C	A	B	C	D	A
191	**192**	**193**	**194**	**195**	**196**	**197**	**198**	**199**	**200**
A	B	A	B	D	B	C	C	B	C
201	**202**	**203**	**204**	**205**	**206**	**207**	**208**	**209**	**210**
D	C	C	B	C	A	B	D	C	A

211	212	213	214	215	216	217	218	219	220
C	A	D	A	A	D	B	C	B	B
221	222	223	224	225	226	227	228	229	230
D	B	C	B	C	B	D	A	D	A
231	232	233	234	235	236	237	238	239	240
B	A	D	C	A	A	D	C	A	A
241	242	243	244	245	246	247	248	249	250
B	D	D	D	D	C	D	B	C	D
251	252	253	254	255	256	257	258	259	260
A	A	B	D	A	B	A	B	C	A
261	262	263	264	265	266	267	268	269	270
C	B	C	C	C	C	D	D	A	C

CHEMISTRY

1	2	3	4	5	6	7	8	9	10
A	A	B	D	B	D	A	C	A	B
11	12	13	14	15	16	17	18	19	20
C	B	B	D	C	C	C	C	A	D
21	22	23	24	25	26	27	28	29	30
B	C	B	B	A	C	B	B	A	C
31	32	33	34	35	36	37	38	39	40
D	C	B	C	C	B	B	D	B	C
41	42	43	44	45	46	47	48	49	50
A	A	D	B	C	D	D	A	A	B
51	52	53	54	55	56	57	58	59	60
C	A	A	D	A	D	B	D	C	B
61	62	63	64	65	66	67	68	69	70
B	B	C	A	A	C	C	B	A	C
71	72	73	74	75	76	77	78	79	80
B	C	A	D	D	B	A	A	C	D
81	82	83	84	85	86	87	88	89	90
B	C	D	C	B	B	D	C	A	D
91	92	93	94	95	96	97	98	99	100
C	B	A	C	C	C	A	B	D	B
101	102	103	104	105	106	107	108	109	110
D	C	C	A	D	A	A	D	A	C
111	112	113	114	115	116	117	118	119	120
A	A	A	B	A	A	B	D	D	B
121	122	123	124	125	126	127	128	129	130
D	A	B	A	C	D	D	C	B	D
131	132	133	134	135	136	137	138	139	140
C	D	D	C	C	D	B	A	B	A
141	142	143	144	145					
D	D	A	D	D					

BIOLOGY

1	2	3	4	5	6	7	8	9	10
B	A	C	B	A	D	A	A	C	C
11	**12**	**13**	**14**	**15**	**16**	**17**	**18**	**19**	**20**
A	A	D	C	D	B	C	C	A	B
21	**22**	**23**	**24**	**25**	**26**	**27**	**28**	**29**	**30**
B	C	D	C	C	C	A	B	A	A
31	**32**	**33**	**34**	**35**	**36**	**37**	**38**	**39**	**40**
B	**A**	**A**	**C**	**D**	**C**	**B**	**A**	**B**	**A**
41	**42**	**43**	**44**	**45**	**46**	**47**	**48**	**49**	**50**
D	D	B	D	B	A	A	A	B	D
51	**52**	**53**	**54**	**55**	**56**	**57**	**58**	**59**	**60**
C	C	B	C	C	B	A	B	A	C
61	**62**	**63**	**64**	**65**	**66**	**67**	**68**	**69**	**70**
D	B	B	B	A	A	C	B	C	B
71	**72**	**73**	**74**	**75**	**76**	**77**	**78**	**79**	**80**
B	C	A	C	D	D	B	B	B	D
81	**82**	**83**	**84**	**85**	**86**	**87**	**88**	**89**	**90**
B	B	D	B	C	C	D	D	C	D
91	**92**	**93**	**94**	**95**	**96**	**97**	**98**	**99**	**100**
B	C	C	A	D	C	A	D	C	A
101	**102**	**103**	**104**	**105**	**106**	**107**	**108**	**109**	**110**
D	A	A	C	B	D	C	C	A	C
111	**112**	**113**	**114**	**115**	**116**	**117**	**118**	**119**	**120**
B	A	B	B	C	C	C	C	A	D
121	**122**	**123**	**124**	**125**	**126**	**127**	**128**	**129**	**130**
A	C	C	A	C	A	C	B	D	C
131	**132**	**133**	**134**	**135**	**136**	**137**	**138**	**139**	**140**
B	C	C	C	B	A	B	B	B	C
141	**142**	**143**	**144**	**145**	**146**	**147**	**148**	**149**	**150**
A	A	B	A	C	A	D	A	D	B
151	**152**	**153**	**154**	**155**	**156**	**157**	**158**	**159**	**160**
A	D	B	D	D	C	D	C	C	A

REASONING & GENERAL INTELLIGENCE

1. LETTER SERIES

In letter series, the letters follow a definite order. The given series of letters can be in natural order or in reverse order or combination of both. The letters may be skipped or repeated or consecutive. The given series may be single or may even comprise of two different series merged at alternate positions. While attempting questions on letter series one should note the pattern of alphabet series.

Alphabets in natural series are :

A B C D E F G H I J K L M N O P Q R S T U V W X Y Z

A ↓ 1st, E ↓ 5th, J ↓ 10th, O ↓ 15th, T ↓ 20th, Y ↓ 25th

Alphabets in reverse series are :

Z Y X W V U T S R Q P O N M L K J I H G F E D C B A

Z ↓ 1st, V ↓ 5th, Q ↓ 10th, L ↓ 15th, G ↓ 20th, B ↓ 25th

Note : On reaching Z, the series restarts from A and on reaching A, it restarts from Z.

EXERCISE

Directions : *In each of the following series determine the order of the letters. Then from the given options select the one which will complete the given series.*

1. B Y C X D W E ?
(*a*) S (*b*) T
(*c*) U (*d*) V

2. B A F E J I P O ? U
(*a*) V (*b*) T
(*c*) S (*d*) Q

3. B A D C ? H G J I
(*a*) E F (*b*) F E
(*c*) F G (*d*) D F

4. ADG, XVT, BEH, WUS, ?
(*a*) VTR (*b*) CFI
(*c*) DFJ (*d*) STU

5. GMSY, IOUA, KQWC, ?
(*a*) MSYE (*b*) NSYE
(*c*) MTYE (*d*) MSYF

6. ADG, GJM, ?, SVY
(*a*) MPS (*b*) MQR
(*c*) MQS (*d*) SPM

7. XYZ, UVW, ?, OPQ
(*a*) RST (*b*) STU
(*c*) QRS (*d*) TUV

8. JOBS, KMEO, LKHK, ?, NGNC
(*a*) MJLH (*b*) LIKG
(*c*) MIKG (*d*) MNGM

9. AZ, GT, MN, ?, YB
(*a*) KF (*b*) TS
(*c*) RX (*d*) SH

10. BMY, DNW, FOU, ?
(*a*) HPT (*b*) HPS
(*c*) HQS (*d*) GPS

11. AZ, CX, EV, ?
(*a*) HU (*b*) GS
(*c*) GT (*d*) HT

EXPLANATORY ANSWERS

1. (*d*) : There are two alternate series.

+1 +1 +1

B Y C X D W E V

−1 −1 −1

Series I : BCDE (natural order)
Series II : YXWV (reverse order)

2. (*a*) : Each vowel (AEIOU) is preceded by the letter that comes next to it in the natural alphabetical series.

B A F E J I P O V U

3. (*b*) : The letters in natural series are divided into sections of two letters each. The letters in each section are written backward.
BA DC FE HG JI

4. (*b*) : There are two alternate series.

ADG XVT BEH WUS CFI

Series I : ADG BEH CFI

+1 +1
+1 +1
+1 +1

Series II : XVT WUS

−1
−1
−1

5. (*a*) : The series is formed by moving each letter two steps forward from one group to the next.

GMSY IOUA KQWC MSYE

+2 +2 +2
+2 +2 +2
+2 +2 +2
+2 +2 +2

(The series restarts from A on reaching Z)

6. (*a*) : In each group of three letters the alphabet is in the succession of +3. The next group begins with the last alphabet of the previous group.

A D G G J M M P S S V Y

+3 +3 +3 +3 +3 +3 +3 +3

7. (*a*) : The alphabet from one group to the next are in recession of −3, *i.e.,*

XYZ UVW RST OPQ

−3 −3 −3
−3 −3 −3
−3 −3 −3

8. (*c*) : The alphabets in each group follow the pattern +1, −2, +3 and −4 respectively from one group to the next group.

JOBS KMEO LKHK MIKG NGNC

+1 +1 +1 +1
−2 −2 −2 −2
+3 +3 +3 +3
−4 −4 −4 −4

9. (*d*) : The letters in one group correspond to the letters in the next group in the manner +6, −6 respectively, *i.e.,*

AZ GT MN SH YB

+6 +6 +6 +6
−6 −6 −6 −6

10. (*b*) : The letters in one group correspond to the letters in the next group in the manner +2, +1, -2 respectively, *i.e.,*

BMY DNW FOU HPS

+2 +2 +2
+1 +1 +1
−2 −2 −2

11. (*c*) : The letters in each group correspond to the letters in the next group in the manner +2, −2 respectively, *i.e.,*

AZ CX EV GT

+2 +2 +2
−2 −2 −2

2. WRONG LETTER SERIES

In this type of series, the candidates are not required to find the letter or group of letters which will complete the given series but, they have to identify the letter or number which is wrong or misfit in the given series.

SOLVED EXAMPLE

1. Which of the following letters in the given series is wrong?
J M P T V Y
(*a*) J (*b*) P (*c*) T (*d*) Y

Ans. (*c*) : The letters in this series are moved three steps forward, *i.e.*,

J M P S V Y
+3 +3 +3 +3 +3

Letter 'T' should have been 'S'.

EXERCISE

Directions : *Which letter(s) in each of the following series is wrong or is misfit in the series?*

1. AEHOU
(*a*) U (*b*) O
(*c*) H (*d*) E

2. CHMSWB
(*a*) C (*b*) S
(*c*) B (*d*) W

3. XSNICY
(*a*) Y (*b*) C
(*c*) S (*d*) I

4. ZAWBXC
(*a*) D (*b*) C
(*c*) X (*d*) W

5. MLONQPR
(*a*) R (*b*) O
(*c*) Q (*d*) L

EXPLANATORY ANSWERS

1. (*c*) : The series is made with vowels only. AEIOU. I should be in place of H.

2. (*b*) : The letters in the series are moved five steps forward.

C H M R W B
+5 +5 +5 +5 +5

R should be in place of S
(The series restarts from A on reaching Z)

3. (*b*) : The pattern in the series is –5, *i.e.*,

X S N I D Y
–5 –5 –5 –5 –5

D should be in place of C.

4. (*d*) : There are two alternate series

+1 +1
Z A Y B X C
–1 –1

Series I : ZYX (reverse series)
Series II : ABC (natural series)
Y should be in place of W.

5. (*a*) : Two consecutive letters are written backwards.

ML ON QP SR

S should be in place of R.

3. REPEAT SERIES

In this type of series, small letters of the alphabet are used to make a set of letters which are repeated. The candidate has to find the set of letters which will fit the blanks left in the given series in such a manner that one section of the series is further repeated in the same manner.

SOLVED EXAMPLE

1. Which of the following groups of letters will complete the given series?
ba-b-aab-a-b
(*a*) baab (*b*) abba (*c*) abaa (*d*) babb

Ans. (*b*) : The series is baab, baab, baab. Here the section 'baab' is repeated in the series.

***Solving steps* :** The candidate has to look for clues to solve such series pattern. 'aab' in the Series indicates that 'b' in this series is preceded by two 'a' so, the first blank and the last blank will be filled by 'a'. Now the first set is formed, *i.e.,* 'baab' in the beginning. This set is repeated, so the second and third blanks will have 'b' filling them. Now, solve the exercise given below to know the different ways in which these series are formed.

EXERCISE

Directions : *Which of the following groups of letters will complete the given series?*

1. ab---b-bbaa-
(*a*) babba (*b*) abaab
(*c*) abbab (*d*) baaab

2. aa-ab--aaa-a
(*a*) baaa (*b*) abab
(*c*) aaab (*d*) aabb

3. -baa-aab-a-a
(*a*) baab (*b*) abab
(*c*) aaba (*d*) aabb

4. -a cca-ccca-acccc-aaa
(*a*) ccaa (*b*) acca
(*c*) caac (*d*) caaa

5. c-bbb--abbbb-abbb-
(*a*) abccb (*b*) bacbb
(*c*) aabcb (*d*) abacb

6. ac-cab-baca-aba-acac
(*a*) bcbb (*b*) aacb
(*c*) babb (*d*) acbc

7. --aba--ba-ab
(*a*) abbab (*b*) bbaba
(*c*) baabb (*d*) abbba

8. --babbba-a--
(*a*) bbaba (*b*) babbb
(*c*) baaab (*d*) ababb

9. k-mk-lmkkl-kk-mk
(*a*) lklm (*b*) lkmk
(*c*) lkmm (*d*) lkml

10. abc-d-bc-d-b-dd
(*a*) decdb (*b*) dadac
(*c*) cdabe (*d*) bacde

EXPLANATORY ANSWERS

1. (*d*) : The series is abbaab, abbaab.
2. (*c*) : The series is aaaaba, aaaaba.
3. (*b*) : The series is aba, aba, aba, aba.
4. (*d*) : The series is c,a,cc,aa, ccc, aaa, cccc, aaaa.
5. (*a*) : The series is cabbbb, cabbbb, cabbbb.
6. (*b*) : The series is acac, abab, acac, abab, acac.
7. (*a*) : The series is ab, ab, ab, ab, ab, ab.
8. (*b*) : The series is bababb, bababb.
9. (*d*) : The series is klmk, klmk, klmk, klmk.
10. (*b*) : The series is abcdd, abcdd, abcdd.

4. NUMBER SERIES

In this type of series, the set of given numbers in a series are related to one another in a particular pattern or manner. The relationship between the numbers may be (i) consecutive odd/even numbers; (ii) consecutive prime numbers; (iii) squares/cubes of some numbers with/without variation of addition or subtraction of some number; (iv) sum/product/difference of preceding numbers; (v) addition/subtraction/multiplication/division by some number; and (vi) many more combinations of the relationships given above.

EXERCISE

Directions : *In the following questions, select the number(s) from the given options for completing the given series.*

1. 7776, 1296, 216, 36, 6, ?
(*a*) 6 (*b*) 0
(*c*) 3 (*d*) 1

2. 29282, 2662, 242, 22, ?
(*a*) 1 (*b*) 2
(*c*) 0 (*d*) 11

3. 1, 2, 2, 4, 16, ?, 65536
(*a*) 276 (*b*) 64
(*c*) 256 (*d*) 198

4. 3, 5, 9, 15, 23, ?, 45
(*a*) 37 (*b*) 35
(*c*) 31 (*d*) 33

5. 7, 21, 35, 49, 63, ?
(*a*) 70 (*b*) 77
(*c*) 81 (*d*) 108

6. 10, 14, 23, 39, 64, ?, 149
(*a*) 78 (*b*) 128
(*c*) 103 (*d*) 100

7. 6, 24, 29, 116, 121, ?, 489
(*a*) 468 (*b*) 484
(*c*) 243 (*d*) 363

EXPLANATORY ANSWERS

1. (*d*) : The numbers in this sequence are divided by 6 each time.

2. (*b*) : The numbers in the series are divided by 11 at each step.

3. (*c*) : The number in the series is product of all the numbers preceding it.

1 2 2 4 16 256 65536

(1×2)

(1×2×2)

(1×2×2×4)

(1×2×2×4×16)

(1×2×2×4×16×256)

4. (*d*) : The difference between consecutive numbers increases by 2 at each step.

3 5 9 15 23 33 45

+2 +4 +6 +8 +10 +12

5. (*b*) : The series is multiplication of 7 by odd numbers starting from 3.

7 21 35 49 63 77

× 3

× 5

× 7

× 9

× 11

6. (*d*) : The number plus the square of numbers in natural order starting from 2 gives the next number in the series.

10 14 23 39 64 100 149

$+2^2$ $+3^2$ $+4^2$ $+5^2$ $+6^2$ $+7^2$

7. (*b*) : The sequence in the series is ×4, +5, which is repeated.

5. WRONG NUMBER SERIES

In this type of series, the given series may be complete but what needs to be identified is the number in the given completed series which is disturbing the sequential pattern of that series and does not fit in with the relationship shared between the other numbers.

EXERCISE

Directions : *In the given series find the number which is wrong.*

1. 5, 25, 120, 625, 3125, 15625
(*a*) 15625 (*b*) 625
(*c*) 120 (*d*) 5

2. 4, 8, 11, 22, 18, 36, 24, 50
(*a*) 8 (*b*) 22
(*c*) 36 (*d*) 24

3. 2, 4, 12, 24, 72, 142, 432
(*a*) 432 (*b*) 12
(*c*) 142 (*d*) 72

4. 2, 3, 4, 4, 6, 8, 9, 12, 16
(*a*) 3 (*b*) 9
(*c*) 6 (*d*) 12

5. 97, 91, 86, 83, 79, 77, 76, 76
(*a*) 86 (*b*) 76
(*c*) 91 (*d*) 83

6. 7, 11, 11, 9, 15, 7, 19, 5, 23, 1
(*a*) 5 (*b*) 7
(*c*) 1 (*d*) 9

7. 3, 7, 12, 28, 48, 118, 192, 448
(*a*) 12 (*b*) 118
(*c*) 28 (*d*) 7

8. 10, 100, 1100, 11000, 111000, 1210000
(*a*) 1210000 (*b*) 11000
(*c*) 100 (*d*) 111000

9. 24576, 6144, 1536, 386, 96, 24
(*a*) 386 (*b*) 6144
(*c*) 96 (*d*) 1536

10. 11, 13, 15, 17, 19, 23, 29, 31, 37
(*a*) 13 (*b*) 23
(*c*) 15 (*d*) 31

11. 36, 43, 49, 54, 60, 61, 63, 64
(*a*) 60 (*b*) 63
(*c*) 54 (*d*) 43

12. 3, 10, 41, 206, 1236, 8660
(*a*) 10 (*b*) 41
(*c*) 206 (*d*) 1236

13. 17, 25, 37, 50, 65, 82, 101
(*a*) 25 (*b*) 17
(*c*) 101 (*d*) 65

14. 12, 20, 38, 42, 56, 72
(*a*) 20 (*b*) 38
(*c*) 56 (*d*) 72

15. 5, 6, 11, 22, 42, 88, 176
(*a*) 5 (*b*) 42
(*c*) 176 (*d*) 11

EXPLANATORY ANSWERS

1. (*c*) : The numbers in the series are multiplied by 5 to get the next number.
∴ 125 should be in place of 120.

2. (*d*) : Two numbers form a pair. The first number increases by 7 for the next pair and the second number is the double of first number.

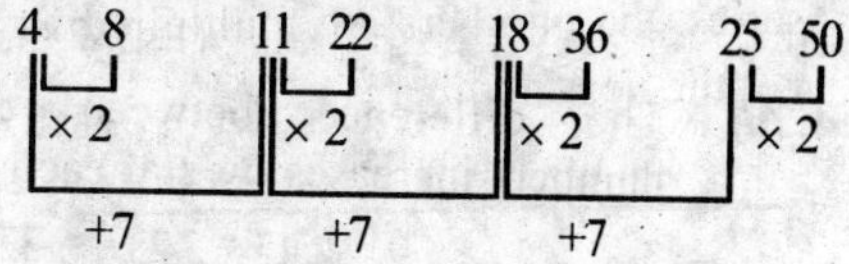

∴ 25 should be in place of 24.

3. (*c*) : There are two alternate series and in each series, the numbers are multiplied by 6 to get the next number.

× 6 × 6 × 6

2 4 12 24 72 144 432

× 6 × 6

∴ 144 should be in place of 142.

4. (*b*) : There are three alternate series and in each series, the numbers are multiplied by 2 to get the next number.

× 2 × 2

2 3 4 4 6 8 8 12 16

× 2 × 2

× 2 × 2

Series I : 2, 4, 8 *Series II* : 3, 6, 12

Series III : 4, 8, 16

∴ 8 should be in place of 9.

5. (*d*) : The difference between the consecutive numbers in the series decreases by 1 at each step.

97 91 86 82 79 77 76 76

–6 –5 –4 –3 –2 –1 –0

∴ 82 should be in place of 83.

6. (*c*) : There are two alternate series :

+4 +4 +4 +4

7 11 11 9 15 7 19 5 21 3

–2 –2 –2 –2

Series I : 7, 11, 15, 19, 23 (addition of 4)

Series II : 11, 9, 7, 5, 3 (subtraction of 2)

∴ 3 should be in place of 1.

7. (*b*) : There are two alternate series and in each series, the numbers are multiplied by 4 to get the next number.

× 4 × 4 × 4

3 7 12 28 48 112 192 448

× 4 × 4 × 4

∴ 112 should be in place of 118.

8. (*d*) : The numbers in this series are multiplied by 10 and 11 alternately is, *i.e.*, × 10, × 11.

10 100 1100 11000 121000 1210000

× 10 × 11 × 10 × 11 × 10

∴ 121000 should be in place of 111000.

9. (*a*) : The numbers in this series are divided by 4 to get the next number.

24576 6144 1536 384 96 24

÷ 4 ÷ 4 ÷ 4 ÷ 4 ÷ 4

∴ 384 should be in place of 386.

10. (*c*) : The series comprises of prime numbers in increasing order. Only 15 is an exception.

11. (*a*) : The difference between two consecutive numbers is decreasing by 1 at each step.

36 43 49 54 58 61 63 64

+7 +6 +5 +4 +3 +2 +1

∴ 58 should be in place of 60.

12. (*d*) : The sequence followed in this series is :

3 × 3 + 1 = 10, 10 × 4 + 1 = 41

41 × 5 + 1 = 206, 206 × 6 + 1 = 1237; and

1237 × 7 + 1 = 8660

∴ 1237 should be in place of 1236.

13. (*a*) : The numbers in the series are 1 plus the squares of numbers in natural order starting from 4.

17 26 37 50 65 82 101

↓ ↓ ↓ ↓ ↓ ↓ ↓

$4^2 + 1$ $5^2 + 1$ $6^2 + 1$ $7^2 + 1$ $8^2 + 1$ $9^2 + 1$ $10^2 + 1$

∴ 26 should be in place of 25.

14. (*b*) : The sequence followed in this series is :

3 × 4 = 12, 4 × 5 = 20, 5 × 6 = 30,

6 × 7 = 42, 7 × 8 = 56, 8 × 9 = 72

∴ 30 should be in place of 38.

15. (*b*) : The numbers in the series are the sum of all the numbers preceding them.

5 6 11 22 44 88 176

(5 + 6)

(5 + 6 + 11)

(5 + 6 + 11 + 22)

(5 + 6 + 11 + 22 + 44)

(5 + 6 + 11 + 22 + 44 + 88)

∴ 44 should be in place of 42.

6. WORD ANALOGY

In Analogy Tests, the relationship between two given words is established and then applied to the other words. The type of relationship may vary, so while attempting such questions the first step is to identify the type of relationship, which can be any one of the following.

EXERCISE

Directions : *In the questions given below one term is missing. Based on the relationship of the two given words find the missing term from the given options.*

1. HUNGER : FOOD : : THIRST : ?
(*a*) Water (*b*) Drink
(*c*) Tea (*d*) Coffee

2. HUNTER : GUN : : WRITER : ?
(*a*) Book (*b*) Pen
(*c*) Poem (*d*) Page

3. WOOL : SHEEP : : SILK : ?
(*a*) Saree (*b*) String
(*c*) Silkworm (*d*) Moth

4. FOOD : STOMACH : : FUEL : ?
(*a*) Engine (*b*) Automobile
(*c*) Rail (*d*) Aeroplane

5. WATER : SAND : : OCEAN : ?
(*a*) Island (*b*) River
(*c*) Desert (*d*) Waves

6. ADULT : BABY : : FLOWER : ?
(*a*) Seed (*b*) Bud
(*c*) Fruit (*d*) Butterfly

7. WRITER : READER : : PRODUCER : ?
(*a*) Creator
(*b*) Contractor
(*c*) Creature
(*d*) Consumer

8. ENTRANCE : EXIT : : LOYALTY : ?
(*a*) Treachery (*b*) Patriotism
(*c*) Fidelity (*d*) Reward

9. MOTHER : MATERNAL : : FATHER : ?
(*a*) Eternal
(*b*) Detrimental
(*c*) Paternal
(*d*) Formidable

10. PEARL : NECKLACE : : FLOWER : ?
(*a*) Plant (*b*) Garden
(*c*) Petal (*d*) Bouquet

EXPLANATORY ANSWERS

1. *(a)* : Hunger is satiated by food, thirst by water.

2. *(b)* : Weapon of a hunter is a gun, weapon of a writer is a pen.

3. *(c)* : Wool is obtained from sheep, silk is obtained from silkworm.

4. *(a)* : Food is consumed in stomach, fuel is consumed in engine.

5. *(c)* : The related words are near opposites.

6. *(b)* : The youngone of an adult is a baby and that of a flower is a bud.

7. *(d)* : A writer aims to please the readers by his writings, a producer aims to please the consumers by his products.

8. *(a)* : The related words are opposites.

9. *(c)* : Relations on the mother's side are maternal and on the father's side paternal.

10. *(d)* : Many pearls make a necklace, many flowers make a bouquet.

7. NUMBER ANALOGY

In number analogy also, the relationship between the given numbers is detected and then applied to the second part to find the missing numbers. This relationship between the numbers can be based on any of the following patterns : *(i)* numbers can be odd/even/prime numbers; *(ii)* numbers can be multiples of one number; *(iii)* numbers can be squares/cubes of different numbers; *(iv)* some numbers can be added to/ subtracted from/multiplied to/divided into the first number to get the second number; *(v)* the second number can be the sum/product/difference of the digits of first number; and *(vi)* combinations of any mathematical calculations given above can apply to the relationship between the two given numbers.

EXERCISE

Directions : *In the following questions, select the number from the given options which follows the same relationship as shared between the first two numbers.*

1. 1 : 11 : : 2 : ?

(*a*) 20 (*b*) 22

(*c*) 24 (*d*) 44

2. $\frac{1}{7} : \frac{1}{14} :: \frac{1}{9} : ?$

(*a*) $\frac{1}{88}$ (*b*) $\frac{1}{80}$

(*c*) $\frac{1}{81}$ (*d*) $\frac{1}{18}$

3. 0.16 : 0.0016 : : 1.02 : ?

(*a*) 10.20 (*b*) 0.102

(*c*) 0.0102 (*d*) 1.020

4. 663 : 884 : : 221 : ?

(*a*) 332 (*b*) 554

(*c*) 773 (*d*) 442

5. 16 : 0.16 : : ?

(*a*) 2 : 0.02 (*b*) 7 : 0.007

(*c*) 1.3 : 0.13 (*d*) 0.01 : 0.001

EXPLANATORY ANSWERS

1. *(b)* : The first number is repeated to obtain the second number.

2. *(d)* : The first fraction is multiplied by half to obtain the second fraction.

$$\frac{1}{7} : \frac{1}{14} :: \frac{1}{9} : \frac{1}{18}$$

(each pair: $\times \frac{1}{2}$)

3. *(c)* : The decimals are divided by 100.

0.16 : 0.0016 : : 1.02 : 0.0102

(each pair: ÷ 100)

4. *(d)* : The digits at tens and hundreds place is same but the digit at the units place is half the other identical digits.

663 : 884 : : 221 : 442

5. *(a)* : Of the two related numbers, the second number is the result of first number divided by 100.

16 : 0.16 : : 2 : 0.02

(each pair: ÷ 100)

8. ODD ONE OUT

In this type of classification, four words are given out of which three are almost same in matter or meaning and only one word is different from the common three. One has to find out the word which is different from the rest.

EXERCISE

Directions : *In each of the following questions, three words are alike in some manner. Spot the odd one out.*

1. (*a*) Green (*b*) Red (*c*) Colour (*d*) Orange
2. (*a*) Stable (*b*) Hole (*c*) Canoe (*d*) Sty
3. (*a*) Nose (*b*) Eyes (*c*) Skin (*d*) Teeth
4. (*a*) Venus (*b*) Moon (*c*) Pluto (*d*) Mars
5. (*a*) Happy (*b*) Gloomy (*c*) Lively (*d*) Cheerful

Directions : *Three of the following four in each question are alike in a certain way and so form a group. Select the group of letters that does not belong to that group.*

6. (*a*) ACE (*b*) LOR (*c*) GIK (*d*) VXZ
7. (*a*) TSR (*b*) LKJ (*c*) PQO (*d*) HGF
8. (*a*) EF LM (*b*) KJ SR (*c*) XW HG (*d*) ED YX
9. (*a*) JOPK (*b*) BOPC (*c*) QOPR (*d*) TOPS
10. (*a*) DfH (*b*) MoQ (*c*) UwY (*d*) lnO

Directions : *In each of the following questions, there are four options. Three numbers, in these options, are alike in certain manner. Only one number does not fit in. Choose the one which is different from the rest.*

11. (*a*) 1948 (*b*) 2401 (*c*) 966 (*d*) 1449
12. (*a*) 182 (*b*) 169 (*c*) 130 (*d*) 158
13. (*a*) 129 (*b*) 130 (*c*) 131 (*d*) 132
14. (*a*) 3215 (*b*) 9309 (*c*) 4721 (*d*) 2850
15. (*a*) 1776 (*b*) 2364 (*c*) 1976 (*d*) 3776

Directions : *In the following questions select the pair which is different from the other three.*

16. (*a*) Chair - Furniture
    (*b*) Shirt - Garment
    (*c*) Necklace - Jewellery
    (*d*) Bogie - Engine
17. (*a*) Crayon - Paper
    (*b*) Pencil - Lead
    (*c*) Pen - Ink
    (*d*) Brush - Paint
18. (*a*) War - Peace
    (*b*) Real - Natural
    (*c*) Premiere - First
    (*d*) Wrath - Anger
19. (*a*) Finger - Thimble
    (*b*) Head - Cap
    (*c*) Waist - Tiara
    (*d*) Foot - Shoe
20. (*a*) Day - Night
    (*b*) Clever - Foolish
    (*c*) Clear - Blurred
    (*d*) Arrive - Come

Directions : *In the following questions, which of the following pair of letters is different from the other three?*

21. (*a*) FGH - HIJ (*b*) PQR - RST (*c*) MNO - OPQ (*d*) CDE - DEF

22. (*a*) JuM - jUm (*b*) iLo - Ilo (*c*) PSa - psA (*d*) ZeX - zEx

23. (*a*) NQT - JMP (*b*) CFI - RUX (*c*) ADG - FGH (*d*) SVY - ORU

24. (*a*) DXD - XDX (*b*) KUK - UKU (*c*) FHF - EHE (*d*) RSR - SRS

25. (*a*) AYT - BZU (*b*) FNG - EMF (*c*) RWO - QVN (*d*) HJD - GIC

EXPLANATORY ANSWERS

1. (c) : All others are types of colour.

2. (c) : Canoe is a boat. Others are resting places of birds/animals.

3. (d) : All others are sense organs.

4. (b) : All others are planets.

5. (b) : All others are expressions of joy.

6. (b) : The sequence in each group is +2. Only option (*b*) has sequence in +3, *i.e.,*

ABCDE: +2 +2 ; LMNOPQR: +3 +3

GHIJK: +2 +2 ; VWXYZ: +2 +2

7. (c) : The sequence of alphabet in each group is in reverse order. Only option (*c*) has sequence in disturbed order.

8. (a) : Two consecutive alphabet in each group are in reverse sequence (–1), *i.e.,*

KJ SR; XW HG; ED YX

–1 –1 –1 –1 –1 –1

Only in option (*a*) the sequence is in natural order (+1), *i.e.,*

E F: +1 ; L M: +1

9. (d) : In each group, letters 'OP' are common. The two corner alphabet are in natural order (+1); *i.e.,*

JOPK: +1 ; BOPC: +1 ; QOPR: +1

Only in option (*d*) they are in reverse order (–1); *i.e.,*

TOPS: –1

10. (d) : In other groups, only the alphabet in the centre is of lower case. In this option letter 'L' on the left is also in lower case.

11. (a) : Other numbers are divisible by 7.

12. (d) : Other numbers are multiples of 13.

13. (c) : 131 is a prime number.

14. (b) : In other numbers, no digit is repeated.

15. (b) : In other numbers, the last two digits are same.

16. (d) : Bogie is a part of train which is a type of conveyance. Chair, Shirt and Necklace are types of furniture, garment and jewellery respectively.

17. (a) : The medium used for writing with pencil is lead, with pen it is ink and with brush, it is paint. With crayon it should be wax.

18. (a) : The pair of words are opposite. Other pairs are synonyms.

19. (c) : Tiara is worn on the head.

20. (d) : Other words are opposite to each other.

21. (d) : In all other groups, the letters are in natural series and the last letter of first part is the first letter of the second part.

22. (b) : In all other groups, only the vowel is in lower case in the first part and in second part the case is reversed.

23. (c) : In all other groups, the letters jump two letters in between them.

24. (c) : In all other groups, the single letter in first part is repeated in the second and vice versa.

25. (a) : In all other groups, the letters in the first part are one step forward than the corresponding letters in the second part.

9. CODING AND DECODING

Coding is a secretive language which is used to change the representation of the actual term/word/value. This coded language can be framed by *(i)* moving the letters one or more steps forward or backward; *(ii)* substituting numbers for letters and vice–versa; *(iii)* writing the letters of the given word in reverse order in part or in whole; and *(iv)* replacing the letters in their natural series by the same positioned letters in their reverse series.

There is variety in ways of coding. Coding language is not only for words and numbers but also for hiding a group of words, statements or even sentences. This form of coding pattern may appear to be confusing but after solving only a few questions it is very easy to understand. Questions based on this coding pattern require no moving of steps or straining efforts of calculations, but only quick tallying or comparing ability. The codes can be letters or numbers.

EXERCISE

Directions : *In the following questions select the right option which indicates the correct code for the word or letter given in the question.*

1. If MUSK is coded as 146816, then ZERO will be coded as :
   (*a*) 113811 (*b*) 122912
   (*c*) 15915 (*d*) 2651815
2. If BAD is coded as 7, HIS as 9, LOW will be coded as :
   (*a*) 50 (*b*) 8
   (*c*) 23 (*d*) 5
3. In a certain code LIBERATE is written as 56403170, TRIBAL will be written in the same code as :
   (*a*) 734615 (*b*) 736415
   (*c*) 136475 (*d*) 034615
4. In certain military code, SYSTEM is written as SYSMET, and NEARER as AENRER, what will be the code for FRACTION?
   (*a*) CRAFNOIT (*b*) FRCAITNO
   (*c*) CARFNOIT (*d*) FRACNOIT
5. If CRUDE is written as BSTED, then MOIST will be coded as :
   (*a*) NNJRU (*b*) LNHRS
   (*c*) NPJTU (*d*) LPHTS
6. In a certain code ALPACA is written as ACAPLA. How will ANIMAL be written in that code?
   (*a*) LAMINA (*b*) ALAMIN
   (*c*) LAMNIA (*d*) AAMLIN
7. In a certain code FINGER is written as DGLECP. What will be the code for KIDNEY?
   (*a*) IGBLCW (*b*) IGCLBW
   (*c*) IBCGLE (*d*) IGBKCV
8. In a certain code QUESTION is written as NXBVQLLQ. How will REPLY be coded?
   (*a*) YHMOV (*b*) OBMVI
   (*c*) VHSOB (*d*) OHMOV

EXPLANATORY ANSWERS

1. (*b*) : The coded number signifies the position of the alphabet in its reverse order of the alphabetical series (ZYXW...)

M	U	S	K	→ MUSK
↓	↓	↓	↓	
14th	6th	8th	16th	→ 146816

Similarly,

Z	E	R	O	→ ZERO
↓	↓	↓	↓	
1st	22nd	9th	12th	→ 122912

2. (*d*) : The coded number is the sum of number digits signifying the position of the alphabet in the natural order.

B	A	D		
↓	↓	↓		
2nd	1st	4th	*i.e.*, 2 + 1 + 4	= 7

Similarly,

H	I	S		
↓	↓	↓		
8th	9th	19th	*i.e.*, 8 + 9 + 19	= 36
			further, 3 + 6	= 9

Also,

L	O	W		
↓	↓	↓		
12th	15th	23rd	*i.e.*, 12 + 15 + 23	= 50
			further, 5 + 0	= 0

3. *(b)* : The letters of the word TRIBAL are picked from LIBERATE. So will be the coded numbers.

L I B E R A T E → given word
5 6 4 0 3 1 7 0 → codes

Similarly,

T R I B A L → word to be coded
7 3 6 4 1 5 → answer codes

4. *(c)* : The word is divided into two equal parts and the letters of each part are written in reverse order.

SYS TEM SYS MET NEA RER AEN RER

Similarly,

FRAC TION CARF NOIT

5. *(d)* : The code is formed by moving the letters one step backwards and one step forward alternately.

CRUDE BSTED

−1, +1, −1, +1, −1

Similarly,

MOIST LPHTS

−1, +1, −1, +1, −1

6. *(a)* : The letters of the word are written backwards.

ALPACA ACAPLA

Similarly,

ANIMAL LAMINA

7. *(a)* : The word is coded by moving the letters two steps backwards.

FINGER DGLECP

−2, −2, −2, −2, −2, −2

Similarly,

KIDNEY IGBLCW

−2, −2, −2, −2, −2, −2

8. *(d)* : The letters of the word are coded by moving three steps backward and three steps forward alternately.

QUESTION NXBVQLLQ

−3, +3, −3, +3, −3, +3, −3, +3

Similarly,

REPLY OHMOV

−3, +3, −3, +3, −3

10. STATEMENT ANALYSIS

In these type of questions, a few statements are given. Certain facts are broken up and mentioned in these statements. What is required is to analyse the statements, arrange and sort out the given facts and then answer the questions related to the given statements.

EXERCISE

1. Among five friends, A is heavier than B; C is lighter than D; B is lighter than D but heavier than E. Who among them is the heaviest?

(*a*) B (*b*) C
(*c*) A (*d*) Can't say

2. Pune is bigger than Jhansi, Sitapur is bigger than Chittor. Raigarh is not as big as Jhansi, but is bigger than Sitapur. Chittor is not as big as Sitapur. Which is the smallest?

(*a*) Jhansi (*b*) Pune
(*c*) Chittor (*d*) Sitapur

3. Ajay works more than Ram. Alok works as much as Raju. Pankaj works less than Alok. Ram works more than Alok. Who works the most of all?

(*a*) Ajay (*b*) Ram
(*c*) Alok (*d*) Raju

4. Among five friends P, Q, R, S and T, who is the youngest? To arrive at the answer which of the following information given in the statements (A) and (B) is sufficient?

(A) R is younger than P and T.
(B) S is younger than Q.

(*a*) Only A alone is sufficient
(*b*) Either A or B is sufficient
(*c*) Both A and B together are needed
(*d*) Both A and B together are not sufficient

5. A is elder to B while C and D are elder to E who lies between A and B. If C be elder to B, which one of the following statements is necessarily true?

(*a*) E is elder to B
(*b*) A is elder to C
(*c*) C is elder to D
(*d*) D is elder to C

6. Suresh is as much older than Kamal as he is younger than Prabodh. Navin is as old as Kamal. Which of the following statements is wrong?

(*a*) Suresh is older than Navin
(*b*) Kamal is younger than Suresh
(*c*) Prabodh is not the oldest
(*d*) Navin is younger than Prabodh

Directions (Qs. 7 to 9) : *Ram, Sohan and Mohan play football, hockey and cricket. Ram, Ramesh and Mohan play hockey, cricket and basketball. Ram, Sohan, Rahim and Mohan play football and cricket. Now answer the following questions based on the above statements :*

7. Which game is played by all the boys?

(*a*) Football (*b*) Hockey
(*c*) Cricket (*d*) Basketball

8. Which two boys play all the games?

(*a*) Ram, Sohan (*b*) Ram, Ramesh
(*c*) Sohan, Mohan (*d*) Ram, Mohan

9. Who does not play football?

(*a*) Ramesh (*b*) Sohan
(*c*) Rahim (*d*) Mohan

Directions (Qs. 10 to 12) : *Read the following directions and answer the questions given below :*

There are five persons in a group. Out of these two are men. Only three persons know swimming, of

which one is a man. There is a couple, of which the husband knows swimming. A is the younger sister of D and B is the husband of E. C is a swimming champion.

10. Who is the other man in the group?
(*a*) C (*b*) B
(*c*) A (*d*) D

11. The two women who know how to swim are:
(*a*) A and C (*b*) C and D
(*c*) D and E (*d*) A and E

12. The two persons who do not know how to swim are :
(*a*) B and D (*b*) D and E
(*c*) A and E (*d*) A and D

Directions (Qs. 13 to 15) : *Read the following statements and answer the questions given below :*

Rajat, Sushil and Nagesh play football, hockey and cricket. Rajat, Ramu and Nagesh play hockey, cricket and basketball. Rajat, Sushil, Mayank and Nagesh play football and cricket.

13. Which game is played by all the boys?
(*a*) Hockey (*b*) Basketball
(*c*) Football (*d*) Cricket

14. Who does not play football?
(*a*) Rajat (*b*) Nagesh
(*c*) Sushil (*d*) Ramu

15. Which of the following two boys play all the games?
(*a*) Nagesh, Rajat (*b*) Mayank, Ramu
(*c*) Ramu, Nagesh (*d*) Sushil, Mayank

EXPLANATORY ANSWERS

1. *(d)* : The five friends in descending order of weight are : A/D, B/C, E or A/D, B, C/E. Either A or D is the heaviest.

2. *(c)* : The order of cities in descending order of size is : Pune, Jhansi, Raigarh, Sitapur, Chittor.

3. *(a)* : On the basis of doing work, the descending order will be : Ajay, Ram, Alok/Raju, Pankaj.

4. *(d)* : Statements are not inter-related.

5. *(a)* : The order in descending seniority will be : A/C/D, E, B.

6. *(c)* : On the basis of age the descending order will be : Prabodh, Suresh, Kamal/Navin.

Chart for Answers 7 to 9

Boy	*Games Played*
Ram	Football, Hocky, Cricket, Basketball
Sohan	Football, Hockey, Cricket
Mohan	Football, Hockey, Cricket, Basketball
Ramesh	Hockey, Cricket, Basketball
Rahim	Football, Cricket.

7. *(c)* **8. *(d)*** **9. *(a)***

For Answers 10 to 12 the information chart will be :

A. Woman ((younger sister of D); knows swimming.

B. Man (husband of E); knows swimming

C. Woman; Swimming champion

D. Man (brother of A)

E. Woman (wife of B)

From the couple B & E, B (husband) knows swimming. C is a swimming champion. Three persons know how to swim of which only B is a man. So, the two women who know how to swim are C and A (the younger sister of D). There are two men in the group of five. One is B and the other will be D.

10. *(d)* **11. *(a)*** **12. *(b)***

Chart for Answers 13 to 15

Boy	*Games Played*
Rajat	— Football, Hockey, Cricket, Basketball
Sushil	— Football, Hockey, Cricket, Basketball
Nagesh	— Football, Hockey, Cricket, Basketball
Ramu	— Hockey, Cricket, Basketball
Mayank	— Football, Cricket

13. *(d)* **14. *(d)*** **15. *(a)***

11. PLACE ARRANGEMENT

Place arrangement generally refers to the positioning of persons or objects in a manner indicated by set of information given. One has to understand the order of placement and then attempt questions following the given information.

EXERCISE

Directions : *In the following questions, understand the arrangement pattern and then select the right answer from the given options :*

1. Five boys are sitting in a row. Raghu is not adjacent to Shyam or Amit. Ajay is not adjacent to Shyam. Raghu is adjacent to Mayank. If Mayank is at the middle in the row, then Ajay is adjacent to whom out of the following?

(*a*) Amit (*b*) Raghu
(*c*) Mayank (*d*) Shyam

2. Mini is to the right of Rajni but to the left of Ananta. Saya is to the right of Mini but to the left of Jaya. Who is on the extreme left if all the girls are facing North?

(*a*) Jaya (*b*) Mini
(*c*) Rajni (*d*) Saya

3. O, P, Q, R, S and T are standing on a bench according to their height. P is taller than O but shorter than S. Only S is taller than T. R is shorter than P but taller than Q. Who is the shortest?

(*a*) O (*b*) Q
(*c*) P (*d*) Cannot be said

4. Five personalities are living in a multistoried building. Mr. Effortless lives in a flat above Mr. Active, Mr. Charge lives in a flat below Mr. Diligent, Mr. Active lives in a flat above Mr. Diligent and Mr. Behaved lives in a flat below Mr. Charge. Who lives in the topmost flat?

(*a*) Mr. Charge (*b*) Mr. Diligent
(*c*) Mr. Effortless (*d*) Mr. Behaved

EXPLANATORY ANSWERS

1. (*b*) : The order of sitting is :
Amit, Shyam, Mayank, Ajay, Raghu
or
Ajay, Raghu, Mayank, Amit, Shyam

2. (*c*) : The order in which the girls are positioned is :
Rajni, Mini, Ananta, Saya, Jaya
or
Saya, Jaya, Ananta
or
Saya, Ananta, Jaya

3. (*d*) : In descending order of height, the standing positions are :

	or	
S		S
T		T
P		P
R		R
O		Q
Q		O

Either O or Q is the shortest. The information given is not enough to clarify the answer.

4. (*c*) : The personalities living in flats in multi-storied building are in order given below :
Mr. Effortless
Mr. Active
Mr. Diligent
Mr. Charge
Mr. Behaved

12. DIRECTION SENSE

In these type of tests, the directions in questions needs to be perceived. Such questions are based on the direction chart.

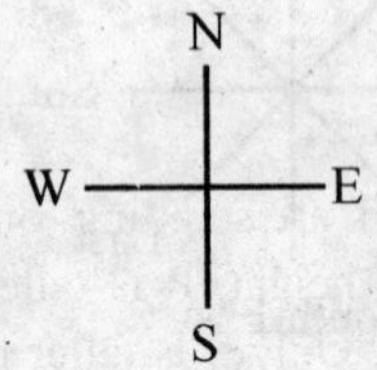

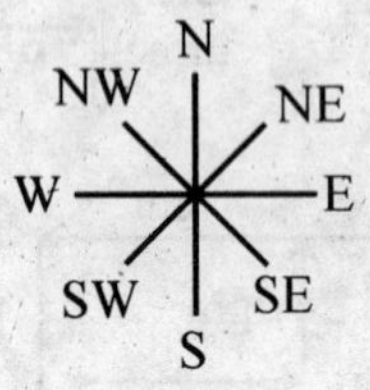

N = North S = South E = East W = West

The sense of the different directions are guided by the left and right turns or angular turns.

EXERCISE

Directions : *In the following questions, select the right answer from the given options to depict the correct direction/distance.*

1. Kittu walks towards East and then towards South. After walking some distance he turns towards West and then turns to his left. In which direction is he walking now?
(*a*) North (*b*) South
(*c*) East (*d*) West

2. A person is driving towards West. What sequence of directions should he follow so that he is driving towards South?
(*a*) left, right, right
(*b*) right, right, left
(*c*) left, left, left
(*d*) right, right, right

3. Richa drives 8 km to the South, turns left and drives 5 km. Again, she turns left and drives 8 km. How far is she from her starting point?
(*a*) 3 km (*b*) 5 km
(*c*) 8 km (*d*) 13 km

4. Dingi runs 40 km towards North then turns right and runs 50 km. He turns right and runs 30 km, and once again turns right and runs 50 km. How far is he from his starting point?
(*a*) 90 km (*b*) 50 km
(*c*) 10 km (*d*) 5 km

5. If North is called North-West, North-West is called West, West is called South-West and so on. What will South-East be called?
(*a*) East (*b*) West
(*c*) North-East (*d*) South-East

6. A man travels 100 km towards South. From there he turns right and travels 100 km and again turns right to travel 50 km. Which direction is he in from his starting point?
(*a*) North (*b*) North-East
(*c*) East (*d*) South-West

7. A train runs 120 km in West direction, 30 km in South direction and then 80 km in east direction before reaching the station. In which direction is the station from the train's starting point?
(*a*) South-West (*b*) North-West
(*c*) South-East (*d*) South

8. Facing the West direction, Priya jogs for 20 m, turns left and goes further 40 m. She turns left again and jogs for 20 m. Then she turns right to go 20 m to reach the park. How far is the park from her starting point and in which direction?
(*a*) 20 m South (*b*) 40 m West
(*c*) 60 m South (*d*) 100 m East

EXPLANATORY ANSWERS

1. (b) :

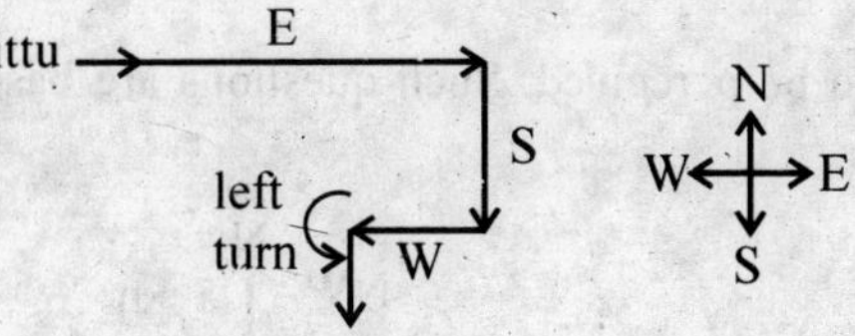

2. (d) :

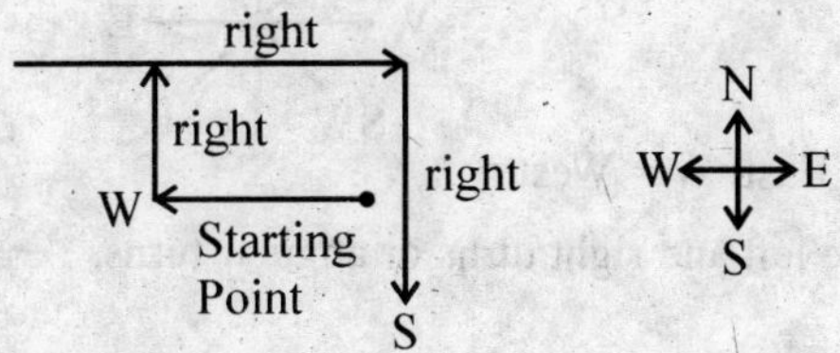

3. (b) :

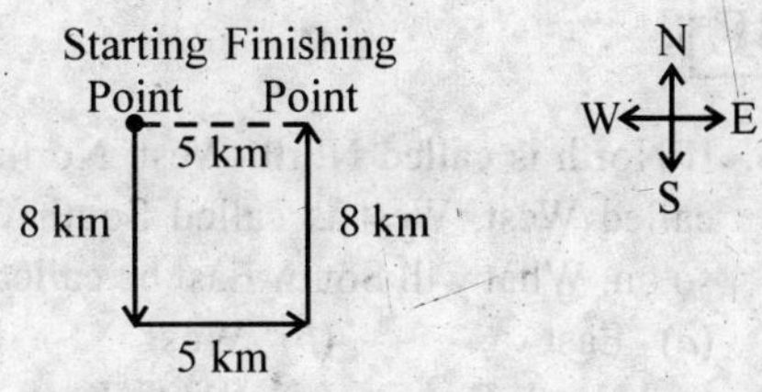

4. (c) :

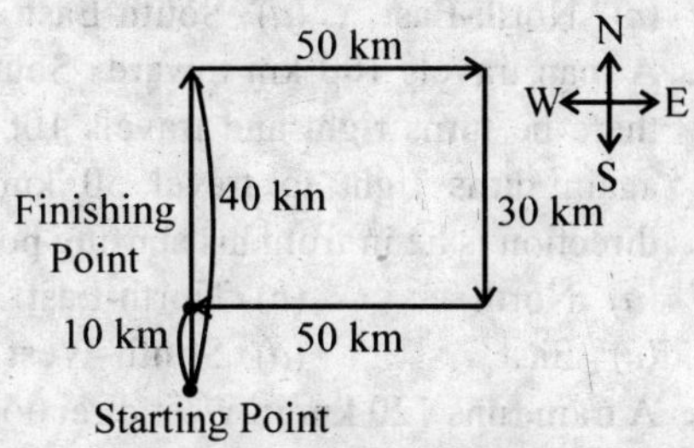

5. (a) :

Original Directions

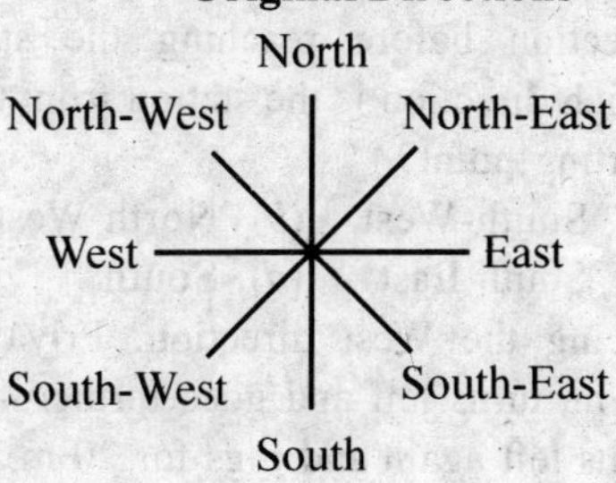

Changed Directions

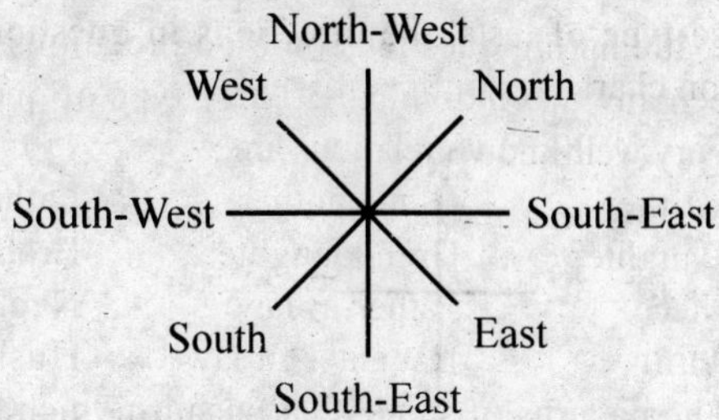

6. (d) :

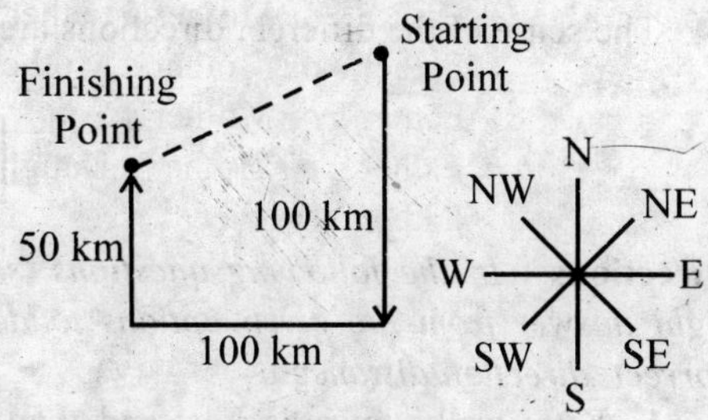

7. (a) :

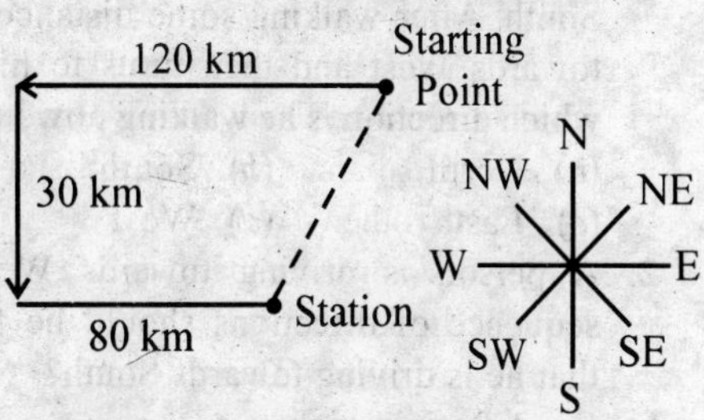

8. (c) : (40 + 20) = 60 metres South

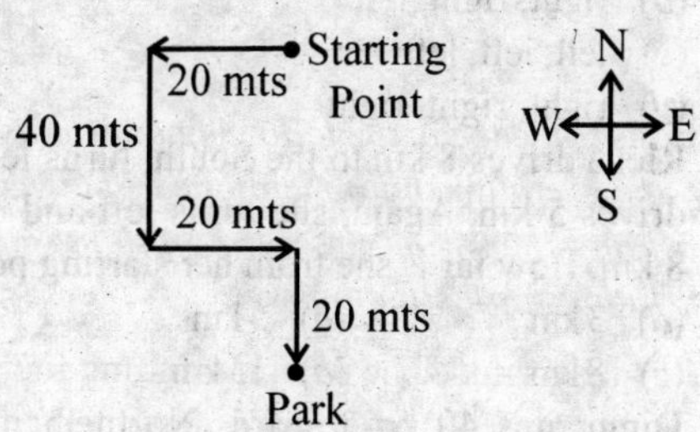

13. BLOOD RELATIONSHIPS

While attempting questions on blood relations, one should be clear of all the relation patterns that can exist between any two individuals. These type of questions are given mainly to test one's relationship ability.

Very well-known relations are :

Mother	Grandmother	Father	Grandfather	Son	Grandson
Daughter	Granddaughter	Brother	Brother-in-law	Sister	Sister-in-law
Niece	Father-in-law	Nephew	Mother-in-law	Uncle	Son-in-law
Aunt	Daughter-in-law	Husband	Cousin	Wife	

The patterns of some relationships which help in solving questions in these tests are :

Father's *or* Mother's Father	—	Grandfather (Paternal *or* Maternal)
Father's *or* Mother's Mother	—	Grandmother (Paternal *or* Maternal)
Father's *or* Mother's Son	—	Brother
Father's *or* Mother's Daughter	—	Sister
Father's Brother	—	Paternal Uncle
Father's Sister	—	Paternal Aunt
Mother's Brother	—	Maternal Uncle
Mother's Sister	—	Maternal Aunt
Uncle *or* Aunt's Son *or* Daughter	—	Cousin
Son's Wife	—	Daughter-in-law
Daughter's Husband	—	Son-in-law
Husband's *or* Wife's Brother	—	Brother-in-law
Husband's *or* Wife's Sister	—	Sister-in-law
Brother's Wife	—	Sister-in-law
Sister's Husband	—	Brother-in-law
Brother's Son	—	Nephew
Brother's Daughter	—	Niece

EXERCISE

Directions : *In each of the following questions keenly study the relationship mentioned between the persons, and then from the given options select the right relationship as the answer.*

1. A lady said, "The person standing there is my grandfather's only son's daughter". How is the lady related to the standing person?

(*a*) Sister (*b*) Mother
(*c*) Aunt (*d*) Cousin

2. Ajay is the brother of Vijay. Mili is the sister of Ajay. Sanjay is the brother of Rahul and Mehul is the daughter of Vijay. Who is Sanjay's Uncle?

(*a*) Rahul (*b*) Ajay
(*c*) Mehul (*d*) Data inadequate

3. A man introduced the boy coming with him as "He is son of the father of my wife's daughter". What relation did the boy bear to the man?

(*a*) Son-in-law (*b*) Son
(*c*) Brother (*d*) Father

4. If Amit's father is Billoo's father's only son and Billoo has neither a brother nor a

daughter, what is the relationship between Amit and Billoo?

(a) Uncle — Nephew
(b) Father — Daughter
(c) Father — Son
(d) Cousins

5. Pointing to a woman in the photograph a man said, "She is the daughter of my grandmother's only son." How is the woman related to the man?

(a) Mother (b) Daughter
(c) Sister-in-law (d) Sister

EXPLANATORY ANSWERS

1. (a) :

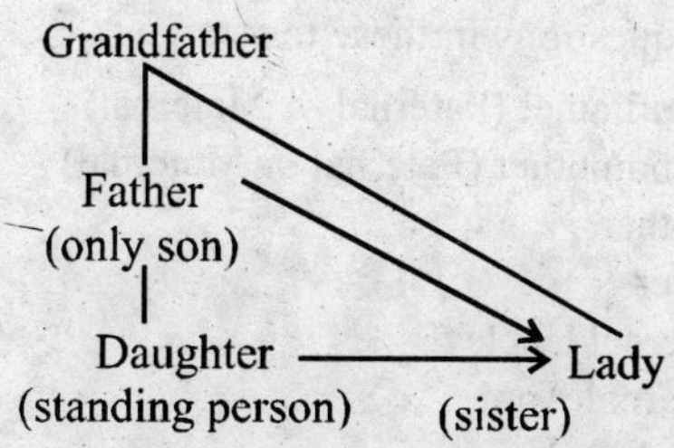

Lady's grandfather's son is lady's father and father's daughter will only be lady's sister.

2. (d) : 1. Mili > Ajay > Vijay
(sister) (brother) ↓
Mehul
(daughter)

2. Sanjay > Rahul
(brother)

There are two sets of relationship. Information given is incomplete and no relation can be established between the two sets.

3. (b) : The relationship chart based on problem is :

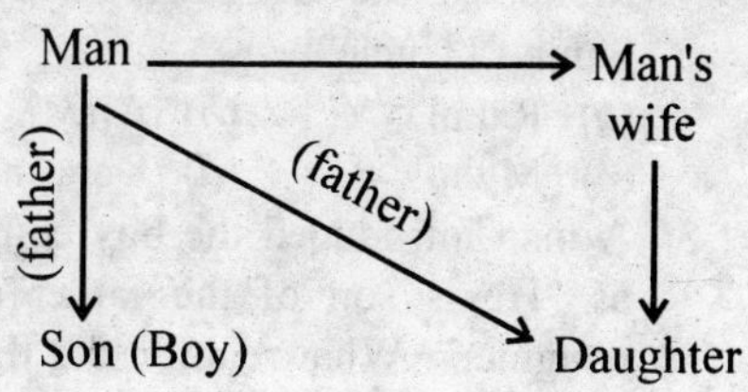

'Father of the man's wife's daughter' is the man himself and the boy in question is the man's son.

4. (c) : The relationship chart based on problem is :

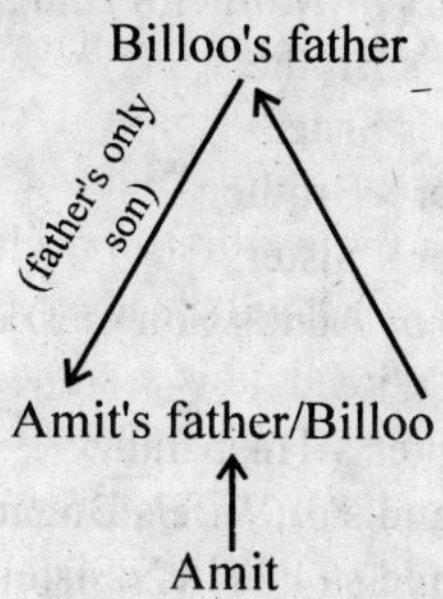

Amit's father is Billoo's father's only son means Billoo is the only son in question also, he is the father of Amit. It must be noted that Billoo has no brother which means he is single and also, when he has no daughter, Amit is his only son.

5. (d) :

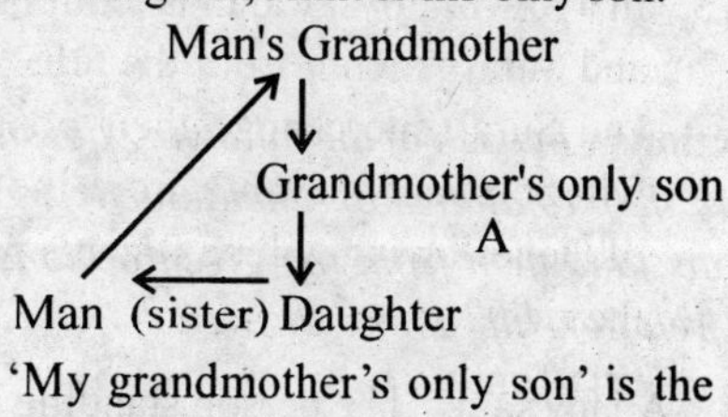

'My grandmother's only son' is the father of the man, and 'daughter of my grandmother's only son' is the sister of the man.

14. ROWS AND RANKS

These type of problems need easy calculations to find out the number of objects in a row, lane or queue or to find a person's rank in a class of certain number of students; or to find the total number of students.

EXERCISE

1. In a row of trees, one tree is fifth from either end of the row. How many trees are in the row?

(*a*) 11 (*b*) 8
(*c*) 10 (*d*) 9

2. Jaya ranks 5th in a class of 53. What is her rank from the bottom in the class?

(*a*) 49th (*b*) 48th
(*c*) 47th (*d*) 50th

3. Mohan ranks twenty-first in a class of sixty-five students. What will be his (Mohan's) rank if the lowest candidate is assigned rank 1?

(*a*) 44th (*b*) 45th
(*c*) 46th (*d*) Data inadequate

4. If Rahul finds that he is 12th from the right in a line of boys and 4th from the left, how many boys should be added to the line such that there are 28 boys in the line?

(*a*) 12 (*b*) 14
(*c*) 20 (*d*) 13

5. In a row of boys, Rajan is tenth from the right and Suraj is tenth from the left. When Rajan and Suraj interchange their positions, Suraj will be twenty-seventh from the left. Which of the following will be Rajan's position from the right?

(*a*) Tenth
(*b*) Twenty-sixth
(*c*) Twenty-ninth
(*d*) None of these

6. Mahesh and Suresh are ranked 11th and 12th respectively from the top in a class of 41 students. What will be their respective ranks from the bottom?

(*a*) 32nd and 33rd
(*b*) 29th and 30th
(*c*) 30th and 31st
(*d*) 31st and 30th

7. Uma ranked 8th from the top and 37th from bottom in a class. How many students are there in the class?

(*a*) 47 (*b*) 46
(*c*) 45 (*d*) None of these

8. In a queue, Sadiq is 14th from the front and Joseph is 17th from the end, while Jane is in between Sadiq and Joseph. If Sadiq be ahead of Joseph and there be 48 persons in the queue, how many persons are there between Sadiq and Jane?

(*a*) 5 (*b*) 6
(*c*) 7 (*d*) 8

9. Rohan ranked eleventh from the top and twenty-seventh from the bottom among the students who passed the annual examination in a class. If the number of students who failed in the examination was 12, how many students appeared for the examination?

(*a*) 48
(*b*) 49
(*c*) 50
(*d*) Cannot be determined

10. Some boys are sitting in a row. P is sitting fourteenth from the left and Q is seventh from the right. If there are four boys between P and Q, how many boys are there in the row?

(*a*) 19 (*b*) 21
(*c*) 25 (*d*) 23

EXPLANATORY ANSWERS

1. (*d*):

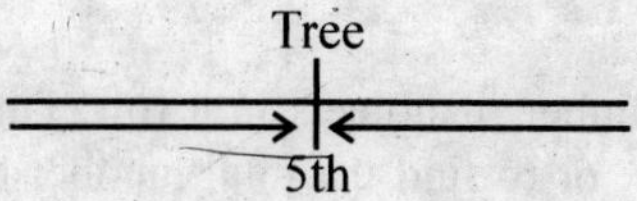

Total number of trees in the row are :
$(5 + 5) - 1 = 9$.

2. (*a*) :

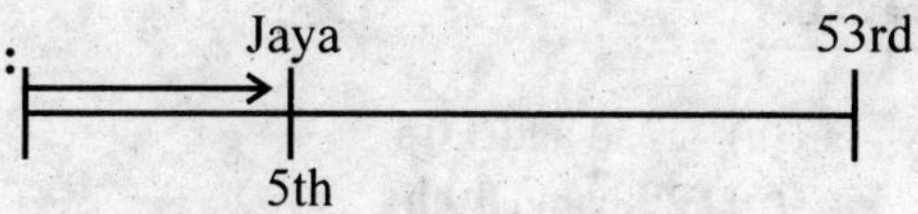

Jaya's rank from the bottom is :
$(53 - 5) + 1 = 49$th.

3. (*b*) :

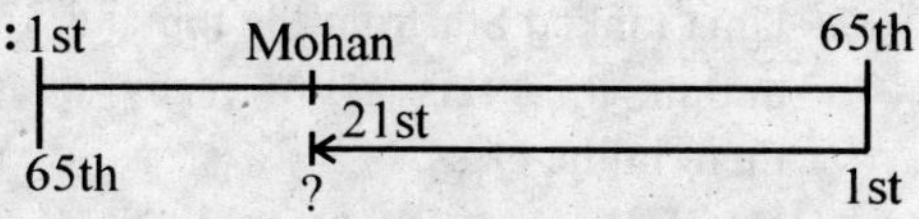

Note : Mohan's rank from the last or the question asked means the same.

Mohan's rank is $(65 - 21) + 1 = 45$th.

4. (*d*) :

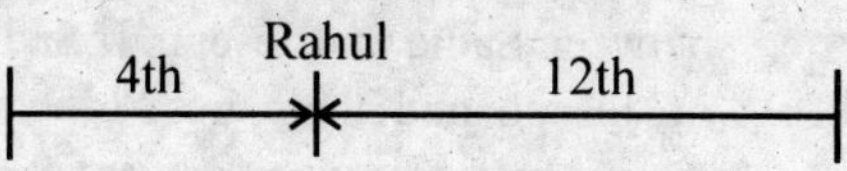

The number of boys in the line are :
$(4 + 12) - 1 = 15$
To make a line of 28 boys, $(28 - 15)$ *i.e.* 13 more boys are needed.

5. (*d*) :

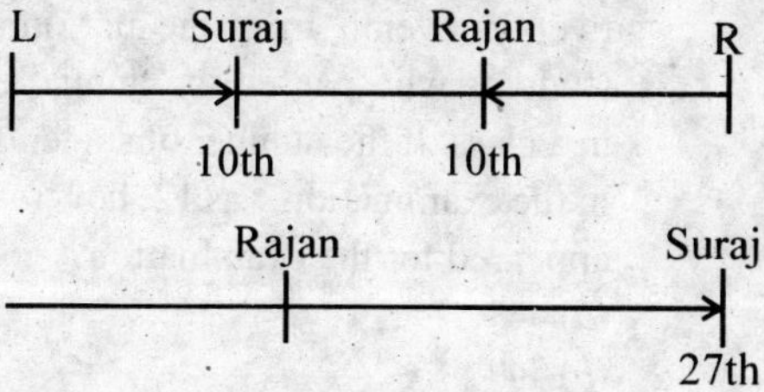

As the position of boys is equal from both ends, Rajan will also be 27th from the right after changing positions.

6. (*d*) :

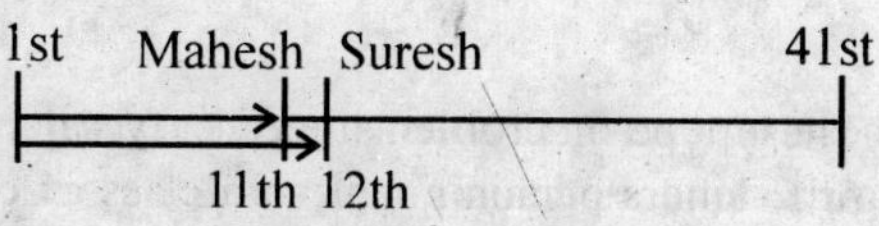

Mahesh's position from bottom is :
$(41 - 11) + 1 = 31$st
Suresh's position from bottom is :
$(41 - 12) + 1 = 30$th.

7. (*d*) :

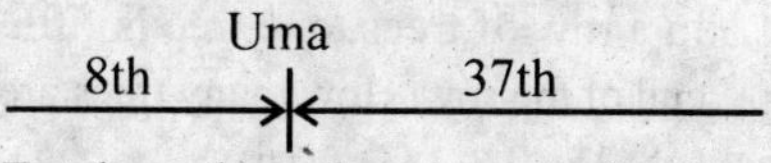

Total number of students in the class are :
$(8 + 37) - 1 = 44$.

8. (*d*) :

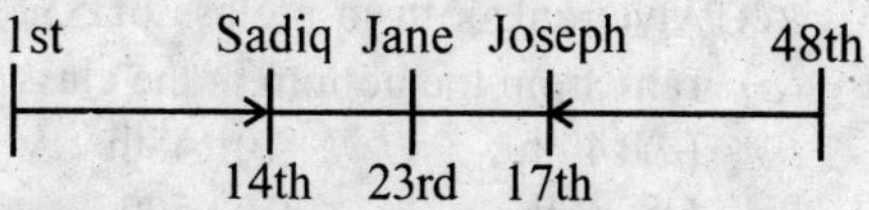

Sadiq's position from front : 14th
Joseph's position from last :
17th or $48 - 17 + 1 = 32$nd from front.
Middle postion between Sadiq & Joseph

$$= \frac{(32 - 14)}{2} + 14 = 23 \text{ rd.}$$

Hence, Jane position is 23rd from front
Person between Sadiq & Jane
$= 23 - 14 - 1 = 8$.

9. (*b*) :

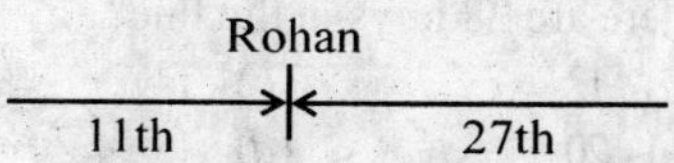

Number of students who passed the examination $(11 + 27) - 1 = 37$
Those who failed = 12
Total number of students who appeared in the examination = $37 + 12 = 49$.

10. (*c*) :

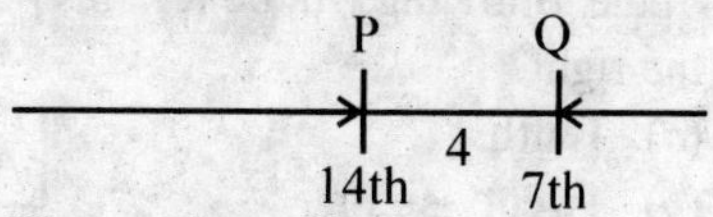

The number of boys in the row are :
$(14 + 4 + 7) = 25$.

15. PERMUTATIONS AND COMBINATIONS

In these type of questions, the only factor essential is alertness. In every question, a word is given. By using the letters of this given word the options are formed. The candidates are required to find from the given options the word *(i)* which cannot be formed by using the letters of the given word or *(ii)* which can be formed by using the letters of the given word.

EXERCISE

Directions : *Find out the one word among the options which cannot be formed by using the letters of the word as given in each question.*

1. ROTATION
   (a) TORN (b) NOTE
   (c) TART (d) RAIN
2. PHILOSOPHY
   (a) SOIL (b) SHIP
   (c) SOLO (d) SPIN
3. SLAVATION
   (a) SNORT (b) LATVIA
   (c) SALIVA (d) AVAIL
4. ACADEMY
   (a) DEMY (b) MACE
   (c) DIRE (d) MADE
5. INCOGNITO
   (a) GOING (b) INACTION
   (c) IGNITION (d) TONGO
6. JUDICIARY
   (a) INJURY (b) CADDY
   (c) DICY (d) ACRID
7. DOCTRINE
   (a) CRUST (b) DOCTOR
   (c) TIRED (d) CREED
8. EDUCATED
   (a) DATE (b) CUTE
   (c) EAST (d) DUCT
9. INSUFFICIENT
   (a) ENTICE (b) SCENT
   (c) SUFFICE (d) THENCE
10. DECEMBER
    (a) REDEEM (b) DECREE
    (c) BRACED (d) MEMBER
11. FUGITIVE
    (a) EXIT (b) FIVE
    (c) GIVE (d) GIFT
12. CATASTROPHE
    (a) TASTE (b) CHEAP
    (c) POUCH (d) STARE
13. TORRENTIAL
    (a) TRAIL (b) MENTAL
    (c) LEARN (d) RETAIL
14. INFRASTRUCTURE
    (a) RAPTURE (b) INSECURE
    (c) CRAFTS (d) STRUCTURE
15. RECOMMEND
    (a) MEND (b) ROME
    (c) CANE (d) OMEN

ANSWERS

1	2	3	4	5	6	7	8	9	10
(b)	(d)	(a)	(c)	(b)	(a)	(a)	(c)	(d)	(c)
11	**12**	**13**	**14**	**15**					
(a)	(c)	(b)	(a)	(c)					

16. SYMBOL SUBSTITUTION

Questions in these category are easy to attempt. Candidates must be quick in substituting symbols and calculations. The common pattern of questions asked are given below.

EXERCISE

1. If "+" means "–"; "–" means "×"; "×"means "÷" and "÷" means "+", then $15 \times 5 \div 10 + 5 - 3 = ?$

(a) 9.5 *(b)* 0

(c) –2 *(d)* 24

2. If "+" means "×"; "–" means "÷"; "÷"means "+" and "×" means "–", then what will be the value of $20 \div 40 - 4 \times 5 + 6 = ?$

(a) 60 *(b)* 1.67

(c) 150 *(d)* 0

3. If × stands for addition, < for subtraction, + stands for division, > for multiplication, – stands for equal to, ÷ for greater than, and = stands for less than, state which of the following is true?

(a) $5 \times 3 < 7 \div 8 + 4 \times 1$

(b) $3 \times 4 > 2 - 9 + 3 < 3$

(c) $5 > 2 + 2 = 10 < 4 \times 8$

(d) $3 \times 2 < 4 \div 16 > 2 + 4$

4. If → stands for subract, ← stands for add, ● ↑↑ stands for multiply, ↓↓ stands for divide, ↔ for greater than, ⟷ stands for equal to, then which of the following alternatives is true?

(a) 4 ← 6 ↑↑ 2 ⟷ 3 → 12 ← 12

(b) 10 ↓↓ 5 ↑↑ 5 ⟷ 9 → 3 ← 4

(c) 15 ↑↑ 2 → 5 ⟷ 12 ↓↓ 4 ← 3

(d) 13 ↓↓ 13 ← 1 ↔ 20 → 5 ↑↑ 2

5. If Δ denotes =; + denotes >, – denotes <, □ denotes ≠, × denotes > and ÷ denotes < then a + b – c denotes

(a) b Δ c □ a *(b)* b □ a ÷ c

(c) a ÷ b × c *(d)* b – a + c

EXPLANATORY ANSWERS

1. *(c)*: $15 \div 5 + 10 - 5 \times 3$
$3 + 10 - 15 = -2$

2. *(d)*: $20 + 40 \div 4 - 5 \times 6$
$20 + 10 - 30 = 0$

3. *(c)*: *(a)* $5 + 3 - 7 > 8 \div 4 + 1$
$1 > 3$

(b) $3 + 4 \times 2 = 9 \div 3 - 3$
$11 = 0$

(c) $5 \times 2 \div 2 < 10 - 4 + 8$
$5 < 14$

(d) $3 + 2 - 4 > 16 \times 2 \div 4$
$1 > 8$

4. *(b)*: *(a)* $4 + 6 \times 2 = 3 - 12 + 12$
$16 = 3$

(b) $10 \div 5 \times 5 = 9 - 3 + 4$
$10 = 10$

(c) $15 \times 2 - 5 = 12 \div 4 + 3$
$25 = 6$

(d) $13 \div 13 + 1 > 20 - 5 \times 2$
$2 > 10$

5. *(d)*: What is given is a > b < c

The equations are :

(a) b = c ≠ a which is wrong

(b) b ≠ a < c which is wrong

(c) a < b > c which is wrong

(d) b < a > c which is correct

Therefore, *(d)* is the answer.

17. MISSING NUMBERS

Playing with numbers and mathematical skills are needed to attempt these type of tests. The candidates have to work out the right combination of arithmetical symbols to arrive at the answer options which will take the place of the interrogation sign in the given questions.

EXERCISE

Directions: *In each question given below which one number can be placed at the sign of interrogation?*

1.

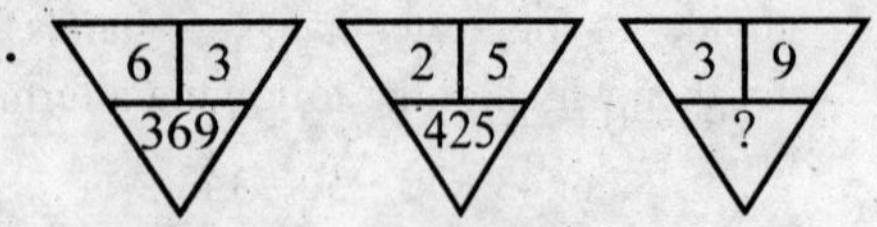

(*a*) 693 (*b*) 939
(*c*) 981 (*d*) 993

2.

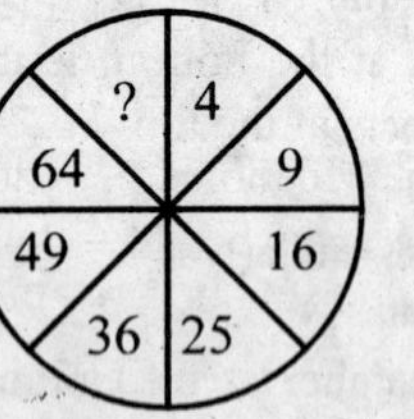

(*a*) 68 (*b*) 100
(*c*) 72 (*d*) 81

3.

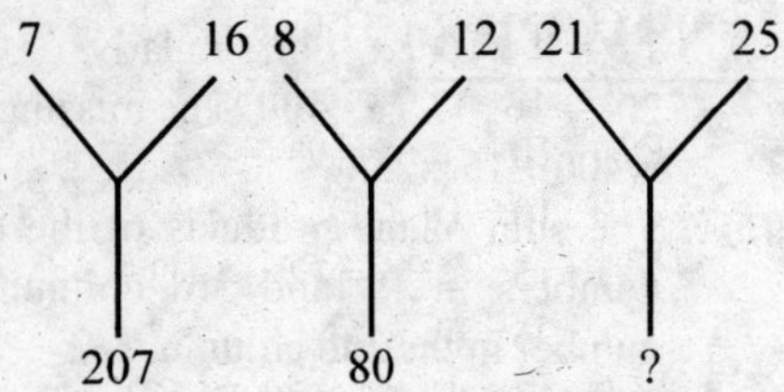

(*a*) 425 (*b*) 184
(*c*) 241 (*d*) 210

4.

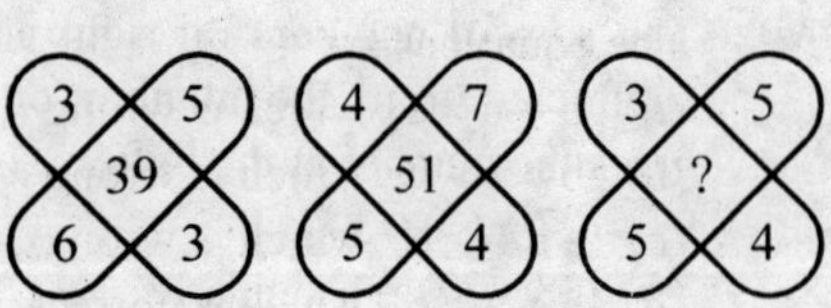

(*a*) 35 (*b*) 37
(*c*) 45 (*d*) 48

5.

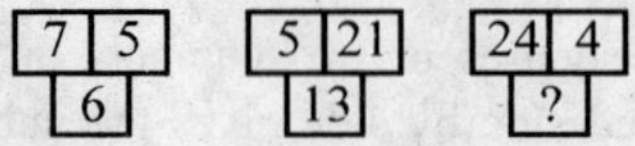

(*a*) 4 (*b*) 8
(*c*) 20 (*d*) 14

6.

14	9	4
12	7	2
10	5	0
16	11	?

(*a*) 9 (*b*) 6
(*c*) 3 (*d*) 7

7.

(*a*) 69 (*b*) 49
(*c*) 50 (*d*) 60

8.

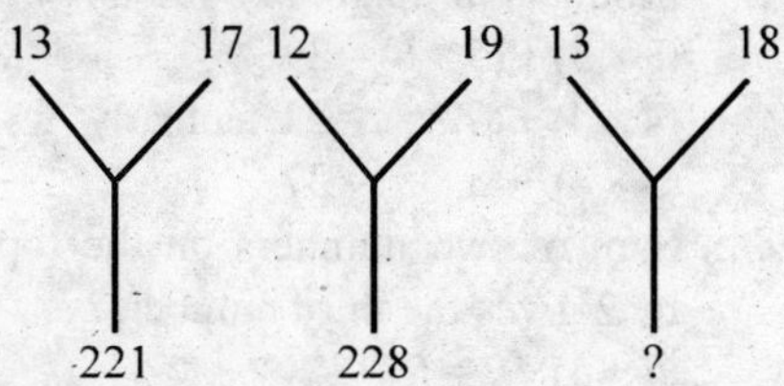

(*a*) 31 (*b*) 229
(*c*) 234 (*d*) 312

9.

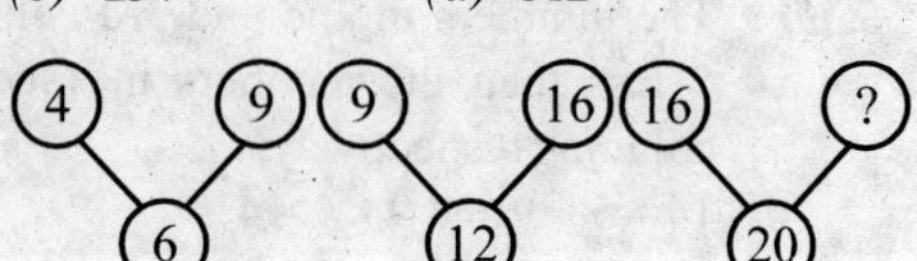

(*a*) 21 (*b*) 25
(*c*) 50 (*d*) 60

10.

51	(11)	61
64	(30)	32
35	(?)	43

(a) 25 *(b)* 27
(c) 32 *(d)* 37

11.

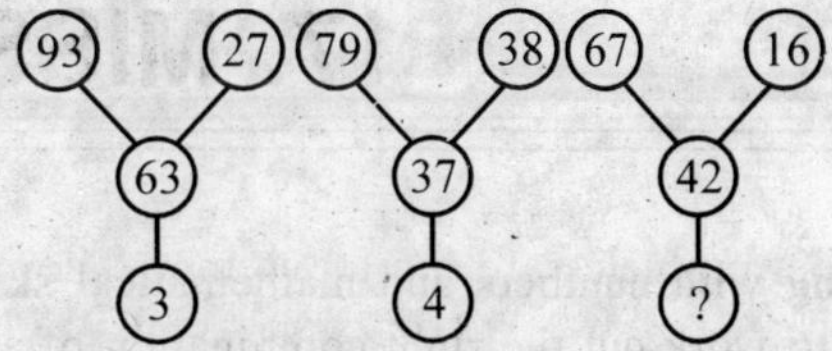

(a) 5 *(b)* 6
(c) 8 *(d)* 9

EXPLANATORY ANSWERS

1. *(c)* : The squares of two numbers on the top placed side by side gives the number inside the bottom triangle, *i.e.*,
6^2 and $3^2 = 369$
2^2 and $5^2 = 425$, similarly
3^2 and $9^2 = 981$.

2. *(d)* : Starting from number 4 the numbers are the squares of numbers in natural order *i.e.*,
$2^2 = 4, 3^2 = 9, 4^2 = 16 \ldots\ldots 9^2 = 81$.

3. *(b)* : The number at the bottom is the difference of the squares of two numbers at the top, *i.e.*,
$16^2 - 7^2 = 256 - 49 = 207$
$12^2 - 8^2 = 144 - 64 = 80$, similarly
$25^2 - 21^2 = 625 - 441 = 184$.

4. *(b)* : The number in the centre is the sum of the products of diagonal numbers, *i.e.*,
$(3 \times 3) + (5 \times 6) = 39$
$(4 \times 4) + (7 \times 5) = 51$, similarly
$(3 \times 4) + (5 \times 5) = 37$.

5. *(d)* : Sum of two numbers on the top divided by 2 gives the third number, *i.e.*,
$(7 + 5) \div 2 = 6$
$(5 + 21) \div 2 = 13$, similarly
$(24 + 4) \div 2 = 14$.

6. *(b)* : The numbers in 2nd and 3rd columns are 5 less than the numbers in 1st and 2nd columns respectively, *i.e.*,
$14 - 5 = 9$ and $9 - 5 = 4$
$12 - 5 = 7$ and $7 - 5 = 2$, . . . similarly
$16 - 5 = 11$ and $11 - 5 = 6$.

7. *(a)* : The sum of 3 numbers in each line in one figure is same, *i.e.*,
$29 + 80 + 43$ or $39 + 80 + 33$
or $45 + 80 + 27 = 152$
$29 + 70 + 44$ or $42 + 70 + 31$
or $43 + 70 + 30 = 143$,
similarly $59 + 80 + 20$ or $39 + 80 + 40 = 159$.
The missing number is :
$159 - (80 + 10) = 69$.

8. *(c)* : The number at the bottom is the product of two numbers at the top, *i.e.*,
$13 \times 17 = 221$
$12 \times 19 = 228$, similarly
$13 \times 18 = 234$.

9. *(b)* : Square of number at the bottom is equal to the product of two numbers at the top, *i.e.*,
$6^2 = 4 \times 9$, *i.e.*, 36
$12^2 = 9 \times 16$, *i.e.*, 144, similarly
$20^2 = 16 \times ?$, *i.e.*, 400. The missing number is $400 \div 16 = 25$.

10. *(b)* : The sum of the products of the digits of numbers in 1st and 3rd columns is the number in the 2nd column, *i.e.*,
$(5 \times 1) + (6 \times 1) = 11$
$(6 \times 4) + (3 \times 2) = 30$, similarly
$(3 \times 5) + (4 \times 3) = 27$.

11. *(d)* : The sum of numbers on right and centre subtracted from the number on the left gives the number at the bottom, *i.e.*,
$93 - (27 + 63) = 3$
$79 - (38 + 37) = 4$, similarly
$67 - (16 + 42) = 9$.

18. ALPHABET PROBLEMS

Alphabet problems are fun to attempt. They are based on alphabetical series in natural as well as reverse order.

Natural Order

A B C D E F G H I J K L M N O P Q R S T U V W X Y Z

Reverse Order

Z Y X W V U T S R Q P O N M L K J I H G F E D C B A

> **Note :** The series starts from A on reaching Z and from Z on reaching A. Of these A E I O U are vowels and the rest are consonants.

EXERCISE

1. Which letter should be ninth letter to the left of ninth letter from the right if the first half of the alphabet is reversed?

(a) I *(b)* D
(c) F *(d)* E

2. Starting from the fifth letter from the left, if twelve letters are written in reverse order, then which letter will be the seventh to the left of the fourteenth letter from the right?

(a) N *(b)* H
(c) L *(d)* O

3. What letter will come in the centre of sixth letter from the right and thirteenth letter from the left?

(a) Q *(b)* R
(c) P *(d)* S

4. If in the word "DISTURBANCE", the first letter is interchanged with the last letter, the second letter is interchanged with the tenth letter and so on, which letter would come after the letter "T" in the newly formed word?

(a) I *(b)* U
(c) N *(d)* S

5. If it is possible to make a meaningful word with the third, the fifth, the seventh and the tenth letters of the word PROJECTION. If no such word can be made, give 'O' as the answer. If more than one such word can be made, give 'M' as the answer.

(a) T *(b)* N
(c) O *(d)* M

EXPLANATORY ANSWERS

1. *(d)* : MLKJIGHFEDCBANOPQRSTUVWXYZ

9th 9th

2. *(d)* : ABCDPONMLKJIHGFEQRSTUVWXYZ

7th 14th

3. *(a)* :

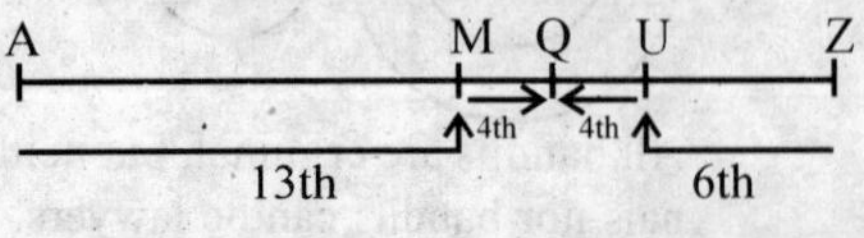

13th letter from left is 'M' and 6th letter from right is 'U'. The letter in the centre of 'M' and 'U' is 'Q'.

4. *(d)* : E C N A B R U T S I D

5. *(d)* : P R O J E C T I O N

The 3rd, 5th, 7th and 10th letters are OETN.

The words formed are TONE and NOTE.

19. LOGICAL DIAGRAM

In these type of questions, a set of five different figures is given as options. Each figure represents a logical pattern of certain groups of related words wherein each word represents a class. One has to identify the most appropriate logical figure for the set of words given. Some of the relationships represented by these diagrams are given below. Understand the relationship patterns and then attempt the exercise following the explanation.

EXERCISE

Directions : *From the five logical Diagrams, select one which best illustrates the relationship among three given classes in the questions 1 to 5.*

(a)

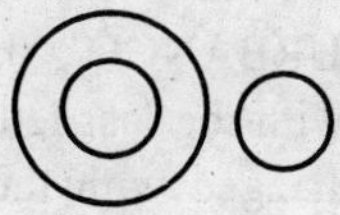

(b)

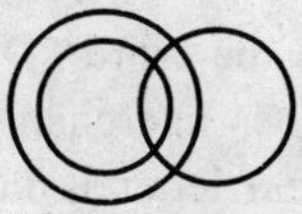

(c)

(d)

(e)

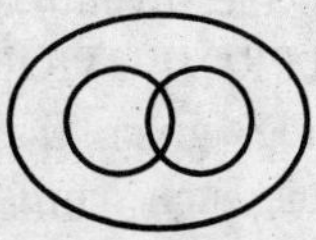

1. Birds, fruits, mangoes
2. Criminals, lawyers, bandits
3. Swimmers, bachelors, men
4. Smart, engineers, women
5. Vegetables, potatoes, brinjals

Directions : *From the five logical diagrams select one which best illustrates the relationship among three given classes in questions 6 to 10.*

(a)

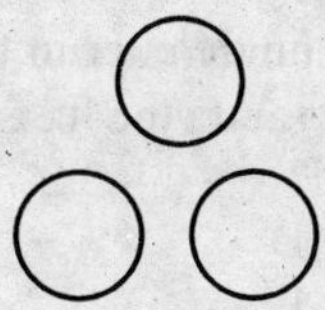

(b)

(c)

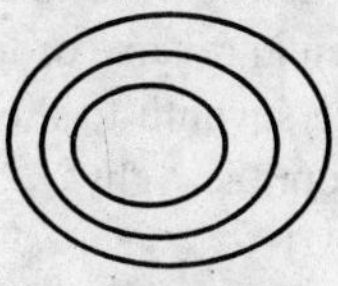

(d)

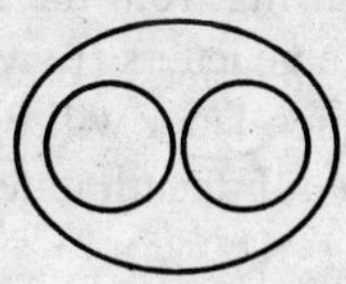

(e)

6. Ink, crayons, red
7. Canines, dogs, pups
8. Table, chair, stool
9. Ripe, mangoes, basket
10. Scholars, studious, illiterates

EXPLANATORY ANSWERS

1. ***(a)* :**

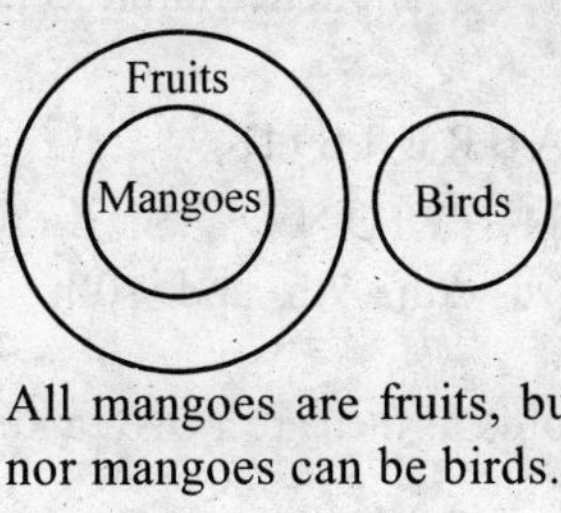

All mangoes are fruits, but neither fruits, nor mangoes can be birds.

2. ***(a)* :**

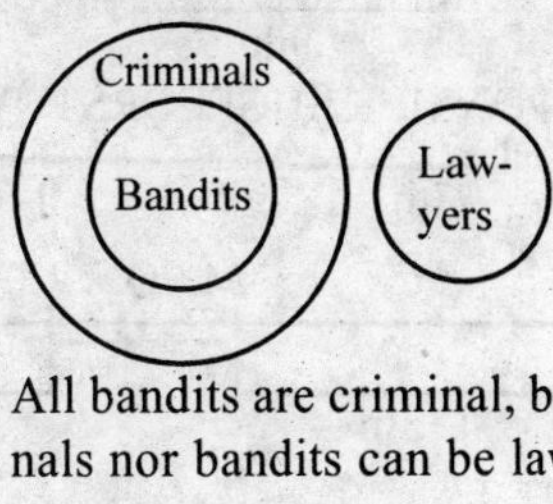

All bandits are criminal, but neither criminals nor bandits can be lawyers.

3. ***(b)*** **:**

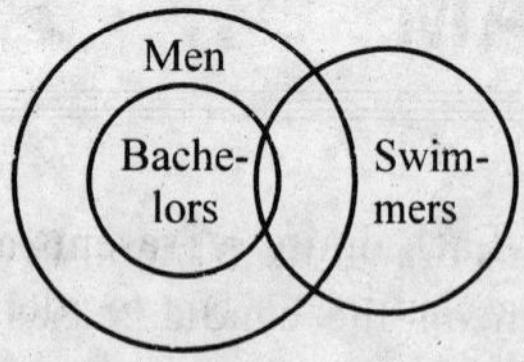

All bachelors are men and some men and bachelors can be swimmers.

4. ***(c)*** **:**

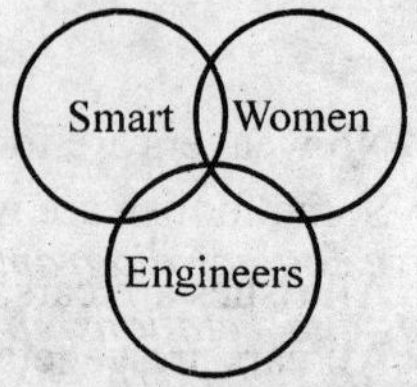

Some women can be smart and some women can be engineers and vice–versa. Some engineers can be women and some engineers can be smart and vice–versa.

5. ***(d)*** **:**

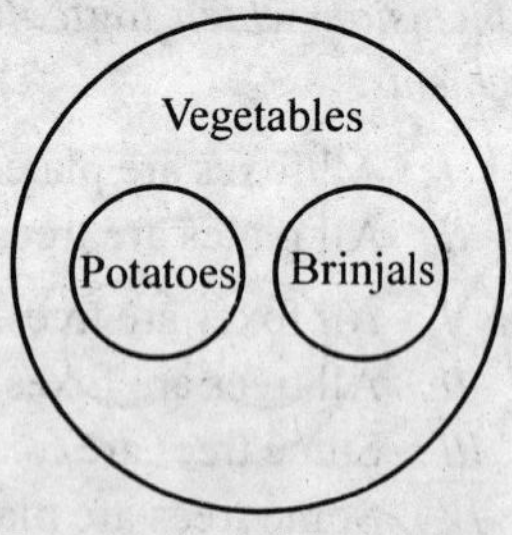

Potatoes and brinjals are vegetables but they have nothing in common. Some vegetables are potatoes and some are brinjals.

6. ***(b)*** **:**

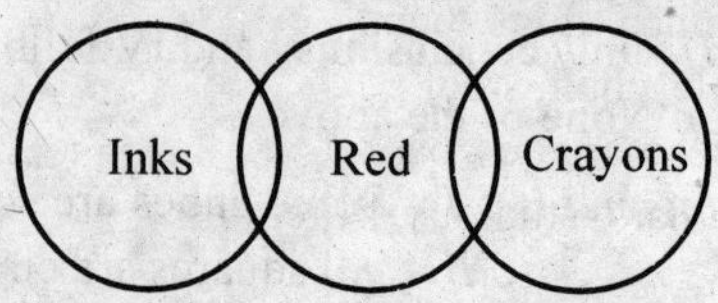

Some ink and some crayons can be red and some red units can be inks and crayons, but ink and crayon have nothing in common.

7. ***(c)*** **:**

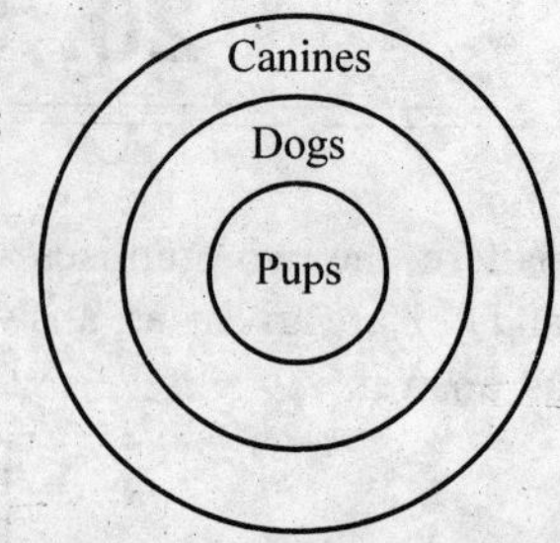

All pups are dogs and all dogs are canines. Some canines are dogs, of which some are pups.

8. ***(a)*** **:**

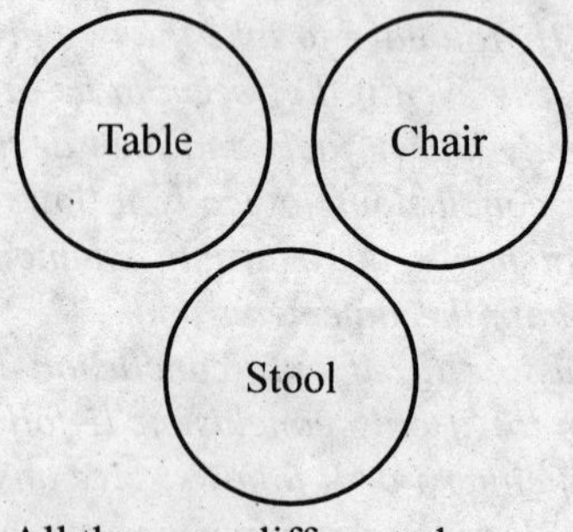

All three are different classes.

9. ***(e)*** **:**

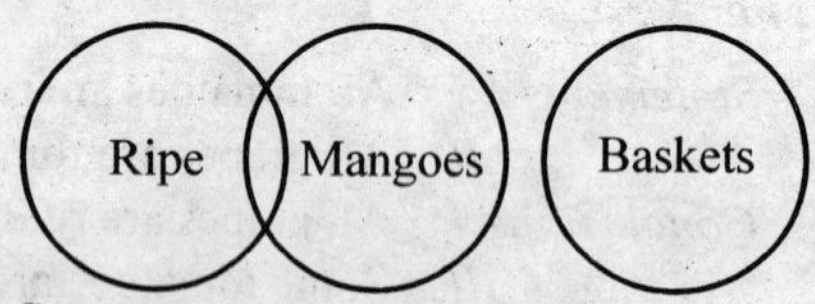

Some mangoes are ripe and some ripe units are mangoes, but neither ripe units nor mangoes can be baskets.

10. ***(e)*** **:**

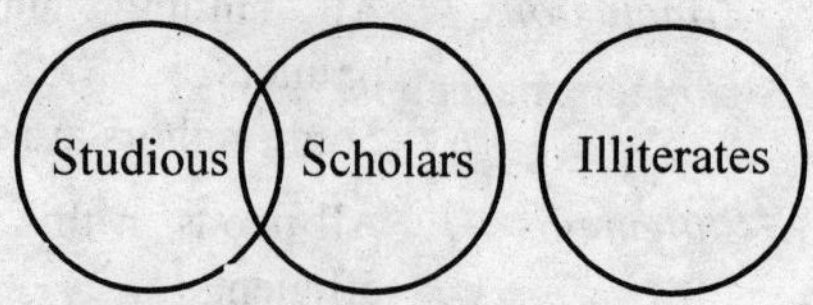

Some studious can be scholars and some scholars can be studious, but neither studious nor scholars can be illiterates.

20. SYLLOGISM

In this reasoning pattern, the two premises are followed by two conclusions drawn from them. Five options *(a)*, *(b)*, *(c)*, *(d)* and *(e)* are given as answers. Based on the two statements the candidate has to select the right option as answer.

EXERCISE

Directions (Qs. 1-5): *In each question below are given two statements followed by two conclusions numbered I and II. You have to take the two given statements to be true even if they seem to be at variance from commonly known facts and then decide which of the given conclusions logically follows from the two given statements, disregarding commonly known facts. Read both the statements and—*

Give answer (a) if only conclusion I follows; give answer (b) if only conclusion II follows; give answer (c) if either I or II follows; give answer (d) if neither I nor II follows and give answer (e) if both I and II follows.

1. *Statements* *I:* All tomatoes are red.
II: All grapes are tomatoes.
Conclusions *I:* All grapes are red.
II: Some tomatoes are grapes.

2. *Statements* *I:* All painters are smilling.
II: Some authors are painters.
Conclusions *I:* All smiling authors are painters.
II: Some authors are smiling.

3. *Statements* *I:* All peons in this office are efficient.
II: Ramu is not efficient.
Conclusions *I:* Ramu is not peon in this office.
II: Ramu should be more efficient.

4. *Statements* *I:* All weavers are hard working.
II: No hard working men are foolish.
Conclusions *I:* No weavers are foolish.
II: Some foolish are weavers.

5. *Statements* *I:* All fishes are cars.
II: All cars are vegetables.
Conclusions *I:* Some vegetables are cars.
II: Some vegetables are fishes.

Directions (Qs. 6 and 7): *In the following questions, select the set of conclusion which logically follows from the given statements.*

6. *Statements* *I:* All foxes are plates.
II: All plates are trees.
Conclusions *I:* All foxes are trees.
II: All trees are foxes.
III: Some trees are foxes.
IV: Some trees are plates.
(a) All conclusions are correct.
(b) Only conclusions I, III, and IV follow.
(c) Only conclusions II, III, and IV follow.
(d) Only conclusions I and IV follow.
(e) None of the above.

7. *Statements* *I:* Some cubes are squares.
II: All squares are circles.
Conclusions *I:* All cubes are circles.
II: Some circles are cubes.
III: Some circles are squares.
IV: All squares are cubes.
(a) Only conclusion I follows.
(b) Only conclusion I, II and III follow.
(c) All conclusions are correct.
(d) Only conclusions II and III follow.
(e) None of the above.

EXPLANATORY ANSWERS

1. *(e)* **:** When all tomatoes are red and all grapes are tomatoes, then all grapes are also red. When all grapes are tomatoes, then some tomatoes must be grapes. Therefore, both conclusions I and II are correct.

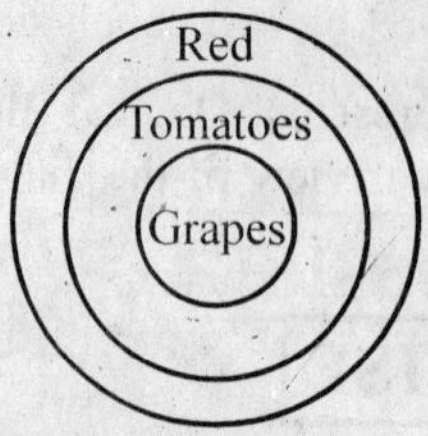

2. *(b)* **:** When all painters are smiling and some authors are painters, then some authors are smiling. Therefore, only conclusion II is correct.

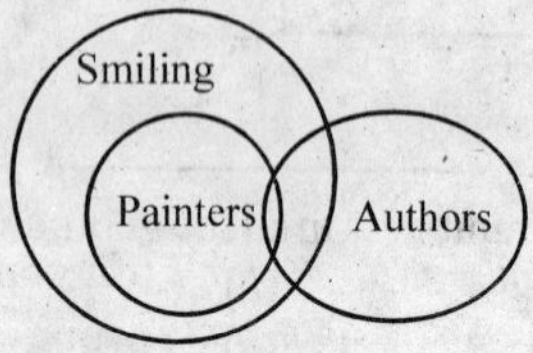

3. *(a)* **:** When all the peons of the office are efficient, then Ramu cannot be a peon in this office. Therefore, only conclusion I is correct.

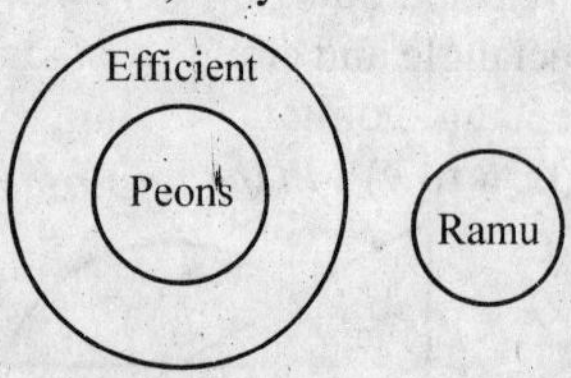

4. *(a)* **:** When all weavers are hardworking and no hardworking men are foolish, then no weavers are foolish. Therefore, only conclusion I is correct.

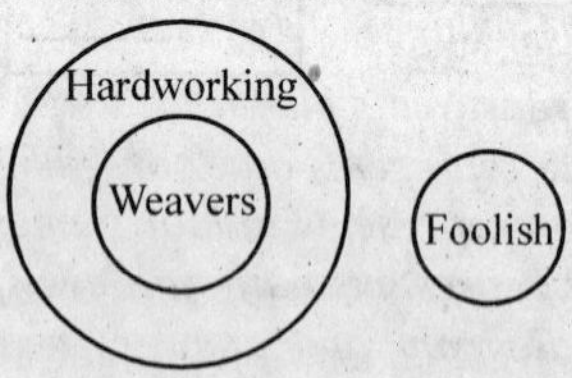

5. *(e)* **:** When all fishes are cars and all cars are vegetables, then all fishes will naturally be vegetables. This means that some vegetables are fishes. And when all cars are vegetables, then some vegetables will be cars naturally. Therefore, both the conclusions I and II are correct.

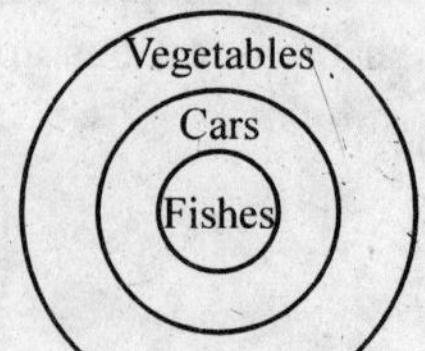

6. *(b)* **:**

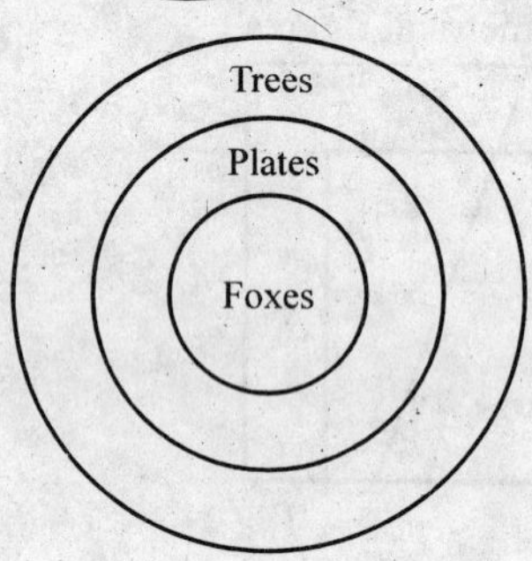

When all foxes are plates and all plates are trees, then naturally all foxes will be trees and some trees will then have to be foxes. And when all plates are trees then some trees will have to be plates. Therefore, only conclusions I, III and IV are correct.

7. *(d)* **:** When it is given that some cubes are squares and all squares are circles, then some cubes will naturally be circles, though all cubes cannot be circles. When some cubes are circles, then some circles will have to be cubes. And when all squares are circles, then some circles will have to be squares. As per given statement II, all squares are circles. Therefore all squares cannot be cubes. As such only conclusions II and III are correct.

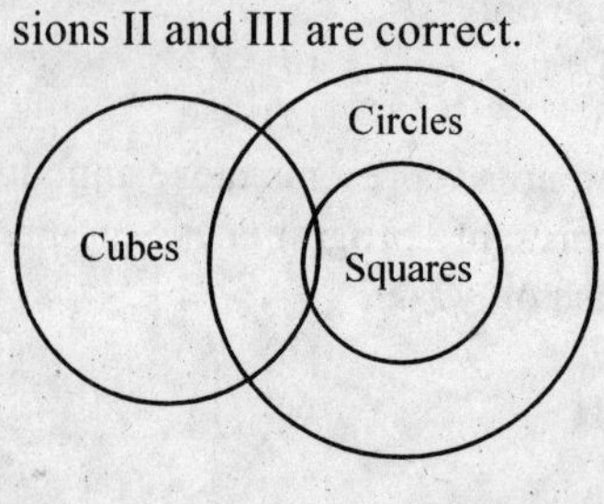

21. VENN DIAGRAMS

In these type of questions, diagrammatic representation presents a logical illustration of particular class or statements based on which the questions are asked. A clear view of the diagram makes the concepts clear for attempting such questions.

EXERCISE

1. What is the number which is common to only two geometrical figures?

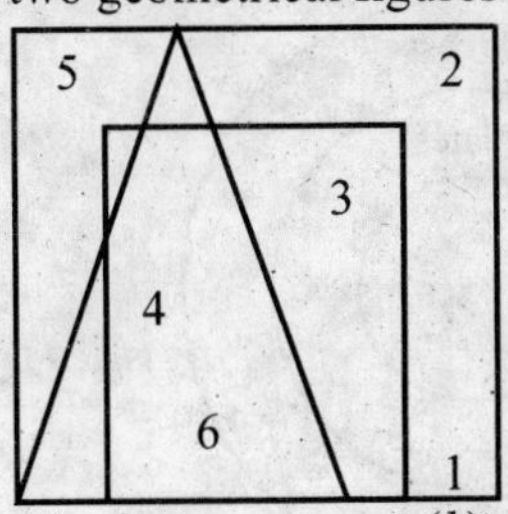

(*a*) 4 (*b*) 3
(*c*) 5 (*d*) 2

Directions (Qs. 2 and 3) : *In the following diagram, rectangle represents Hindi Announcers, circle represents English Announcers, square represents French Announcers, and triangle represents German Announcers.*

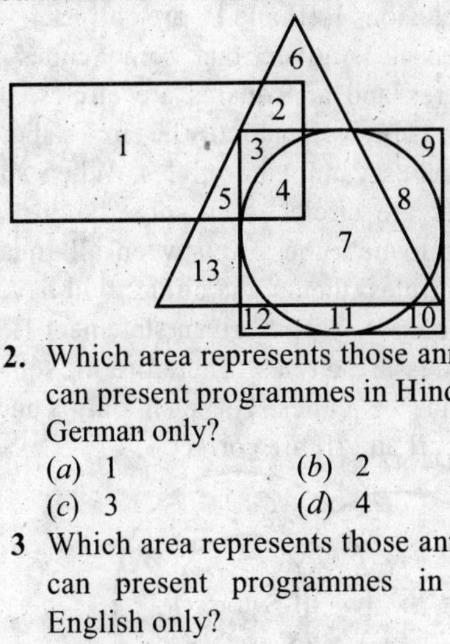

2. Which area represents those announcers who can present programmes in Hindi, French and German only?
(*a*) 1 (*b*) 2
(*c*) 3 (*d*) 4

3 Which area represents those announcers who can present programmes in French and English only?
(*a*) 7 (*b*) 9
(*c*) 11 (*d*) 13

Directions (Qs. 4 and 5) : *Study the diagram to answer these questions.*

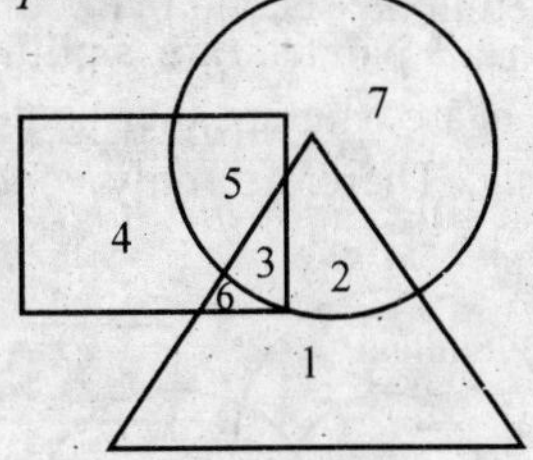

4. Which number is in all the geometrical figures?
(*a*) 5 (*b*) 6
(*c*) 2 (*d*) 3

5. Number 6 is in :
(*a*) Rectangle and triangle
(*b*) Circle and traingle
(*c*) Rectangle and circle
(*d*) Rectangle only

Directions (Qs. 6 to 9) : *In the following diagram*

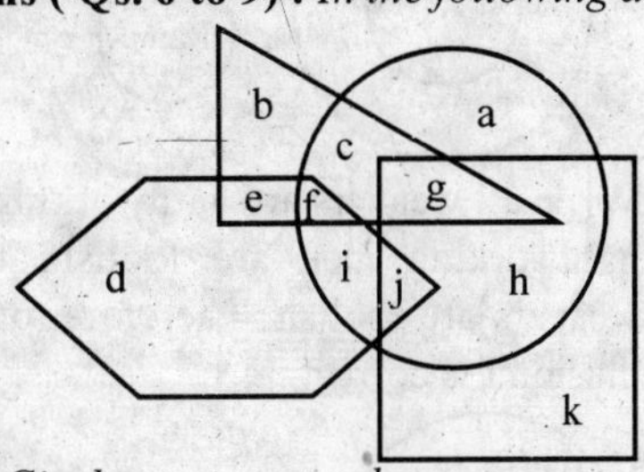

The Circle represents players
The Triangle represents outdoor games
The Hexagon represents indoor games and
The Square represents national level players
Study the diagram and answer the questions given below :

6. The letter in the section representing the players who play indoor games at national level is :
(*a*) f (*b*) i
(*c*) j (*d*) g

7. The letter representing the section of outdoor as well as indoor game players who do not play at the national level is :

(*a*) c (*b*) f
(*c*) e (*d*) i

8. The section representing national level players who do not play either outdoor or indoor games but still come under the category of players is :

(*a*) k (*b*) g
(*c*) c (*d*) h

9. Persons who play outdoor games but do not come under the category of players are represented in the section marked :

(*a*) b (*b*) c
(*c*) a (*d*) d

Direction (Qs. 10) : *Study the diagram given below.*

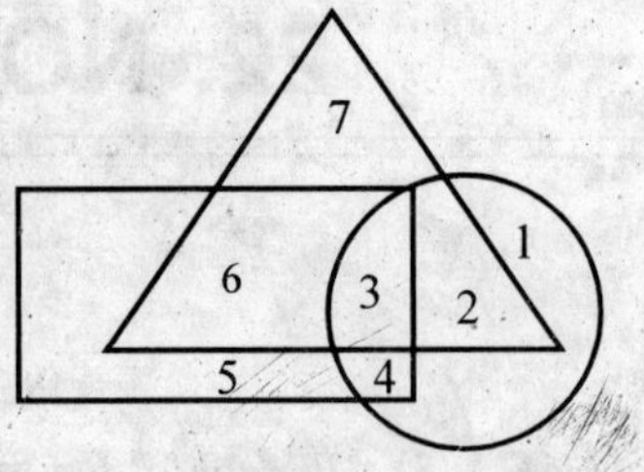

A college provides three different activities, students union represented by triangle, literary society represented by rectangle and social service league represented by circle.

10. Those who take part in both literary society and social service league but not in students union are represented by :

(*a*) 3 & 4 (*b*) 5 & 6
(*c*) 5 & 1 (*d*) 4

EXPLANATORY ANSWERS

1. ***(b)* :**

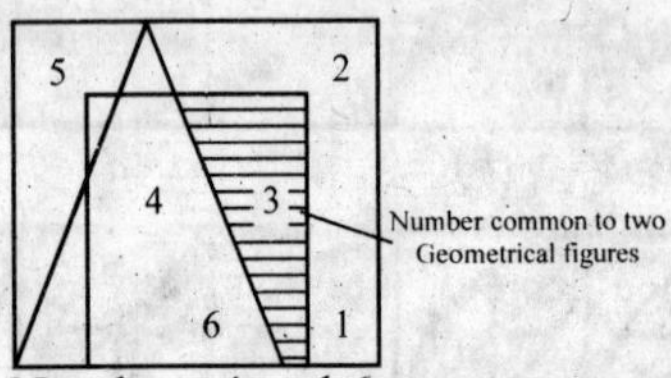

Note : Numbers 4 and 6 are common to all three geometrical figures.

2. ***(c)*,** **3.** ***(c)* :**

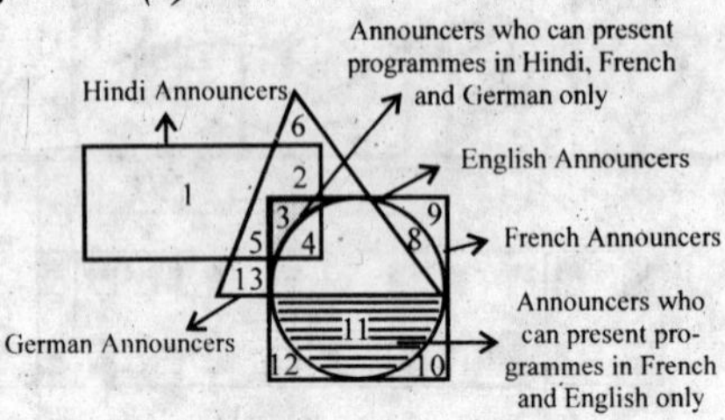

4. ***(d)*,** **5.** ***(a)* :**

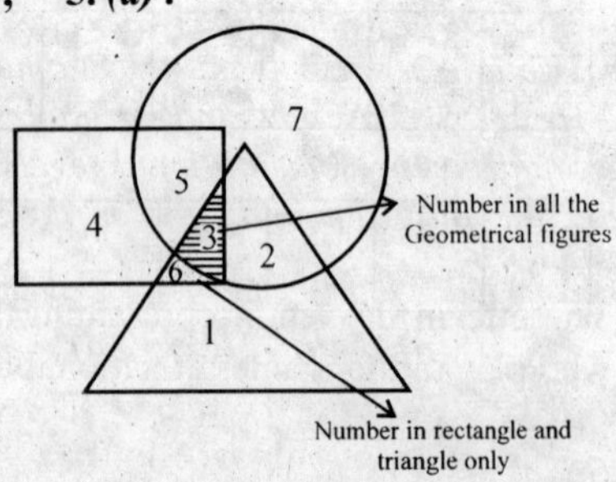

6. ***(c)*,** **7.** ***(b)*,** **8.** ***(d)*,** **9.** ***(a)* :**

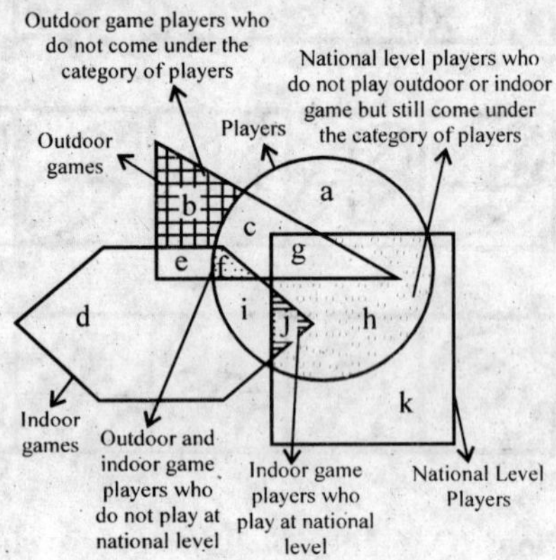

10. ***(d)***

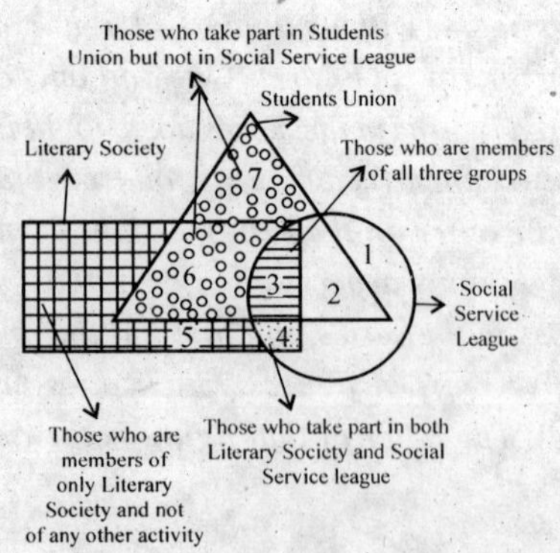

22. NON-VERBAL SERIES

EXERCISE

Directions (Q. 1–5) : *In each of the following questions which one of the five answer figures given below should come after the problem figures if the sequence are continued?*

Problem Figures | **Answer Figures**

1.

(a) (b) (c) (d) (e)

2.

(a) (b) (c) (d) (e)

3.
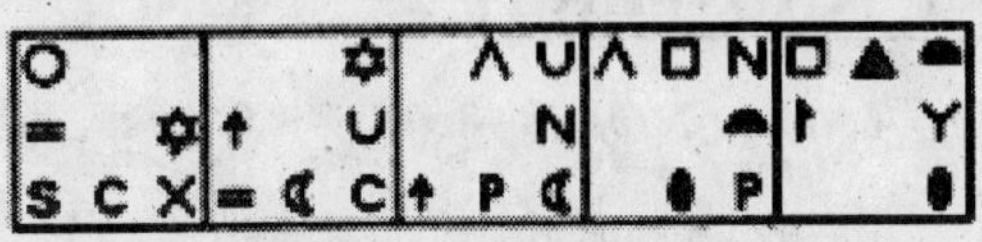

(a) (b) (c) (d) (e)

4.

(a) (b) (c) (d) (e)

5.

(a) (b) (c) (d) (e)

Directions (Q. 6-10) : *In each of these questions, a series begins with an unmarked figure on the extreme left in the row of figures. One and only one of the five lettered figures in the series does not fit into the series. The two unmarked figures, one on the extreme left and the other on the extreme right fit into the series. Take as many aspects into account as possible of the figures in the series and find out the one and only of the five marked figures which does not fit into the series. The letter of that figure is the answer.*

6.
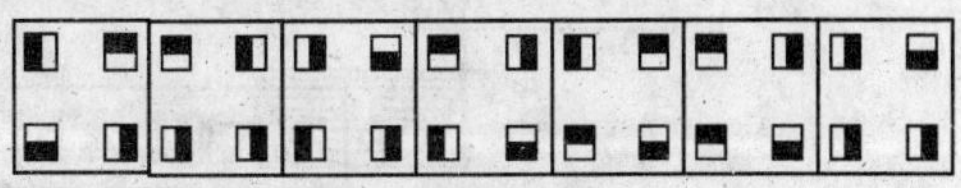
(a) (b) (c) (d) (e)

7.
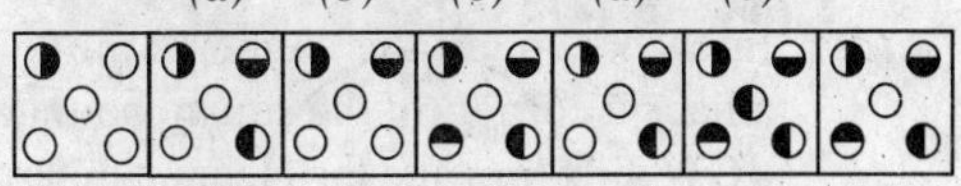
(a) (b) (c) (d) (e)

8.
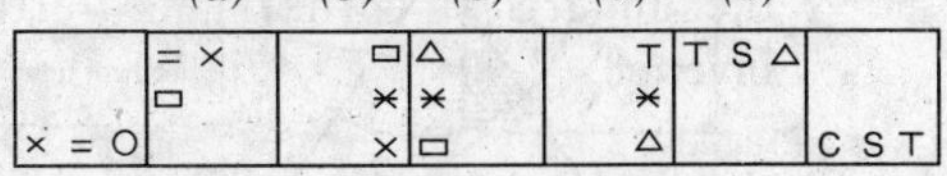
(a) (b) (c) (d) (e)

9. 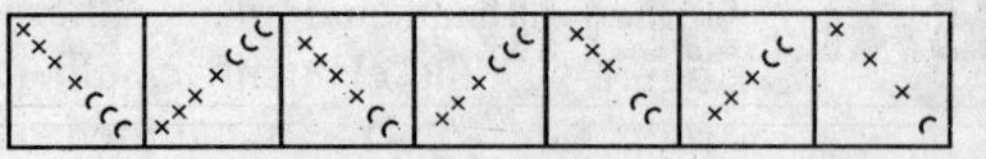

(a) (b) (c) (d) (e)

10. 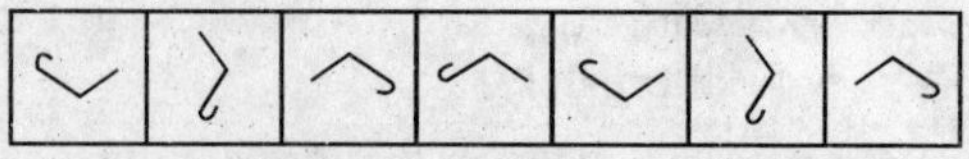

(a) (b) (c) (d) (e)

Directions (Q. 11–15) : *Each of the following questions consist of problem figures followed by answer figures. Select a figure from amongst the answer figures which will continue the same series or pattern as established by the problem figures.*

Problem Figures / **Answer Figures**

11. 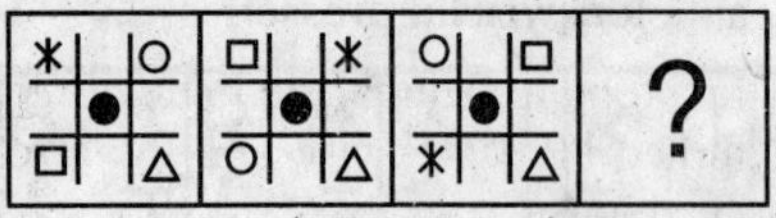 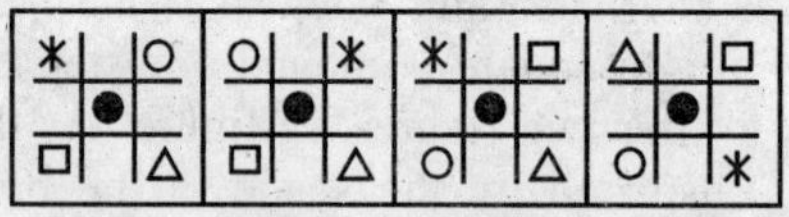

(a) (b) (c) (d)

12. 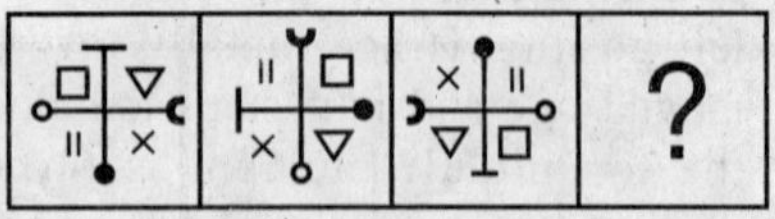 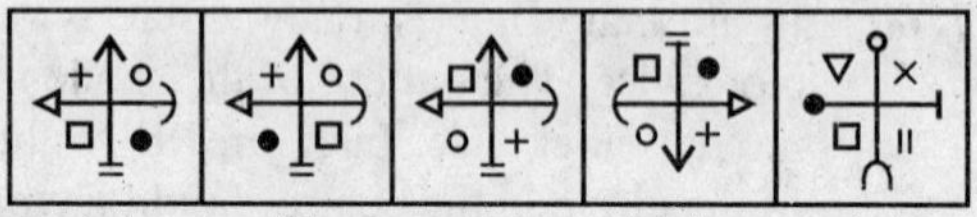

(a) (b) (c) (d) (e)

13. 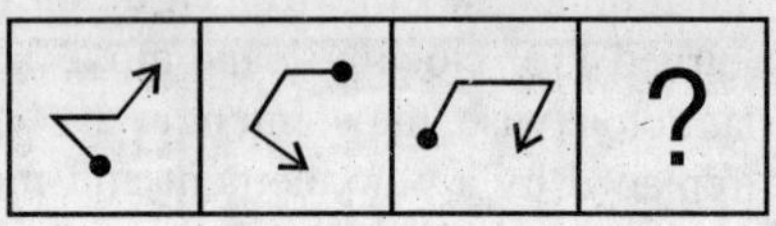 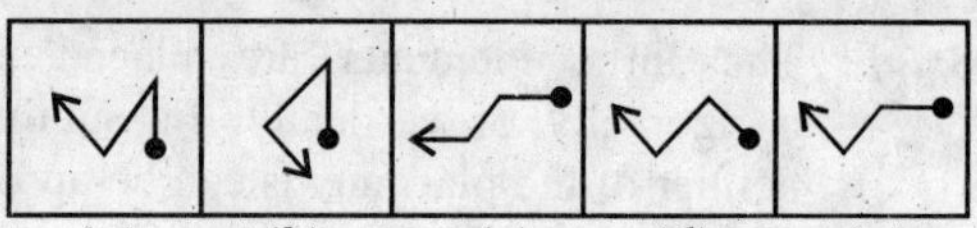

(a) (b) (c) (d) (e)

14. 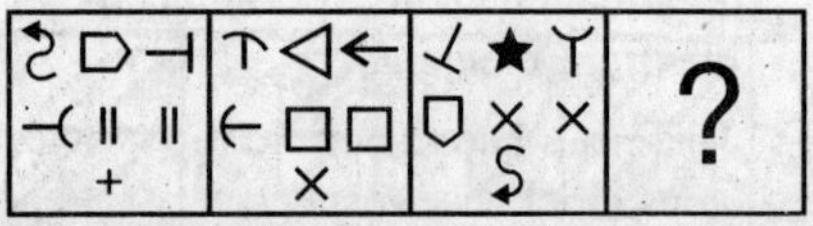 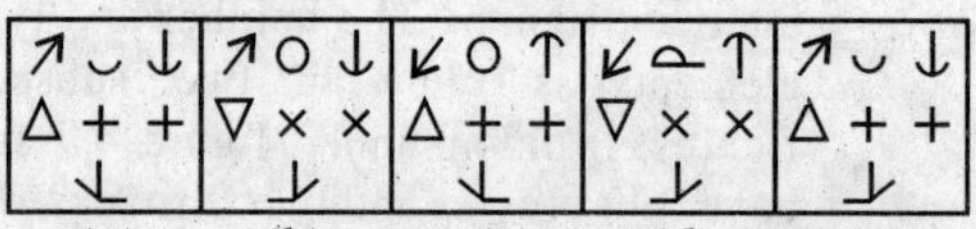

(a) (b) (c) (d) (e)

15. 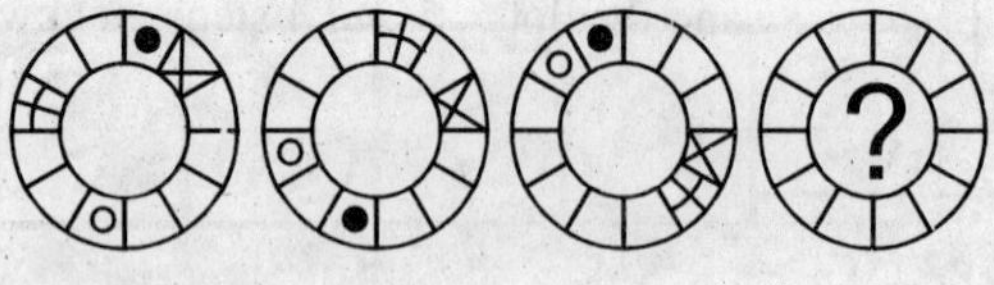 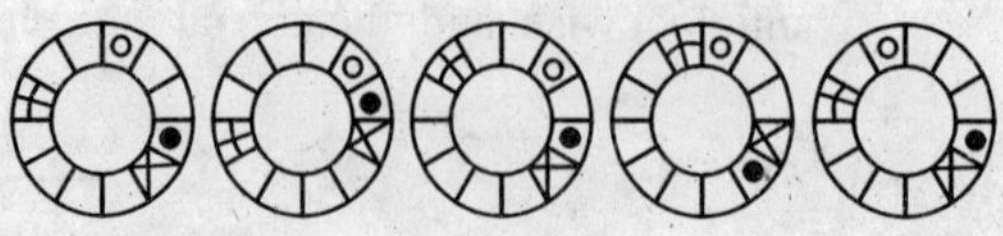

(a) (b) (c) (d) (e)

EXPLANATORY ANSWERS

1. *(d)* : In each step, all the elements move to the adjacent corner (of the square boundary) in a CW direction and the element that reaches the upper-left corner gets vertically inverted.

2. *(c)* : We can label the arcs as shown . The arcs get inverted in the sequence (1 & 2), (3, 4 & 5), (6 & 1), (2, 3 & 4), (5 & 6), ...

3. *(d)* : All the elements move half-a-side of the square boundary in ACW direction in each step. Also, first, third and fifth elements are replaced by new elements in one step and second, fourth and sixth elements are replaced by new elements in the next step. The two steps are repeated alternately.

4. *(a)* : In each step, the dot moves one space CW and the arrow moves two spaces CW.

5. *(c)*: One arc and four arcs get inverted alternately.

6. *(a)*: The shade in the top left square is moved one step clockwise till figure B and then reversed, the process is repeated. The shade in the top right square is moved one step anticlockwise till figure D and then reversed. The shade in the bottom left square is moved one step clockwise in alternate figures and the shade in bottom right square is moved one step clockwise after two figures. In figure 'A' the rule is isolated by the shade in the bottom left square.

7. *(e)*: In alternate figures a new circle is shaded clockwise. The pattern of the shade is also moved clockwise. In figure 'E' right half of the circle in the centre should have been shaded.

8. *(a)*: The three elements are placed either horizontally or vertically. In option 'A' neither of the placements can be applied.

9. *(c)*: The placement of elements is same in alternate figures. The number and type of elements is same in two subsequent figures. In this manner, figure 'C' should have four crosses and two C shapes.

10. *(c)*: The element is moved one step anticlockwise and the arc at one end is turned outside and inside alternately. In figure 'C' the element should be on the right side with the arc turned outside on the top side.

11. *(a)*: The places of star, circle and square are moved one step clockwise at each step.

12. *(e)*: The elements in the four quadrants are moved one step clockwise and the elements at the ends of the cross are moved one step anticlockwise in this series.

13. *(a)*: In alternate figures, the line with the dot is turned 90° clockwise and the arrow 180° clockwise.

14. *(e)*: In alternate figures, the element in the top left position is horizontally inverted and moved one and half steps anticlockwise, the top middle element is turned 90° clockwise and moved one step anticlockwise, the top right element is turned 135° clockwise and moved one step anticlockwise, the element at the bottom is replaced by a new element and moved to the top middle position, and the two identical elements are replaced by two new identical elements.

15. *(a)*: The cross and the circle move one and two steps clockwise respectively (at each step), the plus moves 3, 4 and 5 steps clockwise, and the dot 6, 5 and 4 steps clockwise.

23. NON-VERBAL ANALOGY

EXERCISE

TYPE-I

Directions (Q. 1-10): *The second figure in the first unit of the Problem Figures bears a certain relationship to the first figure. Similarly, one of the figures in the Answer Figures bears the same relationship to the first figures in the second unit of the Problem Figures. Locate the figure which would fit the questions marks.*

Problem Figures | **Answer Figures**

1. 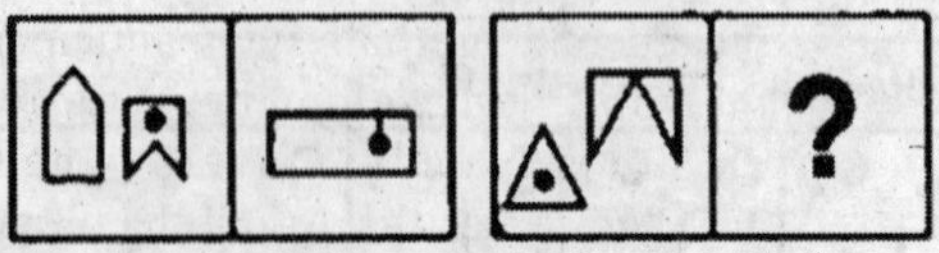
1 2 3 4

(a) (b) (c) (d) (e)

2. 
1 2 3 4

(a) (b) (c) (d) (e)

3. 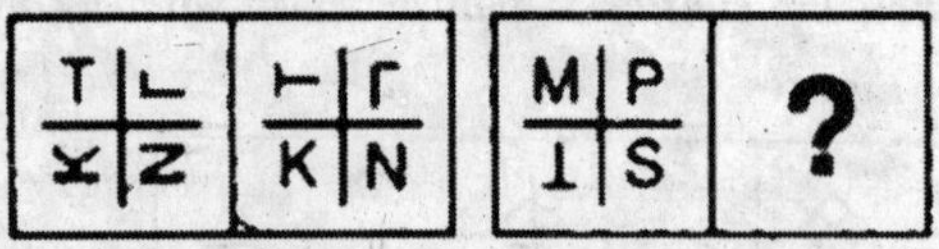
1 2 3 4
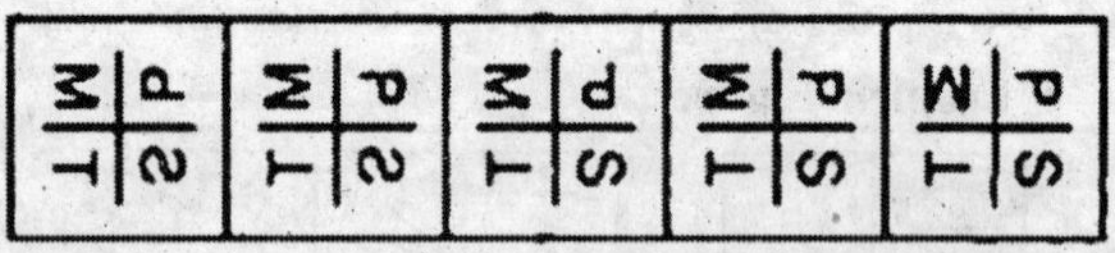
(a) (b) (c) (d) (e)

4. 
1 2 3 4

(a) (b) (c) (d) (e)

5. 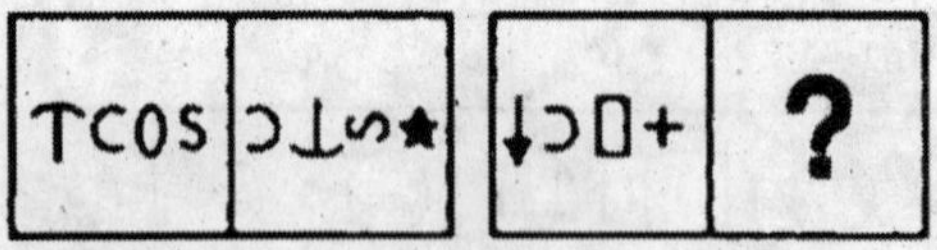
1 2 3 4
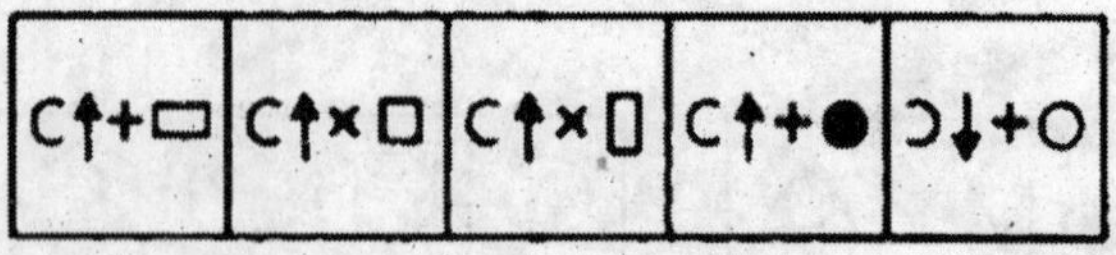
(a) (b) (c) (d) (e)

6. 
1 2 3 4

(a) (b) (c) (d) (e)

Problem Figures **Answer Figures**

7. 

1 2 3 4 (a) (b) (c) (d) (e)

8. 

1 2 3 4 (a) (b) (c) (d) (e)

9. 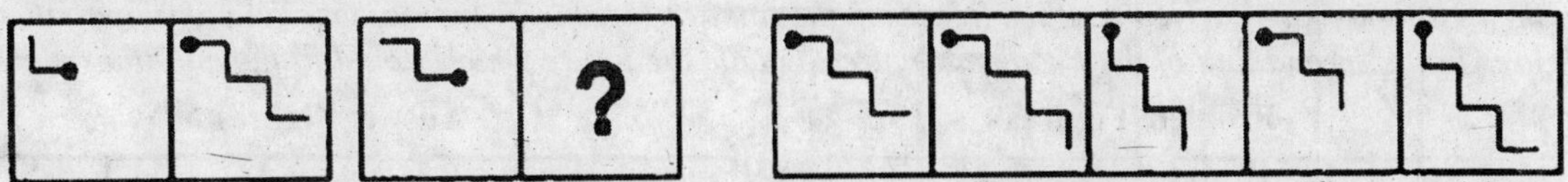

1 2 3 4 (a) (b) (c) (d) (e)

10. 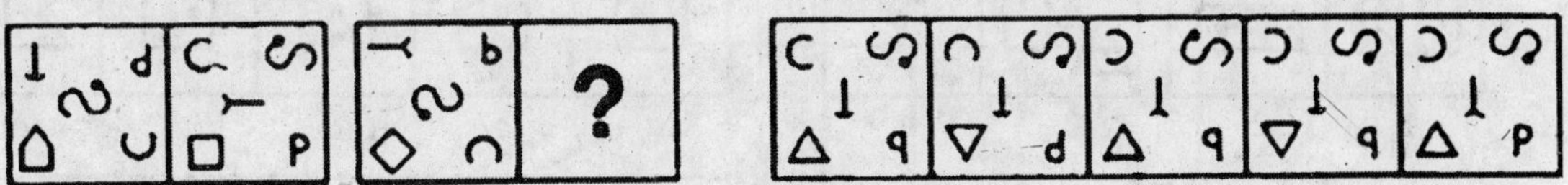

1 2 3 4 (a) (b) (c) (d) (e)

TYPE-II

Directions (Q. 11–20): *In each of the following questions, a related pair of figures is followed by five numbered pairs of figures. Select the pair that has a relationship* ***similar*** *to that in the unnumbered pair.*

Problem Figure **Answer Figures**

11. 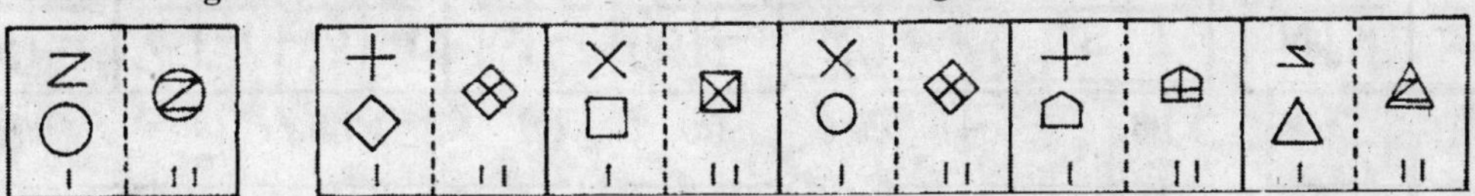

(a) (b) (c) (d) (e)

12. 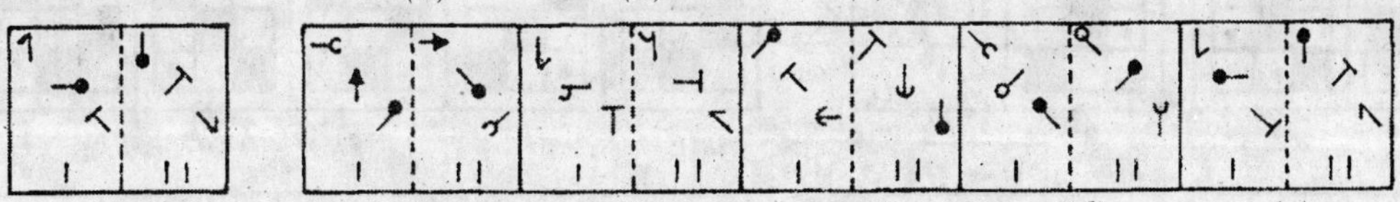

(a) (b) (c) (d) (e)

13. 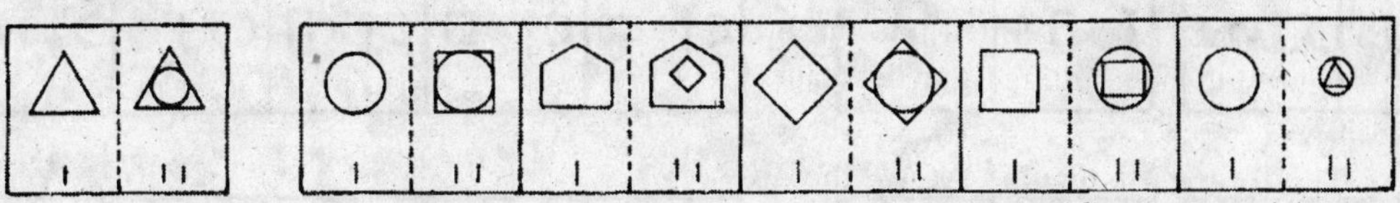

(a) (b) (c) (d) (e)

14. 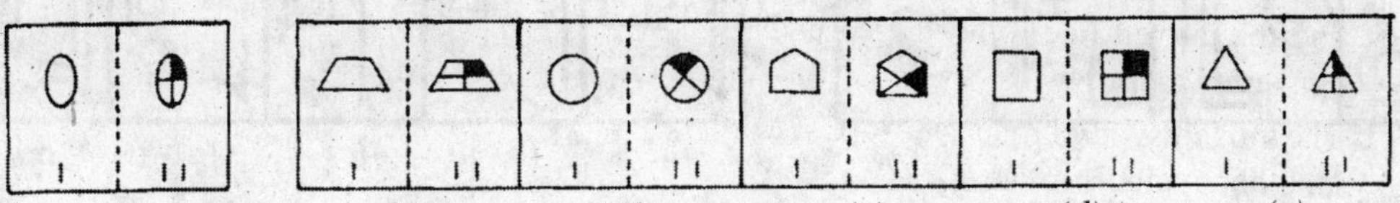

(a) (b) (c) (d) (e)

15. 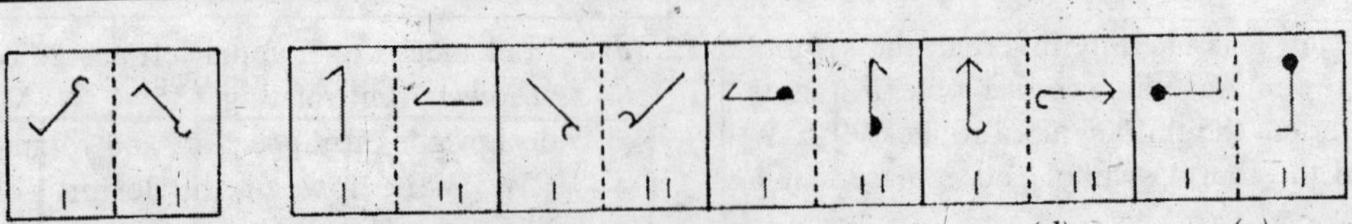

(a) (b) (c) (d) (e)

16. 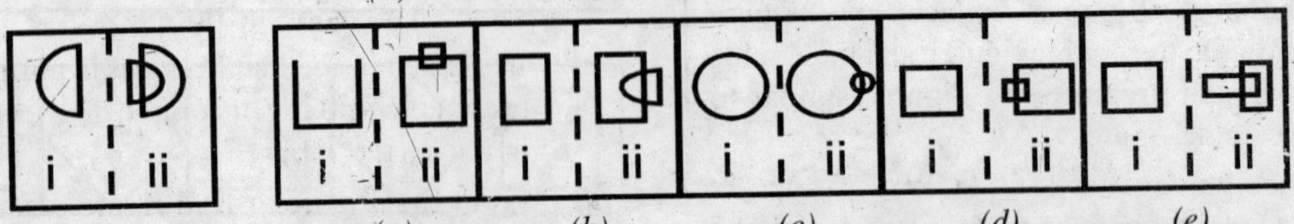

(a) (b) (c) (d) (e)

17. 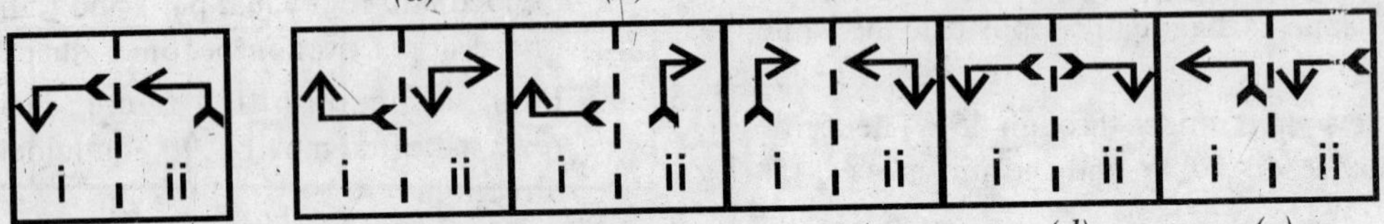

(a) (b) (c) (d) (e)

18. 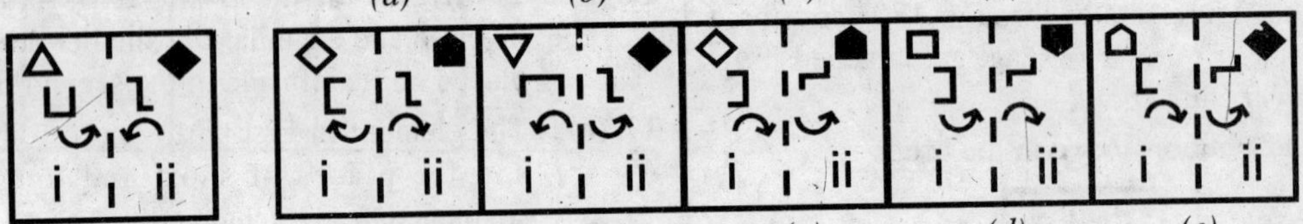

(a) (b) (c) (d) (e)

19. 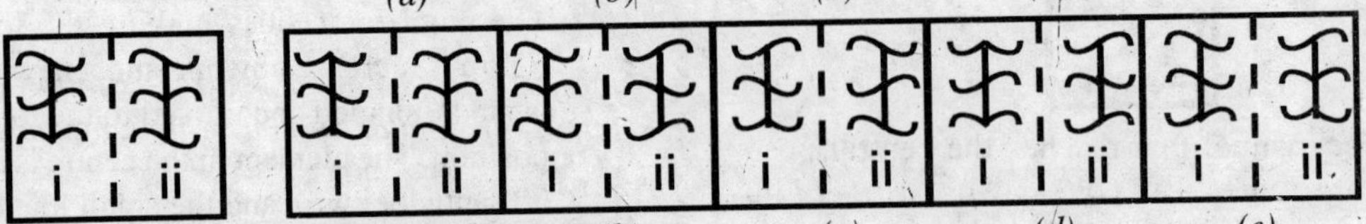

(a) (b) (c) (d) (e)

20. 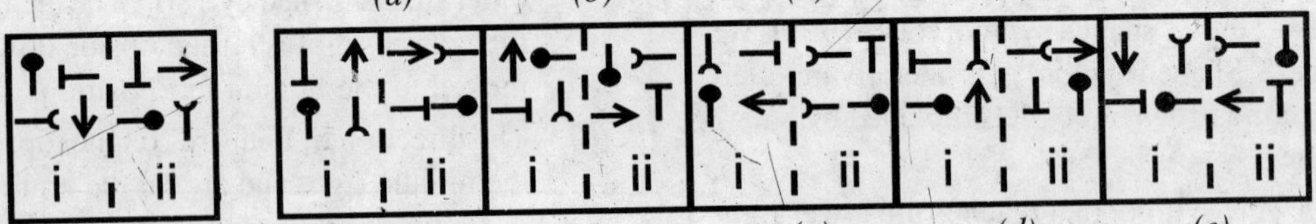

(a) (b) (c) (d) (e)

EXPLANATORY ANSWERS

1. *(b)* : The R.H.S. figure is fitted into the L.H.S. figure and the resulting figure is rotated 90° CW.

2. *(b)* : The figure rotates 45° ACW, the arrow changes to a curved line with dotted ends and the curved lines with dotted ends get converted to arrows.

3. *(d)* : The top left symbol rotates 90° ACW while all other symbols rotate 90° CW.

4. *(e)* : The black portion in top layer moves one step to the right; the black portions in the middle and the lower layers move one step to the left and the dot moves one step upwards.

5. *(d)* : The first and second symbols from the left interchange positions and the other two symbols also interchange positions. The symbol that reaches the first position from

the left gets laterally inverted; the symbol that reaches the second position gets inverted, the third symbol rotates 90° CW and the fourth symbol gets replaced by a new one.

6. ***(d)*** **:** The single figure is replaced by a figure similar to the double figures and the double figures are replaced by figures similar to the single figure.

7. ***(e)*** **:** The figure rotates 135° ACW; a 'T' appears diagonally opposite to the black leaf and a 'Y' appears diagonally opposite to the white leaf.

8. ***(c)*** **:** The square rotates through 45°. The arrow moves 90° ACW and the pin moves 45° ACW.

9. ***(b)*** **:** The figure rotates through 180° and three lines forming a zig-zag, get attached to its lower end.

10. ***(d)*** **:** The symbols move in the order

The symbol that reaches the central position rotates 90° CW and its arc gets inverted; the 'P' shaped symbol rotates through 180°; the 'C' shaped symbol rotates 90° CW; the 'S' Shaped symbol gets laterally inverted and the fifth symbol gets replaced by a new one.

45°, the symbol that reaches the lower right corner rotates 90° ACW and a new symbol appears in middle-left position.

11. ***(b)*** **:** The uppermost design enters into innerside side of the lower design from Ist figure to the IInd figure.

12. ***(a)*** **:** In element I to II upper left design comes at lower right rotating 135° C.W. Middle design goes to upper left and rotates 90° CW. While lower right design goes to middle and it also rotates 90° C.W. The same changes occur in option A.

13. ***(e)*** **:** In element I to II and ellipse is put in the triangle. Similarly in option E a triangle is put in the ellipse.

14. ***(d)*** **:** From first figure to IInd figure, design is divided into four equal parts and right side of the upper portion becomes shaded.

15. ***(e)*** **:** From Ist figure to IInd figure, design is reversed after moving 90° anticlockwise direction.

16. ***(d)*** **:** The figure in the first part is laterally inverted and a similar but smaller design is placed on its left side in the second part.

17. ***(e)*** **:** The element in first part is moved by 90° and the places of short and long line segments are interchanged.

18. ***(c)*** **:** The number of sides making the top left figure is increased by one and a new figure is made, shaded and moved to the top right position. The element in the centre is turned 90° anticlockwise and the small line on the other side is turned by 180°. The element in the bottom right is turned upside down and moved to the bottom left position.

19. ***(a)*** **:** The direction of both arcs on the top, are on the middle right and arc on the bottom left in first part are turned to the other side in the second part.

20. ***(b)*** **:** From part one to part two, the element in the top left is turned 90° clockwise and the other three 90° anticlockwise, also the elements are moved one step anticlockwise.

24. ODD MAN OUT

In this type of reasoning a statement is followed by inferences drawn from it. From these inferences only one definitely follows which is the hidden proposition of the sentence and it is the right answer to the question.

EXERCISE

Directions (Q. 1–5) : *In each question below five figures are given. Four are similar in a certain way and so form a group. The question is— which one of the figures* ***does not*** *belong to that group?*

1. 

(a) (b) (c) (d) (e)

2. 

(a) (b) (c) (d) (e)

3. 

(a) (b) (c) (d) (e)

4. 

(a) (b) (c) (d) (e)

5. 

(a) (b) (c) (d) (e)

Directions (Q. 6–10) : *In each of the following questions, in four out of the five figures, element I is related to element II in the same particular way. Find out the figure in which the element I is* ***not*** *so related to element II.*

6. 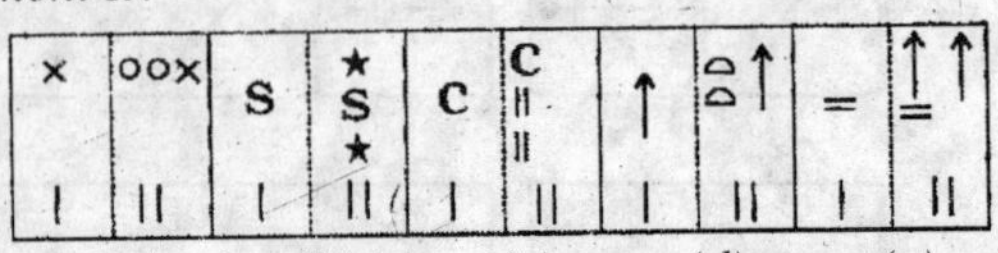

(a) (b) (c) (d) (e)

7. 

(a) (b) (c) (d) (e)

8. 

(a) (b) (c) (d) (e)

9. 

(a) (b) (c) (d) (e)

10. 

(a) (b) (c) (d) (e)

Directions (Q. 11–15) : *In each of the following questions, a related pair of figures (unnumbered) is followed by five numbered pairs of figures. Out of these five, four have relationship similar to that in the unnumbered pair. Only one pair of figures does not have similar relationship. Select that pair of figures which does not have a similar relationship to that in the unnumbered pair. Number of that pair is your answer.*

11. 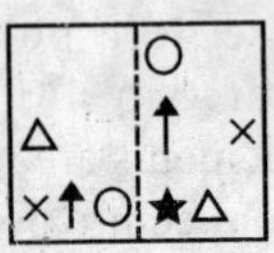 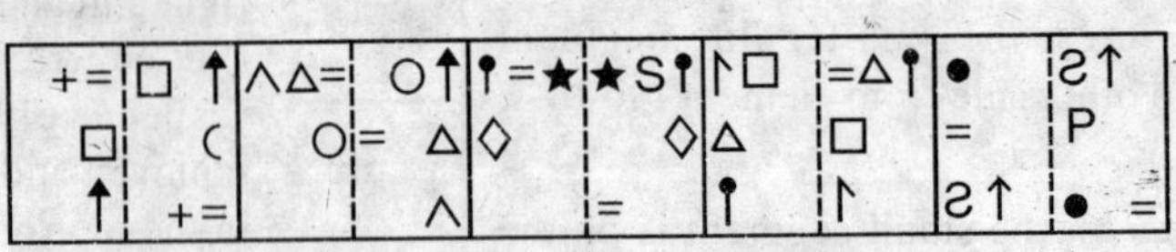

(a) (b) (c) (d) (e)

12. 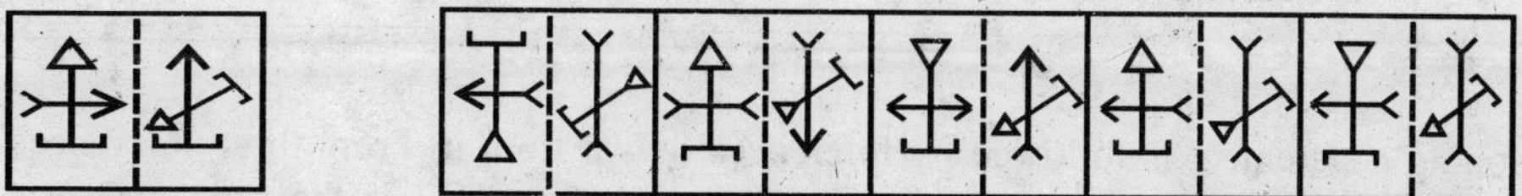

(a) (b) (c) (d) (e)

13. 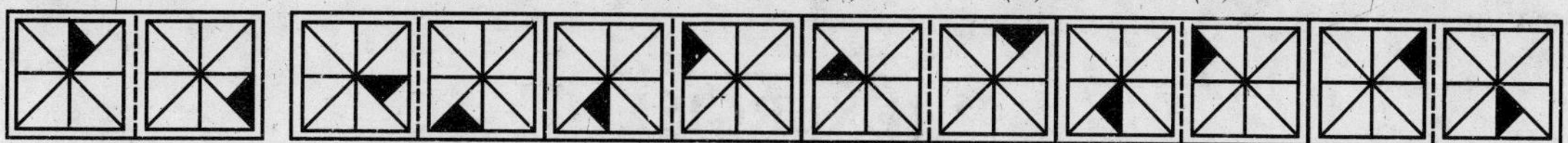

(a) (b) (c) (d) (e)

14. 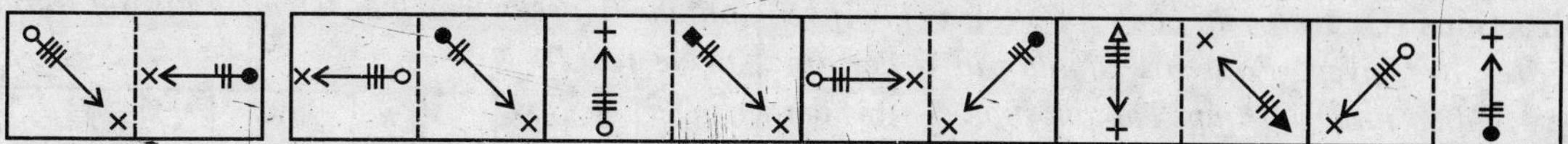

(a) (b) (c) (d) (e)

15. 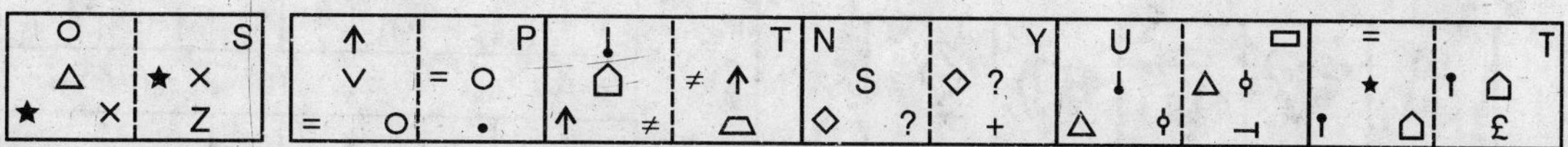

(a) (b) (c) (d) (e)

EXPLANATORY ANSWERS

1. *(d)* : In all other figures, the arrow and the + sign lie towards the black end of the main figure.

2.*(a)* : The pins, equal in number of sides in the main figure are attached to the midpoint of a side of the main figure in case of figures (*b*), (*c*), (*d*) and (*e*). In figure (*a*), these pins are attached to a vertex of the main figure.

3.*(c)* : In all other figures, the dot appears in the angle formed between the arrow and the pin.

4.*(a)* :

5.*(c)* : All other figures have at least one line of symmetry.

6.*(e)* : Except in figure (*b*), in all other figures, from element I to II two new designs are added in one side of the main design.

7.*(c)* : In each figure from element I to II the main design rotates through 135° clockwise or anticlockwise. Except in figure (*c*), in all other figures, the smaller line segment moves to other side from element I to II.

8.*(a)* :

9.*(b)* : In figure (*b*), the small segment is on the same side as that of the half shaded circle in both the elements.

10.*(d)* : The first design is inverted and moved to third place, the second design is moved to the fourth place, third design to the first place and fourth design is inverted and moved to the second place. Option (*d*) violates this.

11.*(d)* : From element I to element II clockwise the first unit is moved 2 steps forward, the second unit 1 step forward, the third unit 2½ steps forward and the fourth unit 3 steps forward. In option '*d*' the third unit violates the rule.

12. *(e)* :

13.*(e)* : In element II, the shade is moved two sections clockwise and shifted from the centre to the base. In option '*e*' it is not so.

14.*(a)* : In element II, the arrow is turned 135° clockwise. In option '*a*' it is turned anticlockwise.

15.*(b)* : From element I to element II, the bottom right unit and bottom left unit are moved to the centre and middle left position respectively. The other two units are removed and two new elements are placed in the top right and bottom centre position respectively. In option '*b*' the placement of bottom right and left elements is not right.

GENERAL KNOWLEDGE

INDIAN HISTORY

ANCIENT INDIA

INDUS VALLEY CIVILISATION (2500-1750 BC)

- The earliest excavations in the Indus valley were done at Harappa in the West Punjab and Mohenjodaro in Sindh. Both places are now in Pakistan.

Important Sites

- The most important sites are Kot Diji in Sindh, Kalibangan in Rajasthan, Ropar in the Punjab, Banawali in Haryana, Lothal, Surkotada and Dhaulavira, all the three in Gujarat.
- Mohenjodaro is the largest of all the Indus cities and it is estimated to have spread over an area of 200 hectares.

Indus Valley Civilisation : An Objective Study

Major Sites	*Excavators*	*Year*	*River*	*Location*	*Important Findings*
1. Harappa	D.R. Sahni	1921	Ravi	West Punjab (Pakistan)	Granaries, Virgin Goddess, Cemetery, Stone symbol of Lingam and Yoni
2. Mohenjodaro	R.D. Banerjee	1922	Indus	Sindh (Pakistan)	Great Bath, Great Granary, Assem bly Hall, Proto-Shiva, Brick Kilns, Mesopotamian seals
3. Chanhudaro	N.G. Mazumdar	1931	Indus	Sindh (Pakistan)	Bronze toy cart, Ink-pot, Lipstick, City without a citadel
4. Kalibangan	B.B. Lal & B.K. Thapar	1953	Ghaggar	Ganganagar (Rajasthan)	Decorated bricks, ploughed field surface, Firealtars
5. Lothal	S.R. Rao	1957	Bhogwa	Ahmedabad (Gujarat)	Dockyard, Rice husk, Fire altars, Double burial
6. Banawali	R.S. Bist	1973	Ghaggar	Hissar (Haryana)	Toy plough, Gridiron pattern of Town planning.
7. Dholavira	R.S. Bist	1990	Luni	Kutchh (Gujarat)	A Large well & a bath, A stadium
8. Surkotada	J. Joshi	1964	—	Gujarat	Bones of Horse, Pot burials

Salient Features of the Harappan Culture

- The Harappan Civilization was primarily Urban.
- Mohenjodaro and Harappa were the planned cities.
- The large-scale use of burnt bricks in almost all kinds of constructions are the important characteristics of the Harappan culture.
- Another remarkable feature was the underground drainage system connecting all houses to the street drains which were covered by stone slabs or bricks.
- The most important public place of Mohenjodaro is the Great Bath measuring 39 feet length, 23 feet breadth and 8 feet depth.

- Agriculture was the most important occupation. In the fertile soils, farmers cultivated two crops a year. They were the first who had grown paddy.
- Wheat and barley were the main crops grown besides sesame, mustard and cotton.
- Animals like sheep, goats and buffalo were domesticated. The use of horse is not yet firmly established.
- Bronze and copper vessels are the outstanding examples of the Harappan metal craft.
- A large number of seals numbering more than 2000 have been discovered.

Social Life

- Jewelleries such as bangles, bracelets, fillets, girdles, anklets, ear-rings and finger rings were worn by women. These ornaments were made of gold, silver, copper, bronze and semi precious stones.
- Fishing was a regular occupation while hunting and bull fighting were other pastimes.
- Manufacture of terracotta (burnt clay) was a major industry of the people.
- Figures of animals such as sacred bull and dove were discovered. The figures of Mother Goddesses were used for religious purposes.
- Most of the inscriptions were engraved on seals. It is interesting to note that the Indus script has not yet been deciphered.
- The Pipal tree was used as a religious symbol.
- The origin of the '*Swastika*' symbol can be traced to the Harrapan Civilization.
- The chief male deity was Pasupati, (proto-Siva) represented in seals as sitting in a yogic posture with three faces and two horns.

THE VEDIC PERIOD

RIG VEDIC AGE (1500 - 1000 B.C.)

- The Early Vedic period is known from the *Rig Veda*.
- The *Rig Veda* refers to Saptasindhu or the land of seven rivers. This includes the five rivers of the Punjab, namely, Jhelum, Chenab, Ravi, Beas and Sutlej along with the Indus and Saraswati.
- Historians view that the Aryans came from Central Asia. They entered India through the Khyber pass between 2000 B.C. and 1500 B.C. They first settled in seven places in the Punjab region which they called Sapta Sindhu. Slowly, they moved towards the Gangetic Valley.
- The Aryan Civilisation was a rural civilisation.

Vedic Literature

- The word 'Veda' is derived from the root 'vid', which means to know and signifies 'superior knowledge'.
- The Vedic literature consists of the four Vedas – Rig, Yajur, Sama and Atharva.
- The *Rig Veda* is the earliest of the four Vedas divided into 10 mandalas and it consists of 1028 hymns. The hymns were sung by *Hotri* in praise of various gods.
- The *Yajur Veda* consists of various details of rules to be observed at the time of sacrifice. Its hymns were recited by *Adharvayus.*
- The *Sama Veda* is set to tune for the purpose of chanting during sacrifice. It is called the book of chants and the origins of Indian music are traced in it. Its hymns were recited by *Udgatri.*
- The *Atharva Veda* contains details of rituals.
- Besides the Vedas, there are other sacred works like the Brahmanas, the Aranyakas, the Upanishads, and the epics Ramayana and Mahabharata.

Political Organisation

- During this period, the kingdom was tribal in character. Each tribe formed a separate kingdom.
- The basic unit of political organisation was *kula* or family.
- The highest political unit was called *jana* or tribe.
- There were several tribal kingdoms during the Rig Vedic period such as Bharatas, Matsyas, Yadus and Purus. The head of the kingdom was called as *rajan* or king.
- There were two popular bodies called the *Sabha* and *Samiti*. The former seems to have been a

council of elders and the latter, a general assembly of the entire people.

Social Life

- Family was the basis of the society.
- The head of the family was known as *grihapathi*.

Economic Condition

- The Rig Vedic Aryans were pastoral people and their main occupation was cattle rearing. Their wealth was estimated in terms of their cattle.
- Carpentry was another important profession.

RELIGION

- The important Rig Vedic gods were Prithvi (Earth), Agni (Fire), Vayu (Wind), Varuna (Rain) and Indra (Thunder).
- Indra was the most popular among them during the early Vedic period.
- There were also female gods like Aditi and Ushas. There were no temples and no idol worship during the early Vedic period.

Rigvedic Rivers

River	Name in Rigveda
Indus	Sindhu
Jhelum	Vitasta
Chenab	Asikni
Ravi	Parushini
Beas	Vipasa
Sutlej	Sutudri
Gomati	Gomal
Saraswati	Sarasvati
Ghaggar	Prishadavati

LATER VEDIC PERIOD (1000–600 B.C.)

- This age is also called as the Epic Age because the two great epics the Ramayana and Mahabharata were written during this period.
- The Sama, Yajur, Atharva Vedas, Brahmanas, Aranyakas, Upanishads and the two epics are the sources of information for this period.

Political Organisation

- Larger kingdoms were formed during the later Vedic period.
- The king performed various rituals and sacrifices to strengthen his position. They include Rajasuya (consecration ceremony), Asvamedha (horse sacrifice) and Vajpeya (chariot race).
- Kingship became hereditary.
- Kings assumed titles like Ekrat, Samrat and Sarvabhauma.

Economic Condition

- Iron was used extensively in this period and this enabled the people to clear forests and to bring more land under cultivation. Agriculture became the chief occupation.
- Taxes like Bali, Sulk and Bhaga were collected from the people.
- Wealth was calculated in terms of cows.

Social Life

- The four divisions of society (Brahmins, Kshatriyas, Vaisyas and Sudras) or the Varna system was thoroughly established during the Later Vedic period.
- The Ashrama system was formed to attain 4 purusharthas. They were *Dharma*, *Artha*, *Kama* and *Moksha*.

Religion

- Gods of the Early Vedic period like Indra and Agni lost their importance. Prajapathi (the creator), Vishnu (the protector) and Rudra (the destroyer) became prominent during the Later Vedic period.

JAINISM AND BUDDHISM

JAINISM

- Jainism originated in the 6th century B.C. It rejected Vedic religion and avoided its rituals.
- Founded by Rishabha Deva. Rishabha Deva was succeeded by 23 Thirthankaras (prophets). Mahavira was the 24th Thirthankara.

Vardhamana Mahavira (540-468 B.C.)

- Vardhamana was born in a village called Kundagrama near Vaishali in Bihar.
- His father was *Siddhartha*. He was the head of a famous Kshatriya clan.

- His mother was *Trisala*. She was a princess of the Lichchhavi clan. She was the sister of the ruler of Vaishali.
- Vardhamana was married to *Yasoda,* a princess. They had a daughter.
- At the age of 30, he left his home and family. He became an ascetic (monk). He wandered from place-to-place in search of truth for 12 years.
- In the 13th year of his penance, he attained the highest spiritual knowledge called Kevalya or Jnana. Thereafter, he was called Mahavira and Jina. His followers were called Jains and his religion Jainism.
- He died at the age of 72 in 468 B.C. at a place called Pavapuri near modern Rajgir in Bihar.

Teachings of Jainism

- The three principles of Jainism, also known as Triratnas (three gems), are:
  1. right faith.
  2. right knowledge.
  3. right conduct.
- Mahavira preached his disciples to follow the five principles. They are:
  1. Ahimsa—not to injure any living beings
  2. Satya—to speak the truth
  3. Asteya—not to steal
  4. Tyag—not to own property
  5. Brahmacharia—to lead a virtuous life.

Spread of Jainism

- Mahavira preached his religion in Prakrit language which was the language of the masses.
- Chandragupta Maurya, Kharavela of Kalinga and the royal dynasties of south India such as the Gangas, the Kadambas, the Chalukyas and the Rashtrakutas patronised Jainism.
- Jainism was divided into two sects after Vallabhi Council, namely *Svetambaras* (wearing white dresses) under Sthulbhadra and *Digambaras* (naked) under Bhadrabahu.
- The first Jain Council was convened at Pataliputra by Sthulabahu, the leader of the *Digambaras*, in the beginning of the 3rd century B.C.
- The second Jain Council was held at Vallabhi in 5th century A.D. The final compilation of Jain literature called *Twelve Angas* was completed in this council.

BUDDHISM

Gautama Buddha (563-483 B.C.)

- Buddha's original name was *Siddhartha*.
- Siddhartha was born in the Lumbini Garden near Kapilavastu in Nepal. His father was Suddhodana. He was a Sakya chief of Kapilavastu. His mother, Mayadevi, died when Siddhartha was only seven days old. He was brought up by his step mother Mahaprajapati Gauthami.
- At the age of sixteen Siddhartha, married Yasodhara and gave birth to a son, Rahul.
- The sight of an old man, a diseased man, a corpse and an ascetic turned him away from worldly life. He left home at the age of twenty-nine in search of Truth.
- He wandered for seven years and at last, he sat under a bodhi tree at Bodh Gaya in Bihar and did intense penance, after which he got Enlightenment (Nirvana) at the age of thirty-five. Since then, he became known as the Buddha or 'the Enlightened One'.
- Buddha delivered his first sermon at Sarnath near Banaras (now Varanasi).
- He died at the age of 80 in 483 B.C. at Kushinagar in Uttar Pradesh.

Teachings of Buddha

- The Four Noble Truths of Buddha are:
  1. The world is full of suffering.
  2. The cause of suffering is desire.
  3. If desires are get rid off, suffering can be removed.
  4. This can be done by following the Eightfold Path.
- The Eightfold Path consists of:
  1. Right Thought.
  2. Right Belief.
  3. Right Speech.

4. Right Action.
5. Right Living.
6. Right Efforts.
7. Right Knowledge.
8. Right Meditation.

Buddhist Literature

- In Pali language.
- Buddhist scriptures in Pali are commonly referred to as *Tripitakas, i.e.*, 'Three Baskets'.
- ***Vinaya Pitaka:*** Rules of discipline in Buddhist monasteries.
- ***Sutta Pitaka:*** Largest, contains collection of Buddha's sermons.
- ***Abidhamma Pitaka:*** Explanation of the philosophical principles of the Buddhist religion.

Main Buddhist Councils

Buddhist Council	Time	Place	Chairman	Patron
First	483 BC	Rajagriha	Mahakashyapa	Ajatasatru
Second	383 BC	Vaishali	Sabakamuni	Kalashoka
Third	250 BC	Patliputra	Moggaliputta Tissa	Ashoka
Fourth	AD 72	Kundalvana	Vasumitra, Ashwaghosa	Kanishka

The Mahajanapadas

Mahajanapadas	Capital
1. Kashi	Varanasi
2. Kosala	Shravasti
3. Anga	Champanagri
4. Magadh	Girivraj or Rajgriha
5. Vajji	Vaishali
6. Malla	Kushinagar and Pavapuri
7. Chedi	Shuktimati
8. Vatsa	Kaushambi
9. Kuru	Hastinapur, Indraprastha and Isukara
10. Panchal	Ahichhatra and Kampilya
11. Matsya	Viratnagar
12. Surasen	Mathura
13. Asmaka	Paudanya
14. Avanti	Ujjaini
15. Gandhara	Taxila
16. Kamboj	Rajpur (Hatak)

DYNASTIES OF ANCIENT INDIA

HARYANKA DYNASTY

- Bimbisara was the founder of Haryanka Dynasty.
- He was a contemporary of both Vardhamana Mahavira and Gautama Buddha.
- During his rule, Darius I, the Achaemenian emperor, conquered the Indus Valley area.
- Ajatasatru imprisoned his father Bimbisara.
- The first Buddhist Council was convened by Ajatasatru at Rajgir.
- The immediate successor of Ajatasatru was Udayin.
- Udayin laid the foundation of the new capital at Pataliputra situated at the confluence of the two rivers, the Ganges and the Sone.
- Shishunaga was the founder of Shishunaga dynasty.
- After Shishunaga, the mighty empire began to collapse. His successor was Kakavarman or Kalasoka. During his reign, the second Buddhist Council was held at Vaishali.
- Kalasoka was killed by the founder of the Nanda dynasty.

NANDAS

- The fame of Magadha scaled new heights under the Nanda dynasty.
- Mahapadmananda was the founder of Nanda rule in Magadha.
- The last Nanda ruler was Dhana Nanda. Alexander invaded India during his rule.

MAURYAN EMPIRE

CHANDRAGUPTA MAURYA (322–298 B.C.)

- Chandragupta Maurya was the founder of the Mauryan Empire. He overthrew Nanda dynasty with the help of Chanakya.
- Chandragupta defeated Seleukos Nikator, the Greek general of Alexander, in a battle in 305 B.C.
- Seleukos sent Megasthenes as Greek Ambassador to the Court of Chandragupta. Megasthenes wrote *Indica*.
- Chandragupta was a follower of Jainism.
- He came to Sravana Belgola, near Mysore with a Jain monk called Bhadrabahu. The hill in which he lived until his death is called Chandragiri.
- Chanakya served as prime minister during the reigns of Chandragupta and Bindusara.

BINDUSARA (298–273 B.C.)

- Chandragupta Maurya was succeeded by his son Bindusara.
- Bindusara was called by the Greeks as "*Amitraghatha*" meaning, slayer of enemies.

ASHOKA (273–232 B.C.)

- Ashoka was the most famous ruler of the Mauryan dynasty.
- The most important event of Ashoka's reign was his victorious war with Kalinga in 261 B.C.
- Ashoka convened the Third Buddhist Council at Pataliputra around 250 B.C. in order to strengthen the *Sangha*. It was presided over by Moggaliputta Tissa.
- Ashoka's edicts and inscriptions were deciphered by James Prinsep in 1837.
- The last Mauryan king, Brahadratha was killed by his minister Pushyamitra Sunga. It put an end to the Mauryan Empire.

SUNGAS

- The founder of the Sunga dynasty was *Pushyamitra Sunga*, who was the commander-in-chief under the Mauryas.
- He ascended the throne of Magadha in 185 B.C.
- Pushyamitra was a staunch follower of Brahmanism. He performed two asvamedha sacrifices.
- After the death of Pushyamitra, his son Agnimitra became the ruler.
- Agnimitra was a great conqueror. He was also the hero of the play *Malavikagnimitram* written by Kalidasa.

KANVA

- The last Sunga ruler was Devabhuti, who was murdered by his minister Vasudeva Kanva, the founder of the *Kanva dynasty*.
- The Kanva dynasty ruled for 45 years. After the fall of the Kanvas, the history of Magadha was a blank until the establishment of the Gupta dynasty.

SATAVAHANAS

- The founder of the Satavahana dynasty was Simuka.
- The greatest ruler of the Satavahana dynasty was *Gautamiputra Satakarni*.
- The greatest port of the Satavahanas was Kalyani on the west Deccan. Gandakasela and Ganjam on the east coast were the other important seaports.
- The fine painting at Amaravathi and Nagarjunakonda caves belong to this period.

SANGAM AGE (300 B.C. TO A.D. 300)

- The Sangam Age constitutes an important chapter in the history of South India.
- According to Tamil legends, there existed three Sangams (Academy of Tamil poets) in ancient Tamil Nadu popularly called Muchchangam. These Sangams flourished under the royal patronage of the Pandyas.
- *The first Sangam*, held at then Madurai, chaired by Agastya.
- *The second Sangam* was held at Kapadapuram, chaired by Tolkappiyar.
- *The third Sangam* at Madurai was founded by Mudathirumaran.

Political History

- The Tamil country was ruled by three dynasties namely the Chera, Chola and Pandyas during the Sangam Age.

CHERAS

- The Cheras ruled over parts of modern Kerala. Their capital was Vanji and their important seaports were Tondi and Musiris.
- The greatest Chera King was *Senguttuvan*.

CHOLAS

- The Chola kingdom of the Sangam period extended from modern Tiruchi district to southern Andhra Pradesh.
- Their capital was first located at Uraiyur and then shifted to Puhar. Kaveripattinam served as their port.

GUPTA PERIOD

- The Gupta period is considered as the *Golden Age* in the history of India because this period witnessed all round developments in Religion, Literature, Science, Art and Architecture.

CHANDRAGUPTA I (320-334 A.D.)

- In the beginning of the 4th Century A.D., Sri Gupta established a small Kingdom at Pataliputra. He is considered as the founder of the Gupta dynasty.
- The first notable ruler of the Gupta dynasty was Chandragupta I. He assumed the title *Maharajadhiraja*. The Meherauli Iron Pillar inscription mentions his extensive conquests.
- Chandragupta I is considered to be the founder of the Gupta era which starts with his accession in A.D. 320.

SAMUDRAGUPTA (335-380 A.D.)

- Samudragupta was the greatest of the rulers of the Gupta dynasty. The Allahabad Pillar inscription provides a detailed account of his reign.
- Because of his military achievements, Samudragupta was hailed as '*Indian Napoleon*'.

CHANDRAGUPTA II (380-414 A.D.)

- Samudragupta was succeeded by his son Chandragupta II Vikramaditya.
- The greatest of the military achievements of Chandragupta II was his war against the Saka *satraps* of western India.
- The famous Chinese pilgrim, Fahien visited India (A.D. 399 - A.D. 414) during the reign of Chandragupta II.

SUCCESSORS OF CHANDRAGUPTA II

- Kumaragupta (415-455) was the son and successor of Chandragupta II. His reign was marked by general peace and prosperity.
- Kumaragupta was the founder of the Nalanda University.
- Kumaragupta was followed by *Skandagupta* who ruled from A.D. 456 to A.D. 468.
- After Skandagupta's death, many of his successors like Purugupta, Narasimhagupta, Buddhagupta and Baladitya could not save the Gupta empire from the Huns. Ultimately, the Gupta power totally disappeared due to the Hun invasions and later by the rise of Yasodharman in Malwa.

PUSHYABHUTI DYNASTY (600 - 647 A.D.)

- The greatest king was *Harshavardhana*, son of Prabhakar Vardhana of Thaneshwar. He shifted the capital to *Kannauj*.
- *Hieun Tsang* visited during his reign.
- He established a large monastery at Nalanda. Banabhata adorned his court, wrote Harshacharita and Kadambari. Harsha himself wrote three plays–Priyadarshika, Ratnawali and Nagananda.

PALLAVAS

- The Pallavas established their kingdom in Tondaimandalam by Simhavishnu with its capital at Kanchipuram.
- Other great Pallava rulers were Mahendravarman I, Narasimhavarman I, and Narasimhavarman II.
- The *Kailasanatha temple* at Kanchipuram is the greatest architectural masterpiece of the Pallava art.

CHALUKYAS (543-755 A.D.)

- Pulakesin I was the founder of the Chalukya dynasty. He established a small kingdom with Vatapi or Badami as its capital.
- The structural temples of the Chalukyas exist at Aihole, Badami and Pattadakal (Virupaksha temple). Cave temple architecture was also famous under the Chalukyas. Their cave temples are found in Ajanta, Ellora and Nasik.

RASHTRAKUTAS (755-975 A.D.)

- The art and architecture of the Rashtrakutas were found at Ellora and Elephanta.

CHOLAS

- Cholas became prominent in the ninth century and established an empire comprising the major portion of South India. Their capital was Tanjore.
- The founder of the Chola kingdom was Vijayalaya.
- Rajaraja Chola built the famous Brihadeeswara temple at Tanjore.
- *Dancing Figure of Shiva* (Nataraja) belong to Chola period.

MEDIEVAL INDIA

ARAB CONQUEST OF SIND

- In 712 A.D., Muhammad bin Quasim invaded Sind. Quasim defeated Dahir, the ruler of Sind and killed him in a well-contested battle.

Mahmud of Ghazni

- In 1024, Mahmud marched from Multan across Rajaputana, defeated the Solanki King Bhimadeva I, plundered Anhilwada and sacked the famous temple of Somanatha. This was his last campaign in India. Mahmud died in 1030 A.D.
- Mahmud patronized art and literature. *Firdausi* was the poet-laureate in the court of Mahmud.

Muhammad Ghori

- Prithviraj Chauhan defeated Ghori in the first battle of Tarain near Delhi in 1191 A.D.
- In the Second Battle of Tarain in 1192, Muhammad Ghori thoroughly routed the army of Prithiviraj, who was captured and killed.
- After his brilliant victory over Prithviraj at Tarain, Muhammad Ghori returned to Ghazni leaving behind his favourite general Qutb-ud-din Aibak to make further conquests in India.

SULTANATE PERIOD

SLAVE DYNASTY (1206-1290)

- The Slave dynasty was also called Mamluk dynasty. Mamluk was the Quranic term for slave.

Qutb-ud-din Aibak

- Qutb-ud-din Aibak was a slave of Muhammad Ghori, who made him the Governor of his Indian possessions.
- After the death of Ghori in 1206, Aibak declared his independence. He assumed the title Sultan and made Lahore his capital.
- Muslim writers call Aibak Lakh Baksh or giver of lakhs because he gave liberal donations to them.
- He built the famous Quwat-Ul-Islam mosque at Delhi. He began the construction of the famous Qutb Minar at Delhi but did not live long to complete it. It was later completed by Iltutmish.

Iltutmish (1210-1236 A.D.)

- Iltutmish belonged to the Ilbari tribe and hence his dynasty was named as Ilbari dynasty.
- He shifted his capital from Lahore to Delhi.
- He organised the *Iqta system* and introduced reforms in civil administration and army.

Raziya (1236-1240 A.D.)

- She appointed an Abyssinian slave Yakuth as Master of the Royal Horses.
- In 1240, Altunia, the governor of Bhatinda revolted against her. She went in personally to

suppress the revolt but Altunia killed Yakuth and took Raziya prisoner.

- Bahram Shah, son of Iltutmish killed her.

Balban (1266-1286 A.D.)

- Balban introduced rigorous court discipline and new customs such as prostration and kissing the Sultan's feet to prove his superiority over the nobles.
- He also introduced the Persian festival of *Nauroz* to impress the nobles and people with his wealth and power.
- He established a separate military department - *diwan-i-arz* – and reorganized the army.

KHILJI DYNASTY (1290-1320 A.D.)

- The founder of the Khilji dynasty was Jalaluddin Khilji.
- Ala-ud-din Khilji was the greatest ruler of the Khilji Dynasty.
- He was the first Muslim ruler to extend his empire right upto Rameshwaram in the South.
- The Sultan had built a new city called Siri near Delhi.
- Amir Khusrau the great Persian poet, patronised by Balban, continued to live in Ala-ud-din Khilji's court also.
- He introduced the system of *dagh* (branding of horses) and prepared *huliya* (descriptive list of soldiers).
- Ala-ud-din Khilji maintained a large permanent standing army and paid them in cash from the royal treasury.

TUGHLAQ DYNASTY

- Ghiyas-ud-din Tughlaq was the founder of the Tughlaq dynasty.
- To have the capital at the centre of the empire and safe from the Mongol raids, Tughlaq chose Devagiri as his new capital in A.D. 1327. The Sultan renamed the new capital Daulatabad.
- In 1329-30, Muhammad-bin-Tughlaq introduced a token currency.
- Firoz Shah Tughlaq became Sultan after the death of Muhammad-bin-Tughlaq in A.D. 1351.
- He was the first Sultan to impose irrigation tax.
- He had built new towns of Firozabad, Jaunpur, Hissar and Firozpur.
- Timur—Mongol leader of Central Asia, ordered general massacre in Delhi (AD 1398) at the time of Nasiruddin Mahmud (later Tughlaq king).

SAYYID DYNASTY

- Before his departure from India, Timur appointed Khizr Khan as governor of Multan. He captured Delhi and founded the Sayyid dynasty in 1414.
- Mubarak Shah, Mohammed Shah and Alam Shah were some of the other important noteworthy rulers of Sayyid Dynasty.

LODHI DYNASTY

- The Lodhis were Afghans.
- Bahlol Lodhi was the first Afghan ruler while his predecessors were all Turks. He died in 1489 and was succeeded by his son, Sikandar Lodhi.
- In 1504, Sikandar Lodhi founded the city of Agra and transferred his capital from Delhi to Agra.
- Babar marched against Delhi and defeated and killed Ibrahim Lodhi in the first battle of Panipat (1526).

BAHMANI AND VIJAYANAGAR KINGDOMS

- The break up of the Delhi Sultanate provided an opportunity for the rise of a number of kingdoms in the Deccan.
- After the decline of the Tughlaqs, there arose two important kingdoms in the Deccan. They were the Bahmani and Vijayanagar kingdoms.

VIJAYANAGAR EMPIRE

- The Vijayanagar Kingdom was set up in A.D. 1336. Its aim was to check the spread of Muslim power and protect Hindu Dharma in South India.
- Four dynasties – Sangama, Saluva, Tuluva and Aravidu – ruled Vijayanagar from A.D. 1336 to 1672.

- Vijayanagar was founded in 1336 by Harihara and Bukka of the Sangama dynasty.
- The Moroccan traveller, Ibn Batuta, Venetian traveller Nicolo de Conti, Persian traveller Abdur Razzak and the Portuguese traveller Domingo Paes were among them who left valuable accounts on the socio-economic conditions of the Vijayanagar Empire.
- The Hampi ruins and other monuments of Vijayanagar provide information on the cultural contributions of the Vijayanagar rulers.

KRISHNA DEVA RAYA (1509-1530)

- The Tuluva dynasty was founded by Vira Narasimha.
- The greatest of the Vijayanagar rulers, Krishna Deva Raya belonged to the Tuluva dynasty.
- Krishna Deva Raya himself authored a Telugu work, *Amukthamalyadha* and Sanskrit works, *Jambavati Kalyanam* and *Ushaparinayam*.
- He built the famous *Vittalaswamy* and *Hazara Ramaswamy* temples at Vijayanagar.
- Krishna Deva Raya renovated Virupaksha temple in A.D. 1510.
- After his death the enemies of Vijayanagar joined together and defeated the Vijayanagar ruler in the battle of Talaikota.

BAHMANI KINGDOM

- The founder of the Bahmani kingdom was Alauddin Bahman Shah also known as Hasan Gangu in 1347. Its capital was Gulbarga.
- Ahmad Wali Shah shifted the capital from Gulbarga to Bidar.
- *Gol Gumbaj* was built by *Muhammad Adil Shah*; it is famous for the so called '*Whispering Gallery*'.
- *Quli Qutub Shah* built the famous *Golcunda Fort*.

MUGHAL EMPIRE (1526-1707 AD)

BABAR (1526-1530 AD)

- Babar was the founder of the Mughal Empire in India.
- On 21st April, 1526 the first Battle of Panipat took place between Babar and Ibrahim Lodhi, who was killed in the battle.
- Babar was the first one to use guns or artillery in a battle on the Indian soil.
- Babar defeated Rana Sanga of Mewar in the battle of Kanwah in A.D. 1527.
- Babar was a soldier-scholar and wrote his own autobiography called Babar Nama in Turkish language.

HUMAYUN (1530-1556 AD)

- Sher Shah defeated Humayun at Chausa in A.D. 1539 and again at Kannauj in A.D. 1540.
- After losing his kingdom, Humayun became an exile for the next fifteen years.
- In 1555, Humayun defeated the Afghans and recovered the Mughal throne. After six months, he died in 1556 due to his fall from the staircase of his library.
- *Gulbadan Begum*, Humayun's half-sister wrote *Humayun-nama*.

SHER SHAH SURI

- The founder of the Sur dynasty was Sher Shah, whose original name was Farid.
- Sher Shah became the ruler of Delhi in 1540.
- Sher Shah organized a brilliant administrative system. The central government consisted of several departments.
- He built a new city on the banks of the river Yamuna near Delhi. Now the old fort called Purana Quila and its mosque is alone surviving.
- He built a Mausoleum at Sasaram, which is considered as one of the master pieces of Indian architecture.

AKBAR (1556-1605 AD)

- When Akbar ascended the throne in A.D. 1556 he was only 14 years old. His guardian Bairam Khan served him as a faithful minister and tutor.
- Bairam Khan, along with Akbar met Hemu in the second Battle of Panipat in 1556. Hemu was initially successful, but lost his consciousness after an arrow hit him. Akbar killed him.

- Battle of Haldighati, was fought between Rana Pratap of Mewar and Mughal army led by Man Singh. Some hisorian say that this battle was indecisive but some say that Rana Pratap was defeated.
- Akbar abolished the pilgrim tax and in 1562, he abolished Jaziya.
- Akbar evolved a new faith called Din-i-Illahi or Divine Faith.

JAHANGIR (1605-1627 AD)

- When Akbar died, Prince Salim succeeded with the title Jahangir (Conqueror of World) in 1605.
- Jahangir's eldest son, Khusrau, rebelled against him. He was arrested and put into prison. *Guru Arjun Dev, the fifth Sikh Guru* was executed by Jahangir.
- In 1611, Jahangir married Mehrunnisa who was known as Nurjahan (Light of World).
- Jahangir died in A.D. 1627.

SHAHJAHAN (1628-1658 AD)

- The reign of Shahjahan is generally considered as the *Golden Age* of the Mughal period.
- Shahjahan is called as the *Prince of Builders*. He had built the Jama Masjid and Red Fort in Delhi and Taj Mahal in Agra.
- Fine arts like painting, music and literature reached high level of development during Shahjahan's time.

AURANGAZEB (1658-1707 AD)

- Aurangazeb was the last great Mughal ruler. He ascended the throne after killing his three brothers Dara, Shuja and Murad in a fratricidal war.
- Aurangazeb defeated Sikandar Shah of Bijapur and annexed his kingdom.
- Aurangazeb was against the Sikhs and he executed the ninth Sikh Guru Tegh Bahadur.
- He was called *Darvesh* or a *Zinda Pir*. He forbade *Sati*. Conquered Bijapur (AD 1686) and Golconda (AD 1687) and reimposed Jaziya and Pilgrim tax in AD 1679.
- He built *Biwi ka Makbara* on the tomb of his queen *Rabaud-Durani* at Aurangabad; *Moti Masjid* within Red Fort, Delhi; and the Jami or Badshahi Mosque at Lahore.
- Aurangazeb died in A.D. 1707.

LATER MUGHALS / FALL OF THE MUGHALS

Bahadur Shah (1707-1712)

- Assumed the title of *Shah Alam I.*

Jahandar Shah (1712-1713)

- First puppet Mughal emperor. He abolished *jaziya.*

Farrukhsiyar (1713-1719)

Mohammad Shah (1719-1748)

- Nadir Shah (*of Iran*) defeated him in the Battle of Karnal (1739) and took away *Peacock throne* and *Kohinoor diamond.*

Ahmad Shah (1748-1754)

Alamgir II (1754-1759),

Shah Alam II (1759-1806)

Akbar II (1806-1837)

- He gave Ram Mohan Roy the title '*Raja*'. He sent Raja Ram Mohan Roy to London to seek a raise in his allowance.

Bahadur Shah II (1837-1857)

- He was confined by the British to the Red Fort. During the revolt of 1857, he was proclaimed the Emperor by the rebels. He was deported to Rangoon after that.

Literature of Mughal Period

Author	Work
Babar	Tuzuk-i-Babari
Abul Fazal	Ain-i-Akbari, Akbarnamah
Jahangir	Tuzuk-i-Jahangiri
Hamid	Padshahnama
Darashikoh	Majm-ul-Bahrain
Mirza Md Qasim	Alamgirnama

THE MARATHAS

SHIVAJI (1627-1680 AD)

- Shivaji was born at Shivner in 1627. His father was Shahji Bhonsle and mother Jija Bai.

- His religious teacher was Samarth Ramdas and guardian was Dadaji Kondadev.
- In 1674, Shivaji crowned himself at Raigarh and assumed the title Chatrapathi.
- *Ashtapradhan* (eight ministers) helped in administration. These were Peshwas, Sar-i-Naubat (Military), Mazumdar or Amatya (Accounts); Waqenavis (Intelligence); Surnavis (Correspondence); *Dabir* or *Sumanta* (Ceremonies); *Nyayadhish* (Justice); and *Panditrao* (Charity).
- Successors of Shivaji were Shambhaji, Rajaram and *Shahu* (fought at Battle of Khed in AD 1708).

THE PESHWAS

- Balaji Vishwanath was the first Peshwa. He began his career as a small revenue official and became Peshwa in 1713.
- Baji Rao I was the eldest son of Balaji Vishwanath. He was considered as the "greatest exponent of guerilla tactics after Shivaji".
- It was during reign of Balaji Baji Rao (Nanasaheb) when the Marathas lost the Third Battle of Panipat.
- Baji Rao II (last Peshwa) was the first Maratha to have fled from the British attacks instead of fighting with them. Baji Rao II surrendered to Sir John Malcom.

THE SIKH

- Guru Nanak Dev was the founder of Sikhism, the religion that draws its elements from both Hinduism and Islam.
- Name of the ten Sikh Gurus and their works are given below:
  1. **Guru Nanak Dev (1469-1539AD):** The founder of Sikhism.
  2. **Guru Angad Dev (1504-1552AD):** Developed Gurmukhi.
  3. **Guru Amar Das (1479-1574AD):** Struggled against Sati system and Purdah system.
  4. **Guru Ram Das (1534-1581AD):** Founded Amritsar, the holy city of Sikhism.
  5. **Guru Arjun Dev (1563-1606AD):** He built the *Swarn Mandir* (Golden Temple).
  6. **Guru Hargobind (1595-1644 AD):** Established Akal Takht.
  7. **Guru Har Rai (1630-1661 AD)**
  8. **Guru Har Krishan (1656-1664 AD)**
  9. **Guru Tegh Bahadur (1621-1675 AD)**
  10. **Guru Gobind Singh (1666-1708 AD):** Founded the Khalsa and Sikh baptism, composed many poems, and nominated the Sikh sacred text as the final and enduring Guru.

MODERN INDIA

THE ADVENT OF THE EUROPEANS

THE PORTUGUESE

- Vasco-da-Gama, a Portuguese explorer, sailed through the route of Cape of Good Hope and reached near Calicut on 20th May 1498 A.D. during the reign of King Zamorin (Hindu King of Calicut).
- Vasco-da-Gama founded a factory at Cannanore on his second visit to India in 1501. In due course, Calicut, Cochin and Cannanore became the Portuguese trading centres.
- Francisco Almeida came to India in 1505. He was the first Governor of Portuguese possessions in India.
- The real founder of Portuguese power in India was *Alfonso de Albuquerque*. He captured Goa from the rulers of Bijapur in 1510. It was made their headquarters.

THE DUTCH

- The United East India Company of the Netherlands founded a factory at Masulipatnam in 1605. They built their first fort on the main land of India at Pulicut in 1609, near Madras (Chennai). They captured Nagapattinam from the Portuguese.
- They made Agra, Surat, Masulipatnam and Chinsura in Bengal as their trading centres.

THE DANES

- The Danish East India Company was established in 1616 in Denmark.
- They came to South India and founded a factory at Tranquebar (Tharangambadi) in 1620. They also made settlements at Serampore near Calcutta (Kolkata).

THE ENGLISH

- The English East India Company was formed in 1599 under a charter granted by Queen Elizabeth in 1600.
- The East India Company sent Sir William Hawkins to the court of the Mughal Emperor Jahangir in 1609 to obtain permission to erect a factory at Surat.
- In 1615, Sir Thomas Roe, another British merchant, came to Jahangir's court. He stayed for three years and succeeded in getting permission to set up their trading centres at Agra, Surat, Ahmedabad and Broach.
- In 1690, the British got permission from Aurangazeb to build a factory on the site of Calcutta. In 1696 a fort was built at that place. It was called Fort William.

THE FRENCH

- The French East India Company was established in 1664 under the inspiring and energetic leadership of Colbert, the economic adviser of the French King Louis XIV.
- In 1667, the first French factory was established at Surat by Francis Caron who was nominated as Director-General.
- French were defeated by English in the *Battle of Wandiwash* (1760).

EAST INDIA COMPANY

- After the Battle of Plassey in 1757 and the Battle of Buxar in 1764, the East India Company became a political power.
- India was under the East India Company's rule till 1858 when it came under the direct administration of the British Crown.
- Robert Clive was the first Governor of Fort William under the Company's rule.

GOVERNOR-GENERALS OF BENGAL

Warren Hastings (1772-85 AD)

- In 1772, the Company appointed Warren Hastings as the Governor of Fort William.
- The Dual System introduced by Robert Clive was abolished by Warren Hastings.
- Warren Hastings was known for his expansionist policy. His administration witnessed the Rohilla War, the First Anglo-Maratha War and the Second Anglo-Mysore War.
- Pitt's India Act (1784) was passed.

Lord Cornwallis (1786-93 AD)

- Cornwallis inaugurated the policy of making appointments mainly on the basis of merit thereby laying the foundation of the Indian Civil Service.
- Lord Cornwallis introduced Permanent Revenue Settlement.
- Tipu Sultan signed the Treaty of Srirangapatnam in 1792 with the British.

Sir John Shore (1793-98 AD)

- Played an important role in the introduction of Permanent Settlement.
- *Battle of Kharda* between the Nizams and the Marathas (1795).

Wellesley (1798-1805)

- Wellesley came to India with a determination to launch a forward policy that he adopted to achieve his object is known as the 'Subsidiary Alliance'.
- The Fourth Anglo-Mysore War started in 1799. The war was short and decisive. Tipu fought till his capital Srirangapatnam was captured and he himself was shot dead.
- Peshwa Baji Rao II signed the *Treaty* of *Bassein* with the British in 1802. It was a subsidiary treaty and the Peshwa was recognized as the head of the Maratha kingdom.
- The Treaty of Deogaon(1803) was signed between Bhonsle and Wellesley.

Lord Minto (1807-1813)

- Lord Minto concluded the Treaty of Amritsar with Ranjit Singh of Punjab in 1809.
- The Charter Act of 1813 was passed during this period.

Lord Hastings (1813-1823)

- Anglo Nepal War (1814-1816) and Treaty of Sugauli (1816).
- Third Maratha War (1817-18), dissolution of Maratha confederacy and creation of Bombay Presidency.
- He encouraged the freedom of the Press and abolished the censorship introduced in 1799.

GOVERNOR-GENERALS OF INDIA

Lord William Bentinck (1828-1835)

- Charter Act of 1833 was passed and he was made the first Governor-General of India. Before him, the designation was Governor-General of Bengal.
- The social reforms of William Bentinck made his name immortal in the history of British India. These include the abolition of *Sati*, the suppression of Thugs and the prevention of female infanticide.
- The Government Resolution in 1835 made English the official and literary language of India.

Lord Metcalfe (1835-36 AD)

- Known as liberator of press in India.

Lord Auckland (1836-42 AD)

- First Afghan War (1838-42), a disaster for the English.

Lord Ellenborough (1842-44 AD)

- Brought an end to Afghan war. War with Gwalior (1843), *Annexation of Sind* by Charles Napier (1843).

Lord Hardinge (1844-48 AD)

- First Anglo-Sikh War (1845-46) and Treaty of Lahore (1846). Gave preference to English educated persons in employment.

Lord Dalhousie (1848-1856)

- The Doctrine of Lapse was applied by Dalhousie.
- The first railway line connecting Bombay with Thane was opened in 1853.

VICEROYS OF INDIA

Lord Canning (1856-62 AD)

- Lord Canning became the first Viceroy of India in 1858.
- Revolt of 1857, Mutiny took place. Indian Penal Code 1860 was passed.

Lord Elgin (1862 AD)

- Wahabi Movement.

Lord John Lawrence (1864-69 AD)

- Established the *High Courts* at Calcutta, Bombay and Madras in 1865.
- Telegraphic communication was opened with Europe. Created the Indian Forest Department.

Lord Northbrooke (1872-76 AD)

- Kuka Rebellion in Punjab, Famine in Bihar.

Lord Lytton (1876-80)

- In 1878, the Vernacular Press Act was passed. This Act empowered a Magistrate to secure an undertaking from the editor, publisher and printer of a vernacular newspaper that nothing would be published against the English Government. This Act crushed the freedom of the Indian press.
- In 1878, the Arms Act was passed. This Act prevented the Indians to keep arms without appropriate license.
- Lord Lytton also held a Darbar at Delhi in 1877 in which Queen Victoria was declared as the Empress of India. This extravagant Darbar cost millions of ruppes.
- In 1878, the Statutory Civil Service was established exclusively for Indians.

Lord Ripon (1880-84 AD)

- Lord Ripon repealed the Vernacular Press Act and earned much popularity among Indians.

- Ripon appointed a Commission in 1882 under the chairmanship of Sir William Hunter.
- The Commission came to be known as the Hunter Commission. The Commission recommended for the expansion and improvement of the elementary education of the masses.
- Ripon was founder of local self-government in modern India.

Lord Dufferin (1884-88 AD)

- *Third Burmese War* (1885-86 AD). Establishment of the Indian National Congress in 1885.

Lord Lansdowne (1888-94 AD)

- Factory Act of 1891 granted weekly holiday and stipulated working hours for women and children.

Lord Elgin II (1894-99 AD)

- Southern uprisings of 1899. Great famine of 1896-1897 and Lyall Commission on famine was established.

Lord Curzon (1899-1905 AD)

- Curzon instituted in 1902, a Universities Commission to go into the entire question of university education in the country.
- On the basis of the findings and recommendations of the Commission, Curzon brought in the Indian Universities Act of 1904, which brought all the universities in India under the control of the government.

Lord Minto (1905-10 AD)

- Swadeshi Movement (1905-08); foundation of Muslim League (1906); Surat Session and split in the Congress (1907). Morley-Minto Reforms (1909).

Lord Hardinge (1910-16 AD)

- Capital shifted from Calcutta to Delhi (1911); Delhi Durbar; Partition of Bengal was cancelled. The Hindu Mahasabha was founded in 1915 by Pandit Madan Mohan Malaviya.

Lord Chelmsford (1916-21 AD)

- Gandhi returned to India (1915) and founded the Sabarmati Ashram (1916), Champaran Satyagraha, Satyagraha at Ahmedabad (1981), Kheda Satyagraha (1918).
- Rowlatt Act (March, 1919) and the Jallianwala Bagh Massacre (13th April, 1919).
- Khilafat Committee was formed and Khilafat Movement started (1919-20).
- Non-Cooperation Movement started (1920-22).

Lord Reading (1921-26)

- Moplah Rebellion (1921) took place. *Kakori Train* Robbery on 1st August, 1925. *Communal Riots* of 1923-25 in Multan, Amritsar, Delhi etc.

Lord Irwin (1926-31 AD)

- Lahore Session of Congress and *Poorna Swaraj* Declaration (1929).
- Simon Commission visited India in 1927.
- Dandi March (12th March, 1930). Civil Disobedience Movement (1930).
- First Round Table Conference was held in England in 1930. Gandhi-Irwin Pact.

Lord Willingdon (1931-36 AD)

- *Second Round Table Conference* in London in 1931 and *third* in 1932.

Lord Linlithgow (1936-43 AD)

- Congress Ministries resignation celebrated as '*Deliverance Day*' by the Muslim League (1939), the Lahore Resolution (23rd March, 1940) of the Muslim League demanding separate state for the Muslims. (It was at this session that Jinnah propounded his Two-Nation Theory). Outbreak of World War II in 1939. Cripps Mission in 1942. Quit India Movement (8th August, 1942).

Lord Wavell (1943-47 AD)

- Cabinet Mission Plan (16th May, 1946).
- First meeting of the Constituent Assembly was held on 9th December, 1946.
- Arranged the Shimla Conference on 25th June, 1945 with Indian National Congress and Muslim League but failed.

Lord Mountbatten (March to Aug, 1947)

- Last viceroy of British India and the first Governor-General of free India.
- Partition of India decided by the 3rd June Plan or Mountbatten Plan.

NATIONAL MOVEMENT (1885-1947)

INDIAN NATIONAL CONGRESS (1885)

- Allan Octavian Hume, a retired civil servant in the British Government took the initiative to form an all-India organization. Thus, the Indian National Congress was founded and its first session was held at Bombay in 1885. W.C. Banerjee was its first president. It was attended by 72 delegates from all over India.
- The second session was held in Calcutta in 1886 and the third in Madras in 1887.
- Between 1885 and 1905, the Congress leaders were moderates. The Moderates had faith in the British justice and goodwill. They were called moderates because they adopted peaceful and constitutional means to achieve their demands.
- In 1905, Gopal Krishna Gokhale founded the Servants of India Society to train Indians to dedicate their lives to the cause of the country.

Partition of Bengal (1905)

- By Lord Curzon on 16th October, 1905 through a royal proclamation, reducing the old province of Bengal in size by creating East Bengal and Assam out of the rest of Bengal.
- The partition of Bengal in 1905 provided a spark for the rise of extremism in the Indian National Movement.
- Curzon's real motives behind this partition were:
  - ❐ To break the growing strength of Bengali nationalism since Bengal was the base of Indian nationalism.
  - ❐ To divide the Hindus and Muslims in Bengal.
  - ❐ To show the enormous power of the British Government in doing whatever it liked.

Swadeshi Movement (1905)

- The Swadeshi Movement involved programmes like the boycott of government service, courts, schools and colleges and of foreign goods. It was both a political and economic movement.
- Lal, Bal, Pal and Aurobindo Ghosh played an important role.

Muslim League (1906)

- In December 1906, Muslim delegates from all over India met at Dacca for the Muslim Educational Conference.
- Taking advantage of this occasion, Nawab Salimullah of Dacca proposed the setting up of an organisation to look after the Muslim interests. The proposal was accepted.
- The All-India Muslim League was finally set up on December 30, 1906.

Minto Morley Reforms (1909)

- Minto, the Viceroy and Morley, the Secretary of State for India jointly proposed reforms to the Indian Councils. An Act, called the Indian Councils Act or the Minto-Morley Reforms Act was passed in 1909.
- A separate communal electorate was introduced for the Muslims.

The Lucknow Pact (1916)

- During the 1916 Congress session at Lucknow two major events occurred. The divided Congress became united. An understanding for joint action against the British was reached between the Congress and the Muslim League and it was called the Lucknow Pact.
- The signing of the Lucknow Pact by the Congress and the Muslim League in 1916 marked an important step in the Hindu-Muslim unity.

The Home Rule Movement (1916)

- Two Home Rule Leagues were established, one by B.G. Tilak at Poona in April 1916 and the other by Mrs. Annie Besant at Madras in September 1916.
- While Tilak's Movement concentrated on

Maharashtra, Annie Besant's Movement covered the rest of the country.

August Declaration

- On 20 August, 1917, Montague, the Secretary of State in England, promised the gradual development of self-governing institutions in India.
- This August Declaration led to the end of the Home Rule Movement.

Rowlatt Act (1919)

- In 1917, a committee was set up under the presidentship of Sir Sydney Rowlatt to look into the militant Nationalist activities. On the basis of its report the Rowlatt Act was passed in March 1919 by the Central Legislative Council. As per this Act, any person could be arrested on the basis of suspicion. No appeal or petition could be filed against such arrests.
- This Act was called the Black Act and it was widely opposed. An all-India hartal was organized on 6 April, 1919.

Jallianwala Bagh Massacre (13 April, 1919)

- On 13th April, the Baisakhi day (harvest festival), a public meeting was organized at the Jallianwala Bagh (garden). Gen. Dyer marched in and without any warning opened fire on the crowd. The firing continued for about 10 to 15 minutes and it stopped only after the ammunition exhausted.
- According to official report 379 people were killed and 1137 wounded in the incident. There was a nationwide protest against this massacre and Rabindranath Tagore renounced his knighthood as a protest.

Khilafat Movement (1920)

- The chief cause of the Khilafat Movement was the defeat of Turkey in the First World War.
- The Muslims in India were upset over the British attitude against Turkey and launched the Khilafat Movement.
- Ali brothers, *Mohd Ali* and *Shaukat Ali* started this movement. It was jointly led by the Khilafat leaders and the Congress.

Non-Co-operation Movement (1920-22)

- Mahatma Gandhi announced his plan to begin Non-Cooperation with the government as a sequel to the Rowlatt Act, Jallianwala Bagh massacre and the Khilafat Movement. It was approved by the Indian National Congress at the Nagpur session in December, 1920.
- The Congress observed the Non-Co-operation movement in 1920. The main aim of this movement was to attain Swaraj through non-violent and peaceful means.
- The whole movement was abruptly called off on 11th February, 1922 by Gandhi following the Chauri-Chaura incident in the Gorakhpur district of U.P. Many top leaders of the country were stunned at this sudden suspension of the Non-Co-operation Movement.
- On 5th February an angry mob set fire to the police station at *Chauri-Chaura* and twenty two police men were burnt to death.

Swaraj Party

- Leaders like Motilal Nehru and Chittranjan Das formed a separate group within the Congress known as the Swaraj Party on 1 January, 1923.
- The Swarajists wanted to contest the council elections and wreck the government from within.

Simon Commission (1927)

- The Act of 1919 included a provision for its review after a lapse of ten years. However, the review commission under the chairmanship of Sir John Simon was appointed by the British Government two years earlier of its schedule in 1927.
- Indian leaders opposed the commission, as there were no Indians in it, they cried *Simon Go Back*.
- The government used brutal repression and at Lahore, *Lala Lajpat Rai* was severely beaten in lathi-charge.

Nehru Report (1928)

- The Secretary of State, Lord Birkenhead, challenged the Indians to produce a Constitution that would be acceptable to all. The challenge

was accepted by the Congress, which convened an all party meeting on 28 February, 1928.

- A committee consisting of eight was constituted to draw up a blueprint for the future Constitution of India. It was headed by Motilal Nehru. The Report published by this Committee came to be known as the Nehru Report.

Lahore Session (1929)

- On Dec. 19, 1929, under the Presidentship of J.L. Nehru, the INC, as its Lahore session, declared Poorna Swaraj (Complete Independence) as its ultimate goal.
- On Dec. 31, 1929, the newly adopted tricolour flag was unfurled and Jan. 26, 1930 was fixed as the First Independence Day, which was to be celebrated every year.

Dandi March (1930)

- On 12th March, 1930, Gandhi began his famous March to Dandi with his chosen 79 followers to break the salt laws. He reached the coast of Dandi on 5 April, 1930 after marching a distance of 200 miles and on 6 April formally launched the Civil Disobedience Movement by breaking the salt laws.

Civil Disobedience Movement

- Countrywide mass participation by women.
- The Garhwal soldiers refused to fire on the people at Peshawar.

Round Table Conference

- The first Round Table Conference was held in November 1930 at London and it was boycotted by the Congress.
- On 8th March, 1931 the Gandhi-Irwin Pact was signed. As per this pact, Mahatma Gandhi agreed to suspend the Civil-Disobedience Movement and participate in the Second-Round Table Conference.
- In September 1931, the Second Round Table Conference was held at London. Mahatma Gandhi participated in the Conference but returned to India disappointed.
- In January 1932, the Civil-Disobedience Movement was resumed.

Poona Pact (1932)

- The idea of separate electorate for the depressed classes was abandoned, but seats reserved for them in the provincial legislature were increased.
- Thus, Poona Pact agreed upon a joint electorate for upper and lower castes.

Demand for Pakistan

- *Chaudhary Rehmat Ali* gave the term *Pakistan* in 1933.
- In March 1940, the Muslim League demanded the creation of Pakistan.

Cripps Mission (1942)

- The British Government in its effort to secure Indian co-operation in the Second World War sent Sir Stafford Cripps to India on 23 March, 1942. This is known as Cripps Mission.
- The main recommendations of Cripps was the promise of Dominion Status to India.
- Congress rejected it. Gandhi called Cripp's proposals as a "Post-dated Cheque".

Quit India Movement (1942-1944)

- The All India Congress Committee met at Bombay on 8th August, 1942 and passed the famous Quit India Resolution. On the same day, Gandhi gave his call of 'do or die'.
- On 8th and 9th August, 1942, the government arrested all the prominent leaders of the Congress. Mahatma Gandhi was kept in prison at Poona. Pandit Jawaharlal Nehru, Abul Kalam Azad, and other leaders were imprisoned in the Ahamednagar Fort.
- Quit India Movement was the final attempt for country's freedom.

Indian National Army (INA)

- On July 2, 1943, Subhash Chandra Bose reached Singapore and gave the rousing war cry of *'Dilli Chalo'*. He was made the President of Indian Independence League and soon became the

supreme commander of the Indian National Army. He gave the country the slogan of *Jai Hind.*

- INA had three fighting brigades named after Gandhi, Azad and Nehru. Rani of Jhansi Brigade was an exclusive women force. INA headquarters were at Rangoon and Singapore.

Cabinet Mission (1946)

- The Cabinet Mission put forward a plan for solution of the constitutional problem. A proposal was envisaged for setting up an Interim Government, which would remain in office till a new government was elected on the basis of the new Constitution framed by the Constituent Assembly.
- Elections were held in July 1946 for the formation of a Constituent Assembly.
- Muslim league observed the *Direct Action Day* on 16 August, 1946.
- An Interim Government was formed under the leadership of Jawaharlal Nehru on 2 September, 1946.

Mountbatten Plan (1947)

- On 20 February 1947, Prime Minister Atlee announced in the House of Commons the definite intention of the British Government to transfer power to responsible Indian hands by a date not later than June 1948.
- Lord Mountbatten armed with vast powers became India's Viceroy on 24 March, 1947. The partition of India and the creation of Pakistan appeared inevitable to him.
- After extensive consultation Lord Mountbatten put forth the plan of partition of India on 3 June, 1947. The Congress and the Muslim League ultimately approved the Mountbatten Plan.

Indian Independence Act, 1947

- The salient features of this Act was the partition of the country into India and Pakistan would come into effect from 15 August, 1947.
- On 15th August, 1947 India, and on the 14th August Pakistan came into existence as two independent states.
- Lord Mountbatten was made the first Governor General of Independent India, whereas Mohammad Ali Jinnah became the first Governor General of Pakistan.
- C. Rajagopalachari became the first and last Indian Governor-General of India. When India became a Republic on 26 January, 1950 Dr. Rajendra Prasad became the first President of our country.

Socio-Religious Movements and Organisation

Name of the Organisation	*Founder*	*Year*	*Place*
Atmiya Sabha	Ram Mohan Roy	1815	Calcutta
Brahmo Samaj	Ram Mohan Roy	1828	Calcutta
Dharma Sabha	Radhakanta Dev	1829	Calcutta
Tattvabodhini Sabha	Debendranath Tagore	1839	Calcutta
Nirankaris	Dayal Das, Darbara Singh, Rattan Chand etc.	1840	Punjab
Manav Dharma Sabha	Durgaram Manchharam	1844	Surat
Paramhansa Mandli	Dadoba Pandurung	1849	Bombay
Namdharis	Ram Singh	1857	Punjab
Radha Swami Satsang	Tulsi Ram	1861	Agra
Brahmo Samaj of India	Keshab Chandra Sen	1866	Calcutta
Dar-ul-Ulum	Maulana Hussain Ahmed	1866	Deoband
Prarthna Samaj	Atmaram Pandurung	1867	Bombay
Arya Samaj	Swami Dayanand Saraswati	1875	Bombay
Theosophical Society	Madam H.P. Blavatsky and Col. H.S. Olcott	1875	New York (USA)
Sadharan Brahmo Samaj	Anand Mohan Bose	1878	Calcutta

Deccan Education Society	G.G. Agarkar	1884	Pune (Poona)
Muhammadan Educational Conference	Syed Ahmad Khan	1886	Aligarh
Indian National Conference	M.G. Ranade	1887	Bombay
Deva Samaj	Shivnarayan Agnihotri	1887	Lahore
Nadwah-ul-Ulama	Maulana Shibli Numani	1894	Lucknow
Ramakrishna Mission	Swami Vivekananda	1897	Belur
Servents of Indian Society	Gopal Krishna Gokhale	1905	Bombay
Poona Seva Sadan	Mrs. Ramabai Ranade and G.K. Devadhar	1909	Pune (Poona)
Social Service League	N.M. Joshi	1911	Bombay
Seva Samiti	H.N. Kunzru	1914	Allahabad

Newspapers and Journals

- *Bengal Gazette* (1780) (India's first newspaper)—James Augustus Hikky
- *Kesari*—B.G. Tilak
- *Maratha*—B.G. Tilak
- *Sudharak*—G.K. Gokhale
- *Amrit Bazar Patrika*—Shishir Kumar Ghosh and Motilal Ghosh
- *Yugantar*—Bhupendranath Datta and Birender Kumar Ghosh
- *Bombay Chronicle*—Firoze Shah Mehta
- *New India (Daily)*—Annie Besant

Books and Authors

- *Causes of the Indian Mutiny*—Sir Syed Ahmed Khan
- *Ghulam Giri*—Jyotiba Phule
- *Anandmath*—Bankim Chand Chatterjee
- *Satyarth Prakash*—Swami Dayanand
- *Unhappy India*—Lala Lajpat Rai
- *India Divided*—Dr. Rajendra Prasad
- *The Discovery of India*—J.L. Nehru
- *Neel Darpan*—Dinbandhu Mitra
- *Hind Swaraj*—M.K. Gandhi
- *What Congress and Gandhi have done to the untouchables*—Dr. B.R. Ambedkar

Important Sayings

- *'Back to Vedas'*—Dayanand Saraswati
- *'Dilli Chalo!'*—Subhash Chandra Bose's battle cry of *Azad Hind Fauj*
- *'Do or Die'*—Mahatma Gandhi (while launching Quit India movement in 1942)
- *'Give me blood and I will give you freedom'*—Subhash Chandra Bose (in his address to soldiers of *Azad Hind Fauj)*
- *'My ultimate aim is to wipe every tear from every eye'*—Jawaharlal Nehru
- *'Swaraj is my birthright and I will have it'*—Bal Gangadhar Tilak
- *'Inqualab Zindabad'*—Bhagat Singh
- *'Jai Jawan, Jai Kisan'*—Lal Bahadur Shastri
- *'Sarfaroshi ki tamanna Ab Hamare Dil mein Hai'*—Ram Prasad Bismill
- *'Saare Jahan Se Achcha,* Hindustan Hamara'—Dr. Mohammed Iqbal
- *'Hindi, Hindu, Hindustan'*—Bhartendu Harishchandra
- *'Vande Mataram'*—Bankim Chandra Chatterjee

❒❒❒

GEOGRAPHY

WORLD GEOGRAPHY

THE UNIVERSE

- Existing matter and energy are together known as **Universe.**

GALAXY

- A galaxy is a huge system of billions of stars and clouds of dust and gases.
- Our solar system is a part of *Milky Way* galaxy.
- There are millions of galaxies that make the Universe.

STARS

- Stars account for 98 per cent of the matter in a galaxy. The stars nearest to the earth are *Proxima Centauri, Alpha Centauri, Barnard's Star, Sirius* and so on. Of these, *Sirius* is the brightest.

LIGHT YEAR

- Light year is the distance travelled by light in one year at a speed of 2,99,792.5 km. per second.

SOLAR SYSTEM

- The Sun, eight planets, satellites and some other celestial bodies known as asteroids and meteoroids form the solar system.

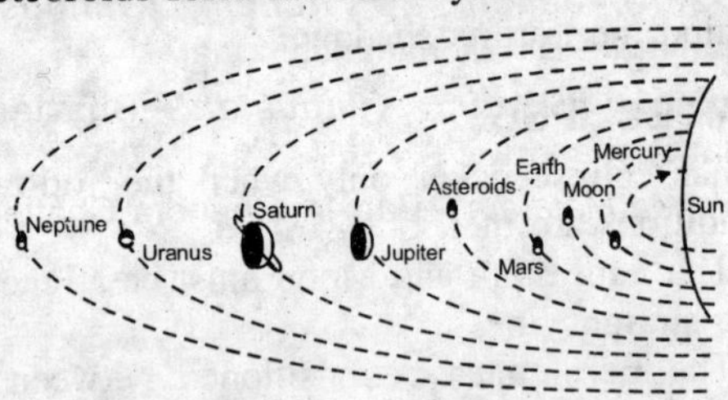

SUN

- The Sun is in the centre of the solar system.
- The Sun is a mixture of gases. It consists of 92% hydrogen, 7.8% helium and 0.2% other gases.
- The Sun is about 150 million km away from the earth.
- The sun is an ultimate source of energy for life on Earth.
- Sunlight takes 8 min 16.6 sec to reach earth.

Facts about Sun

Diameter	—1.392×10^6 km
Volume	—1.304 × 106 times the volume of earth
Temperature	—6000°C at surface and 15 million degree C at the centre
Relative density	—1.4
Gravitational Pull	—28 times the gravitational pull of the earth

Facts about Planets

Closest to Sun	*Mercury*
Farthest from Sun	*Neptune*
Heaviest	*Jupiter*
Hottest	*Venus*
Inner	*Mercury, Venus, Earth, Mars*
Largest	*Jupiter*
Smallest	*Mercury*
Moons, None	*Mercury, Venus*
Moon; Largest	*Ganymede (Jupiter), larger than Mercury*
Nearest to Earth	*Venus*
Orbits; Order	*Mercury (closest to Sun), Venus, Earth, Mars, Jupiter, Saturn, Uranus, Neptune.*
Rings/largest number	*Saturn*
Spin; Backwards	*Venus (East to West)*

COMETS

- It has a head and a tail. Its tail originates only when it gets closer to the sun. The tail can be 20-30 million km long. It always point away from the sun because of the force exerted by solar wind and radiation on the cometory material.

THE EARTH

- The earth is the third nearest planet to the Sun.
- From the outer space, the earth appears blue because its two-thirds surface is covered by water. It is, therefore, called a blue planet.
- It is the densest of all planets.
- Rotation is the movement of the earth on its axis. Due to this rotation, day and night occur.
- The earth takes about 23 hours 56 minutes and 4 seconds to complete one rotation around its axis.
- Earth takes 365¼ days (one year) to revolve around the sun.

THE EARTH: FACTS AND FIGURES

- *Mass of Earth*—5.972 × 10^{21} tonnes
- *Density of Earth*—5.517 times that of water
- *Volume of Earth*—1.083 × 10^{11} cubic km
- *Equatorial circumference*—4.007 × 104 km
- *Polar Diameter*—12,714 km
- *Equatorial Diameter*—12756 km
- *Polar or Meridional circumference*—4.0 × 10^4 km
- *Estimated Age*—At least 4600 million years
- *Land Surface*—148,951,000 sq km
- *Water Surface*—361,150,000 sq km (71 per cent of total area)
- *Highest Point of the land surface*—Mt. Everest (8,848 metres)
- *Lowest point of the land surface*—Shores of the Dead Sea (396 metres below the sea level)
- *Greatest Ocean depth*—Mariana Trench, East of Philippines (11,033 metres below the sea level)

THE MOON

- Earth has only one satellite, that is, the moon.
- Its diameter is only one-quarter that of the earth. It is about 3,84,400 km away from us.
- The moon moves around the earth in about 27 days. It takes exactly the same time to complete one spin. As a result, only one side of the moon (only 59% of its surface) is visible to us on the earth.
- Moonlight takes 1.3 sec. to reach earth.

LATITUDE

- Imaginary lines drawn parallel to the equator. Measured as an angle whose apex is at the centre of the earth.
- The equator represents 0° latitude, while the North Pole is 90°N and the South Pole 90°S.
- 23½°N represents Tropic of Cancer while 23½°S represents Tropic of Capricorn.

LONGITUDE

- It is the angular distance measured from the centre of the earth. On the globe the lines of longitude are drawn as a series of semicircles that extend from the North Pole to the South Pole through the equator. They are also called meridians.
- The distance between any two meridians is not equal. At the equator, 1 degree = 111 km. At 30°N or S, it is 96.5 km. It goes on decreasing this way until it is zero at the poles.

INTERNATIONAL DATE LINE

- It is the 180° meridian running over the Pacific Ocean, deviating at Aleutian Islands, Fiji, Samoa and Gilbert Islands.
- Travellers crossing the Date Line from west to east repeat a day and travellers crossing it from east to west lose a day.

INDIAN STANDARD TIME (IST)

- Indian Standard Time is calculated on the basis of 82.5°E longitude which passes through Uttar Pradesh, Madhya Pradesh, Odisha, Chattisgarh and Andhra Pradesh.

ECLIPSES

- Sun is the only source of light for both the Earth and Moon. Eclipses occur when the light thus received is either blocked by the earth or by the Moon.
- Eclipses occur when either the Earth moves behind the Moon's shadow or the Moon moves behind the Earth's shadow.

LUNAR ECLIPSE

- Lunar eclipse occur only when the following conditions are met.
  1. The Sun, Earth and Moon must be aligned in a straight line.
  2. The Earth must be positioned between the Sun and the Moon.
  3. The Moon must be in its full phase (Full Moon).

SOLAR ECLIPSE

- Solar eclipses occur only when the following conditions are met.
  1. The Sun, Earth and Moon must be aligned in a straight line.

2. The Moon must be positioned between the Sun and the Earth.
3. Must be a New Moon day.

ROCKS

- Rocks are composed of many minerals such as silica, aluminium, iron and magnesium. The nature of the rock is determined by the presence of its minerals.
- Rocks can be classified into three types:
  1. ***Igneous rocks*** are formed by magma that reaches the earth's surface along deep cracks and at volcanic vents. e.g., Mica, Granite etc.
  2. ***Sedimentary rocks*** are formed by the accumulation and cementation of mud, silt, or sand derived from weathered igneous rock fragments. e.g., Gravel, Peat, Gypsum etc.
  3. ***Metamorphic rocks*** are igneous or sedimentary rocks that have been altered by heat and/or pressure, either because they have been buried and folded deep in the crust, or because they have come into contact with molten igneous rock, e.g., Gneiss, Marble, Quartzite etc.

VOLCANOES

Sudden eruption of hot magma (molten rock), gases, ash and other material from inside the Earth to its surface.

- ***Active*** which erupts frequently, e.g., Mauna Loa (Hawaii), Etna (Sicily), Vesuvius (Italy), Stromboli (Mediterranean Sea).
- ***Dormant*** Not erupted for quite sometime, e.g., Fujiyama (Japan), Krakatoa (Indonesia), Barren Island (Andamans).
- ***Extinct*** Not erupted for several centuries, e.g., Arthur's Seat, Edinburgh, Scotland.

EARTHQUAKES

- Earthquakes are a form of wave energy that is transferred through bedrock. It is transmitted from the point of the earthquake focus, as spherical seismic waves. They travel in all directions outward.
- The intensity of earthquake waves is recorded by *Seismograph.*

LANDFORMS

- There are three major landforms: mountains, plateaus and plains.

MOUNTAINS

- A mountain can be defined as an area of land that rises abruptly from the surrounding region.
- There are three types of mountains- *Fold Mountains, Block Mountains* and the ***Volcanic Mountains***.
- Himalayas, Alps, Andes, Rockies, Atlas, etc are examples of Fold Mountains.
- The Aravali range in India is one of the oldest **fold mountain** systems in the world.
- The Rhine valley and the Vosges mountain in Europe are examples of such mountain systems.
- Volcanic mountains are formed due to volcanic activity.
- Mt. Kilimanjaro in Africa and Mt. Fujiyama in Japan are examples of such mountains.

Major Mountain Ranges of the World

Range	Location	Highest Peak (m)	Length (km)
Andes	South America	6,960	7,200
Himalayas-Karakoram-Hindukush	South Central Asia	8,848	4,800
Rockies	North America	4,401	4,800
Great Dividing Range	East Australia	2,228	3,600
Western Ghat	Western India	2,637	1,610
Caucasus	Europe	5,642	1,200
Alaska	USA	6,194	1,130
Alps	Europe	4,808	1,050
Apennines	Europe	2,912	—
Ural	Asia	1,895	—
Atlas	North West Africa	—	1,930

PLATEAUS

- A plateau is an elevated flat land. It is a flat-topped table land standing above the surrounding area.

Principal Mountain Peaks of the World

Mountains	Height in Metres
1. Mount Everest	8,848
2. K-2 (Godwin Austen)	8,611
3. Kanchenjunga	8,597
4. Lhotse	8,511
5. Makalu I	8,481
6. Dhaulagiri I	8,167
7. Mansalu I	8,156
8. Chollyo	8,153
9. Nanga Parbat	8,124
10. Annapurna I	8,091
11. Gasherbrum I	8,068
12. Broad Peak I	8,047
13. Gasherbrum II	8,034
14. Shisha Pangma (Gosainthan)	8,014
15. Gasherbrum III	7,952

PLAINS

- A relatively low-lying and flat land surface with least difference between its highest and lowest points is called a Plain.

OCEANS

- Oceans of the world is classified into four groups: the Pacific, the Atlantic, the Arctic and the Indian.
- The Pacific is the largest ocean, being twice the size of the Atlantic. It covers about a third of the Earth's surface, and contains more than half the water on the planet.

Oceans of the World

Names	Area (Sq. Km.)	Greatest Depth
Pacific	166,240000	Mariana Trench
Atlantic	86,560000	Puerto Rico Trench
Indian	73430000	Java Trench
Arctic	13230000	—

Major Rivers of the World

River	Origin	Falls in	Length (Km.)
Nile	Victoria lake	Mediterranean Sea	6,650
Amazon	Andes (Peru)	Atlantic Ocean	6,428
Yangtze	Tibetan Kiang Plateau	China Sea	6,300
Mississippi Missouri	Itaska lake (USA)	Gulf of Mexico (USA)	6,275
Yenisei	Tannu-Ola Mts.	Arctic Ocean	5,539
Hoang Ho	Kunlun Mts.	Gulf of Chibli	5,464
Ob	Altai Mts., Russia	Gulf of Ob	5,410
Congo	Lualaba & Luapula rivers	Atlantic Ocean	4,700
Amur	Northeast China	Sea of Okhotsk	4,444
Lena	Baikal Mts	Laptev Sea	4,400
Mekong	Tibetan Highlands	South China Sea	4,350
Mackenzie	Great Slave Lake	Beaufort Sea	4,241
Niger	Guinea	Gulf of Guinea	4,200

Major Gulfs of the World

Names	Area (Sq. Km.)	Names	Areas (Sq. Km.)
Gulf of Mexico	15,44,000	Gulf of St. Lawrence	2,37,000
Gulf of Hudson	12,33,000	Gulf of California	1,62,000
Arabian Gulf	2,38,000	English Channel	89,900

Important Straits of the World

Straits	Water Bodies joined	Area
Bab-al-Mandeb	Red Sea & Arabian Sea	Arabia & Africa
Bering	Arctic Ocean & Bering Sea	Alaska & Asia
Bosphorus	Black Sea & Marmara Sea	Turkey
Dover	North Sea & Atlantic Ocean	England & Europe
Florida	Gulf of Mexico & Atlantic Ocean	Florida & Bahamas Islands
Gibralter	Mediterranean Sea & Atlantic Ocean	Spain & Africa
Malacca	Java Sea & Bay of Bengal	India & Indonesia
Palk	Bay of Bengal & Indian Ocean	India & Sri Lanka
Magellan	South Pacific & South Atlantic Ocean	Chile
Sunda	Java Sea & Indian Ocean	Indonesia

Important Lakes of the World

Lake	Location	Area (Sq. Km.)
Caspian	Russia and CIS	371000
Superior	Canada and USA	82414
Victoria	Tanzania (Africa)	69485
Huron	Canada and USA	59596
Michigan	USA	58016
Tanganyika	Africa	32892
Baikal	Russia (CIS)	31502
Great Bear	Canada	31080
Malawi	Malawi (Tanzania)	30044
Great Slave	Canada	28438

Highest Waterfalls of the World

Name(s) (Foreign)	Location
Angel (Salto Angel)	Canaima Nat'l Park, Venezuela
Tugela	Natal Nat'l Park, South Africa
Utigord (Utigordsfoss)	Norway
Monge (Mongefoss)	Marstein, Norway
Gocta Cataracts	Chachapoyas, Peru
Mutarazi (Mtarazi)	Nyanga Nat'l Park, Zimbabwe
Yosemite	Yosemite Nat'l Park, California, U.S.
Espelands (Espelandsfoss)	Hardanger Fjord, Norway
Lower Mar Valley (Ostra Mardolafoss)	Eikesdal, Norway
Tyssestrengene	Odda, Norway

Important Cities on River Banks (World)

City	Country	River
Adelaide	Australia	Torrens
Amsterdam	Netherlands	Amsel
Alexandria	Egypt	Nile
Ankara	Turkey	Kazil
Bangkok	Thailand	Chao Praya
Basra	Iraq	Eupharates and Tigris
Baghdad	Iraq	Tigris
Berlin	Germany	Spree
Bonn	Germany	Rhine
Budapest	Hungary	Danube
Bristol	UK	Avon
Buenos Aires	Argentina	Laplata
Chittagong	Bangladesh	Majyani
Canton	China	Si-Kiang
Cairo	Egypt	Nile
Chung King	China	Yang-tse-kiang
Cologne	Germany	Rhine
Dandzing	Germany	Vistula
Dresden	Germany	Elbe
Dublin	Ireland	Liffy
Hamburg	Germany	Elbe
Kabul	Afghanistan	Kabul
Karachi	Pakistan	Indus
Khortoum	Sudan	Confluence of Blue & White Nile
Lahore	Pakistan	Ravi
Leningrad	Russia	Neva

City	Country	River
Lisbon	Portugal	Tagus
Liverpool	England	Messey
London	England	Thames
Moscow	Russia	Moskva
Montreal	Canada	St. Lawrence
Nanking	China	Yang-tse-kiang
New Orleans	U.S.A.	Mississipi
New York	U.S.A.	Hudson
Ottawa	Canada	Ottawa
Paris	France	Seine
Philadelphia	U.S.A	Delaware
Perth	Australia	Swan
Prague	Czech Republic	Vitava
Quebec	Canada	St. Lawrence
Rome	Italy	Tiber
Rotterdam	The Netherlands	New Moss
Stalingrad	Russia	Volga
Shanghai	China	Yang-tse-kiang
Sidney	Australia	Darling
Saint Louis	U.S.A	Mississippi
Tokyo	Japan	Arakava
Vienna	Austria	Danube
Warsaw	Poland	Vistula
Washington D.C.	U.S.A.	Potomac
Yangoon	Myanmar	Irawaddy

World's Geographical Surnames

City of Sky-scrapers—New York
City of Seven Hills—Rome
City of Dreaming Spires—Oxford
City of Golden Gate—San Francisco
City of Magnificent Buildings—Washington D.C.
City of Eternal Springs—Quito (S. America)
China's Sorrow—Hwang Ho
Cockpit of Europe—Belgium
Dark Continent—Africa
Emerald Isle—Ireland
Eternal City—Rome
Empire City—New York
Forbidden City—Lhasa (Tibet)
Garden City—Chicago
Gate of Tears—Strait of Bab-el-Mandeb
Gift of the Nile—Egypt
Granite City—Aberdeen (Scotland)
Hermit Kingdom—Korea
Herring Pond—Atlantic Ocean
Holy Land—Jerusalem
Island Continent—Australia
Islands of Cloves—Zanzibar
Isle of Pearls—Bahrein (Persian Gulf)
Key to the Mediterranean—Gibralter
Land of Cakes—Scotland
Land of Golden Fleece—Australia
Land of Maple Leaf—Canada
Land of Morning Calm—Korea
Land of Midnight Sun—Norway
Land of the Thousand Lakes—Finland
Land of the Thunderbolt—Bhutan
Land of White Elephant—Thailand
Land of Thousand Elephants—Laos
Land of Rising Sun—Japan
Loneliest Island—Tris an De Gunha (Mid-Atlantic)
Manchester of Japan—Osaka
Pillars of Hercules—Strait of Gibraltar
Pearl of the Antilles—Cuba
Playground of Europe—Switzerland
Quaker City—Philadelphia
Queen of the Adriatic—Venice
Roof of the World—The Pamirs, Central Asia
Sugar bowl of the world—Cuba
Venice of the North—Stockholm
Windy City—Chicago
Whiteman's grave—Guinea Coast of Africa
Yellow River—Huang Ho (China)
Sickman of Europe—Turkey

Important Boundaries

Durand Line	Pakistan & Afghanistan
MacMohan Line	India & China
Radcliff Line	India & Pakistan
Maginot Line	France & Germany
Oder Niesse Line	Germany & Poland
Hindenberg Line	Poland & Germany (at the time of First World War)
38th Parallel	North & South Korea
49th Parallel	USA & Canada

Continents: Some Facts

Continent	Biggest Counrty	Highest Peak	Longest River
Asia	China	Mt. Everest (8848 m)	Yangtze Kiang
Africa	Algeria	Mt. Kilimanjaro (5895 m)	Nile
North America	Canada	Mt. Mckinley (6194 m)	Mississippi Missouri
South America	Brazil	Mt. Acancagua (6960 m)	Amazon
Europe	Russia	Mt. Elbrus (5642 m)	Ob
Australia	Australia	Mt. Coscuisco (2228 m)	Darling
Antarctica	—	Vinson Massif (5140 m)	—

INDIAN GEOGRAPHY

AREA AND LOCATION

- India is in the southern parts of the Asian continent. In the west of India lies the Arabian Peninsula while in the east lies the Indo-China Peninsula.
- India extends between 8°4' N and 37°6' N latitudes and between 68°7' E and 97°2' E longitudes.
- India, has a total geographic area of 32,87,263 sq. km. This is only 2.42 % of the total geographic area of the world but holds 17 per cent of the world's population.
- The 23½°N, which is the Tropic of Cancer, runs across the country.
- India has a length of 3214 km from north to south and 2933 km from east to west. It has a land frontier of 15200 km.
- The total length of the coastline of the mainland, Lakshadweep Islands and Andaman and Nicobar Islands is 7,516.6 km.
- India ranks seventh among the countries of the world, in terms of the geographical extent.
- India is bordered on three sides by water and on one by land, it is also a peninsula.
- India shares its common border with Afghanistan and Pakistan in the north-west, China and Bhutan in the north, and Bangladesh in the east. In the south, Sri Lanka is separated from India by a strait, known as the Palk Strait.
- There are 28 States and 8 Union Territories in India.
- 82°30' E longitude is considered as the Indian Standard Meridian. The local time of this longitude is taken as the Indian Standard Time (IST). This is 5½ hours ahead of the Greenwich Mean Time.

THE INDIAN STATES ON INTERNATIONAL BOUNDARIES ARE:

- ***Bordering Pakistan:*** Jammu and Kashmir, Punjab, Rajasthan, Gujarat.
- ***Bordering China:*** Ladakh, Himachal Pradesh, Uttarakhand, Sikkim, Arunachal Pradesh.
- ***Bordering Nepal:*** Bihar, Uttarakhand, UP, Sikkim, West Bengal.
- ***Bordering Bangladesh:*** West Bengal, Mizoram, Meghalaya, Tripura, Assam.
- ***Bordering Bhutan:*** West Bengal, Sikkim, Arunachal Pradesh, Assam.
- ***Bordering Myanmar:*** Arunachal Pradesh, Nagaland, Manipur, Mizoram.
- ***Bordering Afghanistan:*** Jammu and Kashmir (Pakistan-occupied area).

Important Passes

Jammu and Kashmir	Burzi-La
Himachal Pradesh	Bara La, Cha-La, Shipki-La
Uttarakhand	Niti-La, Lipu-Lekh-La
Sikkim	Jelep-La, Nathu-La
Arunachal Pradesh	Bomdi-La
Ladakh	Joji-La

Heighest Mountain Peaks of India

Peaks	Elevation• (in mts.)
Godwin Austin (K2)	8611
Kanchenjunga	8598*
Nanga Parvat	8126*
Gasherbrum	8068*
Broad Peak	8047*
Dastegil	7885*
Masherbrum (East)	7821*
Nanda Devi	7817
Masherbrum (West)	7806*
Rakoposhi	7788*
Kamet	7756
Saser Kangdi	7672

• *Above mean sea level in metres.*

* *Situated in Pak occupied Kashmir (PoK).*

Towns at River Banks

Town	River
Agra	Yamuna
Prayagraj	Confluence of the Ganges and the Yamuna
Ayodhya	Saryu
Badrinath	The Ganges
Kolkata	Hooghly
Cuttuck	Mahanadi
Delhi	Yamuna
Dibrugarh	Brahmaputra
Ferozepur	Satluj
Guwahati	Brahmaputra
Hardwar	The Ganges
Hyderabad	Musi
Jabalpur	Narmada
Kanpur	The Ganges
Kota	Chambal
Kurnool	Tungbhadra
Lucknow	Gomti
Ludhiana	Sutlej
Nasik	Godavari
Pandharpur	Bhima
Patna	The Ganges
Sambalpur	Mahanadi
Srinagar	Jhelum
Srirangapattam	Cauveri
Surat	Tapti
Varanasi	The Ganges
Vijaywada	Krishna

Waterfalls of India

Waterfall	Hgt (Mt.)	River	State
Jog/Gersoppa	260	Sharavati	Karnataka
Rakim Kund	168	Gaighat	Bihar
Chachai	127	Bihad	Madhya Pradesh
Kevti	98	Mahanadi	Madhya Pradesh
Sivasamudram	90	Cauveri	Karnataka
Kunchikal	455	Varahi	Karnataka

Important Lakes of India

Name of lake	State/UT
Pulicat Lake	Tamil Nadu & Andhra Pradesh Border
Sambhar Lake	Rajasthan
Tso Moriri Lake	Jammu & Kashmir
Vembanad Lake	Kerala
Wular & Dal Lakes	Jammu and Kashmir
Chilka Lake	Odisha
Kolleru Lake	Andhra Pradesh
Loktak Lake	Manipur
Lonar Lake	Maharashtra
Pangong Lake	Jammu and Kashmir

Rivers of India

Name	Originates From	Falls Into
Yamuna	Yamunotri	Ganga
Chambal	Singar Chouri Peak, Vindhyan escarpment	Yamuna
Ghaghara	Matsatung Glacier	Ganga

Name	Originates From	Falls Into
Kosi	Near Gosain Dham Peak	Ganga
Sabarmati	Aravalis	Gulf of Khambat
Krishna	Western Ghats	Bay of Bengal
Godavari	Nasik district in Maharashtra	Bay of Bengal
Caurey	Brahmagir Range of Western Ghats	Bay of Bengal
Tungabharda	Western Ghats	Krishna
Ganges	Combines Sources	Bay of Bengal
Sutlej	Mansarovar Rakas lakes	Chenab
Indus	Near Mansarovar Lake	Arabian Sea
Ravi	Kullu Hills near Rohtang Pass	Chenab
Beas	Near Rohtang Pass	Sutlej
Jhelum	Verinag in Kashmir	Chenab
Son	Amarkantak	Ganga
Brahmaputra	Near Mansarovar Lake	Bay of Bengal
Narmada	Amarkantak	Gulf of Khambat
Tapti	Betul District in Madhya Pradesh	Gulf of Khambat
Mahanadi	Raipur District in Chhattisgarh	Bay of Bengal
Luni	Aravallis	Rann of Kuchchh
Ghaggar	Himalayas	Near Fatehabad
Betwa	Vindhyanchal	Yamuna

Geographical Surnames

Bengal's Sorrow	Damodar River
City of Palaces	Kolkata
Gateway of India	Mumbai
Pink City	Jaipur
Paris of India	Jaipur
Manchester of India	Ahmedabad
Kashmir of South	Kerala
Son of Sea	Lakshadweep
Queen of Mountains	Mussourie
Iron City	Jamshedpur
Hollywood of India	Mumbai
Scotland of East	Meghalaya
City of Nababs	Lucknow
City of Temples & Ghats	Varanasi
Land of Five Rivers	Punjab
City of Golden Temple	Amritsar
Garden of India	Bangaluru
Spice Garden of India	Kerala
City of Lakes	Srinagar
Twin City	Hyderabad-Secunderabad
City of Seven Islands	Mumbai
Diamond Harbour	Kolkata
Switzerland of India	Kashmir
Rice Bowl	Chhattisgarh
Fruit Bowl	Himachal Pradesh
Ganga of South	Cauvery
Pitsburg of India	Jamshedpur
City of Bridges	Srinagar
Residence of God	Allahabad
A Cross-road (Quadrivial) of National Highways	Kanpur
Heart of India	Delhi
Black River	Sharda
City of Festivals	Madurai
Queen of Deccan	Pune
Sorrow of Bihar	Kosi River

Some Major Irrigational and Multipurpose Projects

S.No.	Name of Project	Related State	River
1.	Bargi Project	Madhya Pradesh	Bargi
2.	Beas	Joint Venture of Haryana, Punjab and Rajasthan	Beas
3.	Bhadra	Karnakata	Bhadra
4.	Bhakra Nangal	Haryana, Punjab and Rajasthan	Sutluj
5.	Bhima I	Maharashtra	Pawana
6.	Bhima II	Maharashtra	Krishna
7.	Chambal	Joint Project of M.P. and Rajasthan	Chambal
8.	Damodar Valley Project	West Bengal and Bihar	Damodar
9.	Dulhasti Power Project	Jammu and Kashmir	Chenab
10.	Farakka	West Bengal	Hooghly
11.	Gandak	Bihar and U.P.	Gandak
12.	Ghataprabha	Karnataka	Ghataprabha
13.	Hasdeo Bango Project	Madhya Pradesh, Chhattisgarh	Hasdeo
14.	Hirakud	Odisha	Mahanadi
15.	Jayakwadi	Maharashtra	Godavari
16.	Kakrapara	Gujarat	Tapti
17.	Kangsbati	West Bengal	Kangsbati and Kumari
18.	Karjan	Gujarat	Karjan
19.	Kosi	Bihar	Kosi
20.	Koyana	Maharashtra	Koyana
21.	Krishna Project	Maharashtra	Krishna
22.	Kukadi	Maharashtra	Kukadi
23.	Left Bank Ghagra Canal	Uttar Pradesh	Ghagra
24.	Madhya Ganga Canal.	Uttar Pradesh	Ganga
25.	Mahanadi Delta Scheme	Odisha	(The irrigation scheme will utilise releases from Hirakund Reservoir)
26.	Mahi	Gujarat	Mahi
27.	Malaprabha	Karnataka	Malaprabha
28.	Mayurakshi	West Bengal	Mayurakshi
29.	Nagarjunasagar	Andhra Pradesh	Krishna
30.	Panam	Gujarat	Panam
31.	Parambikulam Aliyar	Tamil Nadu and Kerala	Perimbikulam
32.	Pochampad	Andhra Pradesh	Godavari
33.	Pong Dam	Punjab	Beas
34.	Ramganga	Uttarakhand	Ramganga
35.	Ranjit Sagar Dam (Thein Dam)	Punjab	Ravi
36.	Rihand	Uttar Pradesh	Rihand
37.	Sabarmati	Gujarat	Sabarmati

S.No.	Name of Project	Related State	River
38.	Sharda Sahayak	U.P.	Ghagra
39.	Sone High Level Canal	Bihar	Sone
40.	Tawa	Madhya Pradesh	Tawa
41.	Tehri Dam	Uttarakhand	Bhagirathi
42.	Tungabhadra	Andhra Pradesh and Karnataka	Tungabhadra
43.	Ukai	Gujarat	Tapti
44.	Upper Krishna	Karnataka	Krishna
45.	Upper Penganga	Maharashtra	Penganga
46.	Uri Power Project	Jammu and Kashmir	Jhelum

Major Indian Crops

Crops	Temp(°c)	Water(cm)	States where Produced
Wheat	15°-25°	60-90	Uttar Pradesh, Madhya Pradesh, Punjab, Haryana
Rice	24°-26°	80-200	West Bengal, Uttar Pradesh, Punjab, Andhra Pradesh, Bihar
Maize	18°-21°	50-60	Karnataka, Madhya Pradesh, Maharashtra, Uttar Pradesh
Jowar	20°-35°	40-60	Maharashtra, Madhya Pradesh, Karnataka
Soyabean	25°-27°	50-120	Madhya Pradesh, Maharashtra, Rajasthan
Cotton	20°-30°	80-150	Gujarat, Maharashtra, Telangana, Karnataka, Madhya Pradesh
Tobacco	20°-25°	75-80	Andhra Pradesh, Madhya Pradesh, Gujarat, Karnataka, Maharashtra, Uttar Pradesh
Tea	24°-30°	100-200	Assam, West Bengal, Kerala, Tamil Nadu, Uttar Pradesh
Ground Nut	15°-25°	60-130	Gujarat, Maharashtra

Mineral Wealth at a Glance (Metallic Minerals)

Mineral	Chief Producers
Bauxite	Odisha, Gujarat, Jharkhand
Chromite	Odisha, Karnataka
Coal	Jharkhand, Odisha
Copper	Rajasthan, Madhya Pradesh
Diaspore	Uttar Pradesh, Madhya Pradesh
Gold	Karnataka
Iron	Odisha, Karnataka, Goa
Lead	Rajasthan, Andhra Pradesh
Lignite	Tamil Nadu, Jammu & Kashmir
Manganese	Odisha, Karnataka
Natural Gas	Gujarat, Assam
Petroleum	Gujarat, Assam, Andhra Pradesh
Silver	Rajasthan, Jharkhand, Gujarat
Tungsten	Rajasthan
Zinc	Rajasthan, Maharashtra

Zones and Headquarters of Indian Railways

S.No.	Zone	Headquarters
1.	Central	Mumbai (Victoria Terminus)
2.	Eastern	Kolkata
3.	Northern	New Delhi
4.	North-Eastern	Gorakhpur
5.	North-East Frontier	Maligaon, Guwahati
6.	Southern	Chennai
7.	South-Central	Secunderabad
8.	South-Eastern	Kolkata
9.	Western	Mumbai, Churchgate
10.	East Coast	Bhubaneswar
11.	East Central	Hajipur
12.	North Central	Allahabad
13.	North Western	Jaipur
14.	South Western	Bengaluru (Hubli)
15.	West Central	Jabalpur
16.	South East Central	Bilaspur
17.	Metro Railway	Kolkata
18.	South Coast Railway	Vishakhapatnam (Proposed)

Major National Highways

N H	Connects
NH 1	New Delhi-Ambala-Jalandhar-Amritsar
NH 2	Delhi-Mathura-Agra-Kanpur-Allahabad-Varanasi-Kolkata
NH 3	Agra-Gwalior-Nasik-Mumbai
NH 4	Thane and Chennai *via* Pune and Belgaum
NH 5	Kolkata-Chennai
NH 6	Kolkata-Dhule
NH 7	Varanasi-Kanyakumari (2369 km)
NH 8	Delhi-Mumbai (*via* Jaipur, Baroda and Ahmedabad)
NH 9	Mumbai-Vijaywada
NH 10	Delhi-Fazilka
NH 24	Delhi-Lucknow
NH 26	Lucknow-Varanasi

Major Ports of Country

1. Syama Prasad Mookerjee (Kolkata)
2. Mumbai
3. J.L. Nehru Port (Nhava Sheva)
4. V.O. Chidambarnar (Tuticorin)
5. Chennai
6. Mormugao
7. New Mangalore
8. Paradeep
9. Deendayal (Kandla)
10. Vishakhapatnam
11. Cochin
12. Kamarajar (Ennore).

Major International Airports in India

International Airports	City
Indira Gandhi International Airport	Delhi
Anna International Airport	Chennai
Sri Guru Ram Das Jee International Airport	Amritsar
Rajiv Gandhi International Airport	Hyderabad
Calicut International Airport	Kozhikode
Chhatrapati Shivaji International Airport	Mumbai
Kempegowda International Airport	Bengaluru
Dabolim International Airport in Vasco di Gama City	Goa
Netaji Subash Chandra Bose International Airport	Kolkata
Trivendrum International Airport	Thiruvananthapuram
Lokpriya Gopinath Bordoloi International Airport	Guwahati
Sardar Vallabhbhai Patel International Airport	Ahmedabad

❒ ❒ ❒

INDIAN POLITY

INDIAN CONSTITUTION

- Demand for a Constituent Assembly composed of the people of India officially asserted by the Congress for the first time in 1935.
- The election for Indian Constitution Assembly held in 1946 according to the *Cabinet Mission Plan.*
- The first session of the Assembly was held in New Delhi on December 9, 1946. *Sachidanand Sinha* was elected provisional chairman of the session.
- On December 11, 1946, Dr. Rajendra Prasad was elected as the Permanent Chairman of the Constituent Assembly.
- The Constitution was framed by the Constituent Assembly of India, set-up in December 1946, in accordance with the Cabinet Mission Plan, under the Chairmanship of Sachidanand Sinha, initially.
- The total membership of Constituent Assembly after partition was 299, among them 70 were representatives from the Indian states and others from British India.
- The Chairman of the Drafting Committee was **Dr. BR Ambedkar**, also called the Father of the Constitution.
- The Constituent Assembly took 2 years, 11 months and 18 days to complete the Constitution.
- The Constitution, adopted on 8th November, 1949, contained 395 Articles and Schedules.
- The Constitution was delayed till 26th January because, in 1929, on this day Indian National Congress demanded Poorna Swaraj in Lahore Session under JL Nehru.
- Indian Constitution is a comprehensive document and it is the lengthiest written Constitution in the World.

THE PREAMBLE

- ***The Preamble of the Constitution:*** "We the people of India, having solemnly resolved to Constitute India into a Sovereign, Socialist, Secular Democratic Republic and to secure to all its citizen:

  Justice, Social, economic and political;

  Liberty of thought, expression, belief, faith and worship;

  Equality of status and of opportunity; and to promote among them all;

  Fraternity assuring the dignity of the individual and the unity and integrity of the nation;

  In our Constituent Assembly, this twenty-sixth day of November, 1949, do hereby adopt, enact and give to ourselves this constitution."

Foreign Sources of Indian Constitution

Foreign Sources	*Subject*
Britain	Parliamentary system, collective responsibilities of Cabinet
America	Fundamental right, Independent Judiciary, Judicial review
Canada	Division of powers
Ireland	Directive principles
Germany	Emergency provisions
Russia	Fundamental duties
Australia	Concurrent list

IMPORTANT ARTICLES

PART - I

UNION AND ITS TERRITORIES (ARTICLE 1 - 4)

- The Constitution says, "India, that is Bharat, shall be a Union of States".

- Parliament has the power to create any State, reduce it, change the name of boundaries of any State.

PART - II

CITIZENSHIP (ARTICLE 5 - 11)

- The Constitution provides for a single Citizenship.
- ***Indian Citizenship can be acquire:***

1. by birth
2. by descent
3. by registration
4. by naturalisation
5. by incorporation of territory

- ***Indian Citizenship can be lost by:***

1. renunciation;
2. termination — it takes place if a citizen of India voluntary acquires the citizenship of another country; and
3. deprivation — if the Government terminates the citizenship.

PART - III

FUNDAMENTAL RIGHTS (ARTICLE 12 - 35)

- Following fundamental rights are enjoyed by every Indian citizen, irrespective of caste, colour, creed and sex:

1. ***Right to Equality:*** No special privileges, no distinction on grounds of religion, caste, creed and sex.
2. ***Right to Freedom:*** The right to freedom of expression and speech, the right to choose one's own profession, the right to reside in any part of the Indian Union.
3. ***Right to Freedom to Religion:*** Except when it is in the interest of public order, morality, health or other conditions, everybody has the right to profess, practice and propagate his religion freely.
4. ***Cultural and Educational Rights:*** The Constitution provides that every community can run its own institutions to preserve its own culture and language.
5. ***Right against Exploitation:*** Traffic in human beings and forced labour and the employment of children under 14 years in factories or mines, are punishable offences.
6. ***Rights to Constitutional Remedies:*** When a citizen finds that any of his fundamental rights has been encroached upon, he can move the Supreme Court, which has been empowered to safeguard the fundamental rights of a citizen (Article 32).

PART - IV

DIRECTIVE PRINCIPLES OF STATE POLICY (ARTICLE 36 - 51)

- Directive principles are not enforceable through courts. Main aim of Directive principles is to provide social and economic base of a genuine democracy.

Some Important Directive Principles:

- Provisions for adequate means of livelihood for all citizens (Art. 39).
- Right to work (Art. 41).
- Right to human condition of work and maternity relief (Art. 42).
- Right to a living wage and condition of work ensuring decent standard of life of worker (Art. 43).
- Common Civil Code (Art. 44).
- Prohibit consumption of liquor (Art. 47).
- Prevent slaughter of useful cattle (Art. 48).
- Organise Panchayati Raj (Art. 40).
- Separate the judiciary from the executive (Art. 50).
- Protect and maintain places of historic monuments (Art. 49).
- International peace (Art. 51).

PART - IV A

FUNDAMENTAL DUTIES (ARTICLE 51A)

- The fundamental duties for the Indian citizens have been incorporated in the Constitution through the Constitution (42nd) Amendment Act, 1976. These duties are:

1. to abide by the Constitution and respect its ideals and institutions, the National Flag and the National Anthem;

2. to cherish and follow the noble deeds which inspired our national struggle for freedom;
3. to uphold and protect the sovereignty, unity and integrity of India;
4. to defend the country and render national service when called upon to do so;
5. to promote harmony and the spirit of common brotherhood amongst all the people transcending religious, regional or sectional diversities and to renounce practices derogatory to the dignity of women;
6. to value and preserve the rich heritage of our composite culture;
7. to protect and improve natural environment including forests, lakes, rivers and wildlife, and to have compassion for living creatures;
8. to develop the scientific temper, humanism and the spirit of inquiry and reform;
9. to safeguard public property and to abjure violence;
10. to strive towards excellence in all spheres of individual and collective activity so that the nation constantly rises to higher levels of endeavour and achievement.
11. who is parent or guardian to provide opportunities for education to his child or, as the case may be, ward between age of six and fourteen years.

PART - V

UNION (ARTICLE 52 - 151)

THE PRESIDENT

- The President is the Constitutional head of the Republic of India. He is more or less the titular head of the executive.
- He is the constitutional head but not the real executive. The real power is vested in the hands of the Council of Ministers.
- President is the first citizen of India.
- ***Qualifications:*** (i) Indian citizen, (ii) age not less than 35 years, (iii) should have qualification for election to Lok Sabha, (iv) should not hold any office of profit, (v) should not be a Member of Parliament or State Legislature.
- ***Election:*** Indirectly elected through Electoral College consisting of elected members of both the Houses of the Parliament and elected members of the Legislative Assemblies of the States.
- According to the 70th Amendment Act, 1992, the expression 'States' include the National Capital Territory of Delhi and the Union Territory of Puducherry. Members of the Legislative Councils have no right to vote in the Presidential election.
- ***Powers:*** He makes appointments to all the constitutional posts.
- He can address either House of Parliament and dissolve Lok Sabha.
- All Bills passed by Parliament must receive his assent to become an Act.
- He issues ordinances when Parliament is not in session. No Money Bill can be introduced in Lok Sabha without his recommendation.
- He appoints 12 members of special repute in the Rajya Sabha.
- He has the power of *Pardon* to a criminal in special cases.
- The President holds the office for a period of five years. He is eligible for re-election.
- He is also entitled to rent free official residence called Rashtrapati Bhawan.

VICE-PRESIDENT

- ***Article 63*** of the Constitution stipulates a Vice-President for India.
- The Vice-President acts as the ex-officio Chairman of the Council of States (Rajya Sabha).
- He is elected by an electoral college consisting of the members of both Houses of Parliament in accordance with the system of proportional represen-tation by means of the single trans-ferable vote. He must be a citizen of India, not less than 35 years of age, and should be eligible for election as a member of the Council of States.

- Disputes in connection with election of a president or a vice-president are to be a dealt with in accordance with Article-71. Such disputes shall be decided by the Supreme Court.

Council of Ministers

- The Constitution of India provides for a parliament system of government under which the President is only Constitutional ruler and the real power is exercised by the Council of Ministers, headed by the Prime Minister.
- Council of Ministers is composed of all Union Ministers—the Prime Minister, Cabinet Ministers and Ministers of State.
- The Council of Ministers is Collectively responsible to the Lok Sabha.
- The Prime Minister is a link between the President and the Council of Ministers.

Prime Minister

- The Prime Minister is the leader of the majority party in the Parliament.
- He is appointed by the President. Other Ministers are appointed by the president on his advice.
- The Prime Minister is the head of the Government and the head of the Council of Ministers.
- Jawaharlal Nehru was the first Prime Minister and the longest serving so far.

Union Legislature

- The Legislature of the Union, which is called 'Parliament' consists of the President and the two Houses of Parliament known as the Council of states (Rajya Sabha) and the House of the People (Lok Sabha).

RAJYA SABHA

- The Rajya Sabha is the Upper House of the Parliament and it is constituted of representatives from the States or the Constituent units of the Indian Union.
- It is a permanent body, one third of its members retiring after every two years.
- Its maximum strength is 250. Out of these, twelve members are nominated by the President from well-known personalities in the realm of Science, Art, Literature and Social Service. Rest of 238 representatives of the States and Union Territories are elected.
- Currently, the strength of the Rajya Sabha is 245.

LOK SABHA

- The Lok Sabha whose life is five years, is the Lower House of Parliament and comprises of members directly elected by the people.
- The House of the people (Lok Sabha) at present consists of 543 members directly elected from the states and Union Territories. (By the 104th amendment of the constitution the reservation for two members of Anglo Indian Community nominated by President have been abolished).
- The House of the People shall continue for five years (unless sooner dissolved) from the date of its meeting and no longer and the expiry of the said period of 5 years shall operate as dissolution of the House.

Parliamentary Committees

- There are several Parliamentary Committees to assist the Parliament in its deliberations.
- These are appointed or elected by the respective Houses of Lok Sabha and Rajya Sabha on a motion made or are nominated by their presiding officers.
- Among the Standing Committees, three are financial Committees:
  (*i*) Public Account Committee;
  (*ii*) Estimate Committee;
  (*iii*) Public undertaking Committee.

Speaker of Lok Sabha

- Speaker is elected by the Lok Sabha from among its members.
- The Speaker will have the final power to maintain order within the House of the People and to interpret its rules of procedure.
- A Deputy-Speaker is also elected to officiate in absence of the Speaker.
- *G.V. Mavlankar* was the first Speaker of the Lok Sabha (1952-1956).

Supreme Court

- The Constitution provides for the Supreme Court, which consists of Chief Justice and 33 judges. They are appointed by the President of India.

QUALIFICATION AND TENURE

- Eligibility conditions for a judge of the Supreme Court are that he must be : (i) a citizen of India; (ii) a judge of a high court for a minimum period of 5 years; or (iii) an advocate of a high court for at least ten years or a distinguished jurist.
- Judges hold office till the age of 65.
- They can resign earlier or can be removed by the President on the recommendation of the two Houses of the Parliament by 2/3rd majority of the members present and voting.

Powers

- *Original jurisdiction:* Cases involving Government of India and the states or cases involving the enforcement of Fundamental Rights fall under original jurisdiction.
- *Appellate Jurisdiction:* In cases which are brought to it in the form of appeals against the judgement of the lower courts—It hears appeals in civil and criminal cases.
- *Advisory functions:* the Supreme Court advises the President on the constitutionality of a particular legal matter. However, its advice is not binding on the President.

Other Powers:

1. it is a court of record and can punish for contempt of itself;
2. it can make rules for regulating the practice and procedure of courts with the approval of the President; and
3. it can recommend to the President the removal of chairman and members of the UPSC. Supreme Court enjoys the power of judicial review (right of the court which declares as unconstitutional, the laws passed by the legislature and orders issued by executive) though it is not specifically mentioned in the Constitution.

- The first Chief Justice of India was H.J. Kania (1950-51).

COMPTROLLER AND AUDITOR GENERAL (CAG) (ARTICLE 148-151)

- The Comptroller and Auditor General of India is guardian of the public purse.
- It is his duty to see that not a *paisa* is spent out of consolidated fund of India or of a state without the authority of the appropriate legislature.
- He is appointed by President of India.
- A person with long administrative experience and knowledge of accounts is appointed.
- Holds office for 6 yrs or till 65 yrs of age.
- The President can remove him only on the recommendation of the 2 houses of Parliament (as in case of judge of Supreme Court).
- The CAG submits its reports to the President (in case of accounts relating to the Union Government) or to the State Governors (for State Government Accounts).
- The first CAG of India was *V Narahari Rao* (1948-1954).
- The CAG is not eligible for further office under the Union or State Governments. The expenses of the office of the CAG is charged to the Consolidated Fund of India.

ATTORNEY GENERAL OF INDIA

- The Attorney General of India is the first law officer of the Government of India.
- Though he is not a member of cabinet he has the right to speak in the House of Parliament, but he has no right to vote.
- The Attorney General of India shall be appointed by the President and shall hold office during his pleasure.
- His duty shall be to give advice on such legal matter from time-to-time as may be referred to him by the President.
- To be appointed as Attorney General, a candidate must be qualified to be appointed as a Judge of the Supreme Court.
- The Attorney General can participate in proceedings of the Parliament without the Right to Vote (Article 88).
- The first Attorney General of Independent India was MC Setalvad (1950-1963).

PART - VI

THE STATES (ARTICLE 152 - 237)

The Governor

- The Governor is appointed by the President and holds office during the pleasure of the President.
- Apart from the power to appoint the council of ministers, if the governor finds that the government of state cannot be carried on in accordance with the provisions of the constitution (Art. 356), he may send his report to the President who may assume to himself the functions of the government of the state. (This is popularly known as 'President's Rule').
- Article 161 gives the Governor the power to grant pardons, reprieves, remission of punishment to persons convicted under the state law.
- Article 171 states that the States where Legislative Councils exists, the Governor can nominate some members from amongst those distinguished in literature, science, arts, cooperative movement and social service.

STATES LEGISLATURE (ARTICLE 168 - 212)

- The state legislature consists of Governor and legislative assembly.
- In some state like *Bihar, Maharashtra, Andhra Pradesh, Karnataka, Uttar Pradesh and Telangana* have a legislative council.
- The membership of the council should not be more than *one-third* of the legislative assembly but not less than 40.
- The legislative assembly of each state shall be composed of members chosen by direct election on the basis of adult suffrage and the number of members shall not be more than 500 or less than 60.
- The assembly of Sikkim, Goa, Puducherry and Mizoram have less than 60 members.

HIGH COURTS (ARTICLE 214-232)

- The High Court stands at the apex of the State Judiciary.
- As per the Constitution, there shall be a High Court in each State. But there may be a common High Court for two or more States and Union Territory, if it is provided by a law of the Parliament. For example, the Chennai High Court has its Jurisdiction over the State of Tamil Nadu and the Union Territory of Puducherry.
- The State Government has no control over it.
- There are 25 High Courts in India.
- The Calcutta High Court, established in 1862, is the oldest High Court in India.

THE PANCHAYATS (ARTICLE 243-243 O)

- Panchayati Raj was introduced in India with a view to associate the people with administration at grass-root level.
- It is a three-tier system as recommended by Balwant Rai Mehta Committee.
- Introduced by the 73rd Amendment Act, 1992 which envisaged a three tier system of local governance.

These are:

1. Gram Panchayat at the village level
2. Panchayat Samiti at the block level
3. Zila Parishad at the district level.

Jurisdiction and Seat of High Courts

Name	Year	Territorial Jurisdiction	Seat
Allahabad	1866	Uttar Pradesh	Prayagraj (Bench at Lucknow)
Bombay	1862	Maharashtra, Goa, Dadar and Nagar Haveli and Daman and Diu	Mumbai (Benches at Nagpur, Panaji and Aurangabad)
Calcutta	1862	West Bengal and Andaman & Nicobar	Kolkata (Circuit Benches at Port Blair and Jalpaiguri)
Chhattisgarh	2000	Chhattisgarh	Bilaspur

Name	Year	Territorial Jurisdiction	Seat
Delhi	1966	Delhi	Delhi
Guwahati	1948	Assam, Nagaland, Mizoram and Arunachal Pradesh	Guwahati (Benches at Kohima, Aizawl and Itanagar)
Gujarat	1960	Gujarat	Ahmedabad
Himachal Pradesh	1971	Himachal Pradesh	Shimla
Jammu & Kashmir and Ladakh	1928	Jammu & Kashmir, Ladakh	Srinagar and Jammu
Jharkhand	2000	Jharkhand	Ranchi
Karnataka	1884	Karnataka	Bengaluru (Circuit Benches at Dharwar and Gulbarga)
Kerala	1958	Kerala & Lakshadweep	Kochi (Ernakulam)
Madhya Pradesh	1956	Madhya Pradesh	Jabalpur (Benches at Gwalior and Indore)
Madras	1862	Tamil Nadu & Puducherry	Chennai (Bench at Madurai)
Orissa	1948	Odisha	Cuttack
Patna	1916	Bihar	Patna
Punjab and Haryana	1966	Punjab, Haryana and Chandigarh	Chandigarh
Rajasthan	1949	Rajasthan	Jodhpur (Bench at Jaipur)
Sikkim	1975	Sikkim	Gangtok
Uttarakhand	2000	Uttarakhand	Nainital
Tripura	2013	Tripura	Agartala
Meghalaya	2013	Meghalaya	Shillong
Manipur	2013	Manipur	Imphal
Telangana	2019	Telangana	Hyderabad
Andhra Pradesh	2019	Andhra Pradesh	Amravati

THE MUNICIPALITIES (ARTICLE 243 P-243 ZG)

- Big cities have municipal corporations headed by the elected Mayor.
- For small towns there are elected boards or councils, in turn, elect their Presidents.
- Introduced by the 74th Amendment Act, 1993 which envisages three types of urban local bodies, namely, municipality (nagar palika), city council (nagar panchayat).
- Municipal governance in India was first introduced in Madras in 1688.

PART - XIII

(ARTICLE 301 - 307)

- In this part from Article 301-307 trade, commerce and intercourse within the territory of India are given.

PART - XIV

(ARTICLE 308 - 323)

- In this part services under the union and the states are given.
- ***Article 312:*** *All India Services* and ***Article 315:*** Public Service Commissions for the Union and for the States.
- The first Public Service Commission was set up in 1926, on the recommendations of the Lee Commission.

UNION PUBLIC SERVICE COMMISSION (UPSC)

- This Commission is responsible for:
  1. recruitment to all civil services and posts, under the Union Government by written examinations, interviews and promotions, and
  2. advising the Government on all matters relating to methods of recruitment, principles to be followed in making promotions and transfers. Its Chairman is appointed by the President.

STAFF SELECTION COMMISSION (SSC)

- The Union Government has constituted a Staff Selection Commission for recruitment to non-

technical Class III posts in the central government and in subordinate offices.

- The Administrative Reforms Commission had recommended the setting up of such a Commission.
- The Commission has also been entrusted with the responsibility of making recruitment to Group 'B' services like Assistants' and Stenographers Grade 'C'.
- The Commission has a chairman and two members.

ELECTIONS (ARTICLE 324-329)

- The Constitution provides for an independent election commission to ensure free and fair election to the Parliament, the State legislature and the offices of President and Vice-President.
- Consists of Chief Election Commissioner +2 Election Commissioners. They all enjoy equal powers.
- The Chief Election Commissioner and other Election Commissioners are appointed by the President.
- Election Commissioners are appointed for a term of 5 yrs.
- They are not eligible for re-appointment. Also, they cannot hold any office of profit after their retirement.
- The Election Commission was established on 25th January, 1950 under Article 324 of the Constitution.
- The first Chief Election Commissioner was *Sukumar Sen.*

Functions

- Preparation of electoral rolls and keeping voters list updated.
- Recognition of various political parties and allotment of election symbols.

NITI AAYOG

- The Indian government has replaced Planing Commission with a new institution named **NITI Aayog (National Institution for Transforming India).**
- The Niti Aayog will comprise the following:

1. Prime Minister of India as the Chairperson.
2. Governing Council comprising the Chief Ministers of all the States and Lt. Governors of Territories.
3. Regional Councils will be formed to address specific issues and contingencies impacting more than one state or a region. These will be formed for a specified tenure. The Regional Councils will be convened by the Prime Minister and will comprise of the Chief Ministers of States and Lt. Governors of Territories in the region. These will be chaired by the Chairperson of the NITI Aayog or his nominee.
4. Experts, specialists and practitioners with relevant domain knowledge as special invitees nominated by the Prime Minister.

- The full-time organizational framework will comprise of, in addition to the Prime Minister as the Chairperson:

1. Vice-Chairperson : To be appointed by the Prime Minister.
2. Members : Full-time. : 3
3. Part-time members : Maximum of 2 from leading universities research organizations and other relevant institutions in an ex-officio capacity. Part time members will be on a rotational basis.
4. Ex Officio members : Maximum of 4 members of the Council of Ministers to be nominated by the Prime Minister.
5. Chief Executive Officer : To be appointed by the Prime Minister for a fixed tenure, in the rank of Secretary to the Government of India.
6. Secretariat as deemed necessary.

FINANCE COMMISSION

- The constitution of the Finance Commission is laid down in Art. 280.
- The chairman must be a person having experience in public affairs; and the other four members also having wide experience in financial matters.

- It consists of Chairman and 4 other members.
- It shall be the duty of the Finance Commission to advice the President on matters such as the distribution between the Union and States of the net proceeds of taxes that is required to be shared.
- The Finance Commission is not a permanent body. It is dissolved after it has submitted its recommendations.

Important Amendments to the Constitution

First Amendment, 1951	:	Added Ninth Schedule.
Twenty-second Amendment, 1969	:	Formation of Meghalaya within the state of Assam was facilitated.
Twenty-sixth Amendment, 1971	:	The privy and privileges of the former rulers of Indian States were abolished.
Thirty-first Amendment, 1973	:	The upper limit of representation of states was raised from 500 to 525. The upper limit for representation of the UTs was reduced from 25 to 20.
Thirty-sixth Amendment, 1975	:	Sikkim was made a full-fledged state of Indian Union and it was included in the First Schedule.
Thirty-eight Amendment, 1975	:	This act led to the amendment of Article 123, Article 213 and Article 352 which stated that the satisfaction of President or of Governor contained in these Articles would be called in question in any court of law.
Forty-second Amendment, 1976	:	This amendment was done in accordance with the recommendations of Swaran Singh Committee and included a number of amendments.
Forty-third Amendment, 1977	:	It provided for the restoration of the Jurisdiction of the Supreme Court and High Courts, curtailed by the enactment of the Constitution (Forty-Second Amendment) Act, 1976.
Forty-fourth Amendment, 1978	:	The right to property was deleted as Fundamental Right and was made a legal right.
Fifty-third Amendment, 1986	:	The Act grants statehood to the Union Territory of Mizoram, thus making it the 23rd State of the Indian Unions.
Fifty-sixth Amendment, 1987	:	The UT of Goa converted into Goa state through this amendment whereas Daman and Diu were organised under a new UT.
Seventy-third Amendment, 1992	:	It is concerning Panchayati Raj.
Seventy-fourth Amendment, 1992	:	It is regarding Municipal Boards and Corporations.
Eighty-ninth Amendment, 2003	:	It provides for constitution of a separate National Commission for Scheduled Tribes. (Earlier, there was a combined National Commission for both SC/STs).
Ninety-first Amendment, 2003	:	It is regarding restricting the total number of Ministers including Prime Minister/Chief Minister in Lok Sabha and State Legislatures to 15% of the total number of the Union or State Legislatures.
Ninety-sixth Amendment, 2011	:	Amendment of 8th Schedule, it replaces 'Orissa' with 'Odisha'.
Ninety-eight Amendment, 2013	:	(Insert Article 371 J) To empower the Governor of Karnataka to take steps to develop Hydrabad Karnataka Region.

Ninety-ninth Amendment, 2015	:	The amendment is in toto quashed by Supreme Court on 16 October, 2015.
One hundredth and first Amendment, 2016	:	The act amends the Constitution to introduce "The Goods and Services Tax (GST)."
One hundredth and Third Amendment, 2019	:	The Act providing 10 per cent reservation in government jobs and educational institutions to Economically Weaker Sections (EWS) of General Category, came into effect on January 14, 2019.
One hundredth and Fourth Amendment, 2019	:	This Act ceased the reservation of seats for Anglo-Indians in the Lok Sabha and Legislative assemblies and extended reservations for SCs and STs for up to ten years.

NATIONAL SYMBOLS

STATE EMBLEM

- State Emblem of India is an adaptation from the Sarnath Lion Capital of Ashoka. It was adopted by the Government of India on January 26, 1950. In the adapted form, only three lions are visible, the fourth being hidden from the view.
- The wheel (Dharma Chakra) appears in relief in the centre of the abacus with a bull on the right and a horse on the left.
- The bell-shaped lotus has been omitted. The words ''Satyameva Jayate'' meaning ''Truth alone triumphs'' are inscribed below the Emblem in Devanagari script.

NATIONAL FLAG

- The National Flag of India is a horizontal tricolour of deep saffron (Kesari), white and dark green in equal proportion.
- In the centre of the white band there is a wheel in navy blue colour. It has 24 spokes.
- The ratio of the length and the breadth of the flag is 3 : 2. Its design was adopted by the Constituent Assembly of India on July 22, 1947.

NATIONAL ANTHEM

- Rabindranath Tagore's song 'Jana-gana-mana' was adopted by the Constituent Assembly as the National Anthem of India on January 24, 1950.

Jana-gana-mana-adhinayaka jaya he,
Bharata-bhagya-vidhata
Punjab-Sindh-Gujarat-Maratha-
Dravida-Utkala-Banga
Vindhya-Himachala-Yamuna-Ganga
Uchhala-jaladhi-taranga.
Tava subha name jage,
Tava subha asisa mange,
Gahe tava jaya gatha,
Jana-gana-mangala-dayak,
jaya he Bharata bhagya vidhata,
Jaya he, jaya he, jaya he,
Jaya jaya jaya, jaya he.

NATIONAL SONG

- Bankim Chandra Chatterji's 'Vande Mataram' which was a source of inspiration to the people in their struggle for freedom, has been adopted as National Song. It has an equal status with the National Anthem.

Vande Mataram
Sujalam, suphalam, malayaja-shitalam,
Shasya shyamalam, Mataram
Shubhrajyotsna, pulkita yaminim,
Phulla kusumita drumadalashobhinim,
Subhasinim sumadhura—bhashinim,
Sukhadam, Varadam, Mataram.

- **National Bird and Animal of India:** Peacock and Tiger.
- **National Aquatic Animal:** Dolphin
- **National Flower:** Lotus
- **National Calendar:** It was adopted on March 22, 1957. It has 365 days in the year and the first month of the year is Chaitra.

❑ ❑ ❑

GENERAL SCIENCE

PHYSICS

PHYSICAL QUANTITIES

- Physical quantities may be divided in two classes:
  1. Scalar Quantities 2. Vector Quantities
- A scalar quantity is one which has only magnitude.
- A vector quantity has both magnitude and direction.
- Force, Velocity, Momentum, Acceleration are examples of vector quantities.
- Mass, length, time, volume, speed, energy, work are examples of scalar quantities.

UNITS

- All measurements in physics require standard units.
- In 1960, the General Conference of Weights and Measures recommended that a metric system of measurements called the International System of Units, abbreviated as SI units, be used.

Some Important Units

S.No.	Units	Quantity
1.	Metre	Length
2.	Kilogram	Mass
3.	Second	Time
4.	Ampere	Electric Current
5.	Candela	Luminous Intensity
6.	Newton	Force
7.	Joule	Workdone
8.	Watt	Power
9.	Coulomb	Electric Charge
10.	Volt	Potential Difference
11.	Ohm	Electrical Resistance
12.	Farad	Capacitance
13.	Henry	Inductance
14.	Lumen	Luminous Flux

- Very small distances are measured in micro-meters or (microns) (μm), angstroms (Å), nanometers (nm) and femtometres (fm).

MOTION

- When a body changes its position with respect to something else as time goes on, we say the body is in motion.
- There are two types of motion—translational (linear) and rotational (spin).
- The motion of a car on a road is translational whereas the motion of a top, spinning on its axis is rotational.

SPEED

- It is a scalar form of velocity and is defined as the distance travelled in one second.
- Speed $= \dfrac{\text{distance travelled}}{\text{time required}}$
- SI unit of speed is m/s.

VELOCITY

- The distance covered by an object in a specified direction in unit time interval is called velocity.
- The SI unit of velocity is m/s.
- Velocity is a vector quantity.

ACCELERATION

- The velocity of a body changes due to change in its speed or direction or both. The rate of change of the velocity of a body is called its acceleration.
- Acceleration $= \dfrac{\text{change in velocity}}{\text{time taken}}$

FORCE AND MOTION

GRAVITATIONAL FORCE

- It is the force of attraction between two masses.
- It is gravitational force that holds the moon in its orbit round the earth and the earth in its orbit round the sun.
- *Newton's Law of Universal Gravitation* states that every particle in the universe attracts every other particle with a force that is directly proportional to the product of their masses and inversely proportional to the square of the distance between them.
- The value of G is 6.67×10^{-11} SI units.

CENTRIPETAL FORCE

- The force acting towards the centre on a particle executing uniform circular motion is called centripetal force and is given by

$$F = \frac{mv^2}{r}$$

where, m = Mass of the object
v = Speed
r = Radius of the Circular Path

- In case of the moon, gravitational force between the earth and the moon acts as the centripetal force.
- Centripetal force always acts on the particle performing circular motion.

CENTRIFUGAL FORCE

- The pseudo force that balances the centripetal force in uniform circular motion is called centrifugal force.
- Centrifugal force is directed away from the centre along the radius.
- The centrifugal force is zero exactly at the poles and maximum at the equator.

WEIGHT

- The weight of a body is the force with which the earth attracts the body towards its centre.
- The mass of a body is a constant quantity whereas its weight varies slightly from place-to-place on the earth.
- The weight of a body is maximum at the poles and minimum at the equator. This variation in weight is due to:
  1. the shape of the earth.
  2. the rotation of the earth about its axis.
- The weight of an object is less at high elevations than at sea level.
- At the centre of the earth, the weight of a body would be zero.
- On the surface of the moon the value of the acceleration due to gravity is nearly one-sixth of that on earth and, therefore, an object on the moon would weigh only one-sixth its weight on the earth. The mass of an object on the moon would be the same as on earth.
- The weight of a body would be more if the earth stopped rotating. Conversely, if the speed of rotation were higher, the weight would be less.
- A person weighs more in a lift, which is accelerating upward.
- An astronaut feels weightless in a spaceship because he is not pushing against anything.

FRICTION

- Friction is the force which opposes the relative motion of two surfaces in contact.
- It is friction between the ground and the soles of our shoes that makes walking possible and it is lack of friction that makes our feet slip on highly polished surfaces.
- Friction in machines wastes energy and also causes wear and tear. This friction is reduced by using (1) lubricants, and (2) ball bearings.

NEWTON'S LAWS OF MOTION

First Law

- Every object continues in its state of rest or of uniform motion in a straight line if no net force acts upon it. It is also known as *law of inertia*.
- **Examples:** 1. An unwary passenger in a fast-moving bus falls forward when it stops suddenly. This happens because the feet of the passenger come to rest suddenly whereas his upper part of body continues to be in motion. 2. A person

getting down from a moving bus has to run some distance, in the direction of the bus, before stopping. If he does not run he is bound to fall because his feet come to rest whereas his body continues to be in motion.

Momentum

- The momentum of a body is defined as the product of its mass and velocity.

Second Law

- This law states that "the rate of change of momentum of a body is proportional to the applied force and takes place in the direction of the force."
- If we express force (F) in Newtons, mass (m) in kilograms and acceleration (a) in metres per second squared, we can write the second law as; $F = ma$.
- In travelling the same distance, a car consumes more fuel on a crowded road than on a free road. This happens because the car has to stop and start quite often on a crowded road. The repeated acceleration requires a force (second law), which ultimately comes from the fuel. On a free road the car runs at almost uniform speed requiring fewer accelerations and hence less fuel consumption.

Third Law

- This law states that "to every action there is an equal and opposite reaction."
- When a bullet is fired from a gun, equal and opposite forces are exerted on the bullet and the gun.
- The engine in a jet aeroplane works on the same principle as a rocket but there is a difference in the method of obtaining the high velocity as jet.

IMPULSE

- If a force acts on a body for a very short time, then the product of force and time is called the impulse.

  Impulse= Change in momentum

  = Force × Time

Application of Impulse

1. A cricket player draws his hand back while catching.
2. A person jumping on hard cement floor receives more injuries than a person jumping on muddy or sandy floor.

WORK, POWER AND ENERGY

WORK

- Whenever a force acting on a body displaces it, work is said to be done.

  Work = Force × Distance moved in the direction of force.
- Work is a scalar quantity and its SI unit is Joule (J).

POWER

- Power is defined as the rate of doing work.

$$\text{Power} = \frac{\text{Work done}}{\text{Time taken}}$$

- The SI unit of power is Watt (W) and is also measured in horse power.

  1 HP = 746 W

ENERGY

- Energy is defined as the capacity to do work.

Kinetic Energy

- The energy possessed by an object due to its motion is called kinetic energy and is described by the expression

$$KE = \frac{1}{2}mv^2 \text{; where, m = mass of the object}$$

$$v = \text{speed}$$

Potential Energy

- Potential energy is the energy possessed by the body by virtue of its position, configuration or any condition of stress or strain.
- There are many examples of potential energy. A stone held at some height above the ground has potential energy. Water in an elevated reservoir possesses potential energy.

Transformation of Energy

S.No.	Equipment	Transformation
1.	Dynamo	Mechanical energy into electrical energy
2.	Microphone	Sound energy into electrical energy
3.	Loud Speaker	Electrical energy into sound energy
4.	Electric Bulb	Electrical energy into light and heat energy
5.	Battery	Chemical energy into electrical energy
6.	Electrical Motor	Electrical energy into mechanical energy

CENTRE OF GRAVITY

- The centre of gravity of a body is the point where the whole weight of the body can be considered to act.
- Racing cars are build low and with wide wheel bases to reduce the risk of overturning at sharp bends.
- While crossing a river in a boat, passengers are not allowed to stand. This keeps the CG of the system (boat and passengers) low and ensures stability.

ARTIFICIAL SATELLITES

- In the case of a satellite, the centripetal force is provided by the gravitational pull of the earth.
- If the speed of a satellite is more than 11.2 km/s or 25,000 miles/hour, the satellite would escape the earth entirely and would never come back. This is called escape velocity.
- The existence of gaseous atmosphere on the earth is due to the high value of its escape velocity.

Geostationary Satellites

- Geostationary satellites are stationary with respect to an observer on the earth. Their time period is 24-hour. There height above the surface of earth is 36,000 km. They are always in equatorial plane and their orbits are circular. They are also called parking orbits.

DENSITY AND RELATIVE DENSITY

DENSITY

- The mass per unit volume of a substance is called its density.

$$\text{Density} = \frac{\text{Mass}}{\text{Volume}}$$

- The SI unit of density is kilogram per metre cubed (kg/m^3).
- The relative density of a substance is the ratio of the density of the substance to the density of water.
- Relative density has no unit.

PRESSURE

- Pressure is defined as force acting per unit area.

$$\text{Pressure} = \frac{\text{Force}}{\text{Area}}$$

- The SI unit of pressure is newton per metre squared or pascal.
- Broad wooden sleepers are placed below the rails to reduce the pressure exerted by the weight of a train.
- The pressure of water increases with depth, therefore bottom of a dam is made much thicken than the top.
- The pressure exerted on an enclosed liquid at one place is transmitted equally throughout the liquid. This is called Pascal's Principle.
- Hydraulic presses, hydraulic brakes, hydraulic door closers, etc. are applications of the Pascal's Principle.
- At high attitudes where atmosphere pressure is less nose bleeding may occur due to the greater pressure of blood.
- In an aircraft flying at high altitude, normal atmospheric pressure is maintained by the use of air pumps. If this were not done, the crew and passengers would experience difficulty in breathing and consequently face dangers.
- Atmospheric pressure is measured with an instrument called the *Barometer*.

ARCHIMEDE'S PRINCIPLE

- This principle states that when a body is wholly or partially immersed in a fluid, it experiences an upthrust (upward force) equal to the weight of the fluid displaced.
- An iron nail sinks in water whereas a ship made of iron and steel floats. This is due to the fact that a ship is hollow and contains air and, therefore, its density is less than that of water.
- The density of sea water is more than that of river water, due to this a ship sinks less in sea water. It is for this reason that a ship rises a little when it enters a sea from a river.
- It is because of the higher density of sea water that it is easier to swim in the sea.
- A balloon filled with a light gas, such as hydrogen, rises because the average density of the balloon and the gas is less than that of air. The balloon cannot rise indefinitely because the density of the air decreases with increasing altitude. At a certain height, where the density of air is equal to the average density of the balloon, it ceases to rise and drifts sideways with the wind.
- When an ice block floats in water the water level will remain the same when all the ice melts into water.
- A *hydrometer* is an instrument used for measuring the relative density of liquids.
- A special type of a hydrometer called *Lactometer* is used for testing milk by measuring its density.

SURFACE TENSION

- Surface tension is that property of liquids owing to which they tend to acquire minimum surface area.
- Surface tension is caused by molecular attractions.
- When a paint brush is dipped in water all its hair spread out but when it is taken out it is covered with a thin film of water which contracts due to surface tension and pulls the hair together.
- Liquid drops, such as raindrops, oildrops, drops of molten metals, dewdrops etc. are all spherical because their surface tend to contract in order to have minimum surface area. For a given volume, a sphere has the minimum surface area.
- Soaps and detergents lower the surface tension of water. This increases the wetting power of water or its ability to detach dirt particles from clothes and untensils.
- The force of attraction between unlike molecules is called **adhesion** and that between like molecules **cohesion.**
- The melted wax of a candle is drawn up into the wick by capillary action. Oil rises up a lamp wick for the same reason.
- If one end of a sugar cube is dipped into tea, the entire cube is quickly wet on account of capillary action.

VISCOSITY

- The force which opposes the relative motion between different layers of liquid or gases is called viscous force.
- Viscosity is the property of liquids and gases both.

BERNOULLI'S THEOREM

- According to Bernoulli's theorem, in case of streamline flow of incompressible and non-viscous fluid (ideal fluid) through a tube, total energy (sum of pressure energy, potential energy and kinetic energy) per unit volume of fluid is same at all points.

  1. When a bowler spins a ball, it changes its direction (swings) in the air due to unequal pressure acting on it.

HEAT

- Heat is that form of energy which flows from one body to other body due to difference in temperature between the bodies. The amount of heat contained in a body depends upon the mass of the body.

TEMPERATURE

- The temperature of a body is the quantity that tells how hot or cold it is with respect to some standard body.

MEASUREMENT OF TEMPERATURE

- Temperature is measured by a thermometer.
- A thermometer may be graduated in following scales—
  1. The upper and lower points of centigrade scale are 100°C and 0°C.
  2. The upper and lower points of Fahrenheit scale are 212°F and 32°F.
  3. The upper and lower points of Reaumur scale are 80°R and 0°R.
  4. The upper and lower points of Kelvin scale are 373K and 273K.
  5. The upper and lower points of Rankine scale are 672° Ra and 460° Ra.
- At –40 degrees both celsius and Fahrenheit scales will show identical readings.
- Water cannot be used in a thermometer becaues it freezes at 0°C and also because of its irregular expansion.

THERMAL EXPANSION

- Solids, liquids and gases generally expand when heated and contract when cooled.
- Gaps have to be left in railway tracks to make allowance for expansion, otherwise the rails will buckle. Allowance is made for the expansion of long steel bridges. One end of such bridge is fixed while the other rests on rollers.
- Telephone wires sag more in summer than in winter due to thermal expansion.

EXPANSION OF WATER

- Water has its minimum volume and maximum density at 4°C.

TRANSMISSION OF HEAT

- There are three ways of heat transmission: 1. Conduction; 2. Convection; 3. Radiation.

Conduction

- In this process, heat is transferred from one place to other place by the successive vibration of the particles of the medium without bodily movement of the particles of the medium.
- Conduction takes place mainly in solids.
- Air is a very bad conductor of heat. The good insulating properties of wool, cotton, etc. are mainly due to the air spaces they contain.

Convection

- In this process, heat is transferred by the actual movement of particles of the medium from one place to other place.
- In liquids and gases heat is transmitted by convection.

Radiation

- In this mode of heat transmission heat is transferred from one place to another without effecting the intervening medium.

HEAT CAPACITY

- The heat capacity of a body is defined as the heat required to raise the temperature of the body by 1K. Its SI unit is J/K.

SPECIFIC HEAT CAPACITY

- The specific heat capacity of a substance is the heat required to raise the temperature of a unit mass of the substance by 1K.
- Its SI unit is J/kg K.
- It is because of its high specific heat capacity that water is used as a cooling liquid in car engine.

LATENT HEAT

- It is defined as the amount of heat absorbed or given out by a body during the change of state.
- Each gram of ice that melts absorbs 336 J of heat.

EVAPORATION

- Water can change into the vapour state either by boiling or by evaporation at lower temperatures.
- When sweat evaporates from the skin it draws much heat from the body and produces a cooling sensation.
- In summer, water is stored in pitchers for cooling. Water oozes out of the pores of the pitchers and cools on evaporation.

- The rate of evaporation increases with increase in temperature.

REFRIGERATOR

- In a refrigerator, cooling is produced by the evaporation of a volatile liquid, freon, inside a copper coil (evaporator), which surrounds the freezer.
- The cooling unit (freezer) in a refrigerator is fitted near the top to cool the whole of the interior.

RELATIVE HUMIDITY

- Relative humidity is defined as the ratio of the mass of water vapour in a given volume of air to the mass required for saturating the same volume of air at the same temperature.
- Relative humidity is measured with an instrument called the hygrometer.

PRESSURE COOKER

- The boiling point of a liquid depends on external pressure.
- When the atmospheric pressure is 76 cm of mercury, water boils at 100°C. But when the pressure is increased, the boiling point of water is raised.
- In a pressure cooker, water boils at temperatures higher than 100°C due to increased pressure. The increased boiling temperature allows water to hold more heat which cooks food faster.
- At higher altitudes, atmospheric pressure is reduced. This lowers the boiling point of water and food takes much longer to cook.

WAVE MOTION

- Wave motion may be defined as the transfer of energy without the net transfer of matter.
- If the particles of the medium vibrate perpendicular to the direction of propagation of wave, the wave is called transverse wave.
- Light waves are transverse waves.
- If the particles of the medium vibrate in the direction of propagation of wave, the wave is called longitudinal wave.
- Sound waves are longitudinal waves.

ELECTROMAGNETIC WAVE

- Electromagnetic waves include an enormous range of frequencies—from radio waves with frequencies less than 10^5 Hz to gamma rays having frequencies greater than 10^{20} Hz.
- All electromagnetic wave have the same speed (3×10^8 m/s) in vacuum. The relation $v = n\lambda$ holds good for all electromagnetic waves.

RADIO AND TELEVISION TRANSMISSION

- Radio waves sent out by radio stations are reflected by the ionosphere and can be received anywhere on the earth.
- At night the radio reception improves because the layers of the ionosphere are not exposed to sunlight and are more settled.
- Radar (Radio detection and ranging) employs high frequency radio waves for detecting objects like ships and aeroplanes.
- In microwave oven, when the waves fall on the food, these are absorbed by water, fats, sugars and certain other molecules whose consequent vibrations produce heat. Since heating occurs inside the food, without warming the surrounding air, the cooking time is greatly reduced.
- In microwave oven, food cannot be cooked in metal vessels because the metal blocks out the microwaves.

LIGHT

- Light is a form of energy which is propagated as electromagnetic waves.
- Light is a transverse wave.
- Speed of light in vacuum is 3×10^8 m/s.
- Light takes 8 minute 16.6 second to reach from sun to earth.

REFLECTION

- When light is incident upon a surface, part of it is reflected. But certain surfaces like mirrors and polished metals reflect almost all the light incident upon them.
- The law of reflection states that the angle of incidence is equal to the angle of reflection.

- To see full image in a plane mirror, a person requires a mirror of at least half of his height.

INCLINED MIRROR (NO. OF IMAGES)

- When an object is placed between two inclined mirrors, several images of the object are formed.

CURVED MIRRORS

- There are two types of curved spherical mirrors—1. Concave Mirror, 2. Convex Mirror.
- Concave mirror can concentrate the sun's radiation falling on it at one point, it can be used as a burning glass.
- Concave mirrors are also used in solar cookers.
- Large concave mirrors are used in reflecting telescopes for observing and photographing distant stars and other heavenly bodies.
- Concave mirror is also used as a shaving or make-up mirror.
- Small concave mirrors are used by dentists for examining teeth.
- Concave parabolic mirrors are used in searchlight and headlamps of cars.
- Convex mirrors are also used as rear view mirrors in vehicles.

REFRACTION

- When a ray of light passes from one medium to other it suffers a change in direction at the boundary of separation of two media. This phenomenon is called refraction.
- When a ray passes from one medium to another optically denser medium, e.g., from air to water or glass, it bends towards the normal. Conversely, a ray passing from water or glass into air is bent away from the normal.
- Rivers appear shallow, coin in a beaker filled with water appears raised, due to refraction.
- Another effect of refraction is the apparent upward bending of the immersed portion of a stick when dipped in water.
- It is due to refraction, produced by the earth's atmosphere, that the sun is visible for several minutes after it has set below the horizon. Thus, atmospheric refraction tends to lengthen the day.
- When the sun (or moon) is near the horizon, it appears elliptical, i.e., with the vertical diameter less than the horizontal diameter. This happens because rays from the lower edge of the sun are bent more than those from the upper edge (Atmospheric Refraction).
- One of the most interesting effects of atmospheric refraction and Mirage is a combined effect of atmospheric refraction and total internal reflection.

DISPERSION

- White light consists of seven colours—violet, indigo, blue, green, yellow, orange and red. These colours are called the spectrum of the white light.
- Violet has the minimum wavelength (or maximum frequency) and red the maximum wavelength (or minimum frequency).
- Due to different speeds, the colours are refracted through different angles and therefore, when a narrow beam of white light passes through a glass prism, it is split up into its constituent colours. This separation of light into colours is called dispersion.

COLOUR OF OBJECTS

- We see objects because of the light they reflect.
- When a rose is viewed in white light, its petals appear red and the leaves appear green, because the petals reflect the red part of the white light and leaves reflect the green part. The remaining colours are absorbed. When the same rose is viewed in green light, the petals will appear black and the leaves green. In blue or yellow light both the petals and leaves will appear black.
- Red, blue and green are primary colours.

LENSES

- There are mainly two types of lenses:

  1. Convex or Converging Lens

  2. Concave or Diverging Lens
- Converging or convex lens is used as a magnifying glass.
- Power of a lens is its capacity to deviate a ray.

Power of a lens is measured as the reciprocal of the focal length.

$$P = \frac{1}{f}$$

- SI unit of power of lens is dioptre (D).
- The power of a converging lens is positive and that of a diverging lens is negative.
- For all positions of the object, the images formed by diverging (concave) lens are virtual, erect and diminished.

EYE

- The light entering the eye is focused by the eye-lens to form an image on the retina.
- In front of the eye, lens is the coloured part of eye, called the iris, which automatically adjusts the size of the pupil to the intensity of light falling on it.
- In bright light the iris automatically shuts tighter, reducing the amount of light entering the pupil. This protects the retina from getting damaged.
- When a person enters a dark room after being in bright light, he is not able to see clearly for a while because the iris is unable to dilate the pupil immediately.
- Least distance of distinct vision is 25 cm.

DEFECTS OF VISION

- A person suffering from long sight (hypermetropia) can clearly see objects at infinity but cannot see near objects clearly. This defect is caused by the eyeball being too short and can be corrected by wearing converging lenses.
- In the case of a person suffering from short sight (myopia), the eye ball is too long and distant objects are focused in front of the retina. This defect can be corrected by wearing diverging lenses.
- ***Astigmatism:*** Curvature of cornea becomes irregular and image is not clear. Cylindrical lens is used.

SCATTERING OF LIGHT

- When light falls on atoms and molecules, it is scattered in all directions.
- Scattering of light is maximum for violet colour and minimum for red colour.
- Blue colour of sky is due to scattering of light.
- In the evening, the sun is lower in the sky and its light has to traverse a longer path through the atmosphere to reach an observer. Thus, at sunset, blue, green and other colours having been scattered only red and some orange light reach us and the sun appears a deep orange-red.
- In outerspace, *i.e.,* beyond the atmosphere, there is nothing to scatter the sunlight and therefore the sky appears dark and stars are visible even in the presence of the sun.

INTERFERENCE OF LIGHT

- The superposition of two (or more) waves of the same kind that pass the same point in space at the same time is called interference.
- Beautiful colours seen in soap bubbles and oil films on water are produced due to the interference of white light reflected by these surfaces.
- LASER (Light Amplification by Stimulated Emission of Radiation) is an optical device which produces an intense beam of coherent monochromatic light.
- Examples of Interference of Light: Holography, Laser.

DIFFRACTION OF LIGHT

- When a beam of light passes through a narrow slit or an aperture, it spreads out to a certain extent into the region of geometrical shadow. This is an example of diffraction, *i.e.,* of the failure of light to travel in a straight line.

SOUND

- Sound waves are longitudinal and cannot travel in vacuum. The transmission of sound requires a medium : air, liquid or solid.
- The longitudinal mechanical waves which lie in the frequency range 20 Hz to 20,000 Hz are called audible or sound waves. These waves are sensitive to human ear.

- The longitudinal mechanical waves having frequencies less than 20 Hz are called Infrasonic. These waves are produced by sources of bigger size such as earthquakes, volcanic eruptions, ocean waves etc.
- The longitudinal waves having frequencies greater than 20,000 Hz are called ultrasonic waves. Human ear cannot detect these waves. But some animals such as cats, dogs, bats can detect these waves.

PITCH

- The pitch (shrillness of a sound) depends on its frequency.
- A sound of higher frequency has a higher pitch.
- The pitch of a woman's voice is higher than that of a man.

LOUDNESS

- The relative loudness of a sound is measured in decibels (db).
- All stringed instruments, such as the violin, sitar, guitar, etc. have sound boxes attached to increase the loudness.

SPEED OF SOUND

- The presence of water vapour in the air increases the speed of sound.
- Sound travels faster through warm air than through cold air. The speed of sound is higher on a hot day than on a cold day.
- Thunder is heard much after the flash of lightning is seen because of the wide difference in the speeds of light and sound.

REFLECTION OF SOUND

- When a sound wave is reflected by a distant obstacle, such as a wall or a cliff, an echo is heard.
- To hear echo, the minimum distance between the observer and reflector shou!d be 17 m.
- Exploration of underwater gas and oil is done by detecting the echoes of shock waves produced by explosions on the water surface.
- Bats emit ultrasonic waves of frequencies up to 80,000 Hz and use the reflection of these waves (echoes) to determine the presence and distance of objects on their way and from them respectively.

DOPPLER EFFECT

- The Doppler effect is the change in frequency of a wave (sound or light) due to the motion of the source or observer.
- It is due to the Doppler effect that the whistle of a train appears shriller when it approaches a listener than when it moves away from him.

ELECTRICITY

- Electricity produced by friction between two dissimilar objects is known as static electricity. Depending on the nature of the objects, one acquires a positive charge and the other an equal negative charge. For example, if a glass rod is rubbed with silk, the rod acquires positive charge and the silk an equal negative charge.
- *Lightning* is a gigantic electric discharge occurring between two charged clouds or between a charged cloud and the earth.

CONDUCTOR

- Conductors are those materials which allow electricity (charge) to pass through themselves.
- Metals conduct electricity because they have a large number of conduction or free electrons.

INSULATORS

- Insulators are those materials which do not allow electricity to flow through themselves. Insulators have no free electrons.

SUPER CONDUCTORS

- The resistance of metals to flow of electricity reduces with decreasing temperature. At temperatures near absolute zero, metals have almost zero resistance and became super conductors.

SEMI-CONDUCTORS

- Certain materials, such as silicon and germanium, have electrical resistivity intermediate between those of conductors and insulators. These materials are termed as semi-conductors.

- Semi-conductors are good insulators in their pure crystalline form but their conductivity increases when small amounts of impurities are added to them.

ELECTRIC CURRENT

- Electric current is simply the flow of electric charge. In solid conductors the flow of electrons and in fluids the flow of ions as well as electrons constitute the current.
- SI units of electric current is Ampere (A).

ELECTRICAL RESISTANCE

- When electric current flows through a conductor, e.g., a metallic wire, it offers some obstruction to the current. This obstruction offered by the wire is called its electrical resistance.
- SI unit of Resistance is ohm.

OHM'S LAW

- If physical conditions like temperature, intensity of light etc. remains unchanged then electric current flowing through a conductor is directly proportional to the potential difference across its ends.

ELECTRIC MOTOR

- In an electric motor, electrical energy is converted into mechanical energy.
- Electric fans, mixers, washing machines, etc. work on electric motors.

INVERTER

- An inverter is a device which converts DC to AC. The inverters used in homes and offices are specially designed to:
  1. Convert DC from a battery to AC, and
  2. Charge the battery.

FUSE

- Electric fuse is a protective device used in series with an electric appliance to save it from being damaged due to high current.
- A fuse is a short piece of wire made of a tin-lead alloy, which has a low melting point.
- Fuses are always connected in the live wire in series.

COST OF ELECTRICITY

- The consumption of electrical energy in a house is measured in the unit kWh.
- Kilowatt hour is equal to the energy consumed in the circuit at the rate of 1 kilowatt for 1 hour.

MAGNETISM

- A magnet attracts and holds pieces of iron but does not attract pieces of copper.
- Iron, cobalt, nickel and certain alloys are strongly magnetic whereas copper, wood, glass, etc. are non-magnetic.
- Our earth behaves as a powerful magnet whose south pole is near the geographical north pole and whose north pole is near the geographical south pole.

ATOMIC & NUCLEAR PHYSICS

- Atom consists of three fundamental particles electron, proton and neutron. All the protons and neutrons are present in the central core of atom called nucleus. Electrons revolve around the nucleus.
- The total number of protons in the nucleus is called atomic number (Z).
- The total number of proton and neutrons in the nucleus is called mass number (A).
- Ernest Rutherford, discovered nucleus by the scattering of α-particles from gold foil.

RADIOACTIVITY

- Henry Bacquerel (1896) observed that a photographic plate blackened, when placed near double sulphate of potassium and uranium. He further observed that uranium emitted special kind of rays. They were called Becqueral rays.
- Pierre and Marie Curie observed that the radiation from pitchblende was four times stronger than uranium. In 1898, they finally discovered two new substances—Polonium and Radium. These newly discovered substances were called radioactive substances and this property of these substances was named radioactivity.
- No radioactive substance emits both α and β particles simultaneously.

X-RAYS

- X-rays are electromagnetic radiations having wavelength from a fraction of an Angestrom to about 100Å. They were discovered by Rontgen during his studies on the electrical discharge phenomena in gases—he found that an unknown radiation was produced when electrons collided with the walls of the tubes.

ATOMIC ENERGY

- India today ranks sixth in the atomic energy programmes. It has developed the required know-how and expertise to manufacture nuclear weapons, but it believes in the peaceful uses of atomic power. The Atomic Energy Commission was set-up in the country in 1948 under the Chairmanship of Dr. H. J. Bhabha.
- ***Bhabha Atomic Research Centre (BARC):*** The Bhabha Atomic Research Centre at Trombay near Mumbai (Maharashtra) has four research reactors: (*i*) APSARA—It is the first atomic reactor in Asia; (*ii*) CIRUS—It is a joint Indo-Canadian project; (*iii*) PURNIMA II—a zero energy fast reactor, and (*iv*) DHRUVA—a high power completely indigenous nuclear research reactor with most advanced laboratories in the world. Another fast breeder reactor KAMINI at Kalpakkam has been constructed. Today India is the seventh country in the world and the first developing nation to have mastered the fast breeder reactor technology.
- **Nuclear Power:** Under Nuclear Power Corporation of India Limited (NPCIL) there are seven nuclear power stations in operation in six States: (*i*) Tarapur—Maharashtra, (*ii*) Rawatbhata—Rajasthan, (*iii*) Kalpakkam—Tamil Nadu, (*iv*) Narora—U.P., (*v*) Kakrapara—Gujarat, (*vi*) Kaiga—Karnataka and (*vii*) Kudankulam—Tamil Nadu.
- **Heavy Water:** Heavy water is one of the essential input for Pressurised Heavy Water Reactors (PHWRs) used both as a coolant and moderator. The first heavy water plant was set-up in 1962 in Nangal. Subsequently 7 more plants have been set-up at (*i*) Baroda, (*ii*) Tuticorin, (*iii*) Kota, (*iv*) Talcher, (*v*) Thal, (*vi*) Hazira and (*vii*) Manuguru.
- **Research and Development Centres:** Four research centres namely (*i*) Bhabha Atomic Research Centre, Trombay (Maharashtra), (*ii*) Indira Gandhi Centre for Atomic Research, Kalpakkam (Tamil Nadu), (*iii*) Centre for Advanced Technology, Indore (Madhya Pradesh), (*iv*) Variable Energy Cyclotron Centre at Kolkata (West Bengal) are focal points of research and development work in nuclear energy and related discipline.
- **India's Nuclear Explosions:** On May 18, 1974 India conducted her first underground nuclear explosion at Pokhran (Rajasthan) in the Thar desert, 20 km. away from Jaisalmer, at a depth of more than 100 metres. The successful explosion made India the sixth nuclear nation in the world.
- India conducted 5 nuclear explosion tests at Pokhran in two phases on May 11 and May 13, 1998 and became a nuclear power state.

IMPORTANT INVENTIONS

Name of Invention	Inventor	Nationality	Year
Aeroplane	Orville & Wilbur Wright	U.S.A.	1903
Ball-Point Pen	John J. Loud	U.S.A.	1888
Barometer	Evangelista Torricelli	Italy	1644
Bicycle	Kirkpatrick Macmillan	Britain	1839-40
Bifocal Lens	Benjamin Franklin	U.S.A.	1780
Car (Petrol)	Karl Benz	Germany	1888
Celluloid	Alexander Parkes	Britain	1861
Cinema	Nicolas & Jean Lumiere	France	1895

Name of Invention	*Inventor*	*Nationality*	*Year*
Clock (mechanical)	I-Hsing & Liang Ling-Tsan	China	1725
Diesel Engine	Rudolf Diesel	Germany	1895
Dynamo	Hypolite Pixii	France	1832
Electric Lamp	Thomas Alva Edison	U.S.A.	1879
Electric Motor (DC)	Zenobe Gramme	Belgium	1873
Electric Motor (AC)	Nikola Tesla	U.S.A.	1888
Electro-magnet	William Sturgeon	Britain	1824
Electronic Computer	Dr. Alan M. Turing	Britain	1943
Film (moving outlines)	Louis Prince	France	1885
Film (musical sound)	Dr. Le de Forest	U.S.A.	1923
Fountain Pen	Lewis E. Waterman	U.S.A.	1884
Gramophone	Thomas Alva Edison	U.S.A.	1878
Helicopter	Etienne Oehmichen	France	1924
Jet Engine	Sir Frank Whittle	Britain	1937
Laser	Charles H. Townes	U.S.A.	1960
Lift (Mechanical)	Elisha G. Otis	U.S.A.	1852
Locomotive	Richard Trevithick	Britain	1804
Machine Gun	James Puckle	Britain	1718
Microphone	Alexander Graham Bell	U.S.A.	1876
Microscope	Z. Janssen	Netherlands	1590
Motor Cycle	G. Daimler	Germany	1885
Photography (on film)	John Carbutt	U.S.A.	1888
Printing Press	Johann Gutenberg	Germany	c.1455
Razor (safety)	King C. Gillette	U.S.A.	1895
Refrigerator	James Harrison & Alexander Catlin	U.S.A.	1850
Safety Pin	Walter Hunt	U.S.A.	1849
Sewing machine	Barthelemy Thimmonnier	France	1829
Ship (steam)	J.C. Perier	France	1775
Ship (turbine)	Hon. Sir C. Parsons	Britain	1894
Skyscraper	W. Le Baron Jenny	U.S.A.	1882
Slide Rule	William Oughtred	Britain	1621
Steam Engine (condenser)	James Watt	Britain	1765
Steel Production	Henry Bessemer	Britain	1855
Steel (stainless)	Harry Brearley	Britain	1913
Submarine	David Bushnell	U.S.A.	1776
Tank	Sir Ernest Swinton	Britain	1914
Telegraph	M. Lammond	France	1787
Telegraph Code	Samuel F.B. Morse	U.S.A.	1837
Telephone (perfected)	Alexander Graham Bell	U.S.A.	1876
Television (mechanical)	John Logie Baird	Britain	1926
Television (electronic)	P.T. Farnsworth	U.S.A.	1927
Thermometer	Galileo Galilei	Italy	1593
Transformer	Michael Faraday	Britain	1831
Transistor	Bardeen, Shockley & Brattain	U.S.A.	1948
Washing Machine (elec.)	Hurley Machine Co.	U.S.A.	1907
Zip-Fastener	W.L. Judson	U.S.A.	1891

Important Discoveries

Discovery	*Discoverer*	*Nationality*	*Year*
Aluminium	Hans Christian Oerstedt	Denmark	1827
Atomic number	Henry Moseley	England	1913
Atomic structure of matter	John Dalton	England	1803
Chlorine	C.W. Scheele	Sweden	1774
Electromagnetic induction	Michael Faraday	England	1831
Electromagnetic waves	Heinrich Hertz	Germany	1886
Electromagnetism	Hans Christian Oersted	Denmark	1920
Electron	Sir Joseph Thomson	England	1897
General theory of relativity	Albert Einstein	Switzerland	1915
Hydrogen	Henry Cavendish	England	1766
Law of electric conduction	Georg Ohm	Germany	1827
Law of electromagnetism	Andre Ampere	France	1826
Law of falling bodies	Galileo	Italy	1590
Laws of gravitation & motion	Isaac Newton	England	1687
Laws of planetary motion	Johannes Kepler	Germany	1609-10
Magnesium	Sir Humphry Davy	England	1808
Neptune (Planet)	Johann Galle	Germany	1846
Neutron	James Chadwick	England	1932
Nickel	Axel Cronstedt	Sweden	1751
Nitrogen	Daniel Rutherford	England	1772
Oxygen	Joseph Priestly, C.W. Scheele	England, Sweden	1772
Ozone	Christian Schonbein	Germany	1839
Pluto	Clyde Tombaugh	U.S.A	1930
Plutonium	G.T. Seaborg	U.S.A	1940
Proton	Ernest Rutherford	England	1919
Quantum Theory	Max Planck	Germany	1900
Radioactivity	Antoine Bacquerel	France	1896
Radium	Pierre & Marie Curie	France	1898
Silicon	Jons Berzelius	Sweden	1824
Special theory of relativity	Albert Einstein	Switzerland	1905
Sun as centre of solar system	Copernicus	Poland	1543
Uranium	Martin Klaproth	Germany	1789
Uranus (Planet)	William Herschel	England	1781
X-rays	Wilhelm Roentgen	Germany	1895

Scientific Instruments

Name of Instrument	*Used for*
Altimeter	measuring altitude
Ammeter	measuring strength of an electric current
Anemometer	measuring the velocity of wind
Audiometer	measuring level of hearing
Barometer	measuring atmospheric pressure
Callipers	measuring the internal and external diameters of tubes
Calorimeter	measuring quantity of heat
Compass	finding out direction
Dynamo	converting mechanical energy into electrical energy
Galvanometer	detecting and determining the strength of small electric currents
Hydrometer	measuring specific gravity of a liquid
Hygrometer	measuring the humidity in the atmosphere
Lactometer	measuring the purity of milk
Manometer	measuring the gaseous pressure
Micrometer	measuring minute distances, angles, etc.
Microscope	seeing magnified view of very small objects
Photometer	measuring intensity of light from distant stars
Pyrometer	measuring high temperatures
Radar	detecting and finding the presence and location of moving objects like aircraft, missile, etc.
Radiometer	measuring the emission of radiant energy
Rain Gauge	measuring the amount of rainfall
Seismograph	measuring and recording the intensity and origin of earthquake shocks
Sextant	measuring altitude and angular distances between two objects or heavenly bodies
Spectrometer	measuring the refractive indices
Spherometer	measuring the curvature of spherical objects/surface
Sphygmomanometer	measuring blood pressure
Stethoscope	ascertaining the condition of heart and lungs by listening to their function
Stroboscope	viewing objects that are moving rapidly with a periodic motion as if they were at rest
Tachometer	measuring the rate of revolution or angular speed of a revolving shaft
Telescope	viewing magnified images of distant objects
Thermocouple	measuring the temperature inside furnaces and jet engines
Thermometer	measuring human body temperature
Thermostat	regulating constant temperature
Ultrasonoscope	measuring utrasonic sounds
Viscometer	measuring the viscosity of a fluid
Voltmeter	measuring potential difference between two points.

CHEMISTRY

ELEMENTS

- An element may be defined as a substance which is made by same type of atoms and it can neither be broken into, nor built from two or more simpler substances by any known physical or chemical methods, e.g., copper, silver, hydrogen, carbon, oxygen, nitrogen, gold, iron etc.

COMPOUNDS

- A compound may be defined as a substance which contains two or more elements combined in some fixed proportion by weight and which can be decomposed into two or more elements by any suitable method.
- The properties of a compound are entirely different from those of the elements from which it is made.
- Some common examples of compounds are water, sugar, salt, aspirin, chloroform, alcohol and ether.

MIXTURES

- A material containing two or more elements or compounds in any proportion is a mixture.
- The components of a mixture can be separated by physical means like filtration, sublimation and distillation.

ATOMIC STRUCTURE

ATOM

- Atom is the smallest part of the element that takes part in a chemical reaction. Atom of an element can not be changed into that of another element by a chemical or physical means. It does not exist in free state.

MOLECULE

- A molecule is the smallest part of an element or compound that is capable of existing independently.

ATOMIC WEIGHT (OR ATOMIC MASS)

- The atomic mass of an element is the number of times its atom is heavier than 1/12th of the mass of carbon (C^{12}) atom.
- The unit used to measure atomic mass is called atomic mass unit, *i.e.,* amu.

ELECTRON

- The electron is a fundamental particle of an atom which carries a unit negative charge. It was discovered by J.J. Thomson in 1897.

PROTON

- It is a fundamental particle of an atom carrying a unit positive charge. It was discovered by Rutherford and Goldstein in 1886.

NEUTRON

- It is a fundamental particle of an atom carrying no charge. It was discovered by Chadwick in 1932.

ISOTOPES

- The atoms of the same element having different mass numbers are called isotopes.

ISOBARS

- Elements having the same atomic mass but differ in atomic number are called isobars.

ISOTONES

- Elements having the same number of neutrons are called isotones.

OXIDATION AND REDUCTION

- Oxidation is a process in which a substance adds on oxygen or loses hydrogen. In modern terms, oxidation is the process in which a substance loses electrons.
- Reduction is a process in which a substance adds on hydrogen or loses oxygen. In modern terms, reduction is the process in which a substance gains electrons.
- Oxidation and reduction always occur simultaneously. If one substance is oxidised, another is reduced. The reaction in which this oxidation-reduction process occurs is called a redox reaction.

- Oxidising agents are substances which bring about the oxidation of other substances, e.g., Potassium Permanganate, Potassium Dichromate, Nitric Acid, Hydrogen Peroxide, etc.
- Reducing agents are substances which bring about the reduction of other substances, e.g., hydrogen sulphide, hydrogen, carbon, sulphur dioxide, etc.

ACIDS, BASES AND SALTS

ACID

- An acid is any compound that can react with a base to form a salt, the hydrogen of the acid being replaced by positive metallic ion. According to modern theory, an acid is a compound which yields hydrogen ions (protons) to a base in a chemical reaction. In a water solution, an acid tastes sour, turns blue litmus red and produces free hydrogen ions.

Acid	Sources
Citric Acid	Lemons or Oranges (Citrus Fruits)
Lactic acid	Sour milk
Tartaric acid	Grapes
Acetic acid	Vinegar
Maleic acid	Apples
Oxalic acid	Tomato
Formic acid	Red ants

BASES

- Such compounds which gives salt and water with acid known as bases. Bitter in taste, turns red litmus paper into blue, contains replaceable hydroxyl group.
- Some important bases are sodium hydroxide, potassium hydroxide, sodium carbonate and ammonium hydroxide.
- All alkalies are bases but all bases are not alkalies because all bases are not soluble in water.

SALTS

- Salts are ionic compounds containing a positive ion (cation) and a negative ion (anion).
- When an acid reacts with a base, a salt and water are formed. This reaction is called neutralization since the acid and base neutralize each other's effect.

ELECTROLYSIS

- The process of decomposition of an electrolyte by the passage of an electric current through its molten state or its aqueous solution is called electrolysis.
- Device through which electric current is passed known as electrodes.

METALLURGY

- Metals occur in nature, in the native (in free state) as well as in the combined state.
- Naturally occurring materials containing metals are called minerals.
- A mineral from which a given metal is obtained economically is called an ore.
- The process of extraction of a metal in a pure state on a large scale from its ore by Physical and Chemical means is called metallurgy.
- The rocky and siliceous matter that associated with the ore is known as gangue.
- Substance that is added to ore to remove the gangue is known as flux.
- The process of removal of gangue from the ore is known as concentration.
- Calcination is the heating of the ore in the absence of air. This method is employed for obtaining the metal oxides from carbonates and hydroxides.
- Roasting is the heating of the ore in the presence of air. On roasting, part of the ore is oxidised to form an oxide. This oxide is then reduced to the metal.
- The industrial reduction process for obtaining metal from the treated ore is called smelting.

AMALGUM

- An alloy in which one of the component metals is mercury is known as amalgum.

IRON AND STEEL

- Iron is extracted from its ores by the blast furnace process.

- Iron obtained from blast furnace is called pig iron or cast iron containing about 5% carbon.
- Pure iron is called wrought iron which does not contain carbon more than 0.2%, or any other impurities or constituents.
- Steel contains 0.25% – 2% carbon and varying amounts of other elements.

CARBON AND ITS COMPOUNDS

ALLOTROPY

- Such substances which having the same chemical properties, but differ in physical properties, known as allotropes and this property is called allotropy.

DIAMOND

- Diamond is the purest form of carbon.
- It is non-conductor of heat and electricity.
- It is the hardest natural substance.
- It burns in air at 900°C and gives out CO_2.

GRAPHITE (BLACK LEAD)

- It is good conductor of heat and electricity.
- Graphite is used in making lead pencils.
- Graphite is also used as electrodes, lubricant, moderators, electrotyping and carbon arc.

AMORPHOUS FORMS OF CARBON

1. Wood Charcoal – Obtained from wood
2. Sugar Charcoal – Obtained from cane sugar
3. Bone or Animal Charcoal – Obtained from animal bones
4. Coke Charcoal – Obtained from coal

CARBON MONOXIDE (CO)

- Carbon monoxide is an active poison and is very dangerous as it is a colourless and odourless gas and can not, therefore, be easily detected.
- The extremely poisonous nature of carbon monoxide is a result of its combining with the haemoglobin of the blood to form carboxyhaemoglobin, which is not decompassed by any of the processes in the body.

HYDROCARBONS

- Compounds of carbon and hydrogen are called hydrocarbon.
- A natural source of hydrocarbon is petroleum obtained from sedimentary rocks.
- Compounds having the same molecular formula but differ in properties due to different structural formula known as isomers and this property is called isomerism.

SATURATED HYDROCARBONS (ALKANES)

- Containing single covalent bonds only.
- Such compounds are, in general, called alkanes for instance, Methane, Ethane, Propane, Butane.

UNSATURATED HYDROCARBONS

- Containing multiple bonds.
- Compounds with double bonds are called alkenes, e.g. ethylene, propyene etc. and triple bond containing compounds are called alkynes, e.g. acetylene, propyne etc.
- Benzene is an unsaturated cyclic hydrocarbon with the structure.
- Compounds derived from benzene are called aromatic compounds.

FUELS

Solid Fuels

- These contain carbon and, during combustion, form mainly carbon dioxide and carbon monoxide with a large amount of heat.
- Examples of solid fuels are wood, coal, coke and paraffin wax.

Liquid Fuels

- These are basically mixtures of several hydrocarbons. During combustion, they form carbon dioxide and water.
- Liquid fuels are obtained as different fractions during the distillation of petroleum.
- Examples of liquid fuels are kerosene oil, petrol, diesel oil and alcohol.

Gaseous Fuels

- Gaseous fuels do not leave ash on burning and have high content of heat.
- The main gaseous fuels are liquefied petroleum gas (LPG, mainly a mixture of propane and

butane and used in homes for cooking, water gas ($CO + H_2$), producer gas ($CO + N_2$), coal gas (mixture of hydrogen, methane, ethylene, carbon monoxide, nitrogen, oxygen and carbon dioxide) and natural gas (mixture of methane, ethane, propane and butane with traces of higher hydrocarbons obtained from oil well, above petroleum).

PETROLEUM AND NATURAL GAS

- Natural gas contains about 80% methane and 10% ethane, the remaining 10% being a mixture of higher gaseous hydrocarbons.
- Compressed Natural Gas (CNG) is natural gas filled in cylinders under high pressure.
- The quality of petrol for use in car engines is denoted by their anti-knock properties.
- To increase octane number, tetra ethyl lead (TEL) is added to petrol.

HEAVY WATER

- Chemically heavy water is deuterium oxide.
- Heavy water is used in nuclear reactors as a moderator because it slows the fast moving neutrons.

Hard and Soft Water

- Water which produces lather with soap solution readily is called soft water.
- Water which does not produce lather with soap solution readily is called hard water.
- The hardness of water is due to presence of the bicarbonates, chlorides and sulphates of calcium and magnesium.
- Temporary hardness of water is due to the presence of bicarbonates of calcium and magnesium.
- Permanent hardness of water is due to presence of sulphates, chlorides, nitrates of calcium and magnesium.

GLASS

- Ordinary glass is solid mixture of silica, sodium silicate and calcium silicate.
- Soft glass is a soda-lime silicate glass. It melts at low temperature. It is used in manufacturing of bottles, test tubes etc.
- Hard glass is potash lime silicate and melts at high temperature in comparison to soft glass and is used in manufacturing of flask etc.
- Flint glass is a lead potash silicate and is used in manufacturing of prism, lens and optical instruments.
- Pyrex glass is a mixture of sodium aluminium borosilicates. It is used in manufacturing of high quality equipments in laboratory because it does not melt at very high temperature.
- Safety glass is prepared by placing a layer of transparent plastic glass between two layers of glass by means of a suitable adhesive. It is used in making wind screen of automobiles, aeroplanes, trains etc.

CEMENT

- The approximate composition of Portland cement is:
  1. Calcium Oxide → 62%
  2. Silica → 22%
  3. Alumina → 7.5%
  4. Magnesia → 2.5%
  5. Ferric Oxide → 2.5%
- A small amount of gypsum is added to slow down the setting of cement.
- Cement containing excess amount of lime cracks during setting while cement containing less amount of lime is weak in strength.
- Cement containing no iron is white but hard to burn.

POLYMERS AND PLASTICS

- A polymer is a large molecule, built up from many hundreds of thousands of small unit called monomeric units or monomers.
- The process of formation of polymers from monomers is called polymerization.
- Plastics are cross-linked polymers and very tough.
- Some examples of plastics are — Celluloid, Bakelite and Vinyl Plastics.

RUBBER

- Natural and Synthetic rubbers are examples of polymers.
- Natural rubber is isomer of isoprene.

- When the natural rubber is heated along with sulphur called vulcanisation. The resulting rubber is elastic, hard and strong.
- Synthetic rubbers are made by polymerisation of chloroprene, styrene and butadiene mixtures and isobutylene.

SOAPS

- The soaps are sodium salts of higher fatty acids. They are useful only in soft water as they form an insoluble precipitate in hard water. This precipitate consists of salts of calcium and magnesium of higher fatty acids. No lather or emulsion is formed and washing is not possible.

Some Importants Alloys

Alloys	***Composition***
Brass	Cu, Zn
Bronze	Cu, Sn
Gun metal	Cu, Sn, Zn
Bel metal	Cu, Sn
German silver	Cu, Zn, Ni
Dutch metal	Cu, Zn
Aluminium	Al, Cu
Nichrome	Ni, Fe, Cr, Mn
Chromium steel	Cr, C, Fe

Chemical Formulae, Commercial Name of Chemical Compounds

Commercial Name	**Chemical Compounds**	**Chemical formulae**
Common salt	Sodium chloride	$NaCl$
Baking soda	Sodium bicarbonate	$NaHCO_3$
Washing soda	Sodium carbonate	$Na_2CO_3 \cdot 10H_2O$
Caustic soda	Sodium hydroxide	$NaOH$
Chilli salt peter	Sodium nitrate	$NaNO_3$
Soda ash	Sodium carbonate	Na_2CO_3
Hypo	Sodium thiosulphate	$Na_2S_2O_3 \cdot 5H_2O$

BIOLOGY

BRANCHES OF BIOLOGY

(*a*) **Anthropology:** Deals with the scientific study of man and the mankind.

(*b*) **Agronomy:** Deals with the management of farms and science of crop production.

(*c*) **Apiculture:** Deals with the process of bee keeping for commercial purposes.

(*d*) **Entomology:** Deals with the structure, habits and classification of insects.

(*e*) **Eugenics:** Deals with improving the human race.

(*f*) **Pathology:** Deals with the nature of disease, their causes, symptoms, effects, their cure and control.

(*g*) **Physiotherapy:** Deals with the treatment of diseases, body weakness or defects with the help of massage and exercise etc.

(*h*) **Sericulture:** Deals with the production of raw silk from silkworm.

(*i*) **Pharmacology:** Deals with the knowledge and manufacture of drugs.

(*j*) **Occupational therapy:** Deals with treating the physically handicapped or injured persons through exercise etc.

(*k*) **Psychology:** Deals with the study of human mind, its behaviour and mental qualities.

(*l*) **DNA finger printing:** Technique to help identify a person on the basis of genes.

ANIMALS/PLANTS

- The organisms that closely resemble one another

are placed in one group, the groups which have similarities are combined together into larger groups, and these into still larger ones. The most inclusive category is kingdom. Other major categories, in descending order are: phylum, class, order, family, genus, and species. Man belongs to Animal kingdom, chordata division or phylum, Mammalia class, Primates order, Hominidae family, Homo genus and Sapiens species.

CELL THEORY

- Cell is the basic unit of structure of all living organisms. According to the cell theory, all organism are composed of cells and cell products and growth and development results from the division and differentiation of cells.
- Cells membrane surrounds all living cells.
- Nucleus is the most important cell organelle which controls and coordinates all cell activities and also concerned with the transmission of heredity characters.
- Mitochondria, ribosomes, lysosomes and dictyosomes are present in plant and animal cells.
- Only plant cells have cell wall, chloroplast and vacuole.
- Viruses constitute a difficulty since in many ways they are intermediate between living and dead matter.
- The cell is said to be made up of a substance called Protoplasm which has two main constituents cytoplasm and nucleus, and is bounded by a cell membrane on outside.
- Cells take up the raw materials for metabolism through the cell membrane from extracellular fluid surrounding them.
- Cytoplasm inside is responsible for maintaining the internal distribution of organelles and also for free cell movements.
- Mitochondria inside provides energy for reactions inside the cell. Ribosomes are responsible for the synthesis of proteins.
- The Endoplasmic Reticulum helps in addition of other sugar units to proteins and their transportation to other parts of the cell.

FOOD

- It is a nutritive substance taken by an organism for growth, work, repair and maintaining life processes. It provides energy to do work and maintain body heat, provides materials for the growth of the body, makes necessary materials for reproduction and provides materials for the repair of damaged cells and tissues of our body.
- **Carbohydrates:** For a normal person, 400 to 500 gms of carbohydrates are required daily but for sportspersons, growing children and nursing mothers, it is on higher side.
- **Proteins:** They are complex organic compounds made up of carbon, hydrogen, oxygen and nitrogen. The building blocks of Protein are Amino acids and there are large number of amino acids.
- Proteins are essential for the growth of children and teenagers, and for maintenance and making good the wear and tear of the body tissues in adults.
- An adult needs about 1 gm of protein per kg of body weight.
- **Fats:** They are esters of long chain fatty acids and an alcohol called glycerol. Fats also contain atoms of carbon, hydrogen and oxygen.
- The main function of fats in the body is to provide a steady source of energy and for this purpose, they are deposited within the body.
- One gm of fat gives 37 kilojoules of energy which is more than double of that given by carbohydrates.
- Fats, the richest source of energy to our body, can be stored in the body for subsequent use. Fats, soluble in organic solvents and insoluble in water, also supply fat-soluble vitamins to our body.
- **Minerals:** Some of the important minerals needed by our body are — iron, iodine, calcium, phosphorus, sodium, potassium, zinc, copper, magnesium, chloride, fluoride and sulphur.
- We get most of the minerals in combined form from plant sources. Deficiency of these minerals causes many diseases.
- **Energy Requirements:** The energy requirement of a body varies according to age, sex, lifestyle, occupation, climate and special situations like pregnancy and lactation.

Age	Energy requirements
5 years	6000 kJ per day
11 years	9000 kJ per day
18 years	11000 kJ per day
Adult (normal work)	9600 kJ per day
Adult (heavy work)	12000 kJ per day
Adult (very heavy work)	16000 kJ per day

- **Vitamins:** They act as catalysts in certain chemical reactions of metabolism in our body.
- They don't provide energy to our body nor form body tissues.
- More than 15 types of vitamins are known and only 2 vitamins — D and K can be formed in our body.

Vitamin	Necessity	Source
Vitamin A	For maintaining healthy eyesight, normal skin and hair	Cod liver oil, fish, eggs, milk, carrot, leafy vegetables.
Vitamin B_1	For growth, carbohydrate metabolism, functioning of heart, nerves and muscles.	Milk, soya-food, meat, whole cereals, green vegetables.
Vitamin C	For keeping teeth, gums and joints healthy, for increasing resistance of body to infection	Citrus fruits, guava, tomatoes.
Vitamin D	For normal growth of bones and teeth	Milk, eggs, butter, cod liver oil, sun light.
Vitamin E	For normal reproduction, functioning of muscles and protection of liver	Green leafy vegetables, milk, butter, tomato.
Vitamin K	For normal clotting of blood and normal functioning of liver	Green leafy vegetables, soyabean, tomato.

- **Roughage:** Though it does not provide any energy to the body, yet keeps the digestive system in order, by helping in retaining water in the body and preserving constitution.
- The main source of roughage are salads, cabbage, corn cob, porridge, vegetables and fruits with stems.

DISEASES

COMMUNICABLE DISEASES

- They are the diseases which can be transmitted from reservoirs of infection or infected person to the healthy but susceptible persons.
- The disease causing agent or the pathogen can be transmitted directly or indirectly.

DEFICIENCY DISEASES

- These occur due to deficiency of some nutrients in the diet or some hormone due to hypo activity or damage to endocrine glands.

Diet Deficiency	Disease
Protein	Kwashiorkor
Protein-energy malnutrition	Marasmus
Vitamin A	Night-blindness, Xerophthalmia
Vitamin B_1	Beri-Beri
Vitamin B_2	Cheilosis
Vitamin B_5	Pellagra
Vitamin C	Scurvy
Vitamin D	Rickets (in children), (in adult) Osteomalacia
Vitamin K	Hypothrombinemia
Iron	Anaemia
Iodine	Goitre
Fluoride	Dental caries
Calcium and phosphorus	Affects formation of bones and teeth

Hormone Deficiency	Disease
Insulin	Diabetes
Thyroxine	Cretinism (child), Goitre
STH	Dwarfism, Gigantism

ALLERGIC DISEASE

- In these diseases, body becomes hypersensitive to some foreign agents, allergens, which cause inflammation when come in contact with the body or enter inside the body.

- Foreign agents can be dust, pollens, certain-foods, serum, certain drugs or fabrics.
- The unfavourable response of the body to allergens is called allergic reaction. Asthma and hay fever are allergic diseases.

BACTERIAL DISEASES

- Bacteria are minute organisms which are known to cause a number of diseases:

Disease	Incubation period	Spread through
Tuberculosis	2-10 weeks	Air-borne,droplet infection
Diptheria	2-6 days	Air-borne droplet infection
Cholera	6 hours to 2-3 days	Contaminated food and water. House flies are the vectors
Leprosy	Upto 5 years	Prolonged and intimate contact
Whopping cough	7-14 days	Droplet infection
Tetanus	3-21 days	Entry of cysts through any wound made by sharp object, dog bite or fall on the road
Typhoid	1-3 weeks	Directed and Contact
Plague	2-6 days	Rats and bed-bugs transmit the germs
Pneumonia	1-3 days	Air-borne

VIRAL DISEASES

Disease	Incubation period	Spread through
Chicken-pox	12-20 days	Direct contact with infected persons or infected objects
Smallpox	12 days	Droplet infection
Poliomyalitis	7-14 days	Direct and oral
Measles	10 days	Droplet infection
Mumps	12-26 days	Droplet infection
Rabies	1-3 months	Bite of rabied animal like dogs, monkeys, cats
Influenza	24-28 hours	Air-borne

DISEASES CAUSED BY PROTOZOA

- Amoebiasis (Amoebic dysentery), Malaria, Kala-azar, Trypanosomiasis and Giardiasis are main diseases caused by Protozoans.
- Malaria is a parasitic infection.

SYSTEM OF HUMAN BODY

DIGESTIVE SYSTEM

- The digestive system consists of alimentary canal and digestive glands. Alimentary canal is about 8-10 meters long tube of varying diameter. Food is taken in through mouth.
- The tongue helps in ingestion, chewing, tasting and swallowing of food and mixing of food and saliva.
- Salivary glands secret saliva which helps in digestion of starch. Gastric glands present in the mucosa of the stomach, provide acidic medium for the food digestion.
- Liver, the largest sized, reddish brown gland of body, secrets bile. Liver is present in the right upper part of the abdomen. The bile secreted by the liver is stored in gall bladder. It helps in the emulsification and digestion of fats.
- Pancreas is the second largest gland in human body and secretes pancreatic juices. Intestine also secret juices.

RESPIRATORY SYSTEM

- Oxygen is needed for the oxidation and expelling of carbon dioxide is necessary to avoid its-accumulation. This process of exchange of gases between the environment and the body, is called respiration.
- In some unicellular organisms like aerobic bacteria, amoeba, hydra, etc. there is direct exchange of gases between the carbon dioxide of the body and oxygen of water.
- There is no blood for transport of gases. However, in larger and complex form of animals, specialised respiratory organs are developed.
- Amphibians respire through skin, fishes through gills and mammals, birds and reptiles through lungs.
- A normal adult inspires or expires about 500 ml of gas with each breath and about 72 breathes per minutes.

CIRCULATORY SYSTEM

- Main components of the circulatory system are heart, blood vessels and blood.

- Heart is a thick, muscular, contractile and automatic pumping organ. In birds and mammals, heart is divided into four chambers.
- Arteries are thick walled blood vessels which always carry the blood away from the heart to various body parts.
- Veins are thin walled blood vessels which always carry the blood from various parts generally to the heart.
- In an adult healthy person, the normal rate of heart beat at rest is about 70-72 times per minute.

BLOOD

- It is red, opaque, somewhat sticky and viscous fluid in the body of animals.
- It is slightly alkaline (pH = 7.4), heavier than water (sp gr = 1.05) and five times more viscous than distilled water.
- Blood forms 6 to 10% of the body weight.
- An adult, on average, has about 6.8 litres of blood.
- Blood contains plasma and blood corpuscles with the former occupying 55-60% of the volume.
- Plasma transports food components, metabolic wastes and hormones; keeps constant level of pH of blood, maintains body temperature and helps in blood clotting.
- Erythrocytes or red blood corpuscles (RBCs), leukocytes or white blood corpuscles (WBCs) and blood platelets are other parts of the blood.
- Due to the presence of iron containing pigment haemoglobin, RBCs are red in colour. The RBCs are crucial for ex-change of oxygen and carbon dioxide. WBCs are nucleated and non-pigmented cells. They are larger in size than RBCs but far less in number (1 : 600).
- WBCs play an important role in immune system of the body. Blood platelets cause the coagulation of blood and clot formation to prevent excessive bleeding.
- Human blood is divided into four main Groups— A, B, AB and O.
- The plasma of Group A blood contains an anti-B factor and vice-versa, so that people of Groups A and B cannot accept each other's blood.
- Group AB contains neither anti-A nor anti-B factor and people with this group can receive transfusions from both but can give to neither.
- Group O contains both anti-A and anti-B and can receive blood only from Group O but can donate blood to all Groups. Group O is called universal donor because they can donate to all the Groups.
- Group AB is called universal acceptor because they can accept blood from all Groups.

SKELETON SYSTEM

- The frame or the hard structure of the human body is composed from the bones and the organs of making such frame are called skeleton system.

Bones

- Bone is the hardest tissue of the body and form the largest section of the body weight.
- Bones contain organic as well as inorganic matters. With advancing age, the inorganic matter's share increases, causing the bones to become more brittle.
- Long bones such as humerus and femur are hollow while small bones are solid.

EXCRETORY SYSTEM

- In men, excretory system is formed of one pair of kidneys, one pair of ureters, a urinary bladder and a urethra. Kidney is about 10 cm long, bean shaped, dark-red and slightly flattened structure.
- Sweet glands, oil glands, lungs and liver also act as additional excretory organ.
- In case of kidney failure, a man can treated by hemodialysis or transplantation of a kidney from a donor's body.

NERVOUS SYSTEM

- The system which controls and coordinates the body functions, retains memory and receives and sends signals, is called the nervous system.
- The nervous system comprises brain, spinal cord, nerves and nerve fibres.
- Human brain weighs about 1200 to 1400 gm. Main parts of the brain are cerebrum, cerebellum and medulla oblongata.

- Cerebrum controls voluntary function and is site of intelligence, will power, emotions, etc.
- Cerebellum controls involuntary functions like heart beat, respiration, etc.
- Spinal cord is about 45 cm long and about 35 gm in weight. It conducts impulses to and from the brain and controls reflex actions of the body.
- Various cranial (arising from ending into brain) and spinal nerves (arising from spinal cord) control smell, vision, movements of body parts, taste and hearing.

REPRODUCTION SYSTEM

- In this type of reproduction, there is formation and fusion of sex cells, called gametes.
- Organism develops from the zygote through embryo formation.
- It generally involves two parents — male and female.
- The offsprings are different from the parent as variations appear due to new combinations of genes. So, it plays an important role in evolution.
- All higher plants and animals reproduce sexually.

CHROMOSOMES

- Plants and animals have fixed number of chromosomes per cell.
- Genes are located on chromosomes and are responsible for transfer of characteristics from one cell to the next either in the same organism or from parents to offspring.
- Man has 23 pairs of chromosomes, of which one pair is sex chromosomes.
- Males child inherits X chromosomes from the female parent and Y from the male parent.
- Female child receives a X chromosome each from either of its parents.
- Mendel was the first scientist to explain transmission of units from reproductive cells of the parents to the off-springs.

CLONING

- It is the process of producing genetically identical copies of a biological material, starting from a single cell. The original genes are transplanted and thus one can produce organisms of known and desirable characteristics.

GENETIC ENGINEERING

- It is the method of artificial synthesis of new genes and their subsequent transplantation or methods of correcting the defective genes.
- It has helped in producing plants and animals with specific characters.
- So, crippling hereditary diseases can also be cured like hemophilia etc.

DNA FINGERPRINTING

- It consists of examining repetitive DNA in the genome for variations in the length of restriction fragments.
- Every individual has his own pattern, so that fingerprinting can match blood to a particular person, and patterns are inherited from parent to child, allowing the method to identify relationships between individuals.

IN-VITRO FERTILIZATION

- When a sperm and an egg are made to fertilize outside a living body (usually a test tube), it is called in-vitro fertilization.
- This process has been used to impregnate several females who could not do so through natural means.

Diseases and the Parts of Body they Affect

AIDS—Immune system of body	*Gout*—Joints of bone
Arthritis—Inflammation of joints	*Jaundice*—Liver
Asthma—Lungs	*Meningitis*—Brain or spinal cord
Cataract—Eyes	*Pleurisy*—Pleura (inflammation of)
Conjunctivitis—Eyes	*Polio*—motor neurons
Diabetes—Pancreas	*Pneumonia*—Lungs
Diphtheria—Throat	*Pyorrhoea*—Sockets of teeth
Glaucoma—Eyes	*Tuberculosis*—Lungs
Eczema—Skin	*Typhoid*—Intestine
Goitre—Front of the neck (due to enlargement of thyroid gland)	*Malaria*—Spleen
	Leukaemia—Blood
	Rickets—Bones

SPACE RESEARCH

First in Space

✶ First creator of rules regarding space research	Isaac Newton
✶ First artificial satellite launched in space	Sputnik-1 (1957)
✶ First living being sent in space	Louika (a dog)
✶ Firstever manned spacecraft	Vostok-I
✶ First man in space	Yuri Gagarin U.S.S.R. (1961)
✶ First woman in space	Valentina Tereshkova U.S.S.R. (June 1963)
✶ First man who moved in space out of the spacecraft	Alexi Livonov U.S.S.R. (June 1965)
✶ First person to land on moon	Neil Armstrong, America (21st July, 1969)
✶ First fourwheeled carriage without human being on moon	Leunokhev-I U.S.S.R. (1970)
✶ First space lab in orbit	Skylab (America, 1973)
✶ First space shuttle	Columbia (America, 1981)
✶ First Indian (man) in space	Squadron leader—Rakesh Sharma (13th April, 1984)
✶ First Indian (Woman) in space	Kalpana Chawla (19th Nov., 1997)
✶ First American woman in space	Sailyride (1983)
✶ First spacecraft on Mars	Pathfinder (6 July, 1997)
✶ First woman who lead spacecraft	Allin Collis (America)
✶ First spacecraft without man	Shenzoo, China (20th Nov. 1999)

Indian Space Programme : At a Glance

Satellite	Date	Type	Launch Vehicle	Result
Aryabhatta	19-04-75	Scientific	Cosmos	successful
Bhaskara I	07-06-79	Geosurvey	Cosmos	successful
Rohini	10-08-79	Geosurvey	S.L.V.3	unsuccessful
Rohini D-1	18-07-80	Geosurvey	S.L.V.3	successful
Rohini	31-05-81	Scientific	S.L.V.3	successful
Apple	19-06-81	Communication	Ariane	successful
Bhaskara II	20-11-81	Geosurvey	Cosonos	successful
INSAT-1A	10-04-82	Multipurpose	Delta	unsuccessful
Rohini	17-04-83	Scientific	S.L.V.3	successful
INSAT-1B	30-08-83	Multipurpose	Space Shuttle	successful
SROSS I	24-03-87	Technical	ASLV-D1	unsuccessful
IRS-1A	17-03-88	Remote sensing	Vostok	successful
SROSS II	17-07-88	Technical	ASLV-D2	unsuccessful
INSAT-1C	21-07-88	Multipurpose	Ariane-4	unsuccessful
INSAT-1D	12-06-90	Multipurpose	Delta	successful
IRS-1B	29-08-91	Remote sensing	Vostok	successful
INSAT-2A	10-07-92	Multipurpose	Ariane	successful
INSAT-1D	12-06-90	Multipurpose	Delta	successful
IRS-1B	29-08-91	Remote sensing	Vostok	successful
INSAT-2A	10-07-92	Multipurpose	Ariane	successful
IRS-ID	29-09-97	Remote sensing	PSLV	successful
INSAT-3B	22-03-2000	Multipurpose	Ariane	successful

Satellite	Date	Type	Launch Vehicle	Result
G-SAT-1	18-04-2001	Multipurpose	GSLV-D	successful
INSAT-3E	28-09-2003	Communication	Ariane-5	successful
Cartosat-1 & hamsat	05-05-2005	Maping and Communication	PSLV-C6	successful
CARTOSAT-2	10-01-2007	Communication	PSLV-C7	successful
Chandrayaan-I	22-10-2008	Maping and Scientific	PSLV-C11	successful
Oceansat-2	24-09-2009	Remote Sensing	PSLV-C14	successful
CARTOSAT-2B	12-07-2010	Communication	PSLV-C15	successful
RESOURCESAT-2	20-04-2011	Remote Sensing	PSLV-C16	successful
GSAT-12	15-07-2011	Communication	PSLV-C17	successful
RISAT-1	26-04-2012	Remote Sensing	PSLV-C19	successful
Spot-6	09-09-2012	Remote Sensing	PSLV-C21	successful
Saral	25-02-2013	Scientific	PSLV-C20	successful
GSAT-7	30-08-2013	Defence	Ariane-5	successful
MOM	5-11-2013	Mapping	PSLV-C25	successful
GSAT-14	05-01-2014	Communication	GSLV-D5	successful
IRNSS-1B	04-04-2014	Mapping and Scientific	PSLV-C24	successful
GSAT-16	07-12-2014	Communication	Ariane-5	successful
IRNSS-1D	28-03-2015	Mapping and Scientific	PSLV-C27	successful
GSAT-6	27-08-2015	Communication	GSLV-D6	successful
Astrosat	28-09-2015	Mapping and Scientific	PSLV-C30	successful
IRNSS-1E	20-01-2016	Mapping and Scientific	PSLV-C31	successful
IRNSS-1F	10-03-2016	Mapping and Scientific	PSLV-C32	successful
IRNSS-1G	28-04-2016	Mapping and Scientific	PSLV-C33	successful
Cartosat-2 & others	22-06-2016	Mapping and Scientific	PSLV-C34	successful
insat-3DR	08-09-2016	Meteorology	GSLV-F05	successful
Scatsat-1 & others	26-09-2016	Multipurpose	PSLV-C35	successful
RESOURCESAT-2A	07-12-2016	Remote Sensing	PSLV-C36	successful
CARTOSAT-2 & 103 others	15-02-2017	Multipurpose	PSLV-C37	successful
GSAT-9	06-05-2017	Communication	GSLV MK-II	successful
GSAT-19	05-06-2017	Communication	GSLV MK-III-D1	successful
CARTOSAT-2E	23-06-2017	Earth observation Satellite	PSLV-C38	successful
GSAT-17	29-06-2017	Earth observation Satellite	Ariane-5 ECA	successful
Cartosat-2F & others	12-01-2018	Multipurpose	PSLV-C40	successful
GSAT-6A	29-03-2018	Communication	GSLV-F08	successful
GSAT-7A	19-12-2018	Military Satellite	GSLV-MK-II-F11	successful
Chandrayaan-2	22-07-2019	Lunar Exploration	GSLV MK-III M01	—
Cartosat-3	27-11-2019	Earth Imagine Satellite	PSLV-C47	successful
GSAT-30	17-01-2020	Communication	Ariane-5	successful
EOS-01	07-11-2020	Earth Observation	PSLV-C49	successful
CMS-01/GSAT-12R	17-12-2020	Communication	PSLV-XLC50	successful
Amejonia and 19 others	28-02-2021	Communication	PSLV-C51	successful
EOS-04	14-02-2022	Earth Observation	PSLV-C52	successful
GSAT-24"	23-06-2022	Communication	Ariane-5	successful
DS-E0 and others	30-06-2022	Mapping	PSLV-C53	successful
Oceansat-3 and 8 others	26-11-2022	Earth observation Satellite	PSLV-C54	successful
EOS-07	10-02-2023	Earth observation Satellite	SSLV-02	successful
TeLEOS-2 and LUMILITE-4	22-04-2023	Communication	PSLV-C55	successful
Chandrayaan-3	14-07-2023	Lunar observation	LVM-3	successful
DS-SAR and 6 others	30-07-2023	Earth observation	PSLV-C56	successful
XPoSat	01-01-2024	Earth observation	PSLV-C58	successful

COMPUTER

- The computer is the system of that electronic device through which various informations are processed on the basis of a definite set of instructions called program and mathematical (numerical) and non-mathematical both types of informations are processed.
- The first mechanical computer was composed or fabricated by Blaise Pascal in 1642 and it is called Pascalene.
- But in 1833, Charles Babbage first time conceived an automatic calculator or computer.
- Charles Babbage is called the father of modern computer.
- Herman made an electronic tabulating machine based on punch cards which operates automatically.
- In 1937, first mechanical computer Mark-I was fabricated by Howard Akeen.
- The most outstanding contribution in the development of modern computer goes to John Wan Newmaan who brought the 2nd revolution in the area of computer in 1951.
- He discovered EDVAC (Electronic Discrete Variable Automatic Computer) and utilised the stored program and the binary number system in the computer.

FUNCTIONS OF COMPUTER

- 1. Collection and composition (input) of datas;
  2. Storage of datas.
  3. Processing of datas.
  4. Retrieval or output of the proccessed informations and datas.

UNITS OF COMPUTER

1. Input unit.
2. Central processing unit–CPU.
3. External Memory unit.
4. Output unit.

- The CPU of the computer is called brain of the computer and sometimes CPU is also called Micro Processor of the computer.
- The data is entered through the input unit in the computer and through the central processing unit with the help of External Memory Unit datas are arranged and processed.
- Ultimately by the output unit these datas or informations are issued or released.

PARTS OF COMPUTER

- **Monitor :** The monitor of the computer is like a television in which the picture appears in the form of doted points on the screen and these are called pixels.
- **Hard Disc and Floppy Disc :** The Hard Disc is the permanent disc in the computers while the Floppy Disc is the disc utilised when datas or informations are to be transferred from one computer to another.
- **Mouse :** The mouse of the computer is like the remote control of TV through which computer is directly regulated or controlled without utilising the key-board.
- **Printer :** The printer is a device which prints any documents or processed informations of the computer.

SOME HIGH LEVEL LANGUAGES

1. **FORTRAN :** This language was developed for solving the mathematical formulae very quickly and conveniently.
2. **COBOL :** This language was developed for the commerical purposes. For the processing of this language a group of sentences is selected called paragraph and all paragraphs composed are called a section, while all sections composed are called a division.
3. **BASIC :** In basic a definite part of the prescribed instruction is only inserted in the computer.
4. **ALGOL :** This was basically fabricated and designed for the complex algebraic calculations.
5. **PASCAL :** It is an amplified and modified form of ALGOL.

6. **COMAL :** This computer language is used for the students of secondary level.
7. **LOGO :** This language is used for children and kids for drawing Graphic line diagrams.
8. **PROLOG :** This language is developed in 1973 in France and is used for Artificial Intelligence which is capable and equivalent to the logical program.
9. **FORTH :** This language was invented by Charles Mure which is frequently used in all types of the works in the computer.

COMPUTER VIRUS

- The computer virus is an electronic code which is used to abolish or erradicate the inclusive informations or programs of the computer.
- Some important computer viruses are Micheleanjalo, Dork Avangor, kilo, filip, Macmug, Scores, Casecade, Jeruslem, Date crime, Coloumbs crime, Internet virus, Pachcom, Pach EXE, COM-EXE, Marizuana, C-brain, bloody, Chenge Mungu and Desi etc.

COMPUTER NETWORKING

- There are two types of networkings which are usually occur—Local Area Networking (LAN) and Wide Area Networking (WAN).

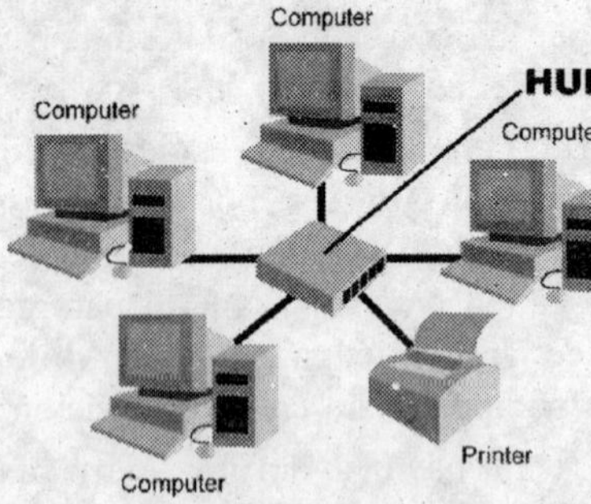

- By LAN all the computers of the same buildings are connected like the computers of university premises, computers of offices etc.
- By WAN all the comptuers of a large area are connected like the computers of all the offices of a city or town etc.
- In India a very large computer network namely INDONET has been installing through which all the main towns and cities has to be interlinked.

COMPUTER TERMINOLOGY

- **Bit :** The bit is a unit of measurement of the electronic data. One bit is either 0 or 1 but not both. On composing 8 bits, 1 byte is formed.
- **Bug :** The Bug is the error in the computer program or system and its eradication is called Debug.
- **Byte :** Total eight bits compose a byte. Thus 8 bits = 1 byte.
- **CD-ROM :** A CD like of music CD in which data can be stored substantially called CD-ROM. In a CD with comparison to floppy extremely more datas can be stored but one problem in it is that one time recorded data can not be deleted or modified.
- **Chip :** It is a thin slice on which by a special mechanism a circuit is designed which is normally made from Silicon.
- **Memory System :** The place where computer data and program are temporarily kept is called Memory system. Usually memory is implied from RAM.
- **Modem :** The device which converts digital signals into analogue signals and vice-versa is called Modem.
- **RAM :** It is Random Access Memory (a place) where datas to be processed are kept temporarily and it is unstable memory.
- **ROM :** It is Read Only Memory and it is stable or Non-valatile memory which doesn't ended after power off.
- **Scanner :** It is a device through which graphic image is transformed to digital image and the scanners are of usually two types one desktop and another hand operating.

PROGRAMING

- Computers perform phenomenal feats of calculation, but they do not do so in a complicated way.

- They actually carry out very simple operations, such as addition and subtraction.
- They achieve their fantastic computing power by carrying out these operations at incredible speed.
- The programme, or set of instructions for operating the computer, is therefore written as a sequence of very simple steps.

Several computer languages have been developed for different applications, including BASIC, COBOL, FORTRAN and PASCAL. Writing programmes is very skilled and time-consuming work.

- But for most typical computer applications ready-written programmes are available, called "packages".

❒ ❒ ❒

GENERAL KNOWLEDGE

FIRST IN THE WORLD

✶ First Chinese visitor to India	*Fahien*
✶ First foreign invader of India	*Alexander, the Great (Greek)*
✶ First person to climb Mt. Everest	*Tenzing Norgay (India) and Edmund Hillary (New Zealand) (1953)*
✶ First atom bomb dropped at	*Hiroshima (Japan)*
✶ First man in the space	*Yuri Gagarin (former USSR)*
✶ First woman in the space	*Valentina Tereshkova (former USSR)*
✶ First person to walk in the space	*Alexei Leonov (former USSR)*
✶ First person to land on the moon	*Neil Armstrong (USA)*
✶ First and the only woman to have climbed Mt. Everest twice	*Santosh Yadav (Indian; May 12, 1992; May 10, 1993)*
✶ First person on Mt. Everest without oxygen	*Phu Dorjee (Indian; May 9, 1984)*
✶ First person to climb Mt. Everest twice	*Nawang Gombu*
✶ First person to climb Mt. Everest maximum times	*Chhewang Nima Sherpa (19 times)*
✶ First President of the USA	*George Washington*
✶ First woman Prime Minister	*Sirimavo Bandaranaike (Sri Lanka)*
✶ First person to swim across English Channel	*Mathew Webb*
✶ First woman to swim across English Channel	*Gertrude Caroline Ederle*
✶ First woman to climb Mt. Everest	*Junko Tabei (Japan)*
✶ First woman to climb Mt. Everest alone and without oxygen supplies	*Alison Hargreaves (Briton: May 13, 1995)*
✶ First Aeroplane to fly around the world without refuelling	*Voyager (Dec. 1986)*
✶ First test-tube Baby	*Louise Brown (UK; 1978)*
✶ First all-talking Film	*Jaz Singer (1927)*
✶ First Secretary-General of the UN	*Trygve Lie (Norway: 1946-53)*
✶ First woman President of the UN General Assembly	*Vijayalakshmi Pandit (India: 1953)*
✶ First woman to reach North Pole	*Ann Bancroft (1986)*
✶ First person to reach North Pole	*Robert Peary*
✶ First person to reach South Pole	*Amundsen (1911)*
✶ First woman to command Spacecraft in Space	*Ellin Collins*

SUPERLATIVES (WORLD)
(The Largest, Biggest, Smallest, Longest, Highest)

Airport	*Largest*	King Fahd International Airport, Dammam (Saudi Arabia)
Animal,	*Tallest*	Giraffe (Average height 6.09 m)
	Largest and Heaviest	Blue Whale (190 tonnes)
	Longest recorded	Boot lace Worm (55 m)
	Fastest	Cheetah (Approximately 100 km/hr)
Bay,	*With max. shore line*	Hudson Bay (Canada: 12268 km)
	With maximum area	Bay of Bengal (India: 217 million hc)
Bridge,	*Highest*	Duge Bridge (China: 1854 ft)
Building,	*Tallest*	Burj Khalifa (Dubai, 818 meter)
Canal,	*Big ship (longest)*	Suez Canal (160 km)
	Busiest	Kiel Canal (North Sea)
Canyon/Gorge,	*Deepest*	Hells Canyon, Snake River (Idaho : 7900 ft)
	Largest	Grand Canyon (Colarado River; USA; 446 km)
Church,	*Largest*	Basilica of St. Peter (Vatican City Rome– Area 23000 sq.m.)
City,	*Largest in Area*	Jiuquan Gansu, China (Area 1,67,996 Sq km)
Continent,	*biggest*	Asia (30,928,605 km^2)
	Smallest	Australia Mainland (Area 8,426,635 km^2)
Country,	*Largest in Population*	China (over 138.5 crore)
	Largest in Area	Russia (17,075,000 sq. km)
	With largest electorate	India (over 90 crores)
	Smallest independent	State of Vatican City (109 acre)
	With most land frontiers	China (16)
Dam,	*Largest (concrete)*	Grand Coulee Dam (1272 m on Columbia River (Washington State, USA)
Delta,	*Largest*	Sundarban's Ganga-Brahmaputra delta (1,05,000 sq. km)
Desert,	*Largest*	Sahara (N. Africa; maximum length 5,150 km EW; maximum width 3,200 km NS)
Dome,	*Largest*	Singapore National Stadium (310 m)
Epic,	*Longest*	Mahabharata
Fish,	*Largest fresh water*	Plabeuk (China, Laos and Thailand)
	Most abundant	Bristle mouth
	Most venomous	Stone Fish (Indo-Pacific Waters)
Film,	*Most Oscars*	Ben Hur (11 Oscars–1959); Titanic (11 Oscars–1998); The Lord of Rings : The Return of the King (11 Oscars—2003).
Fountain,	*Tallest*	King Fahd's Fountain (Jeddah, Saudi Arabia)

Fruit,	*Most nutritive*	Avocado (Vitamins A, C, E and Proteins; Central and South America)
	Least nutritive	Cucumber
Gulf,	*Largest*	Gulf of Mexico (1,544,000 sq. km)
Island,	*Biggest*	Greenland (now known as Kalaatdlit Nunaat–2,175,000 sq km)
Lake,	*Largest*	Caspian Sea (Azerbaijan, Russia, Iran border: 37.18 lakh km^2)
	Deepest	Baikal (Siberia)
	Largest (fresh water)	Superior Lake (USA–Canada border: 82,350 km^2)
Library,	*Biggest*	United States Library of Congress (Washington D.C. founded in 1800, contains 101 million items)
	Biggest non-statutory	New York Public Library
Mountain,	*Highest peak*	Mt. Everest (8848 m; Nepal)
	Highest range	Himalayas, Asia (upto 4200 m)
	Greatest mountain range	Himalaya-Karakoram (96 out of 109 peaks over 7315 m are here)
Museum,	*Largest*	American Museum of Natural History, New York
Ocean,	*Largest and Deepest*	The Pacific (Area: 166,240,000 km^2; Depth: 10,924 m)
Peninsula,	*Largest*	Arabia (3.25 million sq. km)
Places,	*Coldest (annual mean)*	Polus Nedostupnosti (Antarctica –58°C)
	Driest (annual mean)	Desierto de Atacame (near Calama; Chile; rainfall nil)
	Hottest (annual mean)	Dallol (Ethiopia; 34.4°C mean temperature)
	Rainiest (annual mean)	Mowsyrnam near Cherapunji (Meghalaya; India; 11873 mm)
	Windiest	The Commonwealth Bay (Gales reach 320 km/ph)
Planet,	*Biggest*	Jupiter (equatorial diameter 142984 km)
	Brightest, hottest and nearest to Earth	Venus
	Nearest to Sun	Mercury
Plateau,	*Highest*	Tibetan Plateau (Central Asia: 4900 m)
Platform,	*Longest (rail)*	Shree Siddharoodha Swamiji Railway Station Hubballi, Karnataka, India (1507 m. long)
Railway Line,	*Longest*	Trans-Siberian Railway (Moscow-Nakhodka: 9438 km)
Railway Station,	*Largest*	Grand Central Terminal (New York City; 19 hc)
	Highest	Condor (Bolivia; 4786 m)

Religion,	*Oldest*	Hinduism
Religion,	*Largest*	Christianity
Rivers,	*Longest*	(i) Nile (6650 km) (ii) Amazon (6437 km)
Road,	*Longest*	Pan American Highway (from Alaska-Brasila: 24140 km)
Sea,	*Largest*	South China Sea (2,974,600 sq. km)
	Largest (inland)	Mediterranean
Star,	*Brightest*	Sirius A (also called Dog Star)
Swimming	*Longest*	English Channel
Telescope,	*Largest (radio)*	Five Hundred meter Apertune Spherical Telescope (FAST), China.
	Largest (solar)	Kitt Peak National Observatory, (Arizona; USA)
	Largest refractor	At Yerkes observatory (Wisconsin; USA; 18.9 m)
Temple,	*Largest*	Angkor Wat (Cambodia: 402 acres)
Tower,	*Tallest*	Tokyo Sky Tree (634 m.)
Train,	*Fastest*	Japan's magnetically levitated (magler) train (Speed over 500 km/hr)
Tunnel,	*Longest (railway)*	Gotthard Base Rail Tunnel (Switzerland; 57.1 km)
	Largest (road)	Laerdal, Norway (24.51 km)
Volcano	*Greatest concentration in*	Indonesia
	Highest (extinct)	Cerro Aconcagua (6960 m; Andes)
	Highest (dormant)	Volcan Llullaillaco (6723 m; Argentina-Chile)
	Highest (active)	Ojos del Salado (Chile-Argentina)
Waterfall,	*Highest*	Salto-Angel (in Venezuela on a branch of river Carrao, depth 807 m.)
	Largest	Khone Falls (Laos; width 10.8 km)

CAPITAL & CURRENCIES

Country	*Capital*	*Currency*
∗ Afghanistan	Kabul	Afghani
∗ Albania	Tirana	Lek
∗ Algeria	Algiers	Dinar
∗ Angola	Luanda	New Kwanza
∗ Argentina	Buenos Aires	Peso
∗ Armenia	Yeravan	Dram
∗ Australia	Canberra	Dollar
∗ Austria	Vienna	Euro
∗ Azerbaijan	Baku	Manat
∗ Bahrain	Manama	Dinar
∗ Bangladesh	Dhaka	Taka
∗ Barbados	Bridgetown	Dollar
∗ Belarus	Minsk	Ruble
∗ Belgium	Brussels	Euro
∗ Benin	Porto Novo	Franc
∗ Bhutan	Thimphu	Ngultrum[1]
∗ Bolivia	La paz	Dollar
∗ Botswana	Gaborone	Pula

Country	Capital	Currency
∗ Brazil	Brasilia	Real
∗ Bosnia Herzegovina	Sarajevo	Dinar
∗ Bulgaria	Sofia	Lev
∗ Cambodia	Phnom-Penh	Riel
∗ Canada	Ottawa	Dollar
∗ Chile	Santiago	Peso
∗ China	Beijing	Yuan
∗ Colombia	Bogota	Peso
∗ Congo	Brazzaville	Franc
∗ Croatia	Zagreb	Kuna
∗ Cuba	Havana	Peso
∗ Cyprus	Nicosia	Euro
∗ Czech Republic	Prague	Koruna
∗ Denmark	Copenhagen	Krone
∗ Ecuador	Quito	Sucre
∗ Egypt	Cairo	Pound
∗ Estonia	Tallinn	Euro
∗ Ethiopia	Addis Ababa	Birr
∗ Fiji	Suva	Dollar
∗ Finland	Helsinki	Euro
∗ France	Paris	Euro
∗ Georgia	Tbilisi	Lari
∗ Germany	Berlin	Euro
∗ Ghana	Accra	Cedi
∗ Greece	Athens	Euro
∗ Guatemala	Guatemala City	Quetzal
∗ Guyana	George Town	Dollar
∗ Hungary	Budapest	Forint
∗ Iceland	Reykjavik	Krona
∗ India	New Delhi	Rupee
∗ Indonesia	Jakarta	Rupiah
∗ Iran	Teheran	Rial
∗ Iraq	Baghdad	Dinar
∗ Ireland	Dublin	Euro
∗ Israel	Jerusalem	Shekel
∗ Italy	Rome	Euro
∗ Jamaica	Kingston	Dollar
∗ Japan	Tokyo	Yen
∗ Jordan	Amman	Dinar

Country	Capital	Currency
∗ Kazakhstan	Akmola	Tenge
∗ Kenya	Nairobi	Shilling
∗ Korea (S)	Seoul	Won
∗ Korea (N)	Pyongyang	Won
∗ Kyrgyzstan	Bishkek	Som
∗ Kuwait	Kuwait City	Dinar
∗ Laos	Vientiane	Kip
∗ Latvia	Riga	Euro
∗ Lebanon	Beirut	Pound
∗ Liberia	Monrovia	Dollar
∗ Libya	Tripoli	Dinar
∗ Lithuania	Vilnius	Litas
∗ Luxembourg	Luxembourg	Euro
∗ Macedonia	Skopje	Dinar
∗ Malawi	Lilongwe	Kwacha
∗ Malaysia	Kuala Lumpur	Ringgit
∗ Maldives	Male	Rufiyaa
∗ Mali	Bamako	Franc
∗ Mauritius	Port Louis	Rupee
∗ Mexico	Mexico City	Peso
∗ Moldavia	Chisinau	Leu
∗ Mongolia	Ulan Bator	Tugrik
∗ Morocco	Rabat	Dirham
∗ Mozambique	Maputo	Metical
∗ Myanmar	Nay Pyi Taw	Kyat
∗ Namibia	Winohoek	Dollar
∗ Nepal	Kathmandu	Rupee
∗ Netherlands	Amsterdam	Euro
∗ New Zealand	Wellington	Dollar
∗ Nigeria	Abuja	Naira
∗ Norway	Oslo	Krone
∗ Oman	Muscat	Rial
∗ Pakistan	Islamabad	Rupee
∗ Panama	Panama City	Balboa
∗ Peru	Lima	New Sole
∗ Philippines	Manila	Peso
∗ Poland	Warsaw	Zloty
∗ Portugal	Lisbon	Euro
∗ Qatar	Doha	Riyal
∗ Romania	Bucharest	Leu
∗ Russia	Moscow	Ruble

Country	Capital	Currency
∗ Saudi Arabia	Riyadh	Rial
∗ Senegal	Dakar	Franc
∗ Slovakia	Bratislava	Euro
∗ Spain	Madrid	Euro
∗ Sri Lanka	Colombo	Rupee
∗ Sudan	Khartoum	Dinar
∗ Suriname	Paramaribo	Guilder
∗ Sweden	Stockholm	Krona
∗ Switzerland	Berne	Swiss Francs
∗ Syria	Damascus	Pound
∗ South Africa	Capetown (Legislative) Pretoria *(Administrative)*	Rand
∗ Tadzhikistan	Dushanbe	Ruble
∗ Taiwan	Taipei	Dollar
∗ Tanzania	Dodoma	Shilling

Country	Capital	Currency
∗ Thailand	Bangkok	Baht
∗ Tunisia	Tunis	Dinar
∗ Turkey	Ankara	Lira
∗ Turkmania	Ashikabad	Manat
∗ Uganda	Kampala	Shilling
∗ Ukraine	Kiev	Hyrvnia
∗ United Arab Emirates	Abu Dhabi	Dirham
∗ U.K.	London	Pound Sterling
∗ U.S.A.	Washington	Dollar
∗ Uruguay	Montevideo	Peso
∗ Uzbekistan	Tashkent	Som
∗ Venezuela	Caracas	Bolivar
∗ Vietnam	Hanoi	Dong
∗ Yemen	Sana'a	Rial
∗ Zimbabwe	Harare	Dollar
∗ Congo (Zaire)	Kinshasa	Zaire
∗ Zambia	Lusaka	Kwacha

GEOGRAPHICAL EXPLORATIONS/DISCOVERIES

Place	Explorer/Discoverer	Nationality	Year
America	Christopher Columbus	Italy	1492
Hawaii Islands (Sandwich Islands)	Captain James Cook	England	1778
Newfoundland	John Cabot	England	1497
New Zealand	Abel Janszoon Tasman	Holland	1642
North Pole	Robert Peary	USA	1909
Sea Route to India (via Cape of Good Hope)	Vasco da Gama	Portugal	1498
South Pole	Roald Amundsen	Norway	1911

NATIONAL MONUMENTS OF SOME FAMOUS COUNTRIES

Monument	Country	Monument	Country
Great Wall of China	China	Pyramid (Giza)	Egypt
Taj Mahal (Agra)	India	Kinder Disk	Denmark
Emperial Palace (Tokyo)	Japan	Leaning Tower of Pisa	Italy
Opera House (Sydney)	Australia	Statue of Liberty (New York)	USA
Eiffel Tower (Paris)	France	Kremlin (Moscow)	Russia

INTELLIGENCE AGENCIES OF SOME PROMINENT COUNTRIES

Country	Intelligence Agency
∗ India	*Research & Analysis Wing (RAW), Intelligence Bureau (I.B.), Central Bureau of Investigation (C.B.I.)*
∗ Pakistan	*Inter Service Intelligence (I.S.I.)*
∗ U.S.A.	*Central Intelligence Agency (CIA), Federal Bureau of Investigation (FBI)*
∗ Britain	*Military Intelligence (M.I.)-5 and 6, Special Branch, Ultra, Joint Intelligence Organisation*
∗ Israel	*Mosad*
∗ Egypt	*Mukhabarat*
∗ Japan	*Nicho*
∗ Russia	*K.G.B. (Komitel Gosudarstvennoy Bezopasnosty) (Committee for State Security)*
∗ Canada	*Security Intelligence Service (SIS)*
∗ S. Africa	*Bureau of State Security (BSS)*
∗ Iran	*Sabak*
∗ Iraq	*Al-Mukhabarat*
∗ Australia	*Australian Security and Intelligence Organisation (ASIO)*
∗ France	*S.D.E.C.E.*
∗ Spain	*C.E.S.I.D.*

MAJOR LANGUAGES OF THE WORLD AND THEIR SPEAKERS

Listing the languages spoken by approximately 1% of humankind (those spoken by more than 60,000,000 people), this table enumerates speakers of each tongue as a primary language.

Language	Speakers (millions)
∗ Chinese	1,322
∗ Spanish	471
∗ English	369
∗ Arabic	349
∗ Hindi	342
∗ Portuguese	232
∗ Bengali	228
∗ Russian	153
∗ Japanese	126
∗ Lahnda	99
∗ Punjabi (Western)	93
∗ Javanese	84
∗ Marathi	83
∗ Telugu	82
∗ Turkish	82
∗ Malay	81
∗ French	79
∗ Korean	77
∗ Tamil	77
∗ German	76
∗ Vietnamese	76
∗ Urdu	69
∗ Italian	64
∗ Persian	65

Source : The World Almanac 2022

IMPORTANT NEWS AGENCIES OF THE WORLD

Agency	Country
PTI, UNI, UNIVARTA	India
Antara	Indonesia
Tanjug	Serbia
Associated Press (AP)	America
Reuters, NAFEN	United Kingdom
Angence France Press (AFP)	France
TASS	Russia

NAME OF PARLIAMENTS OF SOME COUNTRIES

Country	Name of Parliament	Country	Name of Parliament
Afghanistan	Shora	Norway	Storting
Argentina	National Congress	Poland	Sejm
Australia	Federal Parliament	Russia	Federal Assembly (Council of the Federation and State Duma
Austria	National Assembly	South Africa	National Assembly and Senate
Bangladesh	Jatiya Sansad	Spain	Cortes Generales
India	Lok Sabha and Rajya Sabha	Sweden	Riksdag
Bhutan	Tshogdu (National Assembly)	Switzerland	Federal Assembly (Nationalrat and Standerat)
Britain	House of Commons and House of Lords	North Korea	Supreme People's Assembly
Canada	House of Commons and Senate	South Korea	National Assembly
China	National People Congress	U.S.A.	Congress (Senate and House of Representatives)
Denmark	Folketing	Ethiopia	Federal Council and House of Representatives
Iran	Majlis (Islamic Consultative Assembly)	Iceland	Alpingi
Israel	Knesset	Bulgaria	National Assembly
Japan	Diet	Cuba	National Assembly of People's Power
Myanmar	Pyithu Hluttaw (People's Assembly)		
Nepal	Rashtriya Panchayat		
The Netherlands	States-General		

LARGEST AND SMALLEST COUNTRIES (Top 5)

Largest Country (Area-wise)	Largest Country (Population-wise)	Smallest Country (Area-wise)	Smallest Country (Population-wise)
Russia	China	Vatican City	Vatican City
Canada	India	Monaco	Tuvalu
China	USA	Nauru	Palau
United States	Indonesia	Tuvalu	San Marino
Brazil	Brazil	San Marino	Liechstein

MAJOR RELIGIONS OF THE WORLD

Religion	Member	Percentage	Religion	Member	Percentage
Christianity	2.5 billion	32.2%	Buddhism	545 million	6.9%
Islam	1.9 billion	24.7%	Sikhism	27 million	0.27%
Hinduism	1.0 billion	13.5%	Jews	14 million	0.14%

NATIONAL EMBLEMS OF IMPORTANT COUNTRIES

Country	National Emblem	Country	National Emblem
America	Golden Rod	Australia	Kangaroo
Ireland	Shamrock	Italy	White Lily
Israel	Candelabrum	Iran	Rose
Canada	White Lily	Great Britain	Rose
Chile	Candor and Huemul	Germany	Corn Flower
Japan	Chrysanthemum	Zimbabwe	Zimbabwe Bird
Denmark	Beach	Turkey	Crescent and Star
The Netherlands	Lion	New Zealand	Kiwi, Fern Southern Cross
Norway	Lion	Nepal	Kukri
Pakistan	Crescent	Poland	Eagle
France	Lily	Belgium	Lion
Bangladesh	Water Lily	Mongolia	The Soyombo
Russia	Double headed eagle	Lebanon	Cedar Tree
Sudan	Secretary Bird	Syria	Eagle
India	Lioned Capital		

FIRST IN INDIA

∗ The first Indian to get the Nobel Prize for Literature	*Rabindra Nath Tagore*
∗ The first Indian to get the Nobel Prize for Physics	*C.V. Raman*
∗ The first Indian to get the Nobel Prize for Peace	*Mother Teresa*
∗ The first Indian to get the Nobel Prize for Economics	*Amartya Sen*
∗ The first Indian to get Special Oscar award (1992)	*Satyajit Ray*
∗ The first and the last Indian Governor-General of free India	*C. Rajagopalachari*
∗ The first woman to become the Governor of a State	*Smt. Sarojini Naidu*
∗ The first Indian Chief of the Army Staff*	*General K.M. Cariappa*
∗ The first ever woman to become the Chief Minister of a State	*Smt. Sucheta Kripalani*
∗ The first Indian woman President of UN General Assembly	*Smt. Vijaylakshmi Pandit*
∗ The first Indian to become the President of International Court of Justice	*Dr. Nagendra Singh*
∗ The first Indian woman to swim across the English Channel	*Ms. Aarti Saha*
∗ The first Indian girl to become Miss Universe	*Miss Sushmita Sen*
∗ The first Indian girl to become Miss World	*Rita Faria*
∗ The first Indian to swim across the English Channel	*Mihir Sen*
∗ The first Field Marshal	*S.H.F.J. Manekshaw*
∗ The first Indian recipient of Victoria Cross	*Khudadad Khan*
∗ The first Indian to conquer Mt. Everest	*Sherpa Tenzing (May 29, 1953)*
∗ The first Indian Cosmonaut (man)	*Rakesh Sharma (April 3, 1984)*

∗ The first Indian Cosmonaut (woman)	*Kalpana Chawla (Nov. 19, 1997)*
∗ The first woman to climb Mt. Everest	*Miss Bachendri Pal (May 23, 1984)*
∗ The first ICS	*Satyendranath Tagore*
∗ The first to address the UN General Assembly in Hindi	*Atal Bihari Vajpayee*
∗ The first Newspaper	*Bengal Gazette (Jan 27, 1780)*
∗ The first Postage Stamp issued	*In 1852*
∗ The first Telegraph line laid	*In 1851 (Calcutta-Diamond Harbour)*
∗ The first Railways run	*April 16, 1853 (Bombay-Thane)*
∗ The first Electric Train run	*1925 (Bombay-Kurla)*
∗ The first Atomic Power Station	*Tarapore (Maharashtra)*
∗ The first passenger-cum-cargo ship made in India	*Harshavardhan*
∗ The first Satellite	*Aryabhatta (1975)*
∗ The first President of the Indian National Congress	*W.C. Banerjee*
∗ The first President of Indian Republic	*Dr. Rajendra Prasad*
∗ The first woman judge of the Supreme Court	*Ms Fatima Bibi*
∗ The first to climb Everest without oxygen	*Phu Dorjee (1987)*
∗ The first film (movie)	*Raja Harishchandra*
∗ The first film (talkie)	*Alam Ara*
∗ The first Metro Railway	*Calcutta Metro Railway*
∗ The first Test-tube baby, scientifically documented	*Born on August 6, 1986 at K.E.M. Hospital, Bombay*
∗ The first TV Centre	*At Delhi*
∗ The first Indian to get an Oscar	*Bhanu Athaiya*
∗ The first woman pilot in IAF	*Ms Harita Kaur Deol*
∗ The first woman to get Olympic Medal	*Karnam Malleswari*
∗ The first woman Foreign Secretary	*Chokila Iyer*

SUPERLATIVES (INDIA)

Highest, Biggest, Largest and Longest in India

∗ Award for Gallantry, highest	*Param Vir Chakra*
∗ Award, highest civilian	*Bharat Ratna*
∗ Bank, with largest number of branches	*State Bank of India*
∗ Road Bridge, Longest	*Bhupen Hazarika Bridge, Assam (9.15 km)*
∗ Road and Rail Bridge, Longest	*Bogibeel Bridge, Brahmaputra River, Assam*
∗ Cattle Fair, Largest	*Sonepur (Bihar)*
∗ City, Most Populous	*Mumbai metropolis*
∗ Corridor, Longest	*Rameshwaram Temple corridor (4,000 ft.)*
∗ Desert, Largest	*Thar (Rajasthan)*
∗ Dam, Longest	*Hirakud Dam (Odisha)*
∗ Delta, Largest	*Sunderban's Delta*

✶ Dome, Largest	*Gol Gumbaj (Bijapur)*
✶ Dam, Highest	*Tehri Dam (260 m)*
✶ Gateway, Highest	*Buland Darwaja at Fatehpur Sikri (176 ft.)*
✶ Fresh Water Lake, Largest	*Wular Lake (Kashmir)*
✶ Literacy, Highest	*Kerala (94%)*
✶ Museum, Largest	*Indian Museum (Kolkata)*
✶ Mosque, Biggest	*Jama Masjid (Delhi)*
✶ Peak, Highest**	*K-2 (Pak-Occupied Kashmir)*
✶ Platform, Longest	*Shree Siddharoodha Swamiji Railway Station Hubballi, Karnataka (1507 m. long)*
✶ Railway Bridge, longest	*Vembanad Bridge, Kerala (4.6 km)*
✶ River, Longest***	*The Ganges (2525 Km)*
✶ Rainfall, Highest (annual mean)	*Mowsynram near Cherrapunji (1178 cm)*
✶ Road Longest	*Grand Trunk Road (1,500 miles)*
✶ State, with maximum forest cover	*Madhya Pradesh*
✶ State, with maximum density of population	*Bihar*
✶ Telescope, Largest in Asia	*Vainu Bappu Telescope (at Kavalur: Chennai) 2.34m*
✶ Tunnel, Longest (Road)	*Dr. Shyama Prasad Mukherjee Tunnel (9.28 kms, J & K)*
✶ Tunnel, Longest (Railway)	*Pir Panjal Tunnel, between Qazigund to Banihal (11.21 kms) Jammu & Kashmir.*
✶ Tallest Minaret	*Qutub Minar (Delhi 72.5 m.)*
✶ Waterfall, Highest	*Kunchikal Waterfall (Karnataka: 455 m.)*
✶ Zoo, Largest	*Zoological Gardens (Kolkata)*

** *Highest peak in the world is Mount Everest, which is in Nepal. K-2 is the second highest peak in the world. It is 8,611 metres high.*

*** *Indus and Brahmaputra (each 2900 km). Both of them, however, cover a long distance outside India.*

TABLE OF PRECEDENCE

1. President
2. Vice-President
3. Prime Minister
4. Governors of States within their respective states
5. Former Presidents

5A. Deputy Prime Minister

6. Chief Justice of India, Speaker of Lok Sabha
7. Cabinet Ministers of the Union, Chief Ministers of States within their respective States
   Deputy Chairman NITI Aayog, former Prime Ministers
   Leaders of opposition in Rajya Sabha and Lok Sabha

7A. Holders of the Bharat Ratna Decoration

8. Ambassadors Extraordinary and Plenipotentiary and High Commissioners of Commonwealth Countries accredited to India, Chief Ministers of States outside their respective States
9. Judges of the Supreme Court
10. Deputy Chairman Rajya Sabha, Deputy Chief Minister of States, Deputy Speaker Lok Sabha, Members of the NITI Aayog, Minister of State of the Union and Other Minister in the Ministry of Defence.

BOOKS AND AUTHORS

FOREIGN

Book	Author
✶ As You Like It	*William Shakespeare*
✶ A Tale of Two Cities	*Charles Dickens*
✶ Ben Hur	*Lewis Wallace*
✶ Das Kapital	*Karl Marx*
✶ David Copperfield	*Charles Dickens*
✶ Hamlet	*William Shakespeare*
✶ Iliad	*Homer*
✶ Inferno	*A. Dante*
✶ In Memoriam	*Lord Tennyson*
✶ Ivanhoe	*Walter Scott*
✶ Julius Caesar	*William Shakespeare*
✶ Lady Chatterley's Lover	*D.H. Lawrence*
✶ Lajja	*Taslima Nasreen*
✶ Les Miserable	*Victor Hugo*
✶ Leviathan	*Thomas Hobbes*
✶ Lolita	*V. Nobokov*
✶ Lycidas	*John Milton*
✶ Mein Kampf	*Adolf Hitler*
✶ Moor's Last Sigh	*Salman Rushdie*
✶ Mother	*Maxim Gorky*
✶ Mother India	*Katherine Mayo*
✶ Nana	*Emile Zola*
✶ Odyssey	*Homer*
✶ Origin of Species	*Charles Darwin*
✶ Othello	*William Shakespeare*
✶ Paradise Lost	*John Milton*
✶ Paradise Regained	*John Milton*
✶ Path to Power	*Margaret Thatcher*
✶ Pickwick Papers	*Charles Dickens*
✶ Razor's Edge	*Somerset Maugham*
✶ Republic	*Plato*
✶ The Tempest	*William Shakespeare*
✶ Time Machine	*H.G. Wells*
✶ Tom Sawyer	*Mark Twain*
✶ Treasure Island	*R.L. Stevenson*
✶ Twelfth Night	*William Shakespeare*
✶ Unto This Last	*John Ruskin*
✶ Utopia	*Thomas More*
✶ Wealth of Nations	*Adam Smith*
✶ Wonder that was India	*A.L. Basham*

INDIAN

Book	Author
✶ Ain-i-Akbari	*Abul Fazal*
✶ Anand Math	*Bankim Chandra Chatterjee*
✶ Arthashastra	*Kautilya*
✶ A Suitable Boy	*Vikram Seth*
✶ Bhagwat Gita	*Ved Vyas*
✶ Chidambara	*Sumitranandan Pant*
✶ Devdas	*Sarat Chandra Chatterjee*
✶ Discovery of India	*Jawaharlal Nehru*
✶ Ganadevata	*Tarashankar Bandopadhyaya*
✶ Geet Govind	*Jaya Dev*
✶ Geetanjali	*R. N. Tagore*
✶ Glimpses of World History	*Jawaharlal Nehru*
✶ Godaan	*Prem Chand*
✶ Gul-e-Nagma	*Firaq Gorakhpuri*
✶ Harsh Charita	*Bana Bhatta*
✶ India Divided	*Dr. Rajendra Prasad*
✶ Justice of Peace ke Aansu	Janardan Prasad Singh
✶ The Judgement	*Kuldip Nayyar*
✶ Kadambari	*Bana Bhatta*
✶ Kagaz Te Kanwas	*Amrita Pritam*
✶ Kamayani	*Jai Shankar Prasad*
✶ Kitni Nawon Mein Kitni Bar	*S. H. Vatsyayan*
✶ Kumar Sambhav	*Kalidas*
✶ Mahabharata	*Ved Vyas*
✶ Malgudi Days	*R.K. Narayan*
✶ Meghdoot	*Kalidas*
✶ Mritunjaya	*B.K. Bhattacharya*
✶ Mudrarakshasa	*Vishakhadatta*
✶ Prison Diary	*Jaya Prakash Narayan*
✶ Raghuvansha	*Kalidas*
✶ Rajtarangini	*Kalhana*
✶ Ramayana	*Balmiki*
✶ Ramcharit Manas	*Tulsidas*
✶ Rukh Te Rishi	*Harbhajan Singh*
✶ Satyarth Prakash	*Swami Dayanand*
✶ Sur Sagar	*Surdas*
✶ The Guide	*R.K. Narayan*

IMPORTANT DATES AND DAYS OF THE YEAR

⁎ JANUARY

- **5-11** Road Safety Week
- **12** National Youth Day
- **15** Army Day
- **15-21** Pin Code Week
- **23** National Day of Patriotism
- **26** Republic Day
- **30** Martyr's Day

⁎ FEBRUARY

- **1-14** Oil Conservation Fortnight
- **14** Valentine's Day

⁎ MARCH

- **4** National Safety Day
- **8** International Women's Day
- **15** Consumers' Day
- **16** Immunisation Day
- **21** World Forest Day
- **22** World Day for Water
- **24** World Meteorological Day
- **1-7** Preservation of Blindness Week

⁎ APRIL

- **7** World Health Day
- **7-13** Handloom Week
- **14-20** Fire Service Week
- **18** World Heritage Day
- **22** World Earth Day

⁎ MAY

- **1** May Day
- **5** National Labour Day
- **8** World Red Cross Day
- **11** National Technology Day
- **15** International Day of the Family
- **17** World Telecommunication Day
- **24** Commonwealth Day
- **31** World No-Tobacco Day

⁎ JUNE

- **5** World Environment Day
- **21** World Yoga Day
- **26** International Day against Drug Abuse and Illicit Trafficking

⁎ JULY

- **11** World Population Day

⁎ AUGUST

- **1-7** World Breast feeding Week
- **10** Sanskrit Divas
- **15** Independence Day
- **20** Sadbhavana Divas

⁎ SEPTEMBER

- **1-7** National Nutrition Week
- **5** Teachers' Day
- **8** International Literary Day
- **14** Hindi Diwas
- **23** World Deaf Day
- **27** World Tourism Day

⁎ OCTOBER

- **2** Gandhi Jayanti
  International Day of Non Violence
  Anti-Leprosy Day
- **4** World Animal Day
- **6** World Habitat Day *(Ist Monday)*
- **8** Indian Air Force Day
- **14** World Standard Day
- **15** International Day of Rural Women
- **16** World Food Day
- **24** United Nations Day
- **27** Infantry Day
- **28** World Thrift Day
- **31** Anti-Terrorism Day

⁎ NOVEMBER

- **2** All Saints Day
- **14** Children's Day
- **15-21** National Cooperative Week
- **19-25** Quami Ekta Week
- **20** Child Rights Day
- **26** Constitution Day

⁎ DECEMBER

- **1** World AIDS Day
- **3** World Day for the Disabled
- **4** Naval Day
- **7** Flag Day
- **8** SMRC Day
- **10** Human Rights Day
- **14** National Energy Conservation Day

INDIAN DEFENCE

- The Supreme Command of the Armed Forces is vested in the hands of the President of the Country.
- The responsibility for national defence, however, rests with the Cabinet. All important questions having a bearing on defence are decided by the Cabinet Committee on Political Affairs, which is presided over by the Prime Minister.
- The Defence Minister is responsible to Parliament for all matters concerning the Defence Services.
- All the administrative and operational control of Armed Forces are exercised by the Ministry of Defence. The three services—Army, Navy and Air Force function through their respective service head-quarters headed by the chief of Staff. The post of Chief of Defence Staff (CDS) was created in 2019.

Indian Army Commands

Command	HQ Location
Eastern Command	Kolkata
Western Command	Chandigarh
Northern Command	Udhampur
Southern Command	Pune
Central Command	Lucknow
Training Command	Shimla
South-Western Command	Jaipur

Indian Air Force Commands

Command	HQ Location
Western Air Command	New Delhi
Sout-Western Air Command	Gandhinagar
Central Air Command	Allahabad
Eastern Air Command	Shillong
Southern Air Command	Thiruvananthapuram
Training Command	Bengaluru

Indian Navy Commands

Command	HQ Location
Eastern Naval Command	Vishakhapatnam
Western Naval Command	Mumbai
Southern Naval Command	Cochin

Commissioned Ranks in Defence Services

Army	Navy	Air Force
General	Admiral	Air Chief Marshal
Lieutenant-General	Vice-Admiral	Air Marshal
Major-General	Rear-Admiral	Air Vice-Marshal
Brigadier	Commodor	Air Commodor
Colonel	Captain	Group Captain
Lieutenant-Colonel	Commander	Wing Commander
Major	Lt.Commander	Squadron Leader
Captain	Lieutenant	Flight Lieutenant
Lieutenant	Sub-Lieutenant	Flying Officer

Internal Security Organisations of India

S. No.	Name of Organisation	Year of Creation	Headquarters
1.	Assam Rifles (A.R.)	1835	Shillong
2.	Central Reserve Police Force (CRPF)	1939	New Delhi
3.	Territorial Army	1948	In different States
4.	Indo-Tibetan Border Police	1962	New Delhi
5.	Home Guard	1962	In different States

S. No.	Name of Organisation	Year of Creation	Headquarters
6.	Coast Guard	1978	New Delhi
7.	Border Security Force (B.S.F.)	1965	New Delhi
8.	Central Industrial Security Force (CISF)	1969	New Delhi
9.	National Security Guard	1984	New Delhi
10.	Police	—	In different States

Army Institutes

1.	Sainik Schools upto +2 Level	33 places in India
2.	Rashtriya Indian Military College (prepare for entrance to N.D.A.)	Dehradun
3.	National Defence Academy (three services)	Khadakwasla, Pune
4.	Indian Military Academy (Army)	Dehradun
5.	Officers Training Academy (3 services) Short Courses	Chennai
6.	National Defence College	New Delhi
7.	The College of Combat	Mhow
8.	The College of Military Engineering	Kirkee
9.	Military College of Telecommunication Engineering	Mhow
10.	The Armoured Corps Centre and School	Ahmed Nagar
11.	The School Artillery	Deolali
12.	The Infantry School	Mhow and Belgaum
13.	College of Material Management	Jabalpur

Air Force Institutions

✶ Air Force Academy	Hyderabad	✶ Helicopter Training School	Hakimpet
✶ Flying Instructors School	Tambaram, Chennai	✶ The College of Air Warfare	Secunderabad
✶ Air Force Administrative College	Coimbatore	✶ Air Force Technical College	Jalahalli

UNITED NATIONS (UN)

- The United Nations (UN) is an association of states which have pledged themselves to maintain international peace and security and cooperate in solving international political, economic, social cultural and humanitarian problems towards achieving this end.
- Trygve Lie of Norway (1946-52) was the first Secretary-General of the UN.
- ***Origin:*** UN Charter was signed by 50 members on June 26, 1945. Poland signed the charter later to become one of the original 51 member-states. It officially came into existence on October 24, 1945.
- ***UN Charter:*** The Charter is the Constitution of the UN and contains its aims and objectives and rules and regulations for its functioning.
- ***Aims and Objectives:*** They are security, welfare and human rights.
- ***Headquarters:*** New York.
- ***Flag:*** The flag is light blue in colour, and emblazoned in white, in its centre is the UN symbol—a polar map of world embraced by twin olive branches open at the top.
- ***Official Languages:*** The official languages of the UN are: English, French, Chinese, Russian, Arabic and Spanish. However, working languages are English and French only.

- ***Present Membership:*** At present 193 countries are members of the UN. South Sudan is the latest entrant to this world organisation.
- ***Main Organs of the UN:*** There are six main organs:
  1. General Assembly
  2. Security Council
  3. Economic and Social Council
  4. Trusteeship Council
  5. International Court of Justice, and
  6. Secretariat.

  1. *General Assembly:* It consists of representative of all members of the UN. Each member country has only one vote. It meets once a year and passes UN Budget. It is the main place for discussions and policy making in the UN.
  2. *Security Council:* It is the Executive body of the UN and is mainly responsible for maintaining international peace and security. It has 15 members, 5 of which (USA, UK, France, Russia and China) are permanent members. The 10 non-permanent members are elected by General Assembly for two-year term and are not eligible for immediate re-election.
  3. *Economic and Social Council:* It has 54 members elected by General Assembly.
  4. *Trusteeship Council:* It looks after interest of the people in areas not yet independent and leads them towards self-government.
  5. *International Court of Justice:* It has 15 judges, no two of whom may be nationals of the same state. They are elected by General Assembly and Security Council for a term of 9 years. The Court elects its President and Vice-President for a 3-year term.
  6. *Secretariat:* It is the Secretariat of the UN and is headed by the Secretary General.

Some Important UN Agencies

UN Agencies	Headquarters	Year of Establishment
* United Nations (U.N.)	New York	1945
* International Monetary Fund (I.M.F.)	Washington D.C.	1945
* World Health Organisation (W.H.O.)	Geneva	1948
* Food & Agricultural Organisation (FAO)	Rome	1945
* International Labour Organisation (ILO)	Geneva	1919
* UNESCO	Paris	1946
* Universal Postal Union (UPU)	Berne	1874
* UNIDO	Vienna	1966
* International Atomic Energy Agency (IAEA)	Vienna	1957
* United Nations Development Programme (UNDP)	New York	1965
* UNICEF	New York	1946
* International Maritime Organisation (IMO)	London	1958
* World Meteorological Organisation (WMO)	Geneva	1950
* International Telecommunication Union (ITU)	Geneva	1865
* World Trade Organisation (WTO)	Geneva	1995
* International Development Association (IDA)	Washington D.C.	1960
* World Intellectual Property Organisation (WIPO)	Geneva	1967

Famous International Organisations

International Organisations	Headquarters	Year of Establishment
∗ International Court of Justice	The Hague	1946
∗ International Civil Aviation Organisation (ICAO)	Montreal	1947
∗ International Finance Corporation (IFC)	Washington D.C	1956
∗ Arab League	Cairo	1945
∗ Commonwealth of Nations	London	1949
∗ International Bank for Reconstruction and Development (IBRD)	Washington D.C.	1945
∗ Organisation of Islamic Cooperation (OIC)	Jeddah (Saudi Arabia)	1969
∗ Red Cross	Geneva	1863
∗ Interpol	Lyons	1923
∗ Asian Development Bank (ADB)	Manila	1966
∗ North Atlantic Treaty Organisation (NATO)	Brussels	1949
∗ Association of South East Asian Nations (ASEAN)	Jakarta	1967
∗ South Asian Association for Regional Cooperation (SAARC)	Kathmandu	1985
∗ Asia-Pacific Economic Cooperation (APEC)	Singapore	1989
∗ Organisation for Economic Cooperation and Development (OECD)	Paris	1961
∗ Organisation of Petroleum Exporting Countries (OPEC)	Vienna	1960
∗ Commonwealth of Independent States (CIS)	Minsk	1991
∗ International Olympic Committee (IOC)	Lausanne (Switzerland)	1894
∗ European Union (EU)	Brussels	Changed form of EEC Established in 1958
∗ Amnesty International (AI)	London	1961
∗ Shanghai Cooperation Organisation (SCO)	Beijing	2001
∗ BRICS Development Bank	Shanghai	2014

AWARDS AND HONOURS

NATIONAL AWARDS

BHARAT RATANA

- Bharat Ratna is India's highest Civilian Award. It was first awarded in 1954.
- The actual award is designed in the shape of a *peepal* leaf with Bharat Ratna inscribed in Devanagri script in the Sun Figure.
- This is India's highest civilian award. It is given for exceptional work on art, literature, science and recognition of public service of the highest order.
- The emblem, the Sun and the rim are of platinum. The inscriptions are in burnished bronze.
- Government servants are not eligible for it. The table shows the recipients of the award:

Bharat Ratna Award Winners

No.	Name	Year
1.	Dr. S. Radhakrishnan	1954
2.	C. Rajagopalachari	1954
3.	Dr. C.V. Raman	1954
4.	Dr. Bhagwan Das	1955
5.	Dr. M. Visvesvaraya	1955
6.	Jawahar Lal Nehru	1955
7.	Govind Ballabh Pant	1957
8.	Dr. D.K. Karve	1958
9.	Dr. Bidhan Chandra Roy	1961
10.	Purushottam Das Tandon	1961
11.	Dr. Rajendra Prasad	1962
12.	Dr. Zakir Hussain	1963
13.	Dr. Pandurang Vaman Kane	1963
14.	Lal Bahadur Shastri	1966
15.	Indira Gandhi	1971
16.	V.V. Giri	1975
17.	K. Kamraj	1976
18.	Mother Teresa	1980
19.	Acharya Vinoba Bhave	1983
20.	Khan Abdul Ghaffar Khan	1987
21.	M.G. Ramachandran	1988
22.	Dr. B.R. Ambedkar	1990
23.	Dr. Nelson R. Mandela	1990
24.	Rajiv Gandhi	1991
25.	Sardar Vallabhbhai Patel	1991
26.	Morarji R. Desai	1991
27.	Maulana Abul Kalam Azad	1992
28.	Jehangir Ratanji Dadabhai Tata	1992
29.	Satyajit Roy	1992
30.	Shri Gulzari Lal Nanda	1997
31.	Mrs. Aruna Asaf Ali	1997
32.	Dr. A.P.J. Abdul Kalam	1998
33.	M.S. Subbalakshmi	1998
34.	C. Subramaniam	1998
35.	Jaya Prakash Narayan	1999
36.	Prof. Amartya Sen	1999
37.	Pt. Ravi Shankar	1999
38.	Gopinath Bardoloi	1999
39.	Lata Mangeshkar	2001
40.	Bismillah Khan	2001
41.	Bhimsen Joshi	2009
42.	C.N.R. Rao	2014
43.	Sachin Tendulkar	2014
44.	Pt. Madan Mohan Malaviya	2015
45.	Atal Bihari Vajpayee	2015
46.	Pranab Mukherjee	2019
47.	Bhupen Hazarika	2019
48.	Nanaji Deshmukh	2019

REPUBLIC DAY AWARDS

Padma Awards

They fall in line after the Bharat Ratna. They are also discontinued in 1977 along with the Bharat Ratna and award was started again in 1980.

There are three Padma Awards:

- ***Padma Vibhushan:*** This award is given for exceptional and distinguished service in any field, including service rendered by Govt. servants.
- ***Padma Bhushan:*** This award is given for distinguished service of a high order in any field, including service rendered by Govt. servants.
- ***Padma Shri:*** This award is given for distinguished service in any field, including service rendered by Government servants.

Gallantry Awards

- ***Param Vir Chakra:*** The highest award for bravery or some daring and pre-eminent act of valour or self-sacrifice in the presence of the enemy, whether on land, at sea or in the air.
- ***Mahavir Chakra:*** It is the second highest decoration and is awarded for acts of conspicuous gallantry in the presence of the enemy, whether on land, at sea or in the air.
- ***Vir Chakra:*** It is the third in order of awards given for acts of gallantry in the presence of enemy, whether on land, at sea or in the air.
- ***Ashok Chakra:*** This medal is awarded for the most conspicuous bravery or some daring or pre-eminent act of valour or self-sacrifice on land, at sea or in the air but not in the presence of enemy.
- ***Vishishta Sewa Medal:*** It is awarded to personnel of all the three Services in class I, II and III in recognition of distinguished service of the "most exceptional" and "exceptional" and a "high" order respectively. Prefixes Parma and Ati are added before first two categories of medals respectively.
- ***Jeewan Raksha Padak:*** Awarded for meritorious acts or a series of acts of a human nature displayed in saving life from drowning, fire and rescue operations in mines etc.

OTHER NATIONAL AWARDS

SAHITYA AKADEMI AWARDS

- These prizes are awarded annually to the authors of the most outstanding books of literary merit published in each of the 24 languages recognised by the Akademi.
- There are also two awards for Sanskrit and English. The award, in form of a casket containing an inscribed copper plate and a cheque of ₹ 1 lakh is given to the author or his/her heir.

DADA SAHEB PHALKE AWARD

- The award carries a cash prize of ₹ 10 lakh, a Shawl and Swarna Kamal.
- Mrs Devika Rani Roerich was the first person to receive Dadasaheb Phalke Award in 1969.
- The award for 2021 has been given to famous actress Waheeda Rehman.

BHARATIYA JNANPITH AWARD

- Instituted in 22nd May, 1961, carries a cash prize of ₹ 11 lakh, a citation and a bronze replica of Vagdevi (Saraswati).
- Instituted by a literary organisation in India.

SARASWATI SAMMAN

- Given for outstanding literary works, value ₹ 15 lakh.

INTERNATIONAL AWARDS

NOBEL PRIZES

- These Prizes were instituted in 1901 by a Swedish scientist, Dr. Alfred Nobel; the discoverer of Dynamite.
- Six prizes are awarded annually for (i) Chemistry, (ii) Physics, (iii) Medicine, (iv) Literature, (v) Peace and (vi) Economics —started since 1969.
- **Indians Honoured with Nobel Prize:** So far, following Indians have been honoured with these prizes. Their names are (i) Rabindra Nath Tagore for Literature, for his book 'Gitanjali', in 1913, (ii) Dr. C.V. Raman for Physics in 1930, for his discovery of 'Raman Effect', (iii) Mother Teresa for Peace in 1979, (iv) Prof. Amartya Sen in 1998 for Economics and (v) Kailash Satyarthi for Peace in 2014.

In addition, four non-resident Indians have also been awarded the Nobel Prize. They are: (i) Hargobind Khurana for Medicine in 1968, (ii) Subramanian Chandrasekhar for Physics in 1983, (iii) Venkatraman Ramkrishnan for Chemistry in 2009, (iv) Abhijit Vinayak Banerjee for Economics in 2019.

GANDHI PEACE PRIZE

- The government instituted this ₹ 1 crore prize on the lines of the Nobel Peace Prize in 1995.
- It is the highest Civilian International award by the Govt. of India.

MAN BOOKER PRIZE 2023

- On November 26, 2023, Irish author Paul Lynch won 2023 Booker Prize for his novel, 'Prophet Song' published by Oneworld. He was awarded by Shehan Karunatilaka, the 2022 winner, during a ceremony held at Old Billingsgate, London in the United Kingdom (UK). He received 50,000 Pound sterling and the Iris Trophy for his award winning novel.

INDIRA GANDHI PRIZE FOR PEACE, DISARMAMENT AND DEVELOPMENT

- The award was instituted in the memory of Mrs. Indira Gandhi to foster creative cooperation among nations of the world.

Highest Honours of Some Countries

Country	*Highest Honour*
India	Bharat Ratna
Pakistan	Nishan-e-Pakistan
Kuwait	Mubarak-Al-kabir Medal
Saudi Arabia	Shah Abdul Aziz Medal
Argentina	The Order of Sona Martin
Nicaragua	Augusto-Caesar Sandino Order
Vietnam	The Order of the Golden Star
Hungary	The Order of Banner
Britain	Member of British Empire, Victoria Cross
Japan	Order of Moulovenice Sun
Denmark	Order of Diana Brog
France	Legend of Honour
America	Presidential Medal of Freedom
Germany	Pore Lee Merit Iron Cross
The Netherlands	Netherlands Lion

SPORTS

OLYMPICS

- First of all these games were held by the Greeks in 776 B.C. on Mount Olympus in honour of the Greek God Zeus. In this way, the history of Olympic Games is about twenty eight hundred years old. These games continued to be held every four years until 394 A.D. when these games were stopped by a royal order of the emperor of Rome.
- The modern Olympic Games which started in Athens in 1896, are the result of the devotion and dedication of a French educator Baron Pierre de Coubertin and the first Olympic meet in the modern series was held in 1896 in Athens, the Capital of Greece. Since then, they are being held every four years except for breaks during world wars.
- The Olympic flag is white in colour with five coloured rings, each ring symbolic of a continent. Summer as well as Winter Olympics are held in the same year.
- The 2020 Olympic Games was held at Tokyo, Japan in 2021.
- The official Olympic Motto is *Citius, Altius, Swifter, Higher, Stronger*. The Head Office of International Olympic Committee (IOC) is at Lausanne (Switzerland).

COMMONWEALTH GAMES

- The Commonwealth Games are held every four years, in the year in which Asian Games are held. All the Commonwealth Countries (former colonies of Britain) can take part in it.
- The first Commonwealth Games were held in 1930 at Hamilton (Canada).
- There are currently 54 members of the Commonwealth of Nations, and 71 teams participated in the games.
- The 2022 Commonwealth Games officially known as the XXII Commonwealth Games or Birmingham, 2022 held in Birmingham, UK between July 28 to August 08, 2022.

ASIAN GAMES

- After the Second World War, most of the Asian Countries gained independence. On the lines of Olympic Games, Asian Games were planned every four years.
- India hosted the first Asian Games in 1951.

WORLD CUP CRICKET

- The first Cricket World Cup was organised in England in 1975. A separate women's Cricket World Cup has been held every 4 years since 1973.

List of Cricket World Cup

Year	*Venue*	*Winner/Runner*
1975	England	*West Indies beat Australia*
1979	England	*West Indies beat England*
1983	England	*India beat West Indies*
1987	India & Pakistan	*Australia beat England*
1992	Australia	*Pakistan beat England*
1996	India, Pakistan & Sri Lanka	*Sri Lanka beat Australia*
1999	England	*Australia beat Pakistan*
2003	South Africa	*Australia beat India*
2007	West Indies	*Australia beat Sri Lanka*
2011	India, Sri Lanka, Bangladesh	*India beat Sri Lanka*
2015	Australia, New Zealand	*Australia beat New Zealand*
2019	England	*England beat New Zealand*
2023	India	*Australia beat India*

HOCKEY WORLD CUP

- The first Hockey World Cup was organised in Barcelona (Spain) in 1971. Women's Hockey World Cup has been held since 1974.

FOOTBALL WORLD CUP

- The Football World Cup is organised by FIFA (Federation of International Football Association). The World Cup is called 'Jules Rimet Cup' named after the name of FIFA President Jules Rimet. The first Football World Cup was organised in Uruguay in 1930.
- In 1942 and 1946, the Football World Cup was not played due to World War II.
- Brazil is the only nation to have participated in every World Cup so far. The 2022 Football World Cup held in Qatar. Argentina on December 18, 2022 clinched their third FIFA World Cup title, beating France 4-2 on penalties following a 3-3 stalemate in a thrilling final.

IMPORTANT CUPS & TROPHIES

International

∗ *American Cup* : Yacht Racing
∗ *Ashes* : Cricket
∗ *Davis Cup* : Lawn Tennis
∗ *Derby* : Horse Race
∗ *Grand National* : Horse Streple Chase Race
∗ *Jules Rimet Trophy* : World Soccer Cup
∗ *King's Cup* : Air Races
∗ *Merdeka Cup* : Football
∗ *Swaythling Cup* : Table Tennis (Men)
∗ *Ryder Cup* : Golf
∗ *Thomas Cup* : Badminton
∗ *U. Thant Cup* : Tennis
∗ *Walker Cup* : Golf
∗ *Wightman Cup* : Lawn Tennis
∗ *Rothman's Trophy* : Cricket
∗ *European Champions Cup* : Football
∗ *Grand Prix* : Table Tennis
∗ *Edgbaston Cup* : Lawn Tennis
∗ *Grand Prix* : Lawn Tennis

National

∗ *Agha Khan Cup* : Hockey
∗ *Beighton Cup* : Hockey
∗ *Bombay Gold Cup* : Hockey
∗ *C.K. Naydu Trophy* : Cricket
∗ *Deodhar Trophy* : Cricket
∗ *Duleep Trophy* : Cricket
∗ *Durand Cup* : Football
∗ *Dhyan Chand Trophy* : Hockey
∗ *Dr. B.C. Roy Trophy* : Football (Junior)
∗ *Ezra Cup* : Polo
∗ *Guru Nanak Cup* : Hockey
∗ *Holkar Trophy* : Bridge
∗ *Irani Trophy* : Cricket
∗ *Indira Gold Cup* : Hockey
∗ *Murugappa Gold Cup* : Hockey
∗ *Nehru Trophy* : Hockey
∗ *Nixan Gold Cup* : Football
∗ *Rani Jhansi Trophy* : Cricket
∗ *Ranji Trophy* : Cricket
∗ *Rangaswami Cup* : Hockey
∗ *Ramanujan Trophy* : Table Tennis
∗ *Rene Frank Trophy* : Hockey
∗ *Rohinton Baria Trophy* : Cricket
∗ *Rovers Cup* : Football
∗ *Santosh Trophy* : Football
∗ *Subroto Cup* : Football

SPORTS TERMS

∗ ***Badminton:*** Mixed doubles; Deuce; Drop; Smash; Let; Foot work; Setting.

∗ ***Base Ball:*** Pitcher; Put out, Strike; Home; Bunt.

∗ ***Billiards:*** Cue; Jigger; Pot; Break; In Baulk; In Off; Cannons.

∗ ***Boxing:*** Upper cut; Round; Punch; Bout; Knock down; Hitting below the belt; Ring.

∗ ***Bridge:*** Finesse; Dummy; Revoke; Grand Slam; Little Slam; No Trump; Rubber.

∗ ***Chess:*** Bishop, Gambit; Checkmate; Stalemate.

∗ ***Cricket:*** L.B.W. (leg before wicket); Creases, Popping-creases; Stumped; Bye; Leg-Bye; Googly; Hattrick; Maiden over; Drive; Bowling; Duck; Follow-on; No ball; Leg Break; Silly point; Cover point; Hit-wicket; Late-cut; Slip; Off-spinner; In-swing.

∗ ***Football:*** Off Side; Block; Drop-kick; Penalty-kick (or goal kick); Corner-kick; Free-kick; Dribble; Thrown-in; Foul.

* ***Golf:*** Boggy; Foursome; Stymic; Tee; Put; Hole; Niblic; Caddie; Links; The green; Bunker.
* ***Hockey:*** Carried; Short Corner; Bully; Sticks; Off side; Roll in; Striking Circle; Under-cutting; Dribble.
* ***Horse racing:*** Jockey; Punter.
* ***Polo:*** Bunker; Chukker; Mallet.
* ***Tennis:*** Back hand drive; Volley; Smash; Half-volley; Deuce; Service; Let; Grand Slam.

Stadiums and Places Associated with Sports

Name of Stadium	Sports	Place
Arun Jaitley Stadium	Cricket	Delhi
Jawaharlal Nehru Stadium	Athletics	Delhi
Shivajee Stadium	Hockey	Delhi
National Stadium	Hockey etc.	Delhi
Ambedkar Stadium	Football	Delhi
Brabourne Stadium	Cricket	Mumbai
Wankhede Stadium	Cricket	Mumbai
National Stadium	Hockey etc.	Mumbai
Eden Garden	Cricket	Kolkata
Green Park Stadium	Cricket	Kanpur
Keenan Stadium	Cricket	Jamshedpur
Nehru (Chepauk) Stadium	Cricket	Chennai
Barabati Stadium	Cricket	Cuttack
Lords, Oval, Leeds	Cricket	Britain
Hedingle Manchester	Cricket	Britain
Black Heath	Rugby Football	London
Henley	Boat race	England
Wimbledon	Lawn Tennis	London
Wembley Stadium	Football	London
Narendra Modi Stadium	Cricket	Ahmedabad
White City	Dog-race	England
Aintree	Horse-race	England
Tentbridge	Cricket	England
Patnee Martlake	Boat-race	England
Tibankham	Rugby Football	England
Sandy Lodge	Golf	Scotland
Forest Hill	Tennis	New York
Brooklyn	Baseball	New York
Melbourne	Cricket	Australia

Name of Playing Compound of Different Games

Name of Compound	Related Sports
Court	Lawn Tennis, Badminton, Netball, Hand ball, Volleyball, Squash, Kho-Kho, Kabaddi
Diamond	Baseball
Ring	Boxing, Skating, Wrestling, Circus, Riding display
Course	Golf
Board	Table Tennis
Pool	Swimming
Alley	Bowling
Mat	Judo, Karate II
Arena	Horse Riding
Vellodrum	Cycling
Field	Polo, Football, Hockey
Track	Athletics
Pitch	Cricket, Rugby
Rink	Ice Hockey

❒ ❒ ❒

Multiple Choice Questions

1. Match List-I with List-II and select the correct answer from the codes given below the lists:

List-I

(*a*) Napoleon Bonaparte
(*b*) Jean Jacques Rousseau
(*c*) Croce
(*d*) Madame Roland

List-II

1. 'A history is contemporary history'
2. 'Liberty what crimes are committed in thy name'
3. 'Man is born free but everywhere he is in chains.'
4. 'I am the Child of Revolution'

Codes :

	(*a*)	(*b*)	(*c*)	(*d*)
A.	1	2	3	4
B.	4	3	1	2
C.	3	4	2	1
D.	3	4	1	2

2. Abraham Lincon was elected the President of United States in:
A. 1862 B. 1860
C. 1875 D. 1855

3. Who was known as the 'Prince of Humanists'?
A. Francisco Petrarch B. Dante
C. Boccacio D. Erasmus

4. D-Day is the day when:
A. Germany declared war on Britain
B. US dropped the atom bomb on Hiroshima.
C. Allied Troops landed in Normandy
D. Germany surrendered to the allies

5. Whose teachings inspired the French Revolution?
A. Locke
B. Rousseau
C. Hegel
D. Plato

6. At a time when empires in Europe were crumbling before the might of Napoleon which one of the following Governor-Generals kept the British flag flying high in India?
A. Warren Hastings B. Lord Cornwallis
C. Lord Wellesley D. Lord Hastings

7. Which one of the following statements regarding Fascism in Italy is *not* true?
A. The Fascists came to power as a result of popular uprising
B. In 1926, all political parties except Mussolini's party were banned
C. The Fascists suppressed the Socialist movement
D. The Fascists were hostile to the Communists

8. The fall of Czar Nicholas-II is known as:
A. Bloody Sunday
B. Bolshevik Revolution
C. February Revolution
D. October Revolution

9. Industrial Revolution took place first in:
A. France B. Germany
C. United Kingdom D. Japan

10. The British Prime Minister at the outbreak of World War II was :
A. Churchill B. Baldwin
C. Attlee D. Chemberlain

11. The 'Great Depression' (1929) economic crisis was met by adopting the policy of
A. Stimulus B. Marshall Plan
C. New Deal D. Open Door

12. The slogan "No taxation without representation" was raised during the:
A. American War of Independence
B. Russian Revolution
C. French Revolution
D. Indian Freedom struggle

13. In the nineteenth century the people of Europe started moving from the villages to the cities due to the impact of :
A. Epidemics
B. War
C. Industrialisation
D. Population explosion in villages

14. The important cause of the Civil War in America was:
A. Abolition of slavery
B. Quest for freedom
C. Industrialisation
D. Rebellion by the native Americans

15. Industrial Revolution could not have come about without:
A. Merchant capitalism
B. The Enclosure Movement
C. The services of the proletariat class
D. An agricultural revolution

16. Consider the following statements :
The French Revolution came about mainly due to the :
1. Extreme poverty of the people
2. Impact of the works of great writers
3. Cruelty of the rulers
4. Impact of impulsive reaction
Which of the above statements are correct?
A. 1, 2 and 4 B. 2 and 3
C. 1, 3 and 4 D. 1, 2, 3 and 4

17. Asia's oldest and largest Buddhist monastery is situated in :
A. Tawang (Arunachal Pardesh)
B. Lhasa (Tibet)
C. Trincomallee (Sri Lanka)
D. Ulan Bator (Mongolia)

18. Who was the main architect of the Russian Revolution?
A. Karl Marx B. Lenin
C. Stalin D. Tolstoy

19. V.I. Lenin is associated with :
A. Russian Revolution of 1917
B. Chinese Revolution of 1949
C. German Revolution
D. French Revolution of 1789

20. Which one of the following statements is *not* correct?
A. Voltaire believed in Natural Religion
B. Rousseau wrote *Social Contract*
C. Montesquieu authored *The Spirit of Laws*
D. Necker believed in 'General Will'

21. 6th April, 1930 is well known in the history of India because this date is associated with..........
A. Dandi March by Mahatma Gandhi
B. Quit India Movement
C. Partition of Bengal
D. Partition of India

22. Which ruler enforced the system of 'Price Control' in India?
A. Mohammad Tughlak
B. Razia Begum
C. Alauddin Khilji
D. Sher Shah Suri

23. The concept of 'Din-e-Elahi' was founded by which king?
A. Dara Shikoh B. Akbar
C. Sher Shah Suri D. Shahjahan

24. Who are supposed to be the earliest inhabitants of India? Where did they come from?
A. Aryans from Central Asia
B. Dravidians from Mediterranean
C. Negroids from Africa
D. Bhils and the Santhals from West Asia

25. The one chief characteristic of temple architecture of the Gupta Age was :
A. Absence of dome
B. Huge size
C. Beautiful carvings
D. absence of a covered courtyard for the gathering of worshippers

26. The Rigveda consists of :
A. 1000 hymns B. 2028 hymns
C. 1028 hymns D. 1038 hymns

27. The central point in Ashoka's dharma was :
A. royalty to kings
B. peace and non-violence
C. respect to elders
D. religious tolerance

28. The social evil which was conspicuously absent during ancient India was :

A. *Sati*-System B. *Devadasi*-System
C. Polygamy D. *Purdah*-System

29. Which, among the following, can be accepted as a novelty introduced by Mughal emperors to their buildings?

A. Domes B. Minarets
C. Arches D. Attached gardens

30. The first ruler of India who defeated Muhammud of Ghur was :

A. Mularaja II of Gujarat
B. Prithviraja Chauhan of Delhi
C. Jayachand of Kannauj
D. Parmaldeva of Bundelkhand

31. What important event happened in India in 1911?

A. Bengal was partitioned
B. Non-Cooperation movement was launched
C. India's capital was shifted from Calcutta to Delhi
D. Mahatma Gandhi presided over the Congress session

32. The first phase of the Congress Party (1885-1905) was characterized by its efforts to secure:

A. limited independence
B. complete freedom
C. Indianization of services
D. constitutional reforms

33. The Muslim League demanded a separate homeland for the Indian Muslims openly for the first time at its annual session held in Lahore in the year :

A. 1931 A.D. B. 1936 A.D.
C. 1940 A.D. D. 1941 A.D.

34. Under whose governorship did the East India Company secure the Diwani Rights in Bengal, Bihar and Odisha from Emperor Shah Alam?

A. Lord Cornwallis
B. Lord William Bentinck
C. Lord Clive
D. Lord Wellesley

35. The Simon Commission was generally boycotted by the Indian political parties. What was the reason for this general non-cooperation?

A. the Commission aimed at dividing the people
B. it was an 'all white' Commission
C. it came after the Jallianwala Bagh carnage
D. it was an eye wash

36. Aligarh Muslim University was founded by :

A. Dr. Saifuddin Kitchlu
B. Mohammad Ali Jinnah
C. Sir Syed Ahmed Khan
D. Maulana Mohammad Ali

37. Ibn Batutah was an African traveller visiting India during the time of :

A. Alivardi Khan
B. Ala-ud-din Khalji
C. Iltutmish
D. Mohammad-bin-Tughlaq

38. The battle of Wandiawash was fought in :

A. 1726 B. 1760
C. 1818 D. 1857

39. The abolition of *Sati* by government regulation was at the time of :

A. Warren Hastings B. Lord Wellesley
C. Lord Bentinck D. Lord Ahmerst

40. Pick out the wrong combination :

A. Dilwara Temple : Mt. Abu
B. Pashupati Temple : Kathmandu
C. Padmanabh Temple : Bangalore
D. Minakshi Temple : Madurai

41. Match the following:

(*a*) Chanhudaro (*b*) Kalibangan
(*c*) Lothal (*d*) Surkotada

1. Alleged discovery of the skeleton of horse.
2. Bead making.
3. Traces of a dock and ship on seal.
4. Evidence of ploughing the fields.

The Correct code is :

	(*a*)	(*b*)	(*c*)	(*d*)
A.	2	4	3	1
B.	2	1	3	4
C.	1	2	3	4
D.	2	1	4	3

42. Match the Harappan settlements with the banks of rivers on which they were located :

(*a*) Harappa	1. Ravi
(*b*) Mohenjodaro	2. Indus
(*c*) Ropar	3. Sutlej
(*d*) Kalibangan	4. Ghaggar
(*e*) Lothal	5. Bhogava

Codes :

	(*a*)	(*b*)	(*c*)	(*d*)	(*e*)
A.	1	2	3	4	5
B.	1	2	3	5	4
C.	2	1	3	5	4
D.	2	1	4	3	5

43. The Goddess 'Kannagi' whose many temples were erected during the 'Sangam Age' was the goddess of :

A. Chastity B. Love
C. Prowess D. Wisdom

44. The Jain goal of life is to attain deliverance from the fetters of mudane existence, the way to which lies through three jewels. Which one of the following was not included among the 'three jewels' of Jainism?

A. Right faith B. Right action
C. Right knowledge D. Right conduct

45. The most striking feature of the Ashokan pillar is polish. Name the Ashokan pillar which is considered to be the most graceful of all Ashokan pillars.

A. Sarnath
B. Rampurva
C. Laurya-Nandangarh
D. Rummindei

46. Which are the correct statements?

1. The land grants, started in Satavahana period, paved the way for feudal developments in India.
2. Silk and spices were the Chief Indian export articles of Indo-Roman trade.
3. The Guptas issued the largest number of gold coins in ancient India.
4. The first memorial of a 'SATI' dated 510 A.D. is found at Eran in Madhya Pradesh.

A. 1 and 2 B. 1, 3, and 4
C. 1 and 4 D. 1, 2, 3 and 4

47. Who among the following patronised the 'Gandhara' (Indo-Greek style) School of Art?

A. Ashoka, the Great
B. Harsha Vardhana
C. Kanishka
D. Chandragupta Vikramaditya

48. The Sultanate of Delhi had five ruling dynasties. The dynasty having longest and shortest period were :

A. Ilbari and Khalji
B. Tughlaq and Khalji
C. Tughlaq and Sayyid
D. Ilbari and Lodis

49. Which one of the following events took place at the last during reign of Muhammad-bin-Tughlaq?

A. Introduction of token currency
B. Increase of land-revenue in Doab
C. Transfer of Capital from Delhi to Devagiri.
D. Conquest of Khurasan and Iraq

50. The most learned medieval Muslim ruler who was well versed in various branches of learning including astronomy, mathematics and medicine was :

A. Jalaluddin Khilji
B. Sikander Lodi
C. Ghiyasuddin Tughlaq
D. Muhammad-bin-Tughlaq

51. The 'Sufis' had 12 silsilas. They propounded the idea of Union with God through:

A. Love B. Rituals
C. Fasts D. Prayers

52. Match the following:

(*a*) Peshwa	1. Foreign affairs
(*b*) Panditrao	2. Audit and accounts
(*c*) Amatya	3. Providing grants to scholars
(*d*) Sumant	4. General supervision
	5. Military affairs

Select the correct code :

	(*a*)	(*b*)	(*c*)	(*d*)
A.	2	3	4	5
B.	4	1	2	3
C.	4	3	2	1
D.	3	1	4	2

53. The Regulating Act of 1773 can be regarded as the first measure to :
A. assert the right of British Parliament to legislate for India
B. separate the legislature from the executive
C. separate the judiciary from the executive
D. centralise law-making

54. What was the exact constitutional status of the Indian Republic on 26th January, 1950?
A. A Democratic Republic
B. A Sovereign, Democratic Republic
C. A Sovereign, Secular, Democratic Republic
D. A Sovereign, Socialist, Secular, Democratic Republic

55. When the British obtained the grant of Diwani of Bengal, Bihar and Odisha they acquired the right to :
A. maintain law and order in these territories
B. administer civil justice and collect revenue in these territories
C. collect revenue and establish revenue administration in these territories
D. militarily defend these territories

56. Which of the following were responsible for the growth of nationalism in India during the British rule?
1. Economic exploitation of India.
2. Impact of western education.
3. Role of the Press.
Select the correct answer using the codes given below :
Codes:
A. 1, 2 and 3 B. 1 and 2
C. 2 and 3 D. 1 and 3

57. Which one of the following nationalist leaders has been described as being radical in politics but conservative on social issues?
A. G.K. Gokhale
B. B.G. Tilak
C. Lala Lajpat Rai
D. Madan Mohan Malviya

58. Provincial Autonomy in British India was envisaged by the :
A. Act of 1909 B. Act of 1919
C. Act of 1935 D. Act of 1947

59. Dyarchy means :
A. double government
B. a government in which the centre is very powerful
C. a government based on division of power between centre and provinces
D. None of the above

60. The Indian National Congress observed 'Independence Day' for the first time on 26th January in :
A. 1920 B. 1925
C. 1930 D. 1947

61. ....is situated near the banks of Sabarmati River
A. Bhavnagar B. Aurangabad
C. Ahmedabad D. Rajkot

62. Sericulture is:
A. science of the various kinds of serum
B. artificial rearing of fish
C. art of silkworm breeding
D. study of various cultures of a community

63. The most abundant constituents of earth's crust are:
A. Igneous rocks
B. Sedimentary rocks
C. Metamorphic rocks
D. Granite

64. Indian Standard Time is based on:
A. 80°E longitude B. 82½°E longitude
C. 110°E longitude D. 25°E longitude

65. Tides in the oceans are caused by :
A. Gravitational pull of the moon on the earth's surface including sea water
B. Gravitational pull of the sun on the earth's surface only and not on the sea water
C. Gravitational pull of the moon and the sun on the earth's surface including the sea water
D. None of these

66. Nagarjunasagar Project is situated on the river:
A. Tungabhadra
B. Cauvery
C. Krishna
D. Godavari

67. The difference between the Indian Standard Time and the Greenwich Mean Time is:
A. – 3½ hours B. + 3½ hours
C. – 5½ hours D. + 5½ hours

68. Which of the following dams is not on Narmada river?
A. Indira-Sagar Project
B. Maheshwar Hydel Power Project
C. Jobat Project
D. Koyna Power Project

69. Which of the following statements is **not true** about the availability of water on the earth, the crisis for which is going to increase in the years to come?
A. About 97.5 per cent of the total volume of water available on the earth is salty
B. 80 per cent of the water available to us for use comes in bursts as monsoons
C. About 2.5 per cent of the total water available on the earth is polluted water and cannot be used for human activities
D. Possibility is that some big glaciers will melt in the coming ten-fifteen years and sea level will rise by 3-4 metres all over the earth

70. Which of the following is **not** a cash crop?
A. Jute B. Paddy
C. Cashewnut D. Sugarcane

71. Through which States does Cauvery River flow?
A. Gujarat, M.P., Tamil Nadu
B. Karnataka, Kerala, Tamil Nadu
C. Karnataka, Kerala, Andhra Pradesh
D. M.P., Maharashtra, Tamil Nadu

72. Indian Standard Time is the local time of 82½°E which passes through :
A. Guntur B. Delhi
C. Allahabad D. Kolkata

73. The 17th parallel defines the boundary between:
A. North and South Korea
B. USA and Canada
C. North and South Vietnam
D. China and Russia

74. During the period of south-west monsoon, Tamil Nadu remains dry because:
A. the winds do not reach this area
B. there are no mountains in this area
C. it lies in the rain shadow area
D. the temperature is too high to let the winds cool down

75. Which country does top in producing cocoa?
A. Cote d'Ivoire B. Brazil
C. Ghana D. Nigeria

76. The biggest reserves of thorium are in :
A. India B. China
C. The Soviet Union D. U.S.A.

77. The Girnar Hills are situated in which of the following states?
A. Gujarat B. Karnataka
C. Madhya Pradesh D. Maharashtra

78. During December 22nd the sun is vertically over:
A. Tropic of Cancer
B. Tropic of Capricorn
C. The Equator
D. None of the above

79. Photosphere is described as the :
A. Lower layer of atmosphere
B. Visible surface of the sun from which radiation emanates
C. Wavelength of solar spectrum
D. None of the above

80. Broadly, there are three layers of the earth of the crust, the mantle and the core. The crust forms what percentage of the volume of the earth?
A. 0.5% B. 2.5%
C. 7.5% D. 12.5%

81. The grassland of Argentina is known as :
A. Pampas B. Campos
C. Savanna D. None of the above

82. Different seasons are formed because :
A. Sun is moving around the earth
B. of revolution of the earth around the Sun on its orbit
C. of rotation of the earth around its axis
D. All of the above

83. Eskers and Drumlins are features formed by:
A. underground water
B. running water
C. the action of wind
D. glacial action

84. Match List-I and List-II and select the correct answer using the codes given below the Lists :

List-I *(Rivers)*	**List-II** *(Towns)*
(*a*) Ghaghara	1. Lucknow
(*b*) Brahmaputra	2. Hoshangabad
(*c*) Narmada	3. Ahmedabad
(*d*) Sabarmati	4. Guwahati
	5. Ayodhya

	(*a*)	(*b*)	(*c*)	(*d*)
A.	4	5	1	2
B.	5	4	2	3
C.	5	4	3	1
D.	3	5	2	1

85. Which of the statements as regards the consequences of the movement of the earth is not correct?
A. Revolution of the earth is the cause of the change of seasons.
B. Rotation of the earth is the cause of days and nights.
C. Rotation of the earth causes variation in the duration of days and nights.
D. Rotation of the earth effects the movement of winds and ocean currents.

86. The world is divided into :
A. 12 time zones
B. 20 time zones
C. 24 time zones
D. 36 time zones

87. The 'Kiel' canal links the :
A. Pacific and Atlantic Oceans
B. Mediterranean Sea and Red Sea
C. Mediterranean Sea and Black Sea
D. North Sea and Baltic Sea

88. Match the following :

List-I	**List-II**
(*a*) Himadri	1. Outer Himalayas
(*b*) Shivalik	2. Inner Himalayas
(*c*) Himanchal	3. Middle Himalayas
(*d*) Sahyadri	4. Western Ghats

Codes:

	(*a*)	(*b*)	(*c*)	(*d*)
A.	1	2	3	4
B.	4	2	3	1
C.	2	1	3	4
D.	1	2	3	4

89. The term 'Regur' refers to:
A. Laterite soils
B. Black Cotton soils
C. Red Soils
D. Deltaic Alluvial Soils

90. Location of sugar industry in India is shifting from north to south because of:
A. cheap labour
B. expanding regional market
C. cheap and abundant supply of power
D. high yield and high sugar content in sugarcane

91. Consider the following statements :
1. Ozone is found mostly in the Stratosphere.
2. Ozone layer lies 55-75 km above the surface of the earth.
3. Ozone absorbs ultraviolet radiation from the Sun.
4. Ozone layer has no significance for life on the earth.

Which of the above statements are correct?
A. 1 and 3 B. 2 and 4
C. 2 and 3 D. 1 and 4

92. Match List-I with List-II and select the correct answer using the codes given below the Lists :

List-I *(Crops)*	**List-II** *(Producer)*
(*a*) Banana	1. Brazil
(*b*) Cocoa	2. Cote d'Ivoire
(*c*) Coffee	3. India
(*d*) Tea	4. China

Codes :

	(*a*)	(*b*)	(*c*)	(*d*)
A.	2	3	1	4
B.	3	2	1	4
C.	3	2	4	1
D.	2	3	4	1

93. Darjeeling and Dharamsala would be the right places to visit if one wanted to get a clear view respectively of :
A. Kanchanjunga and Dhauladhar ranges
B. Nandadevi and Dhauladhar ranges
C. Kanchanjunga and Nandadevi ranges
D. Nandadevi and Nanga Parvat

94. Atmosphere exists because:
A. The Gravitational force of the Earth
B. Revolution of the Earth
C. Rotation of the Earth
D. Weight of the gases of atmosphere

95. Victoria lake is located in the continent:
A. Africa
B. Asia
C. North America
D. South America

96. The famous Lagoon Lake of India is :
A. Dal Lake B. Chilka Lake
C. Pulicat Lake D. Mansarover

97. Where are most of the earth's active volcanoes concentrated?
A. Indian Ocean B. Pacific Ocean
C. Aral Sea D. Atlantic Ocean

98. Through which of the following states does the river Chambal flow?
A. U.P., M.P., Rajasthan
B. M.P., Gujarat, U.P.
C. Rajasthan, M.P., Bihar
D. Gujarat, M.P., U.P.

99. Which country is called the sugar bowl of the world?
A. Cuba B. India
C. Argentina D. USA

100. The area covered by forest in India as per ISFR-2021 is:
A. 46% B. 33%
C. 21.71% D. 25.50%

101. A closed economy is the one which :
A. does not permit emigration or immigration
B. permits emigration but no immigration
C. engages in no foreign trade
D. engages in no foreign and domestic trade or transit

102. In a developed economy the major share of employment originates in the :
A. primary sector B. tertiary sector
C. secondary sector D. any of the above

103. The Economic and Social Commission for Asia and Pacific (ESCAP) is located at :
A. Bangkok B. Kuala Lumpur
C. Manila D. Singapore

104. Commercial vehicles are not produced by which of the following companies in India?
A. TELCO B. Ashok Leyland
C. DCM Daewoo D. Birla Yamaha

105. In India, the Public Sector is most dominant in:
A. transport
B. steel production
C. commercial banking
D. organised term-lending financial institutions

106. The main argument advanced in favour of small scale and cottage industries in India is that:
A. cost of production is low
B. they require small capital investment
C. they advance the goal of equitable distribution of wealth
D. they generate a large volume of employment

107. The most serious economic problems of India are:
A. Poverty and unemployment
B. Stagnation, not poverty
C. Unemployment, not poverty
D. Underdevelopment, not poverty

108. Which of the following is not one of the three central problems of an economy?
A. What to produce
B. How to produce
C. When to produce
D. For whom to produce

109. Gender Responsive Budgeting has been adopted in India in the year:
A. 2017 B. 2004
C. 2014 D. 2005

110. In which of the following industries in India are the maximum number of workers employed?
A. Sugar B. Jute
C. Textiles D. Iron and Steel

111. Terrace Cultivation is practiced mostly:
A. in urban areas
B. on slopes of mountains
C. on tops of hills
D. in undulating tracts

112. Which of the following is a Selective Credit Control method?
A. Bank Rate
B. RBI directives
C. Cash Reserve Ratio
D. Open market operations

113. Which of the following taxes is not shared by the Central Government with the States?
A. Union excise duties
B. Customs duty
C. Income tax
D. Estate duty

114. ICICI is the name of a:
A. Financial Institution
B. Chemical Industry
C. Cotton Industry
D. Chamber of Commerce and Industry

115. Structural Unemployment arises due to
A. Deflationary conditions
B. Heavy industry bias
C. Shortage of raw material
D. Inadequate productive capacity

116. Which of the following is the largest single source of the government's earning from tax revenue?
A. Excise duties
B. Customs duties
C. Corporation tax
D. Income tax

117. The largest public sector bank in India is:
A. Central Bank of India
B. Punjab National Bank
C. State Bank of India
D. Indian Overseas Bank

118. Which of the following statements best explains the term contraband goods?
A. Goods produced only for exports
B. Goods produced in joint sector only
C. Goods for the trading of which licence is not required
D. Goods that are forbidden, from export, import or even possession, by law

119. Price in the market is fixed by:
A. Stock exchange rates
B. The demand and supply ruling in the market at a particular time
C. The Finance Minister
D. None of the above

120. Devaluation of currency helps to promote:
A. National Income
B. Savings
C. Imports at lower cost
D. Exports

121. Balanced economic growth can be achieved only if:
A. All the sectors of economy grow at the same rate
B. Population growth is arrested
C. All the inter dependent sectors grow in harmony
D. Basic and heavy industries are assigned highest priority

122. Which one of the following contributes most to the National Income in India?
A. Service Sector
B. Industrial Sector
C. Foreign Trade Sector
D. Agricultural Sector

123. IMF is the result of:
A. Brettonwood conference
B. Rome conference
C. Geneva conference
D. Hawana conference

124. Index 'Residex' is associated with:
A. Share Prices
B. Land Prices
C. Mutual Funds Prices
D. None of the above

125. The term 'devaluation' means:
A. Reducing the value of a currency in terms of another currency
B. Increasing the value of a currency
C. Revising the value of a currency
D. None of the above

126. Per capita net availability of pulses has shown a tendency of:
A. Increase over time
B. Decrease over time
C. Constant over time
D. First increase then decrease

127. National Income is the same as:
A. Net national product at market price
B. Net domestic product at market price
C. Net national product at factor cost
D. Net domestic product at factor cost

128. Which one of the following is not an example of indirect tax?
A. Sales tax B. Excise duty
C. Customs duty D. Expenditure tax

129. The major aim of devaluation is to:
A. encourage imports
B. encourage exports
C. encourage both exports and imports
D. discourage both exports and imports

130. Structural unemployment arises due to:
A. deflationary conditions
B. heavy industry bias
C. shortage of raw materials
D. inadequate productive capacity

131. When was the Family Planning Programme officially started in India?
A. 1950 B. 1952
C. 1956 D. 1962

132. When was the Reserve Bank of India nationalised?
A. 1947 B. 1949
C. 1950 D. 1951

133. Which of the following is *not* a feature of the Indian economy?
A. High rate of population growth
B. Disguised unemployment
C. Lowest rate of adult literacy
D. High rate of exports

134. The 'Relative Deprivation' approach for measuring poverty has been adopted by:
A. developing countries
B. developed countries
C. under-developed countries
D. None of the above

135. One of the main factors that led to rapid expansion of Indian exports is:
A. Imposition of import duties
B. Liberalisation of the economy
C. Recession in other countries
D. Diversification of exports

136. Sustainable economic development means an increase in the rate of growth of real:
A. total and per capita product
B. total and per capita product and level of literacy rate
C. total and per capita product and life expectancy at birth
D. total and per capita product, taking into account the cost of degradation of the quality of environment in this process

137. Functional unemployment occurs when:
A. unemployed have no qualification for job
B. people frequently change their job
C. people were thrown out from job due to recession
D. None of these

138. Which among the following does **not** have a 'free trade zone'?
A. Kandla B. Mumbai
C. Visakhapatnam D. Thiruvanantpuram

139. Sun Belt of USA is important for which one of the following industries?
A. Cotton textile
B. Petrochemicals
C. Hi-tech electronics
D. Food Processing

140. Commercial banking system in India is
A. unit banking B. branch banking
C. mixed banking D. None of the above

141. Who gives recognition to political parties in India?
A. Parliament

B. President
C. Supreme Court
D. Election Commission

142. The Quorum of the Legislative Council is :
A. one-fourth of its total membership
B. one-third of its membership
C. one-tenth of its membership
D. 25

143. The Indian Constitution is:
A. federal
B. unitary
C. a happy mixture of the federal and unitary
D. federal in normal times and unitary in times of emergency

144. Universal adult franchise implies a right to vote to all:
A. adult residents of the State
B. adult male citizens of the State
C. residents of the State
D. adult citizens of the State

145. When a resolution prefering a charge against the President has been passed by a specified majority in the House, it is sent to the other House for investigation. If, as a result of such an investigation, a resolution is passed through a specified majority by the other House, declaring that the charge has been sustained, the President shall leave his office. The specified special majority must not be less than :
A. two-third of the members present and voting
B. one-third of the members present and voting
C. three-fourth of the members present and voting and two-third of the total membership
D. two-third of the total membership

146. Which one of the following judicial powers of the President of India has been *wrongly* listed?
A. he appoints the Chief Justice and other judges of the Supreme Court
B. he can remove the judges of the Supreme Court on grounds of misconduct
C. he can consult the Supreme Court on any question of law or fact which is of public importance
D. he can grant pardon, reprieves and respites to persons punished under Union Law

147. The Vice-president of India can be removed from his office before the expiry of his term if :
A. the Rajya Sabha passes a resolution by a majority of its members and the Lok Sabha agrees with the resolution
B. if the Supreme Court of India recommends his removal
C. the President so desires
D. None of the above

148. The Chief Justice of a High Court in India is appointed by the :
A. Governor of the State
B. Prime Minister of India
C. Chief Justice of the Supreme Court
D. President of India

149. Which of the following statements is constitutionally not true about the passing of the Union Budgets and Finance Bill in India?
1. Under the law, Finance Bill should be adopted by both the Houses of the Parliament within 45 days of its introduction.
2. If the Finance Bill is not adopted within specified period, the government loses its authority to levy the taxes proposed in the budgets.
3. In the absence of full budget, a vote-on-account gives the power to the government to spend.
4. Government cannot raise revenues without a proper approval of the Finance Bill

A. Only 2 B. Only 3
C. Only 4 D. Only 1, 2 and 3

150. Normally, on whose advice the President's Rule is imposed in a State?
A. Chief Minister
B. Legislative Assembly
C. Governor
D. Chief Justice of High Court

151. Which Article of the Indian Constitution deals with Amendment procedure?
A. Article 368 B. Article 358
C. Article 367 D. All of these

152. Government is the agency through which the will of :
A. the state is expressed
B. the people is expressed
C. the head of the state is expressed
D. the majority is expressed

153. In a unitary system of government :
A. The centre is all powerful
B. The centre is weaker than the states
C. The centre and states stand at par
D. The states and centre are supreme in their respective spheres

154. In Cabinet System of Government the real executive authority rests with :
A. The Council of Ministers
B. The Prime Minister
C. The Constitution
D. The Parliament

155. The Head of the State under a parliamentary government:
A. is an elected representative
B. is a hereditary person
C. is a nominated person
D. may be any one of the above

156. In the event of a ministerial proposal being defeated on the floor of the legislature, under the parliamentary system :
A. the government waits for a general no-confidence motion
B. the minister concerned is taken to task by the Prime Minister
C. the minister is forced to resign
D. the whole Council of Ministers resign

157. The "due process of law" is an essential characteristic of the judicial system of:
A. UK B. France
C. USA D. India

158. Under the Constitution it is :
A. obligatory for the President to accept the advice of the Council of Ministers but is not obliged to follow it
B. obligatory for the President to accept the advice of the Council of Ministers
C. not obligatory for the President to seek or accept the advice of the Council of Ministers
D. obligatory for the President to seek the advice of the Council of Ministers if his own party is in power

159. Which one of the following statements is correct?
A. the Presiding Officer of Rajya Sabha is elected every year
B. the Presiding Officer of Rajya Sabha is elected for a term of two years at a time
C. the Presiding Officer of Rajya Sabha is elected for a term of six years
D. the Vice-President of India is the ex-officio Presiding Officer of Rajya Sabha

160. The introduction of "no confidence" motion in the Lok Sabha requires the support of at least:
A. 50 members B. 70 members
C. 60 members D. 80 members

161. The High Court comes under :
A. State List B. Union List
C. Concurrent List D. None of the above

162. Which one of the following has been wrongly listed as a Fundamental Duty of the Indian citizens?
A. to develop scientific temper, humanism and spirit of inquiry and reform
B. to work for raising the prestige of the country in the international sphere
C. to protect and improve the natural environment
D. to strive towards excellence in all spheres of individual and collective activity

163. Which one of the following is not a Fundamental Duty as outlined in Article 51A of the Constitution?
A. to abide by the Constitution and respect its ideals
B. to defend the country and render national service when called upon to do so

C. to work for the moral upliftment of the weaker sections of society
D. to preserve the rich heritage

164. The main characteristics of the Directive Principles of State Policy given in the Indian Constitution are :
A. not enforceable by any court
B. fundamental in the governance of the country
C. 'Like instruments, instructions, political manifesto and a code of moral precepts which have to guide governors of the country'
D. no law can be passed, which is opposed to these principles

165. Of the following which are true?
A. In a State, the Legislative Council is dominant with regard to non-financial bills and the Legislative Assembly with regard to financial (money) bills
B. Vidhan Parishad can virtually block legisla-tion even if the same is passed by the Vidhan Sabha
C. In case of a tie between the two Houses, the Governor is duty-bound to call a joint session of the two Houses to have the issue settled on a majority verdict
D. If a Bill is twice approved by the Vidhan Sabha, it becomes law even if rejected by the Vidhan Parishad

166. Which one of the following types of emergency can be declared by the President?
A. Emergency due to threat of war and external aggresion
B. Emergency due to break-down of constitutional machinery in a State
C. Financial emergency on account of threat to the financial credit of India
D. all the three emergencies

167. The chairman of which of the following parliamentary committees is invariably from the members of ruling party?
A. Committee on public undertakings
B. Public accounts committee
C. Estimates committee
D. Committee on delegated legislation

168. Which of the following is not a formally prescribed device available to the members of parliament?
A. Question hour
B. Zero hour
C. Half-an-hour discussion
D. Short duration discussion

169. Which of the following is not a tool of executive control over public administration?
A. Power of appointment and removal
B. Line agencies
C. Appeal to public opinion
D. Civil services code

170. If the Speaker of the State Legislative Assembly decides to resign, he should submit his resignation to the:
A. Judges of the High Court
B. Deputy Speaker
C. Chief Minister
D. Finance Minister

171. The Constitution of India provides for the nomination of two members of Lok Sabha by the President to represent:
A. the Parsis
B. men of eminence
C. the business community
D. the Anglo-Indian community

172. India is a Federal State because of:
A. dual judiciary
B. dual citizenship prevalent here
C. share of power between the Centre and the States
D. rigid Constitution

173. Residuary Subjects are those subjects which are:
A. contained in the State list
B. contained in the Union list
C. contained in the Concurrent list
D. not covered by any of the three lists

174. Which of the following writs can be issued, by the Supreme Court, to enforce Fundamental Rights?
A. Writ of Habeas Corpus
B. Writ of Mandamus
C. Writ of Quo Warranto
D. All of these

175. When the offices of both the President and the Vice-President of India are vacant, who will discharge their functions?
A. Prime Minister
B. Home Minister
C. Chief Justice of India
D. The Speaker

176. The Supreme Court tenders advice to the President of India on a matter of law or fact:
A. on its own
B. only when such advice is sought
C. only if the matter relates to some basic issue
D. only if the issue poses a threat to the unity and integrity of the country

177. Six months shall **not** intervene between two sessions of the Indian Parliament because :
A. it is the customary practice
B. it is the British convention followed in India
C. it is an obligation under the Constitution of India
D. None of the above

178. The States of the Indian Union can be recognised or their boundaries altered by:
A. the Union Parliament by a simple majority in the ordinary process of legislation
B. two-thirds majority of both the Houses of Parliament
C. two-thirds majority of both the Houses of Parliament and the consent of the legislatures of concerned States
D. an executive order of the Union government with the consent of the concerned State governments

179. The Basic Feature theory of the Constitution of India was propounded by the Supreme Court in the case of :
A. Minerva Mills Vs. Union of India
B. Golaknath Vs. State of Punjab
C. Maneka Gandhi Vs. Union of India
D. Keshavananda Vs. State of Kerala

180. Which one of the following writs is issued by a court in case of illegal detention of a person?
A. Habeas corpus B. Mandamus
C. Certiorari D. Quo-warranto

181. Name the instrument with the help of which a sailor in a submarine can see the objects on the surface of the sea.
A. Telescope B. Periscope
C. Gycroscope D. Stereoscope

182. 'HEMOPHILLIA' is the disease of ....
A. liver B. blood
C. brain D. bones

183. Vitamin A is abundantly found in ....
A. Brinjal B. Tomato
C. Carrot D. Cabbage

184. .... is not soluble in water.
A. Vitamin A B. Vitamin B
C. Vitamin C D. None of these

185. The blood vessels with the smallest diameter are called ....
A. capillaries B. arterioles
C. venules D. lymphatics

186. Out of the following .... has the greatest elasticity.
A. steel B. rubber
C. aluminium D. annealed copper

187. Cooking gas is a mixture of which of the following two gases?
A. Carbon Dioxide and Oxygen
B. Butane and Propane
C. Carbon Monoxide and Carbon Dioxide
D. Methane and Ethylene

188. The substance most commonly used as a food preservative is:
A. sodium carbonate B. tartaric acid
C. acetic acid D. benzoic acid

189. Normally, the substances that fight against diseases in human systems are known as:
A. dioxyribonucleic acids
B. carbohydrates
C. enzymes
D. antibodies

190. The SI unit of temperature is ....
A. Kelvin B. Celsius
C. Fahrenheit D. None of the above

191. One of the common fungal diseases of man is :
A. plague B. ringworm
C. cholera D. typhoid

192. A clear sky is blue because:
A. red light is scattered more than blue
B. ultraviolet light has been absorbed
C. blue light is scattered more than red
D. blue light has been absorbed

193. Jenner introduced the method of making people immune to :
A. small pox B. rabies
C. cholera D. polio

194. The largest cell in the human body is :
A. Nerve cell B. Live cell
C. Muscle cell D. Kidney cell

195. What is the device that steps up or steps down the voltage?
A. Dynamo B. Conductor
C. Inductor D. Transformer

196. The protein deficiency disease is known as :
A. Kwashiorker B. Cirrhosis
C. Eczema D. Clycoses

197. Iron deficiency causes :
A. rickets B. anaemia
C. cirrhosis D. goitre

198. Blood group of an individual is controlled by :
A. Haemoglobin B. Shape of RBC
C. Shape of WBC D. Genes

199. In a normal man the amount of blood pumped out by the heart per minute is about :
A. 1 litre B. 3 litres
C. 4 litres D. 5 litres

200. Red/green colour blindness in man is known as :
A. Protanopia
B. Deutetanopia
C. Both A and B above
D. Marfan's syndrome

201. The blue colour of the water in the sea is due to :
A. Reflection of the blue light by the impurities in sea water
B. Reflection of the blue sky by sea water and scattering of blue light by water molecules
C. Absorption of other colours by water molecules
D. None of the above

202. The image formed on the retina of the eye is:
A. upright and real
B. larger than the object
C. small and inverted
D. enlarged and real

203. Unit of loudness of sound is:
A. bel B. decibel
C. phon D. none of these

204. Oil rises up the wick in a lamp :
A. because oil is volatile
B. due to the capillary action phenomenon
C. due to the surface tension phenomenon
D. because oil is very light

205. The 'stones' formed in human kidney consist mostly of :
A. calcium oxalate
B. sodium acetate
C. magnesium sulphate
D. calcium

206. We hear the sound later, while the light is seen earlier:
A. because light's speed is more than that of sound
B. because lights travel in a straight direction while sound in a zigzag direction
C. because sound's frequency is lower than light
D. All of the above

207. Which part of an eye is transplanted?
A. Cornea
B. Retina
C. Iris
D. Sciera

208. The Universal donor group of blood is:
A. O B. A
C. B D. AB

209. The green colour of the leaf is due to :
A. Presence of Chloroplast
B. Presence of Chromium
C. Presence of Nicoplast
D. Presence of excess of oxygen

210. Voice of a child is more shrill than that of an elderly person because:
A. the pitch of the child's voice is higher than that of the person
B. the pitch is lower
C. the child is more energetic
D. None of the above

211. Camel uses its hump for :
A. storing water
B. storing fat
C. for balancing the body
D. temperature regulation

212. A man standing in a free falling lift releases a ball from his hand. The ball would be :
A. moving down
B. moving up
C. stationary
D. moving up and down

213. To change the quality of sound produced by an instrument we need to vary the:
A. pitch
B. loudness
C. amplitude
D. number of overtonnes

214. The disease caused by Asbestos is:
A. Emphysema B. Paralysis
C. Diarrhoea D. Dysentery

215. Sweetness of a sound depends upon its
A. wavelength
B. frequency
C. amplitude
D. periodicity and regularity

216. Bats can fly in the dark because :
A. they have a better vision in the dark
B. the pupils of their eyes are very big
C. they are guided by ultrasonic waves produced by them
D. any bird can do so

217. Blood is formed in the human adult by the :
A. heart B. spleen
C. kidney D. bone marrow

218. Pencil 'lead' is made up of:
A. graphite B. charcoal
C. lead oxide D. lampblack

219. The deficiency of which one of the following vitamins leads to bleeding of gums and loosening of teeth?
A. Vitamin D B. Vitamin C
C. Vitamin B D. Vitamin A

220. How much blood does a normal person have in his body?
A. 8 litres B. 4 to 5 litres
C. 10 litres D. 2 litres

221. Match List-I with List-II and select the correct answer using the codes given below the Lists :

List-I	**List-II**
(*a*) Visakhadatta	1. Mrichhakatika
(*b*) Shudraka	2. Ritusamhara
(*c*) Kalidasa	3. Kamasutra
(*d*) Vatsyayana	4. Devichandraguptam

Codes :

	(*a*)	(*b*)	(*c*)	(*d*)
A.	1	4	2	3
B.	4	1	3	2
C.	1	4	3	2
D.	4	1	2	3

222. In which one of the following langauges is the *Dalit* writing more conspicuous?
A. Punjabi B. Assamese
C. Marathi D. Odiya

223. The first writer to use Urdu as the medium of poetic expression was:
A. Amir Khusrau
B. Mirza Ghalib
C. Bahadur Shah Zafar
D. Faiz

224. The religious text of the Zoroastrians is named as:
A. Torah B. The Analects
C. Tripatika D. Zend Avesta

225. Name the music duo which composed music for Raj Kapoor's film 'Bobby'?
A. Laxmikant Pyarelal B. Shankar Jaikishen
C. Kalyanji Anandji D. Nadeem Shravan

226. Raja Harishchandra, an early Indian film, was produced by :
A. D.G. Phalke B. Ashok Kumar
C. Ardeshir Irani D. None of the above

227. All films are certificed by .... before they are publicly exhibited.
A. Films Division
B. National Film Development Corporation (NFDC)
C. Directorate of Advertising and Visual Publicity (DAVP)
D. Central Board of Film Certificate (CBFC)

228. Who among the following was the director of the film 'Taal'?
A. Gulzar B. Shekhar Kapoor
C. Satish Shah D. Subhash Ghai

229. Who amongst the following actresses has played the leading role in the film Elizabeth?
A. Gwyneth Paltrow B. Cate Blanchett
C. Simi Garewal D. Kim Basinger

230. The film 'Train to Pakistan' is based on the novel of the same name, written by:
A. Bhishma Sahani
B. Khushwant Singh
C. Amrita Pritam
D. Khwaja Ahmed Abbas

231. Which of the following is a folk dance form of Jharkhand?
A. Pali B. Jhumar
C. Nati D. Chhau

232. The first feature film (talkie) to be produced in India was:
A. Hatimtai B. Alam Ara
C. Pundalik D. Raja Harishchandra

233. Who directed the film "Bombay"?
A. Shyam Benegal B. Meera Nair
C. Shekhar Kapoor D. Mani Ratnam

234. Late Iftekhar Ahmad was famous in which of the following fields?
A. Acting B. Singing
C. Music D. Literature

235. Who among the following is the director of the film 'Kaho Na Pyar Hai'?
A. Subhash Ghai
B. Shekhar Kapoor
C. Ramesh Sippy
D. Rakesh Roshan

236. The character played by Jim Carrey in the movie *Man on Moon* is based on:
A. Andy Kaufman B. Edwin Aldrin
C. John Glenn D. Neil Armstrong

237. A popular Hindi film-based on the famous Sanskrit play *Mrichhakatika*, was titled:
A. Meghadoot B. Amrapali
C. Utsav D. Shakuntala

238. Who composed the song 'Zara Yad Karo Kurbani'?
A. Javed Akhtar
B. Pradeep
C. Nusrat Fateh Ali Khan
D. Raghupati Sahay 'Firaq'

239. Who was the producer of the serial 'Mahabharat'?
A. Shyam Benegal B. B.R. Chopra
C. Ramanand Sagar D. Mani Ratnam

240. Which of the following is a folk dance of Rajasthan?
A. Garba B. Dandya
C. Jhumar D. Kathak

241. 'The Colonel' is the nickname of which Indian Test Cricketer?
A. Colonel C.K. Naidu
B. Rahul Dravid
C. Mohinder Amarnath
D. Dilip Vengsarkar

242. The term 'Grandmaster' is used in which of these games?
A. Judo B. Chess
C. Bridge D. Karate

243. The term "Derby" is related with which of the following?
A. Polo B. Swimming
C. Racing D. Horse Racing

244. With which game is Geet Sethi associated?
A. Basketball B. Chess
C. Snooker D. Tennis

245. Beighton Cup is related with which of the following?
A. Hockey B. Polo
C. Cricket D. Soccer

246. Match List-I with List-II and select the correct answer using the codes given below the Lists :

List-I	List-II
(*a*) Basketball	1. Lob
(*b*) Bridge	2. Revoke
(*c*) Golf	3. Pivot
(*d*) Tennis	4. Bunker

Codes :

	(*a*)	(*b*)	(*c*)	(*d*)
A.	2	3	1	4
B.	2	3	4	1
C.	3	2	1	4
D.	3	2	4	1

247. The head office of the International Cricket Council (ICC) is situated in :
A. Zimbabwe B. Australia
C. South Africa D. UAE

248. Match the following :

List-I	List-II
(*a*) Deodhar Trophy	1. Volleyball
(*b*) Durand Cup	2. Football
(*c*) Davis Cup	3. Cricket
	4. Tennis

Codes:

	(*a*)	(*b*)	(*c*)
A.	3	2	4
B.	3	1	4
C.	2	3	1
D.	1	2	4

249. Which of the following is called 'Grand Slam'?
A. Winning the highest number of medals in the Olympic games
B. Winning the men's singles title in Wimbledon Championship
C. Winning the Wimbledon Singles title successively for two years
D. Winning all the four championships Australian, French, Wimblendon and US

250. With which game is the term 'butterfly stroke' associated?
A. Swimming B. Cricket
C. Gliding D. Skiing

251. Who is the first Indian to win the 'International Grand Master' title in Chess?
A. Anupama Abhayankar
B. Bhagyashree Sathe Thipsay
C. Vishwanathan Anand
D. D.V. Prasad

252. The XXII Commonwealth Games were held in 2022 in:
A. Kuala Lumpur B. Bangkok
C. Victoria D. Birmingham

253. The term 'Tee' is associated with which of the following sports?
A. Golf B. Table Tennis
C. Polo D. Judo

254. The famous woman Tennis player who was stabbed during a match, is
A. Steffi Graf B. Monica Seles
C. Mary Pierce D. Martina Navratilova

255. The term 'Baseline' is related to which of the following?
A. Golf B. Hockey
C. Badminton D. Polo

256. In which Indian State did the game of Polo originate?
A. Manipur B. Rajasthan
C. Gujarat D. West Bengal

257. Narendra Modi Stadium is located at:
A. Hyderabad B. Chennai
C. Ahmedabad D. Prayagraj

258. Rafael Nadal is the well-known player associated with:
A. Hockey B. Cricket
C. Tennis D. Chess

259. Neeraj Chopra is the well-known player associated with :
A. Javelin Throw B. Golf
C. Table Tennis D. Chess

260. Eden Garden, a famous Cricket stadium, is located in :
A. Kanpur B. Kolkata
C. Jamshedpur D. Pune

261. Maharaja Ranjit Singh Trophy is associated with :
A. Golf B. Hockey
C. Soccer D. Tennis

262. Harmanpreet Kaur is a distinguished player in which of the following games?
A. Swimming B. Weightlifting
C. Cricket D. Archery

263. Cricket was an Olympic event at which of the following Olympics?
A. London, 1908 B. Amsterdam, 1928
C. Paris, 1900 D. Melbourne, 1956

264. WISPA competitions are associated with :
A. Squash B. Yatching
C. Boxing D. Billiards

265. Ryder Cup is the famous trophy of :
A. Golf B. Chess
C. Boxing D. Polo

266. Davis Cup is associated with the sport of :
A. Cricket B. Football
C. Tennis D. Hockey

267. 'Volley', 'Chop' and 'Drive Spine' are the term associated with :
A. Lawn Tennis B. Badminton
C. Table Tennis D. Golf

268. Lal Bahadur Shastri Stadium is located at :
A. Hyderabad B. Chennai
C. Ahmedabad D. Varanasi

269. The first winner of "Rajiv Khel Ratna Award" (Now Major Dhyan Chand Khel Ratna Award) was :
A. Geet Sethi
B. Sachin Tendulkar
C. Viswanathan Anand
D. Karnam Malleswari

270. The winner of 2023 Cricket World Cup is:
A. Australia B. Sri Lanka
C. Bangladesh D. England

271. The first team event introduced in 1900 at Paris Olympics was :
A. Hockey B. Football
C. Cricket D. Baseball

272. Which of the following international tennis tournaments is held on grass court?
A. US Open B. French Open
C. Wimbledon D. Australian Open

273. Which cricketer is nicknamed as the pied piper of Punjab?
A. Yuvraj Singh
B. Harbhajan Singh
C. Mohinder Amarnath
D. Navjot Singh Sidhu

274. 'Merdeka Cup' is associated with ....
A. Golf B. Football
C. Squash D. Hockey

275. The first time athletes marched into the stadium behind their nation's flag in Olympics:
A. at St. Louis 1904 B. at London 1908
C. at Antwerp 1920 D. at Paris 1924

276. The "Dronacharya Award" is associated with:
A. Eminent Surgeons B. Famous Sports Person
C. Sport Coaches D. Expert Engineers

277. Which cricketer is nicknamed as 'Jumbo'?
A. Venkatesh Prasad B. Anil Kumble
C. Glenn McGrath D. Shane Warne

278. The first time the Olympic Games were organised by a private company at:
A. Montreal, 1976 B. Los Angeles, 1984
C. Atlanta, 1996 D. Rome, 1960

279. In which Asian Games Cricket was played first?
A. Guangzhou, 2010 B. Doha, 2006
C. Busan, 2002 D. Seoul, 1986

280. The term 'Penalty cick' is used in :
A. Hockey B. Football
C. Baseball D. Golf

281. Which of the following countries is not a member of North Atlantic Treaty Organisation (NATO)?
A. Norway B. United Germany
C. Portugal D. Australia

282. Khmer Rouge is a dictatorial party of :
A. Cambodia B. Indonesia
C. Malaysia D. Thailand

283. Which country is not a member of SAARC?
A. Russia B. Bangladesh
C. Nepal D. Pakistan

284. The headquarters of WTO is located at :
A. Geneva B. Paris
C. The Hague D. Washington

285. The main function of the World Trade Organisation (WTO) is:
A. enforcing of Uruguay Round Agreements
B. facilitating multi-lateral trade relations of member countries and reviewing trade policies
C. administering trade dispute settlement procedures
D. None of the above

286. The Secretary-General of the UNO is appointed by the:
A. General Assembly
B. Security Council
C. Trusteeship Council
D. World Bank

287. The United Nations officially came into existence in 1945 on :
A. November 24 B. October 14
C. October 24 D. November 14

288. Which one of the following is true of the International Court of Justice?
A. The Judges of the Court are appointed according to the discretion of the Secretary General
B. No two Judges may belong to the same country
C. The Court consists of 20 Judges
D. The statute of the International Court of Justice is not an integral part of the UN Charter

289. Which of the following was not among the six founding countries of the European Community?
A. Belgium B. France
C. Germany D. UK

290. The smallest country in South America is:
A. Ecuador B. Guyana
C. Surinam D. Uruguay

291. In which year "Human Rights Resolution" was adopted by the U.N.?
A. 1945 B. 1946
C. 1947 D. 1948

292. Where is the headquarters of INTERPOL located?
A. Berlin B. California
C. Lyons D. Montreal

293. Parliament of which of the following countries is known as Great People's Khural?
A. Malaysia B. Mongolia
C. Thailand D. Indonesia

294. Numbers of major organs of United Nations are:
A. 3 B. 4
C. 5 D. 6

295. When is the UN Day celebrated?
A. October 24 B. January 24
C. June 24 D. September 24

296. Which one of the following organ of United Nations is known as the 'Policeman of the World'?
A. Security Council
B. International Court of Justice
C. The Secretariat
D. General Assembly

297. The members of the NAFTA include:
A. USA, Canada and Mexico
B. USA, Canada, Mexico and UK
C. USA, UK, Russia and Mexicc
D. USA, Canada and Brazil

298. The sits of International Court of Justice is located at :
A. Vienna B. Paris
C. Hague D. New York

299. Which of the following is known as the Constitution of the UN?
A. UN Charter
B. UN Assembly
C. UN Security Council
D. UN Secretariat

300. The Headquarters of the Amnesty International is located at :
A. New York
B. London
C. Geneva
D. Addis-Ababa

301. Who is the author of the book 'PRISON DIARY'?
A. Bal Gangadhar Tilak
B. Rajendra Prasad
C. Jai Prakash Narayan
D. Jawahar Lal Nehru

302. Who is the author of 'Satanic Verses'?
A. Lewis Carrol B. Salman Rushdie
C. Parry Mason D. Mulk Raj Anand

303. Who wrote 'Gitanjali'?
A. Kalidas
B. Gopal Das 'Neeraj'
C. Rabindra Nath Tagore
D. Jawahar Lal Nehru

304. Who, among the following, scholars flourishing during the Gupta Age, was the author of *Dasakumara-Charita?*
A. Asanga B. Dignaga
C. Dandina D. Bhattin

305. The author of *Gitagovinda* was:
A. Halayudha B. Jayadeva
C. Kalhana D. Jona-raja

306. "Ingenious Pain" is a book/novel written by:
A. Andrew Miller B. Santa Monica
C. Ben Johnson D. Bill Gates

307. Who amongst the following is the author of the famous book "An Equal Music"?
A. Salman Rushdie B. Shasthivrata
C. Vikram Seth D. Kamla Markandeya

308. The famous Moorti Devi Award is given for excellence in which of the following fields?
A. Medicine
B. Science & Technology
C. Social Service
D. Literature

309. Who has written "Devdas"?
A. Tarasankar Bandyopadhyay
B. Bankim Chandra Chattopadhyay
C. Rabindranath Tagore
D. Sarat Chandra Chattopadhyay

310. "Ain-i-Akbari" is written by:
A. Todar Mal B. Abul Fazal
C. Sheikh Saadi D. Mirza Ghalib

311. "Alice in Wonderland" is written by :
A. Lewis Carrol B. Chester Bowles
C. Charles Dickens D. Jonathan Swift

312. "Mrichchhakatikam" is written by :
A. Vishakhadatta B. Vatsyayana
C. Sudraka D. Bana Bhatt

313. "My Experiments with Truth" is written by :
A. Jawaharlal Nehru
B. M.K. Gandhi
C. Abul Kalam Azad
D. Rajendra Prasad

314. Who wrote the book "India Wins Freedom"?
A. Maulana Abul Kalam Azad
B. Mahatma Gandhi
C. Sir Mohammad Iqbal
D. Abdul Gaffar Khan

315. Match List-I with List-II and select the correct answer using the codes given below the Lists :

List-I	**List-II**
(*a*) *Emma*	1. Graham Greene
(*b*) *Mother India*	2. E.M. Forster
(*c*) *Human Factor*	3. Jane Austen
(*d*) *Passage to India*	4. Katherine Mayo

Codes :

	(*a*)	(*b*)	(*c*)	(*d*)
A.	2	1	4	3
B.	3	4	1	2
C.	3	1	2	4
D.	4	2	1	3

316. 'Poverty and Un British Rule in India' is written by:
A. R.C. Dutt B. J.L. Nehru
C. D.B. Naoroji D. S.N. Sen

317. Name the author of the book *A Passage to England.*
A. E.M. Forster
B. Nirad C. Choudhuri
C. Vikram Seth
D. Eric Segal

318. The author of the book 'The Struggle in My Life' is:
A. Mandela B. J.L. Nehru
C. Tilak D. Gokhale

319. The Shanti Swarup Bhatnagar Award is given by which of the following organisations?
A. Council for Scientific and Industrial Research
B. Indian Council for Agricultural Research
C. Indian National Science Academy
D. Indian Space Research Organisation

320. Which of the following books is not written by Salman Rushdie?
A. The Satanic Verses
B. Shame
C. Naked Face
D. Midnight's Children

321. The different schools of modern socialism derive their strength primarily from the writings of ....?
A. Joseph Stalin B. Leo Tolstoy
C. Mao Tse-tung D. Karl Marx

322. Baba Amte is famous as a ....
A. Painter B. Singer
C. Politician D. Social Worker

323. Central Government says that .... was received well by citizens as 'imandari ka utsav'.
A. Demonetization
B. Goods and Services Tax
C. E-NAM
D. All of the above

324. Mr. Yehudi Menuhin, was a famous:
A. Sitarist B. Cartoonist
C. Journalist D. Violinist

325. Sundarlal Bahuguna, a famous environmentalist, was associated with :
A. Chipko Movement
B. Narmada Bachao Andolan
C. Satyagraha Movement
D. Anti-corruption Movement

326. Mother Teressa's native place was :
A. Albania B. France
C. Greece D. Italy

327. The live polio vaccine which can be taken by mouth was developed by :
A. Albert Sabin B. Edward Jenner
C. Jonas Salk D. Selman Waksman

328. Which one of the following authors put forth the theory of the Drain of India's resources to England?
A. Raja Rammohan Roy
B. Bankim Chandra Chatterjee
C. G.G. Agarkar
D. Dadabhai Naoroji

329. The "Last Supper" is a famous renaissance painting. It was a masterpiece of :
A. Michael Angelo B. Leonardo da Vinci
C. Titian D. Raphael

330. Dhyanchand is associated with which sports?
A. Badminton B. Hockey
C. Tennis D. Football

331. 'Man is born free, yet every where he is in chains'. This was said by:
A. Voltaire B. John Stuart Mill
C. Rousseau D. Karl Marx

332. Who among the following was a prominent social reformer?
A. Baba Gurmukh Singh
B. Raja Mahendra Pratap
C. Bipin Chandra Pal
D. Jotiba Govind Phule

333. Whose real name was Gadadhar Chhattopadhyaya?
A. Swami Vivekanand
B. Ram Krishna Paramhansa
C. Dayanand Saraswai
D. Raja Ram Mohan Rai

334. Who was known as "Man of Destiny"?
A. Napoleon B. Nehru
C. Hitler D. Mussolini

335. Who discovered that mosquito served as a carrier of malaria?
A. Jonas Salk B. Ronald Ross
C. Louis Pasteur D. Robert Koch

336. Who was the first woman Governor of an Indian State?
A. Sushila Nayar B. Sucheta Kripalani
C. Sarojini Naidu D. Sulochana Modi

337. Who among the following founded the Bhartiya Jana Sangh?
A. Deen Dayal Upadhyaya

B. Veer Savarkar
C. Dr. Ram Manohar Lohia
D. Dr. Shyama Prasad Mukherjee

338. Who among the following President of India held his office for two successive terms?
A. V.V. Giri
B. Dr. Rajendra Prasad
C. Dr. S. Radhakrishnan
D. None of these

339. Ustad Amjad Ali Khan is an exponent of:
A. Flute
B. Sitar
C. Sarod
D. Tabla

340. Who is the first non-Indian to receive the Bharat Ratna?
A. Martin Luther King
B. Zubin Mehta
C. Mother Teressa
D. Khan Abdul Ghaffar Khan

ANSWERS

1	**2**	**3**	**4**	**5**	**6**	**7**	**8**	**9**	**10**
B	C	D	C	B	C	A	C	C	D
11	**12**	**13**	**14**	**15**	**16**	**17**	**18**	**19**	**20**
C	A	C	A	A	D	A	B	A	D
21	**22**	**23**	**24**	**25**	**26**	**27**	**28**	**29**	**30**
A	C	B	C	D	C	B	D	D	B
31	**32**	**33**	**34**	**35**	**36**	**37**	**38**	**39**	**40**
C	D	C	C	B	C	D	B	C	C
41	**42**	**43**	**44**	**45**	**46**	**47**	**48**	**49**	**50**
A	A	A	B	C	D	C	B	B	D
51	**52**	**53**	**54**	**55**	**56**	**57**	**58**	**59**	**60**
A	C	A	B	B	A	B	C	A	C
61	**62**	**63**	**64**	**65**	**66**	**67**	**68**	**69**	**70**
C	C	B	B	C	C	D	D	D	B
71	**72**	**73**	**74**	**75**	**76**	**77**	**78**	**79**	**80**
B	C	C	C	A	A	A	B	B	A
81	**82**	**83**	**84**	**85**	**86**	**87**	**88**	**89**	**90**
A	B	D	B	C	C	D	C	B	D
91	**92**	**93**	**94**	**95**	**96**	**97**	**98**	**99**	**100**
A	B	A	A	A	B	B	A	A	C
101	**102**	**103**	**104**	**105**	**106**	**107**	**108**	**109**	**110**
C	B	A	D	D	D	A	C	D	C
111	**112**	**113**	**114**	**115**	**116**	**117**	**118**	**119**	**120**
B	B	B	A	D	C	C	D	B	D
121	**122**	**123**	**124**	**125**	**126**	**127**	**128**	**129**	**130**
C	A	A	B	A	D	C	D	B	D
131	**132**	**133**	**134**	**135**	**136**	**137**	**138**	**139**	**140**
B	B	D	A	B	D	B	D	D	C
141	**142**	**143**	**144**	**145**	**146**	**147**	**148**	**149**	**150**
D	C	D	D	D	B	A	D	C	C

151	**152**	**153**	**154**	**155**	**156**	**157**	**158**	**159**	**160**
A	B	A	A	A	D	C	B	D	A
161	**162**	**163**	**164**	**165**	**166**	**167**	**168**	**169**	**170**
B	B	C	B	D	D	C	B	B	B
171	**172**	**173**	**174**	**175**	**176**	**177**	**178**	**179**	**180**
D	C	D	D	C	B	C	A	D	A
181	**182**	**183**	**184**	**185**	**186**	**187**	**188**	**189**	**190**
B	B	C	A	A	A	B	D	D	A
191	**192**	**193**	**194**	**195**	**196**	**197**	**198**	**199**	**200**
B	C	A	A	D	A	B	D	D	A
201	**202**	**203**	**204**	**205**	**206**	**207**	**208**	**209**	**210**
B	B	B	B	A	A	A	A	A	A
211	**212**	**213**	**214**	**215**	**216**	**217**	**218**	**219**	**220**
B	A	A	A	D	C	D	A	B	B
221	**222**	**223**	**224**	**225**	**226**	**227**	**228**	**229**	**230**
D	C	A	D	A	A	D	D	B	B
231	**232**	**233**	**234**	**235**	**236**	**237**	**238**	**239**	**240**
D	B	D	A	D	D	C	B	B	C
241	**242**	**243**	**244**	**245**	**246**	**247**	**248**	**249**	**250**
D	B	D	C	A	D	D	A	D	A
251	**252**	**253**	**254**	**255**	**256**	**257**	**258**	**259**	**260**
C	D	A	B	C	A	C	C	A	B
261	**262**	**263**	**264**	**265**	**266**	**267**	**268**	**269**	**270**
B	C	C	A	A	C	C	A	C	A
271	**272**	**273**	**274**	**275**	**276**	**277**	**278**	**279**	**280**
B	C	A	B	A	C	B	B	A	B
281	**282**	**283**	**284**	**285**	**286**	**287**	**288**	**289**	**290**
D	A	A	A	B	A	C	B	D	C
291	**292**	**293**	**294**	**295**	**296**	**297**	**298**	**299**	**300**
D	C	B	D	A	A	A	C	A	B
301	**302**	**303**	**304**	**305**	**306**	**307**	**308**	**309**	**310**
C	B	C	C	B	A	C	D	D	B
311	**312**	**313**	**314**	**315**	**316**	**317**	**318**	**319**	**320**
A	C	B	A	B	C	B	A	A	C
321	**322**	**323**	**324**	**325**	**326**	**327**	**328**	**329**	**330**
D	D	A	D	A	A	C	D	B	B
331	**332**	**333**	**334**	**335**	**336**	**337**	**338**	**339**	**340**
C	D	B	A	B	C	D	B	C	D

❑ ❑ ❑